Alexandria County Virginia

Free Negro Registers

1797–1861

Abstracted and Indexed by
Dorothy S. Provine

HERITAGE BOOKS
2012

HERITAGE BOOKS
AN IMPRINT OF HERITAGE BOOKS, INC.

Books, CDs, and more—Worldwide

For our listing of thousands of titles see our website
at
www.HeritageBooks.com

Published 2012 by
HERITAGE BOOKS, INC.
Publishing Division
100 Railroad Ave. #104
Westminster, Maryland 21157

Copyright © 1990 Dorothy S. Provine

Other Heritage Books by the author:

Alexandria County, Virginia Free Negro Register, 1797–1861

*Compensated Emancipation in the District of Columbia:
Petitions under the Act of April 16, 1862*

District of Columbia Free Negro Registers

District of Columbia Indentures of Apprenticeship, 1801–1893

*District of Columbia Marriage Records Index
June 28, 1877 to October 19, 1885: Marriage Record Books 11 to 20*
Wesley E. Pippenger and Dorothy S. Provine

District of Columbia Marriage Records, 1870–1877

Index to District of Columbia Wills, 1921–1950

All rights reserved. No part of this book may be reproduced or transmitted in any form or by any means, electronic or mechanical, including photocopying, recording or by any information storage and retrieval system without written permission from the author, except for the inclusion of brief quotations in a review.

International Standard Book Numbers
Paperbound: 978-1-55613-416-6
Clothbound: 978-0-7884-3416-7

TO MARGARET VEERHOFF

TABLE OF CONTENTS

Introduction	vii
Table: White, Free Black and Slave Population of Alexandria County	x
Volume 1 1797-1841 (Nos. 1-771)	1
Volume 2 1842-1847 (Nos. 1-386)	105
Volume 3 1847-1850 (Nos. 1-596)	157
1850-1861 (Nos. 1-581)	227
Index	295

INTRODUCTION

The following publication consists of abstracts of entries in the registers for free blacks for Alexandria County (now Arlington County) Virginia for the period 1797 to 1861. The original volumes are located in the Arlington County Courthouse in Arlington, Virginia. A photostatic copy is available at the Lloyd House in Alexandria (220 North Washington St.) and a microfilm copy is located at the Virginia State Library in Richmond and in the Virginia Room of the Arlington County Public Library.

These records were created and maintained by the county or circuit court and were usually signed by the clerk of the court. From February 27, 1801, until the retrocession of Alexandria County to the state of Virginia on September 7, 1846, the Circuit Court of the District of Columbia for Alexandria County, was the agency of origin.

The registers are in three volumes: 1797-1841; 1842-47; and 1847-61. They contain approximately 2,350 numbered entries, but this number is misleading. One entry might relate to one or to several individuals, and many persons were registered more than once. A typical entry gives the name of the person being registered, age, height, color, remarks concerning scars, marks, and other notable physical characteristics, and the basis of the registrant's claim to freedom.

Alexandria County was originally part of Fairfax County, Virginia, until that state ceded the land to the Federal government to form part of the home for the new capital. The United States assumed jurisdiction over the area on February 27, 1801, provided that the laws of Virginia would remain in effect in that area and called that part of the district donated by Virginia "Alexandria County." Alexandria remained a part of the District of Columbia until September of 1846 when it was retroceded to the state of Virginia. It continued to be known as Alexandria County until 1920 when its name was changed to Arlington County.

By 1860, Alexandria County has a population of 12,652 of which 1,415 (11%) were free blacks and 1,386 (11%) were slaves. Although separate figures for town and county are not given in the published census after 1840, there is little doubt but that the over-whelming majority of the free blacks lived in the town. The federal census for 1840, when Alexandria was part of the District of Columbia, presents what is probably a typical picture. In that year, the population of Alexandria County was 1509, of which 235 were free blacks; the population of Alexandria City was 8,459, of which 1,627 were free Negroes.

These registers are a product of the requirement throughout the South (and, indeed, in some non-slave states) that free Negroes prove their claim to freedom before local authorities, become registered, and obtain a freedom certificate which they were to carry with them. A Virginia law of 1793 stipulated that the town clerk was to register free blacks and mulattoes in a volume that recorded the individual's name, age, color, status, and source of freedom, and give a copy of the certificate to the registrant. Theoretically free Negroes were to renew their registration every three years, but this provision of the law was not strictly enforced. The resulting registration books contain valuable information about how free Negroes obtained their freedom, the free black family, as well as genealogical data on individual persons.

One's free status was acquired in several different ways. By the nineteenth century, many Negroes were born of a free mother and were hence born free. The black codes provided that Negroes took their status from their mother--if you were born of a free mother you were born free; if your mother was a white woman you were automatically considered to have been born free.

Many other blacks were freed by manumission, either immediately or after fulfilling certain conditions. The circumstances varied greatly. Some were freed after serving a specified term of years or upon reaching a certain age; others were freed after paying a sum of money (commonly equal to their purchase price); and still others were freed after being purchased by a family member and manumitted.

Some slave owners emancipated their slaves in their wills, either immediately or after they had met certain conditions or reached a certain age. In still other instances, blacks won their freedom by successfully suing in court for their freedom.

Many of the entries in the registers indicate the method by which the registrant received his freedom and contain cross references to other sources of information. Some items refer to deeds of manumission that are recorded in county deed books, wills and probate documents, indentures of apprenticeship, court cases, and registration documents from other jurisdictions. City directories, which occasionally list blacks, and the manuscript of the federal census returns (especially those for 1850 and 1860 when every person living in the household was listed) are also useful research tools.

For additional general information about free blacks in the antebellum period, the reader may wish to consult Ira Berlin's *Slaves without Masters: The Free Negro in the Antebellum South* (New York, 1976), Leonard P. Curry's *The Free Black in Urban America, 1800-1850* (Chicago and London, 1981), and Leon F. Litwack's *North of Slavery: The Negro in the Free States, 1790-1860* (Chicago and London, 1961). For information about the black experience in Virginia and the District of Columbia, see Letitia Woods Brown, *Free Negroes in the District of Columbia, 1790-1846* (New York, 1972); Constance McLaughlin Green, *The Secret City: A History of Race Relations in the Nation's Capital* (Princeton, N.J., 1967); John H. Russell, *The Free Negro in Virginia, 1619-1865* (Baltimore, 1913); Luther Porter Jackson, *Free Negro Labor and Property Holding in Virginia, 1830-1860* (New York, 1942); and Elsa S. Rosenthal, "1790 Names--1970 Faces: A Short History of Alexandria's Slave and Free Black Community" in Elizabeth Hambleton and Marian Van Landingham, *Alexandria: A Composite History*, Vol. I (Alexandria, 1975).

Editorial Method

The entries in the present book are abstracts of the registrations rather than verbatim transcriptions. Every attempt has been made to include all pertinent information about the individual being registered and only notations regarding the delivery of the certificate or obtaining another copy at a later date have been omitted. The documents have been paraphrased closely and the original language has, for the most part, been retained even though few quotation marks have been used. To have used quotes around every exact passage would have resulted in entries that were so chopped-up and disjointed that they would have been extremely difficult to read. (In fact, the documents are so nearly verbatim, that in many cases they have been treated editorially as if they were quotations. Thus when important phrases were omitted, the editor used ellipsis points and when material was inserted, she used brackets). Nor have the documents been edited to clean up offensive expressions that were sometimes used to describe the persons being registered. The language employed in the documents is typical of that used by whites in the nineteenth century and to alter it would be to change the fundamental flavor of the manuscript. Indeed, the words chosen by the clerk of the court to describe the physical appearance of the person being registered are indicative of his, and others of his class', attitudes towards black persons. The editor has made a few concessions to current practice in modernizing spelling ("color" instead of "colour," for example) and in capitalizing the word "Negro."

Handwritten documents present special problems for an editor. For example, the letter "l" ending a word frequently appears to be an "e," so that one is unsure whether an individual's surname is "Hall" or "Hale." In addition, the same name varies in spelling from entry to entry and, in some cases, evolves from one name to another. The user of this book is therefore urged to exercise "creative reading" skills when searching for a particular name.

In many instances, especially in the early years, no surnames were given for Negroes being registered or referred to in the documents. In such cases, the names have been indexed under "Negro" followed by the given name of the individual. The editor has attempted to assign likely surnames whenever possible. In the case of varying spelling of the same name, the editor has tried to link persons by bringing names together under the most likely spelling or by giving both versions of the name in the index (e.g., Townsend/Townshend).

The headings have been supplied by the author and give the number of the registration and the volume and page numbers as they appear in the original registers. The dates given in the heading are as nearly as possible the date that the information was entered in the register. In cases where the registration date was not noted, the date the certificate was delivered or certified or copied (whichever is earlier) has been given. The clerk sometimes made mistakes in numbering both the page and the registration, at times skipping a number, at other times using the same numbers more than once. In a simple cases where numbers are erroneously repeated one following the other, the first is assigned an "a" suffix and the second a "b" suffix. In two instances, however, there is a long sequence of repeated registration numbers: in volume two the clerk repeats the numbers 274 through 293 and in volume three the numbering of the entries begins again with number 1 on page 81 of that volume. When referring to these entries, the page number for the item is given in parentheses following the registration number.

The editor has used ellipsis points (three or four dots) to indicate the omission of a substantive phrase that was illegible, obscured or lost; and has used underlined question marks (??) to show the same thing for a single word or number. She has used a question mark in brackets ([?]), to show that the preceding word is a conjecture on the part of the editor and may be in error. Other remarks within brackets that appear in the text of a document represent material inserted by the editor. Likewise, statements in italics that appear before or after a registration are editorial comments.

With regard to the index, the volume number is given in Roman numerals followed by the registration number. The registration number is underlined if the entry represents the registration of the individual. As indicated above, in cases where there are repeating registration numbers in a volume, the page number is given in parentheses following the registration number.

WHITE, FREE BLACK AND SLAVE POPULATION OF ALEXANDRIA COUNTY*

YEAR	WHITES	FREE BLACKS	SLAVES	TOTAL	% OF WHITES	% OF FREE BLACKS	% OF SLAVES
1800	4,394	383	1,172	5,949	73.9	06.4	19.7
1810	5,734	977	1,841	8,552	67.0	11.4	21.5
1820	6,556	1,290	1,857	9,703	67.5	13.3	19.1
1830	6,391	1,548	1,614	9,573	66.8	16.1	16.9
1840	6,731	1,862	1,374	9,967	67.5	18.6	13.8
1850	7,217	1,409	1,382	10,008	72.1	14.1	13.8
1860	9,851	1,415	1,386	12,652	77.9	11.2	11.0

*Compiled of data from the published federal census returns. Figures include both the town of Alexandria and the county of Alexandria. The percentages have been rounded off with the result that the totals do not always equal 100 percent. Census returns for the years 1810 through 1840 give separate figures for the town and the county. Of the totals in the chart above, the population of the county was: 1810: whites, 831; free blacks, 141; slaves, 353; total, 1,325; 1820: whites, 941; free blacks, 122; slaves, 422; total, 1,485; 1830: whites, 802; free blacks, 177; slaves, 353; total, 1,332; 1840: whites, 973; free blacks, 235; slaves, 300; total, 1508.

VOLUME 1

1797-1841

Volume 1, 1797-1841 1

REGISTRATION NO. 1
(Vol. 1, p. 1)

Negro Hester   27 May 1797

Copy of a manumission from Fredericksburg.

Francis T. Brooke, attorney for John T. Brooke, frees Negro Hester. (27 May 1797)

REGISTRATION NO. 2
(Vol. 1, p. 2)

Margaret Dixon   21 April 1802

Copy of a pass from Charles County, Maryland.

Margaret Dixon is a free mulatto woman, about 36 years old, with black eyes. (21 April 1801)

REGISTRATION NO. 3
(Vol. 1, pp. 3-4)

Elizabeth Johnson   11 May 1802

Rachal Hiday, a white woman, swears that she knows Elizabeth Johnson, a "yellow woman" and her mother, who was a free white woman of Fairfax County. Elizabeth Johnson was born free in Fairfax County.

Johnson is a "bright Mulatto with Black hair of Indian appearance," "thick made," and has an "open Countenance." She has burn on her right hand which has nearly destroyed the little finger and which has drawn the third finger into her hand. Johnson is about 30 years old and is 5 feet 4 inches tall.

REGISTRATION NO. 4
(Vol. 1, p. 4)

Spencer Thomas   1 April 1803

William Lewis swears that Spencer Thomas, a "yellow man" about 53 years old, was born free in the family of his grandfather. He served in Northumberland County until he was 31 years old, the latter part of which time he served with Lewis. Thomas was a "trusty and faithful servant."

REGISTRATION NO. 5
(Vol. 1, pp. 5-6)

Frankey McIntosh   17 November 1803

The bearer, Frankey McIntosh, aged about 16, is the daughter of Molly McIntosh, who was born free. She produced the following certificate signed by David Jamisone, a Justice of the Peace for Culpeper County:

Jamisone states that he has known Mary, aka Molly McIntosh, from the time she was a girl and that she lived in the family of Mr. Argatone Price of Orange County near where he lived. Common report said that Molly was the mulatto bastard child of Ann McIntosh, a Scotch servant woman to Argaton Price. Jamisone knows that Molly lived in the family of Price until she was 31 years old and was then said to be free. Molly has for several years past lived in this county as a free woman and has never been molested on account of any services she owned. Molly appeared and swore that Frankey McIntosh is her daughter. (Signed D Jamisone 17 Nov. 1803)

REGISTRATION NO. 6
(Vol. l, pp. 6-8)

Negro Jenny and children   28 May 1804
Lucy, Sylvia, Sue and Hannah Elizabeth

Thomas G. Addison manumits Jenny and her three daughters: Lucy, Sylvia and Sue. (Signed Prince George's County, Md. 4 July 1800)

District of Columbia:

Jenny is a dark mulatto about 37 years old, of a slim make, who has a small bone raised on the left wrist[?] by rheumatism. Two or three of her upper front teeth are lost.

Lucy is a dark mulatto about 14 years old, 5 feet one-half inch tall, with full black eyes. She has a scar on her right cheek bone from chicken pox.

Sylvia is 9 years old, about 4 feet tall, with black eyes. She is pitted from smallpox, but this is "not to be discovered unless closely examined."

Sue is 5 years old, between 3 and 4 feet tall, with large black eyes.

Hannah Elizabeth is 1 year and 4 months old and has a liver spot on her right shoulder. She was born after the emancipation of Negro Jenny and her three daughters.

REGISTRATION NO. 7
(Vol. 1, pp. 8-9)

Charles Campbell   29 June 1804

William Byrd Page, in consideration of the sum of 5 shillings, manumits Charles Campbell, aged about 34. (Signed Alexandria, 25 July 1799)

Campbell is a dark mulatto, about 39 years old, about 5 feet 8 inches tall, and is stout and broad chested with "projecting lips," a "spreading nose," and "small or moderate eyes" that "are not in strict harmony with the other manly features of his face." He has a "strong masculine voice" and is "active and affable."

REGISTRATION NO. 8
(Vol. 1, pp. 9-10)

Sarah Leucas   10 July 1804

Baldwin Dade certifies that Sarah Leucas, a mulatto woman aged about 40, was born free. She is about 5 feet 8 or 10 inches tall and, to the best of Dade's knowledge, "all her female ancesters were free born particularly her mother who I well know."

REGISTRATION NO. 9
(Vol. 1, pp. 10-11)

Negro Daniel   20 July 1804

Copy of a manumission from Fairfax County.

Jonah Thompson manumits Negro Daniel. (8 Nov. 1790)

Daniel is a dark mulatto about 25 years old, slim made, with an open countenance, and is 5 feet 11 inches tall.

REGISTRATION NO. 10
(Vol. 1, pp. 11-12)

Pompey Primus   23 August 1804

Copy of a manumission from Prince George's County, Maryland.

James Hawkins Baynes, "in consideration of the merit and faithful service of my trusty slave," manumits Pompey Primus, who was born in 1774 and is 29 years old. (17 Apr. 1804)

Pompey Primus is a dark mulatto about thirty years of age, 5 feet 8½ or 9 inches tall, with a small scar on the right side of his breast caused by a pin scratch. The small finger on his left hand is crooked from a cut by a reap[?] hook and he has a large scar on the back of his left arm below the elbow, which was cut in like manner as his finger.

REGISTRATION NO. 11
(Vol. 1, p. 13)

Nicholas Cammel   30 August 1805

John T. Brooks certifies that Nicholas Cammel is a free black man. Cammel is about 35 years old, about 5 feet 7½ inches tall, and has lost the first joint of the little finger of his right hand by frost. He was born in St. Pierre Martinique and came to this city March 1793 in the Ship *Amiable Antonietta* from Havre de Grace. The ship's owners, Misters Forrest and Seaton of this town, sold the boat to William Wilson, Esq., and

Cammel entered into Wilson's service. He continued there for twenty-seven months. Since that time he has married here and sailed constantly out of this town. He has made seven voyages with me, "much to my content and Satisfaction." (29 Aug. 1805)

REGISTRATION NO. 12
(Vol. 1, p. 14)

Sarah Valentine   21 March 1806

Copy of Registration No. 46 from Norfolk.

Sarah Valentine is a black woman about 30 years old and 5 feet 11 inches tall. She was born free. (18 Aug. 1806)

REGISTRATION NO. 13
(Vol. 1, p. 14)

Negro Nanny   21 March 1806

Negro Nanny is 38 years old, 5 feet one-half inch tall, with high cheek bones, and a dimpled, square face. She is "rather white eyed" and has a scar above her eyes.

REGISTRATION NO. 14
(Vol. 1, p. 15)

Negro Congo   21 March 1806

Copy of a manumission from Caroline County.

Charles Clark states that he believes "that all men are by nature equally free and from a dear conviction of the injustice and criminality of depriving my fellow creatures of their natural right & liberty" he emancipates Congo from the first day of August 1794. (8 July 1794)

Congo is described as a dark mulatto about 43 years old with a scar over his right eye.

REGISTRATION NO. 15
(Vol. 1, p. 15)

Negro William   21 March 1806

Negro William is about 38 years old, 5 feet 5 3/4 inches tall, of a very dark complexion, with a small scar over his right cheekbone, and "a tolerable full face." He has lost one of his front teeth and "Speaks tolerable fine."

REGISTRATION NO. 16
(Vol. 1, p. 16)

Negro Nancy   22 March 1806

Negro Nancy is a dark mulatto about 27 years old, 5 feet 4½ inches tall, slender made, with an open countenance. She has two "hare molds," one on each side of her cheek.

REGISTRATION NO. 17
(Vol. 1, pp. 16-17)

Negro Bet or Bett   22 March 1806

Copy of an indenture.

Negro "Bet," a mulatto about 30 years old, "in consideration of having been set free" by John Potts, Jr., by his instrument dated May 24th, voluntarily binds herself as a servant to Potts of Montgomery County, Pennsylvania, to serve him for a term of seven years, after which she is to be free. (26 May 1788)

Negro "Bett" is a bright mulatto about 49 years old, 5 feet 5¼ inches tall, and slender made. She has lost two of her upper teeth and two of her lower teeth.

REGISTRATION NO. 18
(Vol. 1, p. 17)

Negro Rachel   22 March 1806

Negro Rachel is a very bright mulatto about 25 years old, 5 feet 2 inches tall, with dark eyes. She has a scar on her left breast caused by a burn and several small scars on the under side of her right jaw.

REGISTRATION NO. 19
(Vol. 1, p. 17-18)

Mary Lansdale   24 March 1806

John Watts of Alexandria certifies that Mary Lansdale was born free in Charles County, Maryland. Lansdale gave him power of attorney to receive 100 pounds Maryland currency left her by John B. Turner, Esq., Clerk of Charles County. She has received that amount from the executor of Turner's estate.

Mary is a bright mulatto about 22 years old, slender made, and 5 feet 5¼ inches tall. She has a large scar on the under side of her right elbow caused by a burn and has straight black hair.

REGISTRATION NO. 20
(Vol. 1, pp. 18-19)

Negro Sylvia   25 March 1806

Copy of a bill of sale.

John Hubball, for 45 pounds paid to him by Aaron Hewes, sells to Hewes a Negro woman named Sylvia, aged 34, to serve a term of seven years dating from 2 December 1796, after which she is to be free. (23 Aug. 1796)

Sylvia is an African-born woman, 36 years old, and is 5 feet 1 inch tall. She has large lips and a scar on her upper lip.

REGISTRATION NO. 21
(Vol. 1, pp. 19-20)

Betty Handless   21 August 1809

Benjamin Baden certifies that he has known Betty Handless for at least ten years and that during that time she passed as a free woman and he believes that she is a free woman.

William Rhodes certifies that he has known Handless for a number of years and also her mother Betty Cole, both of whom he believes were born free in Fairfax County.

Handless is a straight, well made woman, 5 feet 7½ inches tall, of a tawny color, and is about 53 years old. She has had the little finger on her right hand sprained and has a small lump on her left hand caused by one of the sinews having been drawn.

REGISTRATION NO. 22
(Vol. 1, p. 20-21)

Negro James   24 August 1809

Copy of a manumission from Loudoun County.

John Wren frees Negro man James, aged 24, when he reaches age 31, which will be 1 August 1798. (15 Jan. 1791).

Negro James is about 45 years old, 5 feet 6¼ inches tall, of a tawny color, and has a bald head.

REGISTRATION NO. 23
(Vol. 1, pp. 21-23)

Kitty Jackson   20 December 1810

Copy of a manumission from Prince William County.

Thomas Jacob of Dumfries, Virginia, manumits mulatto woman slave, Kitty, and her child, George, together with all future increase of Kitty. (31 Dec. 1799)

Copy of Registration No. 30 from Prince William County.

This is to certify that a dark mulatto named Kitty, alias Kitty Jackson, was registered on 6th July last. Kitty is about 5 feet 4½ inches tall, 23 years old, and was freed by Thomas Jacob. She has a remarkable scar on the outside of her right arm, a very large round scar on her left arm caused by inoculation for smallpox, also two large pits of the smallpox near the same. (10 Aug. 1804)

REGISTRATION NO. 24
(Vol. 1, p. 23)

William Ennis   15 September 1814

Copy of a registration from Charles County, Maryland.

William Ennis is a bright mulatto man, about 26 years of age, 5 feet 10½ inches tall, well made, with a scar on his lower lip and chin and one on his forehead. He is a free born person, and was born and raised in New Port Parish in Charles County. (15 Sept. 1814).

REGISTRATION NO. 25
(Vol. 1, p. 24)

John Cole   29 May 1815

Copy of registration No. 45 from Prince William County.

John Cole a free black man, and the son of Katy Cole, a free black woman. He is 33 years old, about 5 feet 6 inches tall, with a scar on his right cheek a little below the top of the ear. The end of his left thumb has been cut off. (24 Mar. 1806).

REGISTRATION NO. 26
(Vol. 1, pp. 24-25)

Violett Day   29 May 1815

Copy of Registration No. 28 from Prince William County.

On 14 November 1803 a free Negro named Violett Day was registered according to law. Violett is black, about 5 feet tall, 16 years old, and was ordered to be bound by the Overseers of the Poor on 7 April 1795 to Scarlett Madden. She has a scar on the outside of her left arm nearly half way between her elbow and wrist, and one on her right arm near the wrist. (10 Aug. 1804)

REGISTRATION NO. 27
(Vol. 1, p. 25)

Negro Elick   27 May 1815

Copy of a registration from Calvert County, Maryland.

Negro Elick is about 5 feet 7 inches tall, of a black complexion, with a scar across his knee. He was freed by the will of Peter Hellen late of Calvert County. (3 Jan. 1814).

REGISTRATION NO. 28
(Vol. 1, p. 26)

Ann Fox   27 May 1815

Copy of a registration from Fairfax County.

Ann Fox was freed by the will of Benjamin Burton late of this county which was recorded 16 August 1814. Fox is a black woman about 40 years old, 5 feet 1½ inches tall, of pleasant countenance, and apt to smile when spoken to.

REGISTRATION NO. 29
(Vol. 1, p. 27)

Rachael Shorter and her children,   30 May 1815
Matilda, Ann, Belinda, Catharine,
John, and Barrett

Copy of registration No. 97, Washington County, District of Columbia.

M. H. Rozer certifies that Rachael Shorter and her children, Matilda, Ann, Belinda, Catharine, John and Barrett, obtained their freedom in the month of May, 1795. (30 Sept. 1807).

For the original recording, see D. C. Liber S No. 18, p. 219.

REGISTRATION NO. 30
(Vol. 1, pp. 27-28)

Katy Cole   11 June 1815

Copy of registration No. 61 from Prince William County.

Katy Cole is a free black woman and was registered on 22 May 1810. Cole is about 55 years old, 5 feet 2 inches tall. The top of her nose has been cut off. She was born free in Prince William County. (8 June 1815).

REGISTRATION NO. 31
(Vol. 1, p. 29)

Nelly Cole   11 June 1815

Copy of registration No. 69 from Prince William County.

Nelly Cole is a free black woman about 50 years old, 5 feet 2½ inches tall. She was born free in Prince William County. She has a remarkable burn on her right hand which has caused three of her fingers to grow crooked and a scar on her forehead caused by a cut (5 June 1815)

REGISTRATION NO. 32
(Vol. 1, p. 30)

Negro Hager   4 August 1815

Negro Hager is one of the children mentioned in the within[?] certificate. He was 24 years old on 1 Jan. last, is 5 feet 2 3/4 inches tall, of a "yellow complexion," with a scar caused by a burn on his right shoulder and two scars on his right breast.

REGISTRATION NO. 33
(Vol. 1, p. 30)

Negro Celia   16 October 1815

Robert Brocket[t] of Alexandria swears that between fifteen and twenty years ago he sold to Amos Fisher of Alexandria, a Negro girl named Celia, and that he agreed with Fisher that she should be free at the age of 28 years. She has arrived at that age and is entitled to her freedom. (15 Mar. 1815).

REGISTRATION NO. 34
(Vol. 1, p. 31)

Negro Jacob   Will dated 8 January 1816
Negro Priscilla

Copy of an extract from a will from Northampton County.

The will of Thomas Davis, proved 8 January 1816, provided that Jacob and Priscilla should have their freedom and $30 each, provided there is a sufficiency to pay such legacy.

REGISTRATION NO. 35
(Vol. 1, pp. 31-32)

Ling[?] Nicholls, Henry Nicholls,   23 July 1816
Rachael Nicholls, Mary Nicholls, Asa Nicholls,
George Nicholls, Elizabeth Nicholls,
Kitty Nicholls, Grace Nicholls,
John Ellison Nicholls, Jane (Jenny) Nicholls,
John Nicholls

Copy of a registration from Prince George's County, Maryland.

Ann Nicholls swears that the following are her children: Henry Nicholls, Rachael Nicholls, Mary Nicholls, Asa Nicholls, George Nicholls, Elizabeth Nicholls and Kitty Nicholls. She also swears that Grace Nicholls is the daughter of Mary Nicholls and that John Ellison Nicholls is supposed to be the son of the aforesaid Grace Nicholls, and that Jane Nicholls and John Nicholls are the children of the aforesaid Mary Nicholls.

Ling[?] Nicholls, son of Ann Nicholls, was born May 2, 1775
Henry Nicholls was born August 20, 1777
Grace Nicholls was born August 20, 1776
Rachael Nicholls was born February 18, 1780
Mary Nicholls was born May 21, 1782
Asa Nicholls was born February 1785
John Nicholls was born September 15, 1802
John Nicholls was born March 11, 1802, son of Grace Nicholls
Elizabeth Nicholls, daughter of Ann Nicholls, was born August 14, 1797
Kitty Nicholls was born September 17, 1799
George Nicholls was born March 30, 1789
Jenny Nicholls was born December 10, 1800

(Recorded 2 May 1804. See Liber JRM No. 10, p. 173, Prince George's County Land Records)

REGISTRATION NO. 36
(Vol. 1, p. 32)

Negro Jeffery or Jesse   3 October 1816

Copy of a registration from Frederick County.

Jeffery or Jesse, is a Negro man about 55 years old, 5 feet 10½ inches tall, stout and well made. He was freed by Alexander Henderson of Dumfries in Prince William County by deed dated 6 December 1803 and recorded in Frederick County Court on 6 January 1815.

REGISTRATION NO. 37
(Vol. 1, p. 33)

Henry Morris   11 June 1817

Copy of a document from Prince William County.

At the Court of Quarterly Sessions, Prince William County, 2 June 1817, Henry Morris, a "man of colour" was apprehended and brought before the Court on suspicion of his being a runaway slave. Upon proof of his being a free man, though not an inhabitant of the commonwealth, the Court was of the opinion that he be discharged upon payment of his prison fees, which was accordingly done.

REGISTRATION NO. 38
(Vol. 1, p. 34)

Thomas Cooper, John Cooper, Jr.,   1 August 1817
Edward Cooper, William Cooper,
Edward Younger, Judy Willis,
and Elizabeth Cooper

Copy of an extract from a Deed Book, Prince George's County, Maryland.

At the request of Overton Carr the following manumissions were recorded 9 April 1795:

I hereby emancipate Thomas Cooper, John Cooper, Jr., Edward Cooper, William Cooper, Edward Younger, Judy Willis, and Elizabeth Cooper and their future increase forever. (From Liber JRM No. 3, pp. 434-435)

REGISTRATION NO. 39
(Vol. 1, pp. 35-36)

Negroes Roby, Clem, Anne,   [1817?]
Mordecai, Patty and her two
children, Lilly and her two
children, Frederick, Joe, Mayor,
Isaac, Cloe, Priss, Juda, Rachel,
Charity, Elisha, Betty and her

children, Jenny and her children,
and Sarah

Will of Ann Hutchens of Alexandria.

After her debts and burial expenses are paid, Ann Hutchens frees her "black people," as follows: Toby, Clem, Anne, Mordecai, Patty and her children, Lilly and her two children; and Frederick shall be bound to a trade until he is 21 years old, at which time he shall be free. And she bequeaths to her daughter, Ann Hutchens all title in all the her personal estate, but if she should she die before reaching age 21, all the black people hereafter named shall be free: Joe, Mayor, Isaac, Cloe, Priss, Juda, Rachel, Charity, Elisha, Betty and her children, Jenny and her children, and Sarah. She appoints her brother, Joseph Richardson as her executor and requests that he give her daughter Ann a good education and take Ann to live with him. (Signed 8 July 1814; proved in court 15 Oct. 1814).

REGISTRATION NO. 40
(Vol. 1, pp. 36-38)

Will of Ann Hutchens of Alexandria.

A duplicate of the document in No. 39.

REGISTRATION NO. 41
(Vol. 1, p. 38)

Negro Hannah [1817?]

Copy of a manumission from Fairfax County.

John Wren manumits Hannah, a slave of "yellowish complexion," and her future increase. (Signed 31 Dec. 1801; recorded in Fairfax County Court, 19 June 1815).

REGISTRATION NO. 42
(Vol. 1, p. 39)

Negro Isaac 15 October 1817

Copy of a registration from Washington County, District of Columbia.

James V. Ball manumits his Negro man Isaac, "of sound limbs and pale[?] constitution," aged about 36, who has served him with "great fidelity through periods and difficulties, and by his good conduct has entitled himself to the enjoyment of the blessings of liberty." (Signed at City of New York, 16 Nov. 1816. Recorded in Liber AN 38, folio 393 of Washington County; also apparently recorded in the Clinton Book of Manumission, 18 Dec. 1816, p. 6)

REGISTRATION NO. 43
(Vol. 1, p. 40)

Eleazer Buckner Barnett Ryley 26 October 1818

Copy of a certificate from Winchester.

Milly is a mulatto woman aged about 27 who was freed by Abraham Neill in a deed of emancipation dated 38 June 1799 and recorded in the County Court of Frederick.

Eleazer Buckner Barnett is a small mulatto girl who was 4 years old on 27 February last. She is the daughter of the above named Milly. (2 June 1800.)

The above named Eleazer Buckner Barnett, now Ryley since her marriage, is a bright mulatto aged 21 years and 8 months. She is 5 feet 5¼ inches tall.

REGISTRATION NO. 44
(Vol. 1, pp. 41-42)

Harriet Jane Harris 13 November 1818

Copy of a document from Fairfax County.

Eli[as P.] Legg of Alexandria County, District of Columbia, swears that Harriet Jane Harris, a mulatto woman, is free. She served him in the past, but purchased the residue of her time. Legg releases her and her future increase from all claims. Harris has expressed her desire to go to the western country where her husband resides, and she is at full liberty to do so. (12 Nov. 1818)

Attached is a receipt signed by Eli Legg acknowledging that he has received $100 from Harriet Jane Harris for the residue of her term of service and that she is free. (9 Nov. 1818)

Harris is a bright mulatto and is 5 feet 2½ inches tall.

REGISTRATION NO. 45
(Vol. 1, p. 42)

Thomas Braddock   1 June 1819

Thomas Braddock is a free mulatto, about 34 years old, about 5 feet 11 inches tall, with a yellow complexion, and black bushy hair. He has a large scar on his left hand and has lost a small piece of his right ear.

REGISTRATION NO. 46
(Vol. 1, p. 43)

John Duff   23 August 1819

Margaret Sargent swears that John Duff, a mulatto man about 28 years old, was born free. She states that she knows his father and mother who are free and who lived in Alexandria when Duff was born. Duff was raised in Alexandria.

John Duff is a bright mulatto, about 28 years old, five feet 10½ inches tall, and has hazel eyes.

REGISTRATION NO. 47
(Vol. 1, p. 44)

William Pipsico   25 September 1819

John Pipsico is a free mulatto man and an old resident of Alexandria. He swears that his son, William Pipsico, who is also a mulatto man and is 21 years old, was free born in Fairfax County. William "is now at liberty to travel where his business may Call him, he behaving himself in an Orderly Manner." (24 Sept. 1819)

William is a bright mulatto man, about 21 years old, 5 feet 8½ inches tall, with black eyes, and short curly hair.

REGISTRATION NO. 48
(Vol. 1, pp. 45-46)

Mary Davis   23 October 1819
Sarah James Davis

The Overseers of the Poor of Alexandria County bound Mary Davis, aged 6, as an apprentice to Amos Alexander and Ann his wife in September of 1800.

Amos Alexander certifies that Mary, a bright mulatto of middle size, was bound to him and that she served out her term in a proper manner. He states that he gave her a certificate of her freedom, but she claims that it has been stolen from her. She was free born in Alexandria; her mother was a white woman by the name of "Monacai" [Monica] Davis. (19 May 1818)

Davis is a bright mulatto girl, about 26 years old, and 5 feet 2½ inches tall. She has lost the little finger of her left hand and has a scar between her shoulders. At the same time her daughter, Sarah James, a bright mulatto girl between 2 and 3 years old, was also registered.

REGISTRATION NO. 49
(Vol. 1, p. 46)

Harriet Green Knight   18 December 1819

Harriet Knight, formerly Harriet Green, was manumitted by John Violett. She is a dark mulatto, about 19 years old, 5 feet 8 inches tall, and has light hazel eyes.

REGISTRATION NO. 50
(Vol. 1, p. 47)

Richard Hopes

20 March 1820

Richard Hopes is a dark mulatto man, about 48 years old, and 5 feet 4 inches tall.

REGISTRATION NO. 51
(Vol. 1, p. 47)

Catherine Pipsico

12 May 1820

Catherine Pipsico is a bright mulatto woman, 22 years old, with long black hair.

REGISTRATION NO. 52
(Vol. 1, p. 48)

Negro Letty
Negro Billy

11 July 1820

Negro Letty is a mulatto woman, about 28 years old, and 5 feet 1 inch tall. She was manumitted by Benoni Wheat and registered in Alexandria on 2 June 1820.

Copy of document from Fairfax County certifies that Letty is a mulatto woman, 22 years old, 5 feet 3 inches tall, and slender made. She was lately a slave belonging to George Washington, who by his will left Letty and her children to Martha Washington. Martha freed them by an instrument recorded in this court. (1 Jan. 1801).

Letty's children are: Billy, 4 years; Harry, 3 years; Nila, 3 months.

Billy is a mulatto man, 23 years old, 5 feet 6 inches tall, and has bushy hair. He has the image of a mermaid marked on his left arm. (11 July 1820).

This is a confusing entry. There appear to be two separate registrations. One for Negro Letty, manumitted by Wheat; and an entirely separate one for Negro Billy, a descendant of Negro Letty freed by Martha Washington. Negro Letty is listed in the index as being registered on page 48.

REGISTRATION NO. 53
(Vol. 1, p. 49)

Negro Nila

1 August 1820

Copy of document from Fairfax County.

Letty, a mulatto woman aged 22, and her children listed below, were willed by George Washington to Martha Washington who freed them in a document that is recorded in Fairfax County. Letty is 22 years old, 5 feet 3 inches tall, and slender made. (1 Jan. 1801)

Letty's children are: Billy, 4 years; Har[r]y, 3 years; Nila, 3 months.

Nila is a black woman aged 19 years and 9 months. She is 5 feet 2 inches tall.

See No. 52 directly above.

REGISTRATION NO. 54
(Vol. 1, p. 49-50)

Milly Davis and her children,
Patsey, Sarah, Jane, Eleanor
and William

12 September 1820

Milly Davis is a black woman, about 40 years old, and about 5 feet 1 inch tall. She was manumitted by Anthony Crease, Jr. Milly has five children: Patsey, Sarah, Jane, Eleanor, and William.

REGISTRATION NO. 55
(Vol. 1, p. 50)

Priscilla Pipsico

26 October 1820

Priscilla Pipsico is a very bright mulatto woman, about 25 years old, with black curly hair, and black eyes. She has a small scar on the left side of her underlip and is 5 feet 3 inches tall.

REGISTRATION NO. 56
(Vol. 1, p. 50)

James Wilson [ca. 26 October 1820]

James Wilson, a free black man, has produced evidence of his freedom and has given bond for his good behavior during his residence in Alexandria. Mayor Simms grants him permission and a license to remain in the Town of Alexandria during his good behavior. (6 Aug. 1812)

REGISTRATION NO. 57
(Vol. 1, p. 51)

Alice Fletcher
Mary Fletcher

2 May 1820

E. Brooke, Sr., certifies that Alice Fletcher is a bright mulatto woman, about 25 years old, who was born on the estate of Matthew Whiting, Esq., of Prince William County. Brooke, who is the executor of Whiting, states that her mother was a servant in the family of Whiting and was hired by him as a washer. She served him under indenture for several years but is a free woman born in Ireland. The aforesaid Alice Fletcher is the daughter of the woman who is named Polly Fletcher and she is free. (2 May 1820)

Statement of E. Brooke, Sr., executor of Matthew Whiting, Esq., as follows:

Mary Fletcher is a bright mulatto woman about 40 and was born on the estate of Matthew Whiting, Esq., of Prince William County. Her mother was a servant in the family of said Whiting, being hired by him as a washer. She served him under indentures several years as a free woman born in Ireland. Mary Fletcher is the daughter of that woman, named Polly Fletcher, and was born free and is entitled to a certificate of that fact. (2 May 1820)

REGISTRATION NO. 58
(Vol. 1, p. 52)

James Wilson, Sr., Alice Wilson
Henry Wilson, James Wilson, Jr.,
Mary Wilson

8 December 1820

The following Negroes have been registered: James Wilson is a black man, about 50 years old, 5 feet 5½ inches tall, with a scar on the back of his neck; Alice, wife of James, is a bright mulatto, about 25 years old, 5 feet 2 inches tall; and their 3 children: Henry, a dark mulatto, about 9 years old, with long hair and a scar on the left side of his chin caused by a "scault;" James, a dark mulatto, about 5 years old; and Mary, a dark mulatto about 14 months old.

REGISTRATION NO. 59
(Vol. 1, p. 52)

Mary Fletcher

8 December 1820

Mary Fletcher is a dark mulatto woman, about 40 years old, and 5 feet 2 inches tall.

REGISTRATION NO. 60
(Vol. 1, p. 53)

Negro Milly

13 December 1820

Charles Page certifies that Milly, a black woman, formerly the property of Mr. Adam Craig of Bladensburg, Maryland, is now free according to Craig's will. (30 June 1819).

Milly is 5 feet 2½ inches tall.

REGISTRATION NO. 61
(Vol. 1, p. 53)

Betsey Fletcher [ca. 13 December 1820]

E. Brooke, executor of Matthew Whiting, Esq., states that Betsey Fletcher, a bright mulatto woman about 45 years old, was born on the estate of Matthew Whiting of Prince William County. Her mother, Polly Fletcher, was a servant in Whiting's family, being hired as a washer, and was free after serving him under indentures for several years. She was born in Ireland. Betsey is her daughter and was born free. (2 May 1820)

REGISTRATION NO. 62
(Vol. 1, p. 54)

Betsey Fletcher

14 December 1820

Betsey Fletcher is a bright mulatto woman, 45 years old, 5 feet 2 inches tall, with a scar on her right wrist caused by a cut.

Undoubtedly the same person as the Betsey Fletcher registered in No. 61. There is a mistake in the numbering of the registrations.

REGISTRATION NO. 63
(Vol. 1, p. 54)

Phebe Marsh

[ca. 22 December 1820]

Copy of a document from Montgomery County, Maryland.

Phebe Marsh is a black woman, about 32 years old, and about 5 feet 2 1/8 inches tall. Her right arm is very much disfigured by a burn, and her right hand is very much twisted. She has tolerably high cheeks. Phebe Marsh obtained her freedom in the Montgomery County Court at its November 1791 term. (15 June 1811)

REGISTRATION NO. 64
(Vol. 1, p. 55)

Phebe Marsh

22 December 1820

Phebe Marsh is a black woman, about 41 years old, 5 feet 2 1/8 inches tall. Her right arm very much disfigured by a burn and her right hand very twisted. She has tolerably high cheeks.

A duplicate of No. 63.

REGISTRATION NO. 65
(Vol. 1, p. 55)

Anthony Minor

22 January 1821

Anthony Minor is a thick set black man, about 34 years old, and about 5 feet 4½ inches tall. He was manumitted by Jacob Hoffman.

REGISTRATION NO. 66
(Vol. 1, p. 55)

James Minor

22 January 1821

James Minor is a small black man, about 38 years old, and 5 feet 2¼ inches tall. He was manumitted by Jacob Hoffman.

REGISTRATION NO. 67
(Vol. 1, p. 56)

Blank

REGISTRATION NO. 68
(Vol. 1, p. 56)

Elizabeth Loudoun

29 January 1821

Elizabeth Loudoun is a black girl, about 23 years old, 5 feet 2 3/4 inches tall, with a long scar on the back of her right hand and a small scar on the middle finger of the same hand.

REGISTRATION NO. 69
(Vol. 1, p. 56)

George Loudoun   29 January 1821

George Loudoun is a black man, about 21 years old, and 5 feet 5½ inches tall.

REGISTRATION NO. 70
(Vol. 1, p. 56)

Frederick Loudoun, Nancy Loudoun,   29 January 1821
William Loudoun, Richard Loudoun

Frederick Loudoun is a black boy, about 22 years old, 5 feet 6½ inches tall, with a scar on his left hand above the upper joint of the forefinger. Nancy Loudoun is a black girl, about 16 years old, 5 feet 3 3/4 inches tall. William Loudoun is a black boy, about 14 years old, with a small scar on his left cheek. Richard Loudoun is a black boy, about 15 years old, with a scar on the inside of his right leg, a scar on his forehead, and one over his left eye.

REGISTRATION NO. 71
(Vol. 1, p. 57)

Daniel Dade   20 January 1821

Daniel Dade is a black man, 40 years old, 5 feet 6 1/8 inches tall, with a wen over his right eye in the hair.

REGISTRATION NO. 72
(Vol. 1, p. 57)

David Jarbour   2 February 1821

David Jarbour is a black man, about 33 years old, who has a slight scar on the forefinger of the right hand.

REGISTRATION NO. 73
(Vol. 1, p. 57-58)

Kitty Harris   8 February 1821

Susan Peade, wife of James Peade of Alexandria County, swears that she knew the mother of Kitty Harris who is a free colored woman. Her mother was a white woman who lived in Fairfax County near Occoquan, and Kitty was born free.

The clerk of the Court certifies that Kitty Harris is a bright mulatto, free born woman, 22 years old, 5 feet 3/4 inch tall, with black eyes, and long black hair. She has a small scar on her right cheek caused by the kick of a horse.

REGISTRATION NO. 74
(Vol. 1, p. 58)

John Taylor   27 March 1821

John Taylor is a black man, 21 years and 7 months old, 5 feet 8 inches tall, with a large scar over the left ear.

REGISTRATION NO. 75
(Vol. 1, p. 58)

Elin Fox   [29 May 1821]

Elin Fox is a black woman, 22 years old, and 5 feet 3½ inches tall.

REGISTRATION NO. 76
(Vol. 1, p. 58)

Catharine Turner   30 May 1821

Catharine Turner is a bright mulatto woman, aged about 24 years, with two scars on her right shoulder caused by a burn.

REGISTRATION NO. 77
(Vol. 1, p. 59)

Penny Turner Moody   [30 May 1821?]

Penny Turner, now Moody, is a bright mulatto, about 21 years old, 5 feet 2 inches tall, with long curly hair, and a small scar on the wrist of her right arm caused by a burn.

REGISTRATION NO. 78
(Vol. 1, p. 59)

Arthur Cooper				25 June 1821

Arthur Cooper is a free black man, about 33 years old, 5 feet 6 3/4 inches tall, with a scar on his forehead above the left eye, several scars on his breast and shoulders, and one on each wrist caused by bites.

REGISTRATION NO. 79
(Vol. 1, p. 59)

Robert Roderick				31 July 1821

Benjamin Baden swears that he has known Robert Roderick since 1803, and that he has always been reputed as free born and the son of a free woman of color named Betty Cole, alias Betty Roderick. (31 July 1821).

Roderick is 28 years old, 5 feet 7 3/4 inches tall, with a small scar on his forehead.

REGISTRATION NO. 80
(Vol. 1, p. 60)

Latitia Hepburn				22 August 1821

Latitia Hepburn is a bright mulatto, about 18 years old, 5 feet 4 inches tall, with long black hair.

REGISTRATION NO. 81
(Vol. 1, p. 60)

Negro Nan				28 August 1821

Copy of a registration from Calvert County, Maryland.

Negro Nan is about 48 years old, 5 feet 1 inch tall, has a black complexion, and has a scar on her right wrist caused by a burn. She was manumitted by Mordecai Smith on 7 May 1804. (12 July 1819)

Negro Nan is about 51 years old, 5 feet 1 inch tall, with a scar on her right wrist caused by a burn.

REGISTRATION NO. 82
(Vol. 1, p. 61)

Daniel Taylor				3 September 1821

Daniel Taylor was manumitted by Nancy Cole who purchased him from William Weemes. Taylor was 43 years old on 22 November 1820, is 5 feet 7 3/4 inches tall, and has lost the first joint of his thumb on the right hand.

REGISTRATION NO. 83
(Vol. 1, p. 61-62)

Washington Davis				14 September 1821

Copy of a document from Fauquier County.

Negro Washington was emancipated by the will of James Nelson dated 3 October 1811. (22 Feb. 1819)

Washington Davis is a bright mulatto man, about 25 years old, 5 feet 8½ inches tall, with a small flesh mole under his right ear and a scar on his left thumb caused by a cut. He has black eyes and thick curly hair.

REGISTRATION NO. 84
(Vol. 1, p. 63)

Linny and her children				22 September 1821
Ferdinand, Juliann, and Sally

Copy of an extract from the will of Rachael Wheeler filed in Fairfax County Court.

"Rachael" Wheeler gives to her husband, Ignatius Wheeler, the following Negroes: Scipio, Lem, Mial, Wat, Will, Little Sam, Luie, Linna, Henry, Vina, Priss, Anna and Margery, to serve him during his lifetime. It is Rachael's desire that they be clothed and entitled to their freedom as is also their due.

Jemima Jenkins appeared before a justice of the peace in Alexandria and swore that Linny was manumitted by "Rachel" Wheeler and that her children, Ferdinand, Juliann, and Sally, were born since the manumission.

REGISTRATION NO. 85
(Vol. 1, p. 63)

Linna and her children
Ferdinand, Juliann, and Sally

24 September 1821

Linna was manumitted by the will of Rachael Wheeler. She is 5 feet three-fourths inch tall and about 50 years old. She has three children: Ferdinand, aged about 19, is 5 feet 6 6/8 inches tall, with a scar on his right leg; Juliann, aged about 17, is 5 feet 3½ inches tall, and her left foot is scared by a burn; and Sally, aged about 12 years, is 5 feet one-half inch tall.

REGISTRATION NO. 86
(Vol. 1, pp. 63-64)

William Harris

[ca. 24 September 1821]

Copy of Registration No. 71 from Prince William County.

William Harris is a black man who was born free in Prince William County. Harris is about 21 years old, 5 feet 6 inches tall, with a scar under his chin and on his left cheek, a scar on the first joint of the forefinger of his left hand, a cut on his left foot, and a mole in the palm of his left hand. (2 June 1817)

The clerk of the Prince William County Court states that Harris, a free black boy about 18 or 19 years old, was bound to David Davis as an apprentice and that his master died last December. (8 Jan. 1815).

REGISTRATION NO. 87
(Vol. 1, p. 65)

George Berry

10 October 1821

George Berry is a black man, about 35 years old, 5 feet 6 inches tall, with a scar on his right wrist caused by a burn. He was formerly the property of Daniel McClean and Daniel [F.] Cawood and was manumitted by Daniel McClean and Isaac Robbins by a deed recorded in Liber H No. 2, folio 387.

REGISTRATION NO. 88
(Vol. 1, p. 65)

Henrietta Edwards

11 October 1821

Henrietta, alias Henny Edwards, is a bright mulatto woman, about 33 years old, and 5 feet 2 3/4 inches tall. She was manumitted by Archibald McClean.

REGISTRATION NO. 89a
(Vol. 1, p. 65)

William Armstrong Webster

16 October 1821

Copy of a registration from Prince William County.

Zachariah Ward swears that William Armstrong Webster, a free man of color, is the son of Daniel Webster and Lucy his mother, who are both free and reside at Occoquan Mills in Prince William County. William Armstead is about 22 or 23 years old. (28 Sept. 1821)

Webster is a bright mulatto, 23 years old, and 5 feet 7¼ inches tall. He was born free.

REGISTRATION NO. 89b
(Vol. 1, p. 66)

Negro Sylvia

12 November 1821

Negro Sylvia is a mulatto woman, about 30 years old, 5 feet 3¼ inches tall, with long black hair. She was manumitted by Benoni Wheat by deed recorded in Liber L No. 2, folio 99.

REGISTRATION NO. 90
(Vol. 1, p. 66)

Negro Anthony

26 November 1821

Negro Anthony is a free black man, about 40 years old, 5 feet 4 1/8 inches tall, with short curly hair, and a large scar on the right side of his head. He was manumitted by Hugh Smith by deed recorded in Liber L No. 2, folio 66.

REGISTRATION NO. 91
(Vol. 1, p. 66)

Tristram H. Garner

13 December 1821

Tristram H. Garner is a mulatto man, 30 years old, 5 feet 8½ inches tall, with a slight scar on his right temple, and another over his right eye. He was manumitted by Samuel B. Larmour and John Adam by deed dated 11 December 1821 that is recorded in Liber L, folio 157.

REGISTRATION NO. 92
(Vol. 1, p. 66)

Ann Jones

13 December 1821

Ann Jones is a free black woman, about 30 years old, 5 feet 2 3/4 inches tall, with a scar on her chin and another over her right eye. She was manumitted by Oliver Jones by deed dated 6 September 1821, recorded in Liber L, folio 158.

REGISTRATION NO. 93
(Vol. 1, p. 66)

Jemima Hamilton

20 December 1821

Jemima Hamilton, a black woman about 44 years old and 5 feet 6½ inches tall, was manumitted by James McGuire by deed dated 19 December 1821 and recorded in Liber L No. 2, folio 165.

Hamilton is 43 years old and 5 feet 6 3/4 inches tall.

REGISTRATION NO. 94
(Vol. 1, p. 94*)

Sincai[?] Lee

22 December 1821

Negro Sincai[?] Lee is about 40 years old, 5 feet 3½ inches tall, with scars on the four fingers of her left hand and marks from smallpox. She was manumitted by Richard Libby by deed dated 8 October 1814 recorded in Liber E No. 2, folio 295.

The page numbering gets mixed up at this point, and for a few pages the clerk uses the number of the registration on the page as the number for the page.

REGISTRATION NO. 95
(Vol. 1, p. 94*)

Negro Lydia

28 December 1821

Lydia is a bright mulatto woman, about 24 years old, 5 feet 1 3/4 inches tall. She was manumitted by David Burke and Aquilla Lockwood.

See note to No. 94.

REGISTRATION NO. 96
(Vol. 1, pp. 94-96)

Sarah Moore

12 January 1822

Copies of several documents from Baltimore County, Maryland, are entered to prove Sarah Moore's freedom.

Indenture signed 5 September 1800: Anne Moore, a mulatto woman aged 16, binds herself as a servant to William Walton for a term of six years.

Richard [H.] Litle of Alexandria swears that he is well acquainted with Sarah Moore who lived in his family from the spring or summer of 1815 until last spring, a period of nearly six years, and that he believes from circumstances and from papers he has seen that she is free. Her mother, whose name was Ann Moore, was bound to William Walton of Baltimore for six years. (11 Jan. 1822)

Sarah Moore, a colored girl who was 18 years old last October, is 5 feet 6¼ inches tall, and has a very faint scar on the back of her right hand caused by a burn.

REGISTRATION NO. 97
(Vol. 1, p. 96)

Negro Wesley   12 February 1822

Negro Wesley is a colored man, about 30 years old, and 5 feet 8 inches tall. He was manumitted by the Administrators of the late Anthony Crease, deceased, by deed recorded in Liber L No. 2, folio 192.

REGISTRATION NO. 98
(Vol. 1, p. 96-97)

Charles Pipsico   11 March 1822

John Pipsico, a free mulatto man and a resident of Alexandria, swears that Charles Pipsico, his son, who is also a mulatto, aged 21 years, was born free in Fairfax County and "is now at liberty to travel where his business may call him: he behaving himself in an orderly manner." (11 Mar. 1822)

Charles Pipsico is a free born mulatto man, 21 years of age, 5 feet 6½ inches tall, with a scar on the left side of his head and long black hair. (11 Mar. 1822)

REGISTRATION NO. 99
(Vol. 1, p. 97)

Negro Ben   21 March 1822

Negro Ben is a black man, 5 feet 8 inches tall, who was manumitted by James Lawrason by deed recorded in Liber L No. 2, folio 252.

REGISTRATION NO. 100
(Vol. 1, p. 97)

William Soloman   2 April 1822

William Soloman is about 30 years old, 5 feet 10 inches tall, of a very black complexion, with a scar on his right arm. He was freed by Christopher Frye by deed recorded Liber L No. 2, folio 18.

REGISTRATION NO. 101
(Vol. 1, [p. 98])

Patty Ransom   12 ApriL 1822

Patty Ransom is a Negro woman, 5 feet 2 3/4 inches tall, a thick person, with a dark complexion. She was manumitted 4 May 1815 by Sally Ransom by deed recorded in Liber AA, folio 422.

REGISTRATION NO. 102
(Vol. 1, [p. 98])

Robert Vaughn, Jr.   25 April 1822

Robert Vaughn is a dark mulatto man, about 22 years old, 5 feet 6½ inches tall, with a scar over his left eye. He was manumitted by his father, Robert Vaughn, as will appear by reference to Liber X[?], folio 178.

REGISTRATION NO. 103
(Vol. 1, p. 99)

Negro Henney [Brown?]   2 May 1822

Copy of a manumission from Fairfax County.

John West manumits Negro Henney, aged about 40 years. (2 June 1799)

Negro Henney is about 64 years old, 5 feet 3¼ inches tall, with a very black complexion, and is a "thick person." She was manumitted by John West on 2 June 1799 in Fairfax County.

See No. 104 directly below.

REGISTRATION NO. 104
(Vol. 1, p. 100)

Elizabeth Brown   2 May 1822

Polly Cole swears that she knows Elizabeth Brown and knows that she was born since 1799 or after the manumission of her mother, Negro Henney [Brown?]. (2 May 1822)

Negro Elizabeth is about 22 years old, 5 feet 7 inches tall, with a very black complexion. She was born free.

REGISTRATION NO. 105
(Vol. 1, p. 100)

Fanny Parker   20 May 1822

Fanny Parker is a black girl, 11 years and 2 months old, and 4 feet 8½ inches tall. She is the daughter of George and Jenny Parker.

REGISTRATION NO. 106
(Vol. 1, pp. 101-102)

Hannah Burk   8 June 1822

A copy of court proceedings in the Fairfax County Court, March 1818 term.

Hannah Burk, a pauper, against William P. Richardson, case of trespass, assault and battery and false imprisonment. The jury finds for the plaintiff and assesses her damages to two dollars. And "it is considered by the Court that the said Plaintiff recover her freedom of the said Defendant, and her damages aforesaid by the Jurors" and that her court costs are expended.

No detail is given as to the suit, but Burk was represented by attorney Thomson F. Mason.

Hannah Burk is a black girl, 5 feet 4 inches tall, who obtained her freedom by a suit in the Fairfax County Court against William P. Richardson.

See No. 126 in Book 2 of the registrations for Fairfax County. Hannah Burke is a black woman about 50 years old who was formerly the property of Joseph Riddle, who sold her to William P. Richardson for a term of years to expire in 1816. (Dated 18 August 1834). Donald Sweig (ed.), Registrations of Free Negroes . . . Fairfax County, Virginia *(Fairfax, Virginia, 1977), p. 60. Hereinafter cited as Sweig.*

REGISTRATION NO. 107
(Vol. 1, pp. 102-103)

Sarah Ann Piper Brown   12 June 1822

G. W. West, Charles L. Broadwater, and William Minor certify that Sarah Ann Piper (alias Brown), Milly Piper and Peggy Piper, the daughters of Peggy, were free born. (10 July 1821).

R[obert] J. Taylor states that he has always understood that the within family was free born. He recovered the freedom of Kiezey Piper one of the family and at the trial there was full proof of their descent from a white woman. (June 12, 1822)

Sarah Ann Brown is a light mulatto woman who is 5 feet 7½ inches tall. She was born free.

REGISTRATION NO. 108
(Vol. 1, p. 103)

Milly Payne   12 June 1822

Milly Payne is a dark mulatto woman, about 27 years old, with a tawny complexion, and is 5 feet 4½ inches tall. She was born free.

REGISTRATION NO. 109
(Vol. 1, p. 103)

Margaret Piper Wright   12 June 1822

Margaret Piper (alias Wright) is a bright mulatto woman, nearly 23 years old, 5 feet 4 3/4 inches tall, of a light complexion, with a scar on her right cheek. She was born free.

REGISTRATION NO. 110
(Vol. 1, p. 104)

Sarah Campbell   22 March 1823

Sarah Campbell is a free black woman, about 50 years old, 5 feet 4¼ inches tall, of a very black complexion, with a scar on the back of her right hand more than an inch long. She was manumitted by John Addison, Jr. A certificate of her freedom signed by Mayor George Taylor is dated 13 May 1801 and is filed in the Circuit Court for Alexandria.

REGISTRATION NO. 111
(Vol. 1, p. 104-106)

Rebecca Jarbo Dover, Milly Dover Julius,   15 and 16 May 1823
Samuel Dover, Jr., Lydia Dover,
Celia Dover

James Harris swears that he has known Samuel Dover and Betty his wife for twenty-two years and understood that they were born free. About sixteen years ago he hired their daughter, Cloe Dover, who continued with him five years; and then he hired another daughter, Milly, who lived with him two or three years; and he understands that they are a family of free people and that Rebecca Jarbo is the daughter of Samuel and Betty Dover and that she is free. (21 Mar. 1823)

Joseph Rinker swears that he has known Samuel and Betty Dover and their children for over twenty years and that they have passed for free and he believes them to be free and that Rebecca Jarbo is their daughter. (22 Mar. 1823)

Ezra Kinsey swears that he has known Samuel Dover and Betty, his wife, and their children for over twenty years and they have always been considered free and that Rebecca Dover is their daughter and the wife of David Jarbo. (24 Mar. 1813)

Rebecca Jarbo, late Rebecca Dover, is a black woman, 5 feet 2¼ inches tall, and about 28 years old. (15 May 1823)

Milly Julius, late Milly Dover, is a dark brown woman about 24 years old, 5 feet 3¼ inches tall, with a scar on the left side of her neck. (15 May 1823)

Ezra Kinsey swears that Lydia, Celia and Sam are the children of Samuel and Betty Dover and are free as are their parents. Samuel and Lydia and Celia Dover are brother and sisters of Rebecca Dover. (16 May 1823)

Samuel Dover is 22 years old, 5 feet 7¼ inches tall, of a rather brown color, with a scar on the right side of his face near the mouth. Lydia Dover is 20 years old and of a rather bright color. Celia Dove is 18 years old, of a brown color, and 5 feet 1½ inches high. (16 May 1823)

REGISTRATION NO. 112a
(Vol. 1, pp. 106-107)

Negro Cloe   [ca. 2 June 1823]

Copy of a manumission from Fairfax County.

A manumission from William Bushbey of Fairfax discharged from bondage his slaves on the following terms and conditions: Mary, now aged 25, to go free immediately; Milly, aged 27, to be free in 5 years; Cloe, aged 21, to be free in 7 years; David, now 13, to be free in 12 years; Ned, aged 12, to be free in 13 years; Nancy, aged 8, to be free in 17 years; George, aged 5, to be free in 20 years; Betty, aged 2, to be free in 23 years; and Molly, aged 1, to be free in 24 years. (20 Sept. 1790)

REGISTRATION NO. 112b
(Vol. 1, p. 107)

Negro Rebecca, daughter [ca. 2 June 1823]
of Negro Cloe

Rebecca was aged 24 on 12 March 1823, is 5 feet 4½ inches tall, of a thick form, with a black complexion, thick lips, and several small scars about her body caused by burns. (12 Mar. 1823)

Both Cloe and Rebecca are numbered as Registration 112.

REGISTRATION NO. 113
(Vol. 1, p. 107)

Negro Ruthy, daughter [ca. 2 June 1823]
of Negro Cloe

Ruthy was aged 16 years on 25 August 1822, and is 5 feet 2 inches tall, of a black complexion. She is a thick person with a small scar caused by a burn on her left wrist.

REGISTRATION NO. 114
(Vol. 1, p. 107)

Negro Juliann, daughter 2 June 1823
of Negro Cloe

Juliann was 15 years old on 14 February 1822 and is 5 feet 2½ inches tall. She is a thick person, has a black complexion, and has a burn on the left side of her neck.

REGISTRATION NO. 115
(Vol. 1, p. 107)

Nancy Denty 13 August 1823

Nancy Denty is a free black woman who was manumitted by T. M. A. Vanhavre by an indenture dated 4 June 1803. She is 21 years old, with a scar on her forehead caused by a cut and another on her breast from a burn. Denty is 5 feet 1½ inches tall and has a dark complexion.

REGISTRATION NO. 116
(Vol. 1, p. 107)

Milly Middleton 14 August 1823

Milly Middleton is 29 years old, 5 feet 5 3/4 inches tall, with a scar on the right side of her forehead in her hair. She was manumitted by Letty Minor by deed dated 20 December 1819.

REGISTRATION NO. 117
(Vol. 1, p. 108)

Linney Simpson 19 August 1823

Linney [or "Sinney"?] Simpson is a mulatto woman about 23 years old, 5 feet 1 inch tall, with a scar on her right cheek caused by a rising. She was born free.

REGISTRATION NO. 118
(Vol. 1, p. 108)

Henry Burns 30 August 1823

Henry Burns is a free man of color, 35 years old, 5 feet 8½ inches tall, with a bald head, of a brown complexion, with hazel eyes, and a scar on the inside of his left leg below the calf.

Bryant Johnson, a free white citizen of Alexandria, swears that Henry Burns was born free of a white mother. (30 Aug. 1823)

REGISTRATION NO. 119
(Vol. 1, pp. 108-109)

George Cook 17 September 1823

James Lawras[on] swears that George Cook, a mulatto man about 40 years of age, was sold by Benjamin Dulany to Henry O. Riley and by Riley to William Goddard for a term of ten years, which term has expired. George had in his possession papers which show these facts, but which were lost or mislaid a few days ago in the Mayor's office. Lawrason states that he has seen the papers in the possession of the Mayor and proved before him George Cook's title to his freedom. (17 Sept. 1823)

George Cook is about 40 years old, 6 feet 1 inch tall, with a scar above and in his left eyebrow.

REGISTRATION NO. 120
(Vol. 1, p. 109)

Mary Ann Stoutely

7 September 1823

Negro Mary, alias Mary Ann Stoutely, is about 53 years old, 5 feet 2 inches tall, and of a dark complexion. She has lost the use of her left eye and has a white circle around the pupil of the right eye. She was sold by Jamieson & Anderson about 1791 for the term of ten years, which term is over as appears by a certificate signed by Andrew Jamieson, one of the members of the firm.

REGISTRATION NO. 121
(Vol. 1, pp. 109-110)

Negro Nace, alias
Ignatius Gant

27 October 1823

Negro Nace, alias Ignatius Gant, is 28 or 30 years old, has a dark complexion, about 5 feet 6½ inches tall, with a scar on his left thigh. He was sold by Frances Swann, Administratrix of William T. Swann, to Thomas H. Howland on 29 June 1821 to serve until 12 February 1823. That term has expired and he is entitled to his freedom.

REGISTRATION NO. 122
(Vol. 1, p. 110)

Mary Morgan Reeler

9 November 1823

Esther Halley affirms that she knows Mary Morgan, now Mary Reeler, wife of Samuel Reeler, and that she is the daughter of William and Elizabeth Morgan, free people of color, and that she has known Mary since her childhood and believes that she was born free. Mary Reeler is 5 feet 5 inches tall, 28 years old, and a bright mulatto.

REGISTRATION NO. 123
(Vol. 1, p. 111)

Thomas Julius

25 November 1823

Thomas Julius is a free man of color by birth, aged 25, with thick lips, short, curly hair, a scar on his forehead between his eyes and of a dark complexion. His head is thinner at the top than at the bottom and he is 5 feet 8 inches tall.

REGISTRATION NO. 124
(Vol. 1, p. 111)

Araminta Webster

6 December 1823

Araminta Webster was manumitted by Maria D. Dangerfield. She is a dark mulatto, about 39 years old, 5 feet 3¼ inches tall, and is a large person.

REGISTRATION NO. 125
(Vol. 1, p. 111)

Simon Tate, Sr.

29 January 1824

Simon Tate is a free black man free by birth, and the son of Nanny Tate, a free woman of color, as appears by the certificate of the clerk of Westmoreland County. He is 5 feet 6 1/8 inches tall, 29 years old, with a scar on the cheek under his left eye, and has a high forehead.

REGISTRATION NO. 126
(Vol. 1, pp. 111-112)

William Carmichael

7 May 1824

Copy of a manumission from Westmoreland County.

Henry Toler of Westmoreland County manumits William and Richard, two Negro boys formerly belonging to Winifred Dobyn, deceased, of Richmond County. William is to be free from 1 January 1822 and Richard is to be free from 1 January 1825. (26 Apr. 1812)

William Carmichael is a dark mulatto, about 32 years old, and 5 feet 5 3/4 inches tall. He was manumitted by Henry Toler as appears by a copy of the record from Westmoreland County Court.

REGISTRATION NO. 127
(Vol. 1, p. 112)

William Evans   10 May 1824

William Evans is a mulatto man, free by birth, 41 years old, and 5 feet 9¼ inches tall.

REGISTRATION NO. 128
(Vol. 1, p. 113)

Negro Juliann   17 July 1824

Juliann is a mulatto woman, about 20 years old, 5 feet 4 3/4 inches tall, with her left foot scared by a burn. She is the daughter of Linna who was manumitted by the will of Rachel Wheeler of Fairfax County.

See No. 84 and No. 85 above.

REGISTRATION NO. 129
(Vol. 1, p. 113)

Maria Davis   24 May 1824

Maria Davis was 20 years old on 2 November 1823, is 5 feet 6¼ inches tall, with a scar on the right side of her nose immediately under her eye, and a scar on each wrist. She was manumitted by William Hepburn, now deceased.

REGISTRATION NO. 130
(Vol. 1, p. 113)

Jeremiah Davis   24 November 1824

Jeremiah Davis is a black man who was 23 years old on 16 October 1823. He is 5 feet 9½ inches tall, with a scar on the instep of his right foot. He was manumitted by the will of William Hepburn.

REGISTRATION NO. 131
(Vol. 1, p. 113)

Mary Jacob   27 May 1824

Mary Jacob is the daughter of Kitty Jackson, who was freed by the will of Thomas Jacob of Dumfries by deed 31 December 1799. Mary is about 22 years old, nearly white, and 5 feet 5 3/4 inches tall. She has long black hair, black eyes, a straight figure, and a scar on the right side of her chin.

REGISTRATION NO. 132
(Vol. 1, p. 114)

John Ebb   28 May 1824

Copy of a certificate from the Mayor of Alexandria.

Permission is granted to John Ebb, a free man of color, to reside within the limits of this corporation, he having complied with the law passed 20 January 1821. (1 July 1822)

Attached is a note signed by the Mayor: John Ebb came here from Boston several years back and was put in jail and advertised agreeably to law. No person claimed him as a slave so he was sold for a term of years. That term he has faithfully served out. He has never since been claimed by any person. John states that he was born free and "from every circumstance there is little or no doubt of this." He is therefore granted this license for his protection while he lives within the limits of this Corporation, only subjecting him to the lawful claims of his master or mistress or owner should there be any. (1 July 1822)

John Ebb is a man of brown complexion, 5 feet 4¼ inches tall, about 33 years old, with a scar on his right shoulder caused by a scald. (28 May 1824).

REGISTRATION NO. 133
(Vol. 1, p. 115)

Sina Roberts   9 June 1824

Sina Roberts is a free woman, about 43 years old, of a dark complexion, 5 feet 4 inches tall, with a small scar on her left wrist. She was manumitted by Daniel Dade on 14 May 1824 as will appear by a deed of manumission recorded in Liber N No. 2, folio 323.

REGISTRATION NO. 134
(Vol. 1, p. 115)

John Harriss   6 July 1824

John Harriss is about 29 years old, 5 feet 5¼ inches tall, has a dark complexion, and has a scar over his left eye. He was manumitted by Allan Macrae, as appears by a deed recorded in Liber N No. 2, folio 343.

REGISTRATION NO. 135
(Vol. 1, p. 115)

Negro Bet and children,   3 August 1824
Marcelena and Cincinnatus

Bet is a dark mulatto, about 27 years old, and 5 feet 4½ inches tall. She is scarred from smallpox and has a scar on her forehead over her right eye and a scar on her left arm above the elbow. She was manumitted by Eliza and Mary Dunlap, as will appear by deed recorded in Liber S, folio 288. Her two children are Marcelena, a dark mulatto girl about 12 years old, 4 feet 7½ inches tall, with the mark of two oysters on her left thigh; and Cincinnatus, a bright mulatto boy about 9 years old, with long hair, who is 3 feet 11 inches tall.

REGISTRATION NO. 136
(Vol. 1, p. 116)

Negro Janney   27 August 1824

Janney is a free woman of dark complexion, about 36 years old, and 5 feet tall. She was manumitted by Ambrose Rape[?] on 15 April 1823, as will appear by the deed recorded in Liber N No. 2, folio 315.

REGISTRATION NO. 137a
(Vol. 1, p. 116)

Negro Ann   31 August 1824

Ann is a bright mulatto, 34 years old, 5 feet 6½ inches tall, with high cheek bones. She was emancipated by Wilson Carey Selden, as appears by a deed of emancipation recorded in Loudoun County.

REGISTRATION NO. 137b
(Vol. 1, p. 117-118)

The following statement applies to registrations 137b, 138, and 139: Mary Ann, Lucy, Walter and Douglass Bennett.

William Bennett, a free man of color, of full age, swears that his three children are free. Mary Ann Bennett, about 26, of a bright complexion, about 5 feet 4½ inches tall, with no visible marks; Lucy Bennett, of a bright complexion, about 5 feet tall, aged 22 years, with no visible marks; and Walter Bennett, aged about 20, about 5 feet 8 inches tall, with a scar on his left cheek. These children are the children of his wife, Mary Bennett, who is a free woman of color, as will appear by records from the court of Fairfax County, a copy of which was produced. She was free before the children were born, all of whom were born in Alexandria. In addition, Douglass Bennett, a boy of about 8 years old, about 4 feet 4 inches tall, of a bright complexion, is the son of his above named daughter, Mary Ann Bennett, and was born free in Alexandria. (19 Oct. 1824)

Susan Brown, of full age, swears that she knows that the above named Mary Ann Bennett, Lucy Bennett, and Walter Bennett, are the children of Mary Bennett, a free woman of color, and that they were born free in Alexandria. Also that Douglass Bennett is the son of Mary Ann Bennett, a free woman of color, and was also born in Alexandria. (19 Oct. 1824)

REGISTRATION NO. 137b
(Vol. 1, p. 118)

Mary Ann Bennett
Douglass Bennett

19 October 1824

Mary Ann Bennett, the daughter of William and Mary Bennett, is aged about 26, of a bright complexion, 5 feet 4½ inches tall, with no visible marks or scars. Douglass Bennett, her son, is about 8 years old, 4 feet 4 inches tall, and has a bright complexion.

REGISTRATION NO. 138
(Vol. 1, p. 118)

Lucy Bennett

19 October 1824

Lucy Bennett, daughter of William and Mary Bennett, has a bright complexion, is about 22 years old, 5 feet tall, with no visible scars or marks.

REGISTRATION NO. 139
(Vol. 1, p. 118)

Walter Bennett

19 October 1824

Walter Bennett, son of William and Mary Bennett, is about 20 years old, 5 feet 8 inches tall, with a scar on his left cheek.

REGISTRATION NO. 140
(Vol. 1, p. 118)

Clarissa Selden

3 November 1824

Clarissa Selden is about 29 years old, has a bright complexion, is 5 feet 1½ inches tall, with a "brown Plumb" on her right arm. She was born free.

REGISTRATION NO. 141
(Vol. l, p. 118)

Fanny Harris

3 November 1824

Fanny Harris is about 27 years old, has a bright complexion, is 5 feet 2 inches tall, with a mole on her upper lip. She was born free.

REGISTRATION NO. 142
(Vol. 1, p. 119)

Samuel Pipsicoe

4 November 1824

A justice of the peace certifies that Samuel Pipsicoe, a colored boy about 22 years old, is free and was born of free parents. (4 Nov. 1824)

Pipsicoe is a bright mulatto, about 22 years old, 5 feet 6 inches tall, with light eyes, long curly hair, and a scar on the left side of his upper lip and a scar on his left arm below his elbow.

REGISTRATION NO. 143
(Vol. 1, p. 119)

Catharine Ward

16 April 1825

Catharine Ward is a free woman of dark complexion, about 18 or 20 years old, 5 feet 3½ inches tall, with three small scars on her forehead. She was born free, as appears by the oaths of Thomas Whitington and Benjamin Baden on 4 March 1825.

REGISTRATION NO. 144
(Vol. 1, p. 119)

Harriet Bombay

2 May 1825

Harriet Bombay is a bright mulatto woman, has long hair and black eyes, and is 5 feet 8 inches tall. She was manumitted by John Whiting on 9 September 1822, as will appear by reference to Liber M No. 2, folio 262.

REGISTRATION NO. 145
(Vol. 1, p. 119)

Dennis Lewis [ca. 2 May 1825]

Dennis Lewis is a free man, about 40 years old, with a dark complexion, about 5 feet 7 inches tall, with a scar on his left leg. He was manumitted by Mordecai Miller, as appears by a deed of manumission recorded in Liber C[?] No. 2, folio 115.

REGISTRATION NO. 146
(Vol. 1, p. 120)

David Evans 23 May 1825

David Evans is a free man, as appears by affidavit of Mary Mason. He is about 26 years old, 5 feet 10 inches tall, of a straight form, with a dark complexion.

REGISTRATION NO. 147
(Vol. 1, p. 121)

Mary Ann Nutt 20 July 1825

Mary Ann Nutt is the daughter of Violet Nutt who, with her mother, was liberated by Ellis Price on 13 February 1801, as appears by deed recorded in Liber A, folio 88. She is 25 years old, 5 feet 3 inches tall, and of a dark complexion, not quite black. She has a large smallpox mark on her right arm, is of a stout[?] form and "not of a corpulent make."

REGISTRATION NO. 148
(Vol. 1, p. 122)

Charlotte Cole 20 July 1825

Charlotte Cole was 20 years old on 20 February 1825 and is about 5 feet 2 inches tall. She is of a copper color, has an open countenance, with no visible marks. She was born free and is the daughter of Nancy Cole, deceased, a woman of color who was also born free and has resided in Alexandria for upwards of eighteen years. These facts are certified by the affidavits of John Cole and Daniel Taylor dated 20 July 1825 and on file in this office.

REGISTRATION NO. 149
(Vol. 1, p. 123)

Rebecca Cole Clark 20 July 1825

Rebecca Clark, formerly Rebecca Cole, is the daughter of Nancy Cole, a free woman of color. Rebecca will be 24 on next 24 August, is of a bright dark colour, and about 5 feet 1 inch tall. She has resided in Alexandria more than eighteen years. These facts are certified by affidavits of John Cole and Daniel Taylor.

REGISTRATION NO. 150
(Vol. 1, p. 121)

Isaac Hall, Mary Hall, 29 August 1825
William Hall, John Hall
James Hall

Isaac Hall is 22 years old, about 5 feet 5 inches tall, of a dark complexion, with a small scar on the left side of his mouth and a scar on his left arm; Mary Hall is a bright mulatto 4 feet 11 inches tall, and 19 years old; William Hall is of rather dark complexion, about 5 feet tall and 18 years old; John Hall has a dark complexion, is about 5 feet 3 inches tall, and 15 years old; and James Hall is about 12 years old, about 4 feet 5 inches tall, of rather dark complexion, with two light spots on each side of his face. All of the above were born free and are the children of Letty Hall, a free woman of color, as appears by affidavit of Mrs. Margaret Thompson.

REGISTRATION NO. 151
(Vol. 1, p. 121)

Henry Lenox 10 September 1825

Henry Lenox is about 22 years old, 5 feet 6 inches tall, has a dark complexion, and has a small scar on his left eye. He was born free, as appears by affidavit of William Prout.

REGISTRATION NO. 152
(Vol. 1, p. 122)

William Lyles 20 September 1825

William Lyles is a dark mulatto man, about 30 years old, and 5 feet 11 inches tall. He was manumitted by Samuel Carson, as appears by a deed of manumission recorded in Liber O No. 2.

REGISTRATION NO. 153
(Vol. 1, p. 122)

Negro Fanny 3 October 1825

Fanny is about 60 years old, has a dark complexion, and is 5 feet 5 3/4 inches tall. She was manumitted by Charles Lewis, as appears by deed of manumission recorded in Liber C No. 2, folio 116.

REGISTRATION NO. 154
(Vol. 1, p. 122)

Francis William 3 October 1825

"Frances" [Francis] or Frank is about 22 years old, has a dark complexion, and is 5 feet 8½ inches tall. He was freed by Charles Lewis, as appears by the deed of manumission recorded in Liber C No. 2, folio 116.

See No. 452 on page 279 of Part III: Francis William manumitted by William Lewis.

REGISTRATION NO. 155
(Vol. 1, p. 122)

Benjamin Jones 10 October 1825

Benjamin Jones is about 21 years old, has a dark complexion, is 5 feet 7¼ inches tall, and is marked from the pox. He was born free, as appears by affidavit of Ezra Kinsey made before the mayor of Alexandria.

REGISTRATION NO. 156
(Vol. 1, p. 122)

Henry Colbert 17 November 1825

Henry Colbert is 25 years old, of a dark complexion, 5 feet 6 inches tall, with no visible marks. He was born free, as appears by affirmation of Mordicai Miller.

REGISTRATION NO. 157
(Vol. 1, p. 123)

Hanson Colbert 21 November 1825

Hanson Colbert is about 21 years old, of a dark complexion, 5 feet 6¼ inches tall, with a scar under his left jaw. He was born free, as appears by affirmation of Mordecai Miller.

REGISTRATION NO. 158
(Vol. 1, p. 123)

Henry Grayson 23 November 1825

Henry Grayson is a black boy, 5 years old, and 3 feet 2 inches tall. He was born free, as appears from the certificate of R. S. Chew, clerk of the Court of Hustings for Fredericksburg dated 12 August 1825.

REGISTRATION NO. 159
(Vol. 1, p. 123)

James Shields 9 January 1826

James Shields is a mulatto man, about 22 years old, and 5 feet 9 inches tall. He has a good countenance and a remarkably dark spot on his left arm below the elbow. He was born free, as appears by affidavit of Amos Alexander, Esq.

REGISTRATION NO. 160
(Vol. 1, p. 123)

Letty Edwards 12 January 1826

Letty Edwards is a mulatto girl, about 13 years old, 4 feet 10 inches tall, with no visible marks. She was born free, as appears by affidavit of Ann Adams.

REGISTRATION NO. 161
(Vol. 1, p. 123)

Daniel Edwards

12 January 1826

Daniel Edwards is a mulatto boy, about 10 years 6 months old, 4 feet 9 inches tall, with a dark mole on his left cheek. He was born free, as appears by affidavit of Ann Adams.

REGISTRATION NO. 162
(Vol. 1, p. 124)

Loudon Warner

25 February 1826

Loudon Warner is a free black man who will be about 21 years old on next 22 April. He is about 5 feet 8½ inches tall, is full-faced, with a good countenance, and has no visible marks. He was born free, as appears by affidavit of Amos Alexander.

REGISTRATION NO. 163
(Vol. 1, p. 124)

Elizabeth Hines

27 March 1826

Elizabeth Hines is a free woman of color, about 23 years old, 5 feet 2 inches tall, with a scar under her chin. She was born free, as appears by affidavit of Catherine McRea.

REGISTRATION NO. 164
(Vol. 1, p. 124)

Samuel Bee Wilson

30 March 1826

Samuel Bee Wilson is a man of color, about 19 years old, 5 feet 7¼ inches tall, with a small scar between his eyebrows. He was born free, as appears by affidavit of James Evans.

REGISTRATION NO. 165
(Vol. 1, p. 124)

Negro Maria

5 April 1826

Maria is about 28 years old, 5 feet 1½ inches tall, and much marked by smallpox. She was manumitted by John C. Herbert, as appears by deed recorded in Liber R, folio 333.

REGISTRATION NO. 166
(Vol. 1, p. 125)

Frances Cole

17 April 1826

Frances Cole is about 17 years old, 5 feet 5 inches tall, of a rather dark complexion, with a scar on her left arm below the elbow. She was free born, as appears by affidavits of Mary Ann Cole and Ann L. Morgan, two free woman of color.

REGISTRATION NO. 167
(Vol. 1, p. 125)

Mary Ann Cole

17 April 1826

Mary Ann Cole is about 30 years old, 5 feet 3 inches tall, of a dark complexion, with a mark on her left arm near the hand. She was born free, as appears by affidavit of Benoni E. Harrison.

REGISTRATION NO. 168
(Vol. 1, p. 125)

Ann L. Morgan

5 May 1826

Ann L. Morgan is about 26 years old, 5 feet 1½ inches tall, of a bright complexion, with a large scar on her neck just above her right shoulder, and a long scar on the middle finger of her left hand. She was born free, as appears by affidavit of Amos Alexander.

REGISTRATION NO. 169
(Vol. 1, p. 125)

John Pipsico

15 May 1826

John Pipsico is 37 years old, has a bright complexion, is 5 feet 7¼ inches tall, and has a mole on the right side of his nose. He was liberated by William Adams.

REGISTRATION NO. 170
(Vol. 1, p. 126)

Negro Frank

19 June 1826

Frank is about 50 years old, has a dark complexion, and is 5 feet 10¼ inches tall. He has a scar on his right cheek. The middle joint of the middle finger of his left hand is unusually large, and the little finger of the right hand is crooked. He was manumitted by Benjamin Waters, as appears by Liber N No. 2, folio 348.

REGISTRATION NO. 171
(Vol. 1, p. 126)

John West

28 June 1826

John West is a mulatto man, about 20 years old, of a dark complexion, 5 feet 8 inches tall, with no visible marks. He was born free, as appears by affidavit of Margaret Thompson.

REGISTRATION NO. 172
(Vol. 1, p. 126)

Archibald Beckley

12 July 1826

Archibald Beckley is a dark mulatto, about 25 years old, 5 feet 4 inches tall, with a large scar on the back of his right hand. He was born free, as appears by affidavit of Alexander Henderson.

REGISTRATION NO. 173
(Vol. 1, p. 126)

Negro Amy

14 July 1826

Negro Amy is about 56 years old, of a dark complexion, 5 feet 3 inches tall, with a scar on her left hand. She was purchased from John West by Thomas Preston to serve as a slave from 20 July 1803 until 20 July 1813, and then to be free, as appears by affidavit of Thomas Preston.

REGISTRATION NO. 174
(Vol. 1, p. 127)

Nancy Henson

29 August 1826

Nancy Henson is a mulatto woman, about 21 years old, 5 feet 3 inches tall, with a scar from a burn on the left side of her neck. She was born free, as appears by affidavit of James Harris.

REGISTRATION NO. 175
(Vol. 1, p. 127)

Martha Henson

29 August 1826

Martha Henson is a mulatto girl, aged about 19 years, 5 feet tall, with a wart on the upper side of her tongue. She was born free, as appears by affidavit of James Harris.

REGISTRATION NO. 176
(Vol. 1, p. 127)

Rebecca Henson

29 August 1826

Rebecca Henson is a dark mulatto girl, about 17 years old, 5 feet 1 inch tall, with several moles on the back of her left hand. She was born free, as appears by affidavit of James Harris.

REGISTRATION NO. 177
(Vol. 1, p. 127)

Samuel Evans

29 August 1826

Samuel Evans is a dark mulatto man, about 30 years old, and 5 feet 10 inches tall. He has a small stoppage in his speech but no visible marks. He was born free, as appears by affidavit of James Evans, a free man.

REGISTRATION NO. 178
(Vol. 1, p. 127)

Negro Delila

29 August 1826

Delila is about 29 years old, has a dark complexion, and is about 5 feet 1 3/4 inches tall. She was free born, as appears by affidavit of Kitty Shorter, a free woman.

REGISTRATION NO. 179
(Vol. 1, p. 128)

Eliza Fox

30 August 1826

Eliza Fox is about 24 years old, has a dark complexion, and is 5 feet 5½ inches tall. She was born free, as appears by affidavit of Ann Fulmore.

REGISTRATION NO. 180
(Vol. 1, p. 128)

Nancy Evans

4 September 1826

Nancy Evans is a dark mulatto woman, about 38 years old, and is 5 feet 5 inches tall. She was born free, as appears by affidavit of Dennis Johnston.

REGISTRATION NO. 181
(Vol. 1, p. 128)

Sally Evans

4 September 1826

Sally Evans is a bright mulatto woman, about 25 years old, and is 5 feet 3½ inches tall. She was born free, as appears by affidavit of Dennis Johnston.

REGISTRATION NO. 182
(Vol. 1, p. 128)

Philip Sumby

9 September 1826

Philip Sumby is a bright mulatto man, about 26 years old, 5 feet 7¼ inches tall, with a scar on his right arm near the elbow. He was born free, as appears by affidavit of Dougal McCachran.

REGISTRATION NO. 183
(Vol. 1, p. 128)

Fanny Sumby

9 September 1826

Fanny Sumby is a bright mulatto woman, about 26 years old, and 5 feet three-fourths inch tall. She was born free, as appears by affidavit of Matilda Jeminy.

REGISTRATION NO. 184
(Vol. 1, p. 128)

Betsy Botts

30 October 1826

Betsy Botts is a mulatto girl, about 16 years old, and 5 feet 6 3/4 inches tall. She was born free, as appears by affidavit of John Gird.

REGISTRATION NO. 185
(Vol. 1, p. 129)

John Campbell

1 December 1826

John Campbell is a dark mulatto man, about 26 years old, and 5 feet 11½ inches tall. He was emancipated by William Goddard's will.

REGISTRATION NO. 186
(Vol. 1, p. 129)

Matilda Dilhea and children,
Mary Ann and Francis Montgomery

1 December 1826

Matilda Dilhea is about 27 years old, has a dark complexion, and is 5 feet 3 inches tall. She was emancipated by William Goddard's will, as were her two children, Mary Ann and Francis Montgomery. Mary Ann is 7 years old and Francis is 4 years old.

REGISTRATION NO. 187
(Vol. 1, p. 129)

Henry Weeks

4 December 1826

Henry Weeks is a mulatto man, about 21 years old, and 5 feet 7½ inches tall. He was born free, as appears by affidavit of Sally Weeks.

REGISTRATION NO. 188
(Vol. 1, p. 129)

Nancy Bentley

[ca. 4 December 1826]

Nancy Bentl[e]y is a bright mulatto girl, about 13 years old, and 5 feet 2½ inches tall. She is a free, as appears by a record from the Circuit Court of the District of Columbia, County of Washington, which was produced by Nancy Bentley, wherein Elizabeth Bentley for herself and her children are plaintiffs, and Thomas Kune[?] is the defendant, and by which Nancy Bentley recovered her freedom.

REGISTRATION NO. 189
(Vol. 1, p. 130)

Polly Johnson

5 January 1827

Polly Johnson is a dark mulatto, about 30 years old, 5 feet 10 3/4 inches tall, marked with the scar of a burn on the inside of her right wrist. She was born free, as appears by affidavit of John Adam.

REGISTRATION NO. 190
(Vol. 1, p. 130)

Stephen Scoggins

16 January 1827

Stephen Scoggins is a dark mulatto man, about 22 years old, about 5 feet 10½ inches tall, with two scars on his left wrist caused by a burn. He was born free, as appears by affidavit of Joseph Heston before a justice of the peace in Baltimore County, Maryland.

REGISTRATION NO. 191
(Vol. 1, p. 130)

John Nickens

19 February 1827

John "Nichens" [Nickens] is a bright mulatto, about 23 years old, and 5 feet 5 inches tall. He was born free, as appears by affidavit of Fanny Thomas.

REGISTRATION NO. 192
(Vol. 1, p. 130)

Jane Nickens

19 February 1827

Jane "Nichens" [Nickens] is a bright mulatto girl, about 17 years old, and 5 feet 1 inch tall. She was born free, as appears by affidavit of Fanny Thomas.

REGISTRATION NO. 193
(Vol. 1, p. 131)

William Nickens

19 February 1827

William "Nichens" [Nickens] is a bright mulatto boy, about 23 years old, and 5 feet 5 inches tall. He was born free, as appears by affidavit of Fanny Thomas.

REGISTRATION NO. 194
(Vol. 1, p. 131)

Philip Newell

20 February 1827

Philip Newell is a bright mulatto man, about 30 years old, and 5 feet 1½ inches tall. He was emancipated by Jane Noland.

REGISTRATION NO. 195
(Vol. 1, p. 131)

Negro Rachel and her children,
Jane, Kitty, George, Emily,
and Harriet

22 March 1827

Rachel is a dark mulatto woman, about 32 years old, 5 feet tall, with a scar under her left jaw. She was manumitted by Sarah Baden, as appears by a copy of the deed from Calvert County, Maryland. Jane, about 10 years old, Kitty about 8 years old, George about 6 years old, Emily about 4 years old, and Harriet, about 2 years old, are all children of Rachel and were born free, as appears by affidavit of Benjamin Baden.

REGISTRATION NO. 196
(Vol. 1, p. 131)

Favorite Hall

30 March 1827

Favorite Hall is a dark mulatto woman, about 25 years old, with a scar on her right wrist caused by a burn, and another on her left arm. She was born free, as appears by affidavit of Ann Pritchard.

REGISTRATION NO. 197
(Vol. 1, p. 132)

Mildred Jackson

23 April 1827

Mildred Jackson is about 43 years old, has a rather dark complexion, is 5 feet 2½ inches tall, and has a scar on her right arm. She was liberated by Harriet M[ason] Lloyd.

REGISTRATION NO. 198
(Vol. 1, p. 132)

Mildred, alias Milly Jones

14 May 1827

Mildred, alias Milly Jones, is a free mulatto woman, about 48 years old, and 5 feet 4¼ inches tall. She was manumitted by John Whiting, as appears by deed recorded in Liber K No. 2, folio 42.

REGISTRATION NO. 199
(Vol. 1, p. 132)

Negro Patty

14 May 1827

Patty is a free mulatto woman, about 29 years old, 5 feet 1½ inches tall, with three scars on her right arm, one of them above her elbow and two on her breast. She was emancipated by John C. Herbert, as appears by deed recorded in Liber K, folio 333.

REGISTRATION NO. 200
(Vol. 1, p. 132)

Ellen Cole

14 May 1827

Ellen Cole is a free mulatto woman, about 24 years old, and 5 feet 1 3/4 inches tall. She was manumitted by John Whiting, as appears by deed dated 14 May 1827.

REGISTRATION NO. 201
(Vol. 1, p. 132)

Polly Payne

14 May 1827

Polly Payne is a free black woman, about 34 years old, and 5 feet 4½ inches tall. She is marked with two scars on her right arm, one above and one below the elbow, and a scar on her left arm below the elbow. She was born free, as appears by a certificate from the clerk of King George County Court.

REGISTRATION NO. 202
(Vol. 1, p. 133)

Charlotte Warner

16 May 1827

Charlotte Warner is a mulatto woman, about 43 years old, and 5 feet 7½ inches tall. She is a free woman, as appears by a certificate from Charles County, Maryland.

REGISTRATION NO. 203
(Vol. 1, p. 133)

Lewis Campbell

16 May 1827

Lewis Campbell is a free mulatto man, about 50 years old, and 5 feet 9 inches tall. He is marked with two scars on his right cheek, one on his left cheek, one on his chin, and one on the left side of his mouth. The middle finger of his right hand is deformed. He was manumitted by William Fowle and Henry Dangerfield by deed dated 26 January 1827.

REGISTRATION NO. 204
(Vol. 1, p. 133)

Luke Lee

17 May 1827

Luke Lee is a free black man, about 42 years old, 5 feet 5¼ inches tall, with two scars on the back part of his head. He was manumitted by John Hunter, as appears by deed recorded in Liber M No. 2, folio 463.

REGISTRATION NO. 205
(Vol. 1, p. 133)

Dennis Hacklett

17 May 1827

Dennis Hacklett is a free mulatto man, about 56 years old, 5 feet 8 3/4 inches tall, with a scar on his left cheek, another on the left side of his forehead, and others on his right leg and on both of his feet. He was manumitted by John Hunter, as appears by deed recorded in Liber M No. 2, folio 463.

REGISTRATION NO. 206a
(Vol. 1, p. 134)

Arberilla[Arabella?] Clark

25 May 1827

Arberilla[Arabella?] Clark is a free woman, about 25 years old, 5 feet one-half inch tall, with a double scar on her right arm. She was manumitted by Isaac Clark, as appears by deed recorded in Liber Q, No. 2.

REGISTRATION NO. 206b
(Vol. 1, p. 134)

Negro Lucinda

28 May 1827

Lucinda is a free mulatto woman, about 24 years old, and 5 feet 3½ inches tall. She was emancipated by George W. P. Custis.

REGISTRATION NO. 207
(Vol. 1, p. 134)

Samuel Brown

4 June 1827

Samuel Brown is a free black man, about 54 years old, and 5 feet 11 inches tall. His right eye is out, one joint of the forefinger of his left hand is cut off, the other three fingers on the same hand are deformed, and he is somewhat lame. He was manumitted by John Hunter, as appears by deed recorded in Liber M No. 2, folio 463.

REGISTRATION NO. 208
(Vol. 1, p. 134)

Harriet Haney Rhodes

5 June 1827

Harriet Haney, alias Rhodes, is a free woman of dark complexion, about 23 years old, 5 feet 4½ inches tall, with several scars on her neck and on her right arm. She is a free woman, as appears from her indentures of apprenticeship from the Overseers of the Poor in Fairfax County to William E. Dulin.

REGISTRATION NO. 209
(Vol. 1, p. 135)

Charles Haney Rhodes

5 June 1827

Charles Haney, alias Rhodes, is a free man, about 25 years old, 5 feet 5¼ inches tall, of a dark complexion, with a small scar over his left eye. He is free, as appears by his indentures of apprenticeship from the Overseers of the Poor in Fairfax County to William E. Dulin.

REGISTRATION NO. 210
(Vol. 1, p. 135)

Negro Mary

8 June 1827

Mary is a free woman, has a rather dark complexion, is about 29 years old, is 5 feet 2½ inches tall, and has a small scar near her left eye. She was manumitted by John C. Herbert, as appears by deed recorded in Liber K, folio 333.

REGISTRATION 211
(Vol. 1, p. 135)

Negro Maria

16 June 1827

Maria is a free mulatto woman, with a bright complexion, about 25 years old, and 5 feet 4½ inches tall. She was emancipated by Leonard Marbury by deed recorded in Liber O No. 2, folio 435.

REGISTRATION NO. 212
(Vol. 1, p. 135)

Ambrose Clarke

20 June 1827

Ambrose Clarke is a free man of dark complexion, about 30 years old, and 5 feet 10 inches tall. He was manumitted by his father, Isaac Clarke.

REGISTRATION NO. 213
(Vol. 1, p. 136)

William Dudley

22 June 1827

William Dudley is a free mulatto, aged about 27 years, about 5 feet 7 inches tall, with hazel eyes, curly and short hair, and a scar about two inches long on his right leg caused by an axe. He was born of free parents, as appears by affidavit of William Kesterson and William Forbish.

REGISTRATION NO. 214
(Vol. 1, p. 136)

Hannah Botts

4 July 1827

Hannah Botts is a free mulatto, about 21 years old, and 5 feet 4 inches tall. She was born free, as appears by affidavit of Sarah Gird.

REGISTRATION NO. 215
(Vol. 1, p. 136)

Evelina Butler

20 July 1827

Evelina Butler is a free mulatto woman, about 25 years old, and 5 feet 4 inches tall. She was born free, as appears by affidavit of Davis Bowie.

REGISTRATION NO. 216
(Vol. 1, p. 136)

Gustavus Thomas

3 August 1827

Gustavus Thomas is a free mulatto man, about 32 years old, and 5 feet 5½ inches tall. He is free, as appears by affidavit of Matthew Robinson.

REGISTRATION NO. 217
(Vol. 1, p. 137)

Elizabeth Curry, David Currey,
Mary Ann Currey, Jacob Currey

27 August 1827

Elizabeth Currey, aged about 16 last March; David Currey, aged 14 last February; Mary Ann Currey, aged 12 years next December, and Jacob Currey, aged 7 years, are all the children of Negro Jude who was freed by Seely Bunn. The children were all born after the emancipation of their mother, as appears by a certificate of Jacob Hoffman, former mayor of Alexandria.

REGISTRATION NO. 218
(Vol. 1, p. 137)

Negro Ann   13 August 1827

Ann is a girl of dark complexion, about 20 years old, 4 feet 10½ inches tall, with a scar on the back part of her left leg. She is a free woman, as appears by a bill of sale from Joseph Powell to Mary Davis.

REGISTRATION NO. 219
(Vol. 1, p. 137)

Edward Pleasants   11 September 1827

Edward Pleasants is about 60 years old, has a dark complexion, and is 5 feet 4¼ inches tall. He is a free man, as appears by affidavit of Edward A. Mayfield.

REGISTRATION NO. 220
(Vol. 1, p. 138)

Benjamin Smith   12 Sept. 1827

Benjamin Smith is a free mulatto man, about 22 years old, 5 feet one-half inch tall, with a small scar on the forefinger of his left hand. He was born free, as appears by affidavit of Hannah Smith.

REGISTRATION NO. 221
(Vol. 1, p. 138)

Sarah Lee   12 September 1827

Sarah Lee is 16 years old, about 5 feet tall, and has a rather dark complexion. She was born free, as appears by affidavit of Hannah Smith.

REGISTRATION NO. 222
(Vol. 1, p. 138)

Patty Ferguson   26 September 1827

Patty Ferguson is a free mulatto woman, about 39 years old, 5 feet 4 3/4 inches tall, with black eyes, and black hair, rather of the "Indian kind." She has a scar on the under part of her left arm not far from the wrist. Ferguson was manumitted by Ann Swift.

REGISTRATION NO. 223
(Vol. 1, p. 138)

Negro Hannah   3 October 1827

Hannah is a free woman, about 23 years old, 5 feet tall, with a dark complexion. She was manumitted by John Adam, administrator of Mary Berry, deceased.

REGISTRATION NO. 224
(Vol. 1, p. 139)

Robert Vaughn, Jr.   5 October 1827

Robert Vaughn is a free man, about 26 years old, 5 feet 7 inches tall, with a scar over each eye and one on the back of his neck. He was liberated by his father, Robert Vaughn.

REGISTRATION NO. 225
(Vol. 1, p. 139)

Negro Sophia   5 October 1827

Negro Sophia is a free woman, about 27 years old, of a dark complexion, 5 feet one-fourth inch tall, with a small scar on the left side of her face near her mouth. She was emancipated by John C. Herbert by deed recorded in Liber K, folio 333.

REGISTRATION NO. 226
(Vol. 1, p. 139)

Nancy Smith   8 October 1827

Nancy Smith is about 25 years old, with several scars on her right arm, a scar on her nose, and a white spot on her right eyeball. She was born free, as appears by affirmation of Mordecai Miller.

REGISTRATION NO. 227
(Vol. 1, p. 139)

William Bowles   23 October 1827

William Bowles is about 27 years old, 5 feet 8 inches tall, of a bright complexion, with several scars on his right arm above the elbow. He was born free, as appears by affidavit of Elias P. Legg.

REGISTRATION NO. 228
(Vol. 1, p. 140)

Harriet Butler   24 October 1827

Harriet Butler is about 16 years old, 5 feet 4¼ inches tall, of a black complexion. She was born free, as appears by affidavit of Catharine Allison.

REGISTRATION NO. 229
(Vol. 1, p. 140)

Ann Watson   24 October 1827

Ann Watson is a free woman, about 46 years old, 5 feet 2 inches tall, of a light complexion, with a scar on her left arm. She was born free, as appears by affidavit of Harriet Cockrell.

REGISTRATION NO. 230
(Vol. 1, p. 140)

Elizabeth Bowles   26 October 1827

Elizabeth Bowles is a free mulatto woman, about 23 years old, 5 feet tall, with a scar below her left ear. She was born free, as appears by affidavit of Richard Veitch.

REGISTRATION NO. 231
(Vol. 1, p. 140)

Ann Harris   27 October 1827

Ann Harris is a free mulatto woman about 26 years old, about 5 feet 3 inches tall, with straight hair, and a scar on her left arm. She was born free, as appears by affidavit of John Rollins.

REGISTRATION NO. 232
(Vol. 1, p. 141)

Amy McQuan   27 October 1827

Amy McQuan is a free woman about 39 years old. She has a dark complexion, is 5 feet 5 inches tall, and has two moles, one on the left side of her nose, the other on the left side of her lip. She was born free, as appears by affidavit of Mrs. Kitty McRea.

REGISTRATION NO. 233
(Vol. 1, p. 141)

Betsey Hove   27 October 1827

Betsey Hove has a dark complexion, is about 43 years old, is 5 feet one-fourth inch tall, and has the marks of the smallpox on her face. She is a free woman, as appears by affidavit of Norman R. Fitzhugh.

REGISTRATION NO. 234
(Vol. 1, p. 142)

Clarissa Bowles   1 November 1827

Clarissa Bowles is a light mulatto girl, about 19 years old, 5 feet tall, with a scar on her right arm caused by a burn. She was born free, as appears by affidavit of Davis Bowie.

REGISTRATION NO. 235
(Vol. 1, p. 142)

James Butler   12 November 1827

James Butler is about 18 years old, of a dark complexion, 5 feet 7½ inches tall, with a small mole on his left arm and a cut on his left leg. He was born free, as appears by affidavit of Catherine Allison.

REGISTRATION NO. 236
(Vol. 1, p. 142)

Janney Jackson

17 November 1827

Janney Jackson is about 35 years old and 5 feet 3 inches tall. She was emancipated by Peter Loggins.

REGISTRATION NO. 237
(Vol. 1, p. 142)

John Gibson

20 November 1827

John Gibson is about 21 years old and has a light complexion. He was emancipated by Andrew Ramsay and his wife.

REGISTRATION NO. 238
(Vol. 1, p. 142)

Harriet Brown

22 November 1827

Harriet Brown is about 25 years old, 5 feet 5½ inches tall, of a dark complexion, with a scar on the under part of her right wrist. She was born free, as appears by affidavit of Eliza Butts.

REGISTRATION NO. 239
(Vol. 1, p. 142)

Israel Williams

23 November 1827

Israel Williams is about 20 years old, 5 feet 5½ inches tall, of a dark complexion, with a scar under his left eye and left ear, and also under his right jaw. He was born free, as appears by affidavit of Mrs. Amelia Brocchus.

REGISTRATION NO. 240
(Vol. 1, p. 143)

Gustavus Murray

3 December 1827

Gustavus Murray is about 22 years old and has a bright complexion. He was born free, as appears by certificate of Alexander Moore, a notary public for the County of Alexandria.

REGISTRATION NO. 241
(Vol. 1, p. 143)

Louisa Gaines

3 December 1827

Louisa Gaines is about 24 years old, has a very bright complexion, and is 5 feet one-half inch tall. She was born free, as appears by affidavit of Cath[erine] Allison.

REGISTRATION NO. 242
(Vol. 1, p. 143)

Fanny Frazier

20 December 1827

Fanny Frazier is 21 years old, 5 feet 4 inches tall, with a scar from a burn on her left arm, and another scar on her throat. She was born free, as appears by affidavit of Elizabeth Ann Burgess.

REGISTRATION NO. 243
(Vol. 1, p. 143)

Louisa Santford

24 December 1827

Louisa Santford is about 19 years old, 5 feet tall, of a bright complexion, with a small scar on both lips. She was born free, as appears by affidavit of Davis Bowie.

REGISTRATION NO. 244
(Vol. 1, p. 143)

John Hepburn

28 December 1827

John Hepburn is a free mulatto, about 25 years old, and 5 feet 9 inches tall. He was emancipated by William Hepburn.

REGISTRATION NO. 245
(Vol. 1, p. 144)

James Cole   18 March 1828

James Cole is a bright mulatto man, about 26 years old, 6 feet 1 inch tall, with a scar above his right eye and a scar on his right leg. He was born free, as appears by affidavit of Edmund L. Browne.

REGISTRATION NO. 246
(Vol. 1, p. 144)

Mary Morgan   19 March 1828

Mary Morgan is a dark mulatto woman, about 26 years old, 5 feet 5 inches tall, with a scar a little above her left breast. She was born free, as appears by affidavit of John Muncaster[?].

REGISTRATION NO. 247
(Vol. 1, p. 144)

Robert Henry, Sr.   5 April 1828

Robert Henry is about 25 years old, 5 feet 7½ inches tall, has a dark complexion, and has some small scars on the left side of his face. He was emancipated by John Yates, as appears from records of the Spotsylvania County Court.

REGISTRATION NO. 248
(Vol. 1, p. 144)

Negro Lydia   10 April 1828

Lydia is about 23 years old, 5 feet 4½ inches tall, of a dark complexion, with a scar on her left arm caused by a burn. She was emancipated by John Yates, as appears from records of Spotsylvania County Court.

REGISTRATION NO. 249
(Vol. 1, p. 145)

Negro Sylvia   5 May 1828

Sylvia is about 30 years old, 5 feet 8½ inches tall, of a dark complexion, with her face marked by the smallpox. She was emancipated by Thomas G. Addison, as appears on folio 6 of this book.

See Registration No. 6 in this book.

REGISTRATION NO. 250
(Vol. 1, p. 145)

Jane Ross   8 May 1828

Jane Ross is about 40 years old, 5 feet 6¼ inches tall, of a light complexion, with a scar on her right hand. She was emancipated by Townshend Waugh.

REGISTRATION NO. 251
(Vol. 1, p. 145)

Jacob Bell   15 May 1828

Jacob Bell is about 28 years old, 5 feet 10 3/4 inches tall, and has a dark complexion. He was born free, as appears by affidavit of Henry Tyler.

REGISTRATION NO. 252
(Vol. 1, p. 145)

Eliza Ross   19 May 1828

Eliza Ross is about 16 years old, 5 feet 2½ inches tall, of small statue, and of a bright complexion. She was born free, as appears by affidavit of John Adam.

REGISTRATION NO. 253
(Vol. 1, p. 146)

Mary Sumby   16 June 1828

Mary Sumby is about 23 years old, 5 feet 2 inches tall, of dark complexion, with a white spot on her neck. She was born free, as appears by affirmation of Mordecai Miller.

REGISTRATION NO. 254
(Vol. 1, p. 146)

Lucy Sumby

16 June 1828

Lucy Sumby is about 25 years old, 5 feet 2 3/4 inches tall, of a dark complexion, with a scar on her left cheek caused by a burn. She was born free, as appears by affirmation of Mordecai Miller.

REGISTRATION NO. 255
(Vol. 1, p. 146)

William Noland
Susan Noland
Helin Noland

20 June 1828

William, Susan, and Helin Noland were born free and are the children of Cecelia Noland, now deceased. William Noland was born in August of 1810 and is 18 years old, 5 feet 6 inches tall, with a small scar caused by a burn on the calf of his right leg; Susan Noland was born 27 September 1812, is 5 feet 1¼ inches tall and of a light complexion; Helin Noland was born 17 October 1814, is 4 feet 9 3/4 inches tall, and of a light complexion. They were born of a free woman, as appears by affidavit of Susannah Cannon.

Note dated 26 October 1857: The above named Helin Noland is 5 feet three-fourth inch tall and has a small black mole in her right hand. She was granted a certificate.

REGISTRATION NO. 256
(Vol. 1, p. 147)

Louisa Carter

4 July 1828

Louisa Carter is about 18 years old, 5 feet one-half inch tall, of a light complexion, with a scar on her neck caused by the King's Evil. She was born free, as appears by affidavit of Davis Bowie.

REGISTRATION NO. 257
(Vol. 1, p. 147)

Mary E. Sales

31 July 1828

Mary E. Sales is a dark mulatto girl, about 17 years old, 5 feet 3½ inches tall, of small statue, with a small black mole on her right thumb. She was born free, as appears by affidavit of Susanna Cannon.

REGISTRATION NO. 258
(Vol. 1, p. 147)

Ellen Dtcher [Dutcher?]

4 August 1828

Ellen "Dtcher" [Dutcher?] is a free mulatto girl, about 22 years old, 5 feet 1½ inches tall, with several small scars on her face and a small "back" [black] mole on her right arm. She was born free, as appears by affidavit of Davis Bowie.

REGISTRATION NO. 259
(Vol. 1, p. 147)

Ann Roberts

9 August 1828

Ann Roberts is a dark mulatto woman, about 29 years old, and about 5 feet 4 inches tall. She was born free, as appears by affidavit of Davis Bowie.

REGISTRATION NO. 260
(Vol. 1, p. 148)

Mary Bowles

22 September 1828

Mary Bowles is a mulatto girl, about 21 years old, 5 feet one-half inch tall, with a small scar on her left thumb caused by a cut. She was born free, as appears by affidavit of Will Veitch.

REGISTRATION NO. 261
(Vol. 1, p. 148)

Betsey Ware

24 October 1828

Betsey Ware is about 25 years old, has a dark complexion, and is 5 feet 2½ inches tall. She was born free, as appears by affidavit of Davis Bowie.

REGISTRATION NO. 262
(Vol. 1, p. 148)

John Thomas Cole

1 November 1828

John Thomas Cole is about 16 years old, 5 feet 4 3/4 inches tall, and has a dark complexion. He is the son of Violett Cole, a free born woman of color, as appears from the records in this office.

REGISTRATION NO. 263
(Vol. 1, p. 148)

Eliza Watkins

26 December 1828

Eliza Watkins is about 24 years old, of a dark complexion, 5 feet 6 inches tall, with a small scar caused by a burn on her right arm, and another on her forehead. She was born free, as appears by affidavit of Davis Bowie.

REGISTRATION NO. 264
(Vol. 1, p. 148)

Nanthius Jennings

27 December 1828

Nanthius Jennings is about 24 years old, 5 feet 6¼ inches tall, of a dark complexion, and lame in his left leg. He was born free, as appears by affidavit of John Rheem.

REGISTRATION NO. 265
(Vol. 1, p. 149)

Alexander Butts

3 January 1829

Alexander Butts is a free man of color, 5 feet 8½ inches tall, with two scars on his left leg and a small black mole on his nose. He was emancipated by Reuben Johnston.

There is no registration numbered 266.

REGISTRATION NO. 267
(Vol. 1, p. 149)

Walter Berry (Wat)

27 January 1829

"Wat," alias Walter Berry, is about 37 years old, of a dark complexion, with a scar on his lip caused by a cut. The will of Rachael Wheeler provided that he be devised to Ignatius Wheeler as a slave, but be freed upon the death of Ignatius. Jemima Jenkins swears that Berry is the person referred to as "Wat" in the above will, and states that Ignatius Wheeler has died.

REGISTRATION NO. 268
(Vol. 1, p. 149)

Jane Weeks

Undated

Jane Weeks is a free woman, about 19 years old, 5 feet 2 3/4 inches tall, of a dark complexion. She was born free, as appears by affidavit of Sally Weeks.

REGISTRATION NO. 269
(Vol. 1, p. 149)

Rosetta Barby

17 April 1829

Rosetta Barby is a free mulatto woman, about 33 years old, and 5 feet 4 3/4 inches tall. She sued Benjamin Lewis in *forma pauperis* for her freedom in the Circuit Court of Alexandria and by verdict of a jury recovered damages of one cent from Lewis. She also recovered her freedom and the costs of the suit.

REGISTRATION NO. 270
(Vol. 1, p. 150)

Charles Davis

29 April 1829

Charles Davis is about 29 years old, 5 feet 10½ inches tall, and of a stout build. He produced a copy of a deed of emancipation from the Inferior Court of Common Pleas in the County of Hunterdon, New Jersey from Samuel T. Bellerjean.

REGISTRATION NO. 271
(Vol. 1, p. 150)

Moses Dickson

5 May 1829

Moses Dickson is about 46 years old, 5 feet 7½ inches tall, of a dark complexion, and rather bald on the top of his head. He was manumitted by Benjamin Dawson, Trustee for Robert Carter.

REGISTRATION NO. 272
(Vol. 1, p. 150)

Harriet Ann Dyson

6 May 1829

Harriet Ann Dyson is about 17 years old, 5 feet 2¼ inches tall, and of a dark complexion. She was emancipated by James P. Coleman.

REGISTRATION NO. 273
(Vol. 1, p. 150)

Carolus Anthony Chin

21 May 1829

Carolus Anthony Chin is a mulatto man, about 26 years old, and 5 feet 9½ inches tall. He was emancipated by Charles McKnight by deed dated 5 January 1829.

REGISTRATION NO. 274
(Vol. 1, p. 151)

Julia Gray

25 May 1829

Julia Gray is a dark mulatto woman, about 32 years old, and 5 feet 6 3/4 inches tall. She was emancipated by Delia Clark by deed dated 11 September 1828.

REGISTRATION NO. 275
(Vol. 1, p. 151)

William Jackson

June 1829

William Jackson is about 21 years old, 5 feet 4 inches tall, and has a dark complexion. He was given by John Wise to his granddaughters, Louisa and Ann Maria Seaton, for 14 years, which time expired on 6 April 1829. The affidavit of Henry W. Crea states that it was Wise's intention to free Jackson at the end of his term.

REGISTRATION NO. 276
(Vol. 1, p. 151)

William Dutcher

20 July 1829

William Dutcher is a dark mulatto boy, about 20 years old, 5 feet 8 3/4 inches tall, and stout built. He was born free, as appears by affidavit of Davis Bowie.

REGISTRATION NO. 277
(Vol. 1, p. 151)

Gemima Branham

31 August 1829

Gemima Branham is a bright mulatto woman who is 5 feet tall. She was emancipated by Robert P. Washington by deed recorded in Liber W[possibly "U"], folio 418.

REGISTRATION NO. 278
(Vol. 1, p. 152)

John Thomas Windsor

5 September 1829

John Thomas Windsor is a free mulatto man, about 30 years old, about 5 feet 10 inches tall, with dark eyes and dark hair, and a scar under his chin. He was born of free parents, as appears by affidavit of John Webster, George H. Webster, and Mary Ann Mead.

REGISTRATION NO. 279
(Vol. 1, p. 152)

Hannah Hines

12 October 1829

Hannah Hines is a free mulatto woman, about 30 years old, 5 feet 5¼ inches tall, with black eyes and black hair, and two "perpendicular parallel scars" on the right hand side of her mouth. She is free, as appears by affidavit of Elias [P.] Legg.

REGISTRATION NO. 280
(Vol. 1, p. 152)

Ann Givens

13 October 1829

Ann Givens, the daughter of Hannah "Jinnings" [Jennings], is a free mulatto woman, about 32 years old, about 5 feet 3 3/4 inches tall, of a light mulatto color, black eyes and hair, with a mark or scar above the heel of her right foot, caused by a severe wound. She was born of free parents, as appears by affidavit of John Andrew Rheem.

REGISTRATION NO. 281
(Vol. 1, p. 152)

Sarah Gales

3 November 1829

Sarah Gales is about 20 years old, 5 feet 1½ inches tall, of a dark complexion, with a scar on her left hand above the joint of the forefinger caused by a burn. She was born free, as appears by affidavit of Davis Bowie.

REGISTRATION NO. 282
(Vol. 1, p. 153)

Patty Nelson, Cecelia Nelson,
George Nelson, Martha Nelson

1 December 1829

Patty Nelson is 32 years old, 5 feet 8¼ inches tall. She and her two children, Cecelia Nelson and George Nelson, were emancipated by Maria Blue and Robert and "Britainia" [Britannia] Bell by deed recorded in Liber Q No. 2, folio 329. Her child, Martha, was born after she was freed.

REGISTRATION NO. 283
(Vol. 1, p. 153)

Jefferson Fitzgerald

21 January 1830

Jefferson Fitzgerald is a mulatto man, about 38 years old, 5 feet 6 3/4 inches tall, with a scar on his forehead. He was born free.

REGISTRATION NO. 284
(Vol. 1, p. 153)

Alexander Bryan

38 January 1830

Alexander Bryan is a free mulatto man, about 33 years old, 5 feet 7½ inches tall, with a scar under his left nostril and a mole on his upper lip. He was freed by Elizabeth Turner by deed dated 30 December 1829.

REGISTRATION NO. 285
(Vol. 1, p. 153)

David Thomas

3 February 1830

David Thomas is a free black man, about 21 years old, and 5 feet 7¼ inches tall. He was born free, as appears by affidavit of Rebecca Cooke.

REGISTRATION NO. 286
(Vol. 1, p. 154)

George Pipsico

18 February 1830

George Pipsico is a mulatto man, about 37 years old, 5 feet 5 3/4 inches tall, with a scar on his left hand and another on the crown of his head. He was born of free parents.

REGISTRATION NO. 287
(Vol. 1, p. 154)

Sarah Waugh Sargent

22 March 1830

Sarah Sargent, late Sarah Waugh, is a mulatto woman, about 25 years old, 5 feet 1 3/4 inches tall, very fat and stout, with several small scars on her face. She was born free, as appears by affidavit of James P. Coleman.

REGISTRATION NO. 288
(Vol. 1, p. 154)

George Waugh, Lettia Waugh,
Catharine Waugh, John Thomas Waugh,
Elizabeth Ann Waugh, William Waugh,
James R. Waugh, and Daniel Waugh

22 March 1830

George Waugh, Lettia Waugh, Catharine Waugh, John Thomas Waugh, Elizabeth Ann Waugh, William Waugh, James R. Waugh, and Daniel Waugh are the children of Mary Roderick Waugh, a free mulatto woman. George Waugh is 21 years old, about 5 feet 7 3/4 inches tall, with a large scar on his left cheek.

REGISTRATION NO. 289
(Vol. 1, p. 154)

Sarah Chase

4 May 1830

Sarah Chase is about 21 years old, 5 feet 1½ inches tall, with a small black mole near her right shoulder. She was born free, as appears by affidavit of Mary Wood.

REGISTRATION NO. 290
(Vol. 1, p. 155)

Nelly Hoy Butler

12 May 1830

Nelly Butler, late Nelly Hoy, is about 26 years old, 5 feet 7 inches tall, and has a dark mulatto complexion. She was born free, as appears by affidavit of James Entwisle.

REGISTRATION NO. 291
(Vol. 1, p. 155)

Sarah Reily

20 May 1830

Sarah Reily is a dark mulatto woman, about 20 years old, and 5 feet 6 inches tall. She was born free, as appears by affidavit of Samuel Harrison.

REGISTRATION NO. 292
(Vol. 1, p. 155)

Mary Reily Johnson

20 May 1830

Mary Johnson, formerly Mary Reily, is a dark mulatto woman, about 28 years old, and 5 feet 3 inches tall. She was born free, as appears by affidavit of Samuel Harrison.

REGISTRATION NO. 293
(Vol. 1, p. 155)

Mahala Reily Bird

20 May 1830

Mahala Bird, formerly Mahala Reily, is a dark mulatto woman, about 25 years old, and 5 feet 6¼ inches tall. She was born free, as appears by affidavit of Samuel Harrison.

REGISTRATION NO. 294
(Vol. 1, p. 156)

Dennis Johnson

25 May 1830

Dennis Johnson is about 45 years old and 5 feet 11½ inches tall. He has a dark complexion and a scar on the left side of his forehead caused by the kick of a horse. He was emancipated by William M. McCarty and John M. McCarty by deed dated 6 February 1829, as appears by testimony of Thomson F. Mason, Francis Hall, and Horatio Clagett.

REGISTRATION NO. 295
(Vol. 1, p. 156)

Negro Charles

29 May 1830

Negro Charles is a bright mulatto, about 25 years old, and 5 feet 6 inches tall. He was emancipated by George W. P. Custis.

REGISTRATION NO. 296
(Vol. 1, p. 156)

James Fitzgerald

5 June 1830

James Fitzgerald is about 18 years old, 5 feet 8½ inches tall, and has a dark complexion. He was born free, as appears by affidavit of James Entwisle.

REGISTRATION NO. 297
(Vol. 1, p. 156)

Jane Elizabeth Simpson

10 June 1830

Jane Elizabeth Simpson is about 11 years old and has a slender form. She was emancipated by Harriet Mason Lloyd.

REGISTRATION NO. 298
(Vol. 1, p. 157)

Negro Matilda and
child Sarah Ann

10 June 1830

Matilda is about 29 years old, 5 feet 3 inches tall, and has a very dark complexion. She was emancipated by John C. Herbert by deed recorded in Liber K, folio 333. Her child, Sarah Ann, about 3 years old, was also registered.

REGISTRATION NO. 299
(Vol. 1, p. 157)

John Harris

22 June 1830

John Harris is about 20 years old, 5 feet 7¼ inches tall, of a dark mulatto complexion, with a small scar on his left cheek and a stout build.

REGISTRATION NO. 300
(Vol. 1, p. 157)

Grace Fox

17 July 1830

Grace Fox is a dark mulatto woman, about 17 years old, 5 feet 7½ inches tall, with several scars on her right arm near the wrist. She is a free woman, as appears by affirmation of George Drinker.

REGISTRATION NO. 301
(Vol. 1, p. 158)

William Morrison

7 August 1830

William Morrison, a dark colored man, is 27 years old, 5 feet 7¼ inches tall, with a scar over his left eye and on the back of his head. He was born free, as appears by affidavit of Francis Peyton.

REGISTRATION NO. 302
(Vol. 1, p. 158)

Henny Ann Fitzgerald

16 August 1830

Henny Ann Fitzgerald is a bright mulatto woman, about 22 years old, and 5 feet 4 inches tall. She was born free and is the daughter of Nancy Evans who was also born free, as appears by affidavit of Dennis Johnson.

REGISTRATION NO. 303
(Vol. 1, p. 158)

Mordecai Sombay

4 September 1830

Mordecai Sombay is a dark colored boy, about 18 years old, 5 feet 7½ inches tall, with a small scar on his breast and another on his right leg. He was born free, as appears by affidavit of D. McCatharine.

REGISTRATION NO. 304
(Vol. 1, p. 159)

Maria Craney

November 1830

Maria Craney is a mulatto woman about 19 years old. She was emancipated by Robert H. Miller by deed dated 24 March 1830 and recorded in Liber S No. 2, folio 112.

REGISTRATION NO. 305
(Vol. 1, p. 159)

Essen Lee

13 December 1830

Essen Lee is a free black man, about 31 years old, 5 feet 5 inches tall, with a small scar near his left eye. He was born free.

REGISTRATION NO. 306
(Vol. 1, p. 159)

Dennis Carpenter

27 December 1830

Dennis Carpenter is a free mulatto man, about 31 years old, and 5 feet 9½ inches tall. He was freed by Robert Jamieson by deed dated 27 November 1830.

There is no registration numbered 307.

REGISTRATION NO. 308
(Vol. 1, p. 160)

Alfred Clark

22 February 1831

Alfred Clark is a free mulatto, about 21 years old, 5 feet 6¼ inches tall, with a small scar on his left arm and left hand. He was emancipated by the heirs of Isaac Gibson by deed recorded 5 December 1830.

REGISTRATION NO. 309
(Vol. 1, p. 160)

Maria Morris

6 June 1831

Maria Morris is a free mulatto woman, about 35 years old, 5 feet 2 inches tall, with three small black moles on the right side of her neck and throat. She is fat and corpulent. Morris was emancipated by Maria Blue.

REGISTRATION NO. 310
(Vol. 1, p. 160)

Lewis Miller

11 June 1831

Lewis Miller is about 35 years old, 5 feet 10½ inches tall, of a dark complexion, with a scar on his left hand and another on the left side of his face caused by a cut. Lewis obtained his freedom by court judgement at the November 1830 term in a case in which Miller was the plaintiff and Eloyius Thompson the defendant.

REGISTRATION NO. 311
(Vol. 1, p. 160)

Negro Charles

11 June 1831

Negro Charles is about 40 years old, 5 feet 5 inches tall, and has a black complexion. He was emancipated by Sinah B. Porter.

REGISTRATION NO. 312
(Vol. 1, p. 161)

Armstead Bowling

23 June 1831

Armstead Bowling is about 35 years old, 5 feet 3½ inches tall, of a dark complexion, with a large scar on his left arm caused by a cut and a scar on his face near his mouth. He was emancipated by John Wood by deed recorded 21 April 1819.

REGISTRATION NO. 313
(Vol. 1, p. 161)

Josephine Branham
William Branham

27 June 1831

Josephine and William Branham, the children of Rachael Branham, were born after their mother had been emancipated by Mordecai Miller, as appears by affidavit of Mordecai Miller. Josephine is about 15 years old. William is about 10 years old, and has a bright complexion.

REGISTRATION NO. 314
(Vol. 1, p. 161)

Jane Grayson

25 June 1831

Jane Grayson is about 30 years old, 5 feet 3½ inches tall, of a dark complexion, with a round face, and with a black spot on the back of her left hand. She was emancipated by Henry Darnell by deed dated this day.

REGISTRATION NO. 315
(Vol. 1, p. 161)

Amelia Dutcher

29 June 1831

Amelia Dutcher is a dark mulatto, about 28 years old, and 5 feet 1 3/4 inches tall. She was born free, as appears by affidavit of Davis Bowie.

REGISTRATION NO. 316
(Vol. 1, p. 162)

Kitty Jones

30 June 1831

Kitty Jones is a bright mulatto woman, about 22 years old, and 5 feet 2¼ inches tall. She was emancipated by John Whiting by deed recorded in Liber R No. 2, folio 42.

REGISTRATION NO. 317
(Vol. 1, p. 162)

Emanuel Edwards

2 July 1831

Emanuel Edwards is a bright mulatto man, about 22 years old, and 5 feet 11 3/4 inches tall, with a mole on his breast. He was emancipated by Archibald McLean by deed dated 23 July 1817.

REGISTRATION NO. 318
(Vol. 1, p. 162)

Minny Wheeler

8 July 1831

"Miney" [Minny] Wheeler is a bright mulatto woman, about 30 years old, 5 feet tall, with a dark mole in her left hand. She was born free.

REGISTRATION NO. 319
(Vol. 1, p. 162)

Christopher Harris

16 July 1831

Christopher Harris is a black man, about 32 years old, 5 feet 2 inches tall, with a large scar on his left hand caused by a burn. Harris obtained his freedom by judgement of the Circuit Court issued at its 1830 April term in a suit in which he was the plaintiff and Nelly Alexander the defendant.

See Negro Christopher Harris v. Nelly Alexander, 4 Cranch CC 1.

REGISTRATION NO. 320
(Vol. 1, p. 163)

Anzy Brown

25 July 1831

Anzy Brown is a mulatto girl, about 17 years old, 5 feet 1½ inches tall, with freckles. She was emancipated by Dr. James S. Gunnell by deed recorded in Liber R No. 2, folio 441.

REGISTRATION NO. 321
(Vol. 1, p. 163)

Horatio Jennings

5 September 1831

Horatio Jennings has a yellow complexion, is about 32 years old, 5 feet 8½ inches tall, with three scars on his left hand, one on his right elbow, and one on his left arm. He is a free man, as appears by affidavit of Davis Bowie.

REGISTRATION NO. 322
(Vol. 1, p. 163)

Betsey Triplett

7 September 1831

Betsey Triplett is a Negro girl of dark complexion, about 24 years old, 5 feet 3¼ inches tall, with a small scar on her left wrist. She was emancipated by John Douglass by deed recorded in Liber N No. 2, page 255.

REGISTRATION NO. 323
(Vol. 1, p. 164)

Henry Curtis

8 September 1831

Henry Curtis is a bright mulatto man, about 32 years old, 5 feet 6½ inches tall, with a round scar on his right cheek. He was born free, as appears by a certificate from the mayor of Alexandria.

REGISTRATION NO. 324
(Vol. 1, p. 164)

Clarissa Davis

8 September 1831

Clarissa Davis is a free mulatto girl, about 19 years old, 5 feet 2½ inches tall, with a perpendicular cut on her forehead. She was born free, as appears by affidavit of Thomas Vowell.

REGISTRATION NO. 325
(Vol. 1, p. 164)

Sarah Weston

9 September 1831

Sarah Weston is a free mulatto woman, about 31 years old, 5 feet 2½ inches tall, of a bright complexion, with a large scar on her left breast. She was born free, as appears by affidavit of Thomas Preston.

REGISTRATION NO. 326
(Vol. 1, p. 164)

Israel James

10 September 1831

Israel James is about 30 years old, 5 feet 6 inches tall, of a dark complexion, with several warts on his upper lip. He produced a certificate from Andrew Ramswell[?] late jailor of this county stating that James had been advertised by him as a runaway slave, but that no one came forward to claim him. He was discharged after being hired out for a term in order to pay his jail fees. His term is over and he is free.

REGISTRATION NO. 327
(Vol. 1, p. 165)

Fanny Graham

14 September 1831

Fanny Graham is a mulatto woman, about 21 years old, 5 feet 10½ inches tall, with a large scar on the left side of her neck. She was purchased by her mother, who was a free woman, from Walter Donel[?] and emancipated, as appears by affidavit of Thomas Preston.

REGISTRATION NO. 328
(Vol. 1, p. 165)

Fortune Ann Minor and children,
Richard Henry and James Thomas

15 September 1831

Fortune Ann Minor is a mulatto woman, about 42 years old, 4 feet 10½ inches tall, with a scar across her left eyebrow. She was manumitted by Jacob Hoffman, as appears by deed recorded in Liber R No. 2, folio 398. She has two children: Richard Henry, 4 years and 2 months old, and James Thomas, 9 months old.

REGISTRATION NO. 329
(Vol. 1, p. 165)

Sarah Wyatt

16 September 1831

Sarah Wyat[t] is about 26 years old, 5 feet 2½ inches tall and of a dark complexion. She was born free and is the daughter of Peggy Wyat[t], a free woman of color, as appears by affidavit of Isabella Deakin.

REGISTRATION NO. 330a
(Vol. 1, p. 165)

Julia McIntosh   20 September 1831

Julia McIntosh is a mulatto woman, about 30 years old, 4 feet 10½ inches tall, with a scar on the right side of her mouth. She was emancipated by William Fowle and H[enry] Dangerfield by deed dated 26 January 1827, recorded in Liber Q No. 2, folio 117.

REGISTRATION NO. 330b
(Vol. 1, p. 166)

Nathaniel Hines   26 September 1831

Nathaniel Hines is a dark mulatto man, about 25 years old, 5 feet 7¼ inches tall, with a small scar just over his left eye, as appears by affidavit of Ann Lightfoot.

REGISTRATION NO. 331
(Vol. 1, p. 166)

Ann Maria Smith   27 September 1831

Ann Maria Smith is a bright mulatto girl, about 19 years old, 5 feet one-half inch tall, with a scar and a mole on the right side of her neck. She was born free, as appears by affidavit of Samuel Wheeler.

REGISTRATION NO. 332
(Vol. 1, p. 166)

Tabitha Minor   28 September 1831

Tabitha Minor is a dark mulatto woman, about 32 years old, 4 feet 11 inches tall, with a slight scar on her forehead and a mole on her left arm. She was emancipated by Henry Darnell, as appears by deed recorded in Liber Q, p. 282.

REGISTRATION NO. 333
(Vol. 1, p. 166)

Charles Coats   29 September 1831

Charles Coats is a free black man, about 25 years old, 5 feet 6 3/4 inches tall, with a scar on the left side of his forehead, and a scar on the left side of his chin. He has produced an affidavit by Joseph Smith that he is the person mentioned in a deed of emancipation from John C. Herbert to "sundry negroes by the name of Charles."

REGISTRATION NO. 334
(Vol. 1, p. 167)

Ellen Butler   28 September 1831

Ellen Butler is a black girl, about 17 years old, 5 feet 5 inches tall, with two small scars on her upper lip. She is the daughter of Elizabeth Butler who, as appears by an affidavit from Cornelius Wells, was born free.

REGISTRATION NO. 335
(Vol. 1, p. 167)

Mary Ann Darnell   30 September 1831

Mary Ann Durnell is a bright mulatto, about 23 years old, 5 feet 2 inches tall, with a scar on her right arm near the elbow. She was manumitted by Henry Darnell.

REGISTRATION NO. 336
(Vol. 1, p. 167)

Jerry Banks   30 September 1831

The writing is too faint to make out the details of this item. It appears that Banks was freed by John Childs.

Sarah Jacobs swears that this Jerry is the "Jerry" mentioned in the manumission deed.

REGISTRATION NO. 337
(Vol. 1, p. 167)

William Gibbs

7 October 1831

William Gibbs is about 38 years old, 5 feet 8 inches tall, of a dark complexion, with no visible marks. He was born free, as appears by John G. Gibbs, a white man.

REGISTRATION NO. 338
(Vol. 1, p. 167)

Jane Roseville
John Wilson Parks

8 October 1831

Jane Roseville is a very light mulatto, about 28 years old, 5 feet 3 3/4 inches tall, with straight hair. She was born free, as appears by affidavit of Susan Conner. She has a son, John Wilson Parks, aged 3 years.

REGISTRATION NO. 339
(Vol. 1, p. 168)

Emma Roseville

8 October 1831

Emma Roseville is a very bright mulatto girl, about 15 years old, 5 feet 2 3/4 inches tall, with straight hair. She was born free, as appears by affidavit of Susan Conner.

REGISTRATION NO. 340
(Vol. 1, p. 168)

George Solomon

13 October 1831

George Solomon is about 48 years old, 5 feet 7 3/4 inches tall, of a dark complexion, with a small scar on the right side of his upper lip. He was emancipated by Chr[istopher] Frye, as appears by deed recorded in Liber J[?] No. 2, folio 447.

REGISTRATION NO. 341
(Vol. 1, p. 168)

Jane Morris

15 October 1831

Jane Morris is a mulatto woman, about 35 years old, 5 feet 5 3/4 inches tall, very deaf, with a scar on her forehead near the hair and a defect in each of her fourth fingers. She was manumitted by Josiah Watson by deed dated 15 February 1796 and recorded in Fairfax County.

REGISTRATION NO. 342
(Vol. 1, p. 168)

Jesse Jennings

20 October 1831

Jesse Jennings is a dark mulatto man, about 73 years old, 5 feet 9¼ inches tall, with a defect in both of his little fingers. He is free, as appears by affidavit of William Clark.

REGISTRATION NO. 343
(Vol. 1, p. 169)

Orris Redman and children
Maria, William, and Edward

24 October 1831

Orris Redman is a free woman about 46 years old, 5 feet 4¼ inches tall, and of a dark complexion. She was sold by William Fowle to her husband, William Redman, by bill of sale dated 5 November 1809, in which it was declared that her issue was to be free upon the death of William Redman. Dr. John D. Vowell certifies that the event has taken place. Orris and William Redman have three children: Maria, William and Edward.

REGISTRATION NO. 344
(Vol. 1, p. 169)

Sinah Solomon

26 October 1831

Sinah Solomon is a mulatto woman, about 24 years old, 5 feet 2 3/4 inches tall, with a scar on her forehead over her left eye. She was born free, as appears by affidavit of James Frazier.

REGISTRATION NO. 345
(Vol. 1, p. 169)

Til Berry 26 October 1831

Til Berry is a free man, about 40 years old, 5 feet 6½ inches tall, of a dark complexion, with a small scar on the lid of his right eye, and a scar on the right side of his face. Rachael Wheeler's will devised Berry to Nathaniel Newton during the life of Newton, after which he was to be freed. Jemima Jenkins swears that Newton has died and that Til Berry is free.

REGISTRATION NO. 346
(Vol. 1, p. 170)

William Valentine 7 November 1831

William Valentine is a black man, about 31 years old, 5 feet 10 inches tall, with a small scar on his under lip. He was manumitted by Caesar Valentine by deed dated 5 June 1829.

REGISTRATION NO. 347
(Vol. 1, p. 170)

Sophia Humphries and children, 7 November 1831
Georgeanna and Susanna

Sophia Humphries is a free mulatto woman, about 30 years old, 5 feet 1½ inches tall, with several scars on her throat and neck, and has a stout frame. She has filed in this office a certificate from Alexander Moore, notary public, that she is free. She has two children, Georgeanna, aged 4, and Susanna, aged 3.

REGISTRATION NO. 348
(Vol. 1, p. 170)

Ellen Lomax and children, 8 November 1831
David, Sarah Ann, Margaret,
Ann Eliza, Delilah, Julia,
Caroline, and Hiram

Ellen Lomax is a dark mulatto woman, about 34 years old, 5 feet 8½ inches tall, with a scar on the upper part of her breast. She was emancipated by Isaac Clarke by deed dated 19 October 1831, together with the following children: David, aged 18; Sarah Ann, aged 16; Margaret, aged 13; Ann Eliza, aged 12; Delilah, aged 8; Julia, aged 7; Caroline, aged 3; and Hiram, aged 8 months.

REGISTRATION NO. 349
(Vol. 1, p. 171)

John Henry Deane 10 November 1831

John Henry Deane is a mulatto man, about 29 years old, 5 feet 7½ inches tall, with a scar on his chin, a scar near the left corner of his mouth, a scar on the upper joint of the little finger of his left hand, and two scars on the calf of his left leg. He was born free, as appears by affidavit of the clerk of the Circuit Court of the District of Columbia for the County of Washington.

REGISTRATION NO. 350
(Vol. 1, p. 171)

Kitty Fox 11 November 1831

Kitty Fox is a free black woman, about 40 years old, 5 feet 5 inches tall, and is slender made. She was emancipated by Martha Washington, widow of the late General George Washington, as appears by certification of the clerk of Fairfax County, dated 1 January 1801.

REGISTRATION NO. 351
(Vol. 1, p. 171)

Isaac Fox 11 November 1831

Isaac Fox is a free mulatto man, about 21 years old, 5 feet 6¼ inches tall, with a scar near the corner of his right eye. He was born free, as appears by affidavit of Davis Bowie.

REGISTRATION NO. 352
(Vol. 1, p. 172)

James Butler   17 November 1831

James Butler is about 19 years old, 5 feet 7 3/4 inches tall, with a small scar on the joint of the middle finger of his right hand. He was born free, as appears by affidavit of Catharine Gray.

REGISTRATION NO. 353
(Vol. 1, p. 172)

Calvin Jones   17 November 1831

Calvin Jones is a bright mulatto man, about 24 years old, 5 feet 9 inches tall, with a scar on the joint of his left knee and straight black hair. He was emancipated by Robert Anderson by deed dated 10 May 1830.

REGISTRATION NO. 354
(Vol. 1, p. 172)

Jacob Halley   23 November 1831

Jacob Halley is a black man, about 54 years old, 5 feet 10 inches tall, with a scar on the right side of his face. He was emancipated by William Halley.

REGISTRATION NO. 355
(Vol. 1, p. 172)

Adeline Simpson   2- November 1831

Adeline Simpson is a very bright mulatto, about 19 years old, 5 feet 1 3/4 inches tall, with straight hair, and a scar on her upper lip. She was born free, as appears by affidavit of Davis Bowie.

REGISTRATION NO. 356
(Vol. 1, p. 173)

Lavinia Bailey   30 November 1831

Lavinia Bailey is a dark mulatto, about 56 years old, 5 feet 2¼ inches tall, with a mole on her right cheek. She was emancipated by John Watts by deed dated 1 July 1803.

REGISTRATION NO. 357
(Vol. 1, p. 173)

Elizabeth Honesty   30 November 1831

Elizabeth Honesty is a black woman, about 38 years old, 5 feet 4½ inches tall, with a large scar on her right arm caused by a burn. She was born free, as appears by affidavit of William Minor.

REGISTRATION NO. 358
(Vol. 1, p. 173)

Samuel Hyson   30 November 1831

Samuel Hyson is a black man, about 23 years old, 5 feet 8½ inches tall, with a small scar on his left eyebrow. He was born free, as appears by affidavit of William Minor.

REGISTRATION NO. 359
(Vol. 1, p. 173)

Delilah Hyson   30 November 1831

Delilah Hyson is a black girl, about 25 years old, 5 feet 1½ inches tall, with a scar on her right arm. She was born free, as appears by affidavit of William Minor.

REGISTRATION NO. 360
(Vol. 1, p. 174)

Jack Phenix   7 January 1832

Jack Phenix is a mulatto man, about 58 years old, 5 feet 8 inches tall, with a scar on the front of his right leg about midway between his knee and ankle. He was freed by Elizabeth Washington of Hayfield by deed dated 17 November 1809 recorded in Fairfax County.

REGISTRATION NO. 361
(Vol. 1, p. 174)

Lucinda Lee   12 January 1832

Lucinda Lee is about 24 years old, 5 feet 5 inches tall, of a dark complexion, with a large knot on her left wrist and a scar on the back of her left hand near the wrist. She is a free woman, as appears by affidavit of Lewis "Hipkins" [Hopkins].

REGISTRATION NO. 362
(Vol. 1, p. 174)

Dennis Conner   14 January 1832

Dennis Conner is a bright mulatto man, about 50 years old, 5 feet 9 inches tall, with a large mole on his left ear. He was emancipated by John A. Washington by deed recorded in 1821 in Fairfax County.

REGISTRATION NO. 363
(Vol. 1, p. 174)

Dennis McCarty   27 January 1832

Dennis McCarty is a free black man about 39 years old, 5 feet 8 inches tall, with a piece of his right ear bitten off. He was set free by John C. Herbert by deed dated 24 November 1805.

REGISTRATION NO. 364
(Vol. 1, p. 175)

John Beckley   1 February 1832

John Beckley is a bright mulatto man, about 28 years old, 5 feet 7¼ inches tall. He is a free man, as appears by affidavit of William Meade and the certificate of Mordecai Miller.

REGISTRATION NO. 365
(Vol. 1, p. 175)

Benjamin Harrison   5 March 1832

Benjamin Harrison, a free mulatto man, about 23 years old, has produced satisfactory evidence that he was born free. He is 5 feet 10½ inches tall, has a bright complexion, and has a scar on his left temple.

REGISTRATION NO. 366
(Vol. 1, p. 175)

William Curtis   19 March 1832

William Curtis is a mulatto man, about 24 years old, 5 feet 6¼ inches tall, with a number of scars on his legs caused by fire[?], a scar on his nose caused by a cut, and a round face and stout frame. He was born free, as appears by oath of John Rollings.

REGISTRATION NO. 367
(Vol. 1, p. 175)

Thomas Nickols   29 March 1832

Thomas Nickols is about 35 years old, 5 feet 11½ inches tall, of a dark complexion, with a scar over his right eye, one on his forehead, and one of the calf of his left leg. His hands have been much injured by frostbite. About four years ago, Thomas was taken up as a runaway, and, after remaining in confinement for some time, was released when no one claimed him. He has made application to be registered as a free Negro and that has been done.

REGISTRATION NO. 368
(Vol. 1, p. 176)

George Munay [possibly "Murray"?]   12 April 1832

George Munay[?] is a bright mulatto man, about 24 years old, 5 feet 8½ inches tall, with two scars on his right leg, black hair, and black eyes. He is a free person, as appears by affidavit of Alexander Moore.

REGISTRATION NO. 369
(Vol. 1, p. 176)

Children of Lydia Middleton: 27 April 1832
Ulysses, Chloe Ann,
Thomas Irvin and Richard Henry

The following persons are all children of Lydia Middleton, who was emancipated by A[quilla] Lockwood. Ulysses, aged 10 years and 1 month, with a slight scar on his left cheek; Chloe Ann, aged 8 years and 7 months, with a scar across the upper part of her nose; Thomas Irvin, aged 6 years and 4 months; and Richard Henry, aged 2 years and 3 months. All the children have very bright complexions and light hair.

REGISTRATION NO. 370
(Vol. 1, p. 176))

George Potten 27 April 1832

George Potten is a dark mulatto, about 36 years old, 5 feet 10 3/4 inches tall, with a scar on his breast caused by a knife cut. He has lost the use of his fingers on the right hand. He was committed to the jail as a runaway and advertised as such on 11 March 1831. No one claimed him and he was advertised and sold for a term of 12 months. He has served that period of time and has been discharged. He has applied to be registered and this has been done.

REGISTRATION NO. 371
(Vol. 1, p. 177)

Alfred Halley 1 May 1832

Alfred Halley is a free mulatto man, about 21 years old, 5 feet 11½ inches tall, straight hair, with no visible marks except a small mole on the back of his neck. His mother was a free woman, as appears by affidavit of Patterson Lyles.

REGISTRATION NO. 372
(Vol. 1, p. 177)

John Bowles 2 May 1832

John Bowles is a mulatto man, about 22 years old, 5 feet 8 3/4 inches tall, with a small scar on his left arm. He was born free, as appears by affidavit of Alexander Moore.

REGISTRATION NO. 373
(Vol. 1, p. 177)

John Jones 15 May 1832

John Jones is a mulatto man, about 21 years old, 5 feet 7 inches tall, with black hair, and no visible marks. He was manumitted by John Whiting by deed dated 11 May 1819 and recorded in Liber K No. 2, folio 42. In that deed he was called "Jack" and was 8 years old, and was to gain his freedom on 1 January 1832.

REGISTRATION NO. 374
(Vol. 1, p. 177)

Thacker Jones 15 May 1832
Charles Jones
Louisa Cole

Thacker Jones is a mulatto boy, about 19 years old, and 5 feet 6 inches tall. He was emancipated by John Whiting by deed dated 11 May 1819. Charles Jones, a bright mulatto about 17 years old, was emancipated by the same deed. Thacker and Charles have straight hair. Louisa Cole, a child aged about 7 years, is the daughter of Ellen Cole and was emancipated by deed from John Whiting dated 14 May 1827.

Lucinda Humphries swears that the above persons, John [Jones], Thacker, and Charles, were manumitted by Whiting in a deed dated 11 May 1819, and that Louisa is the daughter of Ellen Cole.

The "John" that Humphries names in the second paragraph is John Jones. See No. 373 directly above. For Ellen Cole's manumission from Whiting, see No. 200 above.

REGISTRATION NO. 375
(Vol. 1, p. 178)

Eveline Vasse 16 May 1832

Eveline Vasse is a mulatto girl, about 18 years old, 5 feet 3 inches tall, with a scar on her neck near the ear. She was emancipated by Ambrose Vasse.

REGISTRATION NO. 376
(Vol. 1, p. 178)

Henry Hoy

24 May 1832

Henry Hoy is a mulatto man, about 24 years old, 5 feet 7½ inches tall, with rather straight hair, and with a scar on the inner side of his right wrist and one on the back of his left hand. He was born free, as appears by affidavit of James Entwisle.

REGISTRATION NO. 377
(Vol. 1, p. 178)

James Bell

29 May 1832

James Bell is about 24 years old, 5 feet 6¼ inches tall, has a dark complexion, and is stout built. He was born free, as appears by affidavit of William Fox[?].

REGISTRATION NO. 378
(Vol. 1, p. 178)

Caroline Koones

11 June 1832

Caroline Koones is a bright mulatto, about 18 years old, 5 feet 3 3/4 inches tall, with straight black hair. She was born free, as appears by affidavit of George W. P. Custis.

REGISTRATION NO. 379
(Vol. 1, p. 179)

Rosanna Bowles

12 June 1832

Rosanna Bowles is a bright mulatto girl, about 16 years old, 5 feet 1¼ inches tall, with a scar on her left arm near the elbow. She was born free, as appears by affidavit of Richard Veitch.

REGISTRATION NO. 380
(Vol. 1, p. 179)

Simon Brown

13 June 1832

Simon Brown is a black man, about 22 years old, 5 feet 7½ inches tall, with a scar on the back of his left hand near the wrist. He was emancipated by Mordecai Miller.

REGISTRATION NO. 381
(Vol. 1, p. 179)

Mary Jane Murray

16 June 1832

Mary Jane Murray is a bright mulatto girl, about 9 years old, 4 feet 5 3/4 inches tall, with a small mole on her left shoulder blade. She was born free, as appears by affidavit of Alexander Moore.

REGISTRATION NO. 382a
(Vol. 1, p. 179)

Jane Deneale

25 June 1832

Jane Deneale is a bright mulatto woman, about 23 years old, 5 feet 2½ inches tall, with a scar on her right arm above the elbow.

REGISTRATION NO. 382b
(Vol. 1, p. 180)

Emeline Barton

3 July 1832

Emeline Barton is a dark mulatto girl, about 16 years old, 5 feet 3½ inches tall, stout built, with a round face, and with a scar on the back of her left hand. Barton has produced a copy of a judgement of the Baltimore City Court that supports her freedom. Sarah Prichard swears that Emeline is the person mentioned in that document.

REGISTRATION NO. 383
(Vol. 1, p. 180)

Cecelia Ramsay

3 July 1832

Cecelia Ramsay is a bright mulatto girl, about 18 years old, and 5 feet one-half inch tall. She has produced a copy of a judgement of the Baltimore City Court that supports her freedom. Sarah Prichard swears that Cecelia is one of the persons mentioned in that document.

REGISTRATION NO. 384
(Vol. 1, p. 180)

William Easton

17 July 1832

William Easton is a bright mulatto man, about 21 years old, 5 feet 6 3/4 inches tall, full face, with a small scar on the right side of his face. He was born free, as appears by affidavit of Chr[istopher] Neale.

REGISTRATION NO. 385
(Vol. 1, p. 180)

Moses Gales

18 July 1832

Moses Gales is about 21 years old, 5 feet 5½ inches tall, of a dark complexion, with a scar on his left arm caused by a cut. He was born free, as appears by affidavit of William P. Milmer

REGISTRATION NO. 386
(Vol. 1, p. 181)

Simon Miller

2 August 1832

Simon Miller, alias Sei[?], is about 25 years old, 5 feet 7½ inches tall, of a dark complexion, with a large scar on his left hand near the thumb caused by a cut. He obtained his freedom by judgement of the Circuit Court at its November 1830 term in which Simon was the plaintiff and Eloysius Thompson the defendant.

REGISTRATION NO. 387
(Vol. 1, p. 181)

Ann Hines

13 August 1832

Ann Hines is a dark mulatto woman, about 32 years old, 5 feet 1½ inches tall, with a large scar on her neck near the right shoulder caused by a burn. She was born free, as appears by affidavit of Ann Ligh[t]foot, a white woman.

REGISTRATION NO. 388
(Vol. 1, p. 181)

Lucy Hepburn

15 September 1832

Lucy Hepburn is a mulatto woman, about 23 years old, 5 feet 3 3/4 inches tall, of a bright complexion, with a small mole on her breast. She was emancipated by Richard H. Clagett by deed dated this day.

REGISTRATION NO. 389
(Vol. 1, p. 181)

Jonathan Waters

17 September 1832

Jonathan Waters is a dark mulatto man, about 30 years old, 5 feet 3½ inches tall, with a large scar on his right temple, and one on his right arm.

REGISTRATION NO. 390
(Vol. 1, p. 182)

William Loudoun

28 November 1832

William Loudoun is a free man, about 23 years old, 5 feet 6 3/4 inches tall, of a dark complexion, with some small scars on his left cheek, and with a round face. (See page 56)

See Registration No. 70 in this volume.

REGISTRATION NO. 391
(Vol. 1, p. 182)

Malvina[?] Barby   7 January 1833

Malvina[?] Barby is the child of Rosetta Barby, a free woman of color (see page 149), and is now about 4 years old. John W. Smith swears that Malvina[?] passes for the child of Rosetta and that he believes her to be such.

Rosetta Barby is registered in No. 269 in this volume.

REGISTRATION NO. 392
(Vol. 1, p. 182)

George Calvin   22 January 1833

George Calvin is a bright mulatto man, about 24 years, and 6 months old. He is 6 feet 1¼ inches tall, with a scar on his forehead. He was born free, as appears by affidavit of John West.

REGISTRATION NO. 393
(Vol. 1, p. 182)

Nelly Jackson   1 February 1833

Nelly Jackson is a mulatto woman, about 47 years old, 5 feet 2¼ inches tall, with a scar on her right cheek near the eye. Full evidence of her freedom appears on the records of this office.

REGISTRATION NO. 394
(Vol. 1, p. 182)

Priscilla Darnell   21 February 1833

Priscilla Darnell is a bright mulatto woman, about 22 years old, and 5 feet three-fourth inch tall. She was manumitted by Henry Darnell.

REGISTRATION NO. 395
(Vol. 1, p. 183)

Robert Butler   7 March 1833

Robert Butler is a black man, about 20 years old, 5 feet 7½ inches tall, with a small black mole in front of his right ear. He was born free, as appears by affidavit of Priscilla Simpson.

REGISTRATION NO. 396
(Vol. 1, p. 183)

Jemima Ross Merricks   8 April 1833

Jemima Ross, alias Jemima Merricks, is a mulatto girl, about 21 years old, 5 feet 3 inches tall, with a small mole on her left breast. She was born free, as appears by affidavit of Rebecca Ross.

REGISTRATION NO. 397
(Vol. 1, p. 183)

Lucinda Berry   2 May 1833

Lucinda Berry is a dark mulatto woman, 25 years old, and 5 feet 3½ inches tall. She was born free, as appears by affidavit of Davis Bowie.

REGISTRATION NO. 398
(Vol. 1, p. 183)

Hannah Dutcher   8 May 1833

Hannah Dutcher is a mulatto girl, about 18 years old, and 5 feet one-fourth inch tall.

REGISTRATION NO. 399
(Vol. 1, p. 184)

Emanuel Weaver   13 May 1833

Emanual Weaver is a black man, about 31 years old, 5 feet 9½ inches tall, with two large scars on his left hand and one on his left leg. He was manumitted by William Newton.

REGISTRATION NO. 400
(Vol. 1, p. 184)

Samson Sumby

15 May 1833

Samson Sumby is a dark mulatto, about 23 years old, and 5 feet 9½ inches tall. He was born free, as appears by affidavit of William H. Miller.

REGISTRATION NO. 401
(Vol. 1, p. 184)

Mary Bennett

14 May 1833

Mary Bennett is a very bright mulatto woman, about 23 years old, 5 feet 4 inches tall, with light hair and eyes and with a scar on her left arm above the elbow.

REGISTRATION NO. 402
(Vol. 1, p. 184)

William Douglas Bennett
James Waters Bennett

15 May 1833

William Douglas Bennett and James Waters Bennett are the children of Mary Bennett. William is about 5 years 6 months old and James is about 2 years old. Both were born free.

REGISTRATION NO. 403
(Vol. 1, p. 185)

Eliza Cole

17 May 1833

Eliza Cole is a dark mulatto girl, about 18 years old, 5 feet 2 3/4 inches tall, with a spot of white hair in her left eyebrow and white hair on the back of her head. Her freedom is proved by affidavit of Mrs. Ann Boothe.

REGISTRATION NO. 404
(Vol. 1, p. 185)

William Beckley

18 May 1833

William Beckley is a dark mulatto man, about 32 years old, 5 feet 5½ inches tall. He has a large scar on his right leg below the knee and a small scar over his right eye. William was born free, as appears by affidavit of Alexander Henderson. (See M. Bonds for the year 1827)

REGISTRATION NO. 405
(Vol. 1, p. 185)

William Briscoe

5 June 1833

William Briscoe is a mulatto man, about 37 years old, 5 feet 5 inches tall, with an oblique scar on the right side of the upper part of his forehead.

REGISTRATION NO. 406
(Vol. 1, p. 185)

David Easton

6 June 1833

David Easton is a mulatto man, about 23 years old, 5 feet 7 inches tall, with a scar above his left knee and a scar over his right eye. He was born free, as appears by affidavit of Alexander Moore.

REGISTRATION NO. 407
(Vol. 1, p. 186)

Maria Easton

15 June 1833

Maria Easton is a bright mulatto girl, about 18 years old, 5 feet 1 inch tall, with a scar on the top of her left foot. She was born free, as appears by affidavit of Alexander Moore.

REGISTRATION NO. 408
(Vol. 1, p. 186)

Daniel Brook

15 June 1833

Daniel Brook is a bright mulatto man, about 33 years old, 5 feet 4 3/4 inches tall, with two crooked fingers on his right hand which were broken. He was emancipated by James M. Stuart by deed recorded in Liber S No. 2, folio 565.

REGISTRATION NO. 409
(Vol. 1, p. 186)

William Syphax   20 June 1833

William Syphax is a mulatto man, about 60 years old, 5 feet 6½ inches tall, with gray and bushy hair, a small black mole under his left eye, and one on his left temple. He was set free by Thomas Brocchus and Samuel Wheeler by deed dated 21 November 1817.

REGISTRATION NO. 410
(Vol. 1, p. 186)

James Carter   24 June 1833

James Carter is about 23 years old, 5 feet 3½ inches tall, and has a bright complexion. He has some dark spots on his forehead and on the right side of his face, and the mark of a cut on the fleshy part of his left hand near the thumb. He is free according to a certificate from the Register of the Orphans' Court.

REGISTRATION NO. 411
(Vol. 1, p. 187)

Daniel Gibson   24 June 1833

Daniel Gibson is a dark mulatto, about 25 years old, 5 feet 6 inches tall, with the mark of a cut on his chin. He was emancipated by Catharine Ramsay and Samuel Miller.

REGISTRATION NO. 412
(Vol. 1, p. 187)

Richard Loudoun   [ca. June or July 1833]

Richard Loudoun is about 26 years old, 5 feet 7 3/4 inches tall, and has a dark complexion. He has a high forehead with a scar on it, and another scar on the inside of his right leg. He was registered on 29 Jan. 1821 in Registration No. 70.

REGISTRATION NO. 413
(Vol. 1, p. 187)

Betty Yorpp   23 July 1833

Betty Yorpp is a dark mulatto woman, about 46 years old, 5 feet 1 inch tall, who has lost her upper teeth. She was emancipated by Richard Veitch by deed dated 22 December 1819. (For the evidence of the freedom of her children, see certificate of Richard Veitch, filed.)

REGISTRATION NO. 414
(Vol. 1, p. 187)

Sally Loggins   25 July 1833

Sally Loggins is a mulatto woman, about 27 years old, 5 feet 1¼ inches tall, with a large burn scar on her right arm near the elbow and a scar from a cut on her right hand between the thumb and forefinger. She was set free by Peter Loggins by deed dated 17 November 1827.

REGISTRATION NO. 415
(Vol. 1, p. 188)

Henry Harris   5 August 1833

Henry Harris is a dark mulatto, about 19 years old, 5 feet 8 inches tall, with two small scars on the knuckles of his left hand. He was born free, as appears by affidavit of Alexander Moore.

REGISTRATION NO. 416
(Vol. 1, p. 188)

Ann Berry   7 August 1833

Ann Berry is a black woman, about 25 years old, 5 feet tall, with a scar on her right wrist. She was manumitted by Frederick Vaccari by deed dated 7 August 1833.

REGISTRATION NO. 417
(Vol. 1, p. 188)

Robert Bell

13 August 1833

Robert Bell is about 21 years old, 5 feet 4½ inches tall, of a dark complexion, with a scar over his left eye and another on his right wrist near the joint. He was born free, as appears by indentures of apprenticeship in his possession by which he was bound by the Orphans' Court of this county to serve Samuel Miller to learn the trade of biscuit baker.

REGISTRATION NO. 418
(Vol. 1, p. 188)

Paul Brown

16 August 1833

Paul Brown is about 17 years old, 5 feet 2 3/4 [possibly 10 3/4 inches] inches tall, and of a dark complexion, with a small scar over his left eye. He is the son of Rachel Brown who was emancipated by Mr. Miller, as appears by a certificate from R[obert] H. Miller filed in this office.

REGISTRATION NO. 419
(Vol. 1, p. 189)

James Lowry

23 August 1833

James Lowry is a bright mulatto man, about 28 years old, 5 feet 9 inches tall, with a small scar on his right wrist and one on his upper lip. He was born free, as appears by a certificate from the clerk of the corporation court of Winchester.

REGISTRATION NO. 420
(Vol. 1, p. 189)

Margaret Stark

14 September 1833

Margaret Stark is a bright mulatto woman, about 22 years old, 5 feet 3 3/4 inches tall, with a scar on the lower edge of her right jaw. She was born free, as appears by affidavit of Charles T. Chapman.

REGISTRATION NO. 421
(Vol. 1, p. 189)

Jesse Williams

18 September 1833

Jesse Williams is a dark mulatto man, about 43 years old, 5 feet 6½ inches tall, with a defect in his right little finger. He obtained his freedom by judgement of the Circuit Court of Alexandria County.

REGISTRATION NO. 422
(Vol. 1, p. 189)

Letty Parnell

24 September 1833

Letty Parnell is a black woman, about 44 years old, and 5 feet 3 inches tall. She has two small black moles on her forehead and is very stout. She was liberated by the will of Col. William Grayson, as appears by a certificate from the clerk of Frederick County.

REGISTRATION NO. 423
(Vol. 1, p. 190)

Benjamin Bowling

26 September 1833

Benjamin Bowling is a black man, about 28 years old, 5 feet 7 inches tall, with a scar on the left side of his face and a large scar on his right hand. He is free, as appears by affidavit of Samuel Wheeler.

REGISTRATION NO. 424
(Vol. 1, p. 190)

James Hall

4 October 1833

James Hall is a mulatto man, about 22 years old, 5 feet 5½ inches tall, with a scar on his forehead and two scars on his right cheek. He was born free, as appears by affidavit of Mrs. Margaret Thompson.

REGISTRATION NO. 425
(Vol. 1, p. 190)

Catharine Starks								14 October 1833

Catharine Starks is about 21 years old, 5 feet one-half inch tall, of a dark complexion, with a round face and a small round scar or mark on her face near her chin. She is free, as appears by affidavit of Davis Bowie. (See bundle of M. licenses 1833).

REGISTRATION NO. 426
(Vol. 1, p. 190)

Sarah Mitchell								16 October 1833

Sarah Mitchell is about 23 years old, 4 feet 11 inches tall, of a dark complexion, with a round and full face. She was emancipated by Christopher Frye by deed dated 28 April 1820 recorded in Liber J[?] No. 2, folio 447. She was identified by Benjamin Waters.

REGISTRATION NO. 427
(Vol. 1, p. 191)

William Henry Barcroft							19 October 1833

William Henry Barcroft is a free mulatto boy, about 18 years old, 5 feet 6¼ inches tall, with a black Indian ink mark resembling an anchor on his left arm. Edmund J. Lee, the clerk of the Circuit Court, states that he knows Barcroft is free.

REGISTRATION NO. 428
(Vol. 1, p. 191)

Emily Evans								13 January 1834

Emily Evans is a mulatto woman, about 50 years old, 5 feet 6 inches tall, with a freckled face and a scar on her right wrist. She was born free, as appears by oath of Davis Bowie.

REGISTRATION NO. 429
(Vol. 1, p. 191)

Daniel Davis								17 January 1834

Daniel Davis is a black man, about 25 years old, 5 feet 7¼ inches tall, with a slight scar on his nose. He was born free, as appears by affidavit of Sarah Harper.

REGISTRATION NO. 430
(Vol. 1, p. 191)

Barney Norris								[ca. January 1834]

Barney Norris is a free mulatto man, about 24 years old, of a very bright complexion, with a mole under his left ear and a mole on the right side of his throat.

REGISTRATION NO. 431
(Vol. 1, p. 192)

William Waugh								7 February 1834

William Waugh is a mulatto man, about 21 years old, 5 feet 7 3/4 inches tall, with a scar from a cut on the inside of his right foot. He was born free, as appears by the affidavit of James Coleman.

REGISTRATION NO. 432
(Vol. 1, p. 192)

James Sumby								8 February 1834

James Sumby is about 20 years old, 5 feet 7½ inches tall, of dark complexion, with a scar on his right wrist. He has a round face and a rather stout frame. He was born free, as appears by a certificate from Robert H. Miller.

REGISTRATION NO. 433
(Vol. 1, p. 192)

Alfred Triplett								12 February 1834

Alfred Triplett is a mulatto boy, about 19 years old, and 5 feet 3¼ inches tall. He was emancipated by Ambrose Vasse by deed recorded in Liber P No. 2, folio 377.

REGISTRATION NO. 434
(Vol. 1, p. 192)

Ellis Barton

25 February 1834

Ellis Barton is about 40 years old, 5 feet 7 inches tall, of a dark complexion, with a scar on her breast near her neck. She obtained her freedom by judgement of the Baltimore City Court. Barton was identified by Sarah Prichard.

REGISTRATION NO. 435
(Vol. 1, p. 192)

Peter Lee

8 March 1834

Peter Lee is a black man, about 37 years old, 5 feet 5 3/4 inches tall, with a scar from a cut on his right forearm near the elbow and another over his right eye.

REGISTRATION NO. 436
(Vol. 1, p. 193)

Dorcas Turley

18 March 1834

Dorcas Turley is a mulatto woman, about 45 years old, 5 feet 2 3/4 inches tall, with a black mole on the lower back part of her neck. She was emancipated by Jonathan Janney.

REGISTRATION NO. 437
(Vol. 1, p. 193)

Maria Turley

18 March 1834

Maria Turley is a very bright mulatto, about 24 years old, 5 feet 4 3/4 inches tall, with a horizontal scar on the brow of her left eye. She was liberated by Jonathan Janney.

REGISTRATION NO. 438
(Vol. 1, p. 193)

Mary Simpson

19 March 1834

Mary Simpson is a mulatto woman, about 20 years old, 5 feet 1 3/4 inches tall, with a mole on her left breast. She was liberated by Mrs. Harriet M[ason] Lloyd by deed dated 12 December 1833.

REGISTRATION NO. 439
(Vol. 1, p. 193)

Patsey Cryer

21 March 1834

Patsey Cryer is a dark mulatto woman, about 22 years old, 4 feet 11 3/4 inches tall, with a small vertical scar on her right eyebrow near her nose. She was born free, as appears by affidavit of Benjamin Cryer.

REGISTRATION NO. 440
(Vol. 1, p. 194)

Betsey Johnson

26 March 1834

Betsey Johnson is about 39 years old, 5 feet 1 3/4 inches tall, and has a dark complexion. She was emancipated by J[ohn] C. Herbert by deed dated 24 November 1805 in which she is described as "Bet daughter of Peg."

REGISTRATION NO. 441
(Vol. 1, p. 194)

William Morrison

7 April 1834

William Morrison is a mulatto man, about 44 years old, and 5 feet 7½ inches tall. He was liberated by William Morgan.

REGISTRATION NO. 442
(Vol. 1, p. 194)

Peter Brown   7 April 1834

Peter Brown is a Negro man, about 30 years old, 5 feet 9½ inches tall, of a dark complexion, with a mark on his right thigh. He was liberated by Robert Jamieson.

REGISTRATION NO. 443
(Vol. 1, p. 194)

Albert Rookard   14 April 1834

Albert Rookard is about 24 years old, 5 feet 7½ inches tall, of a dark complexion, with a large scar over his left eye. He was emancipated by Robert Jamieson by deed dated 10 October 1833.

REGISTRATION NO. 444
(Vol. 1, p. 195)

Douglas Bennett   15 April 1834

Douglas Bennett is a mulatto boy, about 19 years old, 5 feet 7½ inches tall, with the letter "D" marked in blue on his left arm. He was born free.

REGISTRATION NO. 445
(Vol. 1, p. 195)

Isabella Lewis   17 April 1834

Isabella Lewis is a dark mulatto woman, about 18 years old, 5 feet 2½ inches tall, with a scar on the upper part of her forehead. She was born free, as appears by certificates from Samuel Collard and others.

REGISTRATION NO. 446
(Vol. 1, p. 195)

Joseph Feirel   19 April 1834

Joseph Feirel is a dark mulatto man, about 40 years old, and 5 feet 3 1/8 inches tall. He was liberated by Robert Jamieson.

REGISTRATION NO. 447
(Vol. 1, p. 195)

Edward Evans   21 April 1834

Edward Evans is a bright mulatto man, about 21 years old, 5 feet 9¼ inches tall, with a small scar on his nose. He is free, as appears by certificate of Peter Hewitt to whom he was bound as an apprentice to learn the baking business.

REGISTRATION NO. 448
(Vol. 1, p. 196)

Ottoway West   22 April 1834
James West
Robert West

Ottoway West is a dark mulatto, about 14 years old, and is the son of Harriet West, a free woman of color. James West, about 12 years old, of a rather brighter complexion than his brother, and Robert West, a dark mulatto about 9 years old, were also registered.

REGISTRATION NO. 449
(Vol. 1, p. 196)

Catharine Evans and children,   12 May 1834
Sarah Ann and Ann Augustus

Catharine Evans is a mulatto woman, about 32 years old, 5 feet 7½ inches tall, with a small scar on the knuckle of the forefinger of her left hand, and a small black mole on the lower lid of her right eye. She was born free, as appears by affidavit of Davis Bowie. Evans says that she has two children, Sarah Ann, aged 14, and Ann Augustus, aged 4 years.

REGISTRATION NO. 450
(Vol. 1, p. 196)

Sarah Evans   12 May 1834

Sarah Evans is a mulatto woman, about 22 years old, and 5 feet 2¼ inches tall. She was born free, as appears by affidavit of Davis Bowie.

REGISTRATION NO. 451
(Vol. 1, p. 196)

Cynthia Taylor   15 May 1834

Cynthia Taylor is a mulatto woman, about 28 years old, 5 feet 2¼ inches tall, with the upper joint of her right little finger [cut] off by a bone filer. She was liberated by Reuben Johnston.

REGISTRATION NO. 452
(Vol. 1, p. 197)

Richard Middleton   19 May 1834

Richard Middleton is a mulatto man, about 40 years old, 5 feet 6¼ inches tall, with a scar on his right arm near the wrist. He was emancipated by W. H. Quin[?].

REGISTRATION NO. 453
(Vol. 1, p. 197)

Celia Williams and   3 June 1834
son, Junus

Celia Williams is a bright mulatto, about 28 years old, and 4 feet 11½ inches tall. She, with her son, Junus, who is about 1 year and 7 months old, was liberated by Silas [H.] Reed by deed dated 2 June 1834.

REGISTRATION NO. 454
(Vol. 1, p. 197)

Betsey Primus   6 June 1834

Betsey Primus is about 21 years old, 5 feet 4¼ inches tall, and has a dark complexion. She was emancipated by Thomas Brick and others by deed recorded in Liber R No. 2, folio 367.

REGISTRATION NO. 455
(Vol. 1, p. 197)

James Townshend   10 June 1834

James Townshend is a black man, about 38 years old, and 5 feet 7 3/4 inches tall. He was emancipated by Charles McKnight by deed dated 14 November 1828.

REGISTRATION NO. 456
(Vol. 1, p. 198)

Mary Bell   10 June 1834

Mary Bell is a very bright mulatto, about 50 years old, 5 feet 4¼ inches tall, with a scar from a burn about midway on her forearm, and straight hair and hazel eyes. She is free, as appears by affidavit of Charles McKnight.

REGISTRATION NO. 457
(Vol. 1, p. 198)

Simeon Tate, Jr.   17 June 1834
Margaret Ann Tate
Cassandra Tate

"Simion" [Simeon] Tate is a mulatto boy born 12 March 1826; Margaret Ann Tate is a mulatto girl born 26 November 1831. They are both the children of Cassandra Tate and Simon Tate, free people of color. Cassandra is a mulatto woman, about 35 years old, and 5 feet 5 3/4 inches tall. She is free, as appears by affidavit of Chr[istopher] Neale.

REGISTRATION NO. 458
(Vol. 1, p. 198)

Kitty Smith   23 June 1834

Kitty Smith is a black girl, about 6 years old, and 3 feet 7½ inches tall. She was born free, as appears by affidavit of Judith Currie and by certificate of Phebe Butcher.

REGISTRATION NO. 459
(Vol. 1, p. 198)

John Darnell

3 July 1834

John Darnell is a mulatto man, about 19 years old, and 5 feet 5 inches tall. He was born free, as appears by affidavit of Henry Darnell.

REGISTRATION NO. 460
(Vol. 1, p. 199)

Robert Bell

8 July 1834

Robert Bell is a black man, about 21 years old, 5 feet 7 inches tall, with a small scar near the left side of his mouth. He was born free, as appears by affidavit of George Fuddie.

REGISTRATION NO. 461
(Vol. 1, p. 199)

Rachel Walker

19 July 1834

Rachel Walker is a mulatto girl, about 20 years old, 4 feet 11 inches tall, with a scar on the right corner of her mouth, a mark from a burn on her left wrist, and another on the left forearm. She was born free, as appears by affidavit of Townshend D. Fendall.

REGISTRATION NO. 462
(Vol. 1, p. 199)

Jane Ross

22 July 1834

Jane Ross is a very bright mulatto, about 21 years old, 5 feet 2½ inches tall, with a scar on her left cheek. She was born free, as appears by affidavit of John L. Hampson.

REGISTRATION NO. 463
(Vol. 1, p. 199)

George Mitchell

25 July 1834

George Mitchell is a mulatto man, about 24 years old, 5 feet 5 3/4 inches tall, with a scar on his left leg immediately below the knee. He was freed by Christopher Frye.

REGISTRATION NO. 464
(Vol. 1, p. 200)

William Cole

1 September 1834

William Cole is a bright mulatto man, about 23 years old, 5 feet 6½ inches tall, with a small black scar over his right eye and scars on the third and fourth fingers of the left hand. He is free, as appears by affidavit of James Avery.

REGISTRATION NO. 465
(Vol. 1, p. 200)

Sally Gordon

4 September 1834

Sally Gordon is a bright mulatto woman, about 50 years old, 5 feet 4+ inches tall, with a narrow straight scar on the back of her right hand. She is free, as appears by affidavit of James Avery.

REGISTRATION NO. 466
(Vol. 1, p. 200)

Lucretia Gibbs

8 September 1834

Lucretia Gibbs is a black girl, about 20 years old, 5 feet one-half inch tall, with a small mole on her breast. She was born free, as appears by affidavit of Elisa Kennedy.

REGISTRATION NO. 467
(Vol. 1, p. 201)

Francis Washington   17 September 1834

Francis Washington is about 42 years old, 5 feet 4 inches tall, and has a dark complexion The first finger and fingernail of his right hand appear to have been mashed and part of the fingernail cut off. Washington was emancipated by Robert Jamieson by deed recorded in Liber U No. 2, folio 495.

REGISTRATION NO. 468
(Vol. 1, p. 201)

Faith White   26 September 1834

Faith White is about 38 years old, 5 feet one-fourth inch tall, and has a dark complexion. She was born free, as appears by affidavit of Mary Ann Cole.

REGISTRATION NO. 469
(Vol. 1, p. 201)

Dennis and Livinia Wright   3 October 1834
and children, Charles
and Francis

Dennis Wright is about 40 years old and 5 feet 9 3/4 inches tall. The middle finger of his right hand appears to have been cut. He was emancipated by Daniel Parker by deed recorded among the land records of Washington County.

Livinia Wright, wife of Dennis Wright, is a dark mulatto, about 28 years old, 5 feet 1 inch tall, with a black mole on the right side of her neck. She was emancipated by O. H. Dibble by deed recorded among the land records of Washington County.

Dennis and Livinia have two children, Charles and Francis, who are also registered.

REGISTRATION NO. 470
(Vol. 1, p. 202)

Dennis Carpenter   11 October 1834

Dennis Carpenter is a bright mulatto man, about 34 years old, 5 feet 9¼ inches tall, with a scar on the left side of the front part of his head. He was liberated by Robert Jamieson.

REGISTRATION NO. 471
(Vol. 1, p. 202)

Mark Anthony Sumby   11 October 1834

Mark Anthony Sumby is a black man, about 30 years old, 5 feet 8½ inches tall, with large features. He was liberated by Isaac Shreve by deed dated 6 May 1809.

REGISTRATION NO. 472
(Vol. 1, p. 202)

William Stepney   13 October 1834

William "Stephney" [Stepney] is a black man, about 20 years old, 5 feet 6½ inches tall, with a scar on the inner joint of his right second finger. He is free, as appears by affidavit of John L. Hampson.

REGISTRATION NO. 473
(Vol. 1, p. 202)

Robert Carter   17 October 1834

Robert Carter is a bright mulatto man, about 21 years old, 5 feet 5 3/4 inches tall, with a scar on the left side of his face and another on the front of his left thigh.

REGISTRATION NO. 474
(Vol. 1, p. 203)

Lucinda Derrick   18 October 1834

Lucinda Derrick is about 18 years old, 4 feet 10½ inches tall, of a dark mulatto complexion, with a scar on her right cheek caused by a burn. She was born free, as appears by affidavit of William A. Williams.

REGISTRATION NO. 475
(Vol. 1, p. 203)

John Richards

23 October 1834

John Richards is a dark mulatto man, about 21 years old, 5 feet 7 inches tall, with a lump on the back of his head. He is free, as appears by affidavit of William A. Scholfield.

REGISTRATION NO. 476
(Vol. 1, p. 203)

Catharine Lewis

15 November 1834

Catharine Lewis is about 23 years old, 5 feet 2 3/4 inches tall, and has a dark complexion. She was born free, as appears by affidavit of R[obert] H. Miller.

REGISTRATION NO. 477
(Vol. 1, p. 203)

George Bentley

19 November 1834

George Bentley is a bright mulatto man, 21 years of age, 5 feet 9½ inches tall, with a large mark from a burn on the front of his left leg and another from a cut on the front of his right leg. He is free, as appears by oath of John Beckley.

REGISTRATION NO. 478
(Vol. 1, p. 204)

Mary Bremont

23 November 1834

Mary Bremont is a very bright mulatto girl, about 18 years old, 5 feet 1 inch tall, with a small mole on her right shoulder and a slight scar on her left cheek. She was born free, as appears by affidavit of Alexander Moore.

REGISTRATION NO. 479
(Vol. 1, p. 204)

Lewis Lee

16 December 1834

Lewis Lee is 5 feet 8¼ inches tall, of a dark complexion, with a scar caused by a cut on his left arm near the wrist. He obtained his freedom by judgement of the Circuit Court of this county at its April term in 1825 in the suit of Negroes Peter & Lewis against A. W. Preuss *et. al.* The court decided that Lewis was entitled to his freedom when he reached the age of 31 years which would be on 10 December 1834.

See Negroes Peter and Lewis v. D. T. Cureton and A. W. Preuss in 2 Cranch CC 561.

REGISTRATION NO. 480
(Vol. 1, p. 204)

Rosetta Potter and
child, Lydia Ann

23 January 1835

Rosetta Potter is a dark mulatto woman, about 23 years old, 5 feet 1½ inches tall, with a burn scar on her right forearm. She has a child named Lydia Ann who is 2 years old with a burn scar on the right side of her neck. Rosetta and her child were liberated by Joseph C. Moore by deed dated this day.

REGISTRATION NO. 481
(Vol. 1, p. 205)

Henry Lomax

23 February 1835

Henry Lomax is a black man, about 28 years old, 5 feet 5¼ inches tall, with a scar on the middle joint of the forefinger of his left hand. His freedom was proved by certificate from the clerk of Caroline County.

REGISTRATION NO. 482
(Vol. 1, p. 205)

Patsey Evans

6 March 1835

Patsey Evans is a dark mulatto, about 17 years old, 5 feet 2½ inches tall, with a small scar under her left eye caused by a cut.

REGISTRATION NO. 483
(Vol. 1, p. 205)

Emily Hanian

16 March 1835

Emily Hanian is a bright mulatto, about 22 years old, 5 feet 5 3/4 inches tall, with "large front teeth much exposed." She was born free, as appears by affidavit of Nancy Evans.

REGISTRATION NO. 484
(Vol. 1, p. 205)

Adeline Morris and children,
George, Ann Matilda,
and Jane Elisabeth Fortune

25 March 1835

Adeline Morris is a bright mulatto woman, about 29 years old, 5 feet 4 3/4 inches tall, with long straight hair and a small mole on the right side of her breast. Her freedom was proved by affidavit of Hannah Burke along with her children: George, aged 11; Ann Matilda, aged 9; and Jane Elisabeth (alias Fortune), aged 5.

There are no registrations numbered 485-488.

REGISTRATION NO. 489
(Vol. 1, p. 206)

William Henry Weston

26 March 1835

William Henry Weston is a mulatto man, about 24 years old, and 5 feet 7½ inches tall. He was born free (see the record for his mother on page 164).

For his mother, Sarah Weston, see No. 325 above.

REGISTRATION NO. 490
(Vol. 1, p. 206)

Caroline Townshend

4 May 1835

Caroline Townshend is a mulatto woman, about 30 years old, 5 feet 4 3/4 inches tall, with a scar on the back of her right hand about an inch in length. She was liberated by James Townshend.

REGISTRATION NO. 491
(Vol. 1, p. 206)

Winny Gander

4 May 1835

Winny Gander is about 30 years old, 5 feet 5 inches tall, of a dark complexion, with a scar over her right eye caused by a cut. She was emancipated by her husband, Lewis Gander, by deed dated 4 May 1835.

REGISTRATION NO. 492
(Vol. 1, p. 206)

Nancy Dorsey
Martha Dorsey
Sally Ross

8 May 1835

Nancy Dorsey is a mulatto woman, about 37 years old, 5 feet 4 3/4 inches tall, with a mark on the outer joint of her left forefinger and a scar from a burn on the inner joint of her left thumb; Martha Dorsey is a mulatto girl about 18 years old, 5 feet 5½ inches tall, and is the daughter of Nancy; Sally Ross is a very bright mulatto woman about 23 years old, 5 feet 7¼ inches tall, and is also a daughter of Nancy Dorsey. These persons are free, as appears by affidavit of Chr[istopher] Neale, Esq.

REGISTRATION NO. 493
(Vol. 1, p. 207)

Henrietta Taylor

8 May 1835

Henrietta Taylor is a mulatto girl, about 11 years old, 4 feet 7¼ inches tall, with diseased eyes. She was born free, as appears by affidavit of Mrs. Elmira Beale.

REGISTRATION NO. 494
(Vol. 1, p. 207)

Richard Amerger   9 May 1835

Richard Amerger is a dark mulatto man, about 21 years old, 5 feet 9¼ inches tall, with a scar on his right foot and numerous dark spots and moles on his hands and face. He was born free, as appears by affidavit of Venus Humphrey.

REGISTRATION NO. 495
(Vol. 1, p. 207)

Jane Hall   13 May 1835

Jane Hall is a very dark mulatto, about 23 years old, 5 feet one-fourth inch tall, with a mole on the upper edge of her right eyebrow. She was liberated by Elisabeth B. Winter.

REGISTRATION NO. 496
(Vol. 1, p. 207)

Desdemona Brooks   11 May 1835

Desdemona Brooks is a mulatto woman, 30 years old, 5 feet 4 inches tall, with a freckled face and "only one point per tooth." Her mother was a white woman.

REGISTRATION NO. 497
(Vol. 1, p. 208)

William Beckley   15 May 1835

William Beckl[e]y is a bright mulatto boy, about 19 years old, 5 feet 6¼ inches tall, with a scar on the left side of his right leg. He was born free, as appears by affidavit of Pri[s]cilla Simpson.

REGISTRATION NO. 498
(Vol. 1, p. 208)

Betsey Brown Washington   25 May 1835

Betsey Washington (formerly Betsey Brown) is a bright mulatto woman, 39 years old, 5 feet 3 inches tall, with two moles on the back of her neck and one on her left cheek. She was liberated by Mrs. Elisabeth Coke of Fauquier County, as appears by affidavit of Mrs. Jane F. Byrd.

REGISTRATION NO. 499
(Vol. 1, p. 208)

Elizabeth Currie   25 May 1835

"Elisabeth" [Elizabeth] Currie is a mulatto woman, about 24 years old, 4 feet 8 3/4 inches tall, with a small black spot on her left cheek about an inch from her mouth. She was born free as appears by Registration No. 217.

REGISTRATION NO. 500
(Vol. 1, p. 208)

Betty Washington   30 May 1835

Betty Washington is a black woman, about 60 years old, 5 feet 2¼ inches tall, with a scar from a cut on her left cheek. She was liberated by Margaret Garner.

REGISTRATION NO. 501
(Vol. 1, p. 209)

Nelson Harris   5 June 1835

Nelson Harris is a dark mulatto man, about 28 years old, 5 feet 5 3/4 inches tall, with a burn mark on the inside of his right wrist and a scar on his forehead near and in line with his nose. He was liberated by Mary and William Stabler, administrators of the estate of Edward Stabler.

REGISTRATION NO. 502
(Vol. 1, p. 209)

Jane Die   13 June 1835

Jane Die is a bright mulatto woman, about 43 years old, 5 feet 3 inches tall, with a scar at the end of her left eyebrow and a mole on the right side of her neck. She was liberated by Jonathan Janney.

REGISTRATION NO. 503
(Vol. 1, p. 209)

Hetty Tate

30 June 1835

Hetty Tate is a bright mulatto woman, about 35 years old, and 5 feet 3 inches tall. She was liberated by Dr. William F. Alexander.

REGISTRATION NO. 504
(Vol. 1, p. 209)

James Evans

25 July 1835

James Evans is about 35 years old, 5 feet 6 inches tall, with a dark complexion, bushy hair and a scar on the right side of his face. He has filed in this office a certificate stating that he is free signed by the mayor and dated 18 December 1822.

REGISTRATION NO. 505
(Vol. 1, p. 210)

Peyton Hines

10 August 1835

Peyton Hines is a dark mulatto man, about 22 years old, 5 feet 4½ inches tall, with several small scars near the outer corner of his left eye. He obtained his freedom by judgement of the Circuit Court of this county in the case of Peyton Hines v. Peter Hewitt.

See Peyton Hines v. Peter Hewitt, 4 Cranch CC 471.

REGISTRATION NO. 506
(Vol. 1, p. 210)

Leanna Payne

13 August 1835

Leanna Payne is a very bright mulatto woman, about 22 years old, 5 feet 4 3/4 inches tall, with two small moles immediately beneath her chin. She was born free, as appears by affidavit of Mrs. Sinah [B.] Porter.

REGISTRATION NO. 507a
(Vol. 1, p. 210)

Martha Payne

13 August 1835

Martha Payne is a very bright mulatto girl, about 16 years old, 5 feet 1½ inches tall, with a very small mole on her forehead about an inch above the inner end of the left eyebrow. She was born free, as appears by affidavit of Mrs. Sinah [B.] Porter.

REGISTRATION NO. 507b
(Vol. 1, p. 210)

William Minor

14 August 1835

William Minor is a mulatto man, about 21 years old, 5 feet 2¼ inches tall, with a small mole in front of his right shoulder and one in the middle of the root of his neck. He was liberated by Henry Darnell.

REGISTRATION NO. 508
(Vol. 1, p. 211)

Harriet Ann Jones

14 August 1835

Harriet Ann Jones is a very bright mulatto girl, about 21 years old, 5 feet tall, with freckles on her face and a scar on the middle of the inner side of her right forearm caused by a cut. She was born free, as appears by affidavit of William Yeaton.

REGISTRATION NO. 509
(Vol. 1, p. 211)

James Williams

21 August 1835

James Williams is a dark mulatto, aged about 23 years, 6 feet 1¼ inches tall, with a large scar on his left leg below the knee. He is free, as appears by affidavit of Robert Jamieson.

REGISTRATION NO. 510
(Vol. 1, p. 211)

Beverly Botts

22 August 1835

Beverly Botts is a bright mulatto boy, about 20 years old, 5 feet 9 inches tall, with his face marked by smallpox. He was born free, as appears by affidavit of Kitty "Doagan" [Dogan].

REGISTRATION NO. 511
(Vol. 1, p. 211)

Nancy Dudley

22 August 1835

Nancy Dudley is a very bright mulatto woman, 38 years old, 5 feet 7 inches tall, with a mole on her left cheek. She was born free, as appears by affidavit of Mrs. Mary Ann Cole.

REGISTRATION NO. 512
(Vol. 1, p. 211)

Betsey Berry

22 August 1835

Betsey Berry is a very bright mulatto woman, about 40 years old, 5 feet 6½ inches tall, with the nail of her right middle finger split, and with a freckled face. She was born free, as appears by affidavit of Mrs. Mary Ann Cole.

REGISTRATION NO. 513
(Vol. 1, p. 212)

William Cole

22 August 1835

William Cole is a bright mulatto man, about 44 years old, 6 feet tall, with several india ink marks on the back of his left hand and on his left forearm (those on his arm representing, among others, an anchor with the letters "W. C." and "M. C."). He has two moles on his left cheek and one on his left breast. He was born free and is the son of Mary Ann Cole, a white woman now residing in this county.

REGISTRATION NO. 514
(Vol. 1, p. 212)

George Cole

22 August 1835

George Cole is a free mulatto man, about 47 years old, 5 feet 8¼ inches tall, with a curved scar from a cut on the left side upper part of his forehead, and another, also from a cut, on his left wrist. He was born free and is the son of Mary Ann Cole, a white woman now residing in this county.

REGISTRATION NO. 515
(Vol. 1, p. 212)

Jane Noland

1 September 1835

Jane Noland is a bright mulatto woman, about 36 years old, 5 feet 1½ inches tall, with a small mole on her right temple about half an inch from her eyebrow. She was liberated by Robert J. Taylor.

REGISTRATION NO. 516
(Vol. 1, p. 212)

William Slade

1 September 1835

William Slade is a very bright mulatto man, about 21 years old, 5 feet 5 3/4 inches tall, with straight hair and a mole below and near the left corner of his mouth. He was liberated by Robert J. Taylor.

REGISTRATION NO. 517
(Vol. 1, p. 213)

Louisa Gibson

1 September 1835

Louisa Gibson is a very bright mulatto woman, about 26 years old, 5 feet 4¼ inches tall, with a small indentation on the end of her nose and a scar on the outer side of her right ankle. She was born free, as appears by affidavit of Jane Evans.

REGISTRATION NO. 518
(Vol. 1, p. 213)

Thomas Fox

4 September 1835

Thomas Fox is a very dark mulatto, about 22 years old, 5 feet 7¼ inches tall, with a scar on his right temple near the eye. He was born free, as appears by affidavit of Robert Allison.

REGISTRATION NO. 519
(Vol. 1, p. 213)

Mary Ann Payne

9 September 1835

Mary Ann Payne is a very bright mulatto girl, 18 years old, and 5 feet 2¼ inches tall. She has a slightly freckled face and a scar on the inner side of the third finger of her left hand on the joint. She was born free, as appears by affidavit of Mrs. Sinah [B.] Porter.

REGISTRATION NO. 520
(Vol. 1, p. 213)

Thomas Oscar

9 September 1835

Thomas Oscar is 5 feet 7½ inches tall, has a bright complexion, and a freckled face. He has no visible marks. He was emancipated by Bazil H. Davidson by deed dated 13 August 1823 recorded in Liber P No. 2, folio 32.

REGISTRATION NO. 521
(Vol. 1, p. 214)

Dennis Bourbon

10 September 1835

Dennis Bourbon is about 20 years old, 5 feet 5½ inches tall, has a dark complexion, and no visible marks. He was emancipated by Bazil H. Davidson by deed dated 13 August 1823 recorded in Liber P No. 2, folio 32.

REGISTRATION NO. 522
(Vol. 1, p. 214)

David Currie

18 September 1835

David Currie is a Negro man, about 22 years old, 5 feet 6¼ inches tall, with a scar on the back of his left forearm near his wrist, one on his left breast, and one on the lower joint of his right thumb. He was born free, as appears by a certificate from Jacob Hoffman.

REGISTRATION NO. 523
(Vol. 1, p. 214)

Amy Black

24 September 1835

Amy Black is a mulatto woman, about 28 years old, 5 feet 2½ inches tall, with a scar on her right forearm near the elbow and a scar from a burn on the angle of her right jaw reaching to the lower joint of the ear. She is free, as appears by affidavit of John West.

There is no registration numbered 524.

REGISTRATION NO. 525
(Vol. 1, p. 214)

David Williams

9 October 1835

David Williams is a black man, about 42 years old, 5 feet 7 inches tall, with his left forefinger somewhat deformed and disabled and a scar near the outer corner of his left eye. He was liberated by John Wood and Thomas Davey.

REGISTRATION NO. 526
(Vol. 1, p. 215)

William Payne

20 October 1835

William Payne is a bright mulatto man, about 30 years old, and 6 feet one-eighth inch tall. He has a scar from a cut on the hind part of his right leg below the calf, another on the outer side of his leg on a horizontal line with the first from a rising, and another on his left thumb. He was liberated by Sinah B. Porter.

REGISTRATION NO. 527
(Vol. 1, p. 215)

Lucinda Oldham

22 October 1835

Lucinda Oldham is about 20 years old, 5 feet 1 inch tall, with a dark complexion and a large scar on the back of her neck. She was emancipated by Stephen Shinn by deed recorded in Liber U No. 2, folio 410.

REGISTRATION NO. 528
(Vol. 1, p. 215)

Lerue Smith

22 October 1835

Lerue Smith is about 29 years old, 4 feet 10½ inches tall, of a dark complexion, with a small scar over her right eye. She is free, as appears by affidavit of Wesley Carlin.

REGISTRATION NO. 529
(Vol. 1, p. 215)

William Clagett

23 October 1835

William Clagett is a mulatto man, about 27 years old, 5 feet 5½ inches tall. The sinews of his left hand have been burned and are drawn up and he has a scar on the left side of his face. He was emancipated by George Coryell and Silas [H.] Reed.

REGISTRATION NO. 530
(Vol. 1, p. 216)

Mary Bowman

29 October 1835

Mary Bowman is a dark mulatto woman, about 40 years old, 5 feet 4 3/4 inches tall, with a scar on her neck. She was liberated by John W. Smith of Alexandria.

REGISTRATION NO. 531
(Vol. 1, p. 216)

Nancy Williams

3 November 1835

Nancy Williams is a dark mulatto woman, about 45 years old, 5 feet 6½ inches tall, with a freckled face and rather high cheekbones. She is free, as appears by affidavit of Chr[istopher] Neale, Esq.

REGISTRATION NO. 532
(Vol. 1, p. 216)

Ann Elizabeth Brooks

3 November 1835

Ann Elizabeth Brooks is a dark mulatto girl, about 17 years old, 5 feet 1¼ inches tall. She is the daughter of Desdemona Brooks, a free woman of color, as appears by certificate of Mrs. Ann S. Mark.

REGISTRATION NO. 533
(Vol. 1, p. 216)

Samuel T. Williams

9 November 1835

Samuel T. Williams is about 21 years old, 5 feet 11¼ inches tall, with a dark complexion and a small scar on his face near his right eye. He is free, as appears by affidavit of John P. Conman[?].

REGISTRATION NO. 534
(Vol. 1, p. 216)

Mary Bowling Turner and
children, Dick and Hannah

30 November 1835

Mary Turner, formerly Bowling, is about 26 years old, 5 feet 3 3/4 inches tall, of a dark complexion, with a mark from a burn on her left breast. Her freedom, and that of her son Dick, aged 7, and her daughter Hannah, aged about 5, was proved by of oath of Samuel Wheeler.

REGISTRATION NO. 535
(Vol. 1, p. 217)

Hannah Bowling and children
George Henry Isaac and Nancy

30 November 1835

Hannah Bowling is a dark mulatto woman, about 24 years old, 5 feet 4 inches tall, with a burn scar on her left forearm, and a black spot near the right corner of her mouth. Her freedom and that of her son, George Henry Isaac, aged about 7, and her daughter, Nancy, aged about 3, was proved by oath of Samuel Wheeler.

REGISTRATION NO. 536
(Vol. 1, p. 217)

Julia Bowling

30 November 1835

Julia Bowling is about 19 years old, 5 feet 3½ inches tall, and of a dark complexion. Her freedom was proved by oath of Samuel Wheeler.

REGISTRATION NO. 537
(Vol. 1, p. 217)

Rebecca Turner

30 November 1835

Rebecca Turner is a dark mulatto girl, about 9 years old, with a mark from a burn on her left arm near her elbow. She was born free, as appears by affidavit of George Bowling.

REGISTRATION NO. 538
(Vol. 1, p. 217)

Samuel Hopes

1 December 1835

Samuel Hope[s] is a dark mulatto, about 27 years old, 5 feet 6¼ inches tall, with a mark on his belly. He was born free, as appears by a certificate from Alexander Moore, Register of Wills.

REGISTRATION NO. 539
(Vol. 1, p. 218)

Polly Savoy

4 December 1835

Polly Savoy is a nearly black woman, about 38 years old, and 5 feet 4 inches tall. Her freedom was proved by oath of Capt. Robert Brockett.

REGISTRATION NO. 540
(Vol. 1, p. 218)

Daniel Smith, aka Haley

7 December 1835

Daniel Smith, also called Daniel Haley, is a bright mulatto man, about 22 years old, 5 feet 7 inches tall, with an indentation on his right cheek perceptible only when he smiles. He was liberated by Maria Blue and Robert and Britannia Bell by deed recorded in Liber Q No. 2, folio 329.

REGISTRATION NO. 541
(Vol. 1, p. 218)

Ellen Burwell

11 December 1835

Ellen Burwell is a mulatto woman, about 23 years old, 5 feet 2 inches tall, with a scar on the back of her right wrist. She was born free, as appears by affidavit of Alexander Moore.

REGISTRATION NO. 542
(Vol. 1, p. 218)

Moses Bowling

16 December 1835

Moses Bowling is about 29 years old, 5 feet 10 3/4 inches tall, of a dark complexion, with no visible marks. He is free, as appears by oath of William Lanphier, Jr.

REGISTRATION NO. 543
(Vol. 1, p. 219)

William Dutcher

13 January 1836

William Dutcher is a dark mulatto man, about 27 years old, 5 feet 8 3/4 inches tall with the initials of his name marked with india ink on his left arm (M.D.). He is free, as appears by affidavit of Davis Bowie dated 20 July 1829.

See No. 276 above for a previous registration.

REGISTRATION NO. 544
(Vol. 1, p. 219)

Elizabeth Ann Waugh Grymes

16 March 1836

Elizabeth Ann Grymes (formerly Waugh) is a mulatto woman, about 27 years old, 5 feet 5 3/4 inches tall, with the back of her left hand marked slightly by a scald. She was born free, as appears by registration No. 288.

REGISTRATION NO. 545
(Vol. 1, p. 219)

James Wilson, Jr.

21 March 1836

James Wilson is a mulatto boy, about 20 years old, 5 feet 3 3/4 inches tall, with a mark near the outer corner of his left eye and "a mole on the right side of his mole." He is free, as appears by registration No. 58.

REGISTRATION NO. 546
(Vol. 1, p. 220)

Alice Wilson and
son, Samuel

1 March 1836

Alice Wilson is a bright mulatto woman, about 40 years old, 5 feet 1 3/4 inches tall, with a small mole on her upper lip. She is free as appears by registration No. 58. Her son Samuel, aged about 6 years old, was born free.

REGISTRATION NO. 547
(Vol. 1, p. 220)

Mary Ann Lee

7 April 1836

Mary Ann Lee is a dark mulatto woman, about 23 years old, 5 feet 2¼ inches tall, with a scar from a burn on the inner side of the lower joint of the second finger of her left hand. She was freed by Benoni Wheat.

REGISTRATION NO. 548
(Vol. 1, p. 220)

Jane Johnson

11 April 1836

Jane Johnson is a dark mulatto woman, about 40 years old, 5 feet 1 3/4 inches tall, and marked by smallpox.

REGISTRATION NO. 549
(Vol. 1, p. 220)

James Wilson and
sons, Robert and Albert

13 April 1836

James Wilson is about 54 years old, 5 feet 5 inches tall, with a scar on the back of his neck. He has produced satisfactory evidence of his freedom. His two sons, Robert, aged about 14 and Albert, aged about 11 years, were also registered.

REGISTRATION NO. 550
(Vol. 1, p. 221)

Betsy Wheeler

15 April 1836

Betsy Wheeler is a mulatto girl, about 9 years old, 4 feet 2 3/4 inches tall. She was born free and is the daughter of Minny Wheeler, as appears by affidavit of Mrs. Ann Brooks.

REGISTRATION NO. 551
(Vol. 1, p. 221)

Mary Rhodes

6 May 1836

Mary Rhodes is a mulatto girl, about 16 years old, and 5 feet 5 3/4 inches tall. She has a slight semicircular scar on her right cheek and long bushy, nearly straight hair. She was born free, as appears by affidavit of Alexander Moore.

REGISTRATION NO. 552
(Vol. 1, p. 221)

Alfred Hines

10 May 1836

Alfred Hines is a dark mulatto man, about 29 years old, 5 feet 3½ inches tall, with a dark spot on his left cheek and a scar on the inner joint of his right middle finger. He was born free, as appears by affidavit of Mrs. Ann Lightfoot.

REGISTRATION NO. 553
(Vol. 1, p. 221)

Charles Darnell

13 May 1836

Charles Darnell is a bright mulatto man, about 23 years old, 5 feet 6 3/4 inches tall, with his face marked with smallpox. He is free born, as appears by affidavit of P[eter] E. Hoffman.

REGISTRATION NO. 554
(Vol. 1, p. 221)

Henry Darnell

13 May 1836

Henry Darnell is a bright mulatto man, about 22 years old, and 5 feet 5½ inches tall. He was born free, as appears by affidavit of P[eter] E. Hoffman.

REGISTRATION NO. 555
(Vol. 1, p. 222)

Nancy Robinson

21 May 1836

Nancy Robinson is a bright mulatto woman, about 23 years old, with two small brown spots on the back of her left hand. She was liberated by Eleanor Nelson.

REGISTRATION NO. 556
(Vol. 1, p. 222)

Ann Bombray

25 May 1836

Ann Bombray is a bright mulatto girl, aged 14 5/12 years old, 5 feet 2¼ inches tall, with a rather faint scar nearly an inch long across her nose and a scar on the upper part of her forehead at the edge of her hair. She was born of free parents, as appears from the records of this office with the affidavit of Harriet Bombray.

See No. 144 above for Harriet "Bombay."

REGISTRATION NO. 557
(Vol. 1, p. 222)

Mary Robinson
John Robinson

31 May 1836

Mary Robinson is a bright mulatto woman, about 28 years old, 5 feet 4 inches tall, with a mole on the back of her neck near her right shoulder. She was liberated by Eleanor Nelson, as was her son, John Robinson, aged 10, who has a very bright complexion.

REGISTRATION NO. 558
(Vol. 1, p. 222)

Elizabeth Robinson and
daughter, Harriet Elisa

31 May 1836

Elizabeth Robinson is aged about 21 years, is 5 feet 2 inches tall, and is of a dark complexion. Her right arm and cheek are very much scarred by a burn. She was liberated by Eleanor Nelson, together with her daughter, Harriet Elisa, aged 1½ years.

REGISTRATION NO. 559
(Vol. 1, p. 223)

Alfred Gray

7 June 1836

Alfred Gray is a mulatto man, about 24 years old, 5 feet 6½ inches tall, with no visible marks. He was born free, as appears by affidavit of John S. Brown.

REGISTRATION NO. 560
(Vol. 1, p. 223)

Wesley, aka Vester, Hamilton

8 June 1836

Wesley (sometimes called "Vester") Hamilton is about 45 years old, 5 feet 8½ inches tall, with a bald head and a scar on his right eyebrow. He was liberated by the administrators of the estate of Anthony Crease.

REGISTRATION NO. 561
(Vol. 1, p. 223)

Ann Harris

14 June 1836

Ann Harris is a mulatto girl, 19 years old, 4 feet 10 inches tall, with a small scar on her left temple. She is slightly marked with smallpox. She was born free, as appears by the affidavit of Kinsey Ware.

REGISTRATION NO. 562
(Vol. 1, p. 223)

Jane Turley

21 June 1836

Jane Turley is about 37 years old, 5 feet 4¼ inches tall, with a dark complexion, and no visible marks. She was emancipated by Robert Jamieson, Esq., by deed recorded in Liber R No. 2, folio 52.

REGISTRATION NO. 563
(Vol. 1, p. 223)

Mary Ann Carmichael and
child, Elizabeth

25 June 1836

Mary Ann Carmichael is about 35 years old, 5 feet 2 3/4 inches tall, with a small scar on the right side of her face caused by a cut and another on the back of her right hand. She, and her child, Elizabeth, aged about 3 years, were emancipated by William Carmichael by deed recorded in Liber W No. 2, folio 64.

REGISTRATION NO. 564
(Vol. 1, p. 224)

Helin Handless

6 July 1836

Helin Handless is a mulatto woman, about 21 years old, 5 feet one-fourth inch tall, with a dark spot on her left breast near the shoulder. She was born free and is the daughter of Betty (or Eliza) Handless, a free woman of color, as appears by a certificate from Mrs. Elizabeth Quin[?].

REGISTRATION NO. 565
(Vol. 1, p. 224)

Jefferson Duval

18 July 1836

Jefferson Duval is a dark mulatto man, about 29 years old, 5 feet 4 3/4 inches tall, with a scar on his forehead and one on the middle finger of his right hand. He was born free as appears by certificate from Alexander Moore, notary public.

REGISTRATION NO. 566
(Vol. 1, p. 224)

Nancy Botts

18 July 1836.

Nancy Botts is a bright mulatto woman, about 23 years old, 5 feet 2½ inches tall, with a small black mole on the lower part of her throat and one on her left hand near the wrist. She was born free, as appears by affidavit of Kitty Dogan.

REGISTRATION NO. 567
(Vol. 1, p. 224)

James Butler   25 July 1836

James Butler is a bright mulatto man, aged about 22 years, 5 feet 6½ inches tall, with a mole on his left wrist. His freedom was proved by affidavit of John Grantt.

REGISTRATION NO. 568
(Vol. 1, p. 225)

Dennis Ferguson   29 July 1836

Dennis Ferguson is a black man, about 21 years old, 5 feet 8½ inches tall, with grey eyes and a scar on the edge of his chin. His freedom was proved by affidavit of William H. Miller.

REGISTRATION NO. 569
(Vol. 1, p. 225)

Rachel Brent and   30 July 1836
child, George

Rachel Brent is a black woman, about 21 years old, 5 feet 2¼ inches tall, with a scar on the outer edge of her right hand caused by a cut and one of the back of her right wrist from a burn. She was liberated by judgement of the Court at its May term in 1835. She, and her child, named George, aged about 1½ years, are registered.

REGISTRATION NO. 570
(Vol. 1, p. 225)

Louisa Tracey   3 August 1836

Louisa Tracey is a bright mulatto woman, about 23 years old, 5 feet 2 3/4 inches tall, with a full face and hazel eyes. Her freedom was proved by Matthias Snyder.

REGISTRATION NO. 571
(Vol. 1, p. 225)

Ann Elizabeth Brown   3 August 1836

Ann Elizabeth Brown is a bright mulatto woman, about 18 years old, 5 feet 4 inches tall, with a thin face and dark eyes. Edmund J. Lee, clerk of the court, testifies that she is free.

REGISTRATION NO. 572
(Vol. 1, p. 225)

Mary Ann Beckley   16 August 1836

Mary Ann Beckley is a very bright mulatto, about 20 years old, 5 feet 3½ inches tall, with a brown spot on the back of her left forearm about midway up. She was born free, as appears by a certificate from Newton Keene, Esq.

REGISTRATION NO. 573
(Vol. 1, p. 226)

Jane Waugh   30 August 1836

Jane Waugh is a mulatto woman, 5 feet 1 inch tall, with a scar on the back of her right hand and a number of moles on her face. She was born free, as appears by certificate of William Stabler.

REGISTRATION NO. 574
(Vol. 1, p. 226)

Mary Waugh   8 September 1836
Mary Bell or Waugh

Mary Waugh is a bright mulatto woman, about 55 years old, 5 feet 3½ inches tall, who is "large & fleshy." She was born free, as appears by certificate from William Stabler. Her grandchild, Mary Bell (or Waugh), aged about 12, with a bright complexion, was also registered.

REGISTRATION NO. 575
(Vol. 1, p. 226)

Kinsey Ware   14 September 1836

Kinsey Ware is a black man, about 46 years old, 5 feet 8¼ inches tall, with a scar nearly an inch long on his right cheek, three scars on the back of his right hand, and with the end of his little finger of the right hand cut off. His freedom was proved by affidavit of John Jamieson.

REGISTRATION NO. 576
(Vol. 1, p. 226)

Catharine Botts

22 September 1836

Catharine Botts is a mulatto girl, about 16 years old, 5 feet 4½ inches tall, with a red mark over her left eye. She was born free, appears by affidavits of Philip Dogan and Catharine Dogan.

REGISTRATION NO. 577
(Vol. 1, p. 227)

Martha Ann Wright
Mary Jane Wright

22 September 1836

Martha Ann and Mary Jane Wright are mulatto girls and the children of Margaret Wright, a free woman. Martha Ann is about 11 years old and Mary Jane is about 9 years old. Their freedom was proved by a certificate from John D. Simms, Esq.

REGISTRATION NO. 578
(Vol. 1, p. 227)

Philip Smith

30 September 1836

Philip Smith is a black man, about 59 years old and 5 feet 3½ inches tall. He was liberated by the will of Mrs. Jemima Say[? possibly "Lay"] recorded in Fairfax County.

REGISTRATION NO. 579
(Vol. 1, p. 227)

Winny Giverson

7 October 1836

Winny Giverson is a free woman, about 41 years old, 5 feet 5 inches tall, with a dark complexion, and a small scar on her right left wrist. She was emancipated by Simon Summers.

REGISTRATION NO. 580
(Vol. 1, p. 227)

Zilla Henderson

14 October 1836

Zilla Henderson is a free woman, about 35 years old, 5 feet 3½ inches tall, of a dark complexion, with a small mole near her lower lip. She was emancipated by the will of Simon West.

REGISTRATION NO. 581
(Vol. 1, p. 228)

Spencer Seals

14 October 1836

Spencer Seals is a dark mulatto man, about 35 years old, 5 feet 5 3/4 inches tall, with a large mole on his breast. He was the property of Lindsay Hill & Co. and was transferred by them to George Johnson & Co. G. Johnson & Co. transferred him to Lawrence P. Hill & Co. of Mobile from which firm he purchased himself, as appears by the bill of sale and deed of emancipation registered in this office.

REGISTRATION NO. 582
(Vol. 1, p. 228)

Kitty Henry

17 October 1836

Kitty Henry is a black woman, about 30 years old, 4 feet 10 inches tall, with a spot caused by a burn on her left cheek or jaw. Her freedom is proved by a certificate from C. Neale.

REGISTRATION NO. 583
(Vol. 1, p. 228)

Sarah Gray

19 October 1836

Sarah Gray is a mulatto woman, about 38 years old, 5 feet 4 inches tall, with a scar on her breast caused by a burn. Her freedom is proved by oath of Jesse Skidmore.

REGISTRATION NO. 584
(Vol. 1, p. 228)

Amy Gray

19 October 1836

Amy Gray is a bright mulatto woman, about 18 years old, 5 feet 5 inches tall, with a scar on or near her left shoulder. She was born free, as appears by affidavit of Jesse Skidmore.

REGISTRATION NO. 585
(Vol. 1, p. 228)

Anna Gray

19 October 1836

Anna Gray is a mulatto woman, about 21 years old, 5 feet 2½ inches tall, with no visible marks. Her freedom was proved by oath of Jesse Skidmore.

REGISTRATION NO. 586
(Vol. 1, p. 229)

Hannah Lee

28 October 1836

Hannah Lee is a dark mulatto woman, about 43 years old, 5 feet 6 inches tall, with several scars on her body caused by scalds and a mark on the back of her left hand and on her left wrist. She was liberated by Alexander Hunter as appears by deed dated 1 October 1835.

REGISTRATION NO. 587
(Vol. 1, p. 229)

Minty Thomas

1 November 1836

Minty Thomas is a dark mulatto woman, about 45 years old, 5 feet 1¼ inches tall, with the fingernails on her left hand disfigured and a mark on her nose. Her freedom was proved by oath of George Johnson (shoemaker) who states that he has known her for 20 years and that during that time she passed as a free woman.

REGISTRATION NO. 588
(Vol. 1, p. 229)

Jane Darnell

5 November 1836

Jane Darnell is a mulatto girl, about 18 years old, 5 feet 2¼ inches tall, with a large mark under her left jaw and one on the left corner of her mouth. She was born free, as appears by affidavit of John Darnell.

REGISTRATION NO. 589
(Vol. 1, p. 229)

Penny Overtal Cook

17 November 1836

Penny Cook (formerly Overtal) is a dark mulatto woman, about 22 years old, 5 feet 5 inches tall, with the end of the middle finger of her left hand somewhat disfigured from having been mashed and the nail discolored. Her freedom was proved by affidavit of Edward Jacobs.

REGISTRATION NO. 590
(Vol. 1, p. 230)

Richard Henry Reed

18 November 1836

Richard Henry Reed is a bright mulatto boy, about 11 years old, 4 feet 3 inches tall, with nearly straight hair. He was liberated by William H. Irwin on 8 November 1836.

REGISTRATION NO. 591
(Vol. 1, p. 230)

Lucy Ann Reed

18 November 1836

Lucy Ann Reed is a bright mulatto girl, about 7 years old, who has straight hair. She was liberated by William H. Irwin by deed dated 8 November 1836.

REGISTRATION NO. 592
(Vol. 1, p. 230)

Nancy Hall Deane

23 November 1836

Nancy Hall (now Deane) is a mulatto woman, about 23 years old, 5 feet 6 3/4 inches tall, with a large scar on her right arm above the elbow, another on the same arm, several small scars on her forehead, and a mole under her right eye. She was born free, as appears by oath of Barthomew A. Mortimer taken before a justice of the peace in Washington County.

Page 231 is blank.

REGISTRATION NO. 593
(Vol. 1, p. 232)

Susanna Butler   1 December 1836

Susanna Butler is a free mulatto girl, 18 years and 7 months old, 5 feet 6 inches tall, of a bright color, with a scar over her left eye. She was born free, as appears by oath of John Shakes.

REGISTRATION NO. 594
(Vol. 1, p. 232)

Mary Davis   3 December 1836

Mary Davis is a mulatto woman, about 19 years old, and 5 feet 5¼ inches tall. She was born free, as appears by a certificate from Thomas Vowell, Esq.

REGISTRATION NO. 595
(Vol. 1, p. 232)

Jane Williams   14 December 1836

Jane Williams is a dark mulatto woman, about 21 years old, 4 feet 9½ inches tall, with a small scar on her right cheek about an inch from the corner of her nose. She was liberated by Thomas Vowell.

REGISTRATION NO. 596
(Vol. 1, p. 232)

Thacker Jones   19 December 1836

"Thackar" [Thacker] Jones is a bright mulatto man, about 24 years old, 5 feet 9¼ inches tall, with a mark caused by a burn on the outer side of his left leg near the knee. He was liberated by John Whiting by deed dated 11 May 1832.

REGISTRATION NO. 597a
(Vol. 1, p. 232)

Winny Bowling   24 January 1837

Winny Bowling is a black woman, about 37 years old, 5 feet 3 inches tall, with a scar on her left wrist joint and one about midway on her breast. Her freedom was proved by affidavit of Samuel Wheeler.

REGISTRATION NO. 597b
(Vol. 1, p. 233)

Henry Tracy   23 January 1837

Henry Tracy is a bright mulatto man, 26 years, 3 months and 23 days old, and 5 feet 9 inches tall. He has a scar on the left side of his left eye. He was born free, as appears by a certificate from Alexander Moore, notary public.

REGISTRATION NO. 598
(Vol. 1, p. 233)

James Wilson   20 February 1837

James Wilson is a dark mulatto man, about 29 years old, 5 feet 9¼ inches tall, with a scar on his cheek near the right eye, one on his lower lip, and two large scars on the outer side of his right leg near his knee. He was born free, as appears by affidavit of James Evans.

REGISTRATION NO. 599
(Vol. 1, p. 233)

Elisabeth White   20 March 1837

Elisabeth White is a Negro woman, 18 years old, 5 feet 1¼ inches tall, with a small spot on her left cheek and a larger one on the right. She was born of free parents, as appears by affidavit of Charles Ross.

REGISTRATION NO. 600
(Vol. 1, p. 233)

Sarah Ann Bennett and
child, Harrotus Ann

30 March 1837

Sarah Ann Bennett is a free Negro woman, about 29 years old, 5 feet 6¼ inches tall, of a dark complexion, with a mark on the middle of the back of her right hand. She was emancipated by John C. Herbert by deed recorded in Liber K, folio 333, by which she was declared free when she reached age 28. The executors of Joseph Sewall certify that she and her infant child, Harrotus Ann, are free, they having been purchased for a term of years from John C. Herbert.

REGISTRATION NO. 601
(Vol. 1, p. 234)

William Wilson

11 May 1837

William Wilson was liberated by William Sol[o]man, a "man of colour," who purchased him from Margaret Frye, as appears by a deed dated 30 May 1836. Wilson is a black man, aged about 24 years, 5 feet 6 inches tall, with a scar on his forehead.

REGISTRATION NO. 602
(Vol. 1, p. 234)

Robert Mitchell

11 May 1837

Robert Mitchell was liberated by William Soloman who purchased him from Margaret Frye, as appears by a deed recorded 10 June 1836. Mitchell is about 21 years old, 5 feet 5½ inches tall, with a scar on the left side of his face near his nose.

REGISTRATION NO. 603
(Vol. 1, p. 234)

Jane Taylor

11 May 1837

Jane Taylor was liberated by William Stabler. Taylor is a dark mulatto woman, 43 years old, 5 feet 7 inches tall, with a scar caused by a burn on her right arm below the elbow.

REGISTRATION NO. 604
(Vol. 1, p. 234)

Albert Murray

9 June 1837

Albert Murray is a mulatto man, about 26 years old, 5 feet 5 inches tall, who has a wart[?] on the back of his right hand and a large scar on his right arm.

REGISTRATION NO. 605
(Vol. 1, p. 234)

Robert Tenley

9 June 1837

Robert Tenley is about 22 years old, 6 feet tall, of a dark complexion, with several moles on his face. He is free, as appears by affidavit of Robert Jamieson.

REGISTRATION NO. 606
(Vol. 1, p. 235)

Emeline Stepney

7 July 1837

Emeline Stepney was emancipated by Mary S. Handy by deed recorded in Liber Q No. 2, page 370. Stepney is 21 years old, 5 feet 2½ inches tall, of a dark complexion, with a scar over her right eye caused by a cut.

REGISTRATION NO. 607
(Vol. 1, p. 235)

Nace Dorsey

[ca. July 1837]

Nace Dorsey was emancipated by Charles C. Smoot and James E. Smoot by deed dated 5 January 1837. Dorsey is a dark mulatto man, about 36 years old, 5 feet 7 inches tall, with two scars near his left eye, one on the upper part of his nose near the left eye and the other on the left side of his left eye.

REGISTRATION NO. 608
(Vol. 1, p. 235)

Charles Henry Carter   15 August 1837

Charles Henry Carter is a mulatto boy, about 19 years old, 5 feet 7¼ inches tall, with a scar on his back (the mark of a boil), one on his left ear caused by a burn, and several small marks on his breast. He was born free, as appears by oath of Alexander Moore, notary public of Alexandria.

REGISTRATION NO. 609
(Vol. 1, p. 235)

Miriam Seals   16 August 1837

Miriam Seals and her children were liberated by James Irwin[?] by deed dated 6 September 1836[?]. Seals is a bright mulatto woman, about 5 feet 1 3/4 inches tall, with a scar on her right arm on the front side above the elbow caused by a scald.

REGISTRATION NO. 610
(Vol. 1, p. 236)

Lucy Oldham   18 August 1837

Lucy Oldham is a dark mulatto woman, about 41 years old, 5 feet 1 inch tall, with several small scars and one large scar on her right hand. She was liberated by Stephen Shinn, as appears by deed dated 14 October 1833.

REGISTRATION NO. 611
(Vol. 1, p. 236)

William Cooke   7 September 1837

William Cooke is a bright mulatto man, about 31 years old, 5 feet 4 inches tall. He purchased his freedom from Wilson M. Carey, as appears by deed recorded in Liber V No. 2, page 425 from Wilson M. Carey to Orlando Fairfax, Trustee.

REGISTRATION NO. 612a
(Vol. 1, p. 236)

Ellen Brooks   20 September 1837
Sarah Jane Brooks
Mary Georgianna Brooks

Ellen Brooks, Sarah Jane Brooks, and Mary Georgianna Brooks are the daughters of Desdemona Brooks, a free woman of color. Ellen is a bright mulatto girl, about 16 years old, 5 feet one-half inch tall; Sarah Jane is about 12 years and 5 months old and 4 feet 7¼ inches tall; and Mary Georgianna is about 6 years 6 months old and is under 4 feet tall.

REGISTRATION NO. 612b
(Vol. 1, p. 237)

George Parris   22 September 1837

George Parris is a dark mulatto man, about 23 years old, 5 feet 3/4 inches tall, with a scar below his right knee caused by the kick of a horse. He was born free, as appears by oath of Ann Lightfoot.

REGISTRATION NO. 613
(Vol. 1, p. 237)

Celie Brown   27 September 1827

Celie Brown is about 20 years old, 5 feet 5 inches tall, and has a dark complexion. She was born free, as appears by affirmation of Robert H. Miller

REGISTRATION NO. 614a
(Vol. 1, p. 237)

John Cupid, alias John Graham   27 September 1827

John Cupid, alias John Graham, is about 25 years old, 5 feet 7 3/4 inches tall, of a dark complexion, with a small mark under his right eye and a small scar on the back of his right hand. He was emancipated by Mary T. Gordon and Elizabeth Gordon by deed dated 11 August 1837.

REGISTRATION NO. 614b
(Vol. 1, p. 237)

Nelly Taylor and   2 October 1827
daughter, Christy

Nelly Taylor is a dark woman, aged about 48 years, 5 feet 5 inches tall, with a circular scar on her right cheek near the temple and another large scar on her right arm just above the wrist that was caused by a cut. Nelly and her daughter, Christy, were emancipated by deed from Charlotte Howell and John Douglass dated 13 November 1830, recorded in Liber X No. 2.

REGISTRATION NO. 615
(Vol. 1, p. 238)

Louisa Lee Ruston   7 October 1837

Louisa Ruston, formerly Lee, is a dark mulatto woman, about 22 years old, 5 feet 1 inch tall, with a mark from a burn on her left cheek. She was liberated by Benoni Wheat.

REGISTRATION NO. 616
(Vol. 1, p. 238)

Ann Smith   16 October 1827

Ann Smith is a mulatto woman, about 31 years old, 5 feet 4 inches tall, with a small scar on her left ?? caused by a cut and several small black moles on her face. Smith obtained her freedom by a judgement of the Circuit Court at its October 1837 term in which she was the plaintiff and Francis Alexander's administrator the defendant.

REGISTRATION NO. 617
(Vol. 1, p. 238)

Gustavus Williams   20 October 1827

Gustavus William is about 41 years old, 5 feet 7 1/8 inches tall, with the second finger of his right hand having been bent or broken by a wheat fan, and a scar 1½ inches long on the big toe of his left foot. He was liberated by Henry Dangerfield.

REGISTRATION NO. 618
(Vol. 1, p. 238)

Peggy Wyatt   31 October 1837

Peggy Wyatt is 5 feet 1 inch tall and of a dark color. She was liberated by John C. Vowell.

REGISTRATION NO. 619
(Vol. 1, p. 238)

Malinda Wyatt   31 October 1837

Malinda Wyatt is about 29 years old, 5 feet 1½ inches tall, and of a light complexion. She was liberated by John Vowell by deed dated 10 October 1837.

REGISTRATION NO. 620
(Vol. 1, p. 239)

Cecely Bowden   18 November 1837

Cecely Bowden is a bright mulatto woman, about 29 years old, 5 feet 2½ inches tall, with a scar caused by a cut on her left wrist. She was liberated by Jonathan Janney and R[obert] W. Hunter by deed dated 9 January 1835.

REGISTRATION NO. 621
(Vol. 1, p. 239)

Mary Clarke 22 November 1837

Mary Clarke is about 24 years old, 5 feet 2½ inches tall, of a dark complexion, with a scar on her left cheek. She was born free, as appears by affidavit of Mr. J. D. Bryan.

REGISTRATION NO. 622
(Vol. 1, p. 239)

Thomas Dogan 26 November 1837

Thomas Dogan is about 19 years old, 5 feet 4 inches tall, and of a copper color. He is the son of Philip and Flora Dogan, free persons of color. Thomas was born free, as appears by affidavit of Mrs. Elizabeth Ann White, a respectable white woman.

REGISTRATION NO. 623
(Vol. 1, p. 239)

Mark Evans 28 November 1837

Mark Evans is a dark mulatto man, about 24 years old, 5 feet 10 inches tall, with no visible marks. He was born free and identified by Mr. John Diggs as being the son of Emily Evans, a free woman of color.

REGISTRATION NO. 624
(Vol. 1, p. 239)

Charles Hoye 29 November 1837

Charles Hoye is a dark man, about 21 years old, 5 feet 10½ inches tall, who is very scarred from the effects of poison on his face. He was born free and identified by James Entwisle as the son of a free born woman.

REGISTRATION NO. 625
(Vol. 1, p. 240)

Celia Bowden 4 December 1837

Celia Bowden is a light mulatto, about 16 years old, 5 feet 3 3/4 inches tall, with a freckled face. She was emancipated by Jonathan Janney and R[obert] W. Hunter by deed dated 9 January 1835.

REGISTRATION NO. 626
(Vol. 1, p. 240)

Kitty Jackson 4 December 1837

Kitty Jackson is a free mulatto, about 40 years old, 5 feet 3/4 inches tall, with three fingers on her left hand burned. She was emancipated by deed from Jonathan Janney and R[obert] W. Hunter.

REGISTRATION NO. 627
(Vol. 1, p. 240)

Hannah Williams 13 December 1837

Hannah Williams is a mulatto girl, about 19 years old, 5 feet 2 inches tall, who has two extra teeth on each side of her jaw and marks left by the amputation of a sixth finger on each hand. She was born free, as appears by oath of William Minor.

REGISTRATION NO. 628
(Vol. 1, p. 240)

Charity Sarey[?] 22 December 1837

Charity Sarey[?] is a mulatto woman, about 40 years old, 5 feet 7½ inches tall, with a mole on her upper lip and on the right side of her face. She obtained her freedom by judgement of the Circuit Court in its April 1826 term in which she was the plaintiff and Bazil H. Davidson the defendant.

REGISTRATION NO. 629
(Vol. 1, p. 241)

William Savoy 12 March 1838

William Savoy is about 37 years old, 5 feet 10¼ inches tall, of a dark complexion, with two large moles near his left side. He was born free (see B. T. Fendall certificate filed).

REGISTRATION NO. 630
(Vol. 1, p. 241)

Chloe Jarbour   8 May 1838

Chloe Jarbour is a dark mulatto girl, about 16 years old, 5 feet 1½ inches tall, with no particular marks. She was born free, as appears by affidavit of B. C. Milburne.

REGISTRATION NO. 631
(Vol. 1, p. 241)

Jesse Arnett   9 May 1838

Jesse Arnett is a dark mulatto man, about 38 years old, 5 feet 4½ inches tall. The front part of his head is bald and he has a small scar on each side of his face. He was emancipated by Alexander Waugh by deed dated 9 May 1838.

REGISTRATION NO. 632
(Vol. 1, p. 241)

William Evans   26 May 1838

William Evans is a dark mulatto man, about 19 years old, 6 feet 1½ inches tall, with a scar on his left cheek caused by a burn. He is the son of Jane Evans, a free woman, as appears by the records in this office.

REGISTRATION NO. 633
(Vol. 1, p. 242)

Bendett Washington   8 June 1838

Bendett Washington is a bright mulatto man, 62 years old, 5 feet 7½ inches tall, with a one inch scar on his breast. He was liberated by William Bell.

REGISTRATION NO. 634
(Vol. 1, p. 242)

Martha Ann Barker   15 June 1838

Martha Ann Barker is a bright mulatto girl, about 19 years old, 5 feet 5½ inches tall, with a large mole on the right side of her neck. She was born free, as appears by affidavit of John Tatsepaugh.

REGISTRATION NO. 635
(Vol. 1, p. 242)

John McKee   25 June 1838

John McKee is a bright mulatto boy, about 19 years old, 5 feet 4½ inches tall, who is straight built with light colored eyes. He was born free, as appears by oaths of Betsey Beckley and Fanny Beckley.

REGISTRATION NO. 636
(Vol. 1, p. 242)

John Johnson   [25 June 1838]

John Johnson is about 21 years old, 5 feet 7½ inches tall, and of a dark color. He has a small black spot immediately to the left side of his left eye, and a scar on his left leg below the knee caused by a blow from an axe. He is the son of Henny Johnson, a free woman, as appears by affidavit of Mary Denty.

REGISTRATION NO. 637
(Vol. 1, p. 243)

Lydia Ann Butler   25 June 1838

Lydia Ann Butler is a dark colored woman, about 23 years old, 5 feet 2 3/4 inches tall, with no particular marks. She was born free and is the child of Susan Butler, a free woman, as appears by affidavit of Samuel Isaacs.

REGISTRATION NO. 638
(Vol. 1, p. 243)

Elizabeth Beckley, alias Bell   2 July 1838

Elizabeth Beckley, alias Bell, is a free mulatto woman, about 23 years old, 5 feet 2½ inches tall, with large scars on her neck caused by a burn. She was emancipated by George Wise by deed recorded in Liber W No. 2, page 254.

REGISTRATION NO. 639
(Vol. 1, p. 243)

Emeline Logan   5 July 1838

Emeline Logan is about 23 years old, 5 feet one-fourth inch tall, with bushy hair, and a scar on her left arm and a mark under her left eye caused by burns. She was born free, as appears by affidavit of Alexander Moore.

REGISTRATION NO. 640a
(Vol. 1, p. 243)

Ann Payne Barcroft   14 February 1839

Ann Barcroft, formerly Payne, is a free bright mulatto woman, about 22 years old, 5 feet 3½ inches tall, with a mole on the right side of her mouth. She was born free, as appears by affidavit of T[ownshend] D. Fendall.

REGISTRATION NO. 640b
(Vol. 1, p. 244)

Mary Jones   9 July 1838

Mary Jones is a dark mulatto woman, about 20 years old, 5 feet 3½ inches tall, with a mole on the thumb of her left hand and one on the back of her left hand. She was liberated by Oliver Jones by deed recorded in Liber L No. 2, folio 158.

REGISTRATION NO. 641
(Vol. 1, p. 244)

David Garrett   30 July 1838

David Garrett is a bright mulatto man, about 33 years old, 5 feet 1¼ inches tall, with deformed feet that turn inwards. He was liberated by Silas [H.] Reed according to an agreement signed 30 July 1838.

REGISTRATION NO. 642
(Vol. 1, p. 244)

Thomas Gantt   1 August 1838

Thomas Gantt is a dark mulatto man, about 34 years old, 5 feet 2 3/4 inches tall, with several scars on and about his forehead. The middle finger of his right hand has been injured, and he has a speech impediment. He was born free, and bound as an apprentice to Mr. [Thomas] Swayne. He has served his term, as appears by a certificate from the Fairfax County court.

REGISTRATION NO. 643
(Vol. 1, p. 245)

George Humphries   2 August 1838

George Humphries is about 33 years old, 5 feet 7 inches tall, of a dark complexion, with one of the fingers on his left hand missing and the fingernails on his left hand mashed.

REGISTRATION NO. 644
(Vol. 1, p. 245)

Richard Bowles   21 August 1838

Richard Bowles is a dark mulatto man, about 38 years old, 5 feet 4 3/4 inches tall, with a small scar on his forehead. He was born free, as appears by oath of Alexander Moore.

REGISTRATION NO. 645
(Vol. 1, p. 245)

James R. Beckley   20 September 1838

James R. Beckley is a mulatto man, about 21 years old, and 5 feet 5 3/4 inches tall. He was born free, as appears by affidavit of James Phillips.

REGISTRATION NO. 646
(Vol. 1, p. 245)

Alfred Merrick   20 September 1838

Alfred Merrick is a dark mulatto man, about 37 years old, 5 feet 9½ inches tall, with a black spot on the inner side of his left thigh. He was liberated by William Dean of Alexandria by deed dated 16 July 1838.

REGISTRATION NO. 647
(Vol. 1, p. 245)

George Gibson   9 October 1838

George Gibson is a bright mulatto man, about 38 years old, 5 feet 8 3/4 inches tall, with a scar over his left eye and one on the under part of his left arm. He was liberated by Colin Auld and others, executors of M[ordecai] Miller, deceased, by deed recorded in Liber X No. 2, page 488.

REGISTRATION NO. 648
(Vol. 1, p. 246)

Thomas Chin   Recorded 9 October 1838

Thomas Chin is about 60 years old, 5 feet 7 3/4 inches tall, of a dark color, with a scar on the back part of his head and with a rather bald head. He was liberated by John Gadsby of Washington, D. C., as appears by affidavit of Charles McKnight.

REGISTRATION NO. 649
(Vol. 1, p. 246)

Rebecca Lucas   25 October 1838

Rebecca Lucas is a bright mulatto woman, about 30 years old, 5 feet 1 3/4 inches tall, with no visible marks. She was liberated by James McKinzie by deed dated 25 October 1838.

REGISTRATION NO. 650
(Vol. 1, p. 246)

Elisa Taylor   30 October 1838

Elisa Taylor is a mulatto woman, about 35 years old, 5 feet one-fourth inch tall, with a scar on the upper part of her left thumb. She was liberated by Mary T. Gordon by deed filed in Liber T[?] No. 2, page 66.

REGISTRATION NO. 651
(Vol. 1, p. 246)

Alexander Bryan   22 January 1839

Alexander Bryan is a bright mulatto boy, about 17 years and 4 months old, 5 feet 5 3/4 inches tall, with a scar on the top of his left ear. He was born free.

REGISTRATION NO. 652
(Vol. 1, p. 247)

Elisabeth Young   5 March 1839

Elisabeth Young is a mulatto woman, about 23 years old, 5 feet 5 3/4 inches tall and freckled about the nose. She was born free and is the daughter of Ann Young, a free woman, as appears by affidavit of Joanna Markley.

REGISTRATION NO. 653
(Vol. 1, p. 247)

Ann Young   5 March 1839

Ann Young is a dark woman, about 40 years old, 5 feet 4 inches tall, with a scar on her left eyebrow and a black mark extending across her nose. She was freed by the will of Margaret Hutchens and identified by Joanna Markley.

REGISTRATION NO. 654a
(Vol. 1, p. 247)

Samuel White   8 April 1839

Samuel White is about 21 years old, 5 feet 9½ inches tall, of a dark complexion, with a small scar on the back of his left ear. He was born free, as appears by affidavit of Mary Ann Cole.

REGISTRATION NO. 654b
(Vol. 1, p. 247)

Mary Ann Currey   24 April 1839

Mary Ann Currey is a dark mulatto woman, about 24 years old, 5 feet 1 inch tall, with a scar on the front of her left wrist and on the back of the same hand and wrist caused by a burn. She was born free and is the daughter of Jude [Currey] who was freed by deed from Seely Bunn dated 1810 and recorded in Liber T[?], folio 296.

REGISTRATION NO. 655
(Vol. 1, p. 248)

Cowill[?] Rodgers   20 May 1839

Cowill[?] Rodgers is a mulatto man, about 26 years old, 5 feet 7 inches tall, with a small scar on the forefinger of his left hand. He was declared free by decree from the Circuit Court in its May term of 1839 in the suit of William and Cowill[?] Rodgers against Jonathan Janney and Samuel Oldham.

REGISTRATION NO. 656
(Vol. 1, p. 248)

John Thomas Waugh   30 May 1839

John Thomas Waugh is about 21 years old, 5 feet 5¼ inches tall, of a dark complexion, with several scars on the knuckles of his left hand. He was born free.

REGISTRATION NO. 657
(Vol. 1, p. 248)

Rachael Bourbon   5 June 1839

Rachael Bourbon is an almost white girl, about 19 years old, 5 feet 1½ inches tall, with light straight hair. She was liberated by Dennis Bourbon by deed dated June 1839.

REGISTRATION NO. 658
(Vol. 1, p. 248)

Chloe Butler   5 June 1839

Chloe Butler is a bright mulatto girl, about 17 years old, 5 feet tall, with a scar on her left thumb caused by a cut. She was born free.

REGISTRATION NO. 659
(Vol. 1, p. 249)

Henry Rowe   15 June 1839

Henry Rowe is a bright mulatto man, about 21 years old, 5 feet 6 inches tall. He was liberated by Jane A. T. Ramsay by deed recorded in Liber W No. 2, folio 233.

REGISTRATION NO. 660
(Vol. 1, p. 249)

Richard Knight   17 June 1839

Richard Knight is a bright mulatto man, about 24 years old, 5 feet 9 inches tall, of a very light complexion with straight dark hair and a scar on the back of his left hand from a cut. He was liberated by George L. and Eliza Markenheimer[?].

REGISTRATION NO. 661
(Vol. 1, p. 249)

William H. Hatton   26 June 1839

William [H.] Hatton is a mulatto man, about 25 years old, 5 feet 8 inches tall, with several small scars on the back of his left hand and a black mole on the left side of his nose. He was born free, as appears by affidavit of Catharine Evans.

REGISTRATION NO. 662
(Vol. 1, p. 249)

Nathaniel Clark

27 June 1839

Nathaniel Clark is about 26 years old, 5 feet 7 inches tall, of a dark complexion, with his face marked by smallpox and the back of his right hand scarred by a burn. He was emancipated by Silas [H.] Reed by deed recorded in Liber Z No. 2.

REGISTRATION NO. 663
(Vol. 1, p. 250)

Judith Ford

28 June 1839

Judith Ford is a bright mulatto girl, about 19 years old, 5 feet 5 inches tall, with the third finger of her right hand injured at the fingernail, and with sandy colored hair. She was born free, as appears by a certificate from Mrs. Jane C. Washington.

REGISTRATION NO. 664
(Vol. 1, p. 250)

Joseph Williams

3 July 1839

Joseph Williams is about 28 years old, 5 feet 5 inches tall, of a dark complexion, with a small scar on his forehead caused by a cut. He was emancipated by Silas [H.] Reed.

REGISTRATION NO. 665
(Vol. 1, p. 250)

Ellen Mitchell

19 July 1839

Ellen Mitchell is a bright mulatto woman, about 26 years old, 5 feet 4 1/8 inches tall, with very black straight hair. She was liberated by George Brent.

REGISTRATION NO. 666
(Vol. 1, p. 250)

Ann Elisabeth Jones

23 July 1839

Ann Elisabeth Jones is a dark mulatto girl, about 18 years old, and 5 feet tall. She was liberated by deed from Oliver Jones recorded in Liber L[?] No. 2[?], page 158.

REGISTRATION NO. 667
(Vol. 1, p. 250)

Frederick Brooks

29 July 1839

Frederick Brooks is a bright mulatto man, about 24 years old, 5 feet 4 inches tall, with his right eye injured by a burn. He was liberated by Fanny Brooks by deed recorded in Liber L[possibly "T"] No. 2, folio 307.

REGISTRATION NO. 668
(Vol. 1, p. 251)

Richardson Gray

2 August 1839

Richardson Gray is a bright mulatto boy, about 20 years old, 5 feet 6½ inches tall, with the letters "R. G." and the print of an anchor on his right arm, and a small cut on his left knee. He was born free as appears by certificate of George W. P. Custis.

REGISTRATION NO. 669a
(Vol. 1, p. 251)

Helen Simms

26 Aug. 1839

Helen Simms is a bright mulatto girl, about 21 years old, 5 feet 2¼ inches tall. She was born free.

REGISTRATION NO. 669b
(Vol. 1, p. 251)

Elisabeth Julins

[1839]

Elisabeth Julins is a free woman and the daughter of Millie Jackson, formerly Milly Julins.

REGISTRATION NO. 670
(Vol. 1, p. 251)

Henry Sales

3 October 1839

Henry Sales is a mulatto boy, 17 years old, 5 feet 6½ inches tall, with a scar near the left side of his left eye and one on the left side of his chin. He is the son of Harriet Sales and was born free, as appears by a certificate from Charles Scott, a justice of the peace for Alexandria.

REGISTRATION NO. 671
(Vol. 1, p. 252)

Flora Johnson

4 October 1839

Flora Johnson is a dark mulatto woman, about 32 years old, 5 feet 3¼ inches tall. She was liberated by Colin Auld by deed recorded in Liber R No. 2, page 308.

REGISTRATION NO. 672
(Vol. 1, p. 252)

Hannah Reid

8 October 1839

Hannah Reid is a dark mulatto woman, about 36 years old, 4 feet 11½ inches tall, with a scar on the inner side of the forefinger of her left hand. She was emancipated by John D. Harrison by deed recorded in Liber U No. 2.

REGISTRATION NO. 673
(Vol. 1, p. 252)

Joseph Botts

11 October 1839

Joseph Botts is a bright mulatto man, 24 years old, 5 feet 9½ inches tall, with a scar near his right temple and with the little finger of his left hand marked by the loss of the nail. He was born free and is the daughter of Kitty Botts, now Dogan, a free woman.

REGISTRATION NO. 674
(Vol. 1, p. 252)

Lewis West

11 November 1839

Lewis West is a dark mulatto man, about 30 years old, 5 feet 8¼ inches tall, with a large mouth, and a scar from a cut on the back of his left hand in line with his forefinger, and a large scar on the inner side of his left leg at the lower end of his calf. He was liberated by Reuben Johnston by deed dated 3 January 1831.

REGISTRATION NO. 675
(Vol. 1, p. 253)

John Lee

11 November 1839

John Lee is a dark mulatto man, about 23 years old, 5 feet 5 inches tall, with a small scar on his right hand just above the thumb and one on his left cheek just below the ear. He was born free and is the son of Lucy Lee, a free woman.

REGISTRATION NO. 676
(Vol. 1, p. 253)

Alfred Derrick

14 November 1839

Alfred Derrick is a bright mulatto man, about 21 years old, 5 feet 5 inches tall. He was born free, as appears by affidavit of William Simms.

REGISTRATION NO. 677
(Vol. 1, p. 253)

Elvia Taylor

14 November 1839

Elvia Taylor is a bright mulatto girl, about 20 years old, 5 feet 1 inch tall, with a scar on her under lip. She was born free.

The index lists her as Elvia Taylor (Dogan) with another listing under Elvia Dogan (Taylor).

REGISTRATION NO. 678
(Vol. 1, p. 253)

Ann Dogan

14 November 1839

Ann Dogan is a bright mulatto girl, about 18 years old, 5 feet 2 3/4 inches tall. She was born free.

REGISTRATION NO. 679
(Vol. 1, p. 253)

James Gibson

19 November 1839

James Gibson is a bright mulatto man, about 28 years old, 5 feet 7 3/4 inches tall, with a very small scar on the right side of his right eye. He was emancipated by the executors of M[ordecai] Miller.

REGISTRATION NO. 680
(Vol. 1, p. 254)

Thomas Watson

19 November 1839

Thomas Watson is a bright mulatto man, about 26 years old, 5 feet 10¼ inches tall, with a scar on his right foot caused by a burn. He has straight hair and bored ears. He was born free, as appears by affidavit of his mother, Ann Watson.

REGISTRATION NO. 681
(Vol. 1, p. 254)

Francis Talbot

4 December 1839

Francis Talbot is a dark mulatto man, about 42 years old, 5 feet 4 3/4 inches tall. He was emancipated by John McCormack by deed dated 1 December 1839.

REGISTRATION NO. 682
(Vol. 1, p. 254)

Cornelius Brown

5 December 1839

Cornelius Brown is a bright mulatto boy, about 14 years old, and 5 feet 1 inch tall. He was born free, as appears by affidavit of Sarah A. Brown, his mother and a free woman.

REGISTRATION NO. 683
(Vol. 1, p. 254)

William Hines

7 December 1839

William Hines is about 21 years old, 5 feet 4½ inches tall, of a dark complexion, with a small scar over his right eye. He was born free, as appears by affidavit of Ann Lightfoot.

REGISTRATION NO. 684
(Vol. 1, p. 254)

William Henry Lewis

7 December 1839

William Henry Lewis is a bright mulatto man, about 27 years old, 5 feet 7 inches tall, with straight hair and a bald head. He was emancipated by William H. Miller by deed dated 9 November 1839.

REGISTRATION NO. 685
(Vol. 1, p. 255)

George Morris

10 December 1839

George Morris is a bright mulatto boy, about 16 years old, 5 feet 3½ inches tall, with a scar caused by a burn on the right side of his head behind the ear and a mole on his left wrist. He was born free, as appears by affidavit of Adaline Morris.

REGISTRATION NO. 686
(Vol. 1, p. 255)

James Hatton, alias Irwin[?]

24 December 1839

James Hatton, alias Irwin[?], is a bright mulatto man, about 23 years old, 5 feet 3 3/4 inches tall,. His hair is not very dark and "rather straight than is usual with persons of color or mulattoes." For evidence of his freedom, see indentures of apprenticeship of this office. His freedom was further proved by oath of George W. Carson.

REGISTRATION NO. 687
(Vol. 1, p. 255)

Jane Derricks   25 February 1840

Jane Derricks is a dark mulatto girl, about 16 years old, 4 feet 10½ inches tall, with a scar on the left side of her face. She was born free, as appears by affidavit of Mrs. Sally Talbot.

REGISTRATION NO. 688
(Vol. 1, p. 255)

Henry Fisher   28 February 1840

Henry Fisher is a free mulatto man, about 40 years old, and 5 feet 4 inches tall. He was emancipated by Samuel M. Edwards by deed dated 10 September 1825 and recorded in Loudoun County.

REGISTRATION NO. 689
(Vol. 1, p. 255)

Samuel Reeler   23 March 1840

Samuel Reeler is about 40 years old, 5 feet 3/4 inches tall, of a dark complexion with a scar caused by a burn on the back of his left hand and some gray hairs on his head. He obtained his freedom by judgement of the Circuit Court at its November term in 1820.

See Negro Samuel Reeler v. Matthew Robinson, 2 Cranch CC 220.

REGISTRATION NO. 690
(Vol. 1, p. 256)

Emily Robey   31 March 1840

Emily Robey is a very bright mulatto woman, 21 years old, 5 feet 6¼ inches tall, with a scar from a cut on the edge of her left jaw. She was born free, as appears by affidavit of Samuel Isaacs.

REGISTRATION NO. 691
(Vol. 1, p. 256)

Mary Ellen Solomon   22 April 1840
John Thomas Solomon

Mary Ellen Solomon, aged about 16 years old, and John Thomas Solomon, aged about 17 years, are the children of William and Kitty Solomon, free persons of color.

REGISTRATION NO. 692
(Vol. 1, p. 256)

Robert Henry Solomon   22 April 1840

Robert Henry Solomon is about 19 years old, 5 feet 8 3/4 inches tall, and of a dark complexion. He was born free and is the child of William and Kitty Solomon, free persons of color.

REGISTRATION NO. 693
(Vol. 1, p. 256)

Ann Eliza Jenkins   24 April 1840

Ann Eliza Jenkins is a bright mulatto woman, about 21 years old, 5 feet 6 inches tall, with a scar on her upper lip and the letters "AEJ" on her right arm between the elbow and wrist. She was born free, as appears by certificate of Jonathan Batcher.

REGISTRATION NO. 694
(Vol. 1, p. 257)

Mary Tate   19 May 1840

Mary Tate is a dark mulatto woman, about 61 years old, 5 feet 6¼ inches tall, with a dark mark on her right cheek. She was purchased by her husband at the sale of Mrs. Mary Fendall's.

REGISTRATION NO. 695
(Vol. 1, p. 257)

Eliza Palmer   21 May 1840

Eliza Palmer is a mulatto woman, about 36 years old, with a scar on her left cheek. She is free, as appears by certificate from William Fowle.

REGISTRATION NO. 696
(Vol. 1, p. 257)

Ann Bryan   25 May 1840

Ann Bryan is a dark mulatto woman, about 38 years old, 5 feet 3 inches tall, with a scar on her left cheek. She is free, as appears by affidavit of Moses Davis.

REGISTRATION NO. 697
(Vol. 1, p. 258)

Caroline Ware   31 May 1840

Caroline Ware is a mulatto woman, about 39 years old, 5 feet 4 inches tall, with a large scar on her right arm, and another over her right eye. She has lost the sight in her left eye. She was liberated by Lawrence Hough.

REGISTRATION NO. 698
(Vol. 1, p. 258)

Fanny Mack   1 June 1840

Fanny Mack is a black woman, about 31 years old, 5 feet 5½ inches tall, with a scar on her neck. She was liberated by William B[utler] Callicot.

REGISTRATION NO. 699
(Vol. 1, p. 258)

Eliza Easton   11 June 1840

Eliza Easton is a copper-colored mulatto, about 26 years old, 5 feet 5 inches tall, with the mark of a burn on the left side of her neck. She was liberated by Daniel "M Cleod" [McLeod] by deed dated 9 March 1838, recorded on 13 May 1839 in Liber L No. 2, folio 281.

REGISTRATION NO. 700
(Vol. 1, p. 258)

John Colbert   17 June 1840

John Colbert is a black boy, about 18 years old and 5 feet one-half inch tall. He was born free, as appears by affidavit of Hannah Colbert, his grandmother.

REGISTRATION NO. 701
(Vol. 1, p. 258)

Betsy Colbert   17 June 1840

Betsy Colbert is a black girl, about 16 years old, 5 feet 2 inches tall, with a scar between her eyes. She was born free, as was proved by affidavit of her grandmother, Hannah Colbert.

REGISTRATION NO. 702
(Vol. 1, p. 259)

Mary Ann Colbert   17 June 1840

Mary Ann Colbert is a black girl, about 8 years old, 4 feet 6 inches tall. She was born free, as was proved by affidavit of Hannah Colbert, her grandmother.

REGISTRATION NO. 703
(Vol. 1, p. 259)

Martha Colbert   17 June 1840

Martha Colbert is a black girl, about 8 years old, 3 feet 11 inches tall. She was born free, as was proved by affidavit of her grandmother, Hannah Colbert.

REGISTRATION NO. 704
(Vol. 1, p. 259)

Cornelius Watson   25 June 1840

Cornelius Watson is a dark mulatto man, about 35 years old, 5 feet 3½ inches tall, and is bald on the front part of his head. He was emancipated by John Moran.

REGISTRATION NO. 705
(Vol. 1, p. 259)

Richard Lee   30 June 1840

Richard Lee is a mulatto man, about 38 years old, 5 feet three-fourth inch tall, with a scar on the left side of his forehead. He was emancipated by Horatio Clagett by deed dated 29 July 1840.

REGISTRATION NO. 706
(Vol. 1, p. 260)

Alvina Harris   30 June 1840

Alvina Harris is a bright mulatto woman, about 28 years old, and 4 feet 11 inches tall. She was emancipated by Daniel [F.] Cawood on 28 June 1839.

REGISTRATION NO. 707
(Vol. 1, p. 260)

William Evans   4 July 1840

William Evans is a mulatto man, about 22 years old, 5 feet 9½ inches tall, with a scar on his neck. He was born free, as appears by affidavit of James Evans, a free man of color.

REGISTRATION NO. 708
(Vol. 1, p. 260)

John Davis   18 July 1840

John Davis is about 22 years old, 5 feet 6½ inches tall, with a dark complexion. He was bound by the Orphans' Court of Alexandria to Peter Hewitt for four years to learn the business of biscuit baker. His term expired on 5 March 1838 and he is free.

REGISTRATION NO. 709
(Vol. 1, p. 260)

Sandy Taylor   15 August 1840

Sandy Taylor is about 23 years old, 5 feet 6½ inches tall, and of a dark brown color. He is a little pox marked, with a small scar near the corner of his left eye, and with the nail of the small finger on his left hand smashed. He was freed by John Douglass according to papers filed in this office dated 5 June 1838 and 15 August 1840.

REGISTRATION NO. 710
(Vol. 1, p. 261)

Henry Washington   19 August 1840

Henry Washington is a mulatto man, about 26 years old, 5 feet 6 inches tall, with two scars on his left thigh. He is free, as was proved by affidavit of Christopher Neale, Esq.

REGISTRATION NO. 711
(Vol. 1, p. 261)

Fanny Richardson   3 September 1840

Fanny Richardson is about 26 years old, 5 feet 2½ inches tall, of a dark complexion, with a black mole on her neck. She won her freedom by a writ of habeas corpus ex parte Fanny Richardson in the Circuit Court's November 1831 term (bundle 1).

REGISTRATION NO. 712
(Vol. 1, p. 261)

Mary Ann Morton   14 September 1840

Mary Ann Morton is a mulatto woman, about 26 years old, 5 feet 3½ inches tall, with long straight hair that is inclined to curl. She has a scar on the right side of her forehead, under the hair and near the temple, a scar under her right eye, a scar between the wrist and thumb of her right hand, a scar on the first joint near the nail of the forefinger of the same hand, and one of her front upper teeth is out. She was emancipated by the will of Slighter Smith, as appears by testimony of B[ernard] Hooe, executor of Smith's will, which was registered this 14 September 1840.

REGISTRATION NO. 713
(Vol. 1, p. 262)

Charles Buttler   15 September 1840

Charles Buttler is about 21 years old, 5 feet 9½ inches tall, with a black complexion. He has a scar on his right hand and one on his left arm. He is a free man who was born in Alexandria, as appears by affidavit of Delia Simpson.

REGISTRATION NO. 714
(Vol. 1, p. 262)

Margaret Ann Butler   21 September 1840

Margaret Ann Butler is about 26 years old, 5 feet 2 inches tall, of a very dark complexion, with several scars on her left hand and wrist, as well as on her left cheek and on the left side of her head. She was born free, as appears by certificate of Alexander Moore, notary public.

REGISTRATION NO. 715
(Vol. 1, p. 262)

Lucinda Jones   23 September 1840

Lucinda Jones is about 22 years old, 5 feet 1 3/4 inches tall, of a very light complexion (nearly white). She was born free, as appears by affidavit of John W. Smith.

REGISTRATION NO. 716
(Vol. 1, p. 263)

Cecilia Chase   23 September 1840

Cecilia Chase is a mulatto woman, about 25 years old, and 5 feet 3½ inches tall. She was born free, as appears by affidavit of Elvina Jefferson, a white woman.

REGISTRATION NO. 717
(Vol. 1, p. 263)

Robert W. Braddock   25 September 1840

Robert W. Braddock is a mulatto man, about 21 years old, 5 feet 8 inches tall, with a scar over his left eye. He was born free, as appears by affidavit of Rebecca Braddock.

REGISTRATION NO. 718
(Vol. 1, p. 263)

Thomas Braddock   25 September 1840

Thomas Braddock is a mulatto man, about 19 years old, and 5 feet 8 inches tall. He was born free, as appears by affidavit of Rebecca Braddock.

REGISTRATION NO. 719
(Vol. 1, p. 263)

Jesse Hughes   1 October 1840

Jesse Hughes is about 22 years old, 5 feet 6 3/4 inches tall, of a dark complexion, with a black mole under his right eye and a scar over his left eye. He was emancipated by Robert Jamieson, Esq., by deed dated 29 September 1840.

REGISTRATION NO. 720
(Vol. 1, p. 264)

Celia Williams   10 October 1840

Celia Williams is a black woman, about 45 years old, 5 feet 4 inches tall, with a scar on her right arm and a scar on her forehead. She is now free, as appears by a certificate of Charles Scott.

REGISTRATION NO. 721
(Vol. 1, p. 264)

John Bowles   13 October 1840

John Bowles is a black man, about 30 years old, 5 feet 9 inches tall, with a scar on his left arm. He was born free, as appears by a certificate from the Register of Wills.

REGISTRATION NO. 722
(Vol. 1, p. 264)

Esther Gibson   16 October 1840

Esther Gibson is a mulatto woman, about 30 years old, and 5 feet 1½ inches tall. She was emancipated by Jonathan Butcher.

REGISTRATION NO. 723
(Vol. 1, p. 264)

Betsy Jackson   17 October 1840

Betsy Jackson is a mulatto woman, about 34 years old, 5 feet 5 inches tall, with a small scar near her left ear. She was emancipated by Mrs. Caryton[?], as appears by certificate of Mrs. Ann B. Wilmer.

REGISTRATION NO. 724
(Vol. 1, p. 265)

Jacob Currie   21 October 1840

Jacob Currie is about 20 years old, 5 feet 4½ inches tall, of a dark complexion, with a scar on his chin, a scar on his forehead, and a scar on his left arm. He was born free, as appears by a certificate from Jacob Hoffman, formerly mayor of Alexandria, recorded in Registration No. 217. Currie was identified by Davis Herbert as the child of Jude Currie who was emancipated by Seely Bunn.

REGISTRATION NO. 725
(Vol. 1, p. 265)

Richard H. Wheeler   23 October 1840

Richard H. Wheeler is about 17 years old, 5 feet 3 inches tall, of a bright complexion, with a scar below his left eye and another above his left eye. He was born free, as appears by affidavit of Richard Bowles, a free man.

REGISTRATION NO. 726
(Vol. 1, p. 265)

Cassy Yeates   29 October 1840

Cassy Yeates is a mulatto woman, about 54 years old, and 5 feet 4 inches tall. She is now free, as appears by affidavit of Joseph H. Hampson.

REGISTRATION NO. 727
(Vol. 1, p. 265)

Hannah Bruce   11 November 1840
Hannah Ann Bruce
Hannah Elizabeth Bruce

Hannah Bruce is a mulatto woman, about 53 years old, 5 feet 2 3/4 inches tall, with a mole near her lower lip an a scar near her upper lip. She was emancipated by Jesse Scott and James English, by deed recorded in Liber O No. 2, page 491. Hannah Bruce has had two children since her emancipation, who are free: Hannah Ann Bruce, a bright mulatto girl aged about 15; and Hannah Elizabeth Bruce, is a bright mulatto girl about 11 years old.

REGISTRATION NO. 728
(Vol. 1, p. 266)

Elizabeth Williams   10 December 1840

Elizabeth Williams is a mulatto girl, about 16 years old, and 5 feet 1 inch tall. She was born free, as appears by affidavit of William Minor.

REGISTRATION NO. 729
(Vol. 1, p. 266)

Lucy Ann Bull   19 January 1841

Lucy Ann Bull is a mulatto woman, about 34 years old, and 5 feet 3 inches tall. She was born free, as appears by affidavit of Joseph H. Hampson.

REGISTRATION NO. 730
(Vol. 1, p. 266)

Amanda Bull   19 January 1841

Amanda Bull is a mulatto woman, about 17 years old, and 5 feet 3½ inches tall. She was born free, as appears by affidavit of Joseph H. Hampson.

REGISTRATION NO. 731
(Vol. 1, p. 267)

Sicily Carroll   February 4, 1841

"Secily" [Sicily] Carroll is a black woman, about 37 years old, and 5 feet 1½ inches tall. She obtained her freedom by judgement of the Circuit Court in its 1840 October term in the suit of Sicily Carroll v. Lucy Barrett.

REGISTRATION NO. 732
(Vol. 1, p. 267)

Nancy Henderson   19 February 1841

Nancy Henderson is a mulatto woman, about 40 years old, 4 feet 11 inches tall, with several small scars on her face and one on her left arm. She was emancipated by Somerset H. Aubinoe, as appears by deed recorded in Liber B No. 3, folio 62.

REGISTRATION NO. 733
(Vol. 1, p. 267)

William Grymes   20 February 1841
George Andrew Grymes
Thomas Fryer Grymes

William Grymes, George Andrew Grymes, and Thomas Fryer Grymes were born free and are the children of Ann Grymes, a free woman of color, as appears by affidavit of Richard House. William is a mulatto boy about 15 years old, George Andrew is a mulatto about 10 years old, and Thomas Fryer is about 7 years old.

REGISTRATION NO. 734
(Vol. 1, p. 268)

William Davis   26 March 1841

William Davis is a mulatto boy who was 15 years old 1 February. He has a small black mark or mole on the right side of his face near his ear. He was born free, as appears by affidavit of Capt. J. B. F. Russell.

REGISTRATION NO. 735
(Vol. 1, p. 268)

Maria Ann Turley   31 March 1841

Maria Ann Turley is about 23 years old, 5 feet one-half inch tall, of a dark complexion, with a small scar on the right side of her face. She was emancipated by Robert Jamieson, Esq., by deed recorded in Liber R No. 2, page 52.

REGISTRATION NO. 736
(Vol. 1, p. 268)

Mary Jane Cryer

21 March 1841

Mary Jane Cryer is a bright mulatto woman, about 18 years old, 5 feet one-fourth inch tall, with straight black hair. She was emancipated by Peter E. Hoffman by deed recorded in Liber Z[?] No. 2, folio 260.

REGISTRATION NO. 737
(Vol. 1, p. 269)

Alfred Middleton

5 April 1841

Alfred Middleton is a black man, about 22 years old, 5 feet 7 3/4 inches tall, with a long traverse scar from a cut on the back of his left hand extending in the same direction across his forefinger, and a scar on his right thumb about parallel to the foregoing. He was emancipated by Letty Minor, as appears from a deed recorded in Liber J No. 2, folio 360.

REGISTRATION NO. 738
(Vol. 1, p. 269)

Phelicia Burns

26 April 1841

Phelicia Burns is a black woman, about 22 years old, 5 feet 3 inches tall, with woolly hair and a scar on her breast. She was emancipated by the will of Slighter Smith and is identified as the person named in that will by a certificate of Bernard Hooe, Esq., executor of the will.

REGISTRATION NO. 739
(Vol. 1, p. 269)

Elizabeth Brown

26 April 1841

Elizabeth Brown is about 26 years old, 5 feet 6 inches tall, with a dark complexion. She was born free, as appears by affidavit of William H. Harper, Esq.

REGISTRATION NO. 740
(Vol. 1, p. 270)

Arianna Frances

3 May 1841

Arianna Frances is about 52 years old, 5 feet 3 inches tall, with a very bright mulatto complexion. She was emancipated by Ann Clagett.

REGISTRATION NO. 741
(Vol. 1, p. 270)

Adaline Lee

11 May 1841

Adaline Lee is a bright mulatto woman, about 37 years old, 5 feet 3½ inches tall, with a mole on her left hand. She was emancipated by Richard Lee.

REGISTRATION NO. 742
(Vol. 1, p. 270)

Joshua Washington

12 May 1841

Joshua Washington is a bright mulatto man, about 28 years old, 5 feet 7 3/4 inches tall, with a scar on his left cheek. He was emancipated by Sam[uel] and Joseph Harris.

REGISTRATION NO. 743
(Vol. 1, p. 270)

Mary Elizabeth McQueen

28 May 1841

Mary Elizabeth "M. Queen" [McQueen] is a bright mulatto woman, about 19 years old, 5 feet 4¼ inches tall, with the middle finger of her right hand injured so that she cannot straighten it entirely. She was born free, as appears by affidavit of Alexander Moore.

REGISTRATION NO. 744
(Vol. 1, p. 271)

Tamer Jackson

28 May 1841

Tamer Jackson is a bright mulatto woman, about 25 years old, and 5 feet 2½ inches tall. She was emancipated by the Rev. William H. Wilmer, as appears by deed recorded in Liber Q No. 2, folio 56.

REGISTRATION NO. 745
(Vol. 1, p. 271)

Mary Washington   3 June 1841

Mary Washington is a mulatto woman, about 38 years old, 5 feet 3 inches tall, with short hair inclined to curl, and has "about her nose & forehead some marks of a darker & deeper color than her general complexion." She was emancipated by the will of Henrietta Perry.

REGISTRATION NO. 746
(Vol. 1, p. 271)

William Sumby   14 June 1841

William Sumby is the son of Lucy Sumby, as was proved by Robert H. Miller. Lucy is a free woman who is registered in this office. William is about 14 years old, 4 feet 9 inches tall, with a dark complexion.

REGISTRATION NO. 747a
(Vol. 1, p. 271)

George L. Sumby   14 June 1841

George L. Sumby is the son of Lucy Sumby, as was proved by Robert H. Miller, Esq. Lucy is a free woman who is registered in this office. George is about 9 years old, 4 feet 1 inch tall, with a dark complexion.

REGISTRATION NO. 747b
(Vol. 1, p. 272)

Jane Dencole and children,   12 July 1841
Virginia and Josephine

Jane Dencole is a mulatto woman, about 30 years old, 5 feet 3 inches tall, of a very bright complexion with a small scar on her right arm above the elbow. She has two children, Virginia, aged about 12 years, and Josephine, aged about 7 years. They were born free, as appears by affidavit of Alexander Veitch.

REGISTRATION NO. 748
(Vol. 1, p. 272)

Cornelia Ann Lewis   23 July 1841

Cornelia Ann Lewis is about 15 years old, 5 feet 1½ inches tall, of a dark complexion, with a small scar over her left eye and another on her forehead. She was born free, as appears by certificates of Robert H. Miller and Eliza S. Collard.

REGISTRATION NO. 749
(Vol. 1, p. 272)

George Lewis Seaton, Adolphus Seaton,   30 July 1841
Lucinda Seaton, Sarah Seaton,
Martha Seaton, Laura Seaton,
and John Andrew Thomas Seaton

The following are the children of George and Lucinda Seaton, free persons of color, and were born free: George Lewis Seaton, a dark mulatto about 19 years old; Adolphus Seaton, about 17 years old; Lucinda Seaton, about 15 years old; Sarah Seaton, about 13 years old; Martha Seaton, about 11 years old; Laura Seaton, about 9 years old; and John Andrew Thomas Seaton, about 5 years old.

REGISTRATION NO. 750
(Vol. 1, p. 273)

Mary Seaton Rodgers   30 July 1841

Mary Ann Rodgers, formerly Seaton, is about 25 years old, 5 feet 6¼ inches tall, and of a copper complexion. She was born free and is the daughter of George and Lucinda Seaton, free colored persons, the latter of whom was emancipated by General Washington.

REGISTRATION NO. 751
(Vol. 1, p. 273)

Lucinda Seaton   30 July 1841

Lucinda Seaton is a dark mulatto woman, about 42 years old, 5 feet 4 3/4 inches tall, with a slight scar on the back of her left hand caused by a burn. She was emancipated by the late General Washington (see affidavit of Martha Brent filed in this office).

REGISTRATION NO. 752
(Vol. 1, p. 273)

Catharine Seaton Williams   30 July 1841

Catharine Williams, formerly Seaton, is a dark mulatto woman about 23 years old, 5 feet 5¼ inches tall, of a copper complexion, with several small scars on her right hand. She was born free, and is the child of George and Lucinda Seaton, free persons of color, the latter of whom was emancipated by General Washington (see affidavit of Martha Brent and Ann Berry).

REGISTRATION NO. 753
(Vol. 1, p. 273)

Hannah Ann Seaton   30 July 1841

Hannah Ann Seaton is about 32 years old, 5 feet 7 3/4 inches tall, of a copper complexion, with a small black speck in the corner of her right eye. She was born free and is the child of George and Lucinda Seaton, free persons of color (see affidavit of Martha Brent and Ann Berry).

REGISTRATION NO. 754
(Vol. 1, p. 274)

Charity Anderson   10 August 1841

Charity Anderson is about 43 years old, 5 feet 3¼ inches tall, of a dark complexion, with no visible marks. She was emancipated by Samuel Anderson by deed dated 30 September 1818 which is recorded in the Fairfax County court.

REGISTRATION NO. 755
(Vol. 1, p. 274)

Francis Ann Anderson   10 August 1841

Frances Ann Anderson is a bright mulatto girl, about 22 years old, 5 feet 3 3/4 inches tall, with no visible marks. She was born free, and is the child of Charity Anderson, a free woman, as appears by affidavit of John Arrington.

REGISTRATION NO. 756
(Vol. 1, p. 274)

Matilda Warner   17 August 1841

Matilda Warner is a mulatto girl, about 14 years old, 5 feet one-half inch tall, of a bright complexion, with a scar on her right cheek. She was born free, as appears by affidavit of Maria Deshealds.

REGISTRATION NO. 757
(Vol. 1, p. 274)

James Butts   29 September 1841

James Butts is about 15 years old, 4 feet 7 inches tall, of a dark complexion, with two moles on his neck. He was born free, as appears by affidavit of Joseph H. Hampson.

REGISTRATION NO. 758
(Vol. 1, p. 274)

Catherine Foote   11 September 1841

Catherine, alias Kitty, Foote is about 45 years old, 5 feet 2 inches tall, of a very bright complexion. She was emancipated by Robert J. Taylor, Esq., by deed recorded in Liber L No. 2, folio 287.

REGISTRATION NO. 759
(Vol. 1, p. 275)

Mary Jane Billingsly

15 October 1841

Mary Jane Billingsly is about 23 years old, 5 feet 8 inches tall, of a copper complexion, with two moles on her breast, several scars on her left hand, and a left thumb nail that is badly injured. She was emancipated by Aquilla Lockwood by deed dated 1 January 1836 recorded in Liber A No. 3, folio 115.

REGISTRATION NO. 760
(Vol. 1, p. 275)

Sylvia Ann Reeler

19 October 1841

Sylvia Ann Reeler is a bright mulatto woman, about 20 years and 1 month old, 5 feet 2 inches tall, of "a full & corpulent appearance," with a scar or small indentation on the upper part of her nose. She is the daughter of Mary Reeler, a free woman registered in this office.

REGISTRATION NO. 761
(Vol. 1, p. 275)

Margaret Reeler

19 October 1841

Margaret Reeler is a mulatto woman, about 18 years old, 5 feet 11½ inches tall, with a cut on the forefinger of her right hand. She was born free and is the daughter of Mary Reeler, a free woman registered in this office.

REGISTRATION NO. 762
(Vol. 1, p. 275)

Jesse Reeler

19 October 1841

Jesse Reeler is about 13 years old, 4 feet 10½ inches tall, and has a bright complexion. He was born free and is the son of Mary Reeler, a free woman registered in this office.

REGISTRATION NO. 763
(Vol. 1, p. 276)

David Jarbour

29 October 1841

David Jarbour is a black man, about 22 years old, 5 feet 5 3/4 inches tall, of a dark complexion, with a scar from a cut on the elbow of his right arm. He was born free and is the son of Rebecca [Dover] Jarbour, a free woman registered in this office.

REGISTRATION NO. 764
(Vol. 1, p. 276)

Flora E. Morgan

2 November 1841

Flora E. Morgan is a mulatto woman, about 19 years old, 5 feet 4¼ inches tall, with "an affection in the joints of both her thumbs whereby she is prevented from bending them." She was born free, as appears by affidavit of Cassandra L. Cannon. Flora is the daughter of Mary Morgan, a free woman registered in this office.

REGISTRATION NO. 765
(Vol. 1, p. 276)

John Sumby

8 November 1841

John Sumby is about 22 years old, 5 feet 8 3/4 inches tall, of a dark complexion, with a scar on his left leg below the knee. He was born free, as appears by affidavit of Robert W. Hunter, Esq.

REGISTRATION NO. 766
(Vol. 1, p. 276)

Mary Talbert

10 November 1841

Mary Talbert is a very bright mulatto woman, about 25 years old, 5 feet 5½ inches tall, with the back of her neck marked from cupping. She was emancipated by John M. McCartey and others.

REGISTRATION NO. 767
(Vol. 1, p. 277)

Nancy Davis, alias Anderson   10 November 1841

Nancy Davis, alias Anderson, is a bright mulatto woman, about 60 years old, 5 feet 5 inches tall, with several moles on her face, many of which are near her mouth. She was liberated by Thomas Vowell, Esq., of Alexandria, by deed dated 5 October 1841.

Nancy Anderson's age of 60 years is copied correctly, but may be in error. It was illegal to manumit a slave over the age of 45 years.

REGISTRATION NO. 768
(Vol. 1, p. 277)

William Davis   10 November 1841

William Davis is a dark man, about 30 years old, 5 feet 5¼ inches tall, with several moles on his chin. He was liberated by Thomas Vowell, Esq., of Alexandria by deed dated 5 October 1841.

REGISTRATION NO. 769
(Vol. 1, p. 277)

Emeline Davis   10 November 1841

Emeline Davis is a bright mulatto girl, about 17 years old, with a mole on her chin and a small mark on her forehead caused by a fall. She was emancipated by Thomas Vowell, Esq., by deed dated 10 October 1841.

REGISTRATION NO. 770
(Vol. 1, p. 277)

David Blackwell   15 December 1841

David Blackwell is a black man, about 30 years old, 5 feet 10½ inches tall, with a scar on his right elbow. He was emancipated by Elizabeth Gordon, as appears by deed recorded in Liber W No. 2, folio 34.

REGISTRATION NO. 771
(Vol. 1, p. 278)

Betsey Bowles   30 December 1841

Betsey Bowles is a mulatto woman, about 39 years old and 5 feet 1¼ inches tall. She was born free, as appears by affidavit of Thomas Slatford.

VOLUME 2

1842-1847

REGISTRATION NO. 1
(Vol. 2, p. 1)

Louisa Merricks22 March 1842

Louisa Merricks is about 17 years old, 5 feet 2 inches tall, with no visible marks. She was born free, as appears by affidavit of William Dean.

REGISTRATION NO. 2
(Vol. 2, p. 1)

Fanny Crawford6 April 1842

Fanny Crawford is about 24 years old, 5 feet 5 inches tall, of a dark copper complexion, with a small mole over her right eye. She was emancipated by Sarah B. Campbell of Fredericksburg.

REGISTRATION NO. 3
(Vol. 2, p. 1)

David Lee15 April 1842

David Lee is a bright mulatto man, about 52 years old, 5 feet 3 inches tall, with a small scar over his right eye and a mark immediately over his nose. He was liberated by Robert C. Carter, and is free, as appears by affidavit of Christopher Neale.

REGISTRATION NO. 4
(Vol. 2, p. 1)

Fanny Martin20 April 1842

Fanny Martin is about 7 years old, 4 feet 5 inches tall, and has a copper complexion. She was born free, as appears by affidavit of Lawrence B. Taylor.

REGISTRATION NO. 5
(Vol. 2, pp. 1-2)

Louisa Hatton5 May 1842

Louisa Hatton is a bright mulatto woman, about 22 years old, 5 feet 5 inches tall, with a scar from a cut on the fourth finger of her right hand. She was emancipated by Joseph Hatton.

REGISTRATION NO. 6
(Vol. 2, p. 2)

William Anderson7 May 1842

William Anderson is a mulatto man, about 30 years old, 5 feet 10½ inches tall, with smallpox marks on his face. He was emancipated by Sambo Anderson.

REGISTRATION NO. 7
(Vol. 2, p. 2)

Susan Middleton13 May 1842

Susan Middleton is a free woman, about 24 years old, 5 feet 3½ inches tall, of a dark complexion, with a scar on the left side of her face caused by a burn. She was born free, as appears by affidavit of Mary Simmons.

REGISTRATION NO. 8
(Vol. 2, p. 2)

Shederick Greene16 May 1842

Shederick Greene is about 17 years old, 5 feet 3 inches tall, of a dark complexion, with dark curly hair, and a scar on his right forefinger. He was born free, as appears by affidavit of John Russell.

REGISTRATION NO. 9
(Vol. 2, p. 2)

Eliza Anderson23 May 1842

Eliza Anderson is a mulatto woman, about 24 years old, and 5 feet 5¼ inches tall. She was emancipated by Sambo Anderson.

REGISTRATION NO. 10
(Vol. 2, p. 3)

Phillis Taylor and children,
Ann Maria and Mary Ann

10 June 1842

Phillis Taylor is about 21 years old, 5 feet 5 inches tall, of a black complexion, with a scar on her right arm. She was emancipated by the will of Slighter Smith. Taylor has two daughters: Ann Maria, aged about 6 years and 10 months, who was emancipated by Mrs. Elizabeth Monroe, legatee of Slighter Smith; and Mary Ann, about 2 years and 2 months old, who was born free.

REGISTRATION NO. 11
(Vol. 2, p. 3)

William Ross

21 June 1842

William Ross is a dark mulatto man, about 45 years old, 5 feet 7 inches tall. He was emancipated by Thomas Vowell, John C. Vowell, and Samuel B. Larmour, as appears by deed recorded in Liber A No. 3, p. 135.

REGISTRATION NO. 12
(Vol. 2, p. 3)

Jeremiah H. Frazer

25 June 1842

Jeremiah H. Frazer is about 24 years old, 5 feet 2½ inches tall, of a dark complexion, with a small scar on his right hand near the thumb, and a scar or mark caused by a cut near his right eye. He was born free, as appears by affidavit of William Yeates.

REGISTRATION NO. 13
(Vol. 2, p. 4)

Frances Brooks

27 June 1842

Frances Brooks is a mulatto woman, about 24 years old, 4 feet 11 3/4 inches tall, with a scar or black mole under her right jaw. She was born free, as appears by affidavit of James Stewart, Esq. Stewart states that he freed her mother before Frances was born.

REGISTRATION NO. 14
(Vol. 2, p. 4)

Ann Ferguson

29 June 1842

Ann Ferguson is a dark mulatto woman, about 45 years old, 5 feet 2½ inches tall, with a scar under her right jaw. She was emancipated by the will of General George Washington, as appears by affidavit of Mrs. Sarah Cash. Ann was only 2 or 3 years old when Washington died.

REGISTRATION NO. 15
(Vol. 2, p. 4)

Elizabeth Whiting

6 July 1842

Elizabeth Whiting is a bright mulatto child, about 5 years old, 3 feet 6 inches tall, with black straight hair and a scar on her left shoulder caused by a burn. She was born free, and was identified by W. T. Ramsay as the child of Martha Whiting, once Martha Garrett, who was emancipated by Thomas S. Hardy by deed recorded in Liber W No. 2, p. 168.

REGISTRATION NO. 16
(Vol. 2, p. 4)

Maria Butler

14 July 1842

Maria Butler is a mulatto girl, about 20 years old, 5 feet 2 inches tall, with a scar under her left eye. She was born free, as appears by affidavit of Elizabeth Snyder.

REGISTRATION NO. 17
(Vol. 1, p. 5)

Letty Weaver

23 August 1842

Letty Weaver is a dark mulatto woman, about 40 years old, 5 feet 2½ inches tall, with a mole of each side of her face. She was born free, as appears by affidavit of Mrs. Ann Lightfoot.

REGISTRATION NO. 18
(Vol. 2, p. 5)

Margaret Mitchell   28 September 1842

Margaret Mitchell is a mulatto girl about 4 years old. She was born free, as appears by affidavit of George Brent, Esq., who emancipated her mother, Ellen Mitchell, formerly Brown.

REGISTRATION NO. 19
(Vol. 2, p. 5)

Sally Hanson   5 October 1842

Sally Hanson is about 32 years old, 5 feet tall, of a dark complexion, with no visible marks. She was emancipated by William Campbell and John W. Massies[?], executors, by deed recorded in Liber B No. 3, p. 284.

REGISTRATION NO. 20
(Vol. 2, p. 5))

Daniel Waugh   9 November 1842

Daniel Waugh is a light mulatto man, about 21 years old, 5 feet 10¼ inches tall, with two scars above his right knee. He was born free, as appears by oath of Robert Jamieson.

REGISTRATION NO. 21
(Vol. 2, p. 5)

Henry Jackson   17 November 1842

Henry Jackson is about 30 years old, 5 feet 9 inches tall, of a dark complexion, with a scar on the back of his neck and another under his right ear. He was emancipated by William Lanphier[?] by deed recorded in Liber W No. 2, p. 87.

REGISTRATION NO. 22
(Vol. 2, p. 6)

Susan Cryer Reed   24 November 1842

Susan Reed, formerly Susan Cryer, is about 27 years old, 5 feet 4½ inches tall, of a dark complexion, with a scar under her right eye. She was born free, as appears by affidavit of Peter E. Hoffman.

REGISTRATION NO. 23
(Vol. 2, p. 6)

Fanny Fisher   22 December 1842

Fanny Fisher is a bright mulatto, about 42 years old, 5 feet one-fourth inch tall, with a speck in her right eye. She was emancipated by Charles Bennett's executor by deed recorded in Liber L No. 2, page 271.

REGISTRATION NO. 24
(Vol. 2, p. 6)

George Jackson   2 January 1843

George Jackson is a mulatto man, about 47 years old, 5 feet 9¼ inches tall, with a scar or black mark on his left cheek. He was emancipated by Robert Crupper by deed recorded in Liber C No. 3, folio 198.

REGISTRATION NO. 25
(Vol. 2, p. 6)

Joseph Frazer   21 February 1843

Joseph Frazer is a dark mulatto man, about 50 years old, 5 feet 7 3/4 inches tall, with a scar under the right corner of his mouth. He was emancipated by Ezra Lunt by deed recorded in Liber S No. 2, page 363.

REGISTRATION NO. 26
(Vol. 2, p. 6)

Robert Cupet   1 February 1843

Robert Cupet is a bright mulatto boy, about 19 years old, 5 feet 8¼ inches tall, with a scar on his right hand. He was born free.

REGISTRATION NO. 27
(Vol. 2, p. 7)

Amelia Bockett   1843

Amelia Bockett is a bright mulatto girl, about 14 years old, 4 feet 7 inches tall, with no visible marks. She was born free, as appears by affidavit of Stephen Shinn.

There is no registration numbered 28.

REGISTRATION NO. 29
(Vol. 2, p. 7)

Ottaway West   27 April 1843

Ottaway West is 20 years old, 5 feet 5½ inches tall, of a dark complexion, with a scar on the right side of his face caused by a burn. He was born free, as appears by certificate of Mrs. Ann S. Mark. His mother is Harriet West, a free person of color.

Mark's name is given as "Ann H." in No. 30 below.

REGISTRATION NO. 30
(Vol. 2, p. 7)

James West   27 April 1843

James West is a mulatto man, about 21 years old, 5 feet 5½ inches tall, with a scar on his forehead. He was born free and is the son of Harriet West, a free woman of color, as appears by affidavit of Mrs. Ann H. Mark.

Mark's name is given as "Ann S." in No. 29 above.

REGISTRATION NO. 31
(Vol. 2, p. 7)

Jane Eliza Slater   4 May 1843

Jane Eliza Slater is a mulatto woman, about 23 years old, 5 feet 1 3/4 inches tall, with no visible marks. She was born free as appears by affidavit of Mrs. Julia Cox.

REGISTRATION NO. 32
(Vol. 2, p. 8)

Cornelia Morris   8 May 1843

Cornelia Morris is a mulatto woman, about 21 years old, 5 feet 3 inches tall, with no visible marks. She was born free, as appears by oath of James Smart[?].

REGISTRATION NO. 33
(Vol. 2, p. 8)

James Dover   16 May 1843

James Dover is a bright mulatto boy, about 18 years old, 5 feet 9 inches tall with a scar over his left eye caused by a cut. He was emancipated by Jetson Dover.

REGISTRATION NO. 34
(Vol. 2, p. 8)

Fendall Wyatt   17 May 1843

Fendall "Wayatt" [Wyatt] is a bright mulatto boy, about 16 years old, 5 feet one-half inch tall, with no visible marks. He was born free, as appears by affidavit of Isabella Deakin.

Volume 2, 1842-1847

REGISTRATION NO. 35
(Vol. 2, p. 8)

George Anderson Grymes   22 May 1843

George Andrew Grymes is a mulatto boy, about 13 years old, 4 feet 7 inches tall, with no visible marks. He was born free, as appears by certificate from Richard House.

REGISTRATION NO. 36
(Vol. 2, p. 8)

Emily Gibson Hampton   26 May 1843

Emily Hampton, formerly Gibson, is a mulatto woman, about 30 years old, 5 feet 2 3/4 inches tall, with no visible marks. She was emancipated by Henry Gibson.

REGISTRATION NO. 37
(Vol. 2, p. 9)

Clarissa Ann Bruce   6 June 1843

Clarissa Ann Bruce is about 24 years old, 5 feet 4 inches tall, of a dark complexion, with no visible marks. She was born free, as appears by affidavit of Thomas Sanford.

REGISTRATION NO. 38
(Vol. 2, p. 9)

Roxanna Jones   8 June 1843

Roxanna Jones is about 18 years old, 5 feet three-fourth inch tall, of a dark color, with no visible marks. She was born free and was identified by Charles Graham as the child of Ann Jones, a free woman.

REGISTRATION NO. 39
(Vol. 2, p. 9)

Anna Kendall   21 June 1843

Anna Kendall is about 17 years old, 5 feet 1 inch tall, of a dark complexion, with no visible marks. She was born free, as appears by affidavit of Joseph H. Hampson.

REGISTRATION NO. 40
(Vol. 2, p. 9)

James Dorsey   23 June 1843

James Dorsey is about 19 years old, 5 feet 5 inches tall, of a dark complexion, with no visible marks. He was born free, as appears by affidavit of Charles [C.] Smoot.

REGISTRATION NO. 41
(Vol. 2, p. 9)

Mary Bell   14 July 1843

Mary Bell is a bright mulatto girl, about 18 years old, 5 feet 1 inch tall, with no visible marks. She was born free, as appears by affidavit of James P. Coleman.

REGISTRATION NO. 42
(Vol. 2, p. 10)

Grafton Johnson   16 August 1843

Grafton Johnson is about 32 years old, 5 feet 3½ inches tall, of a dark complexion, with a scar on his upper lip caused by a cut. He was born free, as appears by affidavit of Hugh Leddy.

REGISTRATION NO. 43
(Vol. 2, p. 10)

Ann Maria Dougan   16 August 1843

Ann Maria Dougan is a mulatto girl, about 19 years old, 5 feet 8½ inches tall, with no visible marks. She was born free, as appears by a certificate from Mrs. Ann Page.

REGISTRATION NO. 44
(Vol. 2, p. 10)

Phebe Ann Tyler

26 August 1843

Phebe Ann Tyler is a mulatto girl, about 15 years old, 4 feet 9 3/4 inches tall, with no visible marks. She is free, as appears by affidavit of Joseph H. Miller.

REGISTRATION NO. 45
(Vol. 2, p. 10)

Louisa Harris

15 September 1843

Louisa Harris ia a bright mulatto woman, about 23 years old, 5 feet 3 3/4 inches tall, with no visible marks. She was emancipated by Matthias Snyder, Sr.

REGISTRATION NO. 46
(Vol. 2, p. 11)

Ann Elizabeth Jones

28 September 1843

Ann Elizabeth Jones is about 22 years old and 5 feet tall. She was emancipated by Oliver Jones.

REGISTRATION NO. 47
(Vol. 2, p. 11)

Emily Cole Gray

29 September 1843

Emily Gray, late Cole, is a mulatto woman, about 22 years old, 5 feet 4½ inches tall, with a scar on her neck and another on her arm. She was born free, as appears by affidavit of John Chance.

REGISTRATION NO. 48
(Vol. 2, p. 11)

Mary Jane Evans

30 September 1843

Mary Jane Evans is a mulatto woman about 5 feet 3 inches tall. She was born free, and is the daughter of Nancy Evans, a free woman who was also born free, as appears by certificate of Walter Harris.

REGISTRATION NO. 49
(Vol. 2, p. 11)

Sally Syphax

2 October 1843

Sally Syphax is 5 feet 1¼ inches tall, has a dark complexion, with no visible marks. She was emancipated by William Syphax by deed recorded in Liber Z No. 2, page 123.

REGISTRATION NO. 50
(Vol. 2, p. 11)

Judy Syphax

2 October 1843

Judy Syphax is about 5 feet 2 inches tall, has a dark complexion, with no visible marks. She was emancipated by William Syphax by deed recorded in Liber Z No. 2, p. 123.

REGISTRATION NO. 51
(Vol. 2, p. 12)

Violett Day Cole

2 October 1843

Violett Day, alias Cole, is a black woman about 56 years old, and 5 feet 4½ inches tall. She has a scar on the outside of her left arm nearly half way between her elbow and wrist and a scar on her right arm near the wrist. (See Liber A, p. 24).

See Vol. 1, No. 26 for the registration of Violett Day.

REGISTRATION NO. 52
(Vol. 2, p. 12)

Lucian B. L. Pipsico

3 October 1843

Lucian B. L. Pipsico is a bright mulatto boy, about 17 years old, 5 feet 4 inches tall, with no visible marks. He was emancipated by Tristam H. Garner.

REGISTRATION NO. 53
(Vol. 2, p. 12)

Daniel Robinson 12 October 1843

Daniel Robinson is a black man, about 36 years old, 5 feet 3 3/4 inches tall, with no visible marks. He was emancipated by Alexander Waugh.

REGISTRATION NO. 54
(Vol. 2, p. 12)

Lydia Ann Taylor 31 October 1843

Lydia Ann Taylor is about 28 years old, 5 feet 2 3/4 inches tall, and has a dark complexion, with a scar on her nose. She was born free, as appears by affidavit of Hannah S. Wanton.

REGISTRATION NO. 55
(Vol. 2, p. 13)

Charles Bruce 15 November 1843

Charles Bruce is a black man, about 28 years old, 5 feet 4½ inches tall, with no visible marks. He was emancipated by Thomas Sanford.

REGISTRATION NO. 56
(Vol. 1, p. 13)

Jetson Dover 21 November 1843

Jetson Dover is a free mulatto man, about 44 years old, 5 feet 11 inches tall, with a scar on his nose caused by a cut. He was born free, as appears by affidavit of Jesse Ramsay.

REGISTRATION NO. 57
(Vol. 2, p. 13)

Nancy Ages 21 November 1843

Nancy Ages is a black woman, about 32 years old, 5 feet 4½ inches tall, with no visible marks. She was born free, as appears by affidavit of John L. Pascol.

REGISTRATION NO. 58
(Vol. 2, p. 13)

Sarah Taylor Carter 22 November 1843

Sarah Carter, formerly Taylor, is a mulatto woman, about 25 years old, 5 feet tall, with a scar on her nose caused by a cut. She was emancipated by Thomas Birch by deed recorded in Liber R No. 2, folio 367.

REGISTRATION NO. 59
(Vol. 2, p. 13)

Garret Tate 22 November 1843

Garret Tate is a free mulatto man, about 48 years old, 5 feet 4 3/4 inches tall, with no visible marks. He was freed by the will of William Bartleman.

REGISTRATION NO. 60
(Vol. 2, p. 14)

John Hall 1 December 1843

John Hall is a mulatto man, about 32 years old, 5 feet 5 3/4 inches tall, with the little finger of his left hand broken. He was born free, as appears by affidavit of Mrs. Margaret Thompson.

REGISTRATION NO. 61
(Vol. 2, p. 14)

Sarah Jane Brooks 8 February 1844

Sarah Jane Brooks is a bright mulatto girl, about 18 years old, 5 feet 4 inches tall, with no visible marks. She was born free.

REGISTRATION NO. 62
(Vol. 2, p. 14)

Mary Elizabeth Buller

26 February 1844

Mary Elizabeth Buller is a bright mulatto girl, about 19 years old, 5 feet 1 inch tall, with a scar on the left side of her neck caused by a burn. She was born free, as appears by affidavit of John [B.] Hancock.

REGISTRATION NO. 63
(Vol. 2, p. 14)

Ann Matilda Morris

12 March 1844

Ann Matilda Morris is a bright mulatto girl, about 18 years old, 5 feet 5 inches tall, with a scar on the back of her left hand and another in the palm of her right hand. She was proved free by oath of Hannah Buck.

REGISTRATION NO. 64
(Vol. 2, p. 15)

John Crawford

13 March 1844

John Crawford is about 21 years old, 5 feet 8 inches tall, of a dark complexion, with no visible marks. He was emancipated by the will of Sarah B. "Cambell" [Campbell].

REGISTRATION NO. 65
(Vol. 2, p. 15)

Ann Cryer

15 March 1844

Ann Cryer is a mulatto woman, about 24 years old, 5 feet one-half inch tall, with two or three moles on the right side of her face, and two scars on her left arm caused by burns[?]. She was emancipated by Peter E. Hoffman by deed dated 8 May 1839.

REGISTRATION NO. 66
(Vol. 2, p. 15)

Paul Brown

30 April 1844

Paul Brown is about 28 years old, 5 feet 10 inches tall, of a dark complexion, with a scar over his left eye and a scar on his breast caused by a burn. He was emancipated by Mordecai Miller, as appears by affidavit of R[obert] H. Miller.

REGISTRATION NO. 67
(Vol. 2, p. 15)

Jane Brown

30 April 1844

Jane Brown is a dark mulatto woman, about 30 years old, 5 feet 3 inches tall, with a scar on her left arm caused by a burn. She was born free, as appears by affidavit of John L. Smith.

REGISTRATION NO. 68
(Vol. 2, p. 16)

George Chapman

9 May 1844

George Chapman is a bright mulatto man, about 43 years old, 5 feet 10½ inches tall, with a scar on his right leg between the knee and ankle and another on the calf of his right leg caused by a dog bite. He was emancipated by L[awrence] B. Taylor.

REGISTRATION NO. 69
(Vol. 2, p. 16)

James Evans

18 May 1844

James Evans is a dark mulatto man, about 22 years old, 5 feet 8½ inches tall, with a scar on the top of his head caused by the cut of an axe. He was born free, as appears by oath of Patsey Chichester.

REGISTRATION NO. 70
(Vol. 2, p. 16)

Hannah Ann Bruce

30 June 1844

Hannah Ann Bruce is a bright mulatto girl, about 19 years old, 5 feet 1½ inches tall, with a mole on the right side of her face near her lower lip. She was born free, as appears by the papers of her mother, Hannah Bruce, registered in this office on 11 November 1840.

See No. 727 in Vol. 1 for Hannah Bruce.

REGISTRATION NO. 71
(Vol. 2, p. 16)

William E. Tate

8 July 1844

William E. Tate is a dark mulatto man, about 25 years old, 5 feet 6 inches tall, with a scar in the palm of his left hand. He was born free, as appears by oath of John Banks.

REGISTRATION NO. 72
(Vol. 2, p. 17)

Mary Gibbs

23 July 1844

Mary Gibbs is a dark mulatto woman, about 23 years old, 5 feet 5 3/4 inches tall, with a scar on the thumb of her right hand caused by a cut, and a scar on the back of her left hand near her wrist caused by a burn. She was born free, as appears by affidavit of Theodore Meade.

REGISTRATION NO. 73
(Vol. 2, p. 17)

Ann Beckley

5 August 1844

Ann Beckley is a bright mulatto woman, about 29 years old, 5 feet 2½ inches tall, with no visible marks. She has a slight lameness in her right side. She was born free, as appears by affidavit of "Precilla" [Priscilla] Simpson.

REGISTRATION NO. 74
(Vol. 2, p. 17)

Sophia Darnell

7 August 1844

Sophia Darnell is 5 feet 2 3/4 inches tall, of a dark complexion, with a scar on the back of her left hand between the forefinger and her thumb caused by a burn. She was emancipated by Charles McKnight by deed recorded in Liber Z No. 2, folio 279.

REGISTRATION NO. 75
(Vol. 2, p. 17)

Zachariah Handless

21 September 1844

Zachariah "Handlis" [Handless] is about 23 years and 6 months old, 5 feet 6¼ inches tall, with a lump in the small of his back caused by an injury when he was young. He was born free, as appears by affidavit of Mary Ann Cole.

REGISTRATION NO. 76
(Vol. 2, p. 18)

Richard F. Johnson

28 September 1844

Richard F. Johnson is about 20 years old, 5 feet 8 3/4 inches tall, of a dark complexion, with a scar in the center of his upper lip caused by a cut from a shovel and another scar on the outside of the thumb of his right hand. He was born free, as appears by a certificate from Edgar Snowden.

There is no registration numbered 77.

REGISTRATION NO. 78
(Vol. 2, p. 18)

Henry Delly

8 October 1844

Henry Delly is about 26 years old, 6 feet one-half inch tall, with no visible marks. He has a slight lameness in his right side caused by a fall from a horse. He was emancipated by William H. Wilmer by deed recorded in Liber Q No. 2, folio 56.

REGISTRATION NO. 79
(Vol. 2, p. 18)

Presley Wilson

8 October 1844

Presley Wilson is a free man, about 32 years old, 5 feet 7½ inches tall, of a dark complexion, with a scar on his right temple and another on the left side of his face. He was born free, as appears by oath of Patsey Chichester.

REGISTRATION NO. 80
(Vol. 2, pp. 18-19)

Betsy Hall

16 October 1844

Betsy Hall is a mulatto woman, about 23 years old, 4 feet 9¼ inches tall, with a mole on the left side of her face near her nose and a scar on her breast caused by a burn. She was born free, as appears by certificate of Walter Harris.

REGISTRATION NO. 81
(Vol. 2, p. 19)

Sarah Skinner

17 October 1844

Sarah Skinner is a bright mulatto girl about 8 years and 3 months old. She was born free, as appears by certificate of A[nthony] C[harles] Cazenove and William C. Gardner.

REGISTRATION NO. 82
(Vol. 2, p. 19)

Elizabeth Hamilton

22 October 1844

Elizabeth Hamilton is about 21 years old, 5 feet 7½ inches tall and has a dark complexion. She was born free and is the daughter of Ellen Hamilton who was emancipated by the will of Jane Contee before the birth of Elizabeth. Elizabeth was identified by Jane Anne Keith.

REGISTRATION NO. 83
(Vol. 2, p. 19)

Ellen Hamilton Jones

22 October 1844

Ellen Jones, formerly Hamilton, is about 23 years old, 5 feet 2 3/4 inches tall, of a dark complexion, with a scar on her right wrist caused by a burn. She was born free and was identified by Jane Anne Keith as the daughter of Ellen Hamilton who was emancipated by the will of Miss Jane Contee.

REGISTRATION NO. 84
(Vol. 2, p. 20a)

Dicy Brown

22 October 1844

Dicy Brown is about 37 years old, 5 feet 2½ inches tall, of a dark complexion, with a scar over her left eye caused by a cut. She was emancipated by John F. N. Lowe.

REGISTRATION NO. 85
(Vol. 2, p. 20a)

John Henry Brown

7 November 1844

John Henry Brown is a bright mulatto man, about 22 years old, 5 feet 8½ inches tall, with a scar near the left corner of his mouth. He was born free, as appears by affidavit of Sarah Ann Brown, a free woman and his mother.

REGISTRATION NO. 86
(Vol. 2, p. 20a)

Richard Garrett

7 November 1844

Richard Garrett is a bright mulatto man, about 33 years old, 5 feet 7½ inches tall, with a scar over his left eye beginning at the eyebrow. He was emancipated by Silas [H.] Reed, as appears by certificate of Isaac Buckingham.

REGISTRATION NO. 87
(Vol. 2, p. 20a)

Joseph Johnson   25 November 1844

Joseph Johnson is about 21 years old, 5 feet 4¼ inches tall, and has a dark complexion. He was born free, as appears by affidavit of Dr. Orlando Fairfax.

REGISTRATION NO. 88
(Vol. 2, p. 20a)

Sarah Ann Carter   2 December 1844

Sarah Ann Carter is a bright mulatto, about 24 years old, 5 feet 2 inches tall, with a scar behind her left ear. She was born free, as appears by a certificate from Edward Smyth.

REGISTRATION NO. 89
(Vol. 2, p. 20b)

Mary Dover   10 December 1844

Mary Dover is a bright mulatto girl, 5 feet 3¼ inches tall, with straight black hair and is slightly freckled. She was emancipated by Jane A. Ramsay as appears by deed recorded in Liber V No. 2, page 40.

REGISTRATION NO. 90
(Vol. 2, p. 20b)

Mary Sumby   17 December 1844

Mary Sumby is about 40 years old, 5 feet one-half inch tall, of a dark complexion, with a large black mole on the right side of her face a little below her nose. She was emancipated by Sally Thomas by deed dated 24 July 1844.

REGISTRATION NO. 91
(Vol. 2, p. 20b)

Ferdinand Diggs   8 March 1845

Ferdinand Diggs is about 17 years old, 5 feet 4¼ inches tall, of a dark complexion, with no visible marks. He was born free, as appears by affidavit of Ann Brooks.

REGISTRATION NO. 92
(Vol. 2, p. 20b)

James Evans   9 April 1845

James Evans is about 64 years old, 5 feet 7¼ inches tall, of a dark complexion, with a large mark or scar on the inside of his left arm halfway between his wrist and shoulder. He was born free, as appears by affidavit of James Nightingill.

REGISTRATION NO. 93
(Vol. 2, p. 21)

Alfred H. Parry   14 April 1845

Alfred H. Parry is a bright mulatto man, about 39 years old, 5 feet 6 3/4 inches tall, with a scar on his forehead just above his nose caused by a burn. He was born free, as appears by affidavit of Anthony Rhodes.

REGISTRATION NO. 94
(Vol. 2, p. 21)

Sally Fox Parry   14 April 1845

Sally Parry, formerly Fox, is a mulatto woman about 39 years old, 5 feet 5 inches tall, with no visible marks. She was born free, as appears by affidavit of William H. Miller.

REGISTRATION NO. 95
(Vol. 2, p. 21)

Thomas Beckley

7 May 1845

Thomas Beckley is a mulatto man, about 25 years old, 5 feet 9 inches tall, with a scar on his forehead immediately above the left eye, a scar near his right eyebrow caused by a cut, and a large scar caused by a burn on the right side of his forehead almost concealed by his hair. He was born free, as appears by affidavit of "Precilla" [Priscilla] Simpson, a white woman.

REGISTRATION NO. 96
(Vol. 2, p. 21)

Jesse Beckley

7 May 1845

Jesse Beckley is a mulatto man, about 23 years old, 5 feet 8¼ inches tall, with straight black hair and no visible marks. He was born free, as appears by affidavit of "Precilla" [Priscilla] Simpson.

REGISTRATION NO. 97
(Vol. 2, p. 22)

Emily Cryer
Rebecca Frances Cryer
Chloe Ann Cryer

8 May 1845

Emily Cryer is a bright mulatto girl, about 17 years old, 4 feet 10 3/4 inches tall, with a mark on her left arm between the elbow and the wrist; Rebecca Frances Cryer is about 15; and "Cloe" [Chloe] Ann Cryer is about 10. They are the children of Anne Cryer, a free mulatto woman, and were born free, as appears by affidavit of Mrs. Ann Brooks.

REGISTRATION NO. 98
(Vol. 2, p. 22)

Charles Johnson

24 May 1845

Charles Johnson is about 29 years old, 5 feet 5½ inches tall, of a dark complexion, with a scar on his left arm near the elbow caused by a horse bite. Charles is the son of Bet, daughter of Peg, who was emancipated by John C. Herbert by deed dated 24 November 1805 and recorded in Liber K No. 1, folio 333. In that deed it was stated that the future increase of Peg should be free when they reached age of 28. Charles's period of service has expired, and a deed of manumission dated 24 March 1844 has been filed setting forth that he is free.

REGISTRATION NO. 99
(Vol. 2, p. 22)

Francis Brown

30 May 1845

Francis Brown is about 21 years old, 5 feet 4½ inches tall, with a dark complexion, no visible marks and his right thigh has been broken. He is free, as appears by affidavit of John Brown, who states that he has known Francis for upwards of 20 years and that he always passed as a free person. Brown's mother is Matilda Shields, a free woman.

REGISTRATION NO. 100
(Vol. 2, p. 23)

Ephriam Barcroft

9 June 1845

Ephriam Barcroft is about 22 years and 6 months old, 5 feet 9 inches tall, of a dark complexion, with a scar on the inner side of his right arm a little above his wrist. He was born free, as appears by affidavit of John Lawson.

REGISTRATION NO. 101
(Vol. 2, p. 23)

Joseph Gibson

16 June 1845

Joseph Gibson is about 22 years and 1 month old, 5 feet 6¼ inches tall, of a dark complexion, with a scar on the ball of the thumb of his left hand caused by a cut. He was emancipated by William H. and Robert H. Miller, executors of Mordecai Miller, and Richard H. Clagett and William Page, executors of Colin Auld, by deed dated 26 May 1843 recorded in Liber D No. 3, folio 162.

REGISTRATION NO. 102
(Vol. 2, p. 23)

William Dover

24 June 1845

William Dover is about 15 years old, 5 feet 2¼ inches tall, of a light complexion, very much freckled, with no visible marks. He was emancipated by Mrs. Jane A. Ramsay by deed dated 30 May 1835 recorded in Liber V No. 2, folio 360.

REGISTRATION NO. 103
(Vol. 2, p. 23)

Harriet Bruce

25 June 1845

Harriet Bruce is about 16 years old, 5 feet 3½ inches tall, of a light complexion, with no visible marks. She was born free, as appears by affidavit of Mrs. Catharine Ward.

REGISTRATION NO. 104
(Vol. 2, p. 24)

Mary Ellen Johnson

8 July 1845

Mary Ellen Johnson, aged about 18 years and 2 months, 5 feet 2 inches tall, of a dark complexion, with no visible marks. She was born free, as appears by affidavit of Mrs. Martha Ann Taylor.

REGISTRATION NO. 105
(Vol. 2, p. 24)

Mima Dogan

23 July 1845

Mima Dogan is about 43 years old, 5 feet 2½ inches tall, of a dark complexion, with a scar caused by a cut on the right side of her chin just below the lower lip. She was emancipated by David Martin and Sarah Harper by deed dated 6 January 1830. Dogan was identified by Henry Daingerfield as the person named in that deed.

REGISTRATION NO. 106
(Vol. 2, p. 24)

Jane Elizabeth Harris

4 August 1845

Jane Elizabeth Harris is about 18 years 3 months old, 5 feet 2¼ inches tall, of a dark brown complexion, with a scar on her left arm halfway between her elbow and wrist caused by a burn, and a mole near her right eye. She was born free, as appears by affidavit of Mrs. Mary Greenwood, a white citizen.

REGISTRATION NO. 107
(Vol. 2, p. 24)

Andrew Dogan

18 August 1845

Andrew Dogan is about 22 years old, 5 feet 4¼ inches tall, of a dark brown complexion, with no visible marks. He was born free, as appears by affidavit of John B. Hancock.

REGISTRATION NO. 108
(Vol. 2, p. 25)

George Bruce

28 August 1845

George Bruce is 21 years 5 months and 11 days old, of a light complexion, with wavy hair and a black mole on his nose between his eyes. He was emancipated by the will of Colin Auld.

REGISTRATION NO. 109
(Vol. 2, p. 25)

Leanor Evans

30 August 1845

Leanor Evans is about 16 years old, 5 feet one-half inch tall, of a brown complexion, with no visible marks. She was born free, as appears by affidavit of Mrs. Patsy Chichester.

REGISTRATION NO. 110
(Vol. 2, p. 25)

Thomas Turly

2 September 1845

Thomas Turly is about 21 years and 1 month old, 5 feet 7 inches tall, of a dark complexion, with a scar on his throat caused by a burn that extends from his right ear to his chin. He was born free, as appears by a certificate of Robert Jamieson, Esq.

REGISTRATION NO. 111
(Vol. 2, p. 25)

William M. Williams

2 September 1845

William M. Williams is about 22 years old, 5 feet 7¼ inches tall, of a brown complexion, with a scar caused by a burn on his right cheek in a line with his mouth and another, also caused by a burn, on the right side of his cheek. He was emancipated by Colin Auld by deed dated 21 May 1835 recorded in Liber A No. 3, folio 199. Williams was identified by William Page, Esq., as the person mentioned in that will.

REGISTRATION NO. 112
(Vol. 2, p. 26)

Laura Beckley

30 September 1845

Laura Beckley ia about 18 years old, 5 feet 2 inches tall, of a light complexion, with three scars on her forehead directly in line with her nose. She was born free, as appears by the certificate of Edgar Snowden, Esq.

REGISTRATION NO. 113
(Vol. 2, p. 26)

Martha Jackson

4 September 1845

Martha Jackson is about 28 years old, 5 feet 6¼ inches tall, of a dark complexion, with a scar on her right arm near the wrist caused by a burn. She was born free and is the child of Nancy Dorsey, a free woman of color. (See No. 492 in previous book).

See No. 492 in Vol. 1 for Nancy Dorsey.

REGISTRATION NO. 114
(Vol. 2, p. 26)

Richard Madella

4 September 1845

Richard Madella is about 21 years old, 5 feet 7 inches tall, of a dark complexion, with a scar on his left arm near his elbow. He was born free, as appears by affidavit of Josiah H. Davis.

REGISTRATION NO. 115
(Vol. 2, p. 26)

Rebecca Marshall

10 September 1845

Rebecca Marshall is about 16 years old, 5 feet 3 inches tall, of a very light complexion, with a slight scar on her right cheek. She was born free, as appears by affidavit of John Riston.

REGISTRATION NO. 116
(Vol. 2, p. 27)

Martha Tate

30 September 1845

Martha Tate is about 22 years old, 5 feet 4 3/4 inches tall, of a dark complexion, with a slight scar on the wrist of her right hand. She was born free, as appears by affidavit of Mrs. Sinah B. Porter

REGISTRATION NO. 117
(Vol. 2, p. 27)

Julia Roberts

6 October 1845

Julia Roberts is about 36 years old, 5 feet 5 3/4 inches tall, of a dark complexion, with a slight scar on her nose. She obtained her freedom by court judgement at the May 1842 term in the case in which she was the plaintiff and Austin Q. Adams *et. al.* the defendants.

REGISTRATION NO. 118
(Vol. 2, p. 27)

Angelo Harris

13 October 1845

Angelo Harris is about 26 years old, 5 feet 11½ inches tall, of a light complexion, with a slight scar on the back of his left hand. He was emancipated by William Stabler by deed dated 7 January 1845.

REGISTRATION NO. 119
(Vol. 2, p. 27)

William Rodgers

17 October 1845

William Rodgers is a mulatto man, about 39 years old, 5 feet 9½ inches tall, with a scar on his right leg near his ankle. He was declared free by court decree at its May 1839 term in the case of William and Cornell Rodgers *v.* [Jonathan] Janney & [Samuel] Oldham.

REGISTRATION NO. 120
(Vol. 2, p. 28)

Mary Margaret Berry

28 October 1845

Mary Margaret Berry is about 18 years old, 4 feet 9 3/4 inches tall, of a dark brown complexion, with no visible marks. She was emancipated by James Harris, as appears by affidavit of Walter Harris, the son of James.

REGISTRATION NO. 121
(Vol. 2, p. 28)

Chloe Ann Middleton

28 October 1845

Chloe Ann Middleton is about 22 years old, 5 feet 3 3/4 inches tall, of a very light complexion, with a slight scar on the upper part of her nose between her eyes. She was born free, as appears by affidavit of Walter Harris.

REGISTRATION NO. 122
(Vol. 2, p. 28)

William Hamilton

31 October 1845

William Hamilton is about 27 years old, 5 feet 4 3/4 inches tall, of a dark complexion, with a scar on his right arm between the elbow and wrist. He was born free, as appears by affidavit of Wesley Carlin.

REGISTRATION NO. 123
(Vol. 2, p. 28)

Cornelius Madella

22 November 1845

Cornelius Madella is about 18 years old, 5 feet 10 inches tall, of a light complexion, with a scar on his chin and another near and in a line with his right eye. He was born free, as appears by certificate of E. R. and Mary F. Lippitt.

REGISTRATION NO. 124
(Vol. 2, p. 29)

Ellen Bowles

22 November 1845

Ellen Bowles is about 35 years old, 5 feet 2 3/4 inches tall, of a light complexion, with no visible marks. She was emancipated by Mary and Eliza Eaches by deed dated 14 May 1845 recorded in Liber F No. 3, p. 482.

REGISTRATION NO. 125
(Vol. 2, p. 29)

William Henry Bruce

27 January 1846

William Henry Bruce is about 24 years old, 5 feet 6 inches tall, of a light complexion, with a scar on the right side of his face extending from his ear to his chin. He was emancipated by the will of Colin Auld and was identified by William Page, one of the executors of Auld's will.

REGISTRATION NO. 126
(Vol. 2, p. 29)

Oliver Jones

11 February 1846

Oliver Jones is about 24 years old, 5 feet 4 3/4 inches tall, of a dark complexion, with a slight scar under his left eye. He was born free, as appears by affidavit of Charles Graham.

REGISTRATION NO. 127
(Vol. 2, p. 29)

Ann Charlotte Jones

11 February 1846

Ann Charlotte Jones is about 20 years and 4 months old, 5 feet 2½ inches tall, of a dark complexion, with a large black mole on the center of her upper lip and three scars on her right arm between her wrist and her elbow. She was born free, as appears by affidavit of Charles Graham.

REGISTRATION NO. 128
(Vol. 2, p. 30)

Ann Smith

16 February 1846

Ann Smith is about 18 years old, 5 feet 2 inches tall, of a dark complexion, with no visible marks. She was born free, as appears by affidavit of Mrs. Martha Cole.

REGISTRATION NO. 129
(Vol. 2, p. 30)

Robert Brannum

5 March 1846

Robert Brannum is about 22 years and 2 months old, 5 feet 8 3/4 inches tall, of a very light complexion, with no visible marks. He was emancipated by Robert Jamieson by deed dated 7 January 1846.

REGISTRATION NO. 130
(Vol. 2, p. 30)

Hannah Ann Young

23 March 1846

Hannah Ann Young is about 19 years old, 5 feet 1 inch tall, of a light complexion, with a slight scar near her left ear. She was born free, as appears by affidavit of Mrs. Elizabeth Markell.

REGISTRATION NO. 131
(Vol. 2, p. 30)

Richard Henry Gibson

24 March 1846

Richard Henry Gibson is about 28 years old, 6 feet one-half inch tall, of a light complexion, with a scar on the thumb of his right hand. He was emancipated by Colin Auld, William H. Miller, and Robert H. Miller, executors of Mordecai Miller, by deed dated 15 March 1838 recorded in Liber X No. 2, page 513.

REGISTRATION NO. 132
(Vol. 2, p. 31)

Benjamin Crier

26 March 1846

Benjamin Crier is about 46 years old, 5 feet 6 inches tall, of a dark complexion, with a scar over his left eye. He was emancipated by Mary Gordon and Elizabeth Gordon by deed recorded in Liber A No. 3, folio 332.

REGISTRATION NO. 133
(Vol. 2, p. 31)

Charles Dogan

27 March 1846

Charles Dogan is about 40 years old, 5 feet 9 inches tall, of a dark complexion with a large scar on the upper part of his chest. He was born free, as appears by certificate of John B. Daingerfield.

REGISTRATION NO. 134
(Vol. 2, p. 31)

Spencer Day

2 April 1846

Spencer Day is about 38 years old, 5 feet 8 3/4 inches tall, of a brown complexion, with a large mole on the left side of his face above his left eye. He was born free, as appears by affidavit of Mrs. Ann Mason.

REGISTRATION NO. 135
(Vol. 2, p. 31)

Elizabeth Hall and her children, Mary Elizabeth, William, Letticia, and Emma

3 April 1846

Elizabeth Hall is about 32 years old, 5 feet 6¼ inches tall, of a light brown complexion, with a slight scar over her left eye. She was born free, as appears by affidavit of Margaret M. Bangs. Her four children are: Mary Elizabeth, aged 14; William, aged 10 years 7 months; Letticia, aged 8 years; and Emma, aged 4 years.

REGISTRATION NO. 136
(Vol. 2, p. 32)

David Dixon   14 May 1846

David Dixon is about 33 years old, 5 feet 7½ inches tall, of a light complexion, with a slight scar over his left eye and a large scar on the end of the middle finger of his left hand. He was born free, as appears by certificate of John T.[?] Johnson and others.

REGISTRATION NO. 137
(Vol. 2, p. 32)

Ellen Carrell   18 May 1846

Ellen Carrell is about 23 years old, 5 feet 2 3/4 inches tall, of a dark complexion, with several round scars on her face over the left jaw. She was emancipated by Mrs. Rebecca Taylor by deed dated 21 December 1845.

REGISTRATION NO. 138
(Vol. 2, p. 32)

Sally Cotes   30 May 1846

Sally Cotes is about 40 years old, 5 feet tall, and has a dark complexion. She was emancipated by Frederick Cotes by deed dated 25 May 1846.

REGISTRATION NO. 139
(Vol. 2, p. 32)

Emily Adams   30 May 1846

Emily Adams is about 13 years old, 4 feet 10 inches tall, of a dark complexion, with a slight scar under her left eye. She was emancipated by Frederick Cotes by deed dated 25 May 1846.

REGISTRATION NO. 140
(Vol. 2, p. 33)

Susan Slater and   1 June 1846
child, Margaret Ellen

Susan Slater is about 42 years old, 5 feet 3½ inches tall, of a dark complexion, with a scar under her left ear. She was born free, as appears by affidavit of G[eorge] W. P. Custis, as was her child, Margaret Ellen, aged 6.

REGISTRATION NO. 141
(Vol. 2, p. 33)

Elizabeth Ross and   1 June 1846
child, Lucretia

Elizabeth Ross, known as Betty, is 24 years old, 5 feet 4 inches tall, of a brown complexion, with no visible marks. She was born free, as appears by affidavit of W. W. P. Custis, Esq., as was her child, Lucretia, aged about 1 year and 8 months.

REGISTRATION NO. 142
(Vol. 2, p. 33)

William M. Tate   13 June 1846

William M. Tate is about 28 years old, 5 feet 6½ inches tall, of a bright complexion, with a large scar on the inside of his thumb of his left hand. He was emancipated by E. R. Lippitt by deed dated 9 June 1846.

REGISTRATION NO. 143
(Vol. 2, p. 33)

Letitia Darnell   27 June 1846

Letitia Darnell is about 15 years old, 5 feet 2 inches tall, of a bright complexion, with no visible marks. She was born free, as appears by certificate of Dr. John Richards.

REGISTRATION NO. 144
(Vol. 2, p. 34)

Ann Brown

29 June 1846

Ann Brown is about 26 years old, 5 feet 2 3/4 inches tall, of a light complexion, with several large scars on the right side of her throat. She was emancipated by James Vansant by deed recorded in Liber D No. 3, page 403, and was identified by James Vansant.

REGISTRATION NO. 145
(Vol. 2, p. 34)

Lenny Brown

29 June 1846

Lenny Brown is a free woman, about 40 years old, 5 feet 2½ inches tall, of a dark complexion, with no visible marks. She was emancipated by Robert Jamieson by deed recorded in Liber C No. 3, page 53, and was identified by said Jamieson.

REGISTRATION NO. 146
(Vol. 2, p. 34)

Sarah Elizabeth Middleton
Harriet Lockwood Middleton

1 July 1846

Sarah Elizabeth Middleton is about 14 years old and has a light brown complexion; Harriet Lockwood Middleton is about 12 years old and has a very light complexion. They are the children of Lydia Middleton, a free woman, and were born free, as appears by certificate of A[quilla] Lockwood.

REGISTRATION NO. 147
(Vol. 2, p. 35)

Lucy Ann Pipsico

1 July 1846

Lucy Ann Pipsico is about 21 years old, 5 feet 4¼ inches tall, of a brown complexion, with no visible marks. She was born free, as appears by affidavit of Mrs. Anna H. Lloyd.

REGISTRATION NO. 148
(Vol. 2, p. 35)

Sarah Jane Spencer

11 July 1846

Sarah Jane Spencer is about 19 years 6 months old, 5 feet 1½ inches tall, of a dark complexion, with no visible marks. She was born free, as appears by certificate of Margaret A. Shirley.

REGISTRATION NO. 149
(Vol. 2, p. 35)

Robert Spencer

11 July 1846

Robert Spencer is about 22 years 3 months old, 5 feet 7 inches tall, of a dark complexion, with a large scar on the right side of his face. He was born free, as appears by certificate of Mrs. Margaret A. Shirley.

REGISTRATION NO. 150
(Vol. 2, p. 35)

Mary Eliza Ages

11 July 1846

Mary Eliza Ages is about 8 years old and is the daughter of Nancy Ages, a free woman, as appears by certificate of Margaret A. Shirley.

REGISTRATION NO. 151
(Vol. 2, p. 36)

Henry Ross

13 July 1846

Henry Ross is a mulatto man, about 29 years old, 5 feet 9½ inches tall, with a slight scar on his left temple. He was born free, as appears by affidavit of James Dempsey.

REGISTRATION NO. 152
(Vol. 2, p. 36)

William Solomon

15 July 1846

William Solomon is about 24 years 6 months old, 5 feet 7½ inches tall, of a dark complexion, with a slight scar under his left ear. He was born free, as appears by affidavit of Daniel Shryer.

REGISTRATION NO. 153
(Vol. 2, p. 36)

Townshend Solomon   15 July 1846

Townshend Solomon is about 52 years old, 5 feet 8½ inches tall, of a dark complexion. He has lost the first joint of the forefinger of his left hand. He was emancipated by William Solomon by deed dated 13 December 1826 recorded in Liber T No. 2, page 428, and was identified by Daniel Shryer.

REGISTRATION NO. 154
(Vol. 2, p. 36)

Susan Solomon   15 July 1846

Susan Solomon is about 45 years old, 5 feet 4 inches tall, of a dark complexion, with a black mole under her chin. She was emancipated by Thomas G. Addison of Prince George's County, Maryland. Solomon was identified by Daniel Shryer.

REGISTRATION NO. 155
(Vol. 2, p. 37)

James Solomon   15 July 1846

James Solomon is about 22 years old, 5 feet 9 inches tall, of a dark complexion, with a scar on the inner side of his right arm between the wrist and the elbow. He was born free, as appears by affidavit of Daniel Shryer.

REGISTRATION NO. 156
(Vol. 2, p. 37)

Thomas Anderson   30 July 1846

Thomas Anderson is a mulatto man, about 17 years old, 6 feet tall, with a scar under his left eye. He was emancipated by Louisa C. Evans, now Anderson, by deed recorded in Liber F No. 3, page 482.

REGISTRATION NO. 157
(Vol. 2, p. 37)

Lewis Williams   5 August 1846

Lewis Williams is about 50 years old, 5 feet 9 3/4 inches tall, of a dark complexion, with a large scar on his right side. He was emancipated by R. W. Horner by deed recorded in Liber W No. 2, page 98.

REGISTRATION NO. 158
(Vol. 2, p. 37)

Eliza Davis   19 August 1846

Eliza Davis is about 23 years old, 4 feet 11¼ inches tall, of a brown complexion, with no visible marks. She was born free, as appears by affidavit of George Johnson.

REGISTRATION NO. 159
(Vol. 2, p. 38)

Samuel Anderson   27 August 1846

Samuel Anderson is about 19 years 6 months old, 5 feet 7 inches tall, of a dark complexion, with a scar on the forefinger of his left hand. He was born free, as appears by affidavit of Mrs. Rachel Latham.

REGISTRATION NO. 160
(Vol. 2, p. 38)

Lloyd Rozier Dogan   27 August 1846

"Loyd" [Lloyd] Rozier Dogan is about 17 years old, 5 feet 4½ inches tall, of a tawny brown complexion, with several small scars on the back of his left hand near the knuckles of his first and second fingers. He was born free, as appears by affidavit of Mrs. Eliza Clarke.

REGISTRATION NO. 161
(Vol. 2, p. 38)

Clarence Butler
Phineas Butler
Susanna Butler

28 August 1846

Clarence Butler is about 5 years old; Phineas Butler is about 2 years 10 months old; and Susanna Butler is about 5 months old. They are the children of Elizabeth Butler and were born free, as appears by proof of Zenas Kinzey.

REGISTRATION NO. 162
(Vol. 2, pp. 38-39)

Ellen McCoy, William Henry McCoy,
Daniel McCoy, George Fitzgerald McCoy

29 August 1846

Ellen McCoy is about 36 years old, 4 feet 11 inches tall, of a brown complexion, with a small scar on the back part of her right hand. She was born free, as appears by affidavit of Mrs. Mary Ann Cole. She has three children: William Henry McCoy, aged about 15 years 6 months; Daniel McCoy, aged about 12 years 6 months; and George Fitzgerald McCoy, aged about 9.

REGISTRATION NO. 163
(Vol. 2, p. 39)

Mary Ann McCoy

29 August 1846

Mary Ann McCoy is about 18 years 4 months old, 4 feet 11 inches tall, of a dark complexion, with a slight scar on her left cheek. She is the daughter of Ellen McCoy and was born free, as appears by affidavit of Mrs. Mary Ann Cole.

REGISTRATION NO. 164
(Vol. 2, p. 39)

Malvina Pembroke Nokes, Hanson Nokes,
Edward Nokes, Edmonia Nokes,
Mary Ellen Nokes, Hayes Nokes,
and Jesse Nokes, Jr.

29 August 1846

Malvina Nokes is about 34 years old, 5 feet 3 3/4 inches tall, of a light complexion, with a scar over her left eye. She was emancipated by Rosalia Eugenia Webster by deed dated 31 August 1831 and recorded in Frederick County, Virginia, and was identified by William Yeaton as the Malvina Pembroke (now Nokes) emancipated by that deed. Her six children were born free: Hanson Nokes, aged about 14 years 6 months; Edward Nokes, aged about 12 years 2 months; Edmonia Nokes, aged about 9 years; Mary Ellen Nokes, aged about 7 years 10 months; Hayes Nokes, aged about 3 years 6 months; and Jesse Nokes, aged about 4 months.

REGISTRATION NO. 165
(Vol. 2, p. 39)

Jesse Nokes, Sr.

29 August 1846

Jesse Nokes is about 40 years old, 5 feet 7 inches tall, of a dark complexion, with a scar on the wrist of his left hand. He is a free man, as is proved by certificate of R[obert] H. Miller.

REGISTRATION NO. 166
(Vol. 2, p. 40)

Eliza A. Bruce and children,
William Henry, Sarah Clarence,
and Laura

31 August 1846

Eliza A. Bruce is about 24 years old, 5 feet 1 inch tall, of a very light complexion, with a large scar on her left shoulder. She was born free, as appears by oath of Mrs. Martha Johnson. She has three children: William Henry, aged about 7; Sarah Clarence, aged about 5 years 3 months; and Laura, aged about 2 years.

REGISTRATION NO. 167a
(Vol. 2, p. 40)

William Edwards

31 August 1846

William Edwards is about 22 years old, 5 feet 11 inches tall, of a black complexion, with a large scar on his right leg immediately below the knee. He was born free, as appears by oath of Mrs. Ann Lacey.

REGISTRATION NO. 167b
(Vol. 2, p. 40)

Henrietta Bruce Ford
Daniel West Ford

31 August 1846

Henrietta Ford, late Bruce, is about 27 years old, 5 feet 1 inch tall, of a very light complexion, with no visible marks. She was emancipated by the will of Colin Auld, and identified by William Page, one of the executors of Auld's will. She has a child named Daniel West Ford aged about 4 years.

REGISTRATION NO. 168
(Vol. 2, p. 41)

Margaret Lewis

2 September 1846

Margaret Lewis is about 18 years old, 5 feet 3½ inches tall, of a dark complexion, with a scar on her right arm near the bend of the elbow. She was emancipated by Moses Davis and identified by William Veitch.

REGISTRATION NO. 169
(Vol. 2, p. 41)

Martha Elizabeth Bennett

2 September 1846

Martha Elizabeth Bennett is about 9 years and 8 months old and was born free, as appears by a certificate of Mrs. Ewing. Martha is the child of Mary Bennett, a free woman.

REGISTRATION NO. 170
(Vol. 2, p. 41)

Sarah Jane Cooper

4 September 1846

Sarah Jane Cooper is a bright mulatto girl, almost white, about 15 years old, 5 feet 2½ inches tall, with two small scars on the back of her neck. She was born free, as appears by affidavit of Mrs. Elizabeth Stevens.

REGISTRATION NO. 171
(Vol. 2, p. 41)

Kitty Easton

5 September 1846

Kitty Easton is about 19 years old, 5 feet one-half inch tall, of a light brown complexion, with a scar on the back of her neck caused by a burn. She was born free, as appears by affidavit of Mrs. Margaret M. Banks.

REGISTRATION NO. 172
(Vol. 2, p. 42)

Eliza Dudley

8 September 1846

Eliza Dudley is about 17 years old, 5 feet 1 inch tall, of a light complexion, with no visible marks. She was born free, as appears by affidavit of Mrs. Mary Ann Cole.

REGISTRATION NO. 173
(Vol. 2, p. 42)

Orlando Evans

8 September 1846

Orlando Evans is about 12 years old, 4 feet 8½ inches tall, of a light complexion, with several scars on his right leg between the knee and foot. He was born free, as appears by affidavit of Mrs. Mary Ann Cole.

REGISTRATION NO. 174
(Vol. 2, p. 42)

Maria Hall

8 September 1846

Maria Hall is about 22 years old, 5 feet 2 inches tall, of a dark complexion, stout built, with some small scars on her arms near the wrist. She was born free, as appears by affidavit of Theodore Meade.

REGISTRATION NO. 175
(Vol. 2, p. 42)

Rebecca Kane

8 September 1846

Rebecca Kane is a mulatto girl, about 18 years old, 5 feet 1 inch tall, with no visible marks. She was born free, as appears by affidavit of Theodore Meade.

REGISTRATION NO. 176
(Vol. 2, pp. 42-43)

Louisa Davis and children,
Mary and William Henry

11 September 1846

Louisa Davis is about 26 years old, 4 feet 10½ inches tall, of a brown complexion, with a scar on the back of her left hand caused by a burn. She was born free, as appears by affidavit of Mrs. Hannah Wanton. Louisa has two children named Mary, aged 2 years 2 months, and William Henry, aged 7 months.

REGISTRATION NO. 177
(Vol. 2, p. 43)

Sarah Lee and children
Michael Morris, John Wesley,
William Fletcher, Laura Ann,
Philip Andrew, Adam Driver[?],
and Albert.

15 September 1846

Margaret M. Bangs, a white woman, swears that Sarah Lee is a free woman and that her children were born free: Michael Morris, aged about 14; John Wesley, aged about 12; William Fletcher, aged about 9; Laura Ann, aged about 7; Philip Andrew, aged about 5; Adam Driver[?], aged about 2; and Albert, aged about 5 months.

REGISTRATION NO. 178
(Vol. 2, p. 43)

John McKinsey Ware

21 September 1846

John McKinsey Ware is about 9 years 6 months old, and was born free, as appears by affidavit of Mrs. Theresa Hall, a white woman.

REGISTRATION NO. 179
(Vol. 2, p. 43)

Rebecca Butts

21 September 1846

Rebecca Butts is about 12 years old, has a dark complexion, and was born free, as appears by affidavit of Joseph H. Hampson.

REGISTRATION NO. 180
(Vol. 2, pp. 43-44)

Maria Payne

23 September 1846

Maria Payne is about 38 years old, 5 feet 2 inches tall, of a dark complexion, with no visible marks. She was emancipated by James Vansant by deed dated 2 October 1843 recorded in Liber D No. 3, page 404. Payne was identified by James Vansant.

REGISTRATION NO. 181
(Vol. 2, p. 44)

Ann Brown

1 October 1846

Ann Brown is about 22 years old, 5 feet 2½ inches tall, of a very dark complexion, with a scar on her right arm between the elbow and the wrist. She was born free, as appears by affidavit of Theodore Meade.

REGISTRATION NO. 182
(Vol. 1, p. 44)

Isaac Clark

2 October 1846

Isaac Clark is about 22 years old, 5 feet 6¼ inches tall, of a dark complexion, with a slight scar over his left eye. He was born free, as appears by affidavit of J. H. Davis, Jr.

REGISTRATION NO. 183
(Vol. 2, p. 44)

George Hawkins   5 October 1846

George Hawkins is about 10 years 4 months old, and was born free, as appears by affidavit of Mrs. Ann Brooks.

REGISTRATION NO. 184
(Vol. 2, p. 44)

Nora Taylor   6 October 1846

Nora Taylor is a free man, about 24 years 6 months old, 5 feet 6 inches tall, of a brown complexion, with a slight scar on his nose between his eyes. He was born free, as appears by certificate of Robert Bell.

REGISTRATION NO. 185
(Vol. 2, p. 45)

Elias Lomax   10 October 1846

Elias Lomax is about 21 years old, 5 feet 7¼ inches tall, and has a dark complexion. He was born free, as appears by affidavit of Mrs. Harriet Jefferson.

REGISTRATION NO. 186
(Vol. 2, p. 45)

Charles Bowles   12 October 1846

Charles Bowles is about 40 years old, 5 feet 5½ inches tall, of a light complexion, with a scar on his forehead over his right eye. He was born free, as appears by affidavit of Theodore Meade.

REGISTRATION NO. 187
(Vol. 2, p. 45)

Adolphus Seaton   19 October 1846

Adolphus Seaton is about 23 years old, 5 feet 10 inches tall, of a brown complexion, with no visible marks. He was born free, as appears by affidavit of Henry Kilbreath.

REGISTRATION NO. 188
(Vol. 2, p. 45)

George W. Turley   19 October 1846

George W. Turley is about 25 years old, 5 feet 5 inches tall, of a dark complexion, with a small scar near the corner of his right eye. He was born free, as appears by affirmation of Mrs. Charlotte Jacobs.

REGISTRATION NO. 189
(Vol. 2, p. 46)

Lucretia Harris   19 October 1846

Lucretia Harris is about 35 years old, 5 feet 2½ inches tall, of a dark complexion, with a scar on her left thumb. She was born free, as appears by affidavit of Mrs. Sarah Vernon.

REGISTRATION NO. 190
(Vol. 2, p. 46)

Charlotte York   20 October 1846

Charlotte York is about 20 years old, 5 feet 1¼ inches tall, of a dark complexion, and has a small scar on her upper lip. She was born free (see the certificate of Rev. Elias Harrison filed).

REGISTRATION NO. 191
(Vol. 2, p. 46)

Martha Smith   22 October 1846

Martha Smith is about 22 years 10 months old, 5 feet 3 inches tall, of a dark brown complexion, with a slight deformity in the forefinger of her right hand. She was born free, as appears by affidavit of Mrs. Winifred Williams.

REGISTRATION NO. 192
(Vol. 2, p. 46)

22 October 1846

Richard Lyles
Turner Lyles

Richard Lyles, aged 12, and Turner Lyles, aged 10, are the sons of Hannah [Smith] Lyles, a free woman, as appears by affidavit of Mrs. Winifred Williams.

REGISTRATION NO. 193
(Vol. 2, pp. 46-47)

22 October 1846

Hannah Smith Lyles

Hannah Lyles, late Smith, is about 46 years old, 5 feet 3¼ inches tall, of a brown complexion, with a scar on her left wrist caused by a burn. She was born free, as appears by affidavit of Mrs. Winifred Williams.

REGISTRATION NO. 194
(Vol. 2, p. 47)

26 October 1846

Chloe Ann Cryer

Chloe Ann Cryer is about 11 years old, 4 feet 9½ inches tall, of a bright complexion, with no visible marks. She was born free, as appears by affidavit of Mrs. Ann Brook[s].

REGISTRATION NO. 195
(Vol. 2, p. 47)

27 October 1846

Daniel C. Webster, Caroline C. Webster,
William Henry Webster, Julia G. Webster,
Isaac A. Webster, Charles E. Webster

Daniel C. Webster is about 14 years old; Caroline C. Webster is about 12 years old; William Henry Webster is about 8 years and 6 months old; Julia G. Webster is 6 years old; Isaac A. Webster is about 3 years and 3 months old; and Charles E. Webster is about 5½ months old. They are the children of Arabella Webster, late Clark, a free woman, as was proved by affidavit of Elizabeth Anderson, a white woman.

REGISTRATION NO. 196
(Vol. 2, p. 47)

31 October 1846

Ann Brown Clagett

Ann Clagett, late Brown, is about 27 years old, 5 feet tall, of a light complexion, with a large scar on her left arm caused by a burn. She was emancipated by James Entwistle.

REGISTRATION NO. 197
(Vol. 2, pp. 47-48)

31 October 1846

Lucy Brown Nickins

Lucy Nickins, late Brown, is about 35 years old, 5 feet 1 inch tall, of a light complexion, with no visible marks. She was emancipated by James Entwistle and his wife by deed recorded in Liber U No. 2, page 64.

REGISTRATION NO. 198
(Vol. 2, p. 48)

31 October 1846

Maria Hamilton

Maria Hamilton is about 37 years old, 5 feet 2 inches tall, of a dark complexion, with a scar on her left cheek. She was this day emancipated by Robert Miller.

REGISTRATION NO. 199
(Vol. 2, p. 48)

4 November 1846

Moses Jones

Moses Young is about 16 years old, 4 feet 8¼ inches tall, of a brown complexion, with a very full face. He was born free, as appears by affidavit of Dr. Sidney Smith.

REGISTRATION NO. 200
(Vol. 2, p. 48)

Aaron Jones   4 November 1846

Aaron Jones is about 16 years old and is the son of Ann Jones, a free woman, as appears by evidence of Charles Graham.

REGISTRATION NO. 201
(Vol. 2, p. 48)

John E. Evans   5 November 1846

John E. Evans is a mulatto man, about 21 years 3 months old, 5 feet 11 inches tall, with a scar on the upper part of his nose. He was born free, as appears by affidavit of Robert Violett.

REGISTRATION NO. 202
(Vol. 2, p. 49)

Alice Phenix   9 November 1846

Alice Phenix is about 28 years old, 5 feet tall, of a light brown complexion, with a large scar near the left corner of her mouth. She was born free, as appears by affidavit of John Douglass.

REGISTRATION NO. 203
(Vol. 2, p. 49)

Letty Butler   10 November 1846

Letty Butler is a mulatto woman, about 34 years old, 4 feet 11½ inches tall, with no visible marks. She is free, as appears by affidavit of Joseph H. Hampson.

REGISTRATION NO. 204
(Vol. 2, p. 49)

Sidney Easton   10 November 1846

Sidney Easton is about 19 years old, 5 feet 4½ inches tall, of a dark complexion, with a scar on his nose. He was born free, as appears by certificate of Joseph H. Hampson.

REGISTRATION NO. 205
(Vol. 2, p. 49)

Annette Easton   10 November 1846

Annette Easton is about 14 years old, 4 feet 10¼ inches tall, of a brown complexion, with a blue vein that is very visible on the right side of her face. She was born free, as appears by affidavit of Joseph H. Hampson.

REGISTRATION NO. 206
(Vol. 2, p. 49)

William Easton   10 November 1846

William Easton is about 16 years old, 5 feet 1½ inches tall, of a dark complexion, with a scar on the left side of his face. He was born free, as appears by affidavit of Joseph H. Hampson.

REGISTRATION NO. 207
(Vol. 2, p. 50a)

Edmonia Ford   11 November 1846
William Westley Ford

Edmonia Ford and William Westley Ford are the children of Louisa Ford, late Hatton, a free woman, as appears by certificate of Mrs. William Muir.

REGISTRATION NO. 208
(Vol. 2, p. 50a)

Elenora Bell   12 November 1846

Elenora Bell is a dark mulatto woman, about 30 years old, 5 feet 5½ inches tall, with a scar on the third finger of her left hand and a scar on the palm of her left hand. She was this day emancipated by Francis L. Smith.

REGISTRATION NO. 209
(Vol. 2, p. 50a)

Julia Derrick

13 November 1846

Julia Derrick is about 32 years old, 4 feet 11 3/4 inches tall, of a dark brown complexion, and has lost the end of the second finger on her left hand. She was born free, as appears by affidavit of Charles J. Stewart.

REGISTRATION NO. 210
(Vol. 2, p. 50a)

Elizabeth Dorsey

13 November 1846

Elizabeth Dorsey is about 40 years old, 5 feet 2¼ inches tall, of a dark brown complexion, with a scar on the forefinger of her left hand. She was born free, as appears by affidavit of Charles J. Stewart.

REGISTRATION NO. 211
(Vol. 2, p. 50b)

Mary E. Waugh

16 November 1846

Mary E. Waugh is 24 years old, 5 feet 3¼ inches tall, of a very light complexion, with a slight scar over her left eye. She was born free, as appears by affidavit of Mrs. Ary Cook.

REGISTRATION NO. 212
(Vol. 2, p. 50b)

Daniel McCoy

18 November 1846

Daniel McCoy is about 39 years old, 5 feet 7½ inches tall, of a dark complexion with a scar over his left eye. He is a free man, as appears by certificate of William H. Miller.

REGISTRATION NO. 213
(Vol. 2, p. 50b)

Julia Ann Foote, Elizabeth Foote,
Henrietta Foote, Henson Foote,
Andrew Foote

19 November 1846

Julia Ann Foote is about 16 years old; Elizabeth Foote, is about 9 years old; Henrietta Foote is about 5 years old; Henson Foote is about 3 years old; and Andrew Foote is about 6 months old. They are the children of Ann Foote, a free woman, as is proved by Daniel Minor.

REGISTRATION NO. 214
(Vol. 2, p. 50b)

Sarah Jane Foote

19 November 1846

Sarah Jane Foote is a mulatto girl, about 20 years old, 5 feet three-fourth inch tall, with a black mole on the right side of her face. She was born free, as appears by the testimony of Daniel Minor.

REGISTRATION NO. 215
(Vol. 2, p. 51)

Cornelia Taylor

23 November 1846

Cornelia Taylor is about 40 years old, 5 feet tall, of a very light complexion, and has lost all of her upper front teeth. She was born free, as appears by affidavit of Mrs. Margaret Nicholson.

REGISTRATION NO. 216
(Vol. 2, p. 51)

Rebecca Taylor

23 November 1846

Rebecca Taylor is about 16 years old, 4 feet 9 3/4 inches tall, of a light complexion, with no visible marks. She was born free, as appears by affidavit of Margaret Nicholson.

REGISTRATION NO. 217
(Vol. 2, p. 51)

William Taylor   23 November 1846

William Taylor is about 14 years old, 4 feet 7½ inches tall, of a brown complexion, with a scar on his left arm about midway between his wrist and elbow. He was born free, as appears by affidavit of Margaret Nicholson.

REGISTRATION NO. 218
(Vol. 2, p. 51)

Mary Warner   25 November 1846

Mary Warner is about 35 years old, 5 feet 4½ inches tall, of a dark complexion, with a large scar on the upper part of her right arm an a small scar on the inner side of the same arm at the bend of the elbow. She was born free, as appears by affirmation of Zenas Kinsey.

REGISTRATION NO. 219
(Vol. 2, p. 52)

Louisa Marshall and children,
Eldridge, Catharine, Sarah,
and Louisa   27 November 1846

Louisa Marshall is about 37 years old, 4 feet 11 inches tall, of a dark complexion, with her face very much pitted from smallpox. She was born free, as appears by affidavit of John Riston. Marshall has four children: Eldridge, aged about 12, Catharine, aged about 8, Sarah, aged 5 years 6 months, and Louisa, aged about 3 years 6 months.

REGISTRATION NO. 220
(Vol. 2, p. 52)

Ann Maria Marshall   27 November 1846

Ann Maria Marshall is about 19 years old, 5 feet 4½ inches tall, of a very light complexion. She was born free, as appears by affidavit of John Riston.

REGISTRATION NO. 221
(Vol. 2, p. 52)

Lucy Ann Thornton Campbell   28 November 1846

Lucy Ann [Thornton] Campbell is about 18 years old, 5 feet 3 inches tall, of a dark brown complexion, with a scar on her right hand extending from the wrist to the junction of her thumb and forefinger. She was born free, as appears by affidavit of John W. Smith.

REGISTRATION NO. 222
(Vol. 2, p. 52)

Laura Jackson   28 November 1846
Thornton Jackson

Laura Jackson is about 4 years old; Thornton Jackson is about 6 months old. They are the children of Harriet Jackson, a free woman, as appears by oath of Turner Dixon.

REGISTRATION NO. 223
(Vol. 2, p. 53)

Lavinia Wiggins   1 December 1846

Lavinia Wiggins is about 55 years old, 4 feet 8¼ inches tall, of a dark complexion, with a large scar on her forehead and another on her left cheek. She was emancipated by Mrs. Rebecca Taylor by deed recorded in Liber E No. 3, page 426.

REGISTRATION NO. 224
(Vol. 2, p. 53)

Sadonia Johnston   3 December 1846

Sadonia Johnston is about 20 years old, 5 feet 3 inches tall, of a very dark complexion, with a scar on her right hand near the wrist. She was born free, as appears by certificate of William Fowle.

REGISTRATION NO. 225
(Vol. 2, p. 53)

Mary Ellen Johnson

7 December 1846

Mary Ellen Johnson is about 25 years old, 5 feet tall, of a dark complexion, with a small black mole near her left ear. She was born free, as appears by affidavit of John Gibson Peach.

REGISTRATION NO. 226
(Vol. 2, p. 53)

William Francis Chace

8 December 1846

William Francis Chace is about 11 years old. He was born free, as appears by affidavit of Mrs. Mary Ann Cole.

REGISTRATION NO. 227
(Vol. 2, pp. 53-54)

George Andrew Chace

8 December 1846

George Andrew Chace is about 25 years old, 5 feet 6¼ tall, of a brown complexion, with two small scars under his right eye. He was born free, as appears by affidavit of Mrs. Mary Ann Cole.

REGISTRATION NO. 228
(Vol. 2, p. 54)

Mary Ann Eliza Chace

8 December 1846

Mary Ann Eliza Chace is about 20 years old, 5 feet 2½ inches tall, of a light brown complexion, with a slight scar on her left thumb. She was born free, as appears by affidavit of Mrs. Mary Ann Cole.

REGISTRATION NO. 229
(Vol. 2, p. 54)

George Washington Cole

8 December 1846

George Washington Cole is a mulatto boy, about 18 years old, 5 feet 5½ inches tall, with a scar on the bridge of his nose. He was born free, as appears by affidavit of Mrs. Mary Ann Cole.

REGISTRATION NO. 230
(Vol. 2, p. 54)

Mary Jane Cole

8 December 1846

Mary Jane Cole is about 19 years 6 months old, 5 feet 2 3/4 inches tall, of a very light complexion, with a scar on the right side of her upper lip. She was born free, as appears by affidavit of Mrs. Mary Ann Cole.

REGISTRATION NO. 231
(Vol. 2, p. 54)

James E. Piper Ramsay

11 December 1846

James E. P[iper] Ramsay is a mulatto man, about 26 years old, 5 feet 3½ inches tall, with no visible marks. He was born free, as appears by affidavit of his mother, Elizabeth Ann P[iper?] Ramsay, a white woman.

REGISTRATION NO. 232
(Vol. 2, p. 55)

William Henry Piper Ramsay

Recorded 11 December 1846

William Henry Piper Ramsay is a mulatto man, about 22 years old, 5 feet 5½ inches tall, with no visible marks. He was born free, as appears by affidavit of his mother, Elizabeth Ann P[iper?] Ramsay, a white woman.

REGISTRATION NO. 233
(Vol. 2, p. 55)

Milly Evans, Monk Evans,
James Evans, Robert Evans

21 December 1846

Milly Evans is about 34 years old, 4 feet 11 inches tall, of a dark complexion, with a slight scar on the lower part of the left side of her face. She was emancipated by Thompson F. Mason by deed recorded in Liber V No. 2, page 418. Her three children, Monk aged about 6, James aged about 3, and Robert Evans, aged about 1, were born free, as proved by certificate of William Harper.

REGISTRATION NO. 234
(Vol. 2, p. 55)

William Lyons

28 December 1846

William Lyons is a mulatto man, about 25 years old, 5 feet 6 3/4 inches tall, with a scar on the inner side of his right thumb. He was born free, as appears by affidavit of William P. Alexander.

REGISTRATION NO. 235
(Vol. 2, p. 55)

George William Roy McDonny

6 January 1847

George William Roy, commonly known as McDonny, is about 21 years old, 5 feet 7 inches tall, with a slight scar on the left side of his face. He was born free, as appears by affidavit of Willis Henderson.

REGISTRATION NO. 236
(Vol. 2, p. 56)

Martha Ann Johnson
William Johnson

9 January 1847

Martha Ann Johnson is about 17 years old; William Johnson is about 14 years old. They were born free and are the children of Patsey Johnson, later Feyerson, a free woman, as was proved by affidavit of Bernard Hooe.

REGISTRATION NO. 237
(Vol. 2, p. 56)

Susan Armstrong Sears

19 January 1847

Susan Armstrong, sometimes known as Susan Sears, is about 19 years old, 5 feet 1½ inches tall, of a dark complexion, with a slight scar on arm between the wrist and elbow. She was born free, as appears by affidavit of John T. Creighton.

REGISTRATION NO. 238
(Vol. 2, p. 56)

Margaret Brown

19 January 1847

Margaret Brown is about 18 years old, 5 feet 3 inches tall, of a light complexion, with a scar on her forehead on a line with her nose. She was born free, as appears by affidavit of Bernard Hooe.

REGISTRATION NO. 239
(Vol. 2, p. 56)

Catharine Brown

19 January 1847

Catharine Brown is about 15 years old, 5 feet 4 3/4 inches tall, of a light complexion, with no visible marks. She was born free, as appears by affidavit of Bernard Hooe.

REGISTRATION NO. 240
(Vol. 2, pp. 56-57)

Calvin Brown

19 January 1847

Calvin Brown is a bright mulatto boy, about 18 years old, 5 feet 8 inches tall, with a scar over his right eye. He was born free, as appears by affidavit of Bernard Hooe.

REGISTRATION NO. 241
(Vol. 2, p. 57)

Adaline Hunter

28 January 1847

Adaline Hunter is about 18 years old, 5 feet 3 3/4 inches tall, of a very bright, almost white, complexion, with a cluster of moles or a mark of some kind on a line with her left eye and between it and her left ear. She was emancipated by the will of Slighter Smith, as was proved by affidavit of Bernard Hooe, Esq.

REGISTRATION NO. 242
(Vol. 2, p. 57)

Harriet Hunter Watson

28 January 1847

Harriet Watson, late Hunter, is about 37 years old, 5 feet 3½ inches tall, of a very bright complexion, with a speck in the pupil of her right eye. She was emancipated by the will of Slighter Smith, as was proved by affidavit of Bernard Hooe, executor of Smith's will.

REGISTRATION NO. 243
(Vol. 2, p. 57)

Edgar Watson, Sarah Watson, and John Watson

28 January 1847

Edgar Watson aged about 6, Sarah, aged about 4, and John, aged about 1 year, are the children of Harriet [Hunter] Watson, a free woman, and were born free, as appears by affidavit of Bernard Hooe.

REGISTRATION NO. 244
(Vol. 2, p. 58)

Mary Yorpp

28 January 1847

Mary Yorpp is about 17 years old, 4 feet 8½ inches tall, of a dark complexion, with no visible marks. She was born free and is the daughter of Betty Yorpp, a free woman, as appears by affidavit of Mrs. Theresa Adam.

REGISTRATION NO. 245
(Vol. 2, p. 58)

Mary Rustin and son, Moses

2 February 1847

Mary Rustin is about 40 years old, 4 feet 10½ inches tall, of a light brown complexion, with a scar over her left eye. She was emancipated by Lewis M. "Kenzie" [McKenzie]. She has an infant son named Moses.

REGISTRATION NO. 246
(Vol. 2, p. 58)

William Townsend

4 February 1847

William "Townzend" [Townsend] is about 22 years old, 5 feet 8 3/4 inches tall, of a dark complexion, with a very large scar above the elbow of his right arm. He was born free, as appears by affidavit of Francis M. Walker.

REGISTRATION NO. 247
(Vol. 2, p. 58)

Eliza Townsend

4 February 1847

Eliza "Townzend" [Townsend] is about 21 years old, 5 feet 1 inch tall, of a dark complexion, with no visible marks. She was born free, as appears by affidavit of Francis M. Walker.

REGISTRATION NO. 248
(Vol. 2, p. 59)

William Dean

10 February 1847

William Dean is a bright mulatto man, about 21 years old, 5 feet 8 inches tall, with several scars on his left leg between the foot and the knee. He was born free, as appears by records of the Orphans' Court.

REGISTRATION NO. 249
(Vol. 2, p. 59)

Jane Elizabeth Servoy

12 February 1847

Jane "Eliz:" Servoy is about 23 years old, 5 feet 4½ inches tall, of a dark complexion, with scars on both her wrists. She was born free, as appears by affidavit of James P. Coleman.

REGISTRATION NO. 250
(Vol. 2, p. 59)

Mary C. Servoy   12 February 1847

Mary C. Servoy is about 21 years old, 5 feet 2½ inches tall, of a dark complexion, with a scar on her left cheek and another on her left thumb. She was born free, as appears by affidavit of James P. Coleman.

REGISTRATION NO. 251
(Vol. 2, p. 59)

Louisa S. Servoy   12 February 1847

Louisa S. Servoy is about 19 years old, 5 feet 2 inches tall, of a dark complexion, with no visible marks. She was born free, as appears by affidavit of James P. Coleman.

REGISTRATION NO. 252
(Vol. 2, pp. 59-60)

Laura V. Servoy   12 February 1847

Laura V. Servoy is about 17 years old, 5 feet 3/4 inches tall, of a dark complexion, with a scar on the left side of her neck. She was born free, as appears by affidavit of James P. Coleman.

REGISTRATION NO. 253
(Vol. 2, p. 60)

George Dover   12 February 1847

George Dover is a dark mulatto boy, about 12 years 6 months old, 4 feet 9½ inches tall, with no visible marks. He was born free, as appears by affidavit of Jesse T. Ramsay.

REGISTRATION NO. 254
(Vol. 2, p. 60)

Sarah C. Dover   13 February 1847

Sarah C. Dover is about 18 years old, 5 feet 5 inches tall, of a light complexion, with no visible marks. She was born free, as appears by affidavit of Jesse T. Ramsay.

REGISTRATION NO. 255
(Vol. 2, p. 60)

Milly Triplett   19 February 1847
Prince Wesley Triplett

Milly Triplett is about 35 years old, 5 feet 3½ inches tall, of a dark complexion, with a large black mole on the right side of her face. She was emancipated by Eliza M. Norris by deed recorded in Liber E No. 3, p. 379. She has a son named Prince Wesley Triplett who is about 3 years 6 months old.

REGISTRATION NO. 256
(Vol. 2, pp. 60-61

Louisa Taylor and children,   20 February 1847
Gertrude Eugenia and Martha Ellen

Louisa Taylor is a mulatto girl, about 19 years old, 5 feet 4 inches tall, with no visible marks. She was born free, as appears by certificate of E. R. Violett. She has two children, Gertrude Eugenia, aged 18 months, and Martha Ellen, aged 2 months.

REGISTRATION NO. 257
(Vol. 2, p. 61)

Susannah Evans   23 February 1847

Susannah Evans is about 22 years old, 5 feet 4½ inches tall, and very much freckled. She was born free, as appears by affidavit of Mrs. [Patsey] Chichester.

REGISTRATION NO. 258
(Vol. 2, p. 61)

Nancy Derricks   23 February 1847

Nancy Derricks is a mulatto woman, about 24 years old, 5 feet 6 inches tall, with no visible marks. She was born free, as appears by affidavit of Mrs. [Patsey] Chichester.

REGISTRATION NO. 259
(Vol. 2, p. 61)

Julia Jones   23 February 1847

Julia Jones is about 35 years old, 5 feet 5½ inches tall, of a dark complexion, with several scars on her face. She was born free, as appears by affidavit of Hugh Wiley.

REGISTRATION NO. 260
(Vol. 2, p. 61)

Letitia Evans   24 February 1847

Letitia Evans is about 33 years old, 5 feet 4½ inches tall, of a light complexion, with no visible marks. She was born free, as appears by affidavit of R[obert] H. Miller.

REGISTRATION NO. 261
(Vol. 2, p. 62)

James Derrick   24 February 1847

James Derrick is about 30 years old, 5 feet 6 inches tall, of a dark complexion, with a slight deformity in the little finger of his right hand. He was born free, as appears by affidavit of Mrs. Sarah Allen.

REGISTRATION NO. 262
(Vol. 2, p. 62)

William Derrick   24 February 1847

William Derrick is about 22 years old, 5 feet 6½ inches tall, of a dark complexion, with a scar on the right side of his neck. He was born free, as appears by affidavit of Mrs. Sarah Allen.

REGISTRATION NO. 263
(Vol. 2, p. 62)

Susan Derrick   24 February 1847

Susan Derrick is about 22 years old, 4 feet 11 inches tall, of a dark complexion, with a deformity in her right ear. She was born free, as appears by affidavit of Mrs. Sarah Allen.

REGISTRATION NO. 264
(Vol. 2, p. 62)

Robert Derrick   24 February 1847

Robert Derrick is about 16 years old, 5 feet 6¼ inches tall, of a dark complexion, with no visible marks. He was born free, as appears by affidavit of Mrs. Sarah Allen.

REGISTRATION NO. 265
(Vol. 2, pp. 62-63)

Maria Derricks   24 February 1847

Maria Derricks is about 21 years old, 5 feet 1½ inches tall, of a dark complexion, with no visible marks. She was born free, as appears by affidavit of Mrs. Sarah Allen.

REGISTRATION NO. 266
(Vol. 2, p. 63)

Jacob Derrick   24 February 1847

Jacob Derrick is about 14 years old, 5 feet 4 inches tall, of a dark complexion, with no visible marks. He was born free, as appears by affidavit of Mrs. Sarah Allen.

REGISTRATION NO. 267
(Vol. 2, p. 63)

Mary Lee

24 February 1847

Mary Lee is about 33 years old, 5 feet 2 3/4 inches tall, of a dark complexion, with a scar on her right hand. She was born free, as appears by affidavit of Mrs. Margaret Wiley.

REGISTRATION NO. 268
(Vol. 2, p. 63)

Caroline Jones

25 February 1847

Caroline Jones is about 24 years old, 5 feet 6 3/4 inches tall, of a very dark complexion, with no visible marks. She was born free, as appears by affidavit of Mrs. Sarah Allen.

REGISTRATION NO. 269
(Vol. 2, p. 63)

Nancy Lee

26 February 1847

Nancy Lee is about 27 years old, 5 feet 2½ inches tall, of a dark complexion, with a scar on her forehead and a large black mole near her nose. She was born free, as appears by the certificate of B[enoni] Wheat.

REGISTRATION NO. 270
(Vol. 2, p. 64)

Sarah Jones, Jane Eliza Jones,
Albert Jones, Benjamin Jones,
Charles Jones, Catharine Jones

26 February 1847

Sarah Jones, aged about 19, Jane Eliza Jones, aged about 16, Albert Jones, aged about 14, Benjamin Jones, aged about 10, Charles Jones, aged about 8, and Catharine Jones, aged about 5, are the children of Susan Jones, a free woman. They were born free, as appears by affidavit of Margaret [M.] Bangs.

REGISTRATION NO. 271
(Vol. 2, p. 64)

Virginia Nelson, John Nelson,
Charlotte Nelson, Georgianna Nelson,
and William Nelson

26 February 1847

Virginia Nelson, aged about 18, John Nelson, aged about 14, Charlotte Nelson, aged about 12, Georgianna Nelson, aged about 9, and William Nelson, aged about 8, are the children of Patty Nelson, a free woman. They were born free, as appears by affidavit of Harriet Jefferson, a white woman.

REGISTRATION NO. 272
(Vol. 2, p. 64)

Helen Parker Chapman and children,
Mary Jane, Harriet, Hellen Maria,
Rebecca, and George P.

27 February 1847

Helen Chapman, late Parker, is about 45 years old, 5 feet 2½ inches tall, of a dark complexion, with a small scar on the right side of her face. She was emancipated by George Parker by deed recorded in Liber M No. 2, page 2. She has five children: Mary Jane, aged about 20; Harriet, aged about 18; Hellen Maria, aged about 16; Rebecca, aged about 14; and George [P.], aged about 12. They were born free, as was proved by oath of Jonathan Ward.

REGISTRATION NO. 273
(Vol. 2, p. 65)

William Rhodes

27 February 1847

William Rhodes is about 10 years old and has a dark complexion. He is the son of Harriet Rhodes, a free woman, and was born free, as appears by affidavit of Mrs. Elizabeth Ferguson.

REGISTRATION NO. 274
(Vol. 2, p. 65)

Mary Rhodes

27 February 1847

Mary Rhodes is a mulatto woman, about 26 years old, and 5 feet 6¼ inches tall. She was born free, as appears by affidavit of Wilmer Corse.

REGISTRATION NO. 275
(Vol. 2, p. 65)

Charles Chapman Fisher   27 February 1847

Charles Chapman Fisher is about 6 years old and is the child of Lucy Ann Pipsico, a free woman. He was born free, as appears by oath of Jonathan Ward, a white man.

REGISTRATION NO. 276a
(Vol. 2, p. 65)

Mary Smith   27 February 1847

Mary Smith is about 35 years old, 5 feet 3½ inches tall, of a light brown complexion, with a scar on the upper part of her nose. She was born free, as appears by affidavit of George Glasscock.

REGISTRATION NO. 276b
(Vol. 2, p. 65)

Fanny Ashton   1 March 1847

Fanny Ashton is about 29 years old, 5 feet 2 inches tall, of a brown complexion, with a mole on the left side of her neck. She was born free, as appears by affidavit of J[ohn] Gibson Peach.

REGISTRATION NO. 277
(Vol. 2, p. 66)

Elias Taylor   1 March 1847

Elias Taylor is about 18 years old, 5 feet 3 inches tall, of a dark complexion, with a slight scar over his right eye. He was born free, as appears by affidavit of Mrs. Margaret Nickolson.

REGISTRATION NO. 278
(Vol. 2, p. 66)

George Calvert   1 March 1847

George Calvert is about 26 years old, 5 feet 3 inches tall, of a dark complexion, with a scar over his left eye. He was born free, as appears by certificate of Charles [C.] Smoot.

REGISTRATION NO. 279
(Vol. 2, p. 66)

Betsey Blackburn   1 March 1847

Betsey Blackburn is about 28 years old, 4 feet 11 inches tall, of a dark complexion, with a mole near the corner of her right eye. She was born free, as appears by certificate of Charles [C.] Smoot.

REGISTRATION NO. 280
(Vol. 2, p. 66)

Charles Gardner Turley   2 March 1847

Charles Gardner Turley is about 12 years old. He was born free, as appears by affidavit of Andrew Jamieson.

REGISTRATION NO. 281
(Vol. 2, p. 66)

Eliza Lee Dorsey   2 March 1847

Eliza Dorsey, late Lee, is about 30 years old, 5 feet 4½ inches tall, of a dark complexion, with a large black mole under her left eye. She was born free, as appears by certificate of Charles Scott.

REGISTRATION NO. 282
(Vol. 2, p. 67)

William Henry McCoy   5 March 1847
Mary Emily McCoy

Laura McCoy

William Henry McCoy is about 12 years old, Mary Emily McCoy is about 9 years old, and Laura McCoy is about 5 years old. They are the children of Annette McCoy, a free woman, and were born free, as appears by affidavit of Dr. [John] Richards.

REGISTRATION NO. 283
(Vol. 2, p. 67)

Jane Robinson and children,
Jane Eliza, George Francis,
and Ann Sophia

5 March 1847

Jane Robinson is about 33 years old, 5 feet 5 inches tall, of a dark complexion, with a scar on her right arm. She was born free, as appears by affidavit of Mrs. [Ann] Sidebottom. Robinson has three children: Jane Eliza, aged about 13; George Francis, aged about 3; and Ann Sophia, aged about 6 months.

REGISTRATION NO. 284
(Vol. 2, p. 67)

Maria Robinson

5 March 1847

Maria Robinson is about 28 years old, 5 feet 3 3/4 inches tall, of a dark complexion, with a scar over her left eye. She was born free, as appears by affidavit of Mrs. Ann Sidebottom.

REGISTRATION NO. 285
(Vol. 2, pp. 67-68)

Cornelia Bond and children,
Hannah and Georgiana

6 March 1847

Cornelia Bond is about 30 years old, 5 feet one-half inch tall, of a dark complexion, with several scars near her right ear. She was emancipated by Henry Cook by deed recorded in Liber F No. 3, page 468. Bond has two children, Hannah, aged about 3, and Georgiana, aged about 2 years.

REGISTRATION NO. 286
(Vol. 2, p. 68)

Sarah Chace
Samuel Chace
Joseph Henry Chace

6 March 1847

Sarah Chace is about 40 years old, 5 feet 2 3/4 inches tall, of a dark complexion, with a scar on the wrist of her left hand. She was born free, as appears by affidavit of John Shackleford. Chace has two children, Samuel Chace, aged about 15, and Joseph Henry Chace, aged about 7 years.

REGISTRATION NO. 287
(Vol. 2, p. 68)

Eliza Craig

9 March 1847

Eliza Craig is a dark mulatto woman, about 55 years old, 5 feet 4½ inches tall, with a scar on the right side of her neck. She was emancipated by O. Y. Ash and his wife, as appears by oath of Washington [C.] Page.

REGISTRATION NO. 288
(Vol. 2, p. 68)

Anna Craig

9 March 1847

Anna Craig is a dark mulatto girl, about 14 years old, 5 feet 2 3/4 inches tall, with no visible marks. She was born free, as appears by affidavit of Washington C. Page.

REGISTRATION NO. 289a
(Vol. 2, pp. 68-69)

John Henry Craig

9 March 1847

John Henry Craig is a mulatto boy, about 13 years old, 4 feet 4 inches tall, with a large scar near his left ear. He was born free, as appears by affidavit of Washington C. Page.

REGISTRATION NO. 289b
(Vol. 1, p. 69)

Lucy Dover   9 March 1847

Lucy Dover is about 45 years old, 5 feet 1¼ inches tall, of a light complexion, and considerably freckled. She was emancipated by Jane A. Ramsay by deed recorded in Liver V No. 2, page 360.

REGISTRATION NO. 290
(Vol. 1, p. 69)

George Berry   11 March 1847

George Berry is a mulatto man, about 23 years old, 6 feet one-half inch tall, with no visible marks. He was born free, as appears by affidavit of Mrs. Mary Cole.

REGISTRATION NO. 291
(Vol. 2, p. 69)

William Berry   11 March 1847

William Berry is a mulatto man, about 20 years and 6 months old, 5 feet 6 3/4 inches tall, with two large moles on the back of his neck. He was born free, as appears by affidavit of Mrs. Mary Cole.

REGISTRATION NO. 292
(Vol. 2, p. 69)

Ann Berry   11 March 1847

Ann Berry is about 18 years old, 5 feet 2 inches tall, of a bright complexion, with no visible marks. She was born free, as appears by affidavit of Mrs. Mary Cole.

REGISTRATION NO. 293
(Vol. 2, p. 70)

Susan Jones   12 March 1847

Susan Jones is about 42 years old, 5 feet 3¼ inches tall, of a dark complexion, with a scar on her right arm. She was born free, as appears by affirmation of Zenas Kinsey.

REGISTRATION NO. 274*
(Vol. 2, p. 70)

Randolph Smith   13 March 1847

Randolph Smith is about 37 years old, 5 feet 10½ inches tall, of a dark complexion, with a scar near his under lip. He was emancipated by Lambert & McKinzie by deed dated 11 March 1847.

*The registration numbers are incorrect. The clerk begins numbering at 274 instead of at 294 and continues that sequence. The numbers from 274-293 on pages 70-75 will be starred to indicate the repetition of numbers. In the index, the page numbers will be given for these items.

REGISTRATION NO. 275*
(Vol. 2, p. 70)

Elizabeth Dogan   13 March 1847

Elizabeth Dogan is a mulatto girl, about 16 years old, 5 feet 3½ inches tall, with a small mole or lump near her right ear. He was born free, as appears by certificate of Henry Daingerfield.

REGISTRATION NO. 276*
(Vol. 2, pp. 70-71)

Sarah Smith and children,   13 March 1847
Philip Andrew, Thomas Daniel,
William Wilson, and Susan Louisa

Sarah Smith is about 42 years old, 5 feet 2½ inches tall, of a dark complexion, with a scar on her right thumb. She was born free, as appears by affidavit of Mrs. Margaret [M.] Banks. Smith has four children: Philip Andrew, aged about 14, Thomas Daniel, aged about 11, William Wilson, aged about 8 years and 3 months, and Susan Louisa, aged about 2 years and 2 months. They were born free.

REGISTRATION NO. 277*
(Vol. 2, p. 71)

Anthony Dogan   15 March 1847

Anthony Dogan is a dark mulatto man, about 48 years old, 5 feet 10½ inches tall, with no visible marks. He was born free, as appears by affidavit of Mrs. Lucy Philips.

REGISTRATION NO. 278*
(Vol. 2, p. 71)

John Smith   15 March 1847

John Smith is about 35 years old, 5 feet 8¼ inches tall, of a brown complexion, with a scar on his nose and another on his left thumb. He was emancipated by Sarah Waters by deed recorded in Liber X No. 2, page 202.

REGISTRATION NO. 279*
(Vol. 2, p. 71)

Mary Elizabeth Chace   15 March 1847

Mary Elizabeth Chace is about 17 years old, 5 feet 2 3/4 inches tall, of a very dark complexion, with a scar on her left little finger. She was born free, as appears by affidavit of John Shackleford.

REGISTRATION NO. 280*
(Vol. 2, p. 72)

Elizabeth Lee   15 March 1847

Elizabeth Lee is about 25 years old, 5 feet 3/4 inches tall, of a brown complexion, with a black mole on the inside of her left hand near the little finger. She was born free, as appears by affidavit of Mrs. Ann Radcliff.

REGISTRATION NO. 281*
(Vol. 2, p. 72)

Cecelia Lee   15 March 1847

Cecelia Lee is about 18 years old, 5 feet 2 inches tall, of a brown complexion with no visible marks. She was born free, as appears by affidavit of Mrs. Ann Radcliff.

REGISTRATION NO. 282*
(Vol. 2, p. 72)

Sarah Gibson   16 March 1847

Sarah Gibson is a mulatto woman, about 28 years old, 5 feet 2½ inches tall, and slightly pitted by smallpox. She was emancipated by William H. Miller by deed recorded in Liber D No. 3, page 162.

REGISTRATION NO. 283*
(Vol. 2, p. 72)

George Gordon   16 March 1847

George Gordon is 20 years old, 5 feet 6 inches tall, of a dark complexion, with very large teeth. She was born free, as appears by affidavit of W[ashington] C. Page.

REGISTRATION NO. 284*
(Vol. 2, p. 73)

Hannah Frances Skinner   16 March 1847

Hannah Frances Skinner is about 5 years old and was born free, as appears by affidavit of A[nthony] C[harles] Cazenove.

REGISTRATION NO. 285*
(Vol. 2, p. 73)

Mary Jane Ross   16 March 1847

Mary Jane Ross is about 24 years and 6 months old, 5 feet½ inches tall, of a bright complexion, with a scar on her left wrist. She was born free, as appears by affidavit of Henry Dye.

REGISTRATION NO. 286*
(Vol. 2, p. 73)

Sarah Ann Frazer

16 March 1847

Sarah Ann Frazer is about 21 years old, 5 feet 3½ inches tall, of a brown complexion, with no visible marks. She was born free, as appears by affidavit of Henry Dye.

REGISTRATION NO. 287*
(Vol. 2, p. 73)

Silas Madella

16 March 1847

Silas Madella is about 16 years old, 5 feet 3 3/4 inches tall, of a dark brown complexion with a scar on his right thumb. He was born free, as appears by affidavit of Henry Dye.

REGISTRATION NO. 288*
(Vol. 2, pp. 73-74)

John Madella

16 March 1847

John Madella is about 14 years and 6 months old, 4 feet 10 3/4 inches tall, of a dark brown complexion, with a black mole on his left thumb. He was born free, as appears by affidavit of Henry Dye.

REGISTRATION NO. 289*
(Vol. 2, p. 74)

Martha Hopkins

16 March 1847

Martha Hopkins is about 28 years old, 5 feet 5½ inches tall, of a very light complexion, with a scar on her left thumb. She was emancipated by deed from Thomas S. Hardy recorded in Liber W No. 2, page 168.

REGISTRATION NO. 290*
(Vol. 2, p. 74)

Peter Hopkins

16 March 1847

Peter Hopkins is a bright mulatto man, about 38 years old, 5 feet 7½ inches tall, with a scar on the middle finger of his right hand. He was emancipated by James Dempsey by deed dated 16 March 1847.

REGISTRATION NO. 291*
(Vol. 2, p. 74)

James Hopkins, Charles Hopkins,
John T. Whiting, Virginia Whiting,
Daniel Hopkins, Albert Hopkins,
and Catharine Hopkins

16 March 1847

John Hopkins is about 14 years old, Charles Hopkins is about 12 years old, John T. Whiting is about 9 years old, Virginia Whiting is about 7 years old, Daniel Hopkins is about 5 years old, Albert Hopkins is about 3 years old, and Catharine Hopkins is about 1 year old. They are the children of free persons and were born free, as was proved by oath of Mrs. Margaret [M.] Bangs.

REGISTRATION NO. 292*
(Vol. 2, p. 75)

Lydia Valentine

17 March 1827

Lydia Valentine is about 52 years old, 5 feet 5 inches tall, of a dark complexion, with a scar on her right hand near the wrist. She is free, as appears by affirmation of Samuel Miller.

REGISTRATION NO. 293*
(Vol. 2, p. 75)

Kitty Barnes Humphries

17 March 1847

Kitty Humphries, late Barnes, is about 29 years old, 5 feet 4¼ inches tall, of a light brown complexion, with a black mole on the thumb of her left hand. She was born free, as appears by affidavit of A[lexander] Moore.

REGISTRATION NO. 294
(Vol. 2, p. 75)

Georgeana Humphries   17 March 1847

Georgeana Humphries is about 20 years old, 5 feet 3½ inches tall, of a dark brown complexion, with several scars on her right arm. She was born free, as appears by certificate of J. R. Riddle.

REGISTRATION NO. 295
(Vol. 2, p. 75)

Susannah Humphries   17 March 1847

Susannah Humphries is about 18 years and 9 months old, 4 feet 11½ inches tall, of a dark brown complexion, with scars over both eyes. She was born free, as appears by certificate of J. R. Riddle.

REGISTRATION NO. 296
(Vol. 2, p. 76)

George Humphries   17 March 1847

George Humphries is 12 years old and was born free, as appears by affidavit of J. R. Riddle.

REGISTRATION NO. 297
(Vol. 2, p. 76)

Rebecca Merricks   17 March 1847

Rebecca Merricks is about 31 years old, 5 feet one-half inch tall, of a dark complexion, with a scar on the back of her neck. She was born free, as appears by affirmation of Zenas Kinsey.

REGISTRATION NO. 298
(Vol. 2, p. 76)

Samuel Jarboe   17 March 1847
Mary Jarboe

Samuel Jarboe is about 18 years old and Mary Jarboe is about 16 years old. They were born free, as appears by affirmation of Zenas Kinsey.

REGISTRATION NO. 299
(Vol. 2, p. 76)

Orlando Webster, Henrietta Webster,
Oliver and Lucy Webster   17 March 1847

Orlando Webster is about 6 years old, Henrietta Webster is about 2 years old, Oliver and Lucy, who are twins, are about 1 year 3 months old. They were born free, as appears by affidavit of Mrs. Mary Grummond.

REGISTRATION NO. 300
(Vol. 2, p. 76)

Cecelia Peters   17 March 1847
Frances Peters

Cecelia Peters, aged 12, and Frances Peters, aged 11, are the children of Lucinda Peters, a free woman. They were born free, as appears by affidavit of A[nthony] P. Gover.

REGISTRATION NO. 301
(Vol. 2, p. 77)

William Henry Davis   17 March 1847

William Henry Davis is the son of Eliza Davis and was born free, as appears by affidavit of Elijah Horseman.

REGISTRATION NO. 302
(Vol. 2, p. 77)

Mary Wade Dogans   17 March 1847

Mary Wade Dogans is about 24 years old, 5 feet 4¼ inches tall, of a light complexion, with a black [mole?] on her upper lip. She was born free, as appears by affidavit of Mrs. Lucy Phillips.

REGISTRATION NO. 303
(Vol. 2, p. 77)

Isabella Dogans

17 March 1847

Isabella Dogans is about 21 years old, 5 feet 9 inches tall, of a light complexion, with no visible marks. She was born free, as appears by affidavit of Mrs. Lucy Phillips.

REGISTRATION NO. 304
(Vol. 2, p. 77)

Elizabeth S. Fitzgerald

18 March 1847

Elizabeth S. Fitzgerald is about 14 years old, 5 feet 1 inch tall, of a light complexion, with no visible marks. She was born free, as appears by affidavit of Mrs. Patsey Chichester.

REGISTRATION NO. 305
(Vol. 2, p. 77-78)

Mary Jane Fitzgerald

18 March 1847

Mary Jane Fitzgerald is about 12 years old, 4 feet 8 inches tall, of a light complexion, with a scar on her right temple. She was born free, as appears by affidavit of Mrs. Patsey Chichester.

REGISTRATION NO. 306
(Vol. 2, p. 78)

Susan Smith

18 March 1847

Susan Smith is a free woman about 37 years old, 5 feet 2 inches tall, of a light complexion, with a black mole on her upper lip. She was emancipated by Zenas Kinsey by deed recorded in Liber A No. 3, page 328.

REGISTRATION NO. 307
(Vol. 2, p. 78)

Patty Webster

18 March 1847

Patty Webster is about 40 years old, 5 feet 1½ inches tall, of a brown complexion, with a small black mole on her left cheek. She was emancipated by Hugh Smith.

REGISTRATION NO. 308
(Vol. 2, p. 78)

Simeon Evans

18 March 1847

Simeon Evans is about 18 years old, 5 feet 5 inches tall, of a dark brown complexion, with no visible marks. He was born free, as appears by affidavit of Peter G. Henderson.

REGISTRATION NO. 309
(Vol. 2, p. 79)

Mary Jane Skinner

18 March 1847

Mary Jane Skinner is about 17 years and 6 months old, 5 feet 4 inches tall, of a very light complexion, with a scar on the little finger of her right hand. She was born free, as appears by certificate on file of Phinias Janney.

REGISTRATION NO. 310
(Vol. 2, p. 79)

Elizabeth Ebbs

18 March 1847

Elizabeth Ebbs is about 22 years old, 5 feet 5 inches tall, of a dark complexion, with a scar on her right hand. She was born free, as appears by certificate on file of Gottlieb Appich.

REGISTRATION NO. 311
(Vol. 2, p. 79)

Mary Tate

18 March 1847

Mary Tate is about 32 years old, 4 feet 11 inches tall, of a light complexion, with three marks over her left eye. She was emancipated by James Entwistle by deed dated this day.

REGISTRATION NO. 312
(Vol. 2, p. 79)

Jane Bell   18 March 1847

Jane Bell is about 28 years old, 5 feet 6½ inches tall, of a light complexion, with a scar on her right wrist. She is free, as appears by affidavit of Sarah Allen.

REGISTRATION NO. 313
(Vol. 2, p. 80)

Mary Ellen Solomon   19 March 1847

Mary Ellen Solomon is about 23 years old, 5 feet 4¼ inches tall, of a dark complexion, with a small scar on the right side of her nose near the eye. She was born free, as appears by affirmation of Zenas Kinsey. Mary Ellen is the child of William and Kitty Solomon, free persons of color.

REGISTRATION NO. 314
(Vol. 2, p. 80)

Lucy Ann Johnson and   19 March 1847
child, Mary Lavinia

Lucy Ann Johnson is about 18 years old, 5 feet 1 inch tall, of a brown complexion, with a scar on the right side of her face. She was born free, as appears by affidavit of Jane Bossart. Johnson has child named Mary Lavinia, aged seven weeks, who is also registered.

REGISTRATION NO. 315
(Vol. 2, p. 80)

Frances Syphax   18 March 1847
Daniel Syphax

"Francis" [Frances] Syphax is about 37 years old, 5 feet three-fourth inch tall, of a dark complexion. She was emancipated by William Syphax by deed dated 3 May 1827. Daniel Syphax is her son and is about 11 years old.

REGISTRATION NO. 316
(Vol. 2, p. 80)

Alfred Bryant   18 March 1847

Alfred Bryant is a mulatto man, about 22 years old, 5 feet 10 inches tall, with a large long scar on his right wrist. He was emancipated by the will of Joseph Lewis of Loudoun County, as appears by a certificate from that county.

REGISTRATION NO. 317
(Vol. 2, p. 81)

Sarah Johnson   19 March 1847

Sarah Johnson is about 13 years old, 5 feet 2 3/4 inches tall, of a dark complexion, with a black mole on the right side of her face near her nose. She was born free, as appears by affidavit of Mrs. Jane Bossart.

REGISTRATION NO. 318
(Vol. 2, p. 81)

Sarah Elizabeth Dover   19 March 1847

Sarah Elizabeth Dover is about 22 years old, 5 feet 1 inch tall, of a brown complexion, with a scar on the back of her neck. She was born free, as appears by affidavit of Mrs. Margaret [M.] Bangs.

REGISTRATION NO. 319
(Vol. 2, p. 81)

Catharine Ann Dover   19 March 1847

Catharine Ann Dover is about 20 years old, 5 feet 1 inch tall, of a brown complexion, with a scar on her neck. She was born free, as appears by affidavit of Mrs. Margaret [M.] Bangs.

REGISTRATION NO. 320
(Vol. 2, p. 81)

Louisa Cooper

19 March 1847

Louisa Cooper is about 16 years old, 5 feet 1½ inches tall, of a brown complexion, with no visible marks. She was born free, as appears by affidavit of Mrs. Margaret [M.] Bangs.

REGISTRATION NO. 321
(Vol. 2, p. 82)

Mary Jane Cooper
Cornelia Ann Cooper
Richard Randolph Lancaster

19 March 1847

Mary Jane Cooper is 13 years old, Cornelia Ann Cooper is 12 years old, and Richard "Randolp" [Randolph] Lancaster is 3 years old. They are the children of Sarah Lancaster, a free woman, and were born free, as appears by affidavit of Mrs. [Margaret M.] Bangs.

REGISTRATION NO. 322
(Vol. 2, p. 82)

Simeon Tate, Jr.

19 March 1847

Simeon Tate is a dark mulatto man, about 21 years old, 5 feet 8¼ inches tall, with no visible marks. He was born free, as appears by Certificate No. 457 [in Vol. 1] dated 17 June 1834.

REGISTRATION NO. 323
(Vol. 2, p. 82)

Amelia Davis

19 March 1847

Amelia Davis is about 21 years old, 5 feet 1½ inches tall, of a dark complexion, with no visible marks. She was born free, as appears by affidavit of Mary Ann Gibbs.

REGISTRATION NO. 324
(Vol. 2, p. 82)

Simeon Tate, Sr.

19 March 1847

Simeon Tate is about 51 years old, 5 feet 6 inches tall, of a dark complexion, with a scar on his left cheek under his eye. He was born free, as appears by Certificate No. 125 [in Vol. 1].

In No. 125, Simeon is called "Simon" Tate.

REGISTRATION NO. 325
(Vol. 2, p. 83)

Mary Jane Chapman

19 March 1847

Mary Jane Chapman is about 20 years old, 5 feet 6 inches tall, of a brown complexion, with a slight defect in her left eye. She was born free, as appears by affidavit of Jonathan Ward.

REGISTRATION NO. 326
(Vol. 2, p. 83)

Harriet Chapman

19 March 1847

Harriet Chapman is about 18 years old, 5 feet 3½ inches tall, of a brown complexion, with a black mole on the left side of her nose. She was born free, as appears by affidavit of Jonathan Ward.

REGISTRATION NO. 327
(Vol. 2, p. 83)

Hellen Maria Chapman

19 March 1847

Hellen Maria Chapman is about 16 years old, 5 feet 5 inches tall, of a light brown complexion, with a mole on the left side of her neck. She was born free, as appears by affidavit of Jonathan Ward.

REGISTRATION NO. 328
(Vol. 2, p. 83)

Sarah Ovelton   19 March 1847

Sarah Ovelton is about 22 years old, 5 feet 4½ inches tall, of a dark complexion, with a scar on the back of her right hand. She was born free, as appears by affidavit of Mrs. Sarah Allen.

REGISTRATION NO. 329
(Vol. 2, p. 84)

Sarah Thompson   19 March 1847

Sarah Thompson is about 21 years old, 5 feet 1¼ inches tall, of a dark complexion, with a large scar on her right arm. She was born free, as appears by affidavit of Zinas Kinsey.

REGISTRATION NO. 330
(Vol. 2, p. 84)

Maria Windsor and child,   19 March 1847
George William

Maria Windsor is about 20 years old, 5 feet 2 3/4 inches tall, of a dark complexion, with a scar on her neck. She was emancipated by the will of Benjamin Baden. She has a child named George William aged about 19 months.

REGISTRATION NO. 331
(Vol. 2, p. 84)

Sylvia Thompson   19 March 1847

Sylvia Thompson is about 42 years old, 5 feet 11 inches tall, of a dark complexion, with a scar on her upper lip. She was born free, as appears by affidavit of John Churchman.

REGISTRATION NO. 332
(Vol. 2, p. 84)

Lucy Ann Chapman Pipsico   19 March 1847

Lucy Ann Pipsico, late Chapman, is the daughter of Helen Chapman who is a free woman.

REGISTRATION NO. 333
(Vol. 2, p. 85)

William Henry Davis   19 March 1847
Rebecca Davis

William Henry Davis is about 3 years old and Rebecca Davis is about 5 months old. They are the children of Amelia Davis, a free woman, and were born free.

REGISTRATION NO. 334
(Vol. 2, p. 85)

Marcelina Johnson and children,   19 March 1847
Marcelina Johnson, James Edmond
Johnson, and Joseph Nathaniel Johnson

Marcelina Johnson is about 30 years old, 5 feet 1½ inches tall, of a dark complexion, with a black mole on her forehead. She was born free, as appears by affidavit of J[ohn] G[ibson] Peach. Johnson has three children: Marcelina Johnson, aged 13; James Edmond Johnson, aged 10; and Joseph Nathaniel Johnson, aged 7; who were born free.

REGISTRATION NO. 335
(Vol. 2, p. 85)

Nancy Muse and children,   19 March 1847
William Henry and Virginia

Nancy Muse is 39 years old, 5 feet 4 inches tall, of a dark complexion, with a scar on the left side of her face. She was born free, as appears by affidavit of J[ohn] G[ibson] Peach. She has two children, William Henry, aged 16, and Virginia, aged about 10 years.

REGISTRATION NO. 336
(Vol. 2, pp. 85-86)

19 March 1847

Grafton Johnson
Mary Elizabeth Ashton
Charles Henry Ashton

Grafton Johnson, aged 20, Mary Elizabeth Ashton, aged 4, and Charles Henry Ashton, aged about 2, are the children of Fanny Ashton, a free woman. They were born free, as appears by evidence of J[ohn] G[ibson] Peach.

REGISTRATION NO. 337
(Vol. 2, p. 86)

19 March 1847

Betsey Payne

Betsey Payne is about 20 years old, 4 feet 6 inches tall, of a brown complexion, with a scar over her right eye. She was born free, as appears by affidavit of Daniel Bayliss.

REGISTRATION NO. 338
(Vol. 2, p. 86)

19 March 1847

Samuel Williams

Samuel Williams is a black man about 40 years old, 5 feet 3¼ inches tall, with a scar on the left side of his face. He was emancipated by Sarah Pickering and Stephen Shinn by deed dated 1 January 1847.

REGISTRATION NO. 339
(Vol. 2, p. 86)

19 March 1847

Harriet Jasper
Martha Jasper

Harriet Jasper is about 35 years old, 5 feet 4 inches tall, of a brown complexion, with a scar on her left thumb. She and her daughter, Martha Jasper, were freed by George Brooks by deed dated 19 March 1847.

REGISTRATION NO. 340
(Vol. 2, pp. 86-87)

19 March 1847

Martha Thompson

Martha Thompson is a dark mulatto woman, about 31 years old, 5 feet one-fourth inch tall, with a scar on her forehead. She was born free, as appears by affidavit of Margaret A. Hodge.

REGISTRATION NO. 341
(Vol. 2, p. 87)

19 March 1847

Sydney Brooks

Sydney Brooks is about 18 years old, 5 feet 9 inches tall, of a light complexion, with no visible marks. He was born free, as appears by affidavit of Joseph [H.] Hampson.

REGISTRATION NO. 342
(Vol. 2, p. 87)

19 March 1847

James Thompson

James Thompson is a mulatto man, about 36 years old, 5 feet 8½ inches tall, with a scar on the left side of his face. He was emancipated by W[ashington] C. Page by deed dated 19 March 1847.

REGISTRATION NO. 343
(Vol. 2, p. 87)

19 March 1847

Sally Ross

Sally Ross is a bright mulatto woman, about 35 years old, 5 feet 7 3/4 inches tall, with very straight black hair. She was born free, as appears by certificate No. 492 [in Vol. 1].

REGISTRATION NO. 344
(Vol. 2, p. 87)

Rachel Lee and children,

Edgar Briscoe, Josephine Briscoe　　　　　　　　　　　　　　　　　　　　　　　　　19 March 1847

Rachel Lee is about 45 years old, 5 feet 11½ inches tall, of a dark complexion, with a scar on her right arm near the elbow. She was emancipated by the will of James Harris. Edgar Briscoe, aged about 7, and Josephine Briscoe, aged about 6, are children of Rachel's and were born free.

REGISTRATION NO. 345
(Vol. 2)*

Robert Rhodes　　　　　　　　　　　　　　　　　　　　　　　　　　　　　　　　　19 March 1847

Robert Rhodes is about 19 years and 3 months old, 5 feet 5 inches tall, of a light complexion, with no visible marks. He was born free, as appears by affidavit of W. W. Adams.

The pages are not numbered after page 87.

REGISTRATION NO. 346
(Vol. 2)

Rachel Brown Bruce　　　　　　　　　　　　　　　　　　　　　　　　　　　　　　19 March 1847

Rachel Bruce, late Brown, is about 22 years old, 5 feet 4 inches tall, of a dark complexion, with a scar on the left side of her neck. She was freed by Robert Jamieson by deed recorded in Liber F No. 3, page 164.

REGISTRATION NO. 347
(Vol. 2)

Caroline Rebecca Taylor　　　　　　　　　　　　　　　　　　　　　　　　　　　　19 March 1847
Josephine Frances Taylor

Caroline Rebecca Taylor, aged 6, and Josephine Frances Taylor, aged about 3, are the children of Ann Taylor, a free woman. They were born free, as appears by certificate of Hannah S. Wanton.

REGISTRATION NO. 348
(Vol. 2)

Henrietta Tate　　　　　　　　　　　　　　　　　　　　　　　　　　　　　　　　　19 March 1847

Henrietta Tate is about 45 years old, 5 feet 2 inches tall, of a dark complexion, with no visible marks. She was emancipated by William F. Alexander by deed recorded in Liver V No. 2, page 241.

REGISTRATION NO. 349
(Vol. 2)

Susan Delly　　　　　　　　　　　　　　　　　　　　　　　　　　　　　　　　　　19 March 1847
Roxana Delly

Susan Delly is about 18 years old, 5 feet tall, and has a dark complexion. Roxana Delly, her sister, is 5 feet 4½ inches tall. They were born free, as appears by certificate of William Brent, Esq., filed in this office.

REGISTRATION NO. 350
(Vol. 2)

Mary Frances Nickins, Martha Ann Nickins,　　　　　　　　　　　　　　　　　　　19 March 1847
John William Nickins, James Edward Nickins

Mary Frances, aged 10, Martha Ann, aged 8, John William, aged 6, and James Edward, aged 3, are all bright mulatto children of Lucy Nickins, a free person of color, as proved by James Vansant, Esq.

REGISTRATION NO. 351
(Vol. 2)

Mary Ann Beale and children,　　　　　　　　　　　　　　　　　　　　　　　　　19 March 1847
John Francis and Frank

Mary Ann Beale is 26 years old, 5 feet tall, of a light complexion, with scars on both hands. She was born free, as appears by affidavit of Mrs. Monica Foy. Mary Ann has two children, John Francis aged 5, and Frank, aged 16 months.

REGISTRATION NO. 352
(Vol. 2)

Ann Elizabeth Shields

19 March 1847

Ann Elizabeth Shields is 16 years old, 5 feet 3 inches tall, of a light complexion, with no visible marks. She was born free, as appears by affidavit of Mrs. Monica Foy.

REGISTRATION NO. 353
(Vol. 2)

James Henry Shields, John Randolph Shields, Emma Shorter Shields, Nora Jenifer Shields

19 March 1847

James Henry Shields, aged 14, John Randolph Shields, aged 11, Emma Shorter Shields, aged 10, and Nora Shields, aged 9 and the children of ?? Shields, a free woman. They were born free, as appears by affidavit of Mrs. M[onica] Foy.

There is no registration numbered 354.

REGISTRATION NO. 355
(Vol. 2)

Julia Ann Williams and children Georgeanna, John Rozier, Laura Virginia, and Sarah Elizabeth

19 March 1847

Julia Ann Williams is a free woman abut 30 years old, 5 feet 3 inches tall, of a brown complexion, with no visible marks. She was born free, as appears by certificate of A[lexander] Moore on file. She has four children: Georgeanna, aged about 10; John Rozier, aged 7; Laura Virginia, aged 6; and Sarah Elizabeth, aged 11 months.

REGISTRATION NO. 356
(Vol. 2)

Benjamin Dorsey, Zachariah Dorsey, Townshend Dorsey, Sarah E. Dorsey, and Julia Dorsey

19 March 1847

Benjamin Dorsey, aged about 16, Zachariah Dorsey, aged about 14, Townshend Dorsey, aged about 9, Sarah E. Dorsey, aged about 7, and Julia Dorsey, aged about 3, are the children of Elizabeth Dorsey, and were born free, as appears by affidavit of Mrs. Jane Rye.

REGISTRATION NO. 357
(Vol. 2)

Elizabeth Hines

19 March 1847

Elizabeth Hines is about 17 years old, 5 feet 3 3/4 inches tall, of a brown complexion, with a scar on her right wrist. She was born free, as appears by affidavit of Mrs. Jane Rye.

REGISTRATION NO. 358
(Vol. 2)

Sarah Clarke

19 March 1847

Sarah Clarke is about 26 years old, 5 feet 8½ inches tall, of a brown complexion, with a scar over her right eye and mole near her mouth. She was born free, as appears by affidavit of Mrs. Jane Rye.

REGISTRATION NO. 359
(Vol. 2)

Sarah Jane Berry

19 March 1847

Sarah Jane Berry is about 17 years old, 5 feet 4 inches tall, of a light complexion, with no visible marks. She was born free, as appears by affidavit of Mrs. Margaret [M.] Bangs.

REGISTRATION NO. 360
(Vol. 2)

William Berry, Patsy Elizabeth Berry,

19 March 1847

Ellen Berry, Sophia Berry,
Celistia Berry, Mary Catharine Berry,
and Harriet Patterson

William Berry, aged about 17, Patsy Elizabeth, aged about 15, Ellen Berry, aged about 11, Sophia Berry, aged about 10, Celistia Berry, aged 8, Mary Catharine Berry, aged about 6, and Harriet Patterson, aged about 3, are the children of Patsy Berry, a free woman. They were born free, as appears by affidavit of Mrs. Margaret [M.] Bangs.

REGISTRATION NO. 361a
(Vol. 2)

William George Lomax, Thomas Lomax,
Mary Frances Lomax, Elizabeth Lomax

19 March 1847

William George Lomax, aged about 13 and of a dark complexion, Thomas Lomax, aged about 12 and of a dark complexion, Mary Frances and Elizabeth Lomax, twin sisters aged about 10 and of dark complexion, are the children of Ellen Lomax a free colored woman. They were born free, as appears by affidavit of "Hayride" [Harriet] Jefferson.

REGISTRATION NO. 361b
(Vol. 2)

Desirlini T. Harris

19 March 1847

Desirlini T. Harris is about 21 years old, 5 feet 8 inches tall, of a dark complexion, with a mole on his upper lip near his nose. He was born free, as appears by certificate of Mrs. Ann Mark on file.

REGISTRATION NO. 362
(Vol. 2)

Octavia V. Harris

19 March 1847

Octavia V. Harris is a mulatto girl, about 19 years old, 5 feet 1 inch tall, with no visible marks. She was born free, as appears by certificate of Mrs. Ann Mark on file.

REGISTRATION NO. 363
(Vol. 2)

Amelia Syphax

19 March 1847

Amelia "Syfax" [Syphax] is about 19 years old, 5 feet 3½ inches tall, of a brown complexion, with no visible marks. She was born free as appears by the evidence of Mrs. Mary Ann Church.

REGISTRATION NO. 364
(Vol. 2)

Eliza Johnson

19 March 1847

Eliza Johnson is about 18 years old, 5 feet 3 inches tall, of a light brown complexion, with a scar on the left side of her chin. She was born free, as appears by affidavit of Mrs. Sarah Jordan.

REGISTRATION NO. 365
(Vol. 2)

William H. Jones

19 March 1847

William H. Jones is about 20 years old, 5 feet 3 3/4 inches tall, of a dark complexion, with no visible marks. He was born free, as appears by affidavit of Charles Graham.

REGISTRATION NO. 366
(Vol. 2)

John L. Jones

19 March 1847

John L. Jones is about 18 years old, 5 feet 3½ inches tall, of a dark complexion, with a scar on his left cheek. He was born free, as appears by affidavit of Charles Graham.

REGISTRATION NO. 367
(Vol. 2)

Richard Lancaster   19 March 1847

Richard Lancaster is a black man, about 34 years old, and 5 feet 8½ inches tall. He was freed by the will of Benjamin Waters of Maryland, as appears by affidavit of Reuben Zimmerman.

REGISTRATION NO. 368
(Vol. 2)

Jane Thompson   19 March 1847

Jane Thompson is about 40 years old, 5 feet 2½ inches tall, and has a dark complexion. She was freed by the will of Joseph Smith.

REGISTRATION NO. 369
(Vol. 2)

Charles Guss   19 March 1847

Charles Guss is a dark mulatto man, about 23 years old, 5 feet 10 inches tall, with no visible marks. He was born free, as appears by certificate of Josiah H. Davis filed in this office.

REGISTRATION NO. 370
(Vol. 2)

Mary Morris   19 March 1847

Mary Morris is about 19 years old, 5 feet 5 inches tall, of a dark brown complexion, with a mole on her upper lip and a scar on her right arm. She was born free, as appears by affidavit of Marian Walker.

REGISTRATION NO. 371
(Vol. 2)

Charles Wright   19 March 1847
Francis Wright
Joseph Wright

Charles Wright, aged about 16, Francis Wright, aged about 14, and Joseph Wright, aged about 8, are the children of Lavinia Wright, a free woman. They were born free, as appears by the evidence of George Johnson filed in this office.

REGISTRATION NO. 372
(Vol. 2)

Mary Wedge   19 March 1847

Mary Wedge is about 35 years old, 5 feet 2 inches tall, of a dark complexion, with a scar on the third finger of her right hand. She obtained her freedom by judgement of the U. S. Circuit Court for Alexandria County at its May 1845 term in a suit in which she was the plaintiff and Kin and Thomas the defendants.

REGISTRATION NO. 373
(Vol. 2)

Susannah Jones   19 March 1847

Susannah Jones is about 17 years old, 5 feet 3¼ inches tall, of a brown complexion, with a scar on her breast. She was born free, as appears by affidavit of Mrs. Sarah Allen.

REGISTRATION NO. 374
(Vol. 2)

Lucinda Dogans   19 March 1847

Lucinda Dogans is a mulatto woman, about 25 years old, 5 feet 3/4 inches tall, with a scar on her right elbow. She was born free, as appears by affidavit of Mrs. Ann Adams.

REGISTRATION NO. 375
(Vol. 2)

Ann Maria Bumbey and children,   19 March 1847
Mary Elizabeth, Laura Virginia,
and Bernard

Ann Maria Bumbey is about 27 years old, 5 feet 2 inches tall, of a light complexion, with a scar on the forefinger of her right hand. She was born free, as appears by affidavit of N. Hicks. Ann Maria was 3 children: Mary Elizabeth, aged about 9; Laura Virginia, aged about 3; and Bernard, aged about 1 year; who were identified by Mrs. John W. Smith.

REGISTRATION NO. 376
(Vol. 2)

Eliza Whiting   19 March 1847

Eliza Whiting is about 33 years old, 5 feet 5¼ inches tall, of a light complexion, with a black mole on her chin. She was born free, as appears by the evidence of W. C. Yeaton.

REGISTRATION NO. 377
(Vol. 2)

Martha Alexander   19 March 1847

Martha Alexander is about 22 years old, 4 feet 11 inches tall, of a dark complexion, with a scar on her right arm. She was born free, as appears by affidavit of Benjamin Waters.

REGISTRATION NO. 378
(Vol. 2)

Catharine Norris and children   19 March 1847
Isaac, David, Laura, Francis,
and Sophia

Catharine Norris is about 36 years old, 5 feet 2½ inches tall, of a dark complexion, with a scar on her forehead. She was born free, as appears by the certificate on file of Willis Anderson. Catharine has 5 children: Isaac, aged about 13; David, aged about 9; Laura, aged about 6; Francis, aged about 3; and Sophia, aged about 2 months. They were born free, as appears by oath of Mrs. Harriet Jefferson.

REGISTRATION NO. 379
(Vol. 2)

Eliza Syphax and children,
Lewis and Douglas   19 March 1847

Eliza Syphax is about 35 years old, 5 feet 5 inches tall, of a dark complexion, with no visible marks. She was emancipated by William Syphax by deed dated 3 May 1827. She has two children: Lewis, aged about 12, and Douglas, aged about 6 years.

REGISTRATION NO. 380
(Vol. 2)

Hannah Middleton   19 March 1847

Hannah Middleton is about 45 years old, 5 feet 4 inches tall, of a dark complexion, with a scar on her left thumb. She is free, as appears by the certificate on file of Mary Wheeler and others.

REGISTRATION NO. 381
(Vol. 2)

Clara Norris   19 March 1847
Catharine Norris
Mary Norris

Clara Norris, aged about 13, Catharine Norris, aged about 9, and Mary Norris, aged about 2, are the children of Rachel Norris, a free woman. They were born free, as appears by affidavit of Mrs. Harriet Jefferson.

REGISTRATION NO. 382
(Vol. 2)

Charles A. Chinn   19 March 1847

Charles A. Chinn is about 21 years old, 5 feet 11 inches tall, of a bright complexion, with a scar on his forehead over his left eye. He was born free, as appears by the affidavit on file of Charles McKnight.

REGISTRATION NO. 383
(Vol. 2)

Whiting Thomas   19 March 1847

Whiting Thomas is about 30 years old, 5 feet 8 inches tall, of a dark complexion, with a small scar on his forehead. He was emancipated by deed of John C. Herbert and was identified by Miss Eliza Herbert.

REGISTRATION NO. 384
(Vol. 2)

Ann Jackson   19 March 1847

Ann Jackson is about 49 years old, 5 feet 6 inches tall, of a dark complexion, with no visible marks. She was born free, as appears by affidavit of Mrs. Jabez Wheeler.

REGISTRATION NO. 385
(Vol. 2)

Octavia Brown   19 March 1847

Octavia Brown is about 30 years old, 5 feet 8 inches tall, of a dark complexion, with a large scar on the back part of her right hand. She was born free, as appears by affidavit of Mrs. Jabez Wheeler.

REGISTRATION NO. 386
(Vol. 2)

Mary Hawkins   19 March 1847
George Hawkins

Mary Hawkins is about 36 years old, 5 feet 1 3/4 in tall, of a dark complexion, with a scar over her right eye. She was freed by the will of Margaret Hutchins. Mary has a son named George Hawkins who is about 11 years old.

VOLUME 3

1847-1861

REGISTRATION NO. 1[1]
(Vol. 3, p. 1)

Rachel Magruder 21 July 1847

Rachel Magruder is about 35 years old, 5 feet 3 1/8 inches tall, of a dark color, with a scar on the first joint of the forefinger of her right hand. She was born free, as appears by oath of John Ball.

REGISTRATION NO. 2
(Vol. 3, p. 1)

Henry Tate, alias Chase 21 July 1847

Henry Tate, alias Chase, is a bright mulatto who was 30 years old on 6 June 1847, 5 feet 7¼ inches tall, with a small scar on the back of the right hand. Tate was emancipated by Henry C. Herbert by deed recorded in Liber K, page 333, and was identified by John Ball.

REGISTRATION NO. 3
(Vol. 3, p. 1)

Ann Turner 21 July 1847

Ann Turner is a dark mulatto, about 50 years old, 5 feet 9¼ inches tall, with her right hand contracted and drawn awry by a burn, the little finger on that hand permanently crooked, the little finger on the other hand also injured and crooked, and a small incision on the top of her left ear. She was born free, as appears by evidence of Walter Harris.

REGISTRATION NO. 4
(Vol. 3, p. 1)

Cassandra Tate 21 July 1847

Cassandra Tate is a bright mulatto woman, about 48 years old, 5 feet 5 3/4 inches tall, with a small scar on her chin. She was born free.

REGISTRATION NO. 5
(Vol. 3, p. 1)

Susanna Webster 21 July 1847

Susanna Webster is a bright mulatto woman who was 55 years old on 5 March 1847. She is 5 feet 3/4 inches tall, cross-eyed, with a small scar on the first knuckle of the thumb of her right hand. She was born free, as appears by oath of Mary Ann Cole.

REGISTRATION NO. 6
(Vol. 3, p. 1)

Frances Ann Lane 21 July 1847

Frances Ann Lane was 33 years old on 7 January 1847, is 5 feet 3 5/8 inches tall, of a darkish mulatto color, with a small slender scar on her right hand between the thumb and forefinger that extends towards the back of her hand. She was born free, as appears by oath of Mary Ann Cole.

REGISTRATION NO. 7
(Vol. 3, p. 1)

Laurinda Handless 21 July 1847

Laurinda Handless was 18 years old on 9 October 1846, is 5 feet 1¼ inches tall, of a darkish mulatto color, with marks from smallpox on her face. She was born free, as appears by oath of Mary Ann Cole.

REGISTRATION NO. 8
(Vol. 3, p. 1)

Cecilia Jackson 21 July 1847

---

[1]In volume 3 the numbering of the registrations begins again at number 1 on page 81 of the volume and continues through number 581. There is no explanation for this duplication of numbers.

Cecilia Jackson is a dark mulatto woman, about 35 years old, 5 feet 3 inches tall, with two slender scars on her right arm below the elbow. She was born free, as appears by oath of Zenas Kinzey.

REGISTRATION NO. 9
(Vol. 3, p. 2)   21 July 1847

John Myers

John Myers is a bright mulatto man, about 27 years old, 5 feet 10 1/8 inches tall, with a scar on his right hand extending from the first joint of the little finger to the middle of the back of his hand, and a scar on the instep of his left foot. He was born free, as appears by oath of Joshua Bradley.

REGISTRATION NO. 10
(Vol. 3, p. 2)   21 July 1847

Milly Bennett

Milly Bennett is about 60 years old, 5 feet 1 3/4 inches tall, of a blackish color, with a mole on the back of her left ear. She was emancipated by John C. Herbert by deed recorded in Liber K, page 333.

REGISTRATION NO. 11
(Vol. 3, p. 2)   21 July 1847

Ann Hamilton

Ann Hamilton was 33 years old on 25 December 1846 and is 5 feet 3 3/4 inches tall. She is a bright mulatto, with two scars, one of which is very long, on the left side of her neck. She was emancipated in the same way as Milly Bennett [i.e., by John C. Herbert's deed recorded in Liber K, page 333.]

REGISTRATION NO. 12
(Vol. 3, p. 2)   21 July 1847

Harriet Washington

Harriet Washington is a bright mulatto who was 33 years old on 25 December 1846, is 5 feet 3 3/4 inches tall, with a long scar extending down her right cheek from her ear to a line even with the corner of her mouth. She was "Emancipated as above."

"Emancipated as above" probably means by deed of John C. Herbert recorded in Liber K, page 333. See No. 11 above.

REGISTRATION NO. 13
(Vol. 3, p. 2)   21 July 1847

Julia Noland

Julia Noland was 29 years old on 20 June 1847, is 5 feet 1¼ inches tall, of a brownish-black color, with a small black spot just above the corner of her left eye. She was born free, as appears by oath of George Bryan.

REGISTRATION NO. 14
(Vol. 3, p. 2)   21 July 1847

Elizabeth King

Elizabeth King was 26 years old on 28 August 1846, is 5 feet seven-eighths of an inch tall, of a brown-black color, with a small indentation at the right corner of her eye. She was born free, as appears by oath of George Bryan.

REGISTRATION NO. 15
(Vol. 3, p. 2)   21 July 1847

Benjamin Bennett

Benjamin Bennett was 24 years old on 4 January 1847, is 5 feet 9 3/4 inches tall, with a small scar across his forehead on the left side of his face near the edge of his hair, and a scar on the ball of his left thumb. He was born free, as appears by evidence of George Bryan.

REGISTRATION NO. 16
(Vol. 3, p. 2)

William Thomas Chinn   21 July 1847

William Thomas Chinn was 15 years old on 22 August 1846, is 5 feet 5 3/4 inches tall, of a brown-black color, with a faint small scar near the middle of his forehead. He was "Emancipated as above."

The statement that he was "Emancipated as above" (i.e., by John C. Herbert by deed in Liber K, page 333?) is probably a mistake. William is likely to be the brother of Georgianna registered below in No. 17. She was born free.

REGISTRATION NO. 17
(Vol. 3, p. 3)

Georgianna Virginia Chinn   22 July 1847

Georgianna Virginia Chinn is a bright mulatto who was 13 years old on 16 August 1846, is 5 feet 3 inches tall, with no visible marks or scars. She was born free.

REGISTRATION NO. 18
(Vol. 3, p. 3)

John Bigsby   22 July 1847

John Bigsby is about 15 years old, 5 feet tall, of a black color, with a small fresh scar just above the lower knuckle of his middle finger on the left hand. He was born free, as appears by evidence of Margaret [M.] Bangs.

REGISTRATION NO. 19
(Vol. 3, p. 3)

Sarah Moore Lancaster   22 July 1847

Sarah Lancaster, late Moore, was 44 years old last October, is a dark mulatto, 5 feet 2 inches tall, with a very faint scar on the back of her right wrist. She was free, as appears by a previous registration.

REGISTRATION NO. 20
(Vol. 3, p. 3)

Eliza Tate   24 July 1847

Eliza Tate is about 60 years old, 4 feet 9 3/4 inches tall, of a brownish-black color, with a scar on the top of her nose. She was born free.

REGISTRATION NO. 21
(Vol. 3, p. 3)

Hany Johnson   24 July 1847

Hany Johnson is about 57 years old, 5 feet three-eighths of an inch tall, of a brown color, with a small mark on his right cheek just below the eye. Johnson was born free.

REGISTRATION NO. 22
(Vol. 3, p. 3)

Eliza Green   24 July 1847

Eliza Green is a dark mulatto, about 36 years old, 5 feet 2 5/8 inches tall, with a small, slender, slightly curved and scarcely perceptible scar on her right cheek, and a black mole in the middle of her forehead. She was emancipated by Lucinda Walton, as appears by evidence of Robert Jamieson.

REGISTRATION NO. 23
(Vol. 3, p. 3)

Prince Hamilton   26 July 1847

Prince Hamilton is about 50 years old, 5 feet 6 5/8 inches tall, of a brownish-black color, with a faint scar on his forehead above the right eye and with the first and second fingers on his right hand injured and disfigured at their ends by frost[?]. He was emancipated by William C. "Garner" [Gardner], as appears by evidence of Samuel Bartle.

REGISTRATION NO. 24
(Vol. 3, p. 4)

Harriet Cupid   26 July 1847

Harriet Cupid is a dark mulatto, about 16 years old, 5 feet 1½ inches tall, with a small black mark in the palm of her right hand. She is the daughter of Linney Cupid and was born free, as appears by oath of William C. Reynolds.

REGISTRATION NO. 25
(Vol. 3, p. 4)

Catharine Cupid   26 July 1847

Catharine Cupid is a dark mulatto girl, 14 years old, 5 feet 1½ inches tall, with a scar just below her left temple. She is the daughter of Linney Cupid and was born free, as appears by oath of William C. Reynolds.

REGISTRATION NO. 26
(Vol. 3, p. 4)

Linney Cupid   26 July 1847

Linney Cupid is a bright mulatto, about 50 years old, 5 feet three-fourth inch tall, with a small scar on the right side of her face, near the lower jaw, and a mole on her cheek near the right nostril. She was born free.

REGISTRATION NO. 27
(Vol. 3, p. 4)

Andrew Butler   26 July 1847

Andrew Butler was 23 years old on 1 January 1846[1847?], is 5 feet 3½ inches tall, of a brownish-black color, with a scar on his left eyebrow and several small scars on the left side of his face. He was born free, as appears by oath of Samuel Miller, who swears he was born after the death of Mrs. Olivia Stone.

REGISTRATION NO. 28
(Vol. 3, p. 4)

Joshua Taylor   26 July 1847

Joshua Taylor is about 50 years old, 5 feet 4 7/8 inches tall, of a brownish-black color, with a bald head from the front to the crown. He was emancipated by the will of Olivia Stone.

REGISTRATION NO. 29
(Vol. 3, p. 4)

Celia Henry   26 July 1847

Celia Henry is about 43 years old, 5 feet 2 7/8 inches tall, of a brownish-black color, with a scar on the side of her left wrist. She was emancipated by the will of Olivia Stone recorded in Fairfax County.

REGISTRATION NO. 30
(Vol. 3, p. 4)

Lucy Ann Henry Jones   26 July 1847

Lucy Ann Jones, late Henry, is the daughter of Celia Henry. She was 21 years old on 22 April 1847, is 5 feet 2 5/8 inches tall, of a black color, and has a small scar on the back of the third finger of her right hand. She was freed by the will of Olivia Stone.

REGISTRATION NO. 31
(Vol. 3, p. 5)

Rosanna Henry   26 July 1847

Rosanna Henry was 20 years old on 9 July 1847, is 5 feet 1 1/8 inches tall, of a brown color, with two scars on the right side of her neck caused by a burn. She was freed by the will of Olivia Stone.

REGISTRATION NO. 32
(Vol. 3, p. 5)

Robert Henry, Jr.   26 July 1847

Robert Henry was 19 years old on 16 January 1847, is 5 feet 8¼ inches tall, of a black color, with a small scar at the outer corner of his left eye and three small scars in a curved line at the top of his collar bone. He was freed by the will of Olivia Stone.

REGISTRATION NO. 33
(Vol. 3, p. 5)

Robert Henry, Sr.　　　　　　　　　　　　　　　　　　　　　　　　　　　　　　26 July 1847

Robert Henry, Sr., was 44 years old on 1 July 1847, is 5 feet 7 1/8 inches tall, of a black color, with a small scar on the top of his nose and a scar on the back of his right hand. He was freed by the will of John Yates, as appears by a previous registration.

REGISTRATION NO. 34
(Vol. 3, p. 5)

Susan Henry　　　　　　　　　　　　　　　　　　　　　　　　　　　　　　26 July 1847

Susan Henry was 16 years old on 8 February 1847, is 5 feet 2 3/4 inches tall, of a black complexion, with a small scar on the back of her right hand. She was freed by the will of Olivia Stone.

REGISTRATION NO. 35
(Vol. 3, p. 5)

James Butler　　　　　　　　　　　　　　　　　　　　　　　　　　　　　　26 July 1847

James Butler is a bright mulatto, about 33 years old, 5 feet 7½ inches tall, with a mole on the side of his left wrist. He was born free.

REGISTRATION NO. 36
(Vol. 3, p. 5)

William Ford　　　　　　　　　　　　　　　　　　　　　　　　　　　　　　27 July 1847

William Ford is a bright mulatto man, about 33 years old, 5 feet 8¼ inches tall, with a scar on his left arm below the elbow caused by a burn. He was born free.

REGISTRATION NO. 37
(Vol. 3, p. 5)

Richard Jackson　　　　　　　　　　　　　　　　　　　　　　　　　　　　　　27 July 1847

Richard Jackson is about 18 years old, 5 feet 7 inches tall, of a brownish-black complexion, with a scar across the left corner of his mouth and a scar at the edge of his hair on the left side of his forehead. He was born free, as appears by evidence of Elihu Stanton.

REGISTRATION NO. 38
(Vol. 3, p. 6)

William Weaver　　　　　　　　　　　　　　　　　　　　　　　　　　　　　　27 July 1847

William Weaver is a bright mulatto man who was 44 years old on 4 March 1847. He is 5 feet 6½ inches tall with marks caused by smallpox and a small scar on the upper joint of his right thumb. Weaver was born free, as appears by evidence of R[obert] H. Miller.

REGISTRATION NO. 39
(Vol. 3, p. 6)

Nancy Brent　　　　　　　　　　　　　　　　　　　　　　　　　　　　　　27 July 1847

Nancy Brent is about 62 years old, 5 feet 1¼ inches tall, of a black complexion, with a small black mole on the left side of her nose and a scar on her left arm below the wrist. She was emancipated by Thomas Vowell by deed recorded in Liber N No. 2, page 252.

REGISTRATION NO. 40
(Vol. 3, p. 6)

Leannah Davis　　　　　　　　　　　　　　　　　　　　　　　　　　　　　　27 July 1847

Leannah Davis is a bright mulatto, about 32 years old, 5 feet 3 inches tall, with a very faint scar near the right corner of her left eyebrow. She was emancipated by the will of Samuel Adams in Fairfax County.

See No. 68 in Book 3 of the Fairfax County registrations. Leannah Johnson is the daughter of Ann Simms and the granddaughter of Milley Brown, who was freed by Samuel Adams in 1792. (Sweig, p. 124) See also No. 247 in Book 2 for Milley Brown. (Sweig, p. 91)

REGISTRATION NO. 41
(Vol. 3, p. 6)

Nathan Butler   28 July 1847

Nathan Butler is about 25 years old, 5 feet 2½ inches tall, of a black complexion, with a small scar on his left hand between the thumb and forefinger and with a stammer. He was freed by the will of Olivia Stone of Fairfax.

REGISTRATION NO. 42
(Vol. 3, p. 6)

John Cole   28 July 1847

John Cole is a dark mulatto, about 44 years old, 5 feet 5 1/8 inches tall, with a scar above his left eye and a long narrow scar on his right thumb between the first and second joints. He was born free, as appears by evidence of John Hollinsberry.

REGISTRATION NO. 43
(Vol. 3, p. 6)

James Bond   28 July 1847

James Bond is a dark mulatto, about 54 years old, 5 feet 5 3/4 inches tall, with his face scarred by an operation for cancer. He was emancipated by Joseph Grimes by deed recorded in Liber Y No. 2, page 174.

REGISTRATION NO. 44
(Vol. 3, p. 6)

Kinsey Ware   28 July 1847

Kinsey Ware was about 57 years old on 10 March 1847, is 5 feet 8 3/4 inches tall, and of a brownish-black complexion. He has a small scar on the back of his right hand at the root of his forefinger, a long circular scar on the same hand at the wrist, and the little finger of the same hand has been partly cut off. He was born free.

REGISTRATION NO. 45
(Vol. 3, p. 7)

Rosetta Wheeler   28 July 1847

Rosetta Wheeler is about 55 years old, 4 feet 11½ inches tall, of a black complexion, with a large scar on her left hand caused by a burn and a scar across her left eyebrow. She was freed by the will of Gabriel D. Childs in Fairfax. Wheeler is identified by Col. William Minor.

REGISTRATION NO. 46
(Vol. 3, p. 7)

Medora Wheeler   28 July 1847

Medora Wheeler is about 25 years old, 5 feet 1¼ inches tall, of a black complexion, with no visible scars or marks. She is the daughter of Rosetta Wheeler and was born free, as appears by evidence of Mrs. Sarah A. Jacobs.

REGISTRATION NO. 47
(Vol. 3, p. 7)

Lydia Ann Wheeler   28 July 1847

Lydia Ann Wheeler is about 18 years old, 5 feet one-fourth inch tall, of a brown-black complexion, with a scar under her left eye. She is the daughter of Rosetta Wheeler and was born free, as appears by evidence of Mrs. Sarah A. Jacobs.

REGISTRATION NO. 48
(Vol. 3, p. 7)

John Wheeler   28 July 1847

John Wheeler is about 21 years old, 5 feet 3 3/4 inches tall, of a black complexion, with a scar on his upper lip, another on his under lip and several small marks or scars scattered over his face and neck. He is the son of Rosetta Wheeler, and was born free, as appears by evidence of Mrs. Sarah A. Jacobs.

REGISTRATION NO. 49
(Vol. 3, p. 7)

Elizabeth Duvall

28 July 1847

Elizabeth Duvall is a bright mulatto, about 45 years old, 5 feet 3¼ inches tall, with a scar on the back of her left hand. She was born free, as appears by a former registration and the oath of Christopher Neale.

REGISTRATION NO. 50
(Vol. 3, p. 7)

Maria Dogan

28 July 1847

Maria Dogan is a bright mulatto, about 45 years old, 5 feet 4 inches tall, with freckles and scars from smallpox on her face. She was freed by Leonard Marbury by deed recorded in Liber O No. 2, page 435.

REGISTRATION NO. 51
(Vol. 3, p. 7)

Martha Ann Fletcher

29 July 1847

Martha Ann Fletcher is a dark mulatto who was 23 years old on 2 December 1846. She is 5 feet 1 inch tall and has a whitish mark on the right side of her neck. She was born free, as appears by evidence of Benjamin Lambert.

REGISTRATION NO. 52
(Vol. 3, p. 8)

Lydia Haney

29 July 1847

Lydia Haney is about 45 years old, 5 feet 1 inch tall, of a brown complexion, with a small scar on the right side of her arm below the elbow. She was born free, as appears by evidence of Zenas Kinzey.

REGISTRATION NO. 53
(Vol. 3, p. 8)

Susannah Dogan

29 July 1847

Sarah Dogan is a bright mulatto who was 18 years old on 7 March 1847, is 5 feet 5 inches tall, with two very small dark moles on her left nostril. She is the daughter of Betsey Duval and was born free, as appears by evidence of Turner Dixon.

REGISTRATION NO. 54
(Vol. 3, p. 8)

Christiana Logan

29 July 1847

Christiana Logan is about 24 years old, 5 feet 1½ inches tall, of a brownish-black complexion, with a dark mark from a burn on her left wrist and a small scar on her right wrist. She was born free, as appears by oath of Elizabeth Ferguson.

REGISTRATION NO. 55
(Vol. 3, p. 8)

Henry Dulaney

29 July 1847

Henry Dulaney is a bright mulatto, about 57 years old, 5 feet 10 inches tall, with a cataract in his left eye and bushy hair. He was born free, as appears by a previous registration.

REGISTRATION NO. 56
(Vol. 3, p. 8)

Joseph Frazier

29 July 1847

Joseph Frazier is a dark mulatto, about 54 years old, 5 feet 7 3/4 inches tall, with a scar just beneath his under lip near the right corner of his mouth. He was emancipated by Ezra Lunt as appears by Liber S No. 2, page 363 and a previous registration.

REGISTRATION NO. 57
(Vol. 3, p. 8)

John Credit   29 July 1847

John Credit is a bright mulatto who was 24 years old on 17 June 1847. He is 6 feet tall with a scar on the first knuckle of the forefinger of his left hand, a scar on the back of the same hand. He is the grandson of a white woman and was born free, as appears by oath of Mary Ann Cole.

REGISTRATION NO. 58
(Vol. 3, p. 8)

Ann Elizabeth Collins   29 July 1847

Ann Elizabeth Collins is a bright mulatto who will be 19 years old on 5 October 1847, is 4 feet 11 inches tall, with a scar over her left eye. She is the daughter of Ann Collins and was born free, as appears by oath of Elizabeth Ferguson.

REGISTRATION NO. 59
(Vol. 3, p. 9)

Ann Collins   29 July 1847

Ann Collins is a bright mulatto who will be 44 years old on 10 September 1847, is 5 feet tall, with a scar caused by a burn on her left cheek and has freckles. She was born free, as appears by information from Peter Hewitt.

REGISTRATION NO. 60
(Vol. 3, p. 9)

Eliza Cole   29 July 1847

Eliza Cole is about 32 years old, 5 feet 3¼ inches tall, of a brownish-black complexion, with a spot of white hair in her left eyebrow and with white hair on the back of her head near her neck. She was born free, as appears by a former registration.

REGISTRATION NO. 61
(Vol. 3, p. 9)

Kitty Smith   29 July 1847

Kitty Smith is about 19 years old, 5 feet 3 1/8 inches tall, of a black complexion, with a scar on the back of her left hand between the thumb and wrist. She was born free, as appears by a previous registration.

REGISTRATION NO. 62
(Vol. 3, p. 9)

Rosetta Craney   29 July 1847

Rosetta Craney is a bright mulatto who was 17 years old on 18 March 1847. She has a red mark on the top of her tongue and a scar on the right side of her neck. She was born free, as appears by oath of William H. Semmes.

REGISTRATION NO. 63
(Vol. 3, p. 9)

Robert H. Dogan   29 July 1847

Robert H. Dogan is a bright mulatto who was 21 years old on 9 April 1847, is 5 feet 7¼ inches tall, with a scar on his right eyebrow and a mole just in front of his left ear. He was born free.

REGISTRATION NO. 64
(Vol. 3, p. 9)

Richard Collins   29 July 1847

Richard Collins is a dark mulatto who will be 22 years old on 11 October 1847, is 5 feet 6 3/4 inches tall, with a scar on his right wrist and another across the back of his left hand made with blue ink. He is the son of Ann Collins and was born free, as appears by evidence of Peter Hewitt.

REGISTRATION NO. 65
(Vol. 3, p. 9)

Eliza Hawkins

29 July 1847

Eliza Hawkins was 37 years old on 15 April 1847, is 5 feet 3¼ inches tall, of a black complexion, with a small scar under her left eye and another on her right arm below the elbow. She was freed by the will of Margaret Hutchins.

REGISTRATION NO. 66
(Vol. 3, p. 10)

Horsley Gibbs

30 July 1847

Horsley Gibbs was 27 years old on 7 February 1847, is 5 feet 5¼ inches tall, of a brownish-black color, with a scar in his left eyebrow and two scars just above on his forehead. He was born free, as appears by oath of Matilda Bangs.

REGISTRATION NO. 67
(Vol. 3, p. 10)

Charity Anderson

30 July 1847

Charity Anderson is about 49 years old, 5 feet 2¼ inches tall, of a black complexion, with the first knuckle of the middle finger of her left hand enlarged and darkened by washing. She was emancipated by Samuel Anderson, as appears by a previous registration.

REGISTRATION NO. 68
(Vol. 3, p. 10)

Fanny Hall

30 July 1847

Fanny Hall is a dark mulatto, about 25 years old, 5 feet 2 3/4 inches tall, with a mole on her right nostril and another on the right side of her neck. She was born free, as appears by oath of William H. Seyton.

REGISTRATION NO. 69
(Vol. 3, p. 10)

Caroline Ware

30 July 1847

Caroline Ware is a dark mulatto, about 46 years old, 5 feet 4 inches tall, with a small scar on her right eyebrow, another above her left eyebrow, and another across her right arm below the elbow. She was emancipated by Lawrence Hooff.

REGISTRATION NO. 70
(Vol. 3, p. 10)

Cecelia Chase

30 July 1847

Cecelia Chase is about 25 years old, 5 feet 3 3/4 inches tall, of a brownish-black color, with no visible scars. She was born free.

REGISTRATION NO. 71
(Vol. 3, p. 10)

Jonathan Waters

30 July 1847

Jonathan Waters will be about 45 years old on 16 August 1847, is 5 feet 3 inches tall, with a large scar on his right temple. He was born free.

REGISTRATION NO. 72
(Vol. 3, p. 10)

Nancy Dudley

30 July 1847

Nancy Dudley is a bright mulatto, about 50 years old, 5 feet 7 inches tall, with a mole on her left cheek. She is the daughter of Mary Ann Cole, a white woman, and was born free.

REGISTRATION NO. 73
(Vol. 3, p. 11)

Mary Ann Cole

30 July 1847

Mary Ann Cole is a bright mulatto who will be 23 years old on 16 September 1847, is 5 feet 4½ inches tall, with a slightly freckled face. She was born free, as appears by oath of Mary Ann Cole, a white woman, who is her grandmother.

REGISTRATION NO. 74
(Vol. 3, p. 11)

Elizabeth Dudley   30 July 1847

Elizabeth Dudley is a bright mulatto who was 16 years old on 26 December 1846, and is 5 feet 2 1/8 inches tall, with a scar on her left eyebrow, a small scar just below that one, and another on her forehead. She was born free, as appears by oath of Mary Ann Cole.

REGISTRATION NO. 75
(Vol. 3, p. 11)

Betsey Henry   30 July 1847

Betsey Henry is about 42 years old, 4 feet 11 5/8 inches tall, of a black complexion, with her left eye out. She was born free, as appears by oath of C. Neale.

REGISTRATION NO. 76
(Vol. 3, p. 11)

Roxalina Ferguson   30 July 1847

Roxalina Ferguson is about 24 years old, 4 feet 11½ inches tall, of a brownish-black color, with two small scars on her forehead. She was born free, as appears by evidence of Sarah Vernon.

REGISTRATION NO. 77
(Vol. 3, p. 11)

Diana Brown   30 July 1847

Diana Brown is about 35 years old, 5 feet one-half inch tall, of a black complexion, with her face badly scarred, especially on her nose, by smallpox. She was born free, as appears by evidence of Mrs. Sarah Vernon.

REGISTRATION NO. 78
(Vol. 3, p. 11)

William Morrison   30 July 1847

William Morrison is a dark mulatto, about 57 years old, 5 feet 7½ inches tall, with no visible scars. He was emancipated by William Morgan.

REGISTRATION NO. 79
(Vol. 3, p. 11)

William Dudley   30 July 1847

William Dudley is a bright mulatto, about 47 years old, 5 feet 7 inches tall, with a scar about two inches long on his right leg caused by the blow of an axe, and hazel eyes. He was born free.

REGISTRATION NO. 80
(Vol. 3, p. 12)

Richard Henry Carter   30 July 1847

Richard Henry Carter is a bright mulatto who was 21 years old on 3 January 1847, is 5 feet 1 3/4 inches tall, and is slightly freckled. He was born free, as appears by information from Peter Hewitt.

REGISTRATION NO. 81
(Vol. 3, p. 12)

Celia Williams   30 July 1847

Celia Williams is about 47 years old, 5 feet 4 inches tall, of a black complexion, with a scar on her right arm below her elbow and another on her forehead. She was emancipated by Charles Scott, as appears by a previous registration.

REGISTRATION NO. 82
(Vol. 3, p. 12)

Mary Williams   30 July 1847

Mary Williams was 17 years old on 19 January 1847, is 5 feet 5¼ inches tall, of a lightish black color, with a small scar over her left eye, another on her upper lip, another on the back of her left hand, and one on her left wrist. She was born free, as appears by evidence of Ann Davis.

REGISTRATION NO. 83
(Vol. 3, p. 12)

Letitia Williams   30 July 1847

Letitia Williams will be 16 years old in October of 1847, is 5 feet 4¼ inches tall, of a brownish-black color, with a small scar at the corner of her left eye. She is the daughter of Celia Williams and was born free, as appears by evidence of James Dudley.

REGISTRATION NO. 84
(Vol. 3, p. 12)

Letty Frazier   30 July 1847

Letty Frazier is a bright mulatto, about 62 years old, 5 feet 3½ inches tall, with a small scar on the back of her left wrist. She was emancipated by Ezra Lunt by deed recorded in Liber S No. 2, page 363.

REGISTRATION NO. 85
(Vol. 3, p. 12)

Delilah Hopes   30 July 1847

Delilah Hopes is a bright mulatto who was about 37 years old on 10 March 1847, and is 5 feet 2 7/8 inches tall, with a small scar on the lower joint of the forefinger of her left hand. She was born free, as appears by evidence of Turner Dixon.

REGISTRATION NO. 86
(Vol. 3, p. 12)

Priscilla Darnell Ware   30 July 1847

Priscilla Ware, late Darnell, is a dark mulatto, about 30 years old, 5 feet one-half inch tall, with no visible marks. She was emancipated by Henry Darnell, as appears by a previous registration.

REGISTRATION NO. 87
(Vol. 3, p. 13)

James Carter   30 July 1847

James Carter is a bright mulatto, about 37 years old, 5 feet 3½ inches tall, with large black spots on his forehead and cheeks and a small scar on the palm of his left hand. He was born free, as appears by a previous registration.

REGISTRATION NO. 88
(Vol. 3, p. 13)

Lucy Jackson   30 July 1847

Lucy Jackson is a bright mulatto who was 48 years old on 11 March 1847. She is 5 feet 4¼ inches tall and has a scar on her right wrist. She was born free, as appears by information from Jonathan Ross.

REGISTRATION NO. 89
(Vol. 3, p. 13)

Nathaniel Jackson   30 July 1847

Nathaniel Jackson was 21 years old on 26 May 1847, is 5 feet 9½ inches tall, of a brownish-black color, with a scar on his right temple and another above his left eye. He was born free, as appears by information from Jonathan Ross.

REGISTRATION NO. 90
(Vol. 3, p. 13)

John Jackson   30 July 1847

John Johnson was 19 years old on 28 June 1847, is 5 feet 6½ inches tall, of a brown-black color, with a scar on the under side of his right hand. He was born free, as appears by information from Jonathan Ross.

REGISTRATION NO. 91
(Vol. 3, p. 13)

William Cupid   30 July 1847

William Cupid is about 24 years old, 5 feet 9¼ inches tall, of a brown-black color, with no visible scars. He is the son of Linney Cupid and was born free, as appears by oath of Josiah A. Davis.

REGISTRATION NO. 92
(Vol. 3, p. 13)

Ann Watson   31 July 1847

Ann Watson is a bright mulatto, about 66 years old, 5 feet 2 inches tall, with a light yellow scar on her left arm. She was born free.

REGISTRATION NO. 93
(Vol. 3, p. 13)

Eliza Weaver   31 July 1847

Eliza Weaver is a bright mulatto who was 38 years old on 13 February 1847, is 5 feet 2 5/8 inches tall, with a small scar over her right eye near the temple and a scar on the back of her left thumb where it joins her hand. She was born free, as appears by affirmation of Mrs. Sarah Bontz.

REGISTRATION NO. 94
(Vol. 3, p. 14)

Sarah Ann Weaver   31 July 1847

Sarah Ann Weaver is a dark mulatto who will be 19 years old on 31 December 1847, is 5 feet 2 3/4 inches tall, with a scar on the left side of her upper lip. She is the daughter of Eliza Weaver and was born free, as appears by affirmation of Mrs. Sarah Bontz.

REGISTRATION NO. 95
(Vol. 3, p. 14)

Ann Hutchinson   31 July 1847

Ann Hutchinson is a bright mulatto, about 40 years old, 5 feet 5/8 inches tall, with six or eight small black moles scattered over her face. She was emancipated by Robert S. Reed.

REGISTRATION NO. 96
(Vol. 3, p. 14)

Nancy Handless   31 July 1847

Nancy Handless is about 48 years old, 5 feet 3 3/4 inches tall, of a brownish-black color, with a black mole over her eye and a scar on her left hand. She was born free.

REGISTRATION NO. 97
(Vol. 3, p. 14)

Salina Stepney   31 July 1847

Selina Stepney is about 58 years old, 5 feet 2 1/8 inches tall, of a black complexion, with a scar on the right side of her chin. She was emancipated by Mrs. Hardy by deed recorded in Liber Q No. 2, page 370.

REGISTRATION NO. 98
(Vol. 3, p. 14)

Joanna Weaver   31 July 1847

Joanna Weaver is a bright mulatto who will be 16 years old on 18 November 1847, is 5 feet 2 inches tall, with a scar at the top of her forehead in the edge of her hair. She is the daughter of Eliza Weaver, and was born free, as appears by evidence of Turner Dixon.

REGISTRATION NO. 99
(Vol. 3, p. 14)

Nancy Beckley   31 July 1847

Nancy Beckley is a bright mulatto who was about 36 years old on 22 June 1847, is 5 feet 2½ inches tall, with a mole on her left lower eyelid. She was born free, as appears by affirmation of Mrs. Sarah Bontz.

REGISTRATION NO. 100
(Vol. 3, p. 14)

Jane Eliza Beckley   31 July 1847

Jane Eliza Beckley is a dark mulatto who will be 16 years old on 9 October 1847, is 4 feet 11½ inches tall, with a narrow scar on her right arm below the elbow. She was born free, as appears by evidence of Turner Dixon.

REGISTRATION NO. 101
(Vol. 3, p. 15)

Orris Redman   31 July 1847

Orris Redman is about 62 years old, 5 feet 4¼ inches tall, of a brown-black color, with no visible scars. She was emancipated by William Fowle.

REGISTRATION NO. 102
(Vol. 3, p. 15)

William Redman   31 July 1847

William Redman is a bright mulatto, about 28 years old, 5 feet 8½ inches tall, with a small scar under his left eye and another on each of his arms and with sandy hair. He was born free.

REGISTRATION NO. 103
(Vol. 3, p. 15)

Henry Lee   31 July 1847

Henry Lee will be 30 years old on 17 October 1847, is 5 feet 5 inches tall, of a brown-black color, with no visible marks. He was emancipated by Robert Hunter and Benoni Wheat, as appears by evidence of Robert W. Hunter.

REGISTRATION NO. 104
(Vol. 3, p. 15)

Nancy Loudoun   31 July 1847

Nancy Loudoun is about 43 years old, 5 feet 5 inches tall, of a brownish-black color, with a mole on the left side of her chin. She was born free, as appears by affirmation of Zenas Kinzey.

REGISTRATION NO. 105
(Vol. 3, p. 15)

Rachel Jarber   31 July 1847

Rachel Jarber is about 47 years old, 5 feet 3 inches tall, of a black complexion, with a scar on her left wrist. She was born free, as appears by affirmation of Zenas Kinzey.

REGISTRATION NO. 106
(Vol. 3, p. 15)

Henrietta Medella   31 July 1847

Henrietta Medella is about 46 years old, 5 feet 3 3/4 inches tall, of a brown-black color, with a mole on the top of her nose on the left side. She was born free, as appears by affirmation of Zenas Kinzey.

REGISTRATION NO. 107
(Vol. 3, p. 15)

John William Stepney   31 July 1847

John William Stepney was 32 years old on 1 May 1847, is 5 feet 6 3/4 inches tall, and has a black complexion. He has a large scar on the side of his left hand, several smaller scars near that one, and the forefinger of his right hand is scarred from having been split at the end. He was emancipated by Mrs. Hardy.

REGISTRATION NO. 108
(Vol. 3, p. 16)

Daniel Monroe

31 July 1847

Daniel Monroe is about 39 years old, 5 feet 3 inches tall, of a black complexion, with a scar on his forehead and a large scar on his left hand of a white and "sealy look." He was emancipated by Margaret S. Keith.

REGISTRATION NO. 109
(Vol. 3, p. 16)

Susan Whitley

31 July 1847

Susan Whitley is a dark mulatto, about 29 years old, 5 feet 3 inches tall, with a film over her left eye and a stiffness in her right arm, with slight marks from smallpox. She was emancipated by Francis Hagan's will.

REGISTRATION NO. 110
(Vol. 3, p. 16)

John Thornton

31 July 1847

John Thornton is a bright mulatto who will be 22 years old on 15 September 1847, is 5 feet 10 3/4 inches tall, with a scar on his right elbow. He was born free, as appears by evidence of Delia Simpson.

REGISTRATION NO. 111
(Vol. 3, p. 16)

William Beckley

31 July 1847

William Beckley is a dark mulatto who was 18 years old on 9 July 1847, is 5 feet 6 inches tall, with two scars on his left cheek. He is the son of Nancy Beckley and was born free, as appears by evidence of Turner Dixon.

REGISTRATION NO. 112
(Vol. 3, p. 16)

Maria Waters

31 July 1847

Maria Waters is a bright mulatto, about 37 years old, 5 feet 3¼ inches tall, with no visible scars, but with all but one of her upper front teeth gone. She is the daughter of Elizabeth Beckley and was born free, as appears by oath of Mary C. Thompson.

REGISTRATION NO. 113
(Vol. 3, p. 16)

Daniel Waters

31 July 1847

Daniel Waters is a dark mulatto who will be 20 years old on 1 April 1848, is 5 feet 3¼ inches tall, with no visible marks. He was born free, as appears by evidence of Elizabeth Ferguson.

REGISTRATION NO. 114
(Vol. 3, p. 16)

Robert Johnson

31 July 1847

Robert Johnson is about 33 years old, 5 feet 10 3/4 inches tall, of a black complexion, with a scar on the top of his head, two small scars on his forehead, and his right little finger is crooked. He was born free, as appears by evidence of Moses O. B. Cawood.

REGISTRATION NO. 115
(Vol. 3, p. 17)

Mary Fox

31 July 1847

Mary Fox is about 60 years old, 5 feet 4 3/4 inches tall, of a black complexion, with a mole under her left eye. She was emancipated by Benjamin Brady's will.

REGISTRATION NO. 116
(Vol. 3, p. 17)

Ann Kennedy

31 July 1847

Ann Kennedy is a bright mulatto, about 52 years old, 5 feet one-fourth inch tall, with a scar on her left cheek and another on the left side of her head. She was born free, as appears by oath of Sarah Moore.

REGISTRATION NO. 117
(Vol. 3, p. 17)

Eliza Noland

31 July 1847

Eliza Noland is about 35 years old, 5 feet 3¼ inches tall, of a brownish-black color, with two scars on the left side of her face. She was born free, as appears by oath of Dolly Williams.

REGISTRATION NO. 118
(Vol. 3, p. 17)

Julia Cooper

31 July 1847

Julia Cooper is a bright mulatto, about 32 years old, 5 feet 2½ inches tall, with a red mark on the lower end of her right cheek. She was born free, as appears by information from Peter Hewitt.

REGISTRATION NO. 119
(Vol. 3, p. 17)

William Robert Hamilton

31 July 1847

William Robert Hamilton was 16 years old on 23 January 1847, is 5 feet 6 3/4 inches tall, of a brownish-black color, with a scar on his left forefinger. He was born free, as appears by evidence of Turner Dixon.

REGISTRATION NO. 120
(Vol. 3, p. 17)

Mary Ann Maria Hamilton

31 July 1847

Mary Ann Maria Hamilton is a bright mulatto who was 14 years old on 30 December 1846, is 5 feet one-fourth inch tall, with a scar on her left cheek and gray eyes. She was born free, as appears by evidence of Turner Dixon.

REGISTRATION NO. 121
(Vol. 3, p. 17)

Patsey Hopes

31 July 1847

Patsey Hopes is a dark mulatto, about 57 years old, 5 feet 2 inches tall, with a mole above the corner of her right eye and with the third finger of her right hand shortened and the fingernail turned over. She was born free, as appears by evidence of Mrs. Jane Rye.

REGISTRATION NO. 122
(Vol. 3, p. 17)

Gracey Quander

4 August 1847

Gracey Quander is about 36 years old, 5 feet one-half inch tall, of a black complexion, with a scar on her left forefinger and another on her left arm. She was born free, as appears by evidence of Elizabeth Semmes. She is the daughter of Nancy, who is now dead, but whose registration is filed.

See No. 137 in Book 2 of the Fairfax County registrations. Gracy Quander is the daughter of Nancy, who was freed by General Washington. (Sweig, p. 63)

REGISTRATION NO. 123
(Vol. 3, p. 18)

Elizabeth Hinds

31 July 1847

Elizabeth Hinds is about 16 years old, 5 feet 3 5/8 inches tall, of a brownish-black color, with a scar on her right wrist. She was born free.

REGISTRATION NO. 124
(Vol. 3, p. 18)

Maria Hinds   31 July 1847

Maria Hinds is about 36 years old, 5 feet 2¼ inches tall, of a black complexion, with a mole on her right thumb. She is the daughter of Agnes who was manumitted by General Washington. Maria was born free, as appears by oath of Mrs. David Allen.

See note accompanying the registration of Maria's sister, Joanna Gowens in Vol. 3, No. 220.

REGISTRATION NO. 125
(Vol. 3, p. 18)

Charles Williams   31 July 1847

Charles Williams is a dark mulatto who was 23 years old on 5 July 1847, is 5 feet 6 inches tall, with a scar above his right eye, two scars or marks on his right cheek, and a scar at the left corner of his mouth. He was born free, as appears by oath of Jesse Skidmore.

REGISTRATION NO. 126
(Vol. 3, p. 18)

Rozier D. Beckley   31 July 1847

Rozier [D.] Beckley is a bright mulatto, about 16 years old, 5 feet 7 inches tall, with a mole on his upper lip. He was born free, as appears by evidence of Mrs. Delia Simpson.

REGISTRATION NO. 127
(Vol. 3, p. 18)

Stephen Stepney   31 July 1847

Stephen Stepney was 18 years old on 30 April 1847, is 5 feet 4 3/4 inches tall, of a black complexion, with no visible scars. He was born free, as appears by oath of John F. Dyer.

REGISTRATION NO. 128
(Vol. 3, p. 18)

Mary Ann Jefferson   31 July 1847

Mary Ann Jefferson is about 36 years old, 5 feet 2 3/4 inches tall, of a black complexion, with no visible scars. She was born free.

REGISTRATION NO. 129
(Vol. 3, p. 18)

Chloe Ann Jefferson   31 July 1847

Chloe Ann Jefferson is a bright mulatto who will be 16 years old in September of 1847, is 5 feet 4 inches tall, with a faint scar at the corner of her left eye. She was born free, as appears by evidence of George McLish.

REGISTRATION NO. 130
(Vol. 3, p. 19)

Robert Kennedy   31 July 1847

Robert Kennedy is a dark mulatto who was 16 years old on 15 February 1847, is 5 feet 2 3/4 inches tall, with a scar on his forehead. He was born free, as appears by evidence of Matilda Moss.

REGISTRATION NO. 131a
(Vol. 3, p. 19)

George Craney   31 July 1847

George Craney is a dark mulatto, about 16 years old, 4 feet 10¼ inches tall, with a mark on his left temple near the eye. He was born free, as appears by oath of William H. Semmes.

REGISTRATION NO. 131b
(Vol. 3, p. 19)

John Henry Hall   31 July 1847

John Henry Hall is a dark mulatto who will be 10 years old on 15 August 1847, is 4 feet 5 3/4 inches tall, with a scar on his left hand between the thumb and forefinger. He was born free, as appears by information and oath of Joanna Lyle.

REGISTRATION NO. 132
(Vol. 3, p. 19)

Sarah Obleton   31 July 1847

Sarah Obleton is about 22 years old, 5 feet 4¼ inches tall, of a brown-black complexion, with two scars on the back of her right hand, another on the thumb of that same hand, and a small spot on her chin. She was born free.

REGISTRATION NO. 133
(Vol. 3, p. 19)

Sally Logan   31 July 1847

Sally Logan is about 39 years old, 5 feet 1¼ inches tall, of a brownish-black color, with a large scar on her right arm near the elbow caused by a burn, another between the thumb and forefinger of her right hand, and a reddish mark on her right cheekbone. She was emancipated by Peter Loggins.

REGISTRATION NO. 134
(Vol. 3, p. 19)

John Logan   31 July 1847

John Logan is about 20 years old, 5 feet 7 inches tall, of a black complexion, with a scar above his left eye and a small knot above his right eye. He was born free, as appears by oath of Elizabeth Ferguson.

REGISTRATION NO. 135
(Vol. 3, p. 19)

William Mills   31 July 1847

William Mills is a dark mulatto, about 24 years old, 5 feet 7 inches tall, with a small scar on the right side of his head and a scar on his forehead near the edge of his hair. He is the son of Rachel Mills and was born free, as appears by evidence of Cornelius Taylor.

REGISTRATION NO. 136
(Vol. 3, p. 20)

Eliza Johnson   31 July 1847

Eliza Johnson is a bright mulatto, about 18 years old, 5 feet 2 3/4 inches tall, with a scar on the left side of her chin and a scar on the right side of her neck. She was born free.

REGISTRATION NO. 137
(Vol. 3, p. 20)

Betsey Smith   2 August 1847

Betsey Smith is about 40 years old, 4 feet 11 3/4 inches tall, of a brownish-black color, with a scar just below the left corner of her mouth. She was emancipated by Richard Davis by deed recorded in Fairfax County.

REGISTRATION NO. 138
(Vol. 3, p. 20)

Daniel Ford   2 August 1847

Daniel Ford is a dark mulatto who was 31[?] years old on 2 June 1847, is 5 feet 7 3/4 inches tall, with a scar in the middle of his forehead and a mole on his left hand near the thumb. He was born free, as appears by a previous registration.

REGISTRATION NO. 139
(Vol. 3, p. 20)

Rebecca Frazier   3 August 1847

Rebecca Frazier will be 19 years old on 17 September 1847, is 5 feet 5½ inches tall, of a brownish-black color, with no visible marks except some warts on the knuckles of her right hand. She was born free, as appears by evidence of John [B.] Hancock.

REGISTRATION NO. 140
(Vol. 3, p. 20)

Daniel Bruce

August, 1847

Daniel Bruce is a bright mulatto who will be 68 years old on 20 August 1847, is 5 feet 4 3/4 inches tall, with a mark on his left wrist. He was emancipated by Colin Auld.

REGISTRATION NO. 141
(Vol. 3, p. 20)

George Solomon

August, 1847

George Solomon is about 57 years old, 5 feet 7 3/4 inches tall, of a black complexion, with a small scar on the right side of his upper lip. He was emancipated by Christopher Frye.

REGISTRATION NO. 142
(Vol. 3, p. 20)

Richard Berry

2 August 1847

Richard Berry is about 41 years old, 5 feet 7 5/8 inches tall, of a brownish-black complexion, with a scar on his right jaw and a very faint scar on his forehead. He was born free.

REGISTRATION NO. 143
(Vol. 3, p. 21)

William Gray

2 August 1847

William Gray is a bright mulatto, about 22 years old, 5 feet 9¼ inches tall, with no visible marks. He was born free, as appears by oath of Jesse Skidmore.

REGISTRATION NO. 144
(Vol. 3, p. 21)

Wesley Darnall

2 August 1847

Wesley Darnall is a dark mulatto, about 22 years old, 5 feet 8½ inches tall, with a scar on the top of his nose, another on his forehead, and another in his left eyebrow. He was born free, as appears by information from Jonathan Ross.

REGISTRATION NO. 145
(Vol. 3, p. 21)

Mary Bennett

2 August 1847

Mary Bennett is a bright mulatto, about 34 years old, 5 feet 4 inches tall, with a scar on her left arm above the elbow. She was born free.

REGISTRATION NO. 146
(Vol. 3, p. 21)

Catharine Stanly Helm

2 August 1847

Catharine Helm, late Stanly, is about 35 years old, 5 feet one-half inch tall, of a brownish-black color, with a small round scar on her chin. She was born free.

REGISTRATION NO. 147
(Vol. 3, p. 21)

Charlotte Burrell

2 August 1847

Charlotte Burrell is a dark mulatto, about 44 years old, 5 feet one-half inch tall, with two small scars on her right thumb. She was emancipated by James Frazer.

REGISTRATION NO. 148
(Vol. 3, p. 21)

Henson Turley   7 September 1847

Henson Turley is a dark mulatto, about 55 years old, 5 feet 5 3/4 inches tall, with a scar on the back of his left hand. He was emancipated by Hannah B. Territt by deed dated 24 August 1847.

REGISTRATION NO. 149
(Vol. 3, p. 21)

Robert Sumby   5 August 1847

Robert Sumby was 33 years old on 8 February 1847, is 5 feet 4¼ inches tall, of a brownish-black color, with a large scar on his breast from a scald, and another on the back of his left hand. He was born free, as appears by evidence from Zenas Kinzey.

REGISTRATION NO. 150
(Vol. 3, p. 21)

Rebecca Dogan   5 August 1847

Rebecca Dogan is a bright mulatto, about 18 years old, 5 feet 4¼ inches tall, with a scar on the third little finger of her left hand and with freckles. She was born free and is the daughter of Jane Dogan who always passed as free, as appears by oath of John Leadbeater.

REGISTRATION NO. 151
(Vol. 3, p. 22)

Nathaniel Oden   2 August 1847

Nathaniel Oden is a bright mulatto, about 26 years old, 5 feet 7 3/4 inches tall, with the mark of a heart on the back of his left hand. He was born free, as appears by oath of Robert W. Hunter.

REGISTRATION NO. 152
(Vol. 3, p. 22)

Alexander Douglas   2 August 1847

Alexander Douglas is a bright mulatto, about 36 years old, 5 feet 7¼ inches tall, with a scar on the knuckles of the second and third fingers of his right hand. He was emancipated by John Hunter, as appears by evidence of Robert W. Hunter.

REGISTRATION NO. 153
(Vol. 3, p. 22)

Alexander Bowden   2 August 1847

Alexander Bowden is a very bright mulatto who will be 21 years old on 18 October 1847, is 6 feet 1 3/4 inches tall, with a scar on the knuckle of the third finger of his right hand, sleepy eyes, and reddish hair. He was born free, as appears by evidence of Robert W. Hunter.

REGISTRATION NO. 154
(Vol. 3, p. 22)

Nancy White   2 August 1847

Nancy White is about 50 years old, 5 feet tall, of a black complexion, with a scar between her eyebrows. She is free, as appears by evidence of Miss Hannah Walton.

REGISTRATION NO. 155
(Vol. 3, p. 22)

Elias Thomson   2 August 1847

Elias Thomson is a bright mulatto, about 34 years old, 5 feet 9¼ inches tall, with a scar on his right cheek on the lower jaw bone. He was born free, as appears by information from Peter Hewitt.

REGISTRATION NO. 156
(Vol. 3, p. 22)

Matilda Shields   2 August 1847

Matilda Shields is about 40 years old, 5 feet 1½ inches tall, of a black complexion, with a scar on her right arm in line with the elbow. He was emancipated by William Goddard, as appears by a previous registration.

REGISTRATION NO. 157
(Vol. 3, p. 22)

Sinah Ann Peters

2 August 1847

Sinah Ann Peters is a dark mulatto, about 26 years old, 5 feet 3 inches tall, with her upper teeth missing. She was born free, as appears by evidence from Richard K. Lee.

REGISTRATION NO. 158
(Vol. 3, p. 23)

Robert Dogan

ca. 2 August 1847

Robert Dogan is a bright mulatto, 21 years old, with a scar on his right eyebrow, and a mole near his left ear. He is the son of Betsey Dogan and was born free, as appears by information from Peter Hewitt. See No. 63 [on page 164].

REGISTRATION NO. 159
(Vol. 3, p. 23)

Charles Bruce

ca. 2 August 1847

Charles Bruce has no visible marks or scars except a small one on his left wrist. See No. 266 [on page 188].

REGISTRATION NO. 160
(Vol. 3, p. 23)

Louisa Lacey

ca. 2 August 1847

Louisa Lacey is a dark mulatto, about 32 years old, 5 feet 2 3/4 inches tall, with a scar on her left cheek, a mole on her right cheek and a scar on her right wrist. She was emancipated by John C. Herbert, as appears by oath of Robert Brocket[t].

REGISTRATION NO. 161
(Vol. 3, p. 23)

Mary Ann Ramsay

3 August 1847

Mary Ann Ramsay will be 29 years old on 29 October 1847, is 5 feet 3 inches tall, of a black complexion, with a scar on her right wrist and another on her left wrist. She was emancipated by John C. Herbert, as appears by oath of Robert Brockett.

REGISTRATION NO. 162
(Vol. 3, p. 23)

Lewis Campbell

3 August 1847

Lewis Campbell is a dark mulatto, about 70 years old, 5 feet 9 inches tall. He has two scars on his right cheek, one reaching the corner of his mouth; one scar on his left cheek; and two others on the same cheek, meeting in a point in front of the [word left out]; and one on his chin. The middle finger of his right hand is crooked and deformed. Campbell was emancipated by William Fowle and Henry Daingerfield, as appears by a previous registration.

REGISTRATION NO. 163
(Vol. 3, p. 23)

Nelly Short

3 August 1847

Nelly Short is a dark mulatto, about 57 years old, 5 feet one-half inch tall, with several light spots on the right side of her face. She was manumitted in Maryland by the will of Arthelia Mullan dated 15 March 1822.

REGISTRATION NO. 164
(Vol. 3, p. 24)

William Evans

3 August 1847

William Evans is a dark mulatto, about 64 years old, 5 feet 9¼ inches tall, with no visible marks. He was born free, as appears by a previous registration.

Volume 3, 1847-1861

REGISTRATION NO. 165
(Vol. 3, p. 24)

William H. Hatton

3 August 1847

William H. Hatton is a bright mulatto, about 33 years old, 5 feet 8 inches tall, with two small scars on the back of his right hand and a black mole on the left side of his nose. He was born free, as appears by a previous registration.

REGISTRATION NO. 166
(Vol. 3, p. 24)

Fanny Mark

4 August 1847

Fanny Mark is a dark mulatto, about 38 years old, 5 feet 5½ inches tall, with a scar on the left side of her neck. She was emancipated by William Butler Callicot, as appears by a previous registration.

REGISTRATION NO. 167
(Vol. 3, p. 24)

Jane Frazier

3 August 1847

Jane Frazier is about 35 years old, 5 feet 4½ inches tall, of a dark color, with a mark at the left corner of her mouth. She was emancipated by Ezra Lunt and identified by Samuel Lunt.

REGISTRATION NO. 168
(Vol. 3, p. 24)

Ann Seals

3 August 1847

Ann Seals is a dark mulatto, about 24 years old, 5 feet 1½ inches tall, with a scar on the left side of her neck. She is the daughter of Susan Seals and was born free, as appears by evidence of Peter [G.] Henderson.

REGISTRATION NO. 169
(Vol. 3, p. 24)

Winny Banks

ca. 3 August 1847

Winny Banks is about 50 years old, 4 feet 11 inches tall, of a black complexion, with a scar over her left eye. She was emancipated by Mrs. Margaret Shreve and identified by Benjamin Dennison.

REGISTRATION NO. 170
(Vol. 3, p. 24)

Samuel Coats

ca. 3 August 1847

Samuel Coats is about 23 years old, 5 feet 5¼ inches tall, with a small scar on his right cheek and another on the back of his left thumb. He is the son of Winny Banks and was born free, as appears by evidence of Benjamin Dennison.

REGISTRATION NO. 171
(Vol. 3, p. 24)

Nancy Johnson

3 August 1847

Nancy Johnson is about 46 years old, 5 feet one-fourth inch tall, of a black complexion, with no visible marks. She was born free, as appears by a previous registration.

REGISTRATION NO. 172
(Vol. 3, p. 25)

Henrietta Taylor

4 August 1847

Henrietta Taylor is a dark mulatto, about 24 years old, 5 feet 3 5/8 inches tall, with a scar on her right arm. She was born free, as appears by a previous registration.

REGISTRATION NO. 173
(Vol. 3, p. 25)

Lydia Ann Taylor

4 August 1847

Lydia Ann Taylor is a dark mulatto, about 32 years old, 5 feet 2 3/4 inches tall, with a scar on her nose caused by a burn. She was born free, as appears by a previous registration.

REGISTRATION NO. 174
(Vol. 3, p. 25)

Jeremiah H. Frazer   3 August 1847

Jeremiah H. Frazier is about 29 years old, 5 feet 2½ inches tall, of a brownish-black color, with a small scar on his right wrist and a scar on his left eyebrow. He was born free, as appears by a previous registration.

REGISTRATION NO. 175
(Vol. 3, p. 25)

Mary Ellen Johnston   ca. 3 August 1847

Mary Ellen Johnston is about 20 years old, 5 feet 2 inches tall, of a brownish-black color, with no visible marks. She was born free, as appears by a previous registration.

REGISTRATION NO. 176
(Vol. 3, p. 25)

George Seaton   3 August 1847

George Seaton is a dark mulatto, about 26 years old, 5 feet 10 3/4 inches tall, with a scar on his right cheek, another just below his under lip, and another on the back of his right hand. He was born free, as appears by oath of Mrs. Jane Rye.

REGISTRATION NO. 177
(Vol. 3, p. 25)

Sarah Brooks   3 August 1847

Sarah Brooks is a bright mulatto, about 23 years old, 5 feet 1 3/4 inches tall, with a large mole on her chin. She was born free, as appears by evidence by Sarah Loveless.

REGISTRATION NO. 178
(Vol. 3, p. 25)

Ann Laws Oden   ca. 3 August 1847

Ann Oden, late Laws, is a very bright mulatto, about 24 years old, 5 feet 3½ inches tall, with a mole on her neck, freckles, and gray eyes. She was emancipated by Nathaniel Oden.

REGISTRATION NO. 179
(Vol. 3, p. 25)

William Williams   4 August 1847

William Williams is about 60 years old, 5 feet 5 inches tall, of a brownish-black color, with his left eye "out nearly." He was manumitted by Colin Auld.

REGISTRATION NO. 180
(Vol. 3, p. 26)

Jemima Harris   2 August 1847

Jemima Harris is a bright mulatto, about 60 years old, 5 feet 2 inches tall, with several small moles near her right eye. She was emancipated by John C. Herbert, as appears by evidence of Peter Hewitt.

REGISTRATION NO. 181
(Vol. 3, p. 26)

Jane Gales   2 August 1847

Jane Gales is a dark mulatto, about 29 years old, 5 feet three-fourths of an inch tall, with a very slight mark on her right arm caused by a burn. She is the daughter of Jemima Harris, and was born free, as appears by Alexander Moore's certificate.

REGISTRATION NO. 182
(Vol. 3, p. 26)

Judith Ford Rogers   3 August 1847

Judith Ford, now Rogers, is a bright mulatto, about 27 years old, 5 feet 5 inches tall, with the third fingernail of her right hand slightly injured and her hair "inclined to a sandy colour." She was born free, as appears by a previous registration.

REGISTRATION NO. 183
(Vol. 3, p. 26)

Nelson Bentley   4 August 1847

Nelson Bentley is a bright mulatto, about 49 years old, 5 feet 8 3/4 inches tall, with a scar on the back of his right hand. He is free, as appears by evidence of Theodore Meade

REGISTRATION NO. 184
(Vol. 3, p. 26)

William Jones   2 August 1847

William Jones is about 29[?] years old, 5 feet 4 inches tall, of a black complexion, with a scar on his left knee caused by a cut. He is the son of Nancy Jones who was emancipated by General Washington. William was born free, as appears by oath of Mrs. David Allen.

REGISTRATION NO. 185
(Vol. 3, p. 26)

Jane Dyson   ca. 2 August 1847

Jane Dyson is about 29 years old, 5 feet one-half inch tall, of a black complexion, with two scars on the back of her left hand that cross each other. She was born free, as appears by oath of James McGuire.

REGISTRATION NO. 186
(Vol. 3, p. 26)

Chloe Ann Grant   ca. 2 August 1847

Chloe Ann Grant is about 30 years old, 5 feet 3¼ inches tall, of a black complexion, with no visible marks. She was born free, as appears by oath of James McGuire.

REGISTRATION NO. 187
(Vol. 3, p. 26)

William E. Tate   4 August 1847

William E. Tate is a dark mulatto, about 28 years old, 5 feet 6 inches tall, with a scar in the palm of his left hand. He was born free, as appears by a previous registration.

REGISTRATION NO. 188
(Vol. 3, p. 27)

Hannah Lee   3 August 1847

Hannah Lee is about 40 years old, 4 feet 10 inches tall, of a black complexion, with a scar on her right arm. She was emancipated by the will of Thomas G. Harden.

REGISTRATION NO. 189
(Vol. 3, p. 27)

Mary Lee   3 August 1847

Mary Lee is a bright mulatto, about 20 years old, 5 feet 1¼ inches tall, with a scar on her right eyebrow and freckles. She is the daughter of Hannah Lee and was born free, as appears by oath of Mrs. Monica Foy.

REGISTRATION NO. 190
(Vol. 3, p. 27)

Louisa Hatton Ford   3 August 1847

Louisa Hatton, now Ford, is a bright mulatto, about 27 years old, 5 feet 5 inches tall, with a scar at the end of the third finger of her right hand. She was emancipated by Joseph Hatton.

REGISTRATION NO. 191
(Vol. 3, p. 27)

John Campbell   3 August 1847

John Campbell is about 45 years old, 5 feet 11 inches tall, of a black complexion, with a scar on his left nostril and another on his left arm. He was emancipated by the will of William Goddard, as appears by evidence of Turner Dixon.

REGISTRATION NO. 192
(Vol. 3, p. 27)

Betsey Campbell   ca. 3 August 1847

Betsey Campbell is about 35 years old, 5 feet 4 3/4 inches tall, of a brownish-black color, with a scar on the left side of her neck. She was born free, as appears by evidence of Thomas Slatford.

There is no registration No. 193.

REGISTRATION NO. 194
(Vol. 3, p. 27)

Corrill Rodgers   ca. 3 August 1847

Corrill Rodgers is a bright mulatto, about 34 years old, 5 feet 7 inches tall, with a small scar on the forefinger of his left hand. He is free, as appears by a previous registration.

REGISTRATION NO. 195
(Vol. 3, p. 27)

George Simms   ca. 3 August 1847

George Simms is a bright mulatto, about 36 years old, 5 feet 10 inches tall, with a scar on the back of his left hand and another on the forefinger of his left hand. He was born free, as appears by a previous registration.

REGISTRATION NO. 196
(Vol. 3, p. 27)

Mary Anderson   3 August 1847

Mary Anderson is a mulatto, about 24 years old, 5 feet 5½ inches tall, with a scar on her forehead. She is slightly freckled with thick lips. Mary is the daughter of Betsey Davis and was born free, as appears by evidence from Ferdinand O'Neale.

REGISTRATION NO. 197
(Vol. 3, p. 28)

Phillis Jackson   3 August 1847

Phillis Jackson is about 40 years old, 5 feet 7¼ inches tall, of a black complexion, with a scar on her right cheek. She was emancipated by the will of Sarah Monroe, by Monroe's executor, W[illiam] N. Mills, as he so swears.

REGISTRATION NO. 198
(Vol. 3, p. 28)

Helen Simms   ca. 3 August 1847

Helen Simms is a bright mulatto, about 28 years old, 5 feet 2¼ inches tall, with a black mole on her left cheek. She was born free, as appears by a previous registration.

REGISTRATION NO. 199
(Vol. 3, p. 28)

Maria Hughes   ca. 3 August 1847

Maria Hughes is about 55 years old, 5 feet 4 inches tall, of a black complexion, with marks on her face from smallpox. She was emancipated by the will of William H. Wilmer dated 27 November 1826 and was identified by Turner Dixon.

REGISTRATION NO. 200
(Vol. 3, p. 28)

Roxana Medella ca. 3 August 1847

Roxana Medella is a dark mulatto, about 16 years old, 5 feet 5 inches tall, with a slight scar on her right eyebrow. She is the daughter of Maria Hughes and was born free, as appears by evidence of Turner Dixon.

REGISTRATION NO. 201
(Vol. 3, p. 28)

Susan Medella 3 August 1847

Susan Medella is a dark mulatto, about 18 years old, 4 feet 11 3/4 inches tall, with no visible marks. She is the daughter of Maria Hughes, and was born free, as appears by evidence of Turner Dixon.

REGISTRATION NO. 202
(Vol. 3, p. 28)

James Tyler Darnall ca. 3 Aug. 1847

James Tyler Darnall is a dark mulatto, about 26 years old, 5 feet 7½ inches tall, with a scar on his under lip. He was born free, as appears by evidence of Jonathan Ross.

REGISTRATION NO. 203
(Vol. 3, p. 28)

Smith Alexander Johnson 3 August 1847

Smith Alexander Johnson is about 22 years old, 5 feet one-fourth inch tall, of a black complexion, with several slight scars on his forehead and a scar on the third finger of his left hand extending on the back of the hand. He was born free, as appears by oath of J[ohn] G[ibson] Peach.

REGISTRATION NO. 204
(Vol. 3, p. 29)

David Hughes 3 August 1847

David Hughes is about 65 years old, 5 feet 6 3/4 inches tall, of a black complexion, with no visible marks. He was emancipated by Hugh "Carolin" [Caroline] by deed dated 1 December 1836 and was identified by Samuel Bartle.

REGISTRATION NO. 205
(Vol. 3, p. 29)

Mary Ann Colbert ca. 3 August 1847

Mary Ann Colbert is about 18 years old, 5 feet one-half inch tall, of a black complexion, with no visible marks. She was born free, as appears by a previous registration.

REGISTRATION NO. 206
(Vol. 3, p. 29)

Patsy Berry 3 August 1847

Polly Berry is a dark mulatto, about 49 years old, 5 feet 1½ inches tall, with three scars on her right arm, one above her elbow, and two on her breast. She was emancipated by John C. Herbert, as appears by a previous registration.

REGISTRATION NO. 207
(Vol. 3, p. 29)

Ely Whitler 3 August 1847

Ely Whitler is about 36 years old, 5 feet 8 inches tall, of a black complexion, with a small scar on each of his eyebrows. He was emancipated by the will of Francis Hagan.

REGISTRATION NO. 208
(Vol. 3, p. 29)

Jane Davis ca. 3 August 1847

Jane Davis is a dark mulatto, about 28 years old, 5 feet 7 3/4 inches tall, with a small scar on her forehead. She was born free, as appears by evidence of Henry "Tates Paugh" [Tatsepaugh].

REGISTRATION NO. 209
(Vol. 3, p. 29)

George Jackson   4 August 1847

George Jackson is about 30 years old, 5 feet 7 3/4 inches tall, of a brownish-black color, with two small, very faint scars on his right cheek and a small scar on the back of his left hand from a burn. He was emancipated by the will of Sarah Monroe by Monroe's executor, William N. Mills, as he so swears.

REGISTRATION NO. 210
(Vol. 3, p. 29)

Daniel Davis   3 August 1847

Daniel Davis is a dark mulatto, about 20 years old, 5 feet 3 3/4 inches tall, with a scar from cupping on the back of his neck and a scar on the back of his left hand. He is the son of Betsey Davis and was born free, as appears by evidence of Ferdinand O'Neale.

REGISTRATION NO. 211
(Vol. 3, p. 29)

Francis Williams   3 August 1847

Francis Williams is about 44 years old, 5 feet 8½ inches tall, of a brownish-black color, with no visible marks. Williams was emancipated by Charles Lewis, as appears by a previous registration.

REGISTRATION NO. 212
(Vol. 3, p. 30)

Arabella Clarke Webster   ca. 3 August 1847

Arabella Webster, late Clarke, is about 36 years old, 5 feet 4 3/4 inches tall, of a brownish-black color, with a mark on her left cheek. She was emancipated by Isaac Clarke.

REGISTRATION NO. 213
(Vol. 3, p. 30)

Fanny Parker Payne   3 August 1847

Fanny Payne, late Parker, is about 48[?] years old, 5 feet 4¼ inches tall, of a black complexion, with a scar on her forehead. She was born free, as appears by a previous register.

REGISTRATION NO. 214
(Vol. 3, p. 30)

Lucy Harris   ca. 3 August 1847

Lucy Harris is a dark mulatto, about 21 years old, 5 feet 3 3/4 inches tall, with several scars from cupping on the back of her neck, a scar on her right elbow, and freckles. She was born free, as appears by affirmation of William Stabler and the certificate of G[eorge] W. P. Custis

REGISTRATION NO. 215
(Vol. 3, p. 30)

Milly Butler   3 August 1847

Milly Butler is about 30 years old, 5 feet 6¼ inches tall, of a brownish-black color, with a small scar below her left temple and a scar on the back of her right hand between her thumb and forefinger. She was emancipated by William Goddard, as appears by evidence of Zenas Kinsey.

REGISTRATION NO. 216
(Vol. 3, p. 30)

George William Darnall   3 August 1847

George William Darnall is about 24 years old, 6 feet one-fourth inch tall, of a copper color, with the right side of his neck scarred. He was born free, as appears by evidence of Jonathan Ross.

REGISTRATION NO. 217
(Vol. 3, p. 30)

Nancy Lee

3 August 1847

Nancy Lee is about 27 years old, 5 feet 7 inches tall, of a brownish-black complexion, with two scars, one above the other, on her breast bone. She was born free, as appears by evidence of Elizabeth Ferguson.

REGISTRATION NO. 218
(Vol. 3, p. 30)

Margaret Doster

ca. 3 August 1847

Margaret Doster is a very bright mulatto, about 24 years old, 5 feet 2¼ inches tall, with a scar on her left wrist, light colored eyes, and straight hair. She was born free, as appears by oath of Mrs. Elizabeth Morris.

REGISTRATION NO. 219
(Vol. 3, p. 30)

Elizabeth Julius Butler

3 August 1847

Elizabeth Butler, late Julius, is a dark mulatto, about 31 years old, 5 feet 3 inches tall, with no visible marks. She was born free, as appears by a previous registration.

REGISTRATION NO. 220
(Vol. 3, p. 31)

Joanna Gowens

ca. 3 August 1847

Joanna Gowens is about 45 years old, 5 feet 1 3/4 inches tall, of a brownish-black color, with a scar at the root of the forefinger of her left hand. She is the daughter of Agnes who was manumitted by General Washington, and was born free, as appears by evidence of Mrs. David Allen.

See No. 17 in Book 2 of the Fairfax County registrations for Joannah, the daughter of Agnes. (Sweig, p. 16). Agnes is registered in No. 16 in Book 2 (Sweig, p. 16). Other of Agnes's children are also registered in the Fairfax books.

REGISTRATION NO. 221
(Vol. 3, p. 31)

Mary Washington

3 August 1847

Mary Washington is a bright mulatto, about 44 years old, 5 feet 3 inches tall, with a dark place from frostbite on each ear and dark spots over her face. She was emancipated by the will of Henrietta Perry, as appears by a previous registration.

REGISTRATION NO. 222
(Vol. 3, p. 31)

Cassa Yates

ca. 3 August 1847

Cassa Yates is a bright mulatto, about 61 years old, 5 feet 4 inches tall, with a mole on the left side of her nose. She was born free, as appears by a previous registration.

REGISTRATION NO. 223
(Vol. 3, p. 31)

Thomas Baker

4 August 1847

Thomas Baker is about 29 years old, 5 feet 7½ inches tall, of a black complexion, with several scars at the corner of his right eye. He was emancipated by Samuel H. Janney, as appears by evidence of John Lawson.

REGISTRATION NO. 224
(Vol. 3, p. 31)

Patty Nelson

2 August 1847

Patty Nelson is a dark mulatto, about 50 years old 5 feet 8¼ inches tall, with no visible marks. She was emancipated by Maria Blue, Robert Bell, and Britannia Bell, as appears by a previous registration.

REGISTRATION NO. 225
(Vol. 3, p. 31)

Cecilia Nelson   ca. 2 August 1847

Cecilia Nelson is a dark mulatto, about 23 years old, 5 feet 4½ inches tall, with a scar on her right eyelid. She is the daughter of Patty Nelson and was born free, as appears by evidence of Turner Dixon.

REGISTRATION NO. 226
(Vol. 3, p. 31)

George Nelson   ca. 2 August 1847

George Nelson is about 22 years old, 5 feet 7½ inches tall, of a brownish-black color, with a scar on the right side of his forehead. He is the son of Patty Nelson and was born free, as appears by evidence of Turner Dixon.

REGISTRATION NO. 227
(Vol. 3, p. 31)

Martha Nelson   3 August 1847

Martha Nelson is about 18 years old, 5 feet 2¼ inches tall, of a brownish-black color, with a scar on her forehead. She is the daughter of Patty Nelson and was born free, as appears by evidence from Turner Dixon.

REGISTRATION NO. 228
(Vol. 3, p. 32)

Sally Fuller   3 August 1847

Sally Fuller is about 35 years old, 5 feet 6 3/4 inches tall, of a brownish-black color, with the top of her nose scarred. She was emancipated by the will of Rachel Wheeler, as appears by evidence from B[ernard] Hooe.

REGISTRATION NO. 229
(Vol. 3, p. 32)

Catharine Gowens   ca. 3 August 1847

Catharine Gowens is about 17 years old, 5 feet one-eighth inch tall, of a black complexion, with a scar on the right side of her neck. She is the daughter of Joanna Gowens and was born free, as appears by oath of Elizabeth Ferguson.

REGISTRATION NO. 230
(Vol. 3, p. 32)

Emily Gowens   ca. 3 August 1847

Emily Gowens is about 16 years old, 4 feet 10 3/4 inches tall, of a black complexion, with a scar on the left side of her forehead. She is the daughter of Joanna Gowens and was born free, as appears by affidavit of Elizabeth Ferguson.

REGISTRATION NO. 231
(Vol. 3, p. 32)

Kitty Turley   3 August 1847

Kitty Turley is a bright mulatto, about 43 years old, 4 feet 11 inches tall, with a slightly freckled face. She was emancipated by D. McChichester by deed in Fairfax County, as appears by a previous register.

See No. 180 in Book 2 of the Fairfax County registrations (Sweig, p. 74). Kitty Turley is probably the Kitty Hathaway freed on 22 April in 1806 by D. McChichester. Sweig states that D. McChichester is probably Daniel McCarty Chichester.

REGISTRATION NO. 232
(Vol. 3, p. 32)

Sinah Solomon   3 August 1847

Sinah Solomon is a dark mulatto, about 42 years old, 5 feet 2 3/4 inches tall, with a scar on her forehead. She was born free, as appears by a previous register.

REGISTRATION NO. 233
(Vol. 3, p. 32)

Sarah Ann Solomon   3 August 1847

Sarah Ann Solomon is a dark mulatto, about 19 years old, 5 feet one-fourth inch tall, with no visible marks. She was born free, as appears by oath of Samuel M. McCormick.

REGISTRATION NO. 234
(Vol. 3, p. 32)

Eleanor Turner   3 August 1847

Eleanor Turner is a bright mulatto, about 38 year old, 5 feet 1 3/4 inches tall, with a scar on the right side of her neck, and a scar between her eyebrows. She was born free, as appears by a registration from New York, and as proved by C. Neale, Esq., who states that she has resided here for 15 or 20 years.

REGISTRATION NO. 235
(Vol. 3, p. 32)

Elizabeth Colston   ca. 3 August 1847

Elizabeth Colston is about 25 years old, of a black complexion, with a scar on the back of her hand. She was born free, as appears by evidence of Mrs. Jane Rye.

REGISTRATION NO. 236
(Vol. 3, p. 33)

Catharine Williams   3 August 1847

Catharine Williams is a dark mulatto, about 29 years old, 5 feet 4½ inches tall, with several scars on her right hand. She was born free, as appears by a previous registration.

REGISTRATION NO. 237
(Vol. 3, p. 33)

Joseph Jones   ca. 3 August 1847

Joseph Jones is about 22 years old, of a black complexion, with no visible marks. He was born free, as appears by evidence of Sinah Cash.

REGISTRATION NO. 238
(Vol. 3, p. 33)

Sarah Jones   3 August 1847

Sarah Jones is about 66 years old, 5 feet 5½ inches tall, of a black complexion, with a mole near and below the left corner of her mouth. She was emancipated by General Washington, as appears by evidence of Sinah Cash.

REGISTRATION NO. 239
(Vol. 3, p. 33)

Caroline Lomax   ca. 3 August 1847

Caroline Lomax is about 60 years old, of a black complexion, with no visible marks. She was emancipated by ??, and is free, as appears by evidence of B[ernard] Hooe.

REGISTRATION NO 240
(Vol. 3, p. 33)

Hannah Lomax   ca. 3 August 1847

Hannah Lomax is about 27 years old, of a black complexion, with a small scar on her right cheek. She was born free, as appears by evidence of B[ernard] Hooe.

REGISTRATION NO. 241
(Vol. 3, p. 33)

Adolphus Adams   3 August 1847

Adolphus Adams is a bright mulatto, about 17 years old, 5 feet 7 3/4 inches tall, with no visible scars. He is the son of Harriet Butler and was born free, as appears by evidence of John Creighton.

REGISTRATION NO. 242
(Vol. 3, p. 33)

Letitia Webster

3 August 1847

Letitia Webster is a bright mulatto, about 29 years old, 5 feet 2 inches tall, with no visible marks. She is the daughter of Haney Edwards and was born free, as appears by evidence of John Creighton.

REGISTRATION NO. 243
(Vol. 3, p. 33)

Daniel Skinner

4 August 1847

Daniel Skinner is a dark mulatto, about 44 years old, 5 feet 9 inches tall, with a scar on his left wrist. He was born free, as appears by a previous register.

REGISTRATION NO. 244
(Vol. 3, p. 34)

Sylvia Lee

3 August 1847

Sylvia Lee is about 49 years old, 5 feet 8½ inches tall, of a black complexion, with her face marked by smallpox. She was emancipated, as appears by a previous registration.

REGISTRATION NO. 245
(Vol. 3, p. 34)

James Collins

ca. 3 August 1847

James Collins is a dark mulatto, about 43 years old, 5 feet 5 3/4 inches tall, with a scar on his under lip, one on the back of his left hand, and another above his left eyebrow. He was born free, as appears by evidence of Zenas Kinzey.

REGISTRATION NO. 246
(Vol. 3, p. 34)

Philip A. Smith

4 August 1847

Philip A. Smith is about 21 years old, 5 feet 5¼ inches tall, of a black complexion, with a scar on his forehead and a large scar on the back and near the thumb of his left hand. He was born free, as appears by a previous register.

REGISTRATION NO. 247
(Vol. 3, p. 34)

Adell Logan

4 August 1847

Adell Logan is about 14 years old, 4 feet 10 3/4 inches tall, of a brownish-black color, with no visible marks. Logan was born free, as appears by evidence of Elizabeth Ferguson.

REGISTRATION NO. 248
(Vol. 3, p. 34)

Reverdy Bowden

ca. 3 August 1847

Reverdy Bowden is a very bright mulatto, about 17 years old, 5 feet 9½ inches tall, with no visible marks. He is slight freckled and has reddish hair. Bowden is the son of Cecily Bowden and was born free, as appears by evidence of Robert W. Hunter.

REGISTRATION NO. 249
(Vol. 3, p. 34)

Cecily Bowden Brooks

3 August 1847

Cecily Bowden, now Brooks, is a bright mulatto, about 39 years old, 5 feet 2¼ inches tall, with a scar on her left wrist. She was emancipated by Jonathan Janney and R[obert] W. Hunter by deed dated 9 January 1835, as appears by a previous registration.

REGISTRATION NO. 250
(Vol. 3, p. 34)

Addison Bowden   ca. 3 August 1847

Addison Bowden is a bright mulatto, about 12 years old, 4 feet 11 inches tall, with his left eye out, several scars on the back of his left hand, and with light colored straight hair. He is the son of Cecily Bowden and was born free, as appears by evidence of Cecily Bowden.

REGISTRATION NO. 251
(Vol. 3, p. 35)

James Pinn, alias Hollis   ca. 3 August 1847

James Pinn, alias Hollis, is about 34 years old, 5 feet 11 3/4 inches tall, of a black complexion, with his front teeth wide apart, a scar on the first joint of his left thumb, a scar on the under side of his left and, and a scar on this eyelid. He is free.

REGISTRATION NO. 252
(Vol. 3, p. 35)

Jane Weeks Thornton   3 August 1847

Jane Weeks, now Thornton, is about 37 years old, 5 feet 2 3/4 inches tall, of a brownish-black color, with no scars or marks. She was born free.

REGISTRATION NO. 253
(Vol. 3, p. 35)

Robert Handless   3 August 1847

Robert Handless is about 31 years old, 5 feet 8½ inches tall, of a black complexion, with his left hand and fingers very scarred. He was born free, as appears by evidence of William Mankins.

REGISTRATION NO. 254
(Vol. 3, p. 35)

Marcelina Nickles   4 August 1847

Marcelina Nickles is a dark mulatto, about 35 years old, 5 feet 1¼ inches tall, with a small scar on the forefinger of her left hand. She was born free, as appears by evidence of George Johnson.

REGISTRATION NO. 255
(Vol. 3, p. 35)

Betsey Green   4 August 1847

Betsey Green is a dark mulatto, about 24 years old, 5 feet 1½ inches tall, with a scar on the back of her left hand, two on her right arm and two on her left arm. She was born free, as appears by certificate of A[lexander] Moore.

REGISTRATION NO. 256
(Vol. 3, p. 35)

Ann Jones   3 August 1847

Ann Jones is about 56 years old, 5 feet 2¼ inches tall, of a black complexion, with a scar on her chin and another under her right eye. She was manumitted by deed from Olivia Jones dated 6 September 1821.

REGISTRATION NO. 257
(Vol. 3, p. 35)

Henry Cavins   3 August 1847

Henry Cavins is a dark mulatto, about 24 years old, 6 feet one-fourth inch tall, with a scar in his right eyebrow, a scar on his left wrist, and many scars on his hands, and a blemish in his right eye. He was born free, as appears by evidence of Moses O. B. Cawood.

REGISTRATION NO. 258
(Vol. 3, p. 36)

Flora Johnson   4 August 1847

Flora Johnson is about 40 years old, 5 feet 3¼ inches tall, with no visible marks. She was emancipated by Colin Auld by deed dated November 1829, as appears by a previous registration.

REGISTRATION NO. 259
(Vol. 3, p. 36)

Henry Watson   4 August 1847

Henry Watson is about 15 years old, 5 feet 5 inches tall, of a black complexion, with no scars or marks. He is the son of Flora Johnson and was born free, as appears by evidence of Mrs. Ann E. Rose[?].

REGISTRATION NO. 260
(Vol. 3, p. 36)

John Harris   3 August 1847

John Harris is a mulatto, about 37 years old, 5 feet 7¼ inches tall, with a small scar on his left cheek and one of his left wrist. He was born free.

REGISTRATION NO. 261
(Vol. 3, p. 36)

Betsey Colbert   2 August 1847

Betsey Colbert is about 23 years old, 5 feet 2¼ inches tall, of a black complexion, with a scar between her eyes. She was born free.

REGISTRATION NO. 262
(Vol. 3, p. 36)

William E. Tate   ca. 2 August 1847

William E. Tate is a dark mulatto, about 28 years old, 5 feet 6 inches tall, with a scar in the palm of his left hand. He was born free, as appears by a former registration.

REGISTRATION NO. 263
(Vol. 3, p. 36)

William Patrick   3 August 1847

William Patrick is about 36 years old, 5 feet 4 inches tall, of a black complexion, with a scar at the corner of his right eye and a scar on his left thumb where it joins his hand. He was born free, as appears by evidence of Moses O. B. Cawood.

REGISTRATION NO. 264
(Vol. 3, p. 36)

John A. Beckley   ca. 3 August 1847

John A. Beckley is a mulatto, about 43 years old, 5 feet 7¼ inches tall, with no visible marks. He was born free, as appears by a previous registration.

REGISTRATION NO. 265
(Vol. 3, p. 37)

Ann Beckley   ca. 3 August 1847

Ann Beckley is a bright mulatto, about 32 years old, 5 feet 2½ inches tall, who is slightly lame in her right side. She was born free, as appears by a previous registration.

REGISTRATION NO. 266
(Vol. 3, p. 37)

Charles Bruce   4 August 1847

Charles Bruce is about 32 years old, 5 feet 4½ inches tall, of a brownish-black color, with a scar on his left wrist. He was emancipated by Thomas Sanford, as appears by a previous registration.

REGISTRATION NO. 267
(Vol. 3, p. 37)

Laura Ann Dundas Gray   4 August 1847

Laura Ann Gray, late Dundas, is a bright mulatto, about 27 years old, 5 feet 5 inches tall, with a scar on her left cheek and one of her right hand. She was emancipated by Jane[?] C. Keith by deed dated 12 October 1837 and identified by the oath of Thomas R. Keith.

REGISTRATION NO. 268
(Vol. 3, p. 37)

Thomas Holland   3 August 1847

Thomas Holland is a mulatto, about 34 years old, 5 feet 9 inches tall, with a long scar on the inside of his left arm below the elbow. He was born free.

REGISTRATION NO. 269
(Vol. 3, p. 37)

Edward Evans   3 August 1847

Edward Evans is a bright mulatto, about 34 years old, 5 feet 9¼ inches tall, with a small scar on his nose. He was born free, as appears by evidence of Peter Hewitt and a previous registration.

REGISTRATION NO. 270
(Vol. 3, p. 37)

Lucy Ann Bull   3 August 1847

Lucy Ann Bull is a very bright mulatto, about 40 years old, 5 feet 3 inches tall, with no visible marks. She was born free, as appears by a previous registration.

REGISTRATION NO. 271
(Vol. 3, p. 37)

Nancy Jones   3 August 1847

Nancy Jones is about 30 years old, of a brownish-black color, with a small scar on the little finger of her right hand. She was born free, as appears by evidence of Elizabeth Carlin.

REGISTRATION NO. 272
(Vol. 3, p. 38)

Elizabeth Brown   4 August 1847

Elizabeth Brown is about 15 years old, 5 feet one-half inch tall, of a brown-black color, with a scar on her right arm above the wrist. She was born free, as appears by evidence of Mrs. Margaret Semmes.

REGISTRATION NO. 273
(Vol. 3, p. 38)

Harriet Turley   4 August 1847

Harriet Turley is about 20 years old, 5 feet 2¼ inches tall, of a brown-black color, with a scar on her right arm. She was born free, as appears by evidence of Mrs. Ann Carmon.

REGISTRATION NO. 274
(Vol. 3, p. 38)

Anderson Hepburn   4 August 1847

Anderson Hepburn is a bright mulatto, about 37 years old, 6 feet 3 3/4 inches tall, with a reddish mark under his right eye, another on his under lip, and another on his upper lip. He was born free, as appears by evidence of Samuel Bartle.

REGISTRATION NO. 275
(Vol. 3, p. 38)

John Ebb   4 August 1847

John Ebb is a dark mulatto, about 60 years old, 5 feet 4¼ inches tall, with a scar on the back of his head and another on his right shoulder. He is free.

REGISTRATION NO. 276
(Vol. 3, p. 38)

Caroline Lomax								4 August 1847

Caroline Lomax is about 18 years old, 5 feet 4¼ inches tall, of a black complexion, with a scar at the corner of her left eye and a scar on the back of her left wrist. She was born free, as appears by evidence of Mrs. Cornelia Patterson.

REGISTRATION NO. 277

There is no registration numbered 277.

REGISTRATION NO. 278
(Vol. 3, p. 38)

Ellen Lomax								4 August 1847

Ellen Lomax is a dark mulatto, about 50 years old, 5 feet 7½ inches tall, with a scar on the upper part of her breast. She was emancipated by Isaac Clark by deed dated 19 October 1831, as appears by a previous registration.

REGISTRATION NO. 279
(Vol. 3, p. 38)

Dennis Bourbon								4 August 1847

Dennis Bourbon is a dark mulatto, about 32 years old, 5 feet 5½ inches tall, with no visible marks. He was emancipated by Bazil H. Davidson by deed dated 13 August 1823.

REGISTRATION NO. 280
(Vol. 3, p. 38)

William Claggett							ca. 4 August 1847

William Claggett is a dark mulatto, about 39 years old, 5 feet 5½ inches tall, with the sinews of his left hand drawn from a burn and with a small scar on the left side of his face. He was emancipated by George Coryell and S[ilas] H. Reed.

REGISTRATION NO. 281
(Vol. 3, p. 39)

Jane Warner								4 August 1847

Jane Warner is a dark mulatto, about 40 years old, 5 feet 4 inches tall, with a dark mark on her left temple and a dark mark on the inner side of her right little finger. She is free, as appears by evidence of Elias Harrison.

REGISTRATION NO. 282
(Vol. 3, p. 39)

Jane Warner								4 August 1847

Jane Warner is about 15 years old, 5 feet 2 inches tall, of a black complexion, with a scar on the back of her left wrist. She is the daughter of Jane Warner and was born free, as appears by evidence of Rev. Elias Harrison.

REGISTRATION NO. 283
(Vol. 3, p. 39)

Hannah Ann Warner							4 August 1847

Hannah Ann Warner is about 17 years old, 5 feet 3¼ inches tall, with a scar on the right cheek and one between her eyes. She was born free, as appears by evidence of Rev. Elias Harrison.

REGISTRATION NO. 284
(Vol. 3, p. 39)

James Webster								3 August 1847

James Webster is a dark mulatto, about 50 years old, with a scar on his left arm near the elbow. He was born free.

REGISTRATION NO. 285
(Vol. 3, p. 39)

Cornelius Wilson   ca. 4 August 1847

Cornelius Wilson is a dark mulatto, about 55 years old, 5 feet 3¼ inches tall, with a bald head. He was emancipated by John Moran by deed dated 19 March 1830.

REGISTRATION NO. 286
(Vol. 3, p. 39)

William Gray, Sr.   ca. 4 August 1847

William Gray, Sr., is a bright mulatto, about 35 years old, 5 feet 2½ inches tall, with a small scar on his left thumb. He was born free.

REGISTRATION NO. 287
(Vol. 3, p. 39)

Henry Rowe   4 August 1847

Henry Rowe is a bright mulatto, about 29 years old, 5 feet 6 inches tall, with a small indentation on his right cheek near the right corner of his mouth. He was freed by Jane A. T. Ramsay.

REGISTRATION NO. 288
(Vol. 3, p. 39)

Celia Bowden Rowe   4 August 1847

Celia Rowe, late Bowden, is a bright mulatto, about 26 years old, 5 feet 4¼ inches tall, with no visible marks. She was emancipated Jonathan Janney and R[obert] W. Hunter by deed dated 9 January 1835, as appears by a previous registration.

REGISTRATION NO. 289
(Vol. 3, p. 40)

Amey Bell Hackett   4 August 1847

Amey Hackett, late Bell, is about 40 years old, 5 feet 4¼ inches tall, of a brownish-black complexion, with several dark spots or moles scattered over her face. She was emancipated by the will of Jane Contee.

REGISTRATION NO. 290
(Vol. 3, p. 40)

Sophia Lee Henry   4 August 1847

Sophia Lee, now Henry, is a bright mulatto, about 45 years old, 5 feet 6 inches tall, with no scars or marks. She was born free.

REGISTRATION NO. 291
(Vol. 3, p. 40)

Charles Henry   4 August 1847

Charles Henry is about 56 years old, 5 feet 9¼ inches tall, of a black complexion, with a scar on the first finger of his left hand and another on the back of his right hand. He was emancipated by George Minor's will recorded in Fairfax.

REGISTRATION NO. 292
(Vol. 3, p. 40)

Rebecca Henry   ca. 4 August 1847

Rebecca Henry is a dark mulatto, about 13 years old, 5 feet one-half inch tall, with no visible marks. She is the daughter of Sophia Henry and was born free, as appears by evidence from Mrs. Margaret [M.] Bangs.

REGISTRATION NO. 293
(Vol. 3, p. 40)

James Townsend   ca. 4 August 1847

James Townsend is about 19 years old, 5 feet 6 inches tall, of a black complexion, with four scars on the left side of his face and neck. He was born free, as appears by evidence of Marion Walker.

REGISTRATION NO. 294
(Vol. 3, p. 40)

Caroline Townsend   ca. 4 August 1847

Caroline Townsend is about 42 years old, 5 feet 4 3/4 inches tall, of a black complexion, with a scar on the back of her right hand about an inch long. She was freed by James Townsend.

REGISTRATION NO. 295
(Vol. 3, p. 40)

Sophia Townsend   ca. 4 August 1847

Sophia Townsend is about 20 years old, 5 feet 3 5/8 inches tall, of a brownish-black color, with a scar on her right cheek. She is the daughter of Caroline Townsend and was born free, as appears by evidence of Marion Walker.

REGISTRATION NO. 296
(Vol. 3, p. 40)

Catharine Townsend   ca. 4 August 1847

Catharine Townsend is about 17 years old, 5 feet 2 inches tall, of a black complexion, with a scar on her right wrist. She was born free, as appears by evidence of Marion Walker.

REGISTRATION NO. 297
(Vol. 3, p. 41)

Sarah Frances Townsend   ca. 4 August 1847

Sarah Frances Townsend is about 14 years old, 5 feet 1 inch tall, of a black complexion, with a scar on her right cheek near her ear. She was born free, as appears by evidence of Marion Walker.

REGISTRATION NO. 298
(Vol. 3, p. 41)

Ellen Hamilton Jones   4 August 1847

Ellen Jones, formerly Hamilton, is about 27 years old, 5 feet 2 3/4 inches tall, of a black complexion, with a scar on her right wrist caused by a burn. She is the daughter of Ellen Hamilton and was born free, as appears by a previous registration.

REGISTRATION NO. 299
(Vol. 3, p. 41)

Anthony Colston   4 August 1847

Anthony Colston is about 32 years old, 5 feet 3¼ inches tall, of a black complexion, with a scar on his left eyebrow, another on his right eyelid, and another on the back of his left hand. He was born free, as appears by evidence of Moses O. B. Cawood.

REGISTRATION NO. 300
(Vol. 3, p. 41)

Marcus Nickler   4 August 1847

Marcus Nickler is a bright mulatto, about 16 years old, 5 feet 1 inch tall, with a few smallpox marks scattered over his face. He was born free, as appears by evidence of Matilda Moss.

REGISTRATION NO. 301
(Vol. 3, p. 41)

Mary Nutt Cole   4 August 1847

Mary Cole, late Nutt, is about 47 years old, 5 feet 1 3/4 inches tall, of a black complexion, with several dark moles on her left cheek and a scar on her right arm over the elbow. She was emancipated by deed from Ellis Price dated 23 February 1801.

REGISTRATION NO. 302
(Vol. 3, p. 41)

George Medella	ca. 4 August 1847

George Medella is about 26 years old, 5 feet 10½ inches tall, of a black complexion, with a scar on his upper lip and another between the knuckles of the first and second finger of his left hand. He was emancipated by deed from William H. Wilmer to Hannah Somers.

REGISTRATION NO. 303
(Vol. 3, p. 42)

Maria Douglas	ca. 4 August 1847

Maria Douglas is a dark mulatto, about 30 years old, 5 feet 1 inch tall, with a scar at the corner of her right eye. She was born free, as appears by evidence of Turner Dixon.

REGISTRATION NO. 304
(Vol. 3, p. 42)

John Nickens	4 August 1847

John Nickens is a bright mulatto, about 43 years old, 5 feet 5 inches tall, with a scar on his right wrist. He was born free, as appears by a previous registration.

REGISTRATION NO. 305
(Vol. 3, p. 42)

Harriet Medella Turner[?] Jackson	ca. 4 August 1847

Harriet Jackson, late Medella or Turner[?], is a bright mulatto, about 32 years old, 5 feet 2 3/4 inches tall, with no visible marks. She was emancipated by deed of William H. Wilmer to Hannah Somers dated 6 October 1817.

REGISTRATION NO. 306
(Vol. 3, p. 42)

Eliza Bruce	4 August 1847

Eliza Bruce is a bright mulatto, about 27 years old, 5 feet three-fourths of an inch tall, with a scar on her right arm in the bend of the elbow. She was born free, as appears by evidence of Turner Dixon.

REGISTRATION NO. 307
(Vol. 3, p. 42)

William Nickens	4 August 1847

William Nickens is a bright mulatto, about 43 years old, 5 feet 5 inches tall, with a scar on the side of his left hand. He was born free, as appears by a previous registration.

REGISTRATION NO. 308
(Vol. 3, p. 42)

Rebecca Lucas Nickens	ca. 4 August 1847

Rebecca Nickens, late Lucas, is a bright mulatto, about 37 years old, 5 feet 1 3/4 inches tall, slightly freckled, with no visible marks. She was manumitted by James McKenzie by deed dated 25 October 1838.

REGISTRATION NO. 309
(Vol. 3, p. 42)

Catharine Hamilton	4 August 1847

Catharine Hamilton is about 50 years old, 5 feet 2 inches tall, of a black complexion, with several small moles on her face, mainly under her left eye. She was emancipated by Margaret S. Keith by deed dated 12 October 1837 and was identified by Thomas [R.] Keith.

REGISTRATION NO. 310
(Vol. 3, p. 42)

James Webster

4 August 1847

James Webster is a bright mulatto, about 30 years old, 5 feet 3 3/4 inches tall, with a scar on his chin, another on the lower knuckle of his left thumb, and another on the back of his left hand. He was born free, as appears by evidence of George Swain.

REGISTRATION NO. 311
(Vol. 3, p. 43)

Mary Kelsick Payne

5 August 1847

Mary Kelsick, now Payne, is about 45 years old, 5 feet 5¼ inches tall, of a black complexion, with a scar on the inner side of the third finger of her right hand. She is free by emancipation.

REGISTRATION NO. 312
(Vol. 3, p. 43)

Hannah Ann Seaton

4 August 1847

Hannah Ann Seaton is about 26 years old, 5 feet 7 3/4 inches tall, of a copper color, with a small black speck in the corner of her right eye. She was born free, as appears by a previous registration.

REGISTRATION NO. 313
(Vol. 3, p. 43)

Lucinda Seaton

4 August 1847

Lucinda Seaton is about 20 years old, 5 feet 7½ inches tall, of a copper color, with a black mole on her left cheek. She was born free.

REGISTRATION NO. 314
(Vol. 3, p. 43)

Martha Ann Seaton

4 August 1847

Martha Ann Seaton is a dark mulatto, about 17 years old, 5 feet 7 inches tall, with a black spot on the left side of the white of her right eye. She was born free.

REGISTRATION NO. 315
(Vol. 3, p. 43)

Laura Virginia Seaton

4 August 1847

Laura Virginia Seaton is a dark mulatto, about 14 years old, 5 feet 3 3/4 inches tall, with a scar on her left cheek and another on her forehead. She is the daughter of Lucinda Seaton and was born free.

REGISTRATION NO. 316
(Vol. 3, p. 43)

Lucinda Seaton, Sr.

4 August 1847

"Lucinda Seaton Sr." is a dark mulatto, about 46 years old, 5 feet 4 inches tall, with a slight scar on the back of her hand and a stammer. She was emancipated by General Washington, as appears by a previous registration.

REGISTRATION NO. 317
(Vol. 3, p. 43)

John Andrew Seaton

4 August 1847

John Andrew Seaton is a dark mulatto, about 12 years old, 5 feet 1½ inches tall, with no scars or marks. He is the son of Lucinda Seaton and was born free.

REGISTRATION NO. 318
(Vol. 3, p. 44)

Louisa Haney

ca. 4 August 1847

Louisa Haney is about 18 years old, 5 feet 2 inches tall, of a black complexion, with a slight scar on her forehead and another on her right hand between her thumb and forefinger. She was born free, as appears by evidence from Zenas Kinzey.

REGISTRATION NO. 319
(Vol. 3, p. 44)

Mary Haney Johnson   ca. 4 August 1847

Mary Johnson, late Haney, is about 24[?] years old, 5 feet 1 3/4 inches tall, of a blackish color, with a scar at the corner of her left eye. She was born free, as appears by evidence of Zenas Kinzey.

REGISTRATION NO. 320
(Vol. 3, p. 44)

Cornelia Jones   ca. 4 August 1847

Cornelia Jones is a bright mulatto, about 25 years old, 5 feet 3½ inches tall, with a scar on the right side of her neck. She was born free, as appears by evidence of Jesse Skidmore.

REGISTRATION NO. 321
(Vol. 3, p. 44)

Hannah Jackson   4 August 1847

Hannah Jackson is about 15 years old, 5 feet 3¼ inches tall, of a brownish-black color, with scars on the back of her neck from cupping. She was born free, as appears by evidence of Zenas Kinzey.

REGISTRATION NO. 322
(Vol. 3, p. 44)

Milly Julius Campbell   4 August 1847

Milly Julius Campbell is about 45 years old, 5 feet three-fourths of an inch tall, of a dark brown color, with a scar on the left side of her neck and smallpox marks on her face. She was born free.

REGISTRATION NO. 323
(Vol. 3, p. 44)

John Paris   5 August 1847

John Paris is about 33 years old, 5 feet 3¼ inches tall, of a black complexion, with a scar on his right knee. He was born free.

REGISTRATION NO. 324
(Vol. 3, p. 44)

George Gibson   4 August 1847

George Gibson is a dark mulatto, about 48 years old, 5 feet 8 3/4 inches tall, with a small scar on the under part of his left arm. He was emancipated, as appears by a previous registration.

REGISTRATION NO. 325
(Vol. 3, p. 45)

Kitty White   ca. 4 August 1847

Kitty White is a dark mulatto, about 49 years old, 5 feet 1 inch tall, with no visible marks. She was emancipated by Robert Jamieson by deed dated 1833.

REGISTRATION NO. 326
(Vol. 3, p. 45)

Mary Butler   4 August 1847

Mary Butler is about 57 years old, 5 feet 5 inches tall, of a black complexion, with two moles near the left corner of her mouth and a mark from pox near the left corner of her left eye. She was emancipated by Catharine Allison's will.

REGISTRATION NO. 327
(Vol. 3, p. 45)

Louis Lewis   ca. 4 August 1847

Louis Lewis is about 43[?] years old, 5 feet 7¼ inches tall, with a scar on his right wrist and who is bald. He was born free, as appears by evidence of R[obert] H. Miller.

REGISTRATION NO. 328
(Vol. 3, p. 45)

Robert Butler   4 August 1847

Robert Butler is about 34 years old, 5 feet 7½ inches tall, of a black complexion, with a small black mole on his right ear. He was born free, as appears by a previous registration.

REGISTRATION NO. 329
(Vol. 3, p. 45)

William Logan   4 August 1847

William Logan is about 19 years old, 5 feet 4¼ inches tall, of a brownish-black color, with a scar on his forehead and a mole on his upper lip. He was born free, as appears by evidence of Elizabeth Ferguson.

REGISTRATION NO. 330
(Vol. 3, p. 45)

Jane Morris Smith   ca. 4 August 1847

Jane Smith, late Morris, is about 57 years old, 5 feet 5 3/4 inches tall, of a brownish-black color, and who is very deaf. She has a scar on her forehead near her hair and a defect in each of her forefingers. She was emancipated by Josiah Watson, as appears by a previous registration.

REGISTRATION NO. 331
(Vol. 3, p. 45)

William Thornton   ca. 4 August 1847

William Thornton is about 64 years old, 6 feet 2¼ inches tall, of a black complexion, with a scar over his right ear and with the middle finger of his left hand straight. He was emancipated by Robert Anderson.

REGISTRATION NO. 332
(Vol. 3, p. 46)

William Savoy   3 August 1847

William Savoy is a dark mulatto, about 47 years old, 5 feet 10¼ inches tall, with a defect in his right eye. He was born free.

REGISTRATION NO. 333
(Vol. 3, p. 46)

Bazil Miles   3 August 1847

Bazil Miles is about 22 years old, 5 feet 6½ inches tall, of a black complexion, with a scar over his right eye and another on his left cheek. He was born free, as appears by evidence of Sarah Vernon.

REGISTRATION NO. 334
(Vol. 3, p. 46)

James Butler   ca. 3 August 1847

James Butler is about 62 years old, 5 feet 8½ inches tall, of a black complexion, with a scar under his left eye, one on his right cheekbone, and another on the forefinger of his right hand. He was emancipated by Catherine Allison's will.

REGISTRATION NO. 335
(Vol. 3, p. 46)

Daniel H. Smith   3 August 1847

Daniel H. Smith is a bright mulatto, about 34 years old, 5 feet 7 inches tall, with an indentation in his right cheek and a mole on the left side of his neck. He was emancipated by Maria Blue, and Robert and Britannia Bell, as appears by a previous registration.

REGISTRATION NO. 336
(Vol. 3, p. 46)

Samuel Williams   3 August 1847

Samuel Williams is about 30 years old, 6 feet 4 inches tall, of a black complexion, with a small scar on his right eyebrow. He was born free, as appears by evidence of Caleb Richards.

REGISTRATION NO. 337
(Vol. 3, p. 46)

Peter Magruder   4 August 1847

Peter Magruder is about 27 years old, 5 feet 8½ inches tall, of a brownish-black color, with a scar on his right thumb. He was born free, as appears by evidence of John Bell.

REGISTRATION NO. 338
(Vol. 3, p. 46)

Harriet Jones   ca. 4 August 1847

Harriet Jones is a dark mulatto, about 18 years old, with a scar in the middle of her forehead and a scar on her left wrist. She was born free, as appears by evidence of Ann Sidebottom.

REGISTRATION NO. 339
(Vol. 3, p. 47)

Julia Morris   ca. 4 August 1847

Julia Morris is a dark mulatto, about 25 years old with a mole on the right side of her chin. She was born free, as appears by evidence of T. M. White and Christopher Neale.

REGISTRATION NO. 340
(Vol. 3, p. 47)

James Tate   ca. 4 August 1847

James Tate is a black man, about 43 years old, with a scar on the knuckle of the middle finger of the right hand and another on each little finger. He was born free.

REGISTRATION NO. 341
(Vol. 3, p. 47)

Charlotte Seymour   5 August 1847

Charlotte Seymour is about 33 years old, 5 feet one-half inch tall, of a black complexion, with a small scar on the forefinger of her right hand. She was emancipated by A. O. Douglas by deed dated 31 July 1847.

REGISTRATION NO. 342
(Vol. 3, p. 47)

Phebe Ann Tyler   4 August 1847

Phebe Ann Tyler is a bright mulatto, about 19 years old, 4 feet 10 inches tall, with several small dark moles scattered over her face and neck. She is free, as appears by a previous registration.

REGISTRATION NO. 343
(Vol. 3, p. 47)

Richard Brooks   ca. 4 August 1847

Richard Brooks is a bright mulatto, about 37 years old, 5 feet 4 inches tall, with his right eye disfigured by a burn. He was freed by Fanny Brooks.

REGISTRATION NO. 344
(Vol. 3, p. 47)

Henry Butler   4 August 1847

Henry Butler is about 28 years old, 5 feet 8 3/4 inches tall, of a black complexion, with two scars on his right cheek near the right corner of his eye and a scar on his right eyebrow. He is free, as appears by evidence of Benjamin Waters.

REGISTRATION NO. 345
(Vol. 3, p. 47)

Ann Sophia Waters

ca. 4 August 1847

Ann Sophia Waters is a dark mulatto, about 15 years old, 4 feet 9 3/4 in tall, with a mole on her left jaw. She was born free, as appears by evidence of Turner Dixon.

REGISTRATION NO. 346
(Vol. 3, p. 48)

Fanny Beckley

4 August 1847

Fanny Beckley is a dark mulatto, about 48 years old, 5 feet tall, with a scar on her right wrist. She was born free, as appears by evidence of Elizabeth Ferguson.

REGISTRATION NO. 347
(Vol. 3, p. 48)

Eleanor Colbert

5 August 1847

Eleanor Colbert is about 40 years old, 5 feet 1 3/4 inches tall, of a black complexion, with a scar on her right wrist. She is free.

REGISTRATION NO. 348
(Vol. 3, p. 48)

Patty Harris

4 August 1847

Patty Harris is a dark mulatto, about 18 years old, 5 feet 1¼ inches tall, with a small scar on the forefinger of her left hand and a scar on her right arm. She is free.

REGISTRATION NO. 349
(Vol. 3, p. 48)

Nanthius Jennings

ca. 4 August 1847

Nanthius Jennings is a dark mulatto, about 43 years old, 5 feet 6¼ inches tall, with a scar on his left hand, another on his right thumb, and who is lame in his left leg. He was born free.

REGISTRATION NO. 350
(Vol. 3, p. 48)

Thomas Colston

ca. 4 August 1847

Thomas Colston is a dark mulatto, about 25 years old, 5 feet 7½ inches tall, with two scars on his forehead and who has a right big toe that is crooked. He was born free, as appears by evidence of William R. Ball.

REGISTRATION NO. 351
(Vol. 3, p. 48)

Benjamin Jones

4 August 1847

Benjamin Jones is about 45 years old, 5 feet 7¼ inches tall, of a brown-black color, with marks from smallpox. He was born free.

REGISTRATION NO. 352
(Vol. 3, p. 48)

George Ellis

4 August 1847

George Ellis is about 28 years old, 5 feet 10 inches tall, of a brownish-black color, with scars from smallpox. He was born free, as appears by evidence of Anthony P. Gover.

REGISTRATION NO. 353
(Vol. 3, p. 48)

John Colbert

4 August 1847

John Colbert is about 25 years old, 5 feet 3½ inches tall, of a jet black color, with a scar at the left corner of his mouth. He was born free.

REGISTRATION NO. 354
(Vol. 3, p. 49)

Margaret Brown   ca. 4 August 1847

Margaret Brown is a dark mulatto, about 25 years old, 5 feet 3 inches tall, with a large scar on her left temple. She was born free, as appears by evidence of Zenas Kinzey.

REGISTRATION NO. 355
(Vol. 3, p. 49)

Samuel Hopes   ca. 4 August 1847

Samuel Hopes is about 39 years old, 5 feet 6¼ inches tall, of a brownish-black color, with a mark on his belly and a bald head. He was born free.

REGISTRATION NO. 356
(Vol. 3, p. 49)

Lucinda Lee Peters   4 August 1847

Lucinda Peters, formerly Lee, is about 39 years old, 5 feet 5 inches tall, of a black complexion, with a scar on the back of her left hand near the wrist. She was born free.

REGISTRATION NO. 357
(Vol. 3, p. 49)

George Mitchell   4 August 1847

George Mitchell is a dark mulatto, about 37 years old, 5 feet 5 3/4 inches tall, with a scar on his left leg below the knee. He was emancipated by Christopher Frye.

REGISTRATION NO. 358
(Vol. 3, p. 49)

Mary Elizabeth McQuan Lewis   4 August 1847

Mary Elizabeth Lewis, formerly McQuan, is a bright mulatto about 25 years old, 5 feet 4¼ inches tall, with the middle finger of her right hand injured and stiff. She was born free.

REGISTRATION NO. 359
(Vol. 3, p. 49)

Amey McQuan Williams   ca. 4 August 1847

Amey McQuan, now Williams, is about 59 years old, 5 feet 5 inches tall, of a black complexion, with two moles, one on the left side of her nose and another on the left side of her upper lip. She was born free.

REGISTRATION NO. 360
(Vol. 3, p. 49)

William Solomon   4 August 1847

William Solomon is about 25 years old, 5 feet 7½ inches tall, of a black complexion, with a slight scar under his left eye. He was born free.

REGISTRATION NO. 361
(Vol. 3, p. 50)

Daniel Gibson   4 August 1847

Daniel Gibson is about 39 years old, 5 feet 6 inches tall, of a brownish-black color, with the mark from a cut on his under lip. He was emancipated by Catharine Ramsay and Samuel Miller.

REGISTRATION NO. 362
(Vol. 3, p. 50)

James Evans   4 August 1847

James Evans is about 47 years old, 5 feet 6 inches tall, of a brownish-black color, with a small scar on the left side of his face. He is free.

REGISTRATION NO. 363
(Vol. 3, p. 50)

William Hinds

4 August 1847

William Hinds is about 29 years old, 5 feet 4½ inches tall, of a brown-black color, with a small scar over his right eye. He was born free.

REGISTRATION NO. 364
(Vol. 3, p. 50)

Edward Dorsey

ca. 4 August 1847

Edward Dorsey is a black man about 60 years old. He is partially bald but has a heft of hair on his forehead. He is free, as appears by evidence of Benjamin Waters.

REGISTRATION NO. 365
(Vol. 3, p. 50)

Oliver Miles

4 August 1847

Oliver Miles is about 25 years old, 5 feet 7½ inches tall, and has a black complexion. He has a scar at the left corner of his left eye and that eye is crooked and imperfect. He was born free, as appears by evidence of Walter Harris.

REGISTRATION NO. 366
(Vol. 3, p. 50)

Fanny Johnston

4 August 1847

Fanny Johnston is about 35 years old, 5 feet 2 3/4 inches tall, of a brown-black color, with a scar on her right arm. She was born free.

REGISTRATION NO. 367
(Vol. 3, p. 50)

Richard Garrett

4 August 1847

Richard Garrett is a very bright mulatto, about 36 years old, 5 feet 7½ inches tall, with a scar over his left eye. He was emancipated by Silas [H.] Reed.

REGISTRATION NO. 368
(Vol. 3, p. 50)

Philip Hamilton

5 August 1847

Philip Hamilton is about 50 years old, 5 feet 7 3/4 inches tall, of a black complexion, with a scar on his upper lip and another on his left eyebrow. He was emancipated by Colin Auld.

REGISTRATION NO. 369
(Vol. 3, p. 51)

Caroline Koones Garrett

ca. 5 August 1847

Caroline Garrett, formerly Koones, is a bright mulatto, about 33 years old, 5 feet 3 3/4 inches tall, who is marked by smallpox and has straight black hair. She was born free.

REGISTRATION NO. 370
(Vol. 3, p. 51)

Rachel Bourbon

5 August 1847

Rachel Bourbon is about 27 years old, 5 feet 1½ inches tall, and is almost white in color. She has no visible marks or scars. She was emancipated by Dennis Bourbon.

REGISTRATION NO. 371
(Vol. 3, p. 51)

Dennis Hackett

5 August 1847

Dennis Hackett is a bright mulatto, about 60 years old, 5 feet 8 3/4 inches tall, with a scar on his left cheek and another on the left side of his forehead. He was manumitted by John Hunter.

REGISTRATION NO. 372
(Vol. 3, p. 51)

Catharine Wiley   5 August 1847

Catharine Wiley is about 17 years old, 5 feet 1 inch tall, of a black complexion, cross-eyed, with no visible scars. She was born free, as appears by evidence of John Henderson.

REGISTRATION NO. 373
(Vol. 3, p. 51)

Luke Lee   5 August 1847

Luke Lee is about 62 years old, 5 feet 4 3/4 inches tall, of a black complexion, with two scars on the back part of his head. He was manumitted by John Hunter.

REGISTRATION NO. 374
(Vol. 3, p. 51)

Philitia Taylor   5 August 1847

Philitia Taylor is about 30 years old, 5 feet 4½ inches tall, of a black complexion, with no visible marks. Taylor is free, as appears by evidence of B[ernard] Hooe.

REGISTRATION NO. 375
(Vol. 3, p. 51)

Philitia Patrick   5 August 1847

Philitia Patrick is about 35 years old, 5 feet 2½ inches tall, of a black complexion, with a small scar on the left upper eyelid. Patrick is free, as appears by evidence of B[ernard] Hooe.

REGISTRATION NO. 376
(Vol. 3, p. 51)

Nancy Franklin   5 August 1847

Nancy Franklin is a dark mulatto, about 50 years old, 5 feet 5¼ inches tall, with a mole on the right side of her nose. She was manumitted by John Goddard.

REGISTRATION NO. 377
(Vol. 3, p. 52)

William Henry Lewis   4 August 1847

William Henry Lewis is a bright mulatto, about 35 years old, 5 feet 7 inches tall, with a "bald head & straight hair." He was emancipated by William H. Miller.

REGISTRATION NO. 378
(Vol. 3, p. 52)

Jacob Bell   4 August 1847

Jacob Bell is about 48 years old, 5 feet 10 3/4[?] inches tall, of a black complexion, with no scars or marks. He is free.

REGISTRATION NO. 379
(Vol. 3, p. 52)

Francis Talbot   5 August 1847

Francis Talbot is a dark mulatto, about 50 years old, 5 feet 4 3/4 inches tall, with no visible marks. Talbot was emancipated by John McCormack.

REGISTRATION NO. 380
(Vol. 3, p. 52)

Charles Butler   5 August 1847

Charles Butler is about 28 years old, 5 feet 9½ inches tall, of a brown-black color, with a scar on his right hand and another on his left arm. He was born free.

REGISTRATION NO. 381
(Vol. 3, p. 52)

Attoway Newman

5 August 1847

Attoway Newman is about 21 years old, 5 feet 2½ inches tall, of a black complexion, with no visible marks. He was born free.

REGISTRATION NO. 382
(Vol. 3, p. 52)

Letty Weaver

5 August 1847

Letty Weaver is a dark mulatto, about 45 years old, 5 feet 2½ inches tall, with three moles on her face and nose that form a triangle. She was born free.

REGISTRATION NO. 383
(Vol. 3, p. 52)

Polly Savoy

5 August 1847

Polly Savoy is about 50 years old, 5 feet 4 inches tall, of a black complexion, with a scar on the back of her left hand. She was born free.

REGISTRATION NO. 384
(Vol. 3, p. 52)

Hannah Miles

5 August 1847

Hannah Miles is about 59 years old, 4 feet 11½ inches tall, of a black complexion, with marks from smallpox. She was emancipated by John Wilson in Maryland.

REGISTRATION NO. 385
(Vol. 3, p. 53)

William Lyles

4 August 1847

William Lyles is a dark mulatto, about 52 years old, 5 feet 9¼ inches tall, with no scars or marks. He was emancipated by Samuel Carson.

REGISTRATION NO. 386
(Vol. 3, p. 53)

Alfred Merrick

4 August 1847

Alfred Merrick is about 45 years old, 5 feet 9 inches tall, of a black complexion, with several small scars fading[?] on his nose. He was emancipated by William Dean.

REGISTRATION NO. 387
(Vol. 3, p. 53)

John Ross

ca. 4 August 1847

John Ross is a dark mulatto, about 28 years old, 5 feet 6 inches tall, with two moles on the right side of his nose and a mole on his under lip. He was born free, as appears by evidence from Josiah H. Davis.

REGISTRATION NO. 388
(Vol. 3, p. 53)

John Daniels

5 August 1847

John Daniels is about 56 years old, 5 feet 7 inches tall, of a black complexion, with his left eye greatly disfigured. He was emancipated by William N. Mills, executor of Sarah Monroe's will, as directed by that will.

REGISTRATION NO. 389
(Vol. 3, p. 53)

Edward Oldham

5 August 1847

Edward Oldham is about 56 years old, 5 feet 8 inches tall, of a black complexion, with a bald head, a mole on his left eyelid, and a scar on his left cheekbone. He was emancipated by Peggy Ashton by deed dated 8 January 1830.

REGISTRATION NO. 390
(Vol. 3, p. 53)

Frederick Loudoun   5 August 1847

Frederick Loudoun is about 48 years old, 5 feet 7½ inches tall, of a brown-black color, with a scar on his left hand above the upper joint of the forefinger, and who is bald. He was born free.

REGISTRATION NO. 391
(Vol. 3, p. 53)

John Davis   5 August 1847

John Davis is about 29 years old, 5 feet 6½ inches tall, of a brown-black complexion, with a scar on his left knee caused by a cut. He was born free.

REGISTRATION NO. 392
(Vol. 3, p. 53)

Emanuel Weaver   5 August 1847

Emanuel Weaver is a dark mulatto, about 45 years old, 5 feet 9½ inches tall, with two scars on the back of his left hand and one on his left leg. He was freed by William Newton.

REGISTRATION NO. 393
(Vol. 3, p. 54)

Robert Bruce   ca. 5 August 1847

Robert Bruce is a bright mulatto, about 28 years old, 5 feet 6½ inches tall, with a scar on his right wrist. He was emancipated by Colin Auld's will.

REGISTRATION NO. 394
(Vol. 3, p. 54)

William Henry Muse   ca. 5 August 1847

William Henry Muse is about 16 years old, 5 feet 9½ inches tall, of a black complexion, with a small scar on the forefinger of his right hand. He was born free, as appears by evidence of J[ohn] Gibson Peach.

REGISTRATION NO. 395
(Vol. 3, p. 54)

Maria Henry   5 August 1847

Maria Henry is about 49 years old, 5 feet 1½ inches tall, of a black complexion, who is much marked by smallpox. She was manumitted by John C. Herbert.

REGISTRATION NO. 396
(Vol. 3, p. 54)

Lucy Lomax   5 August 1847

Lucy Lomax is about 14 years old, 4 feet 10 inches tall, of a black complexion, with a scar at the corner of her left eye and another on her right arm. She was born free.

REGISTRATION NO. 397
(Vol. 3, p. 54)

Benjamin Franklin   5 August 1847

Benjamin Franklin is about 19 years old, 5 feet 10¼ inches tall, of a brown complexion, with a scar on his left hand towards the palm, and two small scars on his left cheek. He is the son of Nancy Franklin, and was born free, as appears by evidence of Turner Dixon.

REGISTRATION NO. 398
(Vol. 3, p. 54)

Isaac Jackson   ca. 5 August 1847

Isaac Jackson is a bright mulatto, about 67 years old, 5 feet 6 inches tall, with light colored, gray eyes. He was emancipated by James O.[?] Ball.

REGISTRATION NO. 399
(Vol. 3, p. 54)

George Humphries

5 August 1847

George Humphries is about 42 years old, 5 feet 7 inches tall, of a brownish-black color, with the third finger and nail of his left hand mashed. He was manumitted by James McGuire.

REGISTRATION NO. 400
(Vol. 3, p. 54)

Mary Jane Jenkins

ca. 5 August 1847

Mary Jane Jenkins is a bright mulatto, about 25 years old, 5 feet three-fourth inch tall, with a scar on her right ear, dark spots on her nose, and a scar on her right wrist. She was born free, as appears by evidence of Jonathan Ross.

REGISTRATION NO. 401
(Vol. 3, p. 55)

Hannah Jennings

5 August 1847

Hannah Jennings is a dark mulatto, about 77 years old, 5 feet 3¼ inches tall, who is blind in her left eye. She was born free.

REGISTRATION NO. 402
(Vol. 3, p. 55)

Lucy Oldham

5 August 1847

Lucy Oldham is about 51 years old, 5 feet 1 inch tall, of a brownish-black color, with several small scars and one large one on her right hand. She was liberated by Stephen Shinn.

REGISTRATION NO. 403
(Vol. 3, p. 55)

Lucinda Oldham

5 August 1847

Lucinda Oldham is about 32 years old, 5 feet 1 inch tall, of a black complexion, with a large scar on the back of her neck. She was liberated by Stephen Shinn.

REGISTRATION NO. 404
(Vol. 3, p. 55)

Phebe Franklin

5 August 1847

Phebe Franklin is about 17[?] years old, 5 feet 5 inches tall, of a brownish-black color, with a small scar on the lower knuckle of the little finger of the left hand. She is the daughter of Nancy Franklin and was born free, as appears by evidence of Turner Dixon.

REGISTRATION NO. 405
(Vol. 3, p. 55)

Mary Ball

ca. 5 Aug. 1847

Mary Ball is about 18 years old, 5 feet 1½ inches tall, of a black complexion, with marks from smallpox. She is the daughter of Eliza Hawkins and was born free.

A notation states that Ball was not certified until January of 1850. Nevertheless, it appears the entry in this book was made in August of 1847 and that the information as to Ball's age is for her age in 1847.

REGISTRATION NO. 406
(Vol. 3, p. 55)

Mary Ann Jackson Beckley

ca. 5 August 1847

Mary Ann Beckley, late Jackson, is a very bright mulatto, about 18 years old, 5 feet 4 inches tall, with a scar over her left eye and a mole on her right cheek. She has sandy straight hair and light eyes. She was born free, as appears by evidence of Theodore Meade.

REGISTRATION NO. 407
(Vol. 3, p. 55)

Nathaniel Clark											ca. 5 August 1847

Nathaniel Clark is about 34 years old, 5 feet 7 inches tall, of a black complexion, with a scar on the back of his right hand and with smallpox marks. He was emancipated by Silas [H.] Reed.

REGISTRATION NO. 408
(Vol. 3, p. 56)

David Norris											3 August 1847

David Norris is about 38 years old, 5 feet 3 3/4 inches tall, of a brownish-black color, with a scar on the third finger of his left hand "which stiffens it." He "speaks quickly." Norris was born free, as appears by evidence of William Armstrong.

REGISTRATION NO. 409
(Vol. 3, p. 56)

Harriet Brooks											3 August 1847

Harriet Brooks is about 56 years old, 5 feet 3 inches tall, of a black complexion, with a scar on the back of her wrist. She was emancipated by John Roberts.

REGISTRATION NO. 410
(Vol. 3, p. 56)

Jetson Dover											ca. 3 August 1847

Jetson Dover is a bright mulatto, about 48 years old, 5 feet 11 inches tall, with a scar on the right side of his nose. He was born free.

REGISTRATION NO. 411
(Vol. 3, p. 56)

Lucy Dover											ca. 3 August 1847

Lucy Dover is a bright mulatto, about 45 years old, 5 feet 1¼ inches tall, who is very freckled. She was emancipated by Jane A. Ramsay.

REGISTRATION NO. 412
(Vol. 3, p. 56)

William Colston											ca. 3 August 1847

William Colston is about 33 years old, 5 feet 4½ inches tall, of a black complexion, with no marks or scars. He was born free, as appears by a certificate from B[ernard] Hooe.

REGISTRATION NO. 413
(Vol. 3, p. 56)

Margaret Ann Tate										ca. 3 August 1847

Margaret Ann Tate is a dark mulatto, about 15 years old, with no visible marks. She was born free.

REGISTRATION NO. 414
(Vol. 3, p. 56)

Albert Bell											ca. 3 August 1847

Albert Bell is about 27 years old, of a black complexion, with a scar on his forehead and another under his left nostril. He is the son of Britannia Bell, and was born free, as appears by evidence of Peter Hewitt.

REGISTRATION NO. 415
(Vol. 3, p. 56)

Hannah Reed											ca. 3 August 1847

Hannah Reed is about 44 years old, 5 feet 11 3/4 inches tall, of a black complexion, with a scar on the inner side of her left hand. She was emancipated by John D. Harrison.

REGISTRATION NO. 416
(Vol. 3, p. 57)

Maria Syphax ca. 3 August 1847

Maria Syphax is a dark mulatto, about 35 years old, 5 feet 4½ inches tall, with no visible marks. She was born free, as appears by evidence of William Stabler.

REGISTRATION NO. 417
(Vol. 3, p. 57)

Eliza Easton 5 August 1847

Eliza Easton is a dark mulatto, about 33 years old, 5 feet 5 inches tall with a mark from a burn on the left side of her neck. She was freed by Daniel McLeod, as appears by a previous registration.

REGISTRATION NO. 418
(Vol. 3, p. 57)

Samuel Banks ca. 5 August 1847

Samuel Banks is about 50 years old, 5 feet 8 inches tall, of a black complexion, with a scar on his upper lip and another on his right cheekbone. He was emancipated by John Childs by deed dated 5 December 1817.

REGISTRATION NO. 419
(Vol. 3, p. 57)

Daniel Brown 4 August 1847

Daniel Brown is about 30 years old, 5 feet 5½ inches tall, of a black complexion, with a scar on his right eyebrow, and another on his left eyebrow. He has a stammer. He was born free, as appears by information from Peter Hewitt.

REGISTRATION NO. 420
(Vol. 3, p. 57)

Charles W. Richardson 5 August 1847

Charles W. Richardson is about 46 years old, 5 feet 5½ inches tall, of a black complexion, with a scar on his left eyebrow and another on the back of the head, and with his left thumb dislocated. He was emancipated by Alexander Hunter.

REGISTRATION NO. 421
(Vol. 3, p. 57)

Thomas Shorter Gray 5 August 1847

Thomas Shorter Gray is about 39 years old, 5 feet 11 inches tall, with a brownish-black color, and a scar on the right side of his face near the corner of his eye. He was born free.

REGISTRATION NO. 422
(Vol. 3, p. 57)

Moses Hepburn 5 August 1847

Moses Hepburn is a dark mulatto, about 38 years old, 5 feet 11½ inches tall, with his left eye and his left cheek scarred. He was born free.

REGISTRATION NO. 423
(Vol. 3, p. 57)

Martha Roman ca. 5 August 1847

Martha Roman is a dark mulatto, about 25 years old, with a large scar on her right arm. She was born free, as appears by evidence of Jabez Wheeler.

REGISTRATION NO. 424
(Vol. 3, p. 58)

Henrietta Edwards 5 August 1847

Henrietta Edwards is a bright mulatto, about 55 years old with no marks or scars. She was emancipated by John Lloyd upon his testimony.

REGISTRATION NO. 425
(Vol. 3, p. 58)

Jeremiah Quanders   ca. 5 August 1847

Jeremiah Quanders is a black man, about 33 years old, with a scar on his left eyebrow and a scar on his upper lip. The little finger of his right hand is scarred. He was born free, as appears by evidence of Elizabeth Simms.

REGISTRATION NO. 426
(Vol. 3, p. 58)

Milly Page   5 August 1847

Milly Page is a mulatto, about 64 years old, 5 feet 3½ inches tall, with a small scar under her left eye. She was emancipated by Col. William Grayson.

REGISTRATION NO. 427
(Vol. 3, p. 58)

Kitty Bockett   5 August 1847

Kitty Bockett is a bright mulatto, about 40 years old, 5 feet 1½ inches tall, with a scar or mark above her left eye. She is the daughter of Milly Page and was born free.

REGISTRATION NO. 428
(Vol. 3, p. 58)

Monica Lucas   ca. 5 August 1847

Monica Lucas is a black woman who is about 70 years old. She has no visible marks or scars.

REGISTRATION NO. 429
(Vol. 3, p. 58)

Jefferson Mayo   5 August 1847

Jefferson Mayo is about 25 years old, 5 feet 3 inches tall, with a black complexion, and a scar on his left cheek. He was born free, as appears by evidence of Francis Key.

REGISTRATION NO. 430
(Vol. 3, p. 58)

John Goings   ca. 5 August 1847

John Goings is about 50 years old, 5 feet 9 inches tall, of a very black complexion, with several small scars on his left arm. He is free.

REGISTRATION NO. 431
(Vol. 3, p. 58)

John Grant   ca. 5 August 1847

John Grant is a dark mulatto, about 54 years old, 5 feet 9 3/4 inches tall, with a scar over his left eye. He was born free.

REGISTRATION NO. 432
(Vol. 3, p. 59)

Martha Colbert   ca. 5 August 1847

Martha Colbert is about 13 years old, 5 feet one-half inch tall, of a black complexion, with no visible marks. She was born free.

REGISTRATION NO. 433
(Vol. 3, p. 59)

Hannah Bruce   6 August 1847

Hannah Bruce is a bright mulatto, about 60 years old, 5 feet 2 3/4 inches tall, with a mole on her face near her lower lip and a white scar at the corner of her mouth. She was emancipated by Jesse Scott and James English.

REGISTRATION NO. 434
(Vol. 3, p. 59)

Hannah Ann Bruce

6 August 1847

Hannah Ann Bruce is a bright mulatto, about 22 years old, 5 feet 1½ inches tall, with a mole near the right corner of her mouth. She was born free.

REGISTRATION NO. 435
(Vol. 3, p. 59)

Isaac Hall

ca. 6 August 1847

Isaac Hall is a dark mulatto, about 42 years old, 5 feet 5¼ inches tall, with a small scar on his lips at the left corner of his mouth. He was born free.

REGISTRATION NO. 436
(Vol. 3, p. 59)

Enoch Doster

ca. 6 August 1847

Enoch Doster is a bright mulatto, about 52 years old, 5 feet 4¼ inches tall, with a large scar on his left leg and bushy or curly hair and gray eyes. He was manumitted by Margaret Thompson's will.

REGISTER NO. 437
(Vol. 3, p. 59)

Maria Doster

ca. 6 August 1847

Maria Doster is a dark mulatto, about 50 years old, 5 feet 1½ inches tall, with no visible marks. She is the wife of Enoch Doster and was manumitted by him.

REGISTRATION NO. 438
(Vol. 3, p. 59)

George H. Berry

ca. 6 August 1847

George H. Berry is about 25 years old, 5 feet 5½ inches tall, of a black complexion, with a mole on his right cheek. He was born free, as appears by evidence of Henry Whittington.

REGISTRATION NO. 439
(Vol. 3, p. 59)

Walter Berry

ca. 6 August 1847

Walter Berry is about 20 years old, 5 feet 2¼ inches tall, of a black complexion, with a small scar at the right corner of his right eye and a scar on his left arm. He was born free, as appears by evidence of Henry Whittington.

REGISTRATION NO. 440
(Vol. 3, p. 60)

William Wilson

6 August 1847

William Wilson is about 34 years old, 5 feet 6¼ inches tall, of a black complexion, with a scar on his forehead at the edge of his hair. He was manumitted by William Solomon, as appears by a deed dated 30 May 1836 recorded in the District of Columbia Circuit Court.

REGISTRATION NO. 441
(Vol. 3, p. 60)

Flora E. Morgan Wilson

ca. 6 August 1847

Flora E. Wilson, late Morgan, is a dark mulatto, about 25 years old, 5 feet 4¼ inches tall, with both thumbs stiffened. She was born free.

REGISTRATION NO. 442
(Vol. 3, p. 60)

James H. Brown   6 August 1847

James H. Brown is about 22 years old, 5 feet 3 inches tall, of a brownish-black color, with several small scars on cheeks, a scar on his nose and two on his left forefinger. He is free, as appears from his indenture in the Orphans' Court.

REGISTRATION NO. 443
(Vol. 3, p. 60)

John Doster   ca. 6 August 1847

John Doster is a bright mulatto, about 30 years old, 5 feet 6 inches tall, with a small scar on his forehead and another on his right arm. He was manumitted by Margaret Thompson's will.

REGISTRATION NO. 444
(Vol. 3, p. 60)

Delia Smith   ca. 6 August 1847

Delia Smith is about 50 years old, 4 feet 11 inches tall, of a black complexion, with a large scar on her right arm from a burn. She was emancipated by Margaret Thompson's will.

REGISTRATION NO. 445
(Vol. 3, p. 60)

John Smith   ca. 6 August 1847

John Smith is about 12 years old, 4 feet 5 inches tall, of a black complexion, with no visible marks. He is the grandson of Delia Smith and was emancipated by Margaret Thompson's will.

REGISTRATION NO. 446
(Vol. 3, p. 60)

Letty Jackson   6 August 1847

Letty Jackson is about 58 years old, 4 feet ?? inches tall, of a black complexion, with a small scar on her right arm. She was manumitted by Thomas Janney by deed dated 10 May 1822.

REGISTRATION NO. 447
(Vol. 3, p. 61)

Charles Haney   6 August 1847

Charles Haney is about 44 years old, 5 feet 5¼ inches tall, of a black complexion, with several of his upper teeth out, two scars over his left eye, a scar on his right cheek, and a small scar on his right hand. He is free.

REGISTRATION NO. 448
(Vol. 3, p. 61)

Eliza Anderson   6 August 1847

Eliza Anderson is a dark mulatto, about 29 years old, 5 feet 5¼ inches tall, with no visible marks. She was emancipated by Sambo Anderson.

REGISTRATION NO. 449
(Vol. 3, p. 61)

Elijah Wedge   5 August 1847

Elijah Wedge is about 49 years old, 5 feet 6½ inches tall, of a black complexion, with a scar over his right eye on his forehead, a scar on the forefinger of his left hand, a scar on his left foot, and a scar in his left eyebrow. He was born free.

REGISTRATION NO. 450
(Vol. 3, p. 61)

John Sumby   5 August 1847

John Sumby is a dark mulatto, about 28 years old, 5 feet 8 3/4 inches tall, with a scar on his left leg below the knee. He was born free.

REGISTRATION NO. 451
(Vol. 3, p. 61)

Lucinda Derrick

7 August 1847

Lucinda "Derick" [Derrick] is about 31 years old, 4 feet 10¼ inches tall, of a brownish-black color, with a scar on her right cheek caused by a burn. She was born free.

REGISTRATION NO. 452
(Vol. 3, p. 61)

Solomon Dixon

7 August 1847

Solomon Dixon is a dark mulatto, about 55 years old, 5 feet 5¼ inches tall, with a small scar above his left eyebrow, and is bald. He is free, as appears by a certificate dated 5 June 1811 signed by the mayor of Alexandria.

REGISTRATION NO. 453
(Vol. 3, p. 61)

Horatio Jennings

ca. 7 August 1847

Horatio Jennings is a dark mulatto, about 50 years old, 5 feet 8½ inches tall, with a scar on his left hand, a scar on his right arm, and a scar on his left arm. He was born free.

REGISTRATION NO. 454
(Vol. 3, p. 62)

Sinah Lee

7 August 1847

Sinah Lee is about 66 years old, 5 feet 2 inches tall, of a black complexion, with scars across the fingers of her left hand and smallpox marks. She was emancipated by Richard Libby by deed dated 8 October 1814.

REGISTRATION NO. 455
(Vol. 3, p. 62)

David Middleton

7 August 1847

David Middleton is about 56 years old, 5 feet 7 inches tall, of a black complexion, with a scar in the palm of his left hand. He is free, as appears by evidence of Samuel Bartle.

REGISTRATION NO. 456
(Vol. 3, p. 62)

Mary Morgan

ca. 7 August 1847

Mary Morgan is a dark mulatto, about 45 years old, 5 feet 5 inches tall, with a scar a little above her left breast, and who is slightly freckled. She was born free.

REGISTRATION NO. 457
(Vol. 3, p. 62)

Hannah Lee Butler

7 August 1847

Hannah Butler, formerly Lee, is about 55 years old, 5 feet 6 inches tall, of a black complexion, with a mark on her left hand and on her left wrist. She was emancipated by Alexander Hunter.

REGISTRATION NO. 458
(Vol. 3, p. 62)

Fanny Starks

7 August 1847

Fanny Starks is about 40 years old, 5 feet 5 inches tall, of a black complexion, with no visible marks. She was emancipated by John Lee by deed recorded in Washington Court [District of Columbia].

REGISTRATION NO. 459
(Vol. 3, p. 62)

Wilson Solomon

7 August 1847

Wilson Solomon is about 21 years old, 6 feet one-fourth inch tall, of a black complexion, with a scar on the middle finger of his right hand. He was born free.

REGISTRATION NO. 460
(Vol. 3, p. 62)

Malvina Mitchell													ca. 7 August 1847

Malvina Mitchell is about 40 years old, of a black complexion, with her left arm scarred from being broken. She was emancipated by Jo[seph] Mitchell by deed dated 1833.

REGISTRATION NO. 461
(Vol. 3, p. 63)

William Curtis													ca. 7 August 1847

William Curtis is a dark mulatto, about 39 years old, 5 feet 6¼ inches tall, with a scar on his nose, one on his upper lip, and another on the forefinger of his right hand. He was born free, as appears by his registration in the District of Columbia.

REGISTRATION NO. 462
(Vol. 3, p. 63)

Benjamin Hughes													7 August 1847

Benjamin Hughes is a dark mulatto, about 50 years old, 5 feet 9 inches tall, with a scar on the back of his right hand and another on his left eyebrow. He is free.

REGISTRATION NO. 463
(Vol. 3, p. 63)

Ann Brown													ca. 7 August 1847

Ann Brown is about 22 years old, 5 feet 2½ inches tall, of a black complexion, with a scar on her right arm between the elbow and wrist. She was born free.

REGISTRATION NO. 464
(Vol. 3, p. 63)

Mahala Reily Bird													ca. 7 August 1847

Mahala [Reily] Bird is a bright mulatto, about 42 years old, 5 feet 6¼ inches tall, with blots or dark spots over her face. She was born free.

REGISTRATION NO. 465
(Vol. 3, p. 63)

Virginia Fuller													6 September 1847

Virginia Fuller is a dark mulatto, about 14 years old, 5 feet 1 inch tall, with a large scar on her neck. She was born free.

REGISTRATION NO. 466
(Vol. 3, p. 63)

Charles Hamilton													6 September 1847

Charles Hamilton is about 25 years old, 5 feet 2¼ inches tall, of a black complexion, with a scar on his left cheek and another on his left hand near the wrist. He was born free, as appears by oath of James S. Scott.

REGISTRATION NO. 467
(Vol. 3, p. 63)

Maria Bryant Seaton													[ca. 6 September 1847]

Maria Seaton, late Bryant, is a bright mulatto, about 23 years old, 5 feet 1 inch tall, with a small scar between the first and second joints of the first finger of her left hand and a small dark mole on her upper lip. She is free, as appears by her registration from Loudoun [County].

REGISTRATION NO. 468
(Vol. 3, p. 64)

Anthony Obleton [ca. 7 September 1847]

Anthony Obleton is about 40 years old, 5 feet 10½ inches tall, of a black complexion, with a scar on his forehead. He was born free, as appears by evidence of Elizabeth Ferguson.

REGISTRATION NO. 469
(Vol. 3, p. 64)

Ellen Obleton 7 September 1847

Ellen Obleton is a dark mulatto, about 36 years old, 5 feet 3¼ inches tall, with a scar on her upper lip and another on her left arm. She was emancipated by Joseph Dodds.

REGISTRATION NO. 470
(Vol. 3, p. 64)

Mary Sumby 7 September 1847

Mary Sumby is about 43 years old, 5 feet one-half inch tall, of a black complexion, with a large black mole on the right side of her face a little below her nose. She was emancipated by Sally Thomas by deed dated 24 July 1844.

REGISTRATION NO. 471
(Vol. 3, p. 64)

Joseph Henry Frazier [ca. 7 September 1847]

Joseph Henry Frazier is a bright mulatto, about 14 years old, 4 feet 7 inches tall, with no visible marks, and with sandy colored hair. He was born free.

REGISTRATION NO. 472
(Vol. 3, p. 64)

James Carter 6 September 1847

James Carter is a bright mulatto, about 26 years old, 5 feet 7 inches tall, with a small scar on his left wrist. He was born free, as appears by oath of C. A. Alexander.

REGISTRATION NO. 473
(Vol. 3, p. 64)

Louisa Myers [ca. 6 September 1847]

Louisa Myers is a bright mulatto, about 24 years old, 5 feet 8½ inches tall, with a scar in the center of the palm of her left hand and a scar under her chin on the throat. She was born free.

REGISTRATION NO. 474
(Vol. 3, p. 64)

Fanny Richardson [ca. 6 September 1847]

Fanny Richardson is about 33 years old, 5 feet 2½ inches tall, of a black complexion, with a small black mole on the right side of her neck. She is free, as appears by former registration No. 711 [in volume 1].

REGISTRATION NO. 475
(Vol. 3, p. 64)

Julia A. Mandeville Carter 6 September 1847

Julia A. Carter, formerly Julia A. Mandeville, is a very bright mulatto, aged about 33 years, 5 feet 3½ inches tall, who is slightly freckled, with no visible scars. She was emancipated by Joseph Humphreys by deed recorded in Liber T No. 2, page 245.

REGISTRATION NO. 476
(Vol. 3, p. 65)

Eleanor Bowles 6 September 1847

Eleanor Bowles is a bright mulatto, about 37 years old, 5 feet 2 inches tall, with several scars on the left side of her nose. She was emancipated by John Skidmore.

REGISTRATION NO. 477
(Vol. 3, p. 65)

George Smith								6 September 1847

George Smith is about 35 years old, of a black complexion, with a scar on his nose between his eyes, another on the left eyebrow, and one of his upper front teeth is missing. He was manumitted by Samuel Shreve and identified by the oaths of James S. Scott and Charles H. Upton.

REGISTRATION NO. 478
(Vol. 3, p. 65)

Harriet Haney Rhodes							6 September 1847

Harriet Haney, alias Rhodes, is about 45 years old, 5 feet 4½ inches tall, of a black complexion, with several scars on her neck and right arm. She is free, as appears by a previous registration.

REGISTRATION NO. 479
(Vol. 3, p. 65)

Mary Ann Stewart							[ca. 6 September 1847]

Mary Ann Stewart is about 33 years old, 4[?] feet 10 3/4 inches tall, of a brown-black color, with a large scar on the left side of her neck. She was emancipated by Col. William Minor.

REGISTRATION NO. 480
(Vol. 3, p. 65)

Angela Fox								[ca. 6 September 1847]

Angela Fox is about 45 years old, 5 feet 3 3/4 inches tall, of a black complexion, with a scar on her forehead and with the end of the third finger on her right hand deformed and crooked. She was emancipated [rest of statement is blank].

REGISTRATION NO. 481
(Vol. 3, p. 65)

Robert Brannum								7 September 1847

Robert Brannum is a very bright mulatto, about 23 years old, 5 feet 8 3/4 inches tall, with no visible marks. He was emancipated by Robert Jamieson, as appears by previous registration No. 129 [in volume 2].

REGISTRATION NO. 482
(Vol. 3, p. 65)

Elizabeth Curtis								7 September 1847

Elizabeth Curtis is a very bright mulatto, about 26 years old, 5 feet 4½ inches tall, with a mole on each side of her neck. She has had her right collar bone broken. Curtis was born free, as appears by a previous registration.

REGISTRATION NO. 483
(Vol. 3, p. 66)

James Cole								4 October 1847

James Cole is a bright mulatto, about 34 years old, 5 feet 7 inches tall, with no visible marks, and straight hair. He was born free, as appears by evidence of John Hollinsberry.

REGISTRATION NO. 484
(Vol. 3, p. 66)

Lydia Ann Hawkins							4 October 1847

Lydia Ann Hawkins is about 21 years old, 5 feet 2 3/8 inches tall, of a brownish-black color, with a scar on the left side of her cheek, and a scar on the knuckles of the first and second fingers of her right hand. She was born free, as appears by evidence of Ann Davis.

REGISTRATION NO. 485
(Vol. 3, p. 66)

Lucy Bennett Richardson

5 October 1847

Lucy Richardson, formerly Lucy Bennett, is about 48 years old, 5 feet tall, of a brown-black complexion, with a scar on the back of her right hand. She is free, as appears by a previous registration.

REGISTRATION NO. 486
(Vol. 3, p. 66)

Henry Brown

[ca. 5 October 1847]

Henry Brown is a bright mulatto, about 57 years old, 5 feet 5 inches tall, with a scar on the back of his left hand and a small scar on his right eyebrow. He is free, as appears by a previous registration.

REGISTRATION NO. 487
(Vol. 3, p. 66)

William Henry Cole

6 October 1847

William Henry Cole is a bright mulatto, about 29 years old, 5 feet 9 inches tall, with a scar on the inner side of his thumb and a scar on his right arm caused by a burn. He was born free, as appears by evidence of Lucien Peyton.

REGISTRATION NO. 488
(Vol. 3, p. 66)

Margaret Lomax

1 November 1847

Margaret Lomax is about 24 years old, 5 feet 1½ inches inches tall, of a brownish-black color, who is slightly cross-eyed, but with no visible marks. She is the daughter of Ellen Lomax, and was born free, as appears by evidence of Lucien Peyton.

REGISTRATION NO. 489
(Vol. 3, p. 66)

Delilah Lomax

1 November 1847

Delilah Lomax is about 22[?] years old, 5 feet 1½ inches tall, of a brownish-black complexion, with no visible scars. She is the daughter of Ellen Lomax, and as born free as appears by evidence of Lucien Peyton.

REGISTRATION NO. 490
(Vol. 3, p. 66)

Julia Lomax

1 November 1847

Julia Lomax is about 20 years old, 5 feet 3 inches tall, of a brownish-black color, with a very slight scar or mark near and a little below the corner of her left eye. She is the daughter of Ellen Lomax, and was born free, as appears by evidence of Delilah Hall.

REGISTRATION NO. 491
(Vol. 3, p. 67)

Gracey Gales Snowden

[ca. 1 November 1847]

Gracey Snowden, late Gracey Gales, is about 37 years old, 5 feet 1 3/4 inches tall, of a brownish-black color, with no visible marks. She was born free.

REGISTRATION NO. 492
(Vol. 3, p. 67)

Albert Cavans

1 November 1847

Albert Cavans is a dark mulatto, about 21 years old, 5 feet 11 3/4 inches tall, with a scar on his left arm above the wrist. He was born free, as appears by oath of James O. C. Hoskins.

REGISTRATION NO. 493
(Vol. 3, p. 67)

Julia Easton

1 November 1847

Julia Easton is a bright mulatto, about 49 years old, 4 feet 11½ inches tall, with a scar at the right corner of her mouth and a dark spot on her left cheek. She was emancipated by Bryan Hampson, as appears by oath of Joseph [H.] Hampson.

REGISTRATION NO. 494
(Vol. 3, p. 67)

Mary London   2 November 1847

Mary London is about 19 years old, 5 feet 2 1/8 inches tall, of a brownish-black complexion, with a scar on the elbow of her left arm caused by a burn. She was born free, as appears by evidence of Turner Dixon.

REGISTRATION NO. 495
(Vol. 3, p. 67)

Ellen Smith   2 November 1847

Ellen Smith is about 19 years old, 4 feet 10 5/8 inches tall, of a black complexion with several light scars or marks on the back of her neck. She was born free, as appears by evidence of Turner Dixon.

REGISTRATION NO. 496
(Vol. 3, p. 67)

Nancy Williams   2 November 1847

Nancy Williams is a dark mulatto about 18 years old, 5 feet 4 3/4 inches tall, with a scar over her left eyebrow near the temple. She was born free.

REGISTRATION NO. 497
(Vol. 3, p. 67)

Mary Wheeler   2 November 1847

Mary Wheeler is about 33 years old, 5 feet 8½ inches tall, of a brownish-black color, with a slight scar on her left cheekbone near her eye. She was born free.

REGISTRATION NO. 498
(Vol. 3, p. 68)

Martha Ann Wheeler   2 November 1847

Martha Ann Wheeler is about 14 years old, 4 feet 11½ inches tall, of a brownish-black color, with a small scar on her right wrist. She was born free.

REGISTRATION NO. 499
(Vol. 3, p. 68)

Samuel Brown   [ca. 2 November 1847]

Samuel Brown is about 23 years old, 5 feet 4¼ inches tall, of a black complexion, with a scar in the eyebrow of his right eye and one on the third finger of his right hand near the fingernail. He was born free.

REGISTRATION NO. 500
(Vol. 3, p. 68)

John Jones, alias John Whiting   6 December 1847

John Jones, alias John Whiting, is a bright mulatto, about 35 years old, 5 feet 7½ inches tall, with a scar over each eyebrow. He was emancipated by John Whiting by deed dated 11 May 1819 recorded in Liber K No. 2, folio 42.

REGISTRATION NO. 501
(Vol. 3, p. 68)

William Syphax   7 December 1847

William Syphax is a mulatto, about 23 years old, 5 feet 11 inches tall, with a scar on his nose between his eyes and a scar at the corner of his left eye. He was emancipated by Edward Stabler's administrators[?], by deed dated 2 June 1845.

REGISTRATION NO. 502
(Vol. 3, p. 68)

Cornelius Dogan

7 December 1847

Cornelius Dogan is a bright mulatto, about 19 years old, 5 feet 11½ inches tall, with a small scar under his left eye. He was born free, as appears by evidence from Elizabeth Ann Piper.

REGISTRATION NO. 503
(Vol. 3, p. 68)

Rachel Haney

[ca. 7 February 1848]

Rachel Haney is a dark mulatto, about 29 years old, 5 feet 3¼ inches tall, with a scar on the back of her right hand just below the left finger. She was emancipated by Edward Daingerfield by deed dated 7 February 1848.

REGISTRATION NO. 504
(Vol. 3, p. 68)

Sally Pitts

6 March 1848

Sally Pitts is about 40 years old, 5 feet 3¼ inches tall, of a brownish-black color, with a scar on the forefinger of her left hand. She was emancipated by Samuel R. Adams by deed dated 8 February 1848.

REGISTRATION NO. 505
(Vol. 3, p. 69)

Martha Pitts

6 March 1848

Martha Pitts is a dark mulatto, about 8 years old, 4 feet high, with a scar from a burn on the right side of her face near the temple. She was emancipated by Samuel R. Adams by deed dated 8 February 1848.

REGISTRATION NO. 506
(Vol. 3, p. 69)

Emily Cole Gray

6 April 1848

Emily Gray, late Cole, is a mulatto, about 27 years old, 5 feet 2½ inches tall, with a small scar on the top of her breast bone and a small scar on her right arm below the elbow. She was born free, as appears by her previous registration.

REGISTRATION NO. 507
(Vol. 3, p. 69)

Mary Hinds

6 April 1848

Mary Hinds is a bright mulatto, about 15 years old, 5 feet one-eighth inch tall, with a small scar over her right eyebrow. She was born free, as appears by evidence of Nancy Jefferson.

REGISTRATION NO. 508
(Vol. 3, p. 69)

Maria Gibson

3 April 1848

Maria Gibson is a mulatto, about 26 years old, 5 feet 3 inches tall, with a scar on her right temple. She was born free.

REGISTRATION NO. 509
(Vol. 3, p. 69)

Mary Ellen Hodge

4 April 1848

Mary Ellen Hodge is a mulatto, about 21 years old, with a scar under her right eye and another on her left wrist. She was born free.

REGISTRATION NO. 510
(Vol. 3, p. 69)

Elizabeth Evans

6 April 1848

Elizabeth Evans is a dark mulatto, about 27 years old, 5 feet 1¼ inches tall, with a scar on the right side of her neck and a scar on three fingers of her left hand. She was born free, as appears by her registration from Fairfax County.

See No. 62 Book 3 of the Fairfax County registrations. (Sweig, p. 123)

REGISTRATION NO. 511
(Vol. 3, p. 69)

James Burrell [ca. 6 April 1848]

James Burrell is about 22 years old, 3[sic?] feet, 11 1/8 inches tall, with a scar on the forefinger of his left hand which made it crooked. He was born free.

REGISTRATION NO. 512a
(Vol. 3, p. 69)

Milly Jones 1 May 1848

Milly Jones is a mulatto about 69 years old, 5 feet 4¼ inches tall, with no visible marks. She was manumitted by John Whiting by deed recorded in Liber K No. 2, page 42.

REGISTRATION NO. 512b
(Vol. 3, p. 70)

William Beckley, Sr. 1 May 1848

William Beckley, Sr., is a dark mulatto, about 47 years old, 5 feet 3½ inches tall, with a large scar on his right leg below his knee, a small scar over his right eye, and another under his left eye. He was born free, as appears by a previous registration.

REGISTRATION NO. 513
(Vol. 3, p. 70)

Amanda Bull Smith 2 May 1848

Amanda Bull, now Smith, is a bright mulatto, about 24 years old, 5 feet 3½ inches tall, with no visible marks. She was born free, as appears by a previous registration.

REGISTRATION NO. 514
(Vol. 3, p. 70)

Zachariah Handless [ca. 2 May 1848]

Zachariah Handless is a dark mulatto, about 27 years old, 5 feet 6¼ inches tall, with a small scar on the left side of his neck and a lump on the small of his back caused by an injury when he was young. He was born free.

REGISTRATION NO. 515
(Vol. 3, p. 70)

Alexis Baker 3 July 1848

Alexis Baker is about 32 years old, 5 feet 10 inches tall, of a black complexion, with scars on her left arm just below the elbow. Alexis was emancipated by Thomas Janney, as appears by of Robert Brockett.

REGISTRATION NO. 516
(Vol. 3, p. 70)

Albert F. Darnall 5 June 1848

Albert F. Darnall is about 17 years old, 5 feet 6½ inches tall, of a brownish-black color, with no visible scars. He was born free, as appears by evidence of Turner Dixon.

REGISTRATION NO. 517
(Vol. 3, p. 70)

George Brooks 6 June 1848

George Brooks is about 60 years old, 5 feet 6¼ inches tall, of a black complexion, with no visible marks. He was emancipated by Harriet Brooks by deed recorded 6 June 1848.

REGISTRATION NO. 518
(Vol. 3, p. 518)

Mary Francis Alexander

3 July 1848

Mary Francis Alexander is a bright mulatto, about 19 years old, 5 feet one-half inch tall, with a scar on the upper lip near the left corner of her mouth and a cross on the back of her right hand near the lower knuckle of her thumb. She was born free.

REGISTRATION NO. 519
(Vol. 3, p. 71)

Daniel Davis

3 July 1848

Daniel Davis is about 40 years old, 5 feet 7 3/4 inches tall, of a black complexion, with a slight scar across the top of his nose. He was born free.

REGISTRATION NO. 520
(Vol. 3, p. 71)

Lucy Ann Turner

5 July 1848

Lucy Ann Turner is a mulatto, about 20 years old, 5 feet 5 inches tall, with a scar on the forefinger of her right hand between the first and second knuckles. She was born free.

REGISTRATION NO. 521
(Vol. 3, p. 71)

James Berry

17 July 1848

James Berry is about 34 years old, 5 feet 2¼ inches tall, of a black complexion, with a scar on each side of his neck, one on his breast, and a scar on each of the fingers of his left hand. He was born free, as appears by evidence of Henry Cryss[?].

REGISTRATION NO. 522
(Vol. 3, p. 71)

Felix Quander

4 September 1848

Felix Quander is about 21 years old, 6 feet tall, of a black complexion, with a scar across his left eyebrow. He was born free, as appears by evidence of Elizabeth Simms.

REGISTRATION NO. 523
(Vol. 3, p. 71)

Bertha Ellen Syphax

9 September 1848

Bertha Ellen Syphax is a bright mulatto, about 25 years old, 5 feet 3 inches tall, with very thin eyebrows. She was emancipated by William Stabler.

REGISTRATION NO. 524
(Vol. 3, p. 71)

William Montgomery Taylor

6 November 1848

William Montgomery Taylor is a very bright mulatto, about 28 years old, 5 feet 7½ inches tall, with a slight scar on the bridge of his nose and straight hair. He was emancipated by Lawrence Hooff's will.

REGISTRATION NO. 525
(Vol. 3, p. 71)

Henry Anderson

6 November 1848

Henry Anderson is about 19 years old, 5 feet 5 3/4 inches tall, with a large black scar on his right arm. He was born free.

REGISTRATION NO. 526
(Vol. 3, p. 71)

Charles Syphax

9 November 1848

Charles Syphax is a mulatto, 19 years old, 5 feet 9½ inches tall, with no visible scars. He was emancipated by George W. P. Custis.

REGISTRATION NO. 527
(Vol. 3, p. 71)

James H. Tate   7 December 1848

James H. Tate is 21 years old, 5 feet 8½ inches tall, of a black complexion, with a scar on his left hand near the wrist. He born free, as appears by a previous registration.

REGISTRATION NO. 528
(Vol. 3, p. 71)

George Washington   [ca. 7 December 1848]

George Washington is about 26[?] years old, 6 feet one-fourth inch tall, of a brownish-black color, with two scars on his forehead, one over his left eyebrow, and another slight scar across his nose. He was born free.

REGISTRATION NO. 529
(Vol. 3, p. 72)

Cecilia Brown   7 February 1849

Cecilia Brown is about 50 years old, 4 feet 10½ inches tall, with a small mole on her chin. She was freed by Benjamin Contee by deed dated 4 December 1848.

REGISTRATION NO. 530
(Vol. 3, p. 72)

Julia Godfrey   7 February 1849

Julia Godfrey is a bright mulatto, about 21 years old, 5 feet tall, with a scar on her right elbow. She was born free, as appears by evidence of John Whaley.

REGISTRATION NO. 531
(Vol. 3, p. 72)

John M. Turley   [ca. 7 February 1849]

John M. Turley is about 22 years old, 5 feet 10¼ inches tall, of a black complexion, with a small scar at the corner of his left eye. He was born free, as appears by evidence of Robert Jamieson.

REGISTRATION NO. 532
(Vol. 3, p. 72)

Mary Chase Digges   29 May 1849

Mary Chase, alias Digges, is a dark mulatto, about 57 years old, 5 feet 2½ inches tall, with a small scar near her left eye. She was emancipated by John C. Herbert by deed recorded in Liber K, folio 333.

REGISTRATION NO. 533
(Vol. 3, p. 72)

Mary Waugh   29 May 1849

Mary Waugh is a bright mulatto, about 65 years old, 5 feet 3½ inches tall, with a cataract in her right eye. She was born free, as appears by a previous registration.

REGISTRATION NO. 534
(Vol. 3, p. 72)

Samson Sumby   30 May 1849

Samson Sumby is a dark mulatto, about 39 years old, 5 feet 10 inches tall, with a small scar just above the left eyebrow and another across his right eyebrow. He was born free, as appears by a previous registration.

REGISTRATION NO. 535
(Vol. 3, p. 72)

Maria Morris   1 June 1849

Maria Morris is a dark mulatto, about 57 years old, 5 feet 2 inches tall, with three small black moles on the right side of her neck. She was emancipated by Maria Blue.

REGISTRATION NO. 536
(Vol. 3, p. 72)

Lucy Haney Davis

26 June 1849

Lucy Davis, late Lucy Haney, is a bright mulatto, about 28 years old, 5 feet 3½ inches tall, with a mole on the center of her [illegible] She was born free, as appears by a previous registration.

REGISTRATION NO. 537
(Vol. 3, p. 73)

Emily Berry

23 July 1849

Emily Berry is about 39 years old, 4 feet 10 3/4 inches tall, of a brownish-black color, with a mole on her chin, another on her forehead, and a slender scar on her left under jaw. She was emancipated by Armistead Ford by deed recorded 4 October 1847.

REGISTRATION NO. 538
(Vol. 3, p. 73)

Catharine Booth

[ca. 23 July 1849]

Catharine Booth is about 20 years old, 5 feet 4½ inches tall, of a black complexion, with a scar on her throat under her chin. She was born free, as appears by evidence from James Padgett[?].

REGISTRATION NO. 539
(Vol. 3, p. 73)

Ann Smith

[ca. 23 July 1849]

Ann Smith is a mulatto, about 23 years old, 4 feet 11 3/4 inches tall, freckled, with no visible marks. She was born free.

REGISTRATION NO. 540
(Vol. 3, p. 73)

Daniel Bennett

27 August 1849

Daniel Bennett is about 21 years old, 5 feet 7 inches tall, of a black complexion, with a very small mole above his right eye. He was born free, as appears by the evidence of George Bryan.

REGISTRATION NO. 541
(Vol. 3, p. 73)

Armistead Medella

27 August 1849

Armistead Medella is about 25 years old, 5 feet 9½ inches tall, of a brownish-black color, with a small scar on his forehead in the edge of his hair and a small scar on the back of his left hand. He was emancipated by William H. Wilmer by a deed to slave Maria[?] and others in the nature of a bill of sale.

REGISTRATION NO. 542
(Vol. 3, p. 73)

George Smith

27 August 1849

George Smith is about 36 years old, 5 feet 2 3/4 inches tall, of a black complexion, with a scar and three moles on his right wrist. He was emancipated by the will of Margaret Shreve and identified by William Minor.

REGISTRATION NO. 543
(Vol. 3, p. 73)

Rozier D. Beckley

24 September 1849

Rozier D. Beckley is a bright mulatto, about 20 years old, 5 feet 9¼ inches tall, with a small mole on his upper lip. He was born free, as appears by evidence of Joseph Carson.

REGISTRATION NO. 544
(Vol. 3, p. 74)

Guy Henry Piper											24 December 1849

Guy Henry Piper is about 40 years old, 6 feet high, of a brownish-black color, with a scar on his right hand near the lower thumb joint and several small scars on his wrist and on the back of the same hand, and a scar over his right eye. He was born free, as appears by his registration from Fairfax County.

REGISTRATION NO. 545
(Vol. 3, p. 74)

Eliza Williams Meredith										[ca. 24 December 1849]

Eliza Meredith, late Williams, is a dark mulatto, about 41 years old, 5 feet 2½ inches tall, with a small scar on her right hand near the thumb. She was born free.

REGISTRATION NO. 546
(Vol. 3, p. 74)

Charles Pearson											[ca. 24 December 1849]

Charles Pearson is a dark mulatto, about 22 years old, 5 feet 11½ inches tall, with several scars on the back and wrist of his left hand and a recent mark made by india ink on that same hand. He is the son of Eliza Meredith and is born free, as appears by oath of Thomas Chinn.

REGISTRATION NO. 547
(Vol. 3, p. 74)

Susannah Pearson										[ca. 24 December 1849]

Susannah Pearson is a dark mulatto, about 21 years old, 5 feet 3½ inches tall, with a scar in the eyebrow of the left eye. She was born free, as appears by evidence of Thomas Chinn.

REGISTRATION NO. 548
(Vol. 3, p. 74)

William Pearson											[ca. 24 December 1849]

William Pearson is a dark mulatto, about 18 years old, 6 feet tall, with some Indian ink recently put on the back of his left hand. He was born free, as appears by oath of Thomas Chinn.

REGISTRATION NO. 549
(Vol. 3, p. 74)

Levi Jones												24 December 1849

Levi Jones is about 37 years old, 5 feet 11 inches tall, with a dark spot on his forehead. He is the son of Elzy[?] Jones and was born free, as appears by a copy of his register taken in.

REGISTRATION NO. 550
(Vol. 3, p. 74)

Lavinia Shavers											24 December 1849

Lavinia Shavers is about 50 years old, 5 feet 2 inches tall, of a brownish-black color, with a large dark spot, now old, on the back of her right hand. She was emancipated by Landon Shavers by deed recorded 3 November 1834.

REGISTRATION NO. 551
(Vol. 3, p. 75)

Peggy Gray Jones											24 December 1849

Peggy Gray, now Peggy Jones, is about 41 years old, 5 feet 4 inches tall, of a light brown color, with a small scar in her right eyebrow. She was born free.

REGISTRATION NO. 552
(Vol. 3, p. 75)

Ann Maria Black											24 December 1849

Ann Maria Black is a bright mulatto, about 18 years old, 5 feet 2 inches tall, with a small scar on the little finger of her left hand. She was born free, as appears by evidence of Elizabeth Horseman.

REGISTRATION NO. 553
(Vol. 3, p. 75)

Joseph Jones

24 December 1849

Joseph Jones is about 40 years old, 5 feet 9 inches tall, of a black complexion, with a scar on his right cheek. He was born free.

REGISTRATION NO. 554
(Vol. 3, p. 75)

Charles Henry

24 December 1849

Charles Henry is about 23 years old, 5 feet 10 inches tall, of a light brown complexion, with scars on his left hand and over his right eyebrow, and one on the left side of his forehead. He was born free, as appears by evidence of William Minor.

REGISTRATION NO. 555
(Vol. 3, p. 75)

Douglas Jones

24 December 1849

Douglas Jones is about 19 years old, 5 feet 5½ inches tall, of a brownish-black color, with a scar on his right temple in the edge of his hair. He is the son of Peggy Jones and was born free, as appears by evidence of [illegible].

REGISTRATION NO. 556
(Vol. 3, p. 75)

Kizzy Roberts

24 December 1849

Kizzy Roberts is about 26 years old, 4 feet 5½ inches tall, of a black complexion, with a lump on top of her head. He was born free, as appears by oath of William H. F. Carlin.

REGISTRATION NO. 557
(Vol. 3, p. 75)

Edward Piper

24 December 1849

Edward Piper is about 23 years old, 6 feet tall, of a brownish-black color, with a scar on the back of each hand. He was born free, as appears by oath of William Minor.

REGISTRATION NO. 558
(Vol. 3, p. 75)

Louis Gibson

24 December 1849

Louis Gibson is about 70 years old, 5 feet 5 inches tall, with a frostbitten foot and a gray beard. He is free, as appears by evidence of William Minor.

REGISTRATION NO. 559
(Vol. 3, p. 76)

Sarah Margaret Gibson

24 December 1849

Sarah Margaret Gibson is a bright mulatto, about 20 years old, 5 feet tall, with a small scar on her forehead. She was born free, as appears by evidence of William Minor.

REGISTRATION NO. 560
(Vol. 3, p. 76)

Oscar Thomas

24 December 1849

Oscar Thomas is about 33 years old, 5 feet 6½ inches tall, of a black complexion, with a scar on his left thumb and with the end of his thumb missing. He is free, as appears by evidence of Carey Selden.

REGISTRATION NO. 561
(Vol. 3, p. 76)

John Sales   24 December 1849

John Sales is a dark mulatto, about 40 years old, 5 feet 6 inches tall, with a spot on the left side of his nose and on his left cheek. He is free, as appears by evidence of Benjamin Thomas.

REGISTRATION NO. 562
(Vol. 3, p. 76)

Barclay Jones   24 December 1849

Barclay Jones is about 25 years old, 5 feet 6 inches tall, of a black complexion, with a scar on his forehead and one on his upper lip and several small bumps on the left side of his throat. He was born free, as appears by evidence of John Ward.

REGISTRATION NO. 563
(Vol. 3, p. 76)

Samuel Hyson   24 December 1849

Samuel Hyson is about 40 years old, 5 feet 9 inches tall, of a black complexion, with his face marked with smallpox, and a scar over his left eye. He was born free.

REGISTRATION NO. 564
(Vol. 3, p. 76)

Frances Coates   24 December 1849

Frances Coates is a dark mulatto, about 33 years old, 5 feet 4 inches tall, with a scar over the left eye. Coates was born free, as appears by evidence of William Minor.

REGISTRATION NO. 565
(Vol. 3, p. 76)

Sanford Williams   24 December 1849

Sanford Williams is a dark mulatto, about 28 years old, 5 feet 9½ inches tall, with a scar on the inside of the fore and middle fingers of his left hand. He was born free, as appears by evidence of William Minor.

REGISTRATION NO. 566
(Vol. 3, p. 76)

Marcellus Williams   24 December 1849

Marcellus Williams is a dark mulatto, about 23 years old, with both little fingers crooked. He was born free, as appears by evidence of William Minor.

REGISTRATION NO. 567
(Vol. 3, p. 76)

Henry Honesty   24 December 1849

Henry Honesty is about 30 years old, 5 feet 5½ inches tall, with a scar on the back of each hand. He was born free, as appears by evidence of William Minor.

REGISTRATION NO. 568
(Vol. 3, p. 77)

Nancy Williams   24 December 1849

Nancy Williams is a bright mulatto, about 21 years old, with a scar over her left eye towards the temple. She was born free, as appears by oath of William Minor.

REGISTRATION NO. 569
(Vol. 3, p. 77)

James Honesty   24 December 1849

James Honesty is about 41 years old, 6 feet tall, of a black color, with a scar above his right eye, a scar on his throat and a scar on his breast. He was emancipated by the will of William Adams of Fairfax County.

See No. 271 in Book 3 of the Fairfax County registrations. (Sweig, p. 151)

REGISTRATION NO. 570
(Vol. 3, p. 77)

Lorenzo Branham

Certified 28 January 1850

Lorenzo Branham is a bright mulatto, about 20 years old, 5 feet 8 inches tall, with several small black moles on his face. He was born free, as appears by oath of William Stabler.

REGISTRATION NO. 571
(Vol. 3, p. 77)

Rosalee Branham

Certified 28 January 1850

Rosalee Branham is a bright mulatto, about 18 years old, 5 feet 2 inches tall, with several small moles on her face. She was born free, as appears by oath of William Stabler.

REGISTRATION NO. 572
(Vol. 3, p. 77)

Rachel Branham

Certified 28 January 1850

Rachel Branham is a bright mulatto, about 16 years old, 5 feet 3 inches tall, with no visible scars. She was born free, as appears by oath of William Stabler.

REGISTRATION NO. 573
(Vol. 3, p. 77)

William Henry Burke

29 January 1850

William Henry Burke is a bright mulatto, about 36 years old, 5 feet 7 inches tall, with a scar across his nose and two scars on his forehead. He was emancipated the will of William H. Fitzhugh and identified by Col. Silas Burke.

REGISTRATION NO. 574
(Vol. 3, p. 78)

Robert Green

29 January 1850

Robert Green is about 40 years old, 5 feet 9 inches tall, of a black complexion, with a large scar on his left hand. He was emancipated by Mary Barton and others recorded 28 January 1850, as appears by evidence of B[enjamin] Barton.

REGISTRATION NO. 575
(Vol. 3, p. 78)

Agnes Gant

29 January 1850

Agnes Gant is about 40 years old, 5 feet 4 inches tall, of a black complexion, with several small scars on her face. She was freed by deed from Mary Barton and others, recorded 28 January 1850, as appears by evidence of B[enjamin] Barton.

REGISTRATION NO. 576a
(Vol. 3, p. 78)

Charlott Hanson

29 January 1850

Charlott Hanson is about 24 years old, 5 feet 2 inches tall, of a brownish-black color, with a scar on her left wrist. She was freed by deed from Mary Barton and others, recorded 28 January 1850, as appears by evidence of B[enjamin] Barton.

REGISTRATION NO. 576b
(Vol. 3, p. 78)

Elizabeth Frances Gant

29 January 1850

Elizabeth Frances Gant is about 14 years old, 4 feet 8½ inches tall, of a brown complexion, with a scar on the third finger of her left hand. She is the daughter of Agnes Gant, and is free by the deed from Mary Barton and others, recorded 28 January 1850, as appears by evidence of Benjamin Barton.

There is no registration numbered 577.

REGISTRATION NO. 578
(Vol. 3, p. 78)

John Brown   29 January 1850

John Brown is a bright mulatto, about 32 years old, 5 feet 9 inches tall, with a small scar on the back of his right hand. He was emancipated by the will of William H. Fitzhugh and identified by Col. Silas "Burk" [Burke].

REGISTRATION NO. 579
(Vol. 3, p. 78)

Jane Jennings   29 January 1850

Jane Jennings is a very bright mulatto, about 27 years old, 5 feet 4 inches tall, with a scar between her eyes. She was born free, as appears by evidence of Dora[?] Meade.

REGISTRATION NO. 580
(Vol. 3, p. 78)

Thornton Hyson   25 February 1850

Thornton Hyson is about 25 years old, 5 feet 7 inches tall, of a black complexion, with a small scar at the left corner of his left eye. He was born free, as appears by oath of James O. Tucker.

REGISTRATION NO. 581
(Vol. 3, p. 79)

Louisa Hyson   25 February 1850

Louisa Hyson is a bright mulatto, about 34 years old, 5 feet 2 inches tall, with a scar on her right temple. She was born free, as appears by oath of James O. Tucker.

REGISTRATION NO. 582
(Vol. 3, p. 79)

Daniel Williams   25 February 1850

Daniel Williams is about 23 years old, 5 feet 9 inches tall, of a brownish-black complexion, with a scar on the forefinger of his left hand. He was born free, as appears by oath of James O. Tucker.

REGISTRATION NO. 583
(Vol. 3, p. 79)

Sarah Piper   25 February 1850

Sarah Piper is a bright mulatto, about 33 years old, 5 feet 5 inches tall, with a small scar in the center of her forehead. She is free, as appears by oath of Col. [William] Minor.

REGISTRATION NO. 584
(Vol. 3, p. 79)

John Colston   25 March 1850

John Colston is about 21 years old, 5 feet 3 inches tall, of a black complexion, with a scar in the center of his forehead. He is free, as appears by oath of John L. Pascoe.

REGISTRATION NO. 585
(Vol. 3, p. 79)

George Washington   25 March 1850

George Washington is about 35 years old, 5 feet 9 inches tall, of a black complexion, with a small scar on the center of his forehead. He is free, as appears by evidence of [James] Entwisle.

REGISTRATION NO. 586
(Vol. 3, p. 79)

Eliza Williams Meredith   25 March 1850

Eliza Meredith, late Williams, is about 29 years old, 5 feet 3 inches tall, of a brown complexion, with a small scar on her right cheek. She was born free, as appears by oath of Joseph E. Birch.

REGISTRATION NO. 587
(Vol. 3, p. 79)

Eliza Benaugh

25 March 1850

Eliza Benaugh is a bright mulatto, about 25 years old, 5 feet 3 inches tall, with a small scar on her forehead. She was born free, as appears by oath of Joseph E. Birch.

REGISTRATION NO. 588
(Vol. 3, p. 80)

Charles Gibson

25 March 1850

Charles Gibson is about 27 years old, 5 feet 9 inches tall, of a black complexion with a scar on his nose. He was born free, as appears by oath of Joseph E. Birch.

REGISTRATION NO. 589
(Vol. 3, p. 80)

Charles Marshall

26 March 1850

Charles Marshall is a bright mulatto, about 28 years old, 5 feet 9 inches tall, with a scar under his left eye. He was emancipated by James Green

REGISTRATION NO. 590
(Vol. 3, p. 80)

Lenobea[?] Harris

[ca. 26 March 1858]

Lenobea[?] Harris is a bright mulatto, about 18 years old, 5 feet 4 inches tall, with marks from smallpox. Harris was born free, as appears by a certificate from Mrs. Ann S. Mark.

REGISTRATION NO. 591
(Vol. 3, p. 80)

Henry Lee

25 June 1850

Henry Lee is about 40 years old, 5 feet 5 3/4 inches tall, of a black complexion, with a scar on his upper and lower lip and a small scar in the middle of his forehead. He is free, as appears by evidence of John Donaldson.

REGISTRATION NO. 592
(Vol. 3, p. 80)

George Colbert

[ca. 25 June 1850]

George Colbert is about 30 years old, 5 feet 2½ inches tall, with a scar across his left eyebrow, another in the center of his forehead, and another on the first knuckle of his left hand.

REGISTRATION NO. 593
(Vol. 3, p. 80)

Moses Austin

22 July 1850

Moses Austin is about 55 years old, 5 ft 5½ inches tall, copper-colored, with two scars on his left knee. He is crippled in his left knee. He is free, as appears by a record from the Jefferson County court and the identification of Francis L. Smith.

REGISTRATION NO. 594
(Vol. 3, p. 80)

Mary J. Jasper

27 August 1850

Mary J. Jasper is about 25 years old, 5 feet 1 3/4 inches tall, of a black complexion, with a scar on her left temple at the corner of her eye and another on her forehead above her right eye. She was born free in Fairfax County.

REGISTRATION NO. 595
(Vol. 3, p. 80)

Martha Gray

[ca. 27 August 1850]

Martha Gray is a bright mulatto, about 5 feet 6 3/4 inches tall, with a scar on her forehead and a crooked small finger on her left hand. She was born free, as appears by oath of James O. C. Hoskins.

REGISTRATION NO. 1[1]
(Vol. 3, p. 81)

Henry Lee   28 October 1850

Henry Lee is about 23 years old, 5 feet 5 3/4 inches tall, of a black complexion, with a scar on his left wrist. He was emancipated by Thomas R. Keith by deed recorded 28 October 1850.

REGISTRATION NO. 2
(Vol. 3, p. 81)

Moses Wright   28 October 1850

Moses Wright is a dark mulatto, about 50 years old, with a scar in the center of his forehead and another on the inside of the lower joint of the thumb on his right hand. He was emancipated by William L. Powell and Robert Jamieson by deed recorded October 1850.

REGISTRATION NO. 3
(Vol. 3, p. 81)

Laura C. Gant   28 October 1850

Laura C. Gant is about 20 years old, 5 feet 1½ inches tall, of a black complexion, with three moles on the back of her left hand. She was emancipated by Mary Barton and others by deed recorded 28 October 1850.

REGISTRATION NO. 4
(Vol. 3, p. 81)

George P. Douglas   ca. 28 October 1850

George P. Douglas is about 27 years old, 5 feet 8 3/4 inches tall, of a black complexion, with a small scar below his right nostril, a scar on the inner side of the little finger of his right hand, a black scar extending across the outer corner of his left eye, a small scar on the root of his left thumb, and a scar on his forehead above the left eye. He was born free, as appears by a previous registration.

REGISTRATION NO. 5
(Vol. 3, p. 81)

Susan Hall   28 October 1850

Susan Hall is a bright mulatto, about 22 years old, 5 feet 6 inches tall, with no visible marks. She was born free in Westmoreland County as appears by a registration from that county.

REGISTRATION NO. 6
(Vol. 3, p. 81)

Louisa Pierce   28 October 1850

Louisa Pierce is a bright mulatto, about 21 years old, 5 feet 2 inches tall, with a small scar on her left wrist. She was born free in Westmoreland County, as appears by a registration from that county.

REGISTRATION NO. 7
(Vol. 3, p. 81)

Matilda Lanham   28 October 1850

Matilda Lanham is a bright mulatto, about 19 years old, 5 feet 2 inches tall, with a scar on the back of her left hand and a small scar on the back of her left forefinger. She was emancipated by Robert W. Hunter by deed recorded October 1850.

REGISTRATION NO. 8
(Vol. 3, p. 82)

---

[1] The numbering of registrations begins again with number 1 on page 81 of the third volume and continues through registration number 581. There is no explanation for this.

William Lee   25 November 1850

William Lee is about 21 years old, 5 feet 8 inches tall, of a black complexion, with a scar on the little finger of his right hand. He was emancipated by Thomas R. Keith by deed recorded 25 November 1850.

REGISTRATION NO. 9
(Vol. 3, p. 82)

Samuel Dundas   25 November 1850

Samuel Dundas is a bright mulatto, about 28 years old, 5 feet 6¼ inches tall, with several black moles on his face and many scars on the back of his left hand and fingers. He was emancipated by Thomas R. Keith by deed recorded 25 November 1850.

REGISTRATION NO. 10
(Vol. 3, p. 82)

Agnes Virginia Semmes   25 November 1850

Agnes Virginia Semmes is a bright mulatto, about 20 years old, 4 feet 10 3/4 inches tall, with freckles on her face and a scar on her right wrist. She was born free, as appears by oath of John W. Smith.

REGISTRATION NO. 11
(Vol. 3, p. 82)

Charles Ward   27 January 1851

Charles Ward is about 30 years old, 5 feet 7 inches tall, of a black complexion, with a scar on the thumb of his right hand, a large scar on the side of the forefinger of his left hand, and a small scar on the side of his nose. He was emancipated by William H. Fitzhugh's will recorded in Fairfax County.

REGISTRATION NO. 12
(Vol. 3, p. 82)

William Norris   28 January 1851

William Norris is about 35 years old, 5 feet 4¼ inches tall, of a copper color, with a scar on the right side of his nose, another on the forefinger of his right hand, and another on his forehead above his left eye. He has two front teeth out. Norris was born free, as appears by oath of Nancy Piles.

REGISTRATION NO. 13
(Vol. 3, p. 82)

Thomas Anderson   ca. 28 January 1851

Thomas Anderson is a mulatto, about 31 years old, 6 feet tall, with a scar under his left eye. He was emancipated by Louisa C. Evans by deed recorded in Liber F No. 3, page 482.

REGISTRATION NO. 14
(Vol. 3, p. 83)

Eliza Payne   3 April 1851

Eliza Payne is about 46 years old, 5 feet 1½ inches tall, of a copper color, with a scar on the left side of her forehead and another on her left hand below the wrist. She was emancipated by Margaret Shreve's will.

REGISTRATION NO. 15
(Vol. 3, p. 83)

Margaret Ann Piper   3 April 1851

Margaret Ann Piper is a bright mulatto, about 4 feet 11 3/4 inches tall, with a scar on her right wrist and a mark on the back of her left hand. She was born free, as appears by evidence of Junius Sleymaker.

REGISTRATION NO. 16
(Vol. 3, p. 83)

Lewis Hyson   23 June 1851

Lewis Hyson is about 35 years old, 5 feet 8 3/4 inches tall, of a black complexion, with two scars on top of his nose. He was born free, as appears by evidence of Col. George Minor.

Volume 3, 1847-1861

REGISTRATION NO. 17
(Vol. 3, p. 83)

Christiana Dunbar   23 June 1851

Christiana Dunbar is about 31 years old, 5 feet 2¼ inches tall, of a black complexion, with a scar on the left side of her neck, another on her left shoulder, and several small scars on the right side of her forehead. She was freed by judgement of the Alexandria Circuit Court rendered 11 June 1831 in her suit against R. B. Alexander.

REGISTRATION NO. 18
(Vol. 3, p. 83)

Sarah Jane Foote   23 June 1851

Sarah Jane Foote is a bright mulatto, about 24 years old, 5 feet 1 inch tall, with a black mole on the right side of her face. She is free, as appears by oath of Daniel Minor.

REGISTRATION NO. 19
(Vol. 3, p. 83)

Julia Ann Foote   23 June 1851

Julia Ann Foote is a bright mulatto, about 20 years old, 5 feet 1½ inches tall, with a scar on her left arm and a mark behind her left ear. She was born free, as appears by evidence of Fendall Hugle.

REGISTRATION NO. 20
(Vol. 3, p. 83)

Sarah Longster   ca. 23 June 1851

Sarah Longster is a bright mulatto, about 20 years old, 5 feet 1 inch tall, with her middle finger of the right hand broken and a scar on the middle finger of her left hand. She was born free, as appears by evidence of T[urner] Dixon.

REGISTRATION NO. 21
(Vol. 3, p. 83)

Thomas Williams   25 August 1851

Thomas Williams is a bright mulatto, about 35 years old, with a scar on his left side where he was gored by an ox. He was emancipated by the will of John West recorded in Fairfax County.

REGISTRATION NO. 22
(Vol. 3, p. 84)

John F. Whitler   25 August 1851

John F. Whitler is a mulatto, about 21 years old, 5 feet 7¼ inches tall, with no visible marks. He was emancipated by the will of Francis Hagan and identified by Monica Foy.

REGISTRATION NO. 23
(Vol. 3, p. 84)

Georgiana Williams   26 August 1851

Georgiana Williams is a mulatto, about 19 years old, 4 feet 8¼ inches tall with a scar on the right side of her chin, another on her left hand at the bend of the thumb, and a long scar on the back of the same hand. She was born free, as appears by oath of Mrs. [Mary Ann] Church.

REGISTRATION NO. 24
(Vol. 3, p. 84)

Kitty Carrol   27 August 1851

Kitty Carrol is about 40 years old, 4 feet 10½ inches tall, of a black complexion, with her left eye out, a scar on her right cheek and another along the back of her right hand. She was freed by the will of John Lawson.

REGISTRATION NO. 25
(Vol. 3, p. 84)

Lewis Medella   Copy delivered 24 November 1851

Lewis Medella is a mulatto, about 25 years old, 5 feet 6 3/4 inches tall, with a small scar in the middle of his forehead. He was manumitted by Miss Hannah Somers' will, as proven by Joseph R. Somers.

REGISTRATION NO. 26
(Vol. 3, p. 84)

Lauretta Jones   Copy delivered ca. 24 November 1851

Lauretta Jones is about 17 years old, 5 feet 2½ inches tall, of a very dark brown color, with a small mole on the left side of her neck. She was born free.

REGISTRATION NO. 27
(Vol. 3, p. 84)

James E. Evans   Copy delivered January 1852

James E. Evans is about 28 years old, 5 feet 8 3/4 inches tall, of a copper color, with a scar on the top of his head and a mole over his left eye. He was born free.

REGISTRATION NO. 28
(Vol. 3, p. 84)

Washington Hawkins   Copy delivered January 1852

Washington Hawkins is about 21 years old, 5 feet 7 inches tall, of a black complexion, with no visible marks. He was born free.

REGISTRATION NO. 29
(Vol. 3, p. 84)

Rachel Mitchell   Copy delivered 24 July 1852

Rachel Mitchell is about 22 years old, 4 feet 11 3/4 inches tall, of a copper color, with a scar on her right cheek. She was emancipated by a deed from Ezra Lunt, and was identified by J[ohn] F. N. Lowe.

REGISTRATION NO. 30
(Vol. 3, p. 84)

Elizabeth Lee   28 May 1852

Elizabeth Lee is about 38 years old, 5 feet 1 3/4 inches tall, of a black complexion, with a scar on her forehead and another on her arm above the elbow. She was born free.

REGISTRATION NO. 31
(Vol. 3, p. 85)

Frances Frazier   Copy delivered 3 June 1852

Frances Frazier is a mulatto, about 23 years old, 5 feet 6¼ inches tall, with a scar on the left breast and many scars on his arms and face. Frazier was born free.

REGISTRATION NO. 32
(Vol. 3, p. 85)

George P. Chapman   Copy delivered 28 May 1852

George P. Chapman is a dark mulatto, about 17 years old, 5 feet 8 inches tall, with no visible scars. He is the son of George Chapman and was born free.

REGISTRATION NO. 33
(Vol. 3, p. 85)

Richard Henry Gibson   Copy delivered 1 July 1852

Richard Henry Gibson is a mulatto, about 34 years old, 6 feet one-half inch tall, with a scar on the thumb of his right hand. He was emancipated by Mordecai Miller's executors.

REGISTRATION NO. 34
(Vol. 3, p. 85)

Octavia V. Harris   Copy delivered 1 July 1852

Octavia [V.] Harris is a mulatto, about 24 years old with no visible marks. She was born free, as appears by a certificate from Mrs. Ann Mark.

REGISTRATION NO. 35
(Vol. 3, p. 85)

Elizabeth Bryant   Copy delivered 3 July 1852

Elizabeth Bryant is a bright mulatto, about 22 years old, 5 feet one-half inch tall, with a scar on the left side of her forehead.

REGISTRATION NO. 36
(Vol. 3, p. 85)

George Bryant   Copy delivered 3 July 1852

George Bryant is a mulatto, about 21 years old, 5 feet 9 inches tall, with a scar on the back of his right hand, one on each cheekbone, and with the little finger of his left hand broken.

REGISTRATION NO. 37
(Vol. 3, p. 85)

Joseph Bryant   Copy delivered 3 July 1852

Joseph Bryant is a mulatto, about 20 years old, 5 feet 3 inches tall, with a scar on the left side of his neck.

REGISTRATION NO. 38
(Vol. 3, p. 85)

William Jones   Copy delivered 8 September 1852

William Jones is about 25 years old, 5 feet 4¼ inches tall, with a scar on his left knee caused by a cut. See page 26.

See No. 184 on page 179.

REGISTRATION NO. 39
(Vol. 3, p. 85)

Lucy Ann Harrison   Copy delivered 23 November 1852

Lucy Ann Harrison is a mulatto, about 44 years old, 5 feet 1 inch tall, of a copper color, with a mole on her left cheek. She was emancipated by R[obert] H. Miller and identified by Rob[ert] H. Miller

REGISTRATION NO. 40a
(Vol. 3, p. 85)

Mary Eliza Butler   Copy delivered 7 March 1853

Mary Eliza Butler is about 34 years old, 5 feet 5 3/4 inches tall, of a copper color, with dark spots on each cheek and on her forehead. She was emancipated by Samuel Lunt's administrators and identified by William N. Naukeley.

REGISTRATION NO. 40b
(Vol. 3, p. 86)

Ann E. Jackson   Copy delivered 3 January 1853

Ann E. Jackson is a bright mulatto, about 16 years old, 5 feet 2 7/8 inches tall, with a scar under her left jaw. She was born free, as appears by oath of Miss Mary Sullivan.

REGISTRATION NO. 41
(Vol. 3, p. 86)

Ann Laws Oden   Delivered 2 May 1853

Ann Oden, late Laws, is a very bright mulatto, about 30 years old, 5 feet 3½ inches tall, with a mole on her cheek, freckles, and gray eyes. She was emancipated by Nathaniel Oden.

REGISTRATION NO. 42
(Vol. 3, p. 86)

James Alexander   Copy delivered 6 June 1853

James Alexander is a dark mulatto, about 22 years old, 5 feet 3¼ inches tall, with a scar on his breast. He was born free, as appears by oath of James W. Atkinson.

REGISTRATION NO. 43
(Vol. 3, p. 86)

Shimuel Evans   Copy delivered 6 June 1853

Shimuel Evans is a mulatto, about 24 years old, 5 feet 6½ inches tall, with a small scar over his left eye. He was born free, as appears by oath of Peter G. Henderson.

REGISTRATION NO. 44
(Vol. 3, p. 86)

William Lyons   Copy delivered ca. 6 June 1853

William Lyons is a dark mulatto, about 32 years old, 5 feet 6 3/4 inches tall, with a scar on the inner part of his right thumb. He is free, as appears by a previous registration.

REGISTRATION NO. 45
(Vol. 3, p. 86)

Henry Hyson   Copy delivered 6 June 1853

Henry Hyson is a mulatto, about 21 years old, 5 feet 3½ inches tall, with a scar on his right cheek. He was born free, as appears by oath of Wesley Carlin.

REGISTRATION NO. 46
(Vol. 3, p. 86)

Moses G. Hepburn   Copy delivered 13 June 1853

Moses G. Hepburn is a bright mulatto, about 17 years old, 5 feet 6¼ inches tall, with a scar on his left hand behind his thumb and a large scar on his right kneecap. He was born free.

REGISTRATION NO. 47
(Vol. 3, p. 86)

Thomas W. Hepburn   Copy delivered 13 June 1853

Thomas W. Hepburn is a bright mulatto, about 13 years old, 4 feet 10 3/4 inches tall, with a scar on the first joint of his left thumb. He was born free.

REGISTRATION NO. 48
(Vol. 3, p. 86)

Prudence C. Hepburn   Copy delivered 13 June 1853

Prudence C. Hepburn is a bright mulatto, about 20 years old, 5 feet 1 1/8 inches tall, with a mole on her neck. She was born free, as appears by evidence of Rebecca Braddock.

REGISTRATION NO. 49
(Vol. 3, p. 86)

Julia A. W. Hepburn   Copy delivered 13 June 1853

Julia A. W. Hepburn is a bright mulatto, about 10 years old, 4 feet 4 inches tall, with no visible marks. She was born free, as appears by evidence of Rebecca Braddock.

REGISTRATION NO. 50
(Vol. 3, p. 86)

Arthur Hepburn   Copy delivered 13 June 1853

Arthur Hepburn is a bright mulatto, about 4 years old, 3 feet 6 inches tall, with no visible marks. He was born free, as appears by evidence of Rebecca Braddock.

REGISTRATION NO. 51
(Vol. 3, p. 87)

Amelia R. Hepburn   Copy delivered 13 June 1853

Amelia R. Hepburn is a very bright mulatto, about 41 years old, 5 feet 3¼ inches tall, with a scar on her left jaw. She was born free, as appears by evidence of Rebecca Braddock.

REGISTRATION NO. 52
(Vol. 3, p. 87)

Ann Jackson   Copy delivered 5 July 1853

Ann Jackson is a bright mulatto, about 20 years old, 5 feet three-fourths of an inch tall, with no visible marks. She was born free, as appears by evidence of Darkey Biggs.

REGISTRATION NO. 53
(Vol. 3, p. 87)

Hirsley Gibbs   Copy delivered ca. 5 July 1853

Hirsley Gibbs is about 27 years old, 5 feet 5¼ inches tall, of a brownish-black color, with a scar in his left eyebrow and two scars just above that eyebrow on his forehead. He was born free, as appears by oath of Matilda Bangs.

REGISTRATION NO. 54
(Vol. 3, p. 87)

Elizabeth Evans   Copy delivered ca. 5 July 1853

Elizabeth Evans is a dark mulatto, about 32 years old, 5 feet one-fourth inch tall, with a scar on the right side of her neck and a scar on three fingers of her left hand. She was born free, as appears by a previous registration.

REGISTRATION NO. 55
(Vol. 3, p. 87)

Charles Hamilton   Copy delivered 1 August 1853

Charles Hamilton is about 30 years old, 5 feet 3¼ inches tall, of a black complexion, with a scar on his left cheek and another on his left hand near the wrist. He was born free, as appears by a previous registration.

REGISTRATION NO. 56
(Vol. 3, p. 87)

Charles Solomon   Copy delivered 1 August 1853

Charles Solomon is about 24 years old, 5 feet 6¼ inches tall, of a black complexion, with a scar on the first finger of his left hand. He was born free, as appears by evidence from Robert H. Miller.

REGISTRATION NO. 57
(Vol. 3, p. 87)

Stella Brannum   Copy delivered 1 August 1853

Stella Brannum is a dark mulatto, about 45 years old, 5 feet 2 3/4 inches tall, with a scar on her forehead and another on her right hand. She was emancipated by George W. P. Custis since 1806.

A Virginia law of 1806 required that manumitted slaves depart the state, but this was seldom enforced. (See Sweig, p. 3).

REGISTRATION NO. 58
(Vol. 3, p. 87)

Angela Brannum   Copy delivered 1 August 1853

Angela Brannum is a dark mulatto, about 17 years old, 5 feet 5½ inches tall, with a scar on her right hand. She was born free, as appears by evidence of George W. P. Custis.

REGISTRATION NO. 59
(Vol. 3, p. 87)

Samuel Brannum   Copy delivered 5 September 1853

Samuel Brannum is a dark mulatto, about 15 years old, 5 feet 6 inches tall, with a scar on the back of his left hand and another over his left eye. He was born free, as appears by evidence of Robert Ball.

REGISTRATION NO. 60
(Vol. 3, p. 87)

Mary Ann Stewart

Copy delivered 5 September 1853

Mary Ann Stewart is about 34 years old, 4 feet 10 3/4 inches tall, of a brownish-black color, with a large scar on the left side of her neck and a scar on the inside of her left hand below the thumb. She was emancipated by Col. William Minor.

REGISTRATION NO. 61
(Vol. 3, p. 88)

Jacob Bell

Copy delivered 5 September 1853

Jacob Bell is about 54 years old, 6 feet 2¼ inches tall, of a black complexion, with no visible marks. He was born free, as appears by a previous registration.

REGISTRATION NO. 62
(Vol. 3, p. 88)

Rosetta Craney

Copy delivered 5 September 1853

Rosetta "Crany" [Craney] is a mulatto, about 23 years old, 5 feet 5½ inches tall, with a scar on the right side of her neck and a red mark on the end of her tongue. She was born free, as appears by oath of William H. Semmes in a former registration.

REGISTRATION NO. 63
(Vol. 3, p. 88)

Lucy Ann Turner

Copy delivered 5 September 1853

Lucy Ann Turner is a bright mulatto, about 25 years old, 5 feet 5½ inches tall, with a scar on the forefinger of her right hand between the first and second knuckles. She was born free.

REGISTRATION NO. 64
(Vol. 3, p. 88)

Griffith Smith

Copy delivered 3 October 1853

Griffith Smith is about 50 years old, 5 feet 5¼ inches tall, of a black complexion, with a scar on his right eyebrow and another on his left ankle. He is free, as appears by evidence of James S. Hallowell.

REGISTRATION NO. 65
(Vol. 3, p. 88)

John Smith

Copy delivered 3 October 1853

John Smith is a very dark mulatto, about 16 years old, 5 feet 4 inches tall, with a scar on the back of his right wrist. He is free, as appears by evidence from James S. Hallowell.

REGISTRATION NO. 66
(Vol. 3, p. 88)

George Gibbons

Copy delivered 3 October 1853

George Gibbons is a bright mulatto, about 32 years old, 5 feet 7 3/4 inches tall, with a scar on the end of the third finger of his right hand. He was emancipated by Margaret Lovejoy's will in Fairfax County.

See No. 245 in Book 3 of the Fairfax County registrations. (Sweig, p. 166)

REGISTRATION NO. 67
(Vol. 3, p. 88)

Negro Caroline

Copy delivered 3 October 1853

Caroline is a dark mulatto, about 32 years old, 5 feet 3¼ inches tall, with no visible marks. She was emancipated by deed recorded in Fairfax County.

See No. 355 in Book 3 of the Fairfax County registrations. Caroline was freed by Anne McKenzie and William M. McCarty by deed dated 14 July 1841. (Sweig, p. 192)

REGISTRATION NO. 68
(Vol. 3, p. 88)

John Lewis Carter   Copy delivered 3 October 1853

John Lewis Carter is about 24 years old, 5 feet 8 inches tall, of a black complexion, with a scar on his nose. He was born free, as appears by evidence of James S. Scott.

REGISTRATION NO. 69
(Vol. 3, p. 88)

James Shields   Copy delivered 3 October 1853

James Shields is a mulatto, about 18 years old, 5 feet 11 inches tall, with a scar on his upper lip and another on his right ankle. He was born free, as appears by evidence of William B. Brown.

REGISTRATION NO. 70
(Vol. 3, p. 89)

Henrietta Bruce Ford   Copy delivered 3 October 1853

Henrietta Ford, late Bruce, is a bright mulatto, about 34 years old, 5 feet 1 inch tall, with no visible marks. With was emancipated by Colin Auld's will, as appears by a previous registration.

REGISTRATION NO. 71
(Vol. 3, p. 89)

Robert Robinson   Copy delivered 4 October 1853

Robert Robinson is a bright mulatto, about 28 years old, 5 feet 8¼ inches tall, with no visible marks. He was emancipated by Robert Jamieson, as appears by a previous registration.

REGISTRATION NO. 72
(Vol. 3, p. 89)

Mary Ann Lee Robinson   Copy delivered 4 October 1853

Mary Ann Robinson, formerly Lee, is a bright mulatto, about 22 years old, 5 feet 2¼ inches tall, with no visible marks. He was born free, as appears by a registration from Richmond City.

REGISTRATION NO. 73
(Vol. 3, p. 89)

Philip Ware   Copy delivered 4 October 1853

Philip Ware is a mulatto, about 28 years old, 5 feet 8 inches tall, with a scar on the third joint of the forefinger of his left hand and another on his right wrist. He was emancipated on 19 December 1852, as appears by evidence of Philip H. Hooff.

REGISTRATION NO. 74
(Vol. 3, p. 89)

Lucy Lomax   Copy delivered 4 October 1853

Lucy Lomax is about 21 years old, 5 feet 4 inches tall, of a black complexion, with a scar at the corner of her left eye and another on her right arm. She was born free, as appears by evidence of George W. Trammell.

REGISTRATION NO. 75
(Vol. 3, p. 89)

Margaret Stepney   Copy delivered 4 October 1853

Margaret Stepney is about 20 years old, 5 feet 3½ inches tall, of a dark brown color, with a scar above her right wrist. She is the daughter of Lucretia Harris and was born free, as appears by evidence of Sarah Vernon.

REGISTRATION NO. 76
(Vol. 3, p. 89)

James Watson   Copy delivered 7 October 1853

James Watson is about 21 years old, 5 feet 4 3/4 inches tall, of a black complexion, with no visible marks. He was born free, as appears by evidence of James Tubman.

REGISTRATION NO. 77
(Vol. 3, p. 89)

Richard Diggs   Copy delivered 7 October 1853

Richard Diggs is a mulatto, about 24 years old, 5 feet 6¼ inches tall, with a scar on his right arm near the wrist. He was born free, as appears by evidence of John Wood.

REGISTRATION NO. 78
(Vol. 3, p. 89)

John Nickens   Copy delivered 7 November 1853

John Nickens is a bright mulatto, about 49 years old, 5 feet 5 inches tall, with a scar on his right wrist. He was born free, as appears by a previous registration.

A notation on page 126 of Volume 3 states that registrations No. 78 through No. 368 were delivered between 7 October and 6 December of 1853.

REGISTRATION NO. 79
(Vol. 3, p. 90)

Henry Tate, alias Chase   Copy delivered 7 Oct. - 6 Dec. 1853

Henry Tate, alias Henry Chase, is a bright mulatto, about 36 years old, 5 feet 7 3/4 inches tall, with a scar on the back of his right hand. He was emancipated by John C. Herbert by deed recorded in Liber K, page 333.

REGISTRATION NO. 80
(Vol. 3, p. 90)

Kitty Easton Dulaney   Copy delivered 7 Oct. - 6 Dec. 1853

Kitty Dulaney, late Easton, is a mulatto about 26 years old, 5 feet 1 inch tall, with a scar on the back of her neck. She was born free, as appears by a previous registration.

REGISTRATION NO. 81
(Vol. 3, p. 90)

Jetson Dover   Copy delivered 7 Oct. - 6 Dec. 1853

Jetson Dover is a bright mulatto, about 53 years old, 5 feet 11 inches tall, with a scar on the right side of his nose. He was born free, as appears by a previous registration.

REGISTRATION NO. 82
(Vol. 3, p. 90)

Richard Berry   Copy delivered 7 Oct. - 6 Dec. 1853

Richard Berry is about 47 years old, 5 feet 7 5/8 inches tall, of a brownish-black color, with a scar on his right jaw and a faint scar on his forehead. He was born free.

REGISTRATION NO. 83
(Vol. 3, p. 90)

John Thornton   Copy delivered 7 Oct. - 6 Dec. 1853

John Thornton is a bright mulatto, about 27 years old, 5 feet 11½ inches tall, with a scar on his right elbow. He was born free.

REGISTRATION NO. 84
(Vol. 3, p. 90)

Patty Harris   Copy delivered 7 Oct. - 6 Dec. 1853

Patty Harris is a dark mulatto, about 24 years old, 5 feet 5¼ inches tall, with a small scar on the forefinger of her left hand and a scar on her right arm. She is free, as appears by a previous registration.

REGISTRATION NO. 85
(Vol. 3, p. 90)

Mary Morris Nash

Copy delivered 7 Oct. - 6 Dec. 1853

Mary Nash, late Morris, is a dark mulatto, about 25 years old, 5 feet 5 inches tall, with a black mole on her upper lip and a scar on her right arm. She was born free, as appears by a previous registration.

REGISTRATION NO. 86
(Vol. 3, p. 90)

John Jones, alias Whiting

Copy delivered 7 Oct. - 6 Dec. 1853

John Jones, alias John Whiting, is a bright mulatto, about 41 years old, 5 feet 7½ inches tall, with a scar over each eyebrow. He was emancipated by John Whiting by deed dated 11 May 1819 and recorded in Liber K No. 2, folio 42.

REGISTRATION NO. 87
(Vol. 3, p. 91)

William Taylor

Copy delivered 7 Oct. - 6 Dec. 1853

William Taylor is a mulatto, about 20 years old, 5 feet 3½ inches tall, with a scar on his left arm and another over his right eye. He was born free, as appears by a previous registration.

REGISTRATION NO. 88
(Vol. 3, p. 91)

Charles A. Chinn

Copy delivered 7 Oct. - 6 Dec. 1853

Charles A. Chinn is a bright mulatto, about 27 years old, 5 feet 11 inches tall, with a scar over his left eye. He was born free, as appears by a previous registration.

REGISTRATION NO. 89
(Vol. 3, p. 91)

Fanny Parker Payne

Copy delivered 7 Oct. - 6 Dec. 1853

Fanny Payne, late Parker, is about 44 years old, 5 feet 4¼ inches tall, of a black complexion, with a scar on her forehead. She was born free.

REGISTRATION NO. 90
(Vol. 3, p. 91)

Jesse Nookes, Sr.

Copy delivered 7 Oct. - 6 Dec. 1853

Jesse Nookes, Sr., is about 46 years old, 5 feet 7 inches tall, of a black complexion, with a scar on his left wrist. He is free, as appears by a previous registration.

REGISTRATION NO. 91
(Vol. 3, p. 91)

Hanson Nookes

Copy delivered 7 Oct. - 6 Dec. 1853

Hanson Nookes is about 21 years old, 5 feet 9½ inches tall, of a black complexion, with a scar on his forehead. He was born free, as appears by evidence of Lawrence B. Taylor.

REGISTRATION NO. 92
(Vol. 3, p. 91)

Malvina Pembroke Nookes

Copy delivered 7 Oct. - 6 Dec. 1853

Malvina [Pembroke] Nookes is a mulatto, about 40 years old, 5 feet 3 3/4 inches tall, with a scar over her left eye. She was emancipated by Rosalia E. Webster by deed dated 31 August 1831 recorded in Frederick County, Virginia, as appears by a previous registration.

REGISTRATION NO. 93
(Vol. 3, p. 91)

Patty Webster

Copy delivered 7 Oct. - 6 Dec. 1853

Patty Webster is a mulatto, about 46 years old, 5 feet 1½ inches tall, with a small black mole on her left cheek. She was emancipated by Hugh Smith, as appears by a previous registration.

REGISTRATION NO. 94
(Vol. 3, p. 91)

William Berry

Copy delivered 7 Oct. - 6 Dec. 1853

William Berry is a bright mulatto, about 27 years old, 5 feet 8 inches tall, with two large moles on the back of his neck and with freckles on his face. He was born free, as appears by a previous registration.

REGISTRATION NO. 95
(Vol. 3, p. 91)

Ann Clagett

Copy delivered 7 November 1853

Ann Clagett is a bright mulatto, about 34 years old, 5 feet tall, with a large scar on her left arm caused by a burn. She is free, as appears by a previous registration.

REGISTRATION NO. 96
(Vol. 3, p. 92)

William Clagett

Copy delivered 7 Oct. - 6 Dec. 1853

William Clagett is a bright mulatto, about 45 years old, 5 feet 3½ inches tall, with the sinews of his left hand drawn from a burn and a small scar on the left side of his face. He was emancipated by George Coryell and S[ilas] H. Reed since 1806.

REGISTRATION NO. 97
(Vol. 3, p. 92)

Julia Godfrey

Copy delivered 7 Oct. - 6 Dec. 1853

Julia Godfrey is a bright mulatto, about 26 years old, 5 feet tall, with a scar on her right elbow. She was born free.

REGISTRATION NO. 98
(Vol. 3, p. 92)

Ann Smith

Copy delivered 7 Oct. - 6 Dec. 1853

Ann Smith is a very bright mulatto, about 26 years old, with freckles on her face. She was born free.

REGISTRATION NO. 99
(Vol. 3, p. 92)

William H. Burrell

Copy delivered 7 Oct. - 6 Dec. 1853

William H. Burrell is about 22 years old, 5 feet 4½ inches tall, of a black complexion, with scars on his right cheek and all about his face. He was born free, as appears by oath of W. T. Harper.

REGISTRATION NO. 100
(Vol. 3, p. 92)

Henry Rowe

Copy delivered 7 Oct. - 6 Dec. 1853

Henry Rowe is a bright mulatto, about 35 years old, 5 feet 6 inches tall, with a small indentation on his right cheek near the right corner of his mouth. He was emancipated by Jane A. T. Ramsay since 1806.

REGISTRATION NO. 101
(Vol. 3, p. 92)

Celia Bowden Rowe

Copy delivered 7 Oct. - 6 Dec. 1853

Celia Rowe, late Celia Bowden, is a very bright mulatto, about 32 years old, 5 feet 4¼ inches tall, with no visible marks. She was emancipated by Jonathan Janney and R[obert] W. Hunter by deed dated 9 January 1835.

REGISTRATION NO. 102
(Vol. 3, p. 92)

James Gibson

Copy delivered 7 Oct. - 6 Dec. 1853

James Gibson is a bright mulatto, about 41 years old, 5 feet 7 3/4 inches tall, with a scar on the right corner of his right eye. He was emancipated by the executors of M[ordecai] Miller, as appears by a former registration.

REGISTRATION NO. 103
(Vol. 3, p. 92)

Robert Henry   Copy delivered 7 Oct. - 6 Dec. 1853

Robert Henry is about 26 years old, 5 feet 8¼ inches tall, with a scar at the outer corner of his left eye and three small scars in a curved line at the top of his collar. He was freed by the will of Olivia Stone recorded in Fairfax County.

REGISTRATION NO. 104
(Vol. 3, p. 92)

Phebe Ann Tyler   Copy delivered 7 Oct. - 6 Dec. 1853

Phebe Ann Tyler is a bright mulatto, about 25 years old, 4 feet 10 3/4 inches tall, with several small scars and dark moles scattered over her face. She is free, as appears by a previous registration.

REGISTRATION NO. 105
(Vol. 3, p. 93)

Alexander Douglass   Copy delivered 7 October 1853

Alexander Douglass is a bright mulatto, about 41 years old, 5 feet 7¼ inches tall, with a scar on the knuckles of his second and third fingers of his right hand. He was emancipated by John Hunter.

REGISTRATION NO. 106
(Vol. 3, p. 93)

Margaret Louisa Johnson   Copy delivered 7 Oct. - 6 Dec. 1853

Margaret Louisa Johnson is a bright mulatto, about 26 years old, 5 feet 4 inches tall, with a large mole on the right side of her neck. She was emancipated by William D. Nutt, executor of Matthew Robinson.

REGISTRATION NO. 107
(Vol. 3, p. 93)

Frederick Brooks   Copy delivered 7 Oct. - 6 Dec. 1853

Frederick Brooks is a bright mulatto, about 36 years old, 5 feet 4 inches tall, with his right eye disfigured by a burn. He was freed by Fanny Brooks, as appears by a previous registration.

REGISTRATION NO. 108
(Vol. 3, p. 93)

William Weaver   Copy delivered 7 Oct. - 6 Dec. 1853

William Weaver is a bright mulatto, about 50 years old, 5 feet 6½ inches tall, with a scar on the upper joint of his right thumb and marked by smallpox. He was born free.

REGISTRATION NO. 109
(Vol. 3, p. 93)

Letty Weaver   Copy delivered 7 Oct. - 6 Dec. 1853

Letty Weaver is a dark mulatto, about 51 years old, 5 feet 2½ inches tall, with three moles on her face and nose that form a triangle. He was born free.

REGISTRATION NO. 110
(Vol. 3, p. 93)

Elizabeth Butler   Copy delivered 7 Oct. - 6 Dec. 1853

Elizabeth Butler is a dark mulatto, about 37 years old, 5 feet 3 inches tall, with no visible marks. She was born free.

REGISTRATION NO. 111
(Vol. 3, p. 93)

Rachel Magruder   Copy delivered 7 Oct. - 6 Dec. 1853

Rachel Magruder is a dark mulatto, about 41 years old, 5 feet 3 1/8 inches tall, with a scar on the first joint of the forefinger of her right hand. She was born free.

REGISTRATION NO. 112
(Vol. 3, p. 93)

Adolphus Adams   Copy delivered 7 Oct. - 6 Dec. 1853

Adolphus Adams is a bright mulatto, about 23 years old, 5 feet 7 3/4 inches tall, with no visible marks. He was born free.

REGISTRATION NO. 113
(Vol. 3, p. 93)

Sylvia Lee   Copy delivered 7 Oct. - 6 Dec. 1853

Sylvia Lee is about 55 years old, 5 feet 8½ inches tall, of a black complexion, with her face marked by smallpox. She is free, as appears by a previous registration.

REGISTRATION NO. 114
(Vol. 3, p. 93)

John A. Beckley   Copy delivered 7 Oct. - 6 Dec. 1853

John A. Beckley is a mulatto, about 49 years old, 5 feet 7¼ inches tall, with no visible marks. He was born free.

REGISTRATION NO. 115
(Vol. 3, p. 94)

Charlotte Burrell   Copy delivered 7 Oct. - 6 Dec. 1853

Charlotte Burrell is a dark mulatto, about 50 years old, 5 feet one-half inch tall, with two small scars on her right thumb. She was emancipated by James Frazer.

REGISTRATION NO. 116
(Vol. 3, p. 94)

Charlotte Nelson   Copy delivered 7 Oct. - 6 Dec. 1853

Charlotte Nelson is about 20 years old, 4 feet 11 3/4 inches tall, of a black complexion, with no visible marks. She was proven free by evidence of Mary Folmare.

REGISTRATION NO. 117
(Vol. 3, p. 94)

Maria Henry   Copy delivered 7 Oct. - 6 Dec. 1853

Maria Henry is about 55 years old, 5 feet 1½ inches tall, of a black complexion and very much marked by smallpox. She was emancipated by John C. Herbert.

REGISTRATION NO. 118
(Vol. 3, p. 94)

Daniel Williams   Copy delivered 7 Oct. - 6 Dec. 1853

Daniel Williams is about 26 years old, 5 feet 9 inches tall, of a brown complexion, with a scar on the forefinger of his left hand. He was born free, as appears by a previous registration.

REGISTRATION NO. 119
(Vol. 3, p. 94)

George Nelson   Copy delivered 7 Oct. - 6 Dec. 1853

George Nelson is about 27 years old, 5 feet 7½ inches tall, of a brownish-black color, with a scar on the right side of his forehead. He is the son of Patty Nelson and was born free.

REGISTRATION NO. 120
(Vol. 3, p. 94)

Elizabeth King Copy delivered 7 Oct. - 6 Dec. 1853

Elizabeth King is about 32 years old, 5 feet seven-eighths of an inch tall, of a brown-black color, with a small dark indentation at the right corner of her eye. She was born free.

REGISTRATION NO. 121
(Vol. 3, p. 94)

Catherine Ann Dover Copy delivered 7 Oct. - 6 Dec. 1853

Catherine Ann Dover is about 26 years old, 5 feet 1 inch tall, of a brown complexion, with a scar on her neck. She was born free, as appears by a previous registration.

REGISTRATION NO. 122
(Vol. 3, p. 94)

Sarah Jane Berry Copy delivered 7 Oct. - 6 Dec. 1853

Sarah Jane Berry is a bright mulatto, about 23 years old, 5 feet 4 inches tall, with no visible marks. She was born free, as appears by a previous registration.

REGISTRATION NO. 123
(Vol. 3, p. 94)

Elizabeth Ebbs Copy delivered 7 Oct. - 6 Dec. 1853

Elizabeth Ebbs is a mulatto, about 28 years old, 5 feet 5 inches tall, with a scar on her right hand. She was born free, as appears by a previous registration.

REGISTRATION NO. 124
(Vol. 3, p. 95)

Cecilia Nelson Copy delivered 7 Oct. - 6 Dec. 1853

Cecilia Nelson is a dark mulatto, about 28 years old, 5 feet 4½ inches tall, with a scar on her right eyelid. She is the daughter of Patty Nelson and was born free.

REGISTRATION NO. 125
(Vol. 3, p. 95)

Lucy Jackson Copy delivered 7 Oct. - 6 Dec. 1853

Lucy Jackson is a bright mulatto, about 54 years old, 5 feet 4¼ inches tall, with a scar on her right wrist. She was born free.

REGISTRATION NO. 126
(Vol. 3, p. 95)

Patsy Berry Copy delivered 7 Oct. - 6 Dec. 1853

Patsy Berry is a dark mulatto, about 55 years old, 5 feet 1½ inches tall, with three scars on her right arm, one above the elbow, and two scars on her breast. She was emancipated by John C. Herbert, as appears by a previous registration.

REGISTRATION NO. 127
(Vol. 3, p. 95)

Rebecca Taylor Copy delivered 7 Oct. - 6 Dec. 1853

Rebecca Taylor is a bright mulatto, about 23 years old, 4 feet 10¼ inches tall, with no visible marks. She was born free, as appears by a previous register.

REGISTRATION NO. 128
(Vol. 3, p. 95)

Cornelia Taylor Copy delivered 7 Oct. - 6 Dec. 1853

Cornelia Taylor is a bright mulatto, about 47 years old, 5 feet tall, who has lost all her front teeth. She was born free, as appears by a previous registration.

REGISTRATION NO. 129
(Vol. 3, p. 95)

Sarah Johnson   Copy delivered 7 Oct. - 6 Dec. 1853

Sarah Johnson is about 20 years old, 5 feet 2 3/4 inches tall, of a black complexion, with a black mole on the right side of her face near her nose. She was born free, as appears by a previous registration.

REGISTRATION NO. 130
(Vol. 3, p. 95)

Adell Logan   Copy delivered 7 Oct. - 6 Dec. 1853

Adell Logan is about 20 years old, 4 feet 10 3/4 inches tall, of a black complexion, with no visible marks. She was born free.

REGISTRATION NO. 131
(Vol. 3, p. 95)

Christianna Logan   Copy delivered 7 Oct. - 6 Dec. 1853

Christianna Logan is about 29 years old, 5 feet 1½ inches tall, of a brownish-black color, with a dark place or mark from a burn on her left wrist and a small scar on her right wrist. She was born free.

REGISTRATION NO. 132
(Vol. 3, p. 95)

William Berry   Copy delivered 7 Oct. - 6 Dec. 1853

William Berry is about 22 years old, 5 feet 3½ inches tall, of a black complexion, with no visible marks. He is the son of Richard Berry and was born free, as appears by evidence of Thomas M. White.

REGISTRATION NO. 133
(Vol. 3, p. 95)

Ann Maria Bumbey   Copy delivered 7 Oct. - 6 Dec. 1853

Ann Maria Bumbey is a bright mulatto, about 34 years old, 5 feet 2 inches tall, with a scar on the forefinger of her right hand. She was born free, as appears by a previous registration.

REGISTRATION NO. 134
(Vol. 3, p. 96)

Julia Fuller   Copy delivered 7 Oct. - 6 Dec. 1853

Julia Fuller is a mulatto, about 18 years old, 5 feet 5 3/4 inches tall, with a mole on the right side of her neck. She was born free, as appears by evidence of Theodore "Mead" [Meade].

REGISTRATION NO. 135
(Vol. 3, p. 96)

Elijah Wedge   Copy delivered 7 Oct. - 6 Dec. 1853

Elijah Wedge is about 56 years old, 5 feet 6¼ inches tall, of a black complexion, with a scar over his right eye, a scar on the forefinger of his left hand, another on his left foot, and another in his left eyebrow. He was born free.

REGISTRATION NO. 136
(Vol. 3, p. 96)

Mary Wedge   Copy delivered 7 Oct. - 6 Dec. 1853

Mary Wedge is about 42 years old, 5 feet 2 inches tall, of a black complexion, with a scar on the third finger of her right hand. She is free by judgement of the Alexandria County Circuit Court in its May 1845 term.

REGISTRATION NO. 137
(Vol. 3, p. 96)

Thomas Colston   Copy delivered 7 Oct. - 6 Dec. 1853

Thomas Colston is a dark mulatto, about 31 years old, 5 feet 7½ inches tall, with two scars on his forehead and with his right big toe crooked. He was born free, as appears by a previous registration.

REGISTRATION NO. 138
(Vol. 3, p. 96)

John Jackson

Copy delivered 7 Oct. - 6 Dec. 1853

John Jackson is a dark mulatto, about 24 years old, 5 feet 6¼ inches tall, with a scar on the underside of his right hand. He was born free, as appears by evidence of Jonathan Ross.

REGISTRATION NO. 139
(Vol. 3, p. 96)

Cornelia Stuart

Copy delivered 7 Oct. - 6 Dec. 1853

Cornelia Stuart is a mulatto, about 22 years old, 5 feet 2 inches tall, with no visible marks. She was born free, as appears by evidence of Judith Henry.

REGISTRATION NO. 140
(Vol. 3, p. 96)

John Credit

Copy delivered 7 Oct. - 6 Dec. 1853

John Credit is a bright mulatto, about 30 years old, 6 feet tall, with a scar on the first knuckle of the forefinger of his left hand and another on the back of the same hand. He is the grandson of a white woman and was born free.

REGISTRATION NO. 141
(Vol. 3, p. 97)

James Webster

Copy delivered 7 Oct. - 6 Dec. 1853

James Webster is a dark mulatto, about 56 years old, 5 feet 7 inches tall, with a scar on his left arm near the elbow. He was born free.

REGISTRATION NO. 142
(Vol. 3, p. 97)

William Derrick

Copy delivered 7 Oct. - 6 Dec. 1853

William Derrick is a dark mulatto, about 28 years old, 5 feet 6½ inches tall, with a scar on the both sides of his neck. He was born free, as appears by a previous registration.

REGISTRATION NO. 143
(Vol. 3, p. 97)

William Lyles

Copy delivered 7 Oct. - 6 Dec. 1853

William Lyles is a dark mulatto, about 57 years old, 5 feet 9¼ inches tall, with no visible marks. He was emancipated by Samuel Carson as appears by a previous registration.

REGISTRATION NO. 144
(Vol. 3, p. 97)

John Davis

Copy delivered 7 Oct. - 6 Dec. 1853

John Davis is about 34 years old, 5 feet 6½ inches tall, of a brown-black color, with a scar on his left knee caused by a cut. He was born free.

REGISTRATION NO. 145
(Vol. 3, p. 97)

Mary Washington

Copy delivered 7 Oct. - 6 Dec. 1853

Mary Washington is a bright mulatto, about 50 years old, 5 feet 3 inches tall, with a dark place caused by frostbite on each ear and dark spots over her face. She was emancipated by Henrietta Perry's will, as appears by a previous registration.

REGISTRATION NO. 146
(Vol. 3, p. 97)

Sally Logan

Copy delivered 7 Oct. - 6 Dec. 1853

Sally Logan is about 44 years old, 5 feet 1¼ inches tall, of a brownish-black color, with a large scar on her right arm near the elbow caused by a burn, a scar between her thumb and forefinger of her right hand, and a reddish mark on her right cheekbone. She was emancipated by Peter Loggins.

REGISTRATION NO. 147
(Vol. 3, p. 97)

James Butler

Copy delivered 7 Oct. - 6 Dec. 1853

James Butler is a bright mulatto, about 38 years old, 5 feet 7½ inches tall, with a mole on the side of his left wrist. He was born free.

REGISTRATION NO. 148
(Vol. 3, p. 97)

Charles Dogan

Copy delivered 7 Oct. - 6 Dec. 1853

Charles Dogan is about 47 years old, 5 feet 9 inches tall, with a large scar on the upper part of his chest. He was born free, as appears by a previous registration.

REGISTRATION NO. 149
(Vol. 3, p. 97)

Patty Nelson

Copy delivered 7 Oct. - 6 Dec. 1853

Patty Nelson is a dark mulatto, about 55 years old, 5 feet 8¼ inches tall, with no visible marks. She was emancipated by Maria Blue, Robert Bell, and Britannia Bell, as appears by a previous registration.

REGISTRATION NO. 150
(Vol. 3, p. 98)

Virginia Nelson

Copy delivered 7 Oct. - 6 Dec. 1853

Virginia Nelson is a dark mulatto, about 20 years old, 5 feet 2 inches tall, with a dark mole on the left side of her face. She was born free, as appears by evidence of William S. Hough.

REGISTRATION NO. 151
(Vol. 3, p. 98)

Georgiana Nelson

Copy delivered 7 Oct. - 6 Dec. 1853

Georgiana Nelson is a dark mulatto, about 16 years old, 5 feet 3¼ inches tall, with a scar on the back side of her right arm. She is free, as is proven by evidence from Mary Folmare.

REGISTRATION NO. 152
(Vol. 3, p. 98)

William Nelson

Copy delivered 7 Oct. - 6 Dec. 1853

William Nelson is a dark mulatto, about 14 years old, 4 feet 11¼ inches tall, with a scar on his left eyebrow. He was proven free by evidence from Mary Folmare.

REGISTRATION NO. 153
(Vol. 3, p. 98)

Louisa Darnall

Copy delivered 7 Oct. - 6 Dec. 1853

Louisa Darnall is a mulatto, about 30 years old, 5 feet 2 3/4 inches tall, with a mole on her right cheek and a small scar on her right arm. She was born free, as appears by evidence of F. L. Brockett.

REGISTRATION NO. 154
(Vol. 3, p. 98)

Eli Nugent

Copy delivered 7 Oct. - 6 Dec. 1853

Eli Nugent is about 21 years old, 5 feet 9 inches tall, of a black complexion, with a scar at the corner of his left eye and another on the forefinger of his left hand. He was born free, as appears by evidence of F. L. Brockett.

REGISTRATION NO. 155
(Vol. 3, p. 98)

Mary Jane Ross   Copy delivered 7 Oct. - 6 Dec. 1853

Mary Jane Ross is a bright mulatto, about 30 years old, 5 feet 5½ inches tall, with a scar on her left wrist. She was born free, as appears by a previous registration.

REGISTRATION NO. 156
(Vol. 3, p. 98)

Sarah Ann Frazer   Copy delivered 7 Oct. - 6 Dec. 1853

Sarah Ann Frazer is a mulatto, about 27 years old, 5 feet 3½ inches tall, with no visible marks. She was born free, as appears by a previous registration.

REGISTRATION NO. 157
(Vol. 3, p. 98)

Mary Jane Cooper   Copy delivered 7 Oct. - 6 Dec. 1853

Mary Jane Cooper is a dark mulatto, about 18 years old, 5 feet 1½ inches tall, with no visible marks. She was born free, as appears by evidence of Benjamin Waters.

REGISTRATION NO. 158
(Vol. 3, p. 98)

Sarah Moore Lancaster   Copy delivered 7 Oct. - 6 Dec. 1853

Sarah Lancaster, late Moore, is a dark mulatto, about 50 years old, 5 feet 2 inches tall, with a very faint scar on the back of her right wrist. She is free, as appears by a previous registration.

REGISTRATION NO. 159
(Vol. 3, p. 98)

Robert H. Dogan   Copy delivered 7 Oct. - 6 Dec. 1853

Robert H. Dogan is a bright mulatto, 5 feet 7¼ inches tall, with a scar on his right eyebrow and a mole in front of his left ear. He was born free.

REGISTRATION NO. 160
(Vol. 3, p. 99)

Wesley Darnall   Copy delivered 7 Oct. - 6 Dec. 1853

Wesley Darnall is a dark mulatto, about 28 years old, 5 feet 8½ inches tall, with a scar on the top of his nose, another on his forehead, and one in his left eyebrow. He was born free.

REGISTRATION NO. 161
(Vol. 3, p. 99)

Benjamin Jones   Copy delivered 7 Oct. - 6 Dec. 1853

Benjamin Jones is about 51 years old, 5 feet 7¼ inches tall, of a brownish-black color, with marks from smallpox. He was born free.

REGISTRATION NO. 162
(Vol. 3, p. 99)

Sarah Ann Credit   Copy delivered 7 Oct. - 6 Dec. 1853

Sarah Ann Credit is a bright mulatto, about 35 years old, 5 feet 2 inches tall, with a scar behind her left ear. She was born free, as appears by a previous registration.

REGISTRATION NO. 163
(Vol. 3, p. 99)

Sinah Ann Peters   Copy delivered 7 Oct. - 6 Dec. 1853

Sinah Ann Peters is a dark mulatto, about 32 years old, 5 feet 3 inches tall, with her front upper teeth knocked out. She was born free.

REGISTRATION NO. 164
(Vol. 3, p. 99)

Armistead Medella

Copy delivered 7 Oct. - 6 Dec. 1853

Armistead Medella is about 29 years old, 5 feet 9½ inches tall, of a brownish-black color, with a small scar on his forehead at the edge of his hair and a small scar on the back of his left hand. He was emancipated by William H. Wilmer.

REGISTRATION NO. 165
(Vol. 3, p. 99)

Betsey Payne Medella

Copy delivered 7 Oct. - 6 Dec. 1853

Betsey Medella, late Payne, is a mulatto, about 26 years old, 4 feet 6 inches tall, with a scar over her right eye. She was born free, as appears by a previous registration.

REGISTRATION NO. 166
(Vol. 3, p. 99)

Dennis Bourbon

Copy delivered 7 Oct. - 6 Dec. 1853

Dennis Bourbon is a dark mulatto, about 38 years old, 5 feet 5½ inches tall, with no visible marks. He was emancipated by Bazil H. Davidson by deed dated 13 August 1833.

REGISTRATION NO. 167
(Vol. 3, p. 99)

Hiram Lomax

Copy delivered 7 Oct. - 6 Dec. 1853

Hiram Lomax is about 24 years old, 6 feet tall, of a black complexion, with no visible marks. He was proven free by evidence of Henry Cryss[?].

REGISTRATION NO. 168
(Vol. 3, p. 99)

John Bigsby

Copy delivered 7 Oct. - 6 Dec. 1853

John Bigsby is about 22 years old, 5 feet 7½ inches tall, of a black complexion, with no visible marks. He was born free, as appears by a previous registration.

REGISTRATION NO. 169
(Vol. 3, p. 100)

Susan Medella

Copy delivered 7 Oct. - 6 Dec. 1853

Susan Medella is a dark mulatto, about 22 years old, 4 feet 11 3/4 inches tall, with no visible marks. She was born free, as appears by a previous registration.

REGISTRATION NO. 170
(Vol. 3, p. 100)

William Cupid

Copy delivered 7 Oct. - 6 Dec. 1853

William Cupid is about 30 years old, 5 feet 9¼ inches tall, with no visible marks. He is the son of Linney Cupid and was born free.

REGISTRATION NO. 171
(Vol. 3, p. 100)

Dennis Hackett

Copy delivered 7 Oct. - 6 Dec. 1853

Dennis Hackett is a bright mulatto, about 66 years old, 5 feet 8 3/4 inches tall, with a scar on his left cheek and one on the left side of his forehead. He was emancipated by John Hunter, as appears by a previous registration.

REGISTRATION NO. 172
(Vol. 3, p. 100)

Amey Bell Hackett

Copy delivered 7 Oct. - 6 Dec. 1853

Amey Hackett, late Amey Bell, is about 46 years old, 5 feet 4¼ inches tall, of a brownish-black color, with several dark spots or moles on her face. He was emancipated by Jane Contee's will, as appears by a previous registration.

REGISTRATION NO. 173
(Vol. 3, p. 100)

Rebecca Lucas Nickens

Copy delivered 7 Oct. - 6 Dec. 1853

Rebecca Nickens, late Lucas, is a bright mulatto, about 5 feet 1 3/4 inches tall, with freckles. She was manumitted by James McKenzie by deed dated 25 October 1838.

REGISTRATION NO. 174
(Vol. 3, p. 100)

William Nickens

Copy delivered 7 Oct. - 6 Dec. 1853

William Nickens is a bright mulatto, about 49 years old, 5 feet 5 inches tall, with a scar on the side of his left hand. He was born free.

REGISTRATION NO. 175
(Vol. 3, p. 100)

Martha Campbell

Copy delivered 7 Oct. - 6 Dec. 1853

Martha Campbell is about 18 years old, 5 feet 3 3/4 inches tall, of a brownish-black complexion, with no visible marks. She was proven free by evidence of Daniel F. Cawood.

REGISTRATION NO. 176
(Vol. 3, p. 100)

Robert Cupid

Copy delivered 7 Oct. - 6 Dec. 1853

Robert Cupid is a bright mulatto, about 29 years old, 5 feet 8¼ inches tall, with a scar on his right hand. He was born free, as appears by a previous registration.

REGISTRATION NO. 177
(Vol. 3, p. 101)

Benjamin Franklin

Copy delivered 7 Oct. - 6 Dec. 1853

Benjamin Franklin is about 25 years old, 5 feet 10¼ inches tall, of a brownish-black color, with a scar on his left hand towards the palm, and two small scars on his left cheek. He was born free.

REGISTRATION NO. 178
(Vol. 3, p. 101)

Mary Elizabeth Chace

Copy delivered 7 Oct. - 6 Dec. 1853

Mary Elizabeth Chace is about 23 years old, 5 feet 2 3/4 inches tall, of a black complexion, with a scar on her left little finger. She was born free, as appears by evidence of John Shackleford from a previous registration.

REGISTRATION NO. 179
(Vol. 3, p. 101)

John Sumby

Copy delivered 7 Oct. - 6 Dec. 1853

John Sumby is a dark mulatto, about 33 years old, 5 feet 9½ inches tall, with a scar on his left leg below the knee. He was born free, as appears by a previous registration.

REGISTRATION NO. 180
(Vol. 3, p. 101)

Wilson Solomon

Copy delivered 7 Oct. - 6 Dec. 1853

Wilson Solomon is about 26 years old, 6 feet one-fourth inch tall, of a black complexion, with a scar on the middle finger of his right hand. He was born free.

REGISTRATION NO. 181
(Vol. 3, p. 101)

John Hepburn

Copy delivered 7 Oct. - 6 Dec. 1853

John Hepburn is a bright mulatto, about 19 years old, 5 feet 8 3/4 inches tall, with the initials of his name in india ink with a cross above on his left arm. He was born free, as appears by evidence of Theodore Meade.

REGISTRATION NO. 182
(Vol. 3, p. 101)

Randolph Smith

Copy delivered 7 Oct. - 6 Dec. 1853

Randolph Smith is a dark mulatto, about 43 years old, 5 feet 10½ inches tall, with a scar near his under lip. He was emancipated by Lambert and McKinzie by deed dated 11 March 1847.

REGISTRATION NO. 183
(Vol. 3, p. 100)

Anna Maria Taylor

Copy delivered 7 Oct. - 6 Dec. 1853

Anna Maria Taylor is about 17 years old, 5 feet 6½ inches tall, of a black complexion, with a scar above her right eye. She was born free, as appears by evidence of P. A. Brenner.

REGISTRATION NO. 184
(Vol. 3, p. 101)

Philitia Taylor

Copy delivered 7 Oct. - 6 Dec. 1853

Philitia Taylor is about 36 years old, 5 feet 4½ in tall, of a black complexion, with no visible marks. She was born free, as appears by a previous registration.

REGISTRATION NO. 185
(Vol. 3, p. 102)

Peggy Carter

Copy delivered 7 Oct. - 6 Dec. 1853

Peggy Carter is about 60 years old, 5 feet 2½ inches tall, of a black complexion, with a small scar on her nose. She is free, as appears by oath of F. L. Brockett.

REGISTRATION NO. 186
(Vol. 3, p. 102)

Linny Cupid

Copy delivered 7 Oct. - 6 Dec. 1853

Linny Cupid is a bright mulatto, about 56 years old, 5 feet three-fourth inch tall, with a small scar on the right side of her face near the jaw and a mole on her cheek. She was born free, as appears by a previous registration.

REGISTRATION NO. 187
(Vol. 3, p. 102)

Catherine Cupid

Copy delivered 7 Oct. - 6 Dec. 1853

Catherine Cupid is a dark mulatto, about 20 years old, 5 feet 3 3/4 inches tall, with a scar just below her left temple. She is the daughter of Linney Cupid and was born free.

REGISTRATION NO. 188
(Vol. 3, p. 102)

Jane Bell Lee

Copy delivered 7 Oct. - 6 Dec. 1853

Jane Lee, late Jane Bell, is a dark mulatto, about 34 years old, 5 feet 6½ inches tall, with no visible marks. She is free, as appears by a previous registration.

REGISTRATION NO. 189
(Vol. 3, p. 102)

Cecily Brooks Gibson

Copy delivered 7 Oct. - 6 Dec. 1853

Cecily Gibson, late Brooks, is a bright mulatto, about 45 years old, 5 feet 2 3/4 inches tall, with a scar on her left wrist. She was emancipated by Jonathan Janney and R[obert] W. Hunter by deed dated 9 January 1835.

REGISTRATION NO. 190
(Vol. 3, p. 102)

Samuel Haney

Copy delivered 7 Oct. - 6 Dec. 1853

Samuel Haney is about 21 years old, 5 feet 6¼ inches tall, of a black complexion, with a scar above his left eye. He was born free, as appears by oath of B. H. Lambert.

REGISTRATION NO. 191
(Vol. 3, p. 102)

Samuel Williams Copy delivered 7 Oct. - 6 Dec. 1853

Samuel Williams is about 46 years old, 5 feet 3½ inches tall, of a black complexion, with a scar on the left side of his forehead. He was emancipated by Sarah Pickering and Stephen Shinn by deed dated 1 January 1847.

REGISTRATION NO. 192
(Vol. 3, p. 102)

George Chapman Copy delivered 7 Oct. - 6 Dec. 1853

George Chapman is a bright mulatto, about 52 years old, 5 feet 10½ inches tall, with a scar on his right leg between the knee and ankle and a scar on the calf of that same leg. He was emancipated by Lawrence B. Taylor.

REGISTRATION NO. 193
(Vol. 3, p. 102)

Hellen Maria Chapman Copy delivered 7 Oct. - 6 Dec. 1853

Hellen Maria Chapman is a mulatto, about 22 years old, 5 feet 5 inches tall, with a mole on the left side of her neck. She was born free, as appears by a previous registration.

REGISTRATION NO. 194
(Vol. 3, p. 103)

Hellen Parker Chapman Copy delivered 7 Oct. - 6 Dec. 1853

Hellen [Parker] Chapman is a dark mulatto, about 51 years old, 5 feet 2½ inches tall, with a small scar on the right side of her face. She was freed by George Parker by deed recorded in Liber M No. 2, page 2.

REGISTRATION NO. 195
(Vol. 3, p. 103)

Lucy Oldham Copy delivered 7 Oct. - 6 Dec. 1853

Lucy Oldham is about 57 years old, 5 feet 1 inch tall, of a brownish-black color, with several small scars and one large scar on her right hand. She was emancipated by Stephen Shinn, as appears by a previous registration.

REGISTRATION NO. 196
(Vol. 3, p. 103)

Edward Oldham Copy delivered 7 Oct. - 6 Dec. 1853

Edward Oldham is about 62 years old, 5 feet 8 inches tall, of a black complexion, with a bald head, a mole on his left eyelid, and a scar on his left cheek bone. He was emancipated by Peggy Ashton by deed dated 8 January 1830.

REGISTRATION NO. 197
(Vol. 3, p. 103)

Harrison Black Copy delivered 7 Oct. - 6 Dec. 1853

Harrison Black is a mulatto, about 38 years old, 5 feet 11 3/4 inches tall, with a scar over his right eye and a scar on the middle finger of his right hand. He was born free, as appears by a previous registration.

REGISTRATION NO. 198
(Vol. 3, p. 103)

Robert Henry, Sr. Copy delivered 7 Oct. - 6 Dec. 1853

Robert Henry, Sr., is about 49 years old, 5 feet 7 inches tall, of a black complexion, with a small scar on the top of his nose and a scar on the back of his right hand. He was freed by the will of John Yates.

REGISTRATION NO. 199
(Vol. 3, p. 103)

Celia Henry Copy delivered 7 Oct. - 6 Dec. 1853

Celia Henry is about 49 years old, 5 feet 2 7/8 inches tall, of a brownish-black color, with a scar on the side of her left wrist. She was emancipated by the will of Olivia Stone recorded in Fairfax County.

REGISTRATION NO. 200
(Vol. 3, p. 103)

Rosana Henry

Copy delivered 7 Oct. - 6 Dec. 1853

Rosana Henry is about 26 years old, 5 feet 1 1/8 inches tall, of a brown complexion, with two scars on the right side of her neck from a burn, the upper one being faint. She was born free, as appears by a previous registration.

REGISTRATION NO. 201
(Vol. 3, p. 103)

Susan Henry

Copy delivered 7 Oct. - 6 Dec. 1853

Susan Henry is about 22 years old, 5 feet 2 3/4 inches tall, of a black complexion, with a small scar on the back of her right hand. She was born free.

REGISTRATION NO. 202
(Vol. 3, p. 104)

Alice Ann Taylor

Copy delivered 7 Oct. - 6 Dec. 1853

Alice Ann Taylor is a dark mulatto, about 24 years old, 5 feet 1½ inches tall, with a small scar on the back of her right hand. She was born free, as appears by a previous registration.

REGISTRATION NO. 203
(Vol. 3, p. 104)

William Williams

Copy delivered 7 Oct. - 6 Dec. 1853

William Williams is about 66 years old, 5 feet 5 inches tall, of a brownish-black color, with his left eye nearly out. He was emancipated by Colin Auld, as appears by a previous registration.

REGISTRATION NO. 204
(Vol. 3, p. 104)

Adeline Simpson

Copy delivered 7 Oct. - 6 Dec. 1853

Adeline Simpson is a mulatto, about 39 years old, 5 feet 1 3/4 inches tall, with a scar on her upper lip. She was born free, as appears by evidence of Davis [Bowie] from a previous registration.

REGISTRATION NO. 205
(Vol. 3, p. 104)

Turner Lyles

Copy delivered 7 Oct. - 6 Dec. 1853

Turner Lyles is a dark mulatto, about 18 years old, 5 feet 10¼ inches tall, with a scar on the middle finger of his right hand and another in the middle of his forehead. He was born free, as appears by a previous registration.

REGISTRATION NO. 206
(Vol. 3, p. 104)

Letitia Evans

Copy delivered 7 Oct. - 6 Dec. 1853

Letitia Evans is a bright mulatto about 39 years old, 5 feet 4½ inches tall, with no visible marks. She was born free, as appears by a previous registration.

REGISTRATION NO. 207
(Vol. 3, p. 104)

Mary C. Servoy

Copy delivered 7 Oct. - 6 Dec. 1853

Mary C. Servoy is about 27 years old, 5 feet 2½ inches tall, of a black complexion, with a scar on her left cheek and another on her left thumb. She was born free, as appears by evidence from James P. Coleman.

REGISTRATION NO. 208
(Vol. 3, p. 104)

Laura V. Servoy   Copy delivered 7 Oct. - 6 Dec. 1853

Laura V. Servoy is about 23 years old, 5 feet three-fourths of an inch tall, of a black complexion, with a scar on the left side of her neck. She was born free, as appears by evidence of James P. Coleman.

REGISTRATION NO. 209
(Vol. 3, p. 104)

Jane Elizabeth Servoy   Copy delivered 7 Oct. - 6 Dec. 1853

Jane Elizabeth Servoy is about 29 years old, 5 feet 4½ inches tall, of a black complexion, with scars on both wrists. She was born free, as appears by evidence of James P. Coleman.

REGISTRATION NO. 210
(Vol. 3, p. 104)

Louisa Harriss, and   Copy delivered 7 Oct. - 6 Dec. 1853
children, John and
Robert Oscar

Louisa Harriss is about 38 years old, 5 feet 2 3/4 inches tall, of a black complexion, with s small scar on the underside of her nose, and another on the third joint of her first finger. She has two children: John and Robert Oscar, who are under 12 years of age. They were born free, as appears by a registration from Fairfax County.

See No. 113, Book 2 of the Fairfax County registrations. Louisa Harris was born free and is the daughter of Rachael Harris. (Sweig, p. 57)

REGISTRATION NO. 211
(Vol. 3, p. 105)

Edmonia Harriss   Copy delivered 7 Oct. - 6 Dec. 1853

Edmonia Harriss is about 14 years of age, 4 feet 11 3/4 inches tall, of a black complexion, with no visible marks. She was born free, as appears by evidence of Henry Eldred.

REGISTRATION NO. 212
(Vol. 3, p. 105)

Adeline Ware   Copy delivered 7 Oct. - 6 Dec. 1853

Adeline Ware is a mulatto, about 20 years old, 5 feet 3½ inches tall, with a scar on the back of her left wrist. She was emancipated by William Hooff.

REGISTRATION NO. 213
(Vol. 3, p. 105)

Philis Jackson   Copy delivered 7 Oct. - 6 Dec. 1853

Philis Jackson is about 46 years old, 5 feet 7¼ inches tall, of a black complexion, with a scar on her right cheek. She was emancipated by the will of Sarah Monroe by William N. Mills, executor of Monroe's will.

REGISTRATION NO. 214
(Vol. 3, p. 105)

William Mills   Copy delivered 7 Oct. - 6 Dec. 1853

William Mills is a dark mulatto, about 29 years old, 5 feet 7 inches tall, with a small scar on the right side of his head and another on his forehead in the edge of his hair. He is the son of Rachel [Mills], and was born free.

REGISTRATION NO. 215
(Vol. 3, p. 105)

Jane Dyson   Copy delivered 7 Oct. - 6 Dec. 1853

Jane Dyson is about 35 years old, 5 feet one-half inch tall, with two scars crossing each other on the back of her left hand. She was born free, as appears by oath of James McGuire.

REGISTRATION NO. 216
(Vol. 3, p. 105)

James Williams   Copy delivered 7 Oct. - 6 Dec. 1853

James Williams is about 17 years old, 5 feet 8¼ inches tall, with a mole at the left corner of his upper lip. He was born free, as appears by evidence of Theodore Meade.

REGISTRATION NO. 217
(Vol. 3, p. 105)

Sophia Lee Henry   Copy delivered 7 Oct. - 6 Dec. 1853

Sophia Lee, now Henry, is a bright mulatto, about 50 years old, 5 feet 6 inches tall, with freckles. She was born free.

REGISTRATION NO. 218
(Vol. 3, p. 105)

John Kinzey Ware   Copy delivered 7 Oct. - 6 Dec. 1853

John Kinzey Ware is a mulatto, about 17 years old, 5 feet 4½ inches tall, with no visible marks. He was born free, as appears by a previous registration.

REGISTRATION NO. 219
(Vol. 3, p. 106)

Alexis Baker   Copy delivered 7 Oct. - 6 Dec. 1853

Alexis Baker is about 37 years old, 5 feet 10 inches tall, of a black complexion, with two scars on the left arm just below the elbow. Baker was emancipated by Thomas Janney.

REGISTRATION NO. 220
(Vol. 3, p. 106)

Rosetta Wheeler   Copy delivered 7 Oct. - 6 Dec. 1853

Rosetta Wheeler is about 61 years old, 4 feet 11½ inches tall, of a black complexion, with a large scar on her left hand caused by a burn and a scar across her left eyebrow. She was emancipated by the will of Gabriel D. Childs in Fairfax County, as appears by a previous registration.

REGISTRATION NO. 221
(Vol. 3, p. 106)

George Mason   Copy delivered 7 Oct. - 6 Dec. 1853

George Mason is a very dark mulatto, about 35 years old, 5 feet 5¼ inches tall, with the little finger on his left hand slightly bent at the end, a scar on the top of the forefinger of the same hand, and a mole on the left part of his neck. He was born free, as appears by a registration from Loudoun County.

REGISTRATION NO. 222
(Vol. 3, p. 106)

Elizabeth Hall   Copy delivered 7 Oct. - 6 Dec. 1853

Elizabeth Hall is a mulatto, about 39 years old, 5 feet 6¼ inches tall, with a slight scar over her left eye. She was born free, as appears by evidence of Margaret M. Bangs.

REGISTRATION NO. 223
(Vol. 3, p. 106)

William Hall   Copy delivered 7 Oct. - 6 Dec. 1853

William Hall is a mulatto, about 18 years old, 5 feet 9½ inches tall, with a cross mark in india ink on the back of his left wrist and a scar on his right hand near the lowest joint of the thumb. He is the son of Elizabeth Hall and was born free, as appears by a previous registration.

REGISTRATION NO. 224
(Vol. 3, p. 106)

Mary Elizabeth Hall   Copy delivered 7 Oct. - 6 Dec. 1853

Mary Elizabeth Hall is a mulatto, about 21 years old, 5 feet 1 3/4 inches tall, with a scar on the back of her neck. She is the daughter of Elizabeth Hall and was born free, as appears by a previous registration.

REGISTRATION NO. 225
(Vol. 3, p. 106)

Letitia Hall

Copy delivered 7 Oct. - 6 Dec. 1853

Letitia Hall is a mulatto, about 15 years old, 5 feet 3 3/4 inches tall, with a scar on the right side of her neck. She is the daughter of Elizabeth Hall and was born free, as appears by a previous registration.

REGISTRATION NO. 226
(Vol. 3, p. 107)

Townsend Solomon

Copy delivered 7 Oct. - 6 Dec. 1853

Townsend Solomon is about 59 years old, 5 feet 8½ inches tall, of a black complexion, who has lost the first joint of the forefinger of his left hand. He was emancipated by William Solomon by deed dated 13 December 1826 and recorded in Liber T No. 2, page 428.

REGISTRATION NO. 227
(Vol. 3, p. 107)

Susan Solomon

Copy delivered 7 Oct. - 6 Dec. 1853

Susan Solomon is about 52 years old, 5 feet 4 inches tall, of a black complexion, with a black mole under her chin. She was emancipated by Thomas G. Addison of Prince George's County, Maryland.

REGISTRATION NO. 228
(Vol. 3, p. 107)

Peter Magruder

Copy delivered 7 Oct. - 6 Dec. 1853

Peter Magruder is about 33 years old, 5 feet 8½ inches tall, of a brownish-black color, with a scar on his right thumb. He was born free.

REGISTRATION NO. 229
(Vol. 3, p. 107)

Joseph Frazier

Copy delivered 7 Oct. - 6 Dec. 1853

Joseph Frazier is a dark mulatto, about 60 years old, 5 feet 7 3/4 inches tall, with a scar just beneath his under lip near his mouth. He was emancipated by deed of Ezra Lunt recorded in Liber S No. 2, page 363.

REGISTRATION NO. 230
(Vol. 3, p. 107)

Rebecca Frazier

Copy delivered 7 Oct. - 6 Dec. 1853

Rebecca Frazier is about 25 years old, 5 feet 5½ inches tall, of a brownish-black color, with some warts on the knuckles of her right hand. She was born free.

REGISTRATION NO. 231
(Vol. 3, p. 107)

Letty Frazier

Copy delivered 7 Oct. - 6 Dec. 1853

Letty Frazier is a bright mulatto, about 68 years old, 5 feet 3½ inches tall, with a small scar on the back of her left wrist. She was emancipated by Ezra Lunt by deed recorded in Liber S No. 2, page 363.

REGISTRATION NO. 232
(Vol. 3, p. 107)

Ellen Lomax

Copy delivered 7 Oct. - 6 Dec. 1853

Ellen Lomax is a dark mulatto, about 56 years old, 5 feet 7½ inches tall, with a scar on the upper part of her breast. She was emancipated by Isaac Clark by deed dated 19 October 1831, as appears by a previous registration.

REGISTRATION NO. 233
(Vol. 3, p. 108)

Bazil Miles

Copy delivered 7 Oct. - 6 Dec. 1853

Bazil Miles is about 28 years old, 5 feet 6½ inches tall, of a black complexion, with a scar over his right eye and a scar on his left cheek. He was born free, as appears by a previous registration.

REGISTRATION NO. 234
(Vol. 3, p. 108)

John Campbell

Copy delivered 7 Oct. - 6 Dec. 1853

John Campbell is about 51 years old, 5 feet 11 inches tall, with a scar on his left nostril and another on his left arm. He was emancipated by the will of William Goddard, as appears by evidence of Turner Dixon.

REGISTRATION NO. 235
(Vol. 3, p. 108)

Daniel Brown

Copy delivered 7 Oct. - 6 Dec. 1853

Daniel Brown is about 36 years old, 5 feet 5½ inches tall, with a scar on each eyebrow, and with a stammer. He was born free.

REGISTRATION NO. 236
(Vol. 3, p. 108)

Eli Whitler

Copy delivered 7 Oct. - 6 Dec. 1853

Eli Whitler is about 42 years old, 5 feet 8 inches tall, of a black complexion, with a small scar on each eyebrow.

REGISTRATION NO. 237
(Vol. 3, p. 108)

George Mitchell

Copy delivered 7 Oct. - 6 Dec. 1853

George Mitchell is a dark mulatto, about 43 years old, 5 feet 5 3/4 inches tall, with a scar on his left leg below the knee. He was emancipated by Christopher Frye, as appears by a copy of his registration.

REGISTRATION NO. 238
(Vol. 3, p. 108)

Ellen Mitchell

Copy delivered 7 Oct. - 6 Dec. 1853

Ellen Mitchell is a bright mulatto, about 40 years old, 5 feet 4 1/8 inches tall, with straight hair. She was emancipated by George Brent, as appears by a previous registration.

REGISTRATION NO. 239
(Vol. 3, p. 108)

Alfred Merrick

Copy delivered 7 Oct. - 6 Dec. 1853

Alfred Merrick is about 51 years old, 5 feet 9 inches tall, with several small fading scars on his nose. He was emancipated by William Dean, as appears by a previous registration.

REGISTRATION NO. 240
(Vol. 3, p. 108)

Rebecca Merrick

Copy delivered 7 Oct. - 6 Dec. 1853

Rebecca Merrick is about 37 years old, 5 feet one-half inch tall, of a black complexion, with a scar on the back of her neck. She was born free, as appears by evidence from Zenas Kinzey.

REGISTRATION NO. 241
(Vol. 3, p. 109)

William Henry Lewis

Copy delivered 7 Oct. - 6 Dec. 1853

William Henry Lewis is a bright mulatto, about 40 years old, 5 feet 7 inches tall, with a bald head and straight hair[?]. He was emancipated by William H. Miller.

REGISTRATION NO. 242
(Vol. 3, p. 109)

Mary Elizabeth McQuan Lewis   Copy delivered 7 Oct. - 6 Dec. 1853

Mary Elizabeth Lewis, formerly McQuan, is a bright mulatto about 30 years old, 5 feet 4¼ inches tall, with the middle finger of her right hand injured and stiff. She was born free.

REGISTRATION NO. 243
(Vol. 3, p. 109)

Martha Ann Colbert   Copy delivered 7 Oct. - 6 Dec. 1853

Martha Ann Colbert is about 18 years old, 5 feet 1 inch tall, of a black complexion, with no visible marks. She is free, as appears by evidence from Zenas Kinzey.

REGISTRATION NO. 244
(Vol. 3, p. 109)

Francis Ann Lane   Copy delivered 7 Oct. - 6 Dec. 1853

Francis Ann Lane is a mulatto, about 37 years old, 5 feet 3 5/8 inches tall, with a small slender scar on her right hand between her thumb and forefinger. She was born free.

REGISTRATION NO. 245
(Vol. 3, p. 109)

James Carter   Copy delivered 7 Oct. - 6 Dec. 1853

James Carter is a bright mulatto, about 43 years old, 5 feet 3½ inches tall, with large dark spots on his forehead and cheeks, and a small scar on the palm of his left hand. He was born free.

REGISTRATION NO. 246
(Vol. 3, p. 109)

Leannah Davis   Copy delivered 7 Oct. - 6 Dec. 1853

Leannah Davis is a bright mulatto, about 36 years old, 5 feet 3 inches tall, with a very faint scar near the right corner of her left eyebrow. She was emancipated by the will of Samuel Adams recorded in Fairfax County.

See the note accompanying No. 40 on page 162.

REGISTRATION NO. 247
(Vol. 3, p. 109)

Susan Jones   Copy delivered 7 Oct. - 6 Dec. 1853

Susan Jones is a dark mulatto, about 48 years old, 5 feet 3¼ inches tall, with a scar on her right arm. She was born free, as appears by evidence of Zenas Kinzey.

REGISTRATION NO. 248
(Vol. 3, p. 110)

Nathaniel Jackson   Copy delivered 7 Oct. - 6 Dec. 1853

Nathaniel Jackson is about 27 years old, 5 feet 9½ inches tall, of a brownish-black color, with a scar on his right temple and another above his left eye. He was born free.

REGISTRATION NO. 249
(Vol. 3, p. 110)

Ann Brown   Copy delivered 7 Oct. - 6 Dec. 1853

Ann Brown is about 28 years old, 5 feet 2½ inches tall, of a black complexion, with a scar on her right arm between her elbow and wrist. She was born free.

REGISTRATION NO. 250
(Vol. 3, p. 110)

Mary Warner   Copy delivered 7 Oct. - 6 Dec. 1853

Mary Warner is about 42 years old, 5 feet 4½ inches tall, of a black complexion, with a large scar on the upper part of her right arm and a small scar on the inner side of the same arm at the bend of the elbow. She was born free, as appears by evidence of Zenas Kinzey.

REGISTRATION NO. 251
(Vol. 3, p. 110)

Israel Williams,
alias Israel Marvel

Copy delivered 7 Oct. - 6 Dec. 1853

Israel Williams, alias Israel Marvel, is about 46 years old, 5 feet 5½ inches tall, of a black complexion, with a scar under his left eye and left ear, and a scar under his right jaw. He was born free, as appears by evidence of Amelia Brocchus from a previous registration.

REGISTRATION NO. 252
(Vol. 3, p. 110)

Hannah Smith Lyles

Copy delivered 7 Oct. - 6 Dec. 1853

Hannah Lyles, late Smith, is a mulatto, about 53 years old, 5 feet 3¼ inches tall, with a scar on her left wrist from a burn. She was born free, as appears by evidence of Mrs. Winifred Williams from a previous registration.

REGISTRATION NO. 253
(Vol. 3, p. 110)

John E. Evans

Copy delivered 7 Oct. - 6 Dec. 1853

John E. Evans is a bright mulatto, about 28 years old, 5 feet 11 inches tall, with a scar on the upper part of his nose. He was born free, as appears by a previous registration.

REGISTRATION NO. 254
(Vol. 3, p. 111)

Louisa Cooper Addison

Copy delivered 7 Oct. - 6 Dec. 1853

Louisa Addison, late Cooper, is a dark mulatto, about 22 years old, 5 feet 1½ inches tall, with no visible marks. She was born free, as appears by a previous registration.

REGISTRATION NO. 255
(Vol. 3, p. 111)

Letitia Rhodes

Copy delivered 7 Oct. - 6 Dec. 1853

Letitia Rhodes is a dark mulatto, about 20 years old, 5 feet 5 3/4 inches tall, with a scar just under her right eye and another on the under part of her right arm between her elbow and wrist. She was born free, as appears by evidence of Ann E. Grimes.

REGISTRATION NO. 256
(Vol. 3, p. 111)

Ann Lomax

Copy delivered 7 Oct. - 6 Dec. 1853

Ann Lomax is a dark mulatto, about 34 years old, 5 feet 2¼ inches tall, with no visible marks. She was born free, as appears by a previous registration.

REGISTRATION NO. 257
(Vol. 3, p. 111)

Charles Dogan

Copy delivered 7 Oct. - 6 Dec. 1853

Charles Dogan is a mulatto, about 47 years old, 5 feet 9 inches tall, with a large scar on the upper part of his chest. He was born free, as appears by a previous registration.

REGISTRATION NO. 258
(Vol. 3, p. 111)

Caroline Solomon

Copy delivered 7 Oct. - 6 Dec. 1853

Caroline Solomon is a dark mulatto, about 17 years old, 5 feet 3/4 inches tall, with no visible marks. She is the daughter of Susan Solomon and was born free.

REGISTRATION NO. 259
(Vol. 3, p. 111)

Jane Ann Solomon   Copy delivered 7 Oct. - 6 Dec. 1853

Jane Ann Solomon is a very dark mulatto, about 19 years old, 5 feet 4 3/4 inches tall, with no visible marks. She is the daughter of Susan Solomon and was born free.

REGISTRATION NO. 260
(Vol. 3, p. 111)

Robert Johnston   Copy delivered 7 Oct. - 6 Dec. 1853

Robert Johnston is about 38 years old, 5 feet 10 3/4 inches tall, with a scar on the top of his head, two small scars in the middle of his forehead, and his right little finger is crooked. He was born free.

REGISTRATION NO. 261
(Vol. 3, p. 111)

Mary Ellen Solomon   Copy delivered 7 Oct. - 6 Dec. 1853

Mary Ellen Solomon is about 29 years old, 5 feet 4½ inches tall, with no visible marks. She was born free.

REGISTRATION NO. 262
(Vol. 3, p. 112)

George W. Turley   Copy delivered 7 Oct. - 6 Dec. 1853

George W. Turley is a dark mulatto, about 32 years old, 5 feet 5 inches tall, with a small scar near the corner of his right eye. He was born free, as appears by a previous registration.

REGISTRATION NO. 263
(Vol. 3, p. 112)

Ellen Hamilton Jones   Copy delivered 7 Oct. - 6 Dec. 1853

Ellen Jones, formerly Hamilton, is about 32 years old, 5 feet 2 3/4 inches tall, with a scar on her right wrist caused by a burn. She is the daughter of Ellen Hamilton and was born free.

REGISTRATION NO. 264
(Vol. 3, p. 112)

Catherine Hamilton   Copy delivered 7 Oct. - 6 Dec. 1853

Catherine Hamilton is about 56 years old, 5 feet 2 inches tall, with several small moles on her face mainly under her left eye. She was emancipated by Margaret S. Keith by deed dated 12 October 1837.

REGISTRATION NO. 265
(Vol. 3, p. 112)

Philip Hamilton   Copy delivered 7 Oct. - 6 Dec. 1853

Philip Hamilton is about 56 years old, 5 feet 7 3/4 inches tall, with a scar on his upper lip and another on his left eyebrow. He was emancipated by Colin Auld.

REGISTRATION NO. 266
(Vol. 3, p. 112)

Harriet Hunter Watson   Copy delivered 7 Oct. - 6 Dec. 1853

Harriet Watson, late Hunter, is a bright mulatto, about 43 years old, 5 feet 3½ inches tall, with a speck in the pupil of her right eye. She was emancipated by the will of Slighter Smith.

REGISTRATION NO. 267
(Vol. 3, p. 112)

Adaline Hunter   Copy delivered 7 Oct. - 6 Dec. 1853

Adaline Hunter is a bright mulatto, about 24 years old, 5 feet 3¼ inches tall, with a cluster of moles or a mark of some kind near her left eye. She was emancipated by the will of Slighter Smith.

REGISTRATION NO. 268
(Vol. 3, p. 112)

Lucinda Lee Peters

Copy delivered 7 Oct. - 6 Dec. 1853

Lucinda Peters, formerly Lee, is about 45 years old, 5 feet 5 inches tall, of a black complexion, with a scar on the back of her left hand near the wrist. She was born free.

REGISTRATION NO. 269
(Vol. 3, p. 113)

Ann Elizabeth Collins

Copy delivered 7 Oct. - 6 Dec. 1853

Ann Elizabeth Collins is a bright mulatto, about 25 years old, 4 feet 11 inches tall, with a scar over her left eye. She is the daughter of Ann Collins and was born free.

REGISTRATION NO. 270
(Vol. 3, p. 113)

Ann Collins

Copy delivered 7 Oct. - 6 Dec. 1853

Ann Collins is a bright mulatto, about 50 years old, 5 feet tall, with a scar caused by a burn on her left cheek and who is slightly freckled. She was born free.

REGISTRATION NO. 271
(Vol. 3, p. 113)

Harriet Brooks

Copy delivered 7 Oct. - 6 Dec. 1853

Harriet Brooks is about 62 years old, 5 feet 11 inches tall, with a scar on the back of her wrist. She was emancipated by John Roberts, as appears by a previous registration.

REGISTRATION NO. 272
(Vol. 3, p. 113)

George Brooks

Copy delivered 7 Oct. - 6 Dec. 1853

George Brooks is about 65 years old, 5 feet 6¼ inches tall, with no visible marks. He was emancipated by Harriet Brooks by deed dated 6 June 1848.

REGISTRATION NO. 273
(Vol. 3, p. 113)

Harriet Jasper

Copy delivered 7 Oct. - 6 Dec. 1853

Harriet Jasper is a mulatto, about 5 feet 4 inches tall, with a scar on her left thumb. She was emancipated by George Brooks by deed dated 19 March 1837.

REGISTRATION NO. 274
(Vol. 3, p. 113)

Alice Clark

Copy delivered 7 Oct. - 6 Dec. 1853

Alice Clark is about 32 years old, 5 feet one-half inch tall, of a dark brown color, with a small scar on each cheek, another on the back of her right hand, another on the first joint of her thumb, and two small scars on the wrist of her left hand. She is free, as appears by a previous registration.

REGISTRATION NO. 275
(Vol. 3, p. 113)

Nancy Johnson

Copy delivered 7 Oct. - 6 Dec. 1853

Nancy Johnson is about 52 years old, 5 feet one-fourth inch tall, with no visible marks. She was born free.

REGISTRATION NO. 276
(Vol. 3, p. 113)

Lucy Ann Johnson

Copy delivered 7 Oct. - 6 Dec. 1853

Lucy Ann Johnson is a dark mulatto, about 22 years old, 5 feet 1 inch tall, with a scar on the right side of her face. She was born free, as appears by a previous registration.

REGISTRATION NO. 277
(Vol. 3, p. 114)

William Evans

Copy delivered 7 Oct. - 6 Dec. 1853

William Evans is a dark mulatto, about 70 years old, 5 feet 9¼ in tall, with no visible marks. He was born free.

REGISTRATION NO. 278
(Vol. 3, p. 114)

Gracey Quander

Copy delivered 7 Oct. - 6 Dec. 1853

Gracey Quander is about 42 years old, 5 feet one-half inch tall, of a black complexion, with a scar on the left forefinger of her left arm. She was born free.

REGISTRATION NO. 279
(Vol. 3, p. 114)

Walter Berry

Copy delivered 7 Oct. - 6 Dec. 1853

Walter Berry is about 26 years old, 5 feet 2¼ inches tall, with no visible marks. He was born free, as appears by evidence of Henry Whittington.

REGISTRATION NO. 280
(Vol. 3, p. 114)

William Ford

Copy delivered 7 Oct. - 6 Dec. 1853

William Ford is a bright mulatto, about 39 years old, 5 feet 8¼ inches tall, with a scar on his left arm below the elbow caused by a burn. He was born free.

REGISTRATION NO. 281
(Vol. 3, p. 114)

Susan Smith

Copy delivered 7 Oct. - 6 Dec. 1853

Susan Smith is a bright mulatto, about 43 years old, 5 feet 2 inches tall, with a black mole on her upper lip. She was emancipated by Zenas Kinzey by deed recorded in Liber A No. 3, page 328.

REGISTRATION NO. 282
(Vol. 3, p. 114)

Kitty Bockett

Copy delivered 7 Oct. - 6 Dec. 1853

Kitty Bockett is a bright mulatto, about 46 years old, 5 feet 1½ inches tall, with a scar or mark above her left eye. She was born free.

REGISTRATION NO. 283
(Vol. 3, p. 114)

Thomas Baker

Ordered[?] November 1853

Thomas Baker is about 35 years old, 5 feet 7½ inches tall, with of a black complexion, with several scars at the corner of his right eye. He was emancipated by Samuel H. Janney, as appears by a previous registration.

REGISTRATION NO. 284
(Vol. 3, p. 114)

Richard Brooks

Copy delivered 7 Oct. - 6 Dec. 1853

Richard Brooks is a bright mulatto, about 5 feet 4 inches tall, with his right eye disfigured by a burn. He was liberated by Fanny Brooks.

REGISTRATION NO. 285
(Vol. 3, p. 115)

Mary Butler

Copy delivered 7 Oct. - 6 Dec. 1853

Mary Butler is about 63 years old, 5 feet 5 inches tall, of a black complexion, with two moles near the corner of her mouth and a mark from pox near the left corner of her left eye. She was emancipated by the will of Catherine Allison, as appears by a previous registration.

REGISTRATION NO. 286
(Vol. 3, p. 115)

Richard Wilson

Copy delivered 7 Oct. - 6 Dec. 1853

Richard Wilson is about 52 years old, 5 feet 8½ inches tall, of a black complexion, with a scar on his right eyebrow. He was born free, as appears by a registration from Fairfax County.

See No. 280 in Book 3 of the Fairfax County registrations. Dick Wilson obtained his freedom by order of the Fairfax Superior Court of Law and Chancery. (Sweig, p. 174)

REGISTRATION NO. 287
(Vol. 3, p. 115)

Sarah Chace

Copy delivered 7 Oct. - 6 Dec. 1853

Sarah Chace is about 46 years old, 5 feet 2 3/4 inches tall, of a black complexion, with a scar on the wrist of her left hand. She was born free, as appears by a previous registration.

REGISTRATION NO. 288
(Vol. 3, p. 115)

Margaret J. Brown

Copy delivered 7 Oct. - 6 Dec. 1853

Margaret J. Brown is a dark mulatto, about 38 years old, 5 feet 3¼ inches tall, with a scar on the left side of her forehead. She was proven free upon evidence of Zenas Kinzey.

REGISTRATION NO. 289
(Vol. 3, p. 115)

Adeline Brown

Copy delivered 7 Oct. - 6 Dec. 1853

Adeline Brown is a dark mulatto, about 17 years old, 4 feet 11½ inches tall, with a scar on her right arm between the wrist and elbow. She was proven free upon evidence of Zenas Kinzey.

REGISTRATION NO. 290
(Vol. 3, p. 115)

Jesse Johnson

Copy delivered 7 Oct. - 6 Dec. 1853

Jesse Johnson is a mulatto, about 19 years old, 5 feet 6 3/4 inches tall, with a long black mark on his right arm near his shoulder. He was born free, as appears by evidence of Henry Peyton.

REGISTRATION NO. 291
(Vol. 3, p. 115)

Joshua Johnson

Copy delivered 7 Oct. - 6 Dec. 1853

Joshua Johnson is about 50 years old, 5 feet 4 7/8 inches tall, of a brownish-black color, with a bald head from the front to the crown. He was emancipated by the will of Olivia Stone.

REGISTRATION NO. 292
(Vol. 3, p. 115)

Mary Anderson

Copy delivered 7 Oct. - 6 Dec. 1853

Mary Anderson is a mulatto, about 24 years old, 5 feet 5½ inches tall, with a scar on her forehead. She is slightly freckled and has thick lips. Mary is the daughter of Betsey Davis and was born free.

REGISTRATION NO. 293
(Vol. 3, p. 116)

Rebecca Chapman

Copy delivered 7 Oct. - 6 Dec. 1853

Rebecca Chapman is a dark mulatto, about 20 years old, 5 feet 7½ inches tall, with no visible marks. She is the daughter of Hellen Chapman and was born free, as appears by a previous registration.

REGISTRATION NO. 294
(Vol. 3, p. 116)

Peter Hopkins

Copy delivered 7 Oct. - 6 Dec. 1853

Peter Hopkins is a bright mulatto, about 44 years old, 5 feet 7½ inches tall, with a scar on the middle finger of his right hand. He was emancipated by James Dempsey by deed dated 16 March 1847.

REGISTRATION NO. 295
(Vol. 3, p. 116)

Julia Noland

Copy delivered 7 Oct. - 6 Dec. 1853

Julia Noland is about 35 years old, 5 feet 1¼ inches tall, of a brownish-black complexion, with a small black spot just above the corner of her left eye. She was born free.

REGISTRATION NO. 296
(Vol. 3, p. 116)

Cecelia Lee

Copy delivered 7 Oct. - 6 Dec. 1853

Cecelia Lee is a mulatto, about 24 years old, 5 feet 2 inches tall, with no visible marks. She was born free, as appears by a previous registration.

REGISTRATION NO. 297
(Vol. 3, p. 116)

Samuel Chase

Copy delivered 7 Oct. - 6 Dec. 1853

Samuel Chase is about 21 years old, 5 feet 4 3/4 inches tall, of a black complexion, with no visible marks. He is free, as appears by evidence of C[harles] C. Smoot.

REGISTRATION NO. 298
(Vol. 3, p. 116)

Benjamin Dorsey

Copy delivered 7 Oct. - 6 Dec. 1853

Benjamin Dorsey is about 21 years old, 5 feet 4 3/4 inches tall, of a black complexion, with no visible marks. He was born free, as appears by evidence of C[harles] C. Smoot.

REGISTRATION NO. 299
(Vol. 3, p. 116)

Zachariah Dorsey

Copy delivered 7 Oct. - 6 Dec. 1853

Zachariah Dorsey is about 19 years old, 4 feet 11½ inches tall, of a black complexion, with a wart on his left ear. He was born free, as appears by evidence of C[harles] C. Smoot.

REGISTRATION NO. 300
(Vol. 3, p. 116)

Emily Gowens

New copy delivered 8 October 1856

Emily Gowens is about 22 years old, 4 feet 10 3/4 inches tall, of a black complexion, with a scar on the left side of her forehead. She is the daughter of Joanna Gowens and was born free, as appears by evidence of Elizabeth Ferguson.

REGISTRATION NO. 301
(Vol. 3, p. 117)

Sarah Dorsey

Copy delivered 7 Oct. - 6 Dec. 1853

Sarah Dorsey is about 16 years old, 4 feet 11 inches tall, of a black complexion, with no visible marks. She was born free, as appears by evidence of C[harles] C. Smoot.

REGISTRATION NO. 302
(Vol. 3, p. 117)

John A. Beckley

Copy delivered 7 Oct. - 6 Dec. 1853

John A. Beckley is a mulatto, about 48 years old, 5 feet 7¼ inches tall, with no visible marks. He was born free.

REGISTRATION NO. 303
(Vol. 3, p. 117)

James W. Collins

Copy delivered 7 Oct. - 6 Dec. 1853

James W. Collins is a bright mulatto, about 5 feet 2 inches tall, with an anchor in india ink on the back of his left hand. He was born free, as appears by evidence of Peter Hewitt.

REGISTRATION NO. 304
(Vol. 3, p. 117)

Copy delivered 7 Oct. - 6 Dec. 1853

James Pinn,
alias James Hollins

James Pinn, alias James Hollins, is about 40 years old, 5 feet 11 3/4 inches tall, of a black complexion, with his front teeth wide apart, a scar on the first joint of his left thumb, a scar on the under side of his left hand, and a scar on the upper eyelid of his left eye. He is free, as appears by a previous registration.

REGISTRATION NO. 305
(Vol. 3, p. 117)

Copy delivered 7 Oct. - 6 Dec. 1853

Luke Lee

Luke Lee is about 67 years old, 5 feet 4 3/4 inches tall, of a black complexion, with two scars on the back of his head. He was manumitted by John Hunter.

REGISTRATION NO. 306
(Vol. 3, p. 117)

Copy delivered 7 Oct. - 6 Dec. 1853

Mary Ellen Johnston

Mary Ellen Johnston is about 26 years old, 5 feet 2 inches tall, of a black complexion, with no visible marks. She was born free, as appears by a previous registration.

REGISTRATION NO. 307
(Vol. 3, p. 117)

Copy delivered 7 Oct. - 6 Dec. 1853

Elizabeth Dorsey

Elizabeth Dorsey is a dark mulatto, about 47 years old, 5 feet 2¼ inches tall, with a scar on the forefinger of her left hand. She was born free, as appears by a previous registration.

REGISTRATION NO. 308
(Vol. 3, p. 118)

Copy delivered 7 Oct. - 6 Dec. 1853

Nace Dorsey

Nace Dorsey is a dark mulatto, about 5 feet 7 inches tall, with two scars near his left eye, one on the upper part of his nose near his left eye and the other on the left side of his eye. He was emancipated by deed from C[harles] C. Smoot and James E. Smoot dated 5 January 1837.

REGISTRATION NO. 309
(Vol. 3, p. 118)

Copy delivered 7 Oct. - 6 Dec. 1853

Hannah Middleton

Hannah Middleton is a dark mulatto, about 51 years old, 5 feet 4 inches tall, with a scar on her left thumb. She is free, as appears by a previous registration.

REGISTRATION NO. 310
(Vol. 3, p. 118)

Copy delivered 7 Oct. - 6 Dec. 1853

John Ebb

John Ebb is a dark mulatto, about 66 years old, 5 feet 4¼ inches tall, with a scar on the back of his head and a scar on his right shoulder. He is free, as appears by a previous registration.

REGISTRATION NO. 311
(Vol. 3, p. 118)

Copy delivered 7 Oct. - 6 Dec. 1853

John Berry

John Berry is a bright mulatto, about 19 years old, 5 feet 8¼ inches tall, with no visible marks. He is free, as appears by evidence of Henry W. Ferguson.

REGISTRATION NO. 312
(Vol. 3, p. 118)

Richard Collins   Copy delivered 7 Oct. - 6 Dec. 1853

Richard Collins is a dark mulatto, about 28 years old, 5 feet 6 3/4 inches tall, with a "scar" [mark] on his right wrist and across the back of his hand made with india ink. He was born free, as appears by evidence of Peter Hewitt.

REGISTRATION NO. 313
(Vol. 3, p. 118)

James W. Noland   Copy delivered 7 Oct. - 6 Dec. 1853

James W. Noland is a dark mulatto, about 15 years old, 4 feet 11¼ inches tall, with no visible marks. He was proven free by Willis E. Henderson.

REGISTRATION NO. 314
(Vol. 3, p. 118)

Amelia E. Noland   Copy delivered 7 Oct. - 6 Dec. 1853

Amelia E. Noland is a dark mulatto, about 14 years old, 5 feet one-half inch tall, with no visible marks. She was proven free by Willis E. Henderson.

REGISTRATION NO. 315
(Vol. 3, p. 119)

Robert Darnall   Copy delivered 7 Oct. - 6 Dec. 1853

Robert Darnall is a mulatto, about 21 years old, 5 feet 10 3/4 inches tall, with no visible marks. He was born free, as appears by evidence of Jacob Roxbury.

REGISTRATION NO. 316
(Vol. 3, p. 119)

John Goings   Copy delivered 7 Oct. - 6 Dec. 1853

John Goings is about 53 years old, 5 feet 9 inches tall, of a black complexion, with several small scars on his left arm. He is free, as appears by a previous registration.

REGISTRATION NO. 317
(Vol. 3, p. 119)

Charles Williams   Copy delivered 7 Oct. - 6 Dec. 1853

Charles Williams is a dark mulatto, about 28 years old, 5 feet 6 inches tall, with a scar above his right eye, two marks or scars on his right cheek and a scar at the left corner of his mouth. He was born free.

REGISTRATION NO. 318
(Vol. 3, p. 119)

John Myers   Copy delivered 7 Oct. - 6 Dec. 1853

John Myers is a bright mulatto, about 33 years old, 5 feet 10 1/8 inches tall, with a scar on his right hand extending from the first joint of his little finger to the middle of the back of his hand and a scar on the instep of his left foot. He was born free.

REGISTRATION NO. 319
(Vol. 3, p. 119)

Lucy Ann Johnson   Copy delivered 7 Oct. - 6 Dec. 1853

Lucy Ann Johnson is a mulatto, about 24 years old, 5 feet 1 inch tall, with a scar on the right side of her face. She was born free, as appears by a previous registration.

REGISTRATION NO. 320
(Vol. 3, p. 119)

Richard Lancaster   Copy delivered 7 Oct. - 6 Dec. 1853

Richard Lancaster is about 40 years old, 5 feet 8½ inches tall, of a black complexion, with a scar on his forehead. He was freed by the will of Benjamin Waters of Maryland.

REGISTRATION NO. 321
(Vol. 3, p. 120)

James Webster

Copy delivered 7 Oct. - 6 Dec. 1853

James Webster is a bright mulatto, about 36 years old, 5 feet 3 3/4 inches tall, with a scar on his chin, another on the lower knuckle of his left thumb and another on the back of his left hand. He was born free.

REGISTRATION NO. 322
(Vol. 3, p. 120)

Letitia Webster

Copy delivered 7 Oct. - 6 Dec. 1853

Letitia Webster is a bright mulatto, about 35 years old, 5 feet 2 inches tall, with no visible marks. She is the daughter of Haney Edwards and was born free.

REGISTRATION NO. 323
(Vol. 3, p. 120)

Catherine Norris Young

Copy delivered 7 Oct. - 6 Dec. 1853

Catherine Young, late Norris, is about 42 years old, 5 feet 2½ inches tall, of a dark brown complexion, with a scar on her forehead. She was born free, as appears by a previous registration.

REGISTRATION NO. 324
(Vol. 3, p. 120)

Malvina Mitchell

Copy delivered 7 Oct. - 6 Dec. 1853

Malvina Mitchell is about 46 years old, 5 feet 5 3/4 inches tall, of a black complexion, with her left arm scarred from having been broken. She was emancipated by Jo[seph] Mitchell in 1833, as appears by a previous registration.

REGISTRATION NO. 325
(Vol. 3, p. 120)

Patsy Elizabeth Berry

Copy delivered 21 November 1853

Patsy Elizabeth Berry is a dark mulatto, about 19 years old, 4 feet 10½ inches tall, with a large scar on her right arm between the elbow and shoulder. She was proven free by evidence of Thomas [M.] White.

REGISTRATION NO. 326
(Vol. 3, p. 120)

Ellen Berry

Copy delivered 21 November 1853

Ellen Berry is a dark mulatto, about 17 years old, 5 feet 1 inch tall, with several scars on the back of her right hand and one of her left wrist. She was proved free by evidence of Thomas [M.] White.

REGISTRATION NO. 327
(Vol. 3, p. 120)

Sophia Berry

Copy delivered 7 Oct. - 6 Dec. 1853

Sophia Berry is a dark mulatto about 15 years old, 5 feet 1 1/8 inches tall, with a small mole between the fingers of her left hand. She was proven free by evidence of Thomas [M.] White.

REGISTRATION NO. 328
(Vol. 3, p. 121)

Celestial Berry

Copy delivered 7 Oct. - 6 Dec. 1853

"Celeshall" [Celestial] Berry is a dark mulatto, about 14 years old, 4 feet 11¼ inches tall, with a mole on the left side of her forehead near her temple. She was proved free by evidence of Thomas [M.] White.

REGISTRATION NO. 329
(Vol. 3, p. 121)

Ann Foote

Copy delivered 7 Oct. - 6 Dec. 1853

Ann Foote is a dark mulatto, about 52 years old, 5 feet 1½ inches tall, with a scar on the middle finger of her left hand, several scars on the left side of her nose and the little finger on her right hand crooked. She was emancipated by Hannah Adams of Fairfax County.

See No. 115, Book 3 of the Fairfax County registrations. (Sweig, p. 137)

REGISTRATION NO. 330
(Vol. 3, p. 121)

Fanny Hall

Copy delivered 7 Oct. - 6 Dec. 1853

Fanny Hall is a dark mulatto, about 31 years old, 5 feet 2 3/4 inches tall, with a mole on her right nostril and another on the right side of her neck. She was born free.

REGISTRATION NO. 331
(Vol. 3, p. 121)

Nelly Shortt

Copy delivered 7 Oct. - 6 Dec. 1853

Nelly Shortt is a dark mulatto, about 57 years old, 5 feet one-half inch tall, with several light spots on the right side of her face. She was manumitted in Maryland by Arthelia Mullan's will dated 15 March 1822, as appears by a previous registration.

REGISTRATION NO. 332
(Vol. 3, p. 121)

Leme Smith

Copy delivered 7 Oct. - 6 Dec. 1853

Leme Smith is a dark mulatto, about 47 years old, 4 feet 10½ inches tall, with a small scar over her right eye. She was born free, as appears by evidence of Wesley Carlin.

REGISTRATION NO. 333
(Vol. 3, p. 121)

Priscilla Valentine

Copy delivered 7 Oct. - 6 Dec. 1853

Priscilla Valentine is a dark mulatto, about 60 years old, 5 feet 6 3/4 inches tall, with a scar on the inside of her right arm near the elbow. She was born free, as appears by evidence of Wesley Carlin.

REGISTRATION NO. 334
(Vol. 3, p. 122)

Margaret Brown

Copy delivered 7 Oct. - 6 Dec. 1853

Margaret Brown is a bright mulatto, about 24 years old, 5 feet 3 inches tall, with a scar on her forehead in line with her nose. She was born free, as appears by evidence of B[ernard] Hooe.

REGISTRATION NO. 335
(Vol. 3, p. 122)

Maria Robinson

Copy delivered 7 Oct. - 6 Dec. 1853

Maria Robinson is a dark mulatto, about 34 years old, 5 feet 3 3/4 inches tall, with a scar over her left eye. She was born free, as appears by evidence of Ann Sidebottom.

REGISTRATION NO. 336
(Vol. 3, p. 122)

John Daniels

Copy delivered 7 Oct. - 6 Dec. 1853

John Daniels is about 62 years old, 5 feet 7 inches tall, of a black complexion, with his left eye greatly disfigured. He was emancipated by William N. Mills, the administrator of Sarah Monroe's will.

REGISTRATION NO. 337
(Vol. 3, p. 122)

Charles Bowles

Copy delivered 7 Oct. - 6 Dec. 1853

Charles Bowles is a bright mulatto, about 47 years old, 5 feet 5½ inches tall, with a scar on his forehead over his right eye. He was born free, as appears by evidence of Theo[dore] Meade.

REGISTRATION NO. 338
(Vol. 3, p. 122)

Dicy Brown

Copy delivered 7 Oct. - 6 Dec. 1853

Dicy Brown is a dark mulatto, about 5 feet 2½ inches tall, with a scar over her left eye caused by a cut. She was emancipated by John F. N. Lowe, as appears by a previous registration.

REGISTRATION NO. 339
(Vol. 3, p. 122)

Lewis Williams

Copy delivered 7 Oct. - 6 Dec. 1853

Lewis Williams is about 57 years old, 5 feet 9 3/4 inches tall, with a large scar on his right side. He was emancipated by R. W. Horner by deed recorded in Liber W No. 2, page 98.

REGISTRATION NO. 340
(Vol. 3, p. 122)

Charles Coats

Copy delivered 7 Oct. - 6 Dec. 1853

Charles Coats is about 47 years old, 5 feet 6 3/4 inches tall, of a black complexion, with a scar on the left side of his forehead and another on his chin. He was emancipated by John C. Herbert, as appears by a previous registration.

REGISTRATION NO. 341
(Vol. 3, p. 123)

Letty Baltus

Copy delivered 7 Oct. - 6 Dec. 1853

Letty Baltus is a bright mulatto, about 51 years old, 4 feet 11½ inches tall, with no visible marks. She is free, as appears by a previous registration.

Her name appears to be spelled "Ballus" in the index.

REGISTRATION NO. 342
(Vol. 3, p. 123)

John Williams

Copy delivered 7 Oct. - 6 Dec. 1853

John Williams is about 22 years old, 5 feet 8¼ inches tall, with a scar on his forehead over his left eye. He was born free, as appears by evidence of William Minor.

REGISTRATION NO. 343
(Vol. 3, p. 123)

Spenser Hyson

Copy delivered 7 Oct. - 6 Dec. 1853

Spenser Hyson is about 37 years old, 5 feet 8½ inches tall, of a black complexion, with no visible marks. He was born free, as appears by evidence of William Minor.

REGISTRATION NO. 344
(Vol. 3, p. 123)

Ann Maria Williams

Copy delivered 7 Oct. - 6 Dec. 1853

Ann Maria Williams is about 18 years old, 5 feet 8½ inches tall, of a black complexion, with the fourth finger of her right hand crooked and a scar on the back of that same hand. She was born free, as appears by evidence of William Minor.

REGISTRATION NO. 345
(Vol. 3, p. 123)

Ann Cornelia Smith

Copy delivered 7 Oct. - 6 Dec. 1853

Ann Cornelia Smith is about 25 years old, 5 feet 2½ inches tall, of a black complexion, with no visible marks. She was born free, as appears by evidence of William Minor.

REGISTRATION NO. 346
(Vol. 3, p. 123)

Jane Williams

Copy delivered 7 Oct. - 6 Dec. 1853

Jane Williams is a dark mulatto, about 37 years old, 5 feet 7 inches tall, with a small scar on her forehead over the right eye and two scars on the outside of her right arm. She was born free, as appears by evidence of William Minor.

REGISTRATION NO. 347
(Vol. 3, p. 123)

John Jones

Copy delivered 7 Oct. - 6 Dec. 1853

John Jones is a mulatto, about 24 years old, 5 feet 8½ inches tall, with a scar on his right arm between the elbow and the wrist, and another near his left temple. He was born free, as appears by evidence of Richard Southson.

REGISTRATION NO. 348
(Vol. 3, p. 123)

Amelia Blackburn

Copy delivered 7 Oct. - 6 Dec. 1853

Amelia Blackburn is a mulatto, about 18 years old, 4 feet 10 3/4 inches tall, with a small scar on her left cheek. She was born free, as appears by evidence of Theo[dore] Meade.

REGISTRATION NO. 349
(Vol. 3, p. 124)

John Rhodes

Copy delivered 7 Oct. - 6 Dec. 1853

John Rhodes is a mulatto, about 33 years old, 5 feet 5¼ inches tall, with a scar on his forehead over his left eye and several scars on the back of his left hand. He was proven free by evidence of William Minor.

REGISTRATION NO. 350
(Vol. 3, p. 124)

William Colston

Copy delivered 7 Oct. - 6 Dec. 1853

William Colston is about 39 years old, 5 feet 4½ inches tall, of a black complexion, with the end of his fourth finger of the left hand disfigured. He was born free, as appears by a previous registration.

REGISTRATION NO. 351
(Vol. 3, p. 124)

James Edward Hyson

Copy delivered 7 Oct. - 6 Dec. 1853

James Edward Hyson is about 22 years old, 5 feet 5¼ inches tall, of a black complexion, with no visible marks. He was born free, as appears by evidence of William Minor.

REGISTRATION NO. 352
(Vol. 3, p. 124)

Samuel Jenkins

Copy delivered 7 Oct. - 6 Dec. 1853

Samuel Jenkins is a bright mulatto, about 54 years old, 5 feet 9½ inches tall. He is blind in one eye and his left hand has been amputated. Jenkins was emancipated by Eleanor A[nn] Harris, alias Jenkins, by deed recorded 5 December 1853.

REGISTRATION NO. 353
(Vol. 3, p. 124)

Eleanor Ann Harris Jenkins

Copy delivered 7 Oct. - 6 Dec. 1853

Eleanor Ann Harris, alias Jenkins, is about 44 years old, 5 feet 5½ inches tall, with no visible marks. She was born free, as appears by evidence of Robert Ball.

REGISTRATION NO. 354
(Vol. 3, p. 124)

Eleanora Bell

Copy delivered 7 Oct. - 6 Dec. 1853

Eleanora Bell is a dark mulatto, about 37 years old, 5 feet 5½ inches tall, with a scar on the third finger of her left hand and another on the palm of her left hand. She was emancipated by Francis L. Smith, as appears by a previous registration.

There is no registration numbered 355.

REGISTRATION NO. 356
(Vol. 3, p. 124)

Sarah Burrell

Copy delivered 7 Oct. - 6 Dec. 1853

Sarah Burrell is a dark mulatto, about 17 years old, 5 feet 4¼ inches tall, with a scar on her right cheek. She was born free, as appears by evidence of Catharine Phillips.

REGISTRATION NO. 357
(Vol. 3, p. 125)

Susannah Burrell

Copy delivered 7 Oct. - 6 Dec. 1853

Susannah Burrell is a dark mulatto, about 14 years old, 5 feet 2 inches tall, with a small scar on the middle of her forehead. She was born free, as appears by evidence of Catharine Phillips.

REGISTRATION NO. 358
(Vol. 3, p. 125)

Ann Hutchinson

Copy delivered 7 Oct. - 6 Dec. 1853

Ann Hutchinson is a bright mulatto, about 46 years old, 5 feet five-eighths of an inch tall, with six or eight small black moles scattered over her face. She was emancipated by Robert S. Reed.

REGISTRATION NO. 359
(Vol. 3, p. 125)

David Middleton

Copy delivered 7 Oct. - 6 Dec. 1853

David Middleton is about 18 years old, 5 feet 5½ inches tall, of a black complexion, with a large scar on the front of his neck. He was born free, as appears by evidence of John L. Bowyer.

REGISTRATION NO. 360
(Vol. 3, p. 125)

Catharine Brown

Copy delivered 7 Oct. - 6 Dec. 1853

Catharine Brown is a bright mulatto, about 21 years old, 5 feet 4 3/4 inches tall, with no visible marks. She was born free, as appears by a previous registration.

REGISTRATION NO. 361
(Vol. 3, p. 125)

Flavus Lane

Copy delivered 7 Oct. - 6 Dec. 1853

Flavus Lane is a bright mulatto, about 19 years old, 5 feet 9½ inches tall, with no visible marks. He is the son of Frances Ann Lane and was born free, as appears by evidence of John Arrington.

REGISTRATION NO. 362
(Vol. 3, p. 125)

Oscar Thomas

Copy delivered 7 Oct. - 6 Dec. 1853

Oscar Thomas is about 43 years old, 5 feet 7 inches tall, of a black complexion, with the thumb of his left hand disfigured. His freedom was proved by evidence of W. T. Harper.

REGISTRATION NO. 363
(Vol. 3, p. 125)

Cornelia Syphax

Copy delivered 7 Oct. - 6 Dec. 1853

Cornelia Syphax is a bright mulatto, about 22 years old, 5 feet 10 inches tall, with a small scar in the middle of her forehead. She was born free, as appears by evidence of G[eorge] W. P. Custis.

REGISTRATION NO. 364
(Vol. 3, p. 125)

James Allen

Copy delivered 7 Oct. - 6 Dec. 1853

James Allen is about 27 years old, 5 feet 7½ inches tall, of a dark brown complexion, with a scar on his right shoulder and one of the back of his left hand. He was emancipated by the will of Joseph Lewis.

REGISTRATION NO. 365
(Vol. 3, p. 126)

William Curtis   Copy delivered 7 Oct. - 6 Dec. 1853

William Curtis is a dark mulatto, about 45 years old, 5 feet 5¼ inches tall, with several scars on each hand, one on his right elbow and one on each thigh. He was born free, as appears by evidence of Wesley Carlin.

REGISTRATION NO. 366
(Vol. 3, p. 126)

John Madella   Copy delivered 7 Oct. - 6 Dec. 1853

John Madella is a dark mulatto, about 20 years old, 5 feet 4½ inches tall, with a black mole on his left thumb. He was born free, as appears by a previous registration.

REGISTRATION NO. 367
(Vol. 3, p. 126)

Jane Frazier   Copy delivered 7 Oct. - 6 Dec. 1853

Jane Frazier is a dark mulatto, about 41 years old, 5 feet 1½ inches tall, with a mark at the left corner of her mouth. She was emancipated by Ezra Lunt.

REGISTRATION NO. 368
(Vol. 3, p. 126)

Dennis Halley   Delivered Oct. 6 - Dec. 6, 1853

Dennis Halley is a mulatto, about 40 years old, 5 feet 8¼ inches tall, with a scar on his nose. He was emancipated by the will of Penelope Stone and identified by Samuel Beach, executor.

REGISTRATION NO. 369
(Vol. 3, p. 126)

Fanny Mitchell   Copy delivered 6 December 1853

Fanny Mitchell is about 60 years old, 4 feet 9 inches tall, with a scar at the left corner of her left eye. She was emancipated by the will of Reuben Potter recorded in June, 1845.

REGISTRATION NO. 370
(Vol. 3, p. 126)

Louisa Myers   Copy delivered 6 December 1853

Louisa Myers is a bright mulatto, about 31 years old, 5 feet 8½ inches tall, with a scar in the center of the palm of her left hand and another under her chin on her throat. She was born free.

REGISTRATION NO. 371
(Vol. 3, p. 126)

Noble Logan   Copy delivered 7 Oct. - 6 Dec. 1853

Noble Logan is about 19 years old, 5 feet 9 inches tall, of a dark brown complexion, with a scar on the left side of his chin. He was born free, as appears by evidence of Elizabeth Ferguson.

REGISTRATION NO. 372
(Vol. 3, p. 126)

Edward Evans   Copy delivered 7 Oct. - 6 Dec. 1853

Edward Evans is a bright mulatto, about 40 years old 5 feet 9¼ inches tall, with a small scar on his nose. He was born free.

REGISTRATION NO. 373
(Vol. 3, p. 127)

Austin Syphax   Copy delivered 7 December 1853

Austin Syphax is a mulatto, about 22 years old, 5 feet 10¼ inches tall, with a small mole near the middle of his forehead. He was born free, as appears by evidence of G[eorge] W. P. Custis.

REGISTRATION NO. 374
(Vol. 3, p. 127)

Rudolph Logan

Copy delivered 7 December 1853

Rudolph Logan is a mulatto, about 12 years old, 4 feet 7 3/4 inches tall, with no visible marks. He was born free, as appears by evidence of Elizabeth Ferguson.

REGISTRATION NO. 375
(Vol. 3, p. 127)

William Logan

Copy delivered 9 December 1853

William Logan is about 25 years old, 5 feet 4¼ inches tall, of a brownish-black color, with a scar on his forehead and a mole on his upper lip. He was born free.

REGISTRATION NO. 376
(Vol. 3, p. 127)

John Nelson

Copy delivered 9 December 1853

John Nelson is a very dark mulatto, about 21 years old, 5 feet 9 3/4 inches tall, with a large scar on his breast from a burn. He was born free, as appears by evidence of Mary Folmare.

REGISTRATION NO. 377
(Vol. 3, p. 127)

Reverdy Bowden

Copy delivered 2 January 1854

Reverdy Bowden is a very bright mulatto, about 23 years old, 6 feet 1 inch tall, with freckles and reddish hair. He is the son of Cecily Bowden and was born free, as appears by evidence of Robert W. Hunter.

REGISTRATION NO. 378
(Vol. 3, p. 127)

Ann Seals

Copy delivered 2 January 1854

Ann Seals is a dark mulatto, about 30 years old, 5 feet 1½ inches tall, with a scar on the left side of her neck. She is the daughter of Susan Seals and was born free.

REGISTRATION NO. 379
(Vol. 3, p. 127)

Mary Ann Cole

Copy delivered 5 July 1854

Mary Ann Cole is a bright mulatto, about 29 years old, 5 feet 4½ inches tall, with her face slightly freckled. She is the granddaughter of Mary Ann Cole, a white woman.

REGISTRATION NO. 380
(Vol. 3, p. 128)

Alexander Bowden

Copy delivered 2 January 1854

Alexander Bowden is a very bright mulatto, about 25 years old, 6 feet 1 3/4 inches tall, with a scar on the knuckle of the third finger of his right hand. He has "sleepy eyes and reddish hair." Bowden was born free.

REGISTRATION NO. 381
(Vol. 3, p. 128)

Henson Turley

Copy delivered 2 January 1854

Hanson Turley is a dark mulatto, about 61 years old, 5 feet 5 3/4 inches tall, with a scar on the back of his left hand. He was emancipated by Hannah B. Lenett[?] by deed dated 24 August 1847.

Hannah's name may be "Senett" or even "Levett."

REGISTRATION NO. 382
(Vol. 3, p. 128)

William H. Hatton   Copy delivered 3 January 1854

William H. Hatton is a bright mulatto, about 38 years old, 5 feet 8 inches tall, with two small scars on the back of his right hand and a black mole on the left side of his nose. He was born free.

REGISTRATION NO. 383
(Vol. 3, p. 128)

George Andrew Chace   Copy delivered 3 January 1854

George Andrew Chace is a dark mulatto, about 32 years old, 5 feet 6¼ inches tall, with two small scars under his right eye. He was born free, as appears by a previous registration.

REGISTRATION NO. 384
(Vol. 3, p. 128)

Govenor Dogans   Copy delivered 3 January 1854

Govenor Dogans is a mulatto, about 21 years old, 5 feet 8½ inches tall, with a mark across his forehead. He was born free, as appears by evidence of Peter Hewitt.

REGISTRATION NO. 385
(Vol. 3, p. 128)

Maria Dogan   Copy delivered 3 January 1854

Maria Dogan is a bright mulatto, about 51 years old, 5 feet 4 inches tall, with freckles and with scars from smallpox on her face. She was freed by Leonard Marbury by deed recorded in Liber O No. 2, p. 435.

REGISTRATION NO. 386
(Vol. 3, p. 128)

Anthony Dogan   Copy delivered 3 January 1854

Anthony Dogan is a dark mulatto, about 55 years old, 5 feet 10½ inches tall, with no visible marks. He was born free, as appears by a previous registration.

REGISTRATION NO. 387
(Vol. 3, p. 129)

Mary Wade Dogan   Copy delivered 3 January 1854

Mary Wade Dogan is a bright mulatto, about 31 years old, 5 feet 4¼ inches tall, with a black mole on the center of her upper lip. She was born free, as appears by a previous registration.

REGISTRATION NO. 388
(Vol. 3, p. 129)

Isabella Dogans   Copy delivered 3 January 1854

Isabella Dogans is a bright mulatto, about 28 years old, 5 feet 9 inches tall, with no visible marks. She was born free, as appears by a previous registration.

REGISTRATION NO. 389
(Vol. 3, p. 129)

Elizabeth Duval   Copy delivered 3 January 1854

Elizabeth Duval is a bright mulatto, about 51 years old, 5 feet 3¼ inches tall, with a scar covering the back of her left hand. She was born free.

REGISTRATION NO. 390
(Vol. 3, p. 129)

Nancy Cole Dudley   Copy delivered 4 January 1854

Nancy Dudley is a bright mulatto, about 56 years old, 5 feet 7 inches tall, with a mole on her left cheek. She is the daughter of Mary Ann Cole, a free white woman, and was born free.

REGISTRATION NO. 391
(Vol. 3, p. 129)

Robert Bell

Copy delivered 4 January 1854

Robert Bell is about 33 years old, 5 feet 5 3/4 inches tall, of a black complexion, with three scars over the top of his left eye. He was born free, as appears by evidence of Samuel Miller.

REGISTRATION NO. 392
(Vol. 3, p. 129)

Robert Butler

Copy delivered 5 January 1854

Robert Butler is about 40 years old, 5 feet 7½ inches tall, of a black complexion,, with a small black mole on his right ear. He was born free.

REGISTRATION NO. 393
(Vol. 3, p. 129)

Ann Elizabeth Brown Piper

Copy delivered 11 January 1854

Ann Elizabeth Piper, late Brown, is a bright mulatto, about 36 years old, 5 feet 4 inches tall, with a thin face and dark eyes. She was born free.

REGISTRATION NO. 394
(Vol. 3, p. 129)

Livinia Wright

Copy delivered 6 February 1854

Livinia Wright is a mulatto, about 48 years old, 5 feet 1 inch tall, with a black mole on the right side of her neck. She was emancipated by O. H. Dibble by deed dated 15 July 1834 recorded in Washington, D. C.

REGISTRATION NO. 395
(Vol. 3, p. 130)

Thomas Greyson

Copy delivered 7 February 1854

Thomas Greyson is a dark mulatto, about 22 years old, 6 feet 1½ inches tall, with a scar in the left corner of his left eye. He was born free and is from Prince William County.

REGISTRATION NO. 396
(Vol. 3, p. 130)

Thomas Cole

Copy delivered 7 February 1854

Thomas Cole is a dark mulatto, about 59 years old, 5 feet 4½ inches tall, with the forefinger of his right hand very disfigured. He was born free and is from Prince William County.

REGISTRATION NO. 397
(Vol. 3, p. 130)

Thomas Williams

Copy delivered 7 February 1854

Thomas Williams is a dark mulatto, about 52 years old, 5 feet 10½ inches tall, with a scar on the right side of his neck. He was born free and is from Prince William County.

REGISTRATION NO. 398
(Vol. 3, p. 130)

Emanuel Cupid

Copy delivered February 7, 1854

Emanuel Cupid is a mulatto, about 20 years old, 5 feet 8½ inches tall, with a black spot near the elbow of his right arm. He was born free, as appears by evidence of J. A. Shinn.

REGISTRATION NO. 399
(Vol. 3, p. 130)

Catharine Harris

Copy delivered 8 February 1854

Catharine Harris is a bright mulatto, about 33 years old, 5 feet 2 3/4 inches tall, with a small scar on her forehead, one across her nose, and two small scars on her neck from burns. She was born free in Prince William County, as appears by a previous registration.

REGISTRATION NO. 400
(Vol. 3, p. 130)

James Webster

Copy delivered 6 March 1854

James Webster is a mulatto, about 25 years old, 5 feet 4½ inches tall, with no visible marks. He was emancipated by Hugh Smith by deed dated after 1806.

REGISTRATION NO. 401
(Vol. 3, p. 130)

Caroline F. Brannum

Copy delivered 6 March 1854

Caroline F. Brannum is a mulatto, about 24 years old, 5 feet 1¼ inches tall, with a small black mole on the right side of her upper lip. She was emancipated by deed from Robert H. Miller dated after 1806.

REGISTRATION NO. 402
(Vol. 3, p. 130)

Charles Berry

Copy delivered 6 March 1854

Charles Berry is about 28 years old, 5 feet 10 inches tall, of a dark copper color, with two scars above his right eye. The forefinger of his left hand is shortened and the little finger on the same hand is crooked. He was born free.

REGISTRATION NO. 403
(Vol. 3, p. 131)

Jemima Evans

Copy delivered ca. 6 March 1854

Jemima Evans is about 50 years old, 5 ft 1¼ inches tall, of a brownish-black color, with a scar under each jaw. She was born free.

REGISTRATION NO. 404
(Vol. 3, p. 131)

Letty Gray

Copy delivered ca. 6 March 1854

Letty Gray is about 42 years old, 5 feet 3 inches tall, of a dark brown complexion, with a scar on her forehead, another on her left eye and another on the right corner of her right eye. She was born free, as appears by a previous registration from Fairfax County.

See No. 212 in Book 3 of the Fairfax County registrations. Letty Gray is the daughter of Tomason Gray, a free woman, and was born free. See also No. 167 in Book 2 for "Tomson" Gray who was freed by General George Washington. Other children of Tomason's are also registered in the Fairfax books. (Sweig, pp. 70, 160)

REGISTRATION NO. 405
(Vol. 3, p. 131)

Lucy Ann Mitchell

Copy delivered 5 April 1854

Lucy Ann Mitchell is about 21 years old, 5 feet 3 3/4 inches tall, of a copper color, with a scar on her left wrist and three scars over her left eye. She was born free, as appears by a previous registration.

REGISTRATION NO. 406
(Vol. 3, p. 131)

Martha Ann Hones

Copy delivered 5 June 1854

Martha Ann Hones is about 27 years old, 5 feet 2 3/4 inches tall, of a black complexion, with a scar on her left arm near the wrist. She was emancipated by Sally Swink since 1806 and was identified by W. R. Birch.

REGISTRATION NO. 407
(Vol. 3, p. 131)

Thomas Lee

Copy delivered 5 June 1854

Thomas Lee is about 18 years old, 5 feet 9½ inches tall, of a black complexion, with a scar on the back of his head and another over his left eye. He was born free, as appears by evidence of Mrs. [Jane] Rye.

REGISTRATION NO. 408
(Vol. 3, p. 131)

Betsey Jackson						Copy delivered 5 July 1854

Betsey Jackson is a mulatto, about 48 years old, 5 feet 5 inches tall, with a small scar near her left ear. She was emancipated by Mrs. Coryton as appears by a certificate from Mrs. Ann B. Wilmer.

REGISTRATION NO. 409
(Vol. 3, p. 131)

Marion E. Jackson					Copy delivered 5 July 1854

Marion E. Jackson is a mulatto, about 7 years old, 4 feet 11 3/4 inches tall, with no visible marks. Jackson was proven to be born free by Mrs. Marion R. Brown.

REGISTRATION NO. 410
(Vol. 3, p. 131)

Emma Hewett						Copy delivered 5 July 1854

Emma Hewett is a very bright mulatto, about 18 years old, 4 feet 11½ inches tall, with no visible marks. She was born free, as appears by evidence of James P. Coleman.

REGISTRATION NO. 411
(Vol. 3, p. 132)

Silvina Johnson						Copy delivered 5 July 1854

Silvina Johnson is a dark mulatto, about 18 years old, 5 feet 1¼ inches tall, with a scar in the middle of her forehead. She was born free, as appears by evidence of Walter Harris.

REGISTRATION NO. 412
(Vol. 3, p. 132)

Alfred Carter						Copy delivered 7 August 1854

Alfred Carter is a mulatto, about 26 years old, 6 feet tall, with a scar on his nose, another in his right eyebrow and a small cut in his right ear. He was born free, as appears by evidence of W. T. Harper.

REGISTRATION NO. 413
(Vol. 3, p. 132)

John Kenny						Copy delivered 8 August 1854

John Kenny is about 31 years old, 5 feet 10 inches tall, of a black complexion, with a scar on the back of his right hand. He is free, as appears by a registration from Orange County "delivered up and destroyed."

A previous registration was destroyed so that it wouldn't fall into the hands of a slave.

REGISTRATION NO. 414
(Vol. 3, p. 132)

Daniel Carmichael					Copy delivered 9 August 1854

Daniel Carmichael is about 30 years old, 5 feet 5 3/4 inches tall, of a dark brown complexion, with no visible marks. He was emancipated by R[obert] H. Miller.

REGISTRATION NO. 415
(Vol. 3, p. 132)

Fendall Wyatt						Copy delivered 11 August 1854

Fendall Wyatt is a bright mulatto, about 27 years old, 5 feet 8½ inches tall, with a scar on his forehead over his left eye. He is free, as appears by a previous registration.

REGISTRATION NO. 416
(Vol. 3, p. 132)

Charlotte Jackson					Copy delivered 4 September 1854

Charlotte Jackson is a mulatto, about 21 years old, 5 feet 3¼ inches tall, with a scar on the back of her right hand. She was emancipated by John Skidmore and identified by Isaac Skidmore.

REGISTRATION NO. 417
(Vol. 3, p. 132)

John Washington   Copy delivered September 1854

John Washington is a mulatto, about 27 years old, 5 feet 4 3/4 inches tall, with no visible marks. He was emancipated by deed from William L. Powell & Son.

REGISTRATION NO. 418
(Vol. 3, p. 132)

Henry Watson   Copy ordered 7 November 1853

Henry Watson is about 20 years old, 5 feet 5 inches tall, of a black complexion, with no visible marks. He is the son of Flora Johnson and was born free.

REGISTRATION NO. 419
(Vol. 3, p. 133)

Lucy Ann Thornton Campbell   Copy delivered 2 October 1854

Lucy Ann Campbell, late Thornton, is about 25 years old, 5 feet 3 inches tall, of a dark brown complexion, with a scar on her right hand extending from the wrist to the junction of the thumb and forefinger. She was born free, as appears by a previous registration.

REGISTRATION NO. 420
(Vol. 3, p. 133)

George Fox   Copy delivered 4 October 1854

George Fox is about 26 years old, 5 feet 9½ inches tall, of a black complexion, with a scar on the middle on his nose and upper lip. He was proven free by John Tatsepaugh.

REGISTRATION NO. 421
(Vol. 3, p. 133)

Jesse Cole   Ordered 1 July 1854

Jesse Cole is about 38 years old, 5 feet 8¼ inches tall, of a black complexion, with a scar on the little finger of his right hand. He was born free, as appears by a registration from Prince William County.

REGISTRATION NO. 422
(Vol. 3, p. 133)

Mary Tate   Ordered 6 November 1854

Mary Tate is about 25 years old, 5 feet 2½ inches tall, of a black complexion, with scars on the inside of both arms near the elbows. She was born free, as appears by evidence of Elizabeth Domain.

REGISTRATION NO. 423
(Vol. 3, p. 133)

Sarah Ellen Grayson   Copy delivered 6 November 1854

Sarah Ellen Grayson is a bright mulatto, about 20 years old, 5 feet 4 inches tall, with a scar on her nose. She was born free, as appears by her registration from Prince William County.

REGISTRATION NO. 424
(Vol. 3, p. 133)

Thornton Check   Copy delivered 5 February 1855

Thornton Check is about 35 years old, 6 feet 2½ inches tall, of a dark brown complexion, with a knot and scar on the top of his left wrist. He was emancipated by Bazil Williams by deed recorded January 1855.

REGISTRATION NO. 425
(Vol. 3, p. 133)

Lewis Check   Copy delivered 5 February 1855

Lewis Check is about 33 years old, 6 feet 1 inch tall, of a dark brown complexion, with a scar in the middle of his forehead. He was emancipated by Bazil Williams by deed recorded January 1855.

REGISTRATION NO. 426
(Vol. 3, p. 133)

Daniel Check

Copy delivered 5 February 1855

Daniel Check is about 30 years old, 5 feet 11 inches tall, of a dark brown color, with a scar on his forehead near the hair and another on the left side of his forehead. He was emancipated by Bazil Williams by deed recorded January 1855.

REGISTRATION NO. 427
(Vol. 3, p. 134)

Jackson Check

Copy delivered 5 February 1855

Jackson Check is about 24 years old, 6 feet three-fourths of an inch tall, of a dark brown complexion, with no visible marks. He was emancipated by Bazil Williams by deed recorded January 1855.

REGISTRATION NO. 428
(Vol. 3, p. 134)

Robert Mahoney

Copy delivered 5 February 1855

Robert Mahoney is about 17 years old, 5 feet 8 inches tall, of a dark brown complexion, with a scar from a burn on his forehead.

REGISTRATION NO. 429
(Vol. 3, p. 134)

Harriet Richardson and
children, John William,
Jane Eliza, Louisa,
and Catharine

Copy delivered 5 February 1855

Harriet Richardson is a bright mulatto, about 36 years old, 5 feet 8 inches tall, with a scar from a burn on her forehead. She and her children, all mulattoes, were manumitted by Bazil Williams by deed recorded January 1855. They are: John William, aged 9; Jane Eliza, aged 7; Louisa, aged about 4; and Catharine, aged about 14 months.

REGISTRATION NO. 430
(Vol. 3, p. 134)

Winney Steele and
children, Elijah,
Emma, and Sarah

Copy delivered 5 February 1855

Winney Steele is about 41 years old, 5 feet 2¼ inches tall, of a dark brown complexion. She and her children: Elijah, aged 6, Emma aged 4, and Sarah, aged one (who are of a dark brown color like their mother) were emancipated by Bazil Williams by deed recorded January 1855.

REGISTRATION NO. 431
(Vol. 3, p. 134)

Sally Richardson and
child, Alice

Copy delivered 5 February 1855

Sally Richardson is about 21 years old, 5 feet 3¼ inches tall, of a dark brown complexion, with no visible marks. She and her child, Alice, a mulatto aged 2 years, were emancipated by Bazil Williams by deed recorded January 1855.

REGISTRATION NO. 432
(Vol. 3, p. 134)

Jane Cole

Copy delivered 6 February 1855

Jane Cole is a bright mulatto, about 45 years old, 5 feet 6¼ inches tall, with a mole over her left eyebrow. She is the wife of Thomas Cole and was born free, as appears by oath of James R. Reid.

Volume 3, 1847-1861

REGISTRATION NO. 433
(Vol. 3, p. 134)

Lucinda Cole   Copy delivered 6 February 1855

Lucinda Cole is a very bright mulatto, about 16 years old, 5 feet 4 inches tall, with a small scar in her left eyebrow. She is the daughter of Thomas and Jane Cole, and was born free, as appears by papers from Prince William County.

REGISTRATION NO. 434
(Vol. 3, p. 135)

Catherine Matthews   Ordered 6 February 1855

Catherine Matthews is a dark mulatto, about 22 years old, 5 feet 3¼ inches tall, with no visible marks. She was born free, as appears by her papers from Page County.

REGISTRATION NO. 435
(Vol. 3, p. 135)

Fanny Butler   Ordered April 1855

Fanny Butler is about 22 years old, 5 feet 3 3/4 inches tall, of a copper color, with a scar on the left side of her forehead [rest of description is too faint to read]. She was emancipated by the will of Basil Williams recorded January Term 1855.

REGISTRATION NO. 436
(Vol. 3, p. 135)

John Butler   Ordered April 1855
Laura Butler
Mary Elizabeth Butler

Fanny Butler's children were emancipated by the will of Basil Williams recorded January term of 1855. They are: John Butler, aged 3 years; Laura Butler, aged 2 years; and Mary Elizabeth Butler, aged 2 months.

REGISTRATION NO. 437
(Vol. 3, p. 135)

John W. Payne   Ordered 2 April 1855

John W. Payne is about 21 years old, 5 feet 8½ inches tall, of a dark brown complexion, with a scar over the right corner of his right eye. He was born free, as appears by evidence of William H. Fowle.

REGISTRATION NO. 438
(Vol. 3, p. 135)

Felicia Daniels   Ordered 2 April 1855

Felicia Daniels is about 35 years old, 4 feet 10 inches tall, of a dark brown complexion, with the forefinger of her right hand disfigured by a bone filer. She was emancipated by Rev. Edward Kingsford.

REGISTRATION NO. 439
(Vol. 3, p. 135)

Mary Frances Evans   Copy ordered 8 November 1853

Mary Frances Evans is a dark mulatto, about 26 years old, 5 feet 4 inches tall, with no visible marks. She was emancipated by Nathaniel Lucas and identified by Benjamin Hallowell

REGISTRATION NO. 440
(Vol. 3, p. 135)

Rebecca Kane Lee   Copy delivered 30 April 1855

Rebecca Lee, late Kane, is a bright mulatto, about 26 years old, 5 feet tall, with no visible marks. She was born free, as appears by a previous registration.

REGISTRATION NO. 441
(Vol. 3, p. 135)

Sally Piper   Ordered 7 May 1855

Sally Piper is a bright mulatto, about 5 feet tall. She was born free, as appears by her papers from Fredericksburg.

REGISTRATION NO. 442
(Vol. 3, p. 135)

William Henry Piper Ramsay

Ordered 7 May 1855

William Henry Piper Ramsay is a mulatto, about 31 years old, 5 feet 5½ inches tall, with no visible marks. He was born free, as appears by a previous registration.

REGISTRATION NO. 443
(Vol. 3, p. 136)

James E. Piper Ramsay

Ordered 7 May 1855

James E. Piper Ramsay is a mulatto, about 35 years old, 5 feet 3½ inches tall, with no visible marks. He was born free, as appears by a previous registration.

REGISTRATION NO. 444
(Vol. 3, p. 136)

John Dogan

Undated

John Dogan is a dark mulatto, about 32 years old, 6 feet one-half inch tall, with no visible marks.

The above entry has been struck through.

REGISTRATION NO. 445
(Vol. 3, p. 136)

Mary Franklin

Ordered 7 May 1855

Mary Franklin is about 18 years old, 5 feet 3 inches tall, of a dark brown complexion, with a scar on the right side of her chin. She was born free, as appears by evidence of Henry Hallowell.

REGISTRATION NO. 446
(Vol. 3, p. 136)

Mary Jane Cole Ware

Ordered 4 June 1855

Mary Jane Ware, formerly Cole, is a bright mulatto, about 28 years old, 5 feet 2 3/4 inches tall, with a scar on the right side of her upper lip. She was born free, as appears by a previous registration.

REGISTRATION NO. 447
(Vol. 3, p. 136)

Martha Smith

Ordered 4 June 1855

Martha Smith is about 29 years old, 5 feet 3½ inches tall, of a dark brown complexion, with a small scar on the right side of her head near her eye. She was born free, as appears by evidence of Mrs. Rachel Risten.

REGISTRATION NO. 448
(Vol. 3, p. 136)

George Kendall

Ordered 5 June 1855

George Kendall is a bright mulatto, about 20 years old, 5 feet 10 inches tall, with no visible marks. He was born free, as appears by evidence of James G. Grimes.

REGISTRATION NO. 449
(Vol. 3, p. 136)

John Williams

Ordered 5 June 1855

John Williams is a bright mulatto, about 19 years old, 6 feet 1 inch tall, with no visible marks. He was born free, as appears by evidence of James G. Grimes.

REGISTRATION NO. 450
(Vol. 3, p. 136)

Cordelia Williams

Ordered 5 June 1855

Cordelia Williams is a very bright mulatto, about 17 years old, 5 feet 4 3/8 inches tall, with a scald mark on the back of her right hand and wrist. She was born free, as appears by evidence of James G. Grimes.

REGISTRATION NO. 451
(Vol. 3, p. 136)

Mary Williams

Ordered 5 June 1855

Mary Williams is a bright mulatto, about 37 years old, 5 feet 7 1/8 inches tall, with a dark spot over her right eye and over her cheek. She was born free, as appears by evidence of James G. Grimes.

REGISTRATION NO. 452
(Vol. 3, p. 136)

Francis Williams

Copy delivered 5 June 1855

"Frances" [Francis] Williams is about 52 years old, 5 feet 8½ inches tall, of a dark brown complexion, with no visible marks. He was emancipated by Charles Lewis, as appears by a previous registration.

REGISTRATION NO. 453
(Vol. 3, p. 137)

Virginia Fuller

Copy delivered ca. 5 June 1855

Virginia Fuller is a dark mulatto, about 22 years old, 5 feet 2 inches tall, with a large scar on the right side of her neck. She was born free, as appears by evidence of Zenas Kinzey.

REGISTRATION NO. 454
(Vol. 3, p. 137)

Margaret Hutchison

Copy delivered 6 August 1855

Margaret Hutchison is a bright mulatto, about 17 years old, 4 feet 10 inches tall, with a small scar over each eye. She was born free, as appears by evidence of Newman Cross.

REGISTRATION NO. 455
(Vol. 3, p. 137)

Sydney Asher

Copy delivered 6 August 1855

Sydney Asher is a bright mulatto, about 39 years old, 4 feet 11½ inches tall, with no visible marks. Sydney was born free as appears by evidence of Thomas T. Hill.

REGISTRATION NO. 456
(Vol. 3, p. 137)

David Syphax

Copy delivered 7 August 1855

David Syphax is a bright mulatto, about 21 years old, 5 feet 10 inches tall, with no visible marks. He was born free, as appears by evidence of R[ichard] H. Stabler.

REGISTRATION NO. 457
(Vol. 3, p. 137)

Jane Norris

Copy delivered 7 August 1855

Jane Norris is about 19 years old, 4 feet 11 3/8 inches tall, of a dark brown complexion, with a small scar on the first joint of her left middle finger. She was born free, as appears by evidence of Margaret Sims.

REGISTRATION NO. 458
(Vol. 3, p. 137)

Robert Franklin

Copy delivered 7 August 1855

Robert Franklin is about 21 years old, 5 feet 8¼ inches tall, of a dark brown complexion, with a small scar on the forefinger of his left hand between the second and third joints. He was born free, as appears by evidence of Joseph Nightingill.

REGISTRATION NO. 459
(Vol. 3, p. 137)

Harriet Bounty

Ordered 3 September 1855

Harriet Bounty is about 29 years old, 5 feet one-eighth of an inch tall, with no visible marks. She was proven free by evidence of Mrs. Sarah Beans.

REGISTRATION NO. 460
(Vol. 3, p. 137)

George Washington

Copy delivered 1 October 1855

George Washington is about 40 years old, 5 feet 9 inches tall, of a black complexion, with a small scar in the center of his forehead. He was emancipated by Eliza Black's will.

REGISTRATION NO. 461
(Vol. 3, p. 137)

Charles Henry Wright

Copy delivered 6 November 1855

Charles Henry Wright is about 24 years old, 5 feet 6 3/4 inches tall, of a dark brown complexion, with a scar on the right side of his forehead in the edge of his hair. He was proved free by evidence of John L. Smith.

REGISTRATION NO. 462
(Vol. 3, p. 138)

Francis Wright

Copy delivered 6 November 1855

Francis Wright is about 22 years old, 5 feet 6 3/4 inches tall, of a dark brown complexion, with a scar on the right arm above the wrist and a scar on the back of the left hand. Wright was proven free by evidence of John L. Smith.

REGISTRATION NO. 463
(Vol. 3, p. 138)

Joseph Wright

Copy delivered 6 November 1855

Joseph Wright is about 16 years old, 4 feet 11¼ inches tall, of a light brown complexion, with a small scar on the back of his right hand above the forefinger. He was proven free by evidence of John L. Smith.

REGISTRATION NO. 464
(Vol. 3, p. 138)

George Turley

Copy delivered 3 March 1856

George Turley is about 17 years old, 5 feet 9 inches tall, of a black complexion, with a bumpy face and with the little finger of his left hand stiff at the joint. He was born free, as appears by evidence of Robert Jamieson.

REGISTRATION NO. 465
(Vol. 3, p. 138)

Milly Triplett

Copy delivered 7 April 1856

Milly Triplett is about 44 years old, 5 feet 3½ inches tall, of a dark brown complexion, with a large black mole on the right side of her nose. She was emancipated by Eliza M. Norris by deed recorded in Liber E No. 3, page 379, as appears by a previous registration.

REGISTRATION NO. 466
(Vol. 3, p. 138)

Catharine Hutchin

Copy delivered 8 April 1856

Catharine Hutchin is a very bright mulatto, about 22 years old, 4 feet 9 3/4 inches tall, with two dark moles on her left cheek and one on her upper lip. She was born free, as appears by evidence of James W. Simpson.

REGISTRATION NO. 467
(Vol. 3, p. 138)

William Lyons

Copy delivered 8 April 1856

William Lyons is a dark mulatto, about 35 years old, 5 feet 6 3/4 inches tall, with a scar on the inner part of his right thumb. He was born free, as appears by a previous registration.

REGISTRATION NO. 468
(Vol. 3, p. 138)

Julia Gaskins

Ordered 7 April 1856

Julia Gaskins is about 32 years old, 5 feet 2 3/4 inches tall, of a light brown complexion, with a small scar on her right hand above the forefinger and a scar on her left wrist. She was born free, as appears by a registration from Prince William County.

REGISTRATION NO. 469
(Vol. 3, p. 138)

Elizabeth Hall

Ordered 7 April 1856

Elizabeth Hall is a bright mulatto, about 17 years old, 5 feet 3½ inches tall, with a scar on the first joint of her left thumb. She was born free, as appears by a registration from Prince William County.

REGISTRATION NO. 470
(Vol. 3, p. 139)

Lorenzo Branham

Copy delivered 5 May 1856

Lorenzo Branham is a bright mulatto, about 26 years old, 5 feet 8 inches tall, with a scar on the back of his right hand. He was born free, as appears by registration No. 570 [on page 224].

REGISTRATION NO. 471
(Vol. 3, p. 139)

Rosalee Branham

Copy delivered 5 May 1856

Rosalee Branham is a bright mulatto, about 24 years old, 5 feet 2 inches tall, with several small black moles over her face. She was born free as appears by registration No. 571 [on page 224].

REGISTRATION NO. 472
(Vol. 3, p. 139)

Lewis Syphax

Copy delivered 6 May 1856

Lewis Syphax is a bright mulatto, about 22 years old, 5 feet 6 3/4 inches tall, with a scar on his left eyebrow. He was born free, as appears by evidence of Gilbert Simpson.

REGISTRATION NO. 473
(Vol. 3, p. 139)

Elizabeth Haney

Copy delivered 14 May 1856

Elizabeth Haney is about 19 years old, 5 feet 1¼ inches tall, of a brown complexion, with a small black mole on the left side of her nose. She was born free, as appears by evidence of John West.

REGISTRATION NO. 474
(Vol. 3, p. 139)

Aaron Burrell

Copy delivered 7 July 1856

Aaron Burrell is a dark mulatto, about 21 years of age, 5 feet 8½ inches tall, with a large scar on his left cheek. He was born free.

REGISTRATION NO. 475
(Vol. 3, p. 139)

Mary Reed

Copy delivered 8 July 1856

Mary Reed is about 17 years old, 4 feet 10 inches tall, of a brown complexion, with a scar on her left cheek near her eye. She was born free, as appears by evidence of Wesley Carlin.

REGISTRATION NO. 476
(Vol. 3, p. 139)

Dennis Halley

Ordered 6 December 1853

Dennis Halley is a light mulatto, about 40 years old, 5 feet 8¼ inches tall, with a scar on the right side of his nose. He was emancipated by Penelope Stone and identified by Samuel Beach, the executor of Stone's will.

REGISTRATION NO. 477
(Vol. 3, p. 140)

Daniel Turner

Copy delivered 4 August 1856

Daniel Turner is a dark mulatto, about 3 [30?] years old, 5 feet 3 inches tall, with a scar in his right eyebrow and one on the lower part of his left forefinger. He was emancipated by the will of Margaret Shreve recorded 28 September 1811.

The dates are copied as they are written. Shreve's will probably provided that the children of her female slaves be freed upon reaching a certain age. See, for example, No. 560 below. Margaret Smith was freed by Shreve's will upon reaching age 28.

REGISTRATION NO. 478
(Vol. 3, p. 140)

Richard Lyles

Copy delivered ca. 4 August 1856

Richard Lyle[s] is a dark mulatto, about 22 years old, 5 feet 7½ inches tall, with no visible marks. He was born free, as appears by evidence of Rachel Riston.

REGISTRATION NO. 479
(Vol. 3, p. 140)

Negro Daniel

Copy delivered 5 August 1856

Daniel is a dark mulatto, about 45 years old, 5 feet 6 inches tall, with his left thumb very disfigured by an accident and a small scar between his eyebrows. He was emancipated by John Hooff by deed dated 13 December 1855 recorded in Liber Q No. 3, page 558.

REGISTRATION NO. 480
(Vol. 3, p. 140)

Hannah Lee

Copy delivered 7 August 1856

Hannah Lee is about 49 years old, 4 feet 10 inches tall, of a black complexion, with a scar on her right arm. She was emancipated by the will of Thomas G. Harden.

REGISTRATION NO. 481
(Vol. 3, p. 140)

Rosetta Lee

Copy delivered 7 August 1856

Rosetta Lee is about 20 years old, 4 feet 8 inches tall, of a black complexion, with a large scar on her right arm at the elbow from a burn. She was born free, as appears by evidence of Sarah A. Peyton.

REGISTRATION NO. 482
(Vol. 3, p. 140)

Andrew Brown

Copy delivered ca. 7 August 1856

Andrew Brown is a light mulatto, about 23 years old, 5 feet 8 1/3 inches tall, with no visible marks. He was emancipated by deed of R. G. Violett dated 17 March 1856, and identified by S[amuel] O. Baggett.

REGISTRATION NO. 483
(Vol. 3, p. 140)

Elizabeth Beckley

Copy delivered ca. 7 August 1856

Elizabeth Beckley is a bright mulatto, about 20 years old, 5 feet 3 inches tall, with no visible marks. She was born free, as appears by evidence of W. W. Harper.

REGISTRATION NO. 484
(Vol. 3, p. 141)

Joanna Thomas

Copy delivered ca. 7 August 1856

Joanna Thomas is a dark mulatto, about 26 years old, 5 feet 1¼ inches tall, with a small scar on her forehead. She was born free, as appears by evidence of Elizabeth Taylor.

REGISTRATION NO. 485
(Vol. 3, p. 141)

Louisa Gray																				Copy delivered ca. 7 August 1856

Louisa Gray is about 20 years old, 5 feet tall, of a light brown complexion, with no visible marks. She was born free, as appears by evidence of John William Skidmore.

REGISTRATION NO. 486
(Vol. 3, p. 141)

Margaret Scott																			Copy delivered 7 October 1856

Margaret Scott is a bright mulatto, about 23 years old, 5 feet 5½ inches tall, with a scar on the right side of her neck. She was born free, as appears by a registration from Albemarle County.

REGISTRATION NO. 487
(Vol. 3, p. 141)

Joseph Hutchin																			Copy delivered ca. 7 October 1856

Joseph Hutchin is a bright mulatto, about 47 years old, 5 feet 2 inches tall, with a scar over his right eye extending into the edge of his hair. He was freed by the will of Sinah B. Porter recorded 8 February 1853.

REGISTRATION NO. 488
(Vol. 3, p. 141)

William Webster																			Ordered 3 November 1856

William Webster is about 26 years old, 5 feet 6¼ inches tall, of a light brown color, with a scar on the thumb of his right hand and with the little finger of that same hand crooked. He was emancipated by Hugh Smith by deed dated 1 January 1840 and recorded in Liber A No. 3, page 109.

REGISTRATION NO. 489
(Vol. 3, p. 141)

Addison Webster																			Ordered 3 November 1856

Addison Webster is about 26 years old, 5 feet 5¼ inches tall, of a light brown color, with a small scar on the second joint of his right thumb. He was emancipated by Hugh Smith by deed dated 1 January 1840 recorded in Liber A No. 3, page 109.

REGISTRATION NO. 490
(Vol. 3, p. 141)

Jane Bell Lee																			Copy delivered 1 December 1856

Jane Lee, late Jane Bell, is a dark mulatto, about 36 years old, 5 feet 6½ inches tall, with no visible marks. She is free, as appears by a registration from Fairfax County.

See No. 448 in Book 3 of the Fairfax County registrations. (Sweig p. 217)

REGISTRATION NO. 491
(Vol. 3, p. 142)

George Franklin																			Copy delivered December 1856

George Franklin is a very dark mulatto, about 21 years old, 5 feet 9 inches tall, with a dark mark on his forehead over his left eye. He was born free, as appears by evidence of Henry Hallowell.

REGISTRATION NO. 492
(Vol. 3, p. 142)

Elizabeth Harris																		Copy delivered 5 January 1857

Elizabeth Harris is about 16 years old, 5 feet 2 inches tall, of a light brown complexion, with several black moles on her cheeks. She was born free, as appears by evidence of Sally Vernon.

REGISTRATION NO. 493
(Vol. 3, p. 142)

Alexander Peters																		Copy delivered 6 January 1857

Alexander Peters is a dark mulatto, about 43 years old, 5 feet 7 inches tall, with a scar on his left eyebrow. He was emancipated by deed from Harriet G. Lamar dated 27 December 1856.

REGISTRATION NO. 494
(Vol. 3, p. 142)

Robert Thornton

Copy delivered 6 January 1857

Robert Thornton is about 56 years old, 5 feet 7 inches tall, of a dark brown complexion, with no visible marks. He was freed by judgement of the Alexandria County Court at its August 1854 term.

REGISTRATION NO. 495
(Vol. 3, p. 142)

John Robinson

Copy delivered 6 January 1857

John Robinson is a bright mulatto, about 27 years old, 5 feet 7¼ inches tall, with a scar near the middle of his forehead. He was born free, as appears by evidence of Joshua Grady.

REGISTRATION NO. 496
(Vol. 3, p. 142)

Thomas Robinson

Copy delivered 6 January 1857

Thomas Robinson is a bright mulatto, about 24 years old, 5 feet 5½ inches tall, with a scar on his left temple and a large scar on the back of his right hand. He was born free, as appears by evidence of Joshua Grady.

REGISTRATION NO. 497
(Vol. 3, p. 142)

William Gray

Copy delivered 2 March 1857

William Gray is a bright mulatto, about 32 years old, 5 feet 9¼ inches tall, with no visible marks. He was born free.

REGISTRATION NO. 498
(Vol. 3, p. 142)

Randolph Whitler

Copy delivered 2 March 1857

Randolph Whitler is a bright mulatto, about 20 years old, 5 feet 5¼ inches tall, with several scars on his left cheek. He was born free, as appears by evidence of Richard C. Barton.

REGISTRATION NO. 499
(Vol. 3, p. 143)

John E. Hyson

Copy delivered 2 March 1857

John E. Hyson is about 22 years old, 5 feet 8¼ inches tall, of a dark brown complexion, with a long narrow scar on his left cheek. He was born free, as appears by evidence of Henry Feeby.

REGISTRATION NO. 500
(Vol. 3, p. 143)

Mary Pitts

Copy delivered 2 March 1857

Mary Pitts is a dark mulatto, about 13 years old, 5 feet 2 inches tall, with a scar on her left eyebrow and two black moles on her left cheek near her nose. She was born free, as appears by evidence of Samuel R. Adams.

REGISTRATION NO. 501
(Vol. 3, p. 143)

John Shields

Copy delivered 6 April 1857

John Shields is a dark mulatto, about 22 years old, 6 feet one-fourth inch tall, with a small scar on the right side of his forehead. he was born free, as appears by evidence of William B. Richards.

REGISTRATION NO. 502
(Vol. 3, p. 143)

Ann M. Curtis

Copy delivered 10 April 1857

Ann M. Curtis is about 23 years old, 5 feet 6 inches tall, of a black complexion, with a scar on her left arm just below her elbow. She was emancipated by Charles Curtis by deed dated 16 May 1855 recorded in Liber R No. 3, page 18, and identified by William Logan.

REGISTRATION NO. 503
(Vol. 3, p. 143)

Adeline Curtis

Copy delivered 10 April 1857

Adeline Curtis is about 22 years old, 5 feet 4 3/4 inches tall, of a black complexion, with no visible marks. She was emancipated by Charles Curtis by deed dated 16 May 1855 recorded in Liber R No. 2, page 18, and identified by William Logan.

REGISTRATION NO. 504
(Vol. 3, p. 143)

John Henry Payne

Ordered 4 May 1857

John Henry Payne is about 45 years old, 5 feet 7 3/4 inches tall, with a scar on his forehead above the right eye. He was emancipated by James H. Simpson by deed dated 2 May 1857.

REGISTRATION NO. 505
(Vol. 3, p. 143)

Frederick Payne

Copy delivered ca. 11 May 1857

Frederick Payne is a bright mulatto, about 30[?] years old, 5 feet 4 inches tall, with light eyes, with his left eye smaller than his right one. He has two scars on his left cheek, one of them extending to his neck. He was freed by the will of Anne Henderson recorded at the May 1857 term of the Alexandria Court.

REGISTRATION NO. 506
(Vol. 3, p. 144)

Mary Ellen Henderson

Copy delivered 7 September 1857

Mary Ellen Henderson is a bright mulatto, about 31 years old, with a scar on the left side of her neck and being very freckled. She was born free.

REGISTRATION NO. 507
(Vol. 3, p. 144)

James Blackburn

Copy delivered 7 September 1857

James Blackburn is about 26 years old, 5 feet 11 3/4 inches tall, with a small scar on the left side of his nose and a large one on the thumb of his left hand. He was born free, as appears by a registration from Fairfax County.

See No. 409 in Book 3 of the Fairfax County registrations. James is the son of Polly Blackburn. See also No. 237 in Book 3. Polly Blackburn appears to be the Polly Harrison freed by George Washington. (Sweig, pp. 165, 206)

REGISTRATION NO. 508
(Vol. 3, p. 144)

William Henry Campbell

Copy delivered 6 October 1857

William Henry Campbell is about 19 years old, 5 feet 6½ inches tall, of a copper color, with a scar under his left jaw and a long scar on his right hand. He was born free.

REGISTRATION NO. 509
(Vol. 3, p. 144)

George Simms

Copy delivered 6 October 1857

George Simms is a bright mulatto, about 46 years old, 5 feet 10 inches tall, with a scar on the back of his left hand and a scar on the forefinger of his left hand. He was born free. (See page 27)

See No. 195 on page 180.

REGISTRATION NO. 510
(Vol. 3, p. 144)

Helen Simms

Copy delivered 6 October 1857

Helen Simms is a bright mulatto, about 38 years old, 5 feet 2¼ inches tall, with a black mole on her left cheek. She was born free. (See page 28)

No. 198 on page 180.

REGISTRATION NO. 511
(Vol. 3, p. 144)

Richard Bailey

Ordered 6 October 1857

Richard Bailey is about 30 years old, 5 feet 5 3/4 inches tall, of a dark copper color, with no visible marks. He was emancipated by the will of Rev. William D. Cairns probated in Russell County, Alabama.

REGISTRATION NO. 512
(Vol. 3, p. 144)

Edmund Lee Bailey

Ordered 6 October 1857

Edmund Lee Bailey is about 26 years old, 5 feet 7¼ inches tall, of a dark copper color, with no visible marks. He was emancipated by the will of Rev. William D. Cairns probated in Russell County, Alabama.

REGISTRATION NO. 513
(Vol. 3, p. 145)

Jesse Johnson

Ordered 2 November 1857

Jesse Johnson is a bright mulatto, about 22 years 6 months old, 5 feet 9 3/4 inches tall, with a long black mark on his right arm near his shoulder. He was born free.

REGISTRATION NO. 514
(Vol. 3, p. 145)

Benjamin F. Reed

Copy delivered 8 December 1857

Benjamin F. Reed is about 23 years old, 5 feet 8½ inches tall, of a "nearly black" color, with a slight scar on his cheekbone, and "affected in the right eye." He was born free, as appears by evidence of William H. Phillips.

REGISTRATION NO. 515
(Vol. 3, p. 145)

James H. Claggett

Copy delivered 6 February 1858

James H. Claggett is a bright mulatto, about 21 years old, 5 feet 3½ inches tall, with an anchor on his right hand and a star on his left hand "prickled in India ink." He was born free, as appears by evidence of Robert Bell.

REGISTRATION NO. 516
(Vol. 3, p. 145)

William H. Ages

Copy delivered 6 February 1858

William H. Ages is about 25 years old, 5 feet 5½ inches tall, of a black complexion, with his two front teeth broken off. He was born free.

REGISTRATION NO. 517
(Vol. 3, p. 145)

Maria V. Ages

Copy delivered 6 February 1858

Maria V. Ages is about 23 years old, 5 feet 1 inch tall, nearly black in color, with a slight scar on her right hand. She was born free.

REGISTRATION NO. 518
(Vol. 3, p. 145)

Martha Ann Seaton

Ordered 1 March 1858

Martha Ann Seaton is a very bright mulatto, about 27 years old, 5 feet 8 inches tall, with a small mark on the white of her right eye. She was born free.

REGISTRATION NO. 519
(Vol. 3, p. 145)

Mary Elizabeth Carmichael　　　　　　　　　　　　　　　　　　　　　　　Copy delivered 5 April 1858

Mary Elizabeth Carmichael is a dark mulatto, about 22 years old, 5 feet 4½ inches tall, with no visible marks. She was born free, as appears by evidence of John Arrington.

REGISTRATION NO. 520
(Vol. 3, p. 145)

Mary Ellen Seymour　　　　　　　　　　　　　　　　　　　　　　　Copy delivered 7 May 1858

Mary Ellen Seymour is a bright mulatto, about 19 years old, 5 feet 1 inch tall, with a small mole on her right cheek. She was emancipated by deed from A. O. Douglas recorded 7 August 1847.

REGISTRATION NO. 521
(Vol. 3, p. 146)

Rebecca Green　　　　　　　　　　　　　　　　　　　　　　　Copy delivered 7 May 1858

Rebecca Green is about 22 years old, 5 feet 4½ inches tall, of a dark brown complexion, with three scars on her left arm. She was born free, as appears by a registration from Fredericksburg, which was destroyed.

REGISTRATION NO. 522
(Vol. 3, p. 146)

John Marrs　　　　　　　　　　　　　　　　　　　　　　　Copy delivered 7 May 1858

John Marrs is about 23 years old, 5 feet 8½ inches tall, of a dark brown complexion, with a scar on his navel and a small scar on his right temple. He was born free, as appears by a registration from Culpeper County, destroyed.

REGISTRATION NO. 523
(Vol. 3, p. 146)

Jacquelin Strange　　　　　　　　　　　　　　　　　　　　　　　Ordered 3 May 1858

Jacquelin Strange is about 21 years old, 5 feet 6 3/4 inches tall, of a dark brown complexion, with no visible marks. Samuel Hartley proved "him" [sic] to be free born.

REGISTRATION NO. 524
(Vol. 3, p. 146)

George W. Walker　　　　　　　　　　　　　　　　　　　　　　　Copy delivered 7 June 1858

George W. Walker is about 20 years old, 5 feet 3 inches tall, of a black complexion, with a large scar on the left side of his head between his ear and forehead. He was born free, as appears by evidence of James H. Monroe.

REGISTRATION NO. 525
(Vol. 3, p. 146)

Georgiana Brown　　　　　　　　　　　　　　　　　　　　　　　Ordered 7 June 1858

Georgiana Brown is a very bright mulatto, about 19 years old, 5 feet 5 inches tall, with no visible marks. She is free by judgement of the Alexandria Circuit Court in its May 1858 term.

REGISTRATION NO. 526
(Vol. 3, p. 146)

Moses Robinson　　　　　　　　　　　　　　　　　　　　　　　Ordered 7 June 1858

Moses Robinson is about 16 years old, 5 feet 6 inches tall, of a black complexion, with a scar under his right eye. He was freed by judgement of the Circuit Court of Alexandria in its May 1858 term.

REGISTRATION NO. 527
(Vol. 3, p. 146)

Thomas Robinson   Ordered 7 June 1858

Thomas Robinson is about 15 years old, 5 feet 1 inch tall, of a light brown complexion, with no visible marks. He was freed by judgement of the Circuit Court of Alexandria in its May 1858 term.

REGISTRATION NO. 528
(Vol. 3, p. 146)

Mary Brown   Ordered 7 June 1858

Mary Brown is a bright mulatto about 11 years old, 4 feet 6½ inches tall, with a mole on the left part of her right eyebrow. She was freed by judgement of the Circuit Court of Alexandria in its May 1858 term.

REGISTRATION NO. 529
(Vol. 3, p. 146)

Helen Payne   Copy delivered 6 July 1858

Helen Payne is about 16 years old, 5 feet 2¼ inches tall, of a light brown complexion, with no visible marks. She was born free, as appears by evidence of Mrs. Ann D. Ratcliff.

REGISTRATION NO. 530
(Vol. 3, p. 146)

Harriet Humphreys   Copy delivered 8 July 1858

Harriet Humphreys is about 22 years old, 4 feet 11¼ inches tall, of a dark brown complexion, with a small scar at the left corner of her mouth. She was emancipated after 1806.

REGISTRATION NO. 531
(Vol. 3, p. 147)

Margaret Peck   Copy delivered 3 August 1858

Margaret Peck is a bright mulatto, about 20 years old, 5 feet 2 inches tall, with no visible marks. She was born free, as appears by a registration from Shenandoah County, destroyed.

REGISTRATION NO. 532
(Vol. 3, p. 147)

Ellen Berry   Ordered 11 August 1858

Ellen Berry is about 30 years old, 5 feet one-half inch tall, of a black complexion, with no visible marks. She was emancipated by deed from Henry Chatham dated 11 August 1858.

REGISTRATION NO. 533
(Vol. 3, p. 147)

William Blackburn   Copy delivered 8 September 1858

William Blackburn is about 17 years old, 5 feet 5½ inches tall, of a dark brown complexion. with no visible marks. He was born free, as appears by evidence of Samuel Beach.

REGISTRATION NO. 534
(Vol. 3, p. 147)

Rebecca Butts   Copy delivered 14 October 1858

Rebecca Butts is about 21 years old, 5 feet three-fourths of an inch tall, of a dark brown complexion, with no visible marks. She was born free, as appears by evidence of F. A. Marbury.

REGISTRATION NO. 535
(Vol. 3, p. 147)

John Burke   Copy delivered 1 November 1858

John Burke is a bright mulatto, about 59 years old, 5 feet 9 inches tall, with his left leg and foot contracted from birth. He was emancipated by the will of William H. Fitzhugh of Fairfax County, destroyed.

See No. 305 in Book 3 of the Fairfax County registrations. (Sweig, p. 180)

REGISTRATION NO. 536
(Vol. 3, p. 147)

Mary Catherine Berry

Copy delivered 3 November 1858

Mary C[atherine] Berry is a bright mulatto, about 16 years old, 5 feet 4¼ inches tall, with no visible marks. She is the daughter of Patsy Berry and was born free, as appears by evidence of George Duffey.

REGISTRATION NO. 537
(Vol. 3, p. 147)

Robert Jackson

Copy delivered 3 January 1859

Robert Jackson is about 26 years old, 5 feet 6½ inches tall, of a dark brown complexion, with no visible marks. He was born free, as appears by evidence of Hugh Latham.

REGISTRATION NO. 538
(Vol. 3, p. 147)

Margaret Mitchell

Copy delivered 5 January 1859

Margaret Mitchell is a bright mulatto, about 20 years old, 5 feet 3¼ inches tall, with no visible marks. She was born free, as appears by a previous registration delivered up.

REGISTRATION NO. 539
(Vol. 3, p. 147)

William Dent

Ordered 5 January 1859

William Dent is about 25 years old, 5 feet 11 inches tall, of a dark brown complexion, with no visible marks. He is free, as appears by evidence of Turner Dixon.

REGISTRATION NO. 540
(Vol. 3, p. 147)

Amelia Gibson

Copy delivered 8 March 1859

Amelia Gibson is about 21 years old, 5 feet 3 3/4 inches tall, of a light brown color, with several scars on the back of her right hand. She was born free.

REGISTRATION NO. 541
(Vol. 3, p. 148)

Sarah Ann Grayson

Copy delivered 6 April 1859

Sarah Ann Grayson is about 28 years old, 5 feet 3 3/4 inches tall, of a light brown color, with a mark or scar from a burn on the front part of her collar bone. She was emancipated by the will of David Betzold.

REGISTRATION NO. 542
(Vol. 3, p. 148)

Catharine Jackson

Ordered 9 April 1859

Catharine Jackson is a bright mulatto, about 22 years old, 5 feet 6¼ inches tall, with a scar on the front of each wrist. She was born free.

REGISTRATION NO. 543
(Vol. 3, p. 148)

William Lomax

Ordered 6 April 1859

William Lomax is about 24 years old, 5 feet 7¼ inches tall, of a light brown color, with a scar on the back of his right hand. He was born free, as appears by evidence of Joseph Padgett.

REGISTRATION NO. 544
(Vol. 3, p. 148)

Hannah Ann Weaver

Ordered 11 April 1859

Hannah Ann Weaver is a bright mulatto, about 18 years old, 5 feet 3 inches tall, with no visible marks. She was born free, as appears by evidence of John J. Walsh.

REGISTRATION NO. 545
(Vol. 3, p. 148)

Charles Henry Weaver

Ordered 11 April 1859

Charles Henry Weaver is about 20 years old, 5 feet 4¼ inches tall, of a light brown color, with a small scar on his chin. He was born free, as appears by evidence of John J. Walsh.

REGISTRATION NO. 546
(Vol. 3, p. 148)

Martha D. Boden

Copy delivered 6 June 1859

Martha D. Boden is a bright mulatto, about 21 years old age, 5 feet 4 3/4 inches tall, with freckles on her face. She was born free.

REGISTRATION NO. 547
(Vol. 3, p. 148)

Sally Dixon

Ordered 8 July 1859

Sally Dixon is a bright mulatto, about 24 years old, 5 feet 2 inches tall, with a small scar on the right corner of her mouth. She was emancipated by William H. Fitzhugh's will.

See No. 309 in Book 3 of the Fairfax County registrations. (Sweig, p. 181)

REGISTRATION NO. 548
(Vol. 3, p. 148)

Ellen Maria Watts

Ordered 8 July 1859

Ellen Maria Watts is a bright mulatto, about 24 years old, 4 feet 11¼ inches tall, with a mole on her right cheek and a scar on her right wrist. She was emancipated by the will of Mary Swann.

REGISTRATION NO. 549
(Vol. 3, p. 148)

Henry Walker

Ordered 2 August 1859

Henry Walker is about 21 years old, of a black complexion, 5 feet 4 3/4 inches tall, with a scar on his right cheek. He was born free.

REGISTRATION NO. 550
(Vol. 3, p. 148)

Rachel Norris

Ordered 5 September 1859

Rachel Norris is about 53 years old, 5 feet 1½ inches tall, of a black complexion, with no visible marks. She was born free.

REGISTRATION NO. 551
(Vol. 3, p. 149)

Rebecca Henry

Ordered 5 September 1859

Rebecca Henry is a bright mulatto, about 25 years old, 5 feet 4 inches tall, with no visible marks. She was born free.

REGISTRATION NO. 552
(Vol. 3, p. 149)

Basheba Harris

Copy delivered 6 September 1859

Basheba Harris is a bright mulatto, about 21 years old and 5 feet 3 3/4 inches tall. Her left eye is smaller than her right one and she has a small mole on her forehead. Harris was born free.

REGISTRATION NO. 553
(Vol. 3, p. 149)

Mary Frances Prior Hove

Ordered 2 August 1859

Mary Frances Hove, late Prior, is a bright mulatto, about 20 years old, 5 feet 1 inch tall, with no visible marks. She was born free, as appears by a registration from King George County, destroyed.

REGISTRATION NO. 554
(Vol. 3, p. 149)

Daniel Carter

Ordered 3 October 1859

Daniel Carter is about 23 years old, 5 feet 8½ inches tall, of a black complexion, with a scar across the back of his left hand. He was born free.

REGISTRATION NO. 555
(Vol. 3, p. 149)

Benjamin Bennett

Copy delivered 4 October 1859

Benjamin Bennett is about 37 years old, 5 feet 9 inches tall, of a light brown color, with a scar on his left leg and one over his left eye. He was born free.

REGISTRATION NO. 556
(Vol. 3, p. 149)

Edmonia Nokes

Copy delivered 5 October 1859

Edmonia Nokes is about 18 years old, 5 feet 1 inch tall, of a light brown color, with no visible marks. She was born free.

REGISTRATION NO. 557
(Vol. 3, p. 149)

Harriet Mans Carroll

Ordered 3 October 1859

Harriet Carroll, formerly Harriet Mans, is about 22 years old, 5 feet 1 inch tall, of a black complexion, with a scar on the upper eyelid of her left eye. She was born free, as appears by a registration from Culpeper County, destroyed.

REGISTRATION NO. 558
(Vol. 3, p. 149)

Mary Johnson

Copy delivered 7 November 1859

Mary Johnson is a bright mulatto, about 21 years old, 5 feet 1½ inches tall, with no visible marks. She was born free.

REGISTRATION NO. 559
(Vol. 3, p. 149)

Philip A. Bell

Copy delivered 5 December 1859

Philip A. Bell is about 21 years old, 5 feet 9 inches tall, with a slight scar under his left eye. He was born free.

REGISTRATION NO. 560
(Vol. 3, p. 149)

Margaret V. Smith

Copy delivered 5 December 1859

Margaret V. Smith is a bright mulatto, about 29 years old, 5 feet 2 inches tall, with a small scar on the back of her right hand. She was emancipated when she reached age 28, as provided by the will of Margaret Shreve.

REGISTRATION NO. 561
(Vol. 3, p. 150)

William Lyons

Copy delivered 3 January 1860

William Lyons is a dark mulatto, about 39 years old, 5 feet 6 3/4 inches tall, with a scar on the inner part of his right thumb. He was born free.

REGISTRATION NO. 562
(Vol. 3, p. 150)

Walter Hyson   Copy delivered 3 January 1860

Walter Hyson is about 22 years old, 5 feet 6½ inches tall, of a black complexion, with several scars on the back of his left hand. He was born free.

REGISTRATION NO. 563
(Vol. 3, p. 150)

Matilda Payne   Copy delivered 4 January 1860

Matilda Payne is a bright mulatto, about 33 years old, 5 feet 1½ inches tall, with a small scar on her left arm and the initials "A. M. B." marked in india ink on her left arm. She was born free.

REGISTRATION NO. 564
(Vol. 3, p. 150)

Lucretia Johnson   Ordered 7 January 1860

Lucretia Johnson is a bright mulatto, about 17 years old, with a small scar over her left eye. She was born free.

REGISTRATION NO. 565
(Vol. 3, p. 150)

Louisa Haney Henderson   Copy delivered 6 February 1860

Louisa Henderson, formerly Louisa Haney, is about 26 years old, 5 feet 2 3/4 inches tall, of a dark complexion, with a small scar on her right hand between the thumb and forefinger. She was born free.

REGISTRATION NO. 566
(Vol. 3, p. 150)

Mary Elizabeth Butler   Copy delivered 7 February 1860

Mary Elizabeth Butler is about 19 years old, 5 feet 2½ inches tall, of a dark complexion, with a scar on the back of her left hand. She was born free.

REGISTRATION NO. 567
(Vol. 3, p. 150)

William Field   Copy delivered 5 March 1860

William Field is about 28 years old, 5 feet 6½ inches tall, of a dark complexion, with a small scar on his right temple and another on his left thumb. He was born free, as appears by a registration from Culpeper County, destroyed.

REGISTRATION NO. 568
(Vol. 3, p. 150)

James Bennett   Copy delivered 5 April 1860

James Bennett is about 24 years old, 5 feet 7 3/4 inches tall, of a dark complexion, with no visible marks. He was born free.

REGISTRATION NO. 569
(Vol. 3, p. 150)

John Williams   Copy delivered 2 July 1860

John Williams is a bright mulatto, about 24 years old, 6 feet 1¼ inches tall, with no visible marks. His registration is renewed from former papers issued by this office. See No. 449 [on page 278].

REGISTRATION NO. 570
(Vol. 3, p. 151)

Joseph Jones   Copy delivered 2 July 1860

Joseph Jones is about 20 years old, 5 feet 7 1/2 inches tall, of a black complexion, with no visible marks. He was born free, as appears by evidence of Samuel O. Baggett.

REGISTRATION NO. 571
(Vol. 3, p. 151)

James Henry Jones   Copy delivered 2 July 1860

James Henry Jones is about 22 years old, 5 feet 7½ inches tall, of a black complexion, with no visible marks. He was born free, as appears by evidence of S[amuel] O. Baggett.

REGISTRATION NO. 572
(Vol. 3, p. 151)

Albert Jones   Copy delivered 2 July 1860

Albert Jones is about 18 years old, 5 feet 7¼ inches tall, of a black complexion, with no visible marks. He was born free, as appears by evidence of S[amuel] O. Baggett.

REGISTRATION NO. 573
(Vol. 3, p. 151)

Catherine Williams   Copy delivered 2 July 1860

Catherine Williams is a bright mulatto about 21 years old, 5 feet 3 inches tall, with no visible marks. She was emancipated by the will of Hayward Foote[?] of Fairfax County since 1806.

REGISTRATION NO. 574
(Vol. 3, p. 151)

Dolly Ann Mitchell   Copy delivered 5 July 1860

Dolly Ann Mitchell is about 21 years old, 5 feet 3½ inches tall, of a light brown color, with two scars on her forehead over her left eye. She was born free, as appears by evidence of John Hart.

REGISTRATION NO. 575
(Vol. 3, p. 151)

James Derrick   Copy delivered 5 July 1860

James Derrick is about 43 years old, 5 feet 6 inches tall, of a dark brown complexion, with a slight deformity in the little finger of his right hand. He was born free, as appears by a previous registration.

REGISTRATION NO. 576
(Vol. 3, p. 151)

Charles William Harrison   Copy delivered 6 October 1860

Charles Williams Harrison is a bright mulatto, about 15 years old, 5 feet 7 inches tall, with the end of the first finger of his right hand cut off. He was manumitted by Robert H. Miller by deed recorded in Liber H No. 3, folio 203.

REGISTRATION NO. 577
(Vol. 3, p. 151)

Douglass Syphax   Ordered 5 November 1860

Douglass Syphax is a bright mulatto, about 19 years old, 5 feet 8 3/4 inches tall, with several scars on the thumb of his left hand. He was born free, as appears by oath of Richard H. Stabler.

REGISTRATION NO. 578
(Vol. 3, p. 151)

Rachael Carmichael   Ordered 9 January 1861

Rachael Carmichael is a bright mulatto, about 40 years old, 5 feet 4 inches tall, with a wen over her right eye. She was manumitted by David Carmichael.

REGISTRATION NO. 579
(Vol. 3, p. 152)

Harriet McGruder   Ordered 4 April 1861

Harriet McGruder is about 35 years old, 4 feet three-fourths of an inch tall, of a dark brown complexion, with a slight protuberance on the middle finger of her right hand. She was manumitted by John Mills.

REGISTRATION NO. 580
(Vol. 3, p. 152)

Lucy Robinson

Copy delivered 6 May 1861

Lucy Robinson is a dark mulatto, about 34 years old, 5 feet 5 inches tall, with a scar on her right arm near the wrist and another at the base of her nose. She was registered agreeably to the certificate of John M. Miller.

REGISTRATION NO. 581
(Vol. 3, p. 152)

Louisa Robinson

Copy delivered 6 May 1861

Louisa Robinson is a bright mulatto, about 41 years old, 5 feet 4 3/4 inches tall, with a scar over her right eye and another on the inside of her right forefinger. She was emancipated by deed from Henry Robinson in Frederick County, and was registered agreeably to the certificate of John M. Miller.

INDEX

Roman numerals refer to volume number; other numbers refer to registration number. Registration numbers that are underlined indicate that the item is the registration for that individual. Registration numbers that are not underlined indicate that the individual is mentioned in the document, but is not the person being registered. Because there are duplicate registration numbers in the third volume (and to a lesser extent in volume 2), the page number that begins the registration is given in parenthesis.

Adam, John
   I: 91, 189, 223, 252
Adam, Theresa
   II: 244
Adams, Adolphus
   III: 241 (p. 185), 112 (p. 240)
Adams, Ann
   I: 160, 161 II: 374
Adams, Austin Q.
   II: 117
Adams, Emily
   II: 139
Adams, Hannah
   III: 329 (p. 264)
Adams, Samuel
   III: 40 (p. 161), 246 (p. 255)
Adams, Samuel R.
   III: 504 (p. 216, 505 (p. 216), 500 (p. 284)
Adams, W. W.
   II: 345
Adams, William
   I: 169 III: 569 (p. 223)
Addison, John Jr.
   I: 110
Addison, Louisa Cooper
   III: 254 (p. 256); see also Louisa Cooper
Addison, Thomas G.
   I: 6, 249 II: 154 III: 227 (p. 253)
Ages, Maria V.
   III: 517 (p. 286)
Ages, Mary Eliza
   II: 150
Ages, Nancy
   II: 57
Ages, William H.
   III: 516 (p. 286)
Alexander, Amos
   I: 48, 159, 162, 168
Alexander, Ann
   I: 48
Alexander, C. A.
   III: 472 (p. 212)
Alexander, Francis
   I: 616
Alexander, James
   III: 42 (p. 231)
Alexander, Martha
   II: 377
Alexander, Mary Francis
   III: 518 (p. 218)
Alexander, Nelly
   I: 319
Alexander, R. B.
   III: 17 (p. 229)

Alexander, William F.
   I: 503 II: 348
Alexander, William P.
   II: 234
Allen, David (Mrs.)
   III: 124 (p. 172), 184 (p. 179), 220 (p. 183)
Allen, James
   III: 364 (p. 268)
Allen, Sarah
   II: 261, 262, 263, 264, 265, 266, 268, 312, 328, 373
Allison, Catharine/Catherine
   I: 228, 235, 241 III: 326 (p. 195), 334 (p. 196), 285 (p. 259)
Allison, Robert
   I: 518
Amerger, Richard
   I: 494
Anderson, Charity
   I: 754, 755 III: 67 (p. 165)
Anderson, Eliza
   II: 9 III: 448 (p. 209)
Anderson, Elizabeth
   II: 195
Anderson, Francis Ann
   I: 755
Anderson, Henry
   III: 525 (p. 218)
Anderson, Louisa C. Evans
   II: 156
Anderson, Mary
   III: 196 (p. 180), 292 (p. 260)
Anderson, Nancy
   See Nancy Davis
Anderson, Robert
   I: 353 III: 331 (p. 196)
Anderson, Sambo
   II: 6, 9 III: 448 (p. 209)
Anderson, Samuel
   I: 754 II: 159 III: 67 (p. 165)
Anderson, Thomas
   II: 156 III: 13 (p. 228)
Anderson, William
   II: 6
Anderson, Willis
   II: 378
Appich, Gottlieb
   II: 310
Armstrong, Susan
   See Susan Sears
Armstrong, William
   III: 408 (p. 205)
Arnett, Jesse
   I, 631

Arrington, John
  I: 755 III: 361 (p. 268), 519 (p. 287)
Ash, O. Y.
  II: 287 (p. 68)
Asher, Sydney
  III: <u>455</u> (p. 279)
Ashton, Charles Henry
  II: <u>336</u>
Ashton, Fanny
  II: <u>276b</u> (p. 138), 336
Ashton, Mary Elizabeth
  II: <u>336</u>
Ashton, Peggy
  III: 389 (p. 202), 196 (p. 249)
Atkinson, James W.
  III: 42 (p. 231)
Aubinoe, Somerset H.
  I: 732
Auld, Colin
  I: 647, 671 II: 101, 108, 111, 125, 131, 167b
  III: 140 (p. 174) 179 (p. 178), 258 (p. 187),
  368 (p. 200), 393 (p. 203), 70 (p. 235), 203
  (p. 250), 265 (p. 257)
Austin, Moses
  III: <u>593</u> (p. 226)
Avery, James
  I: 464, 465
Baden, Benjamin
  I: 21, 79, 143, 195 II: 330
Baden, Sarah
  I: 195
Baggett, Samuel O.
  III: 482 (p. 282), 570 (p. 292), 571 (p. 293),
  572 (p. 293)
Bailey, Edmund Lee
  III: <u>512</u> (p. 286)
Bailey, Lavinia
  I: <u>376</u>
Bailey, Richard
  III: <u>511</u> (p. 286)
Baker, Alexis
  III: <u>515</u> (p. 217), <u>219</u> (p. 252)
Baker, Thomas
  III: <u>223</u> (p. 183), <u>283</u> (p. 259)
Ball, James O.[?]
  III: 398 (p. 203)
Ball, James V.
  I: 42
Ball, John
  III: 1 (p. 157), 2 (p. 157)
Ball, Mary
  III: <u>405</u> (p. 204)
Ball, Robert
  III: 59 (p. 233), 353 (p. 267)
Ball, William R.
  III: <u>350</u> (p. 198)
Ballus/Baltus, Letty
  III: <u>341</u> (p. 266)
Bangs, Margaret M.
  II: 135, 177, 270, 291 (p. 74), 318, 319, 320,
  321, 359, 360 III: 18 (p. 159), 292 (p. 191),
  222 (p. 252)
Bangs, Matilda
  III: 66 (p. 165), 53 (p. 233)
Banks, Jerry
  I: <u>336</u>
Banks, John
  II: 71
Banks, Margaret M.
  II: 171, 276 (p. 70)
Banks, Samuel
  III: <u>418</u> (p. 206)
Banks, Winny
  III: <u>169</u> (p. 177), 170 (p. 177)
Barby, Malvina[?]
  I: <u>391</u>
Barby, Rosetta
  I: <u>269</u>, 391
Barcroft, Ann Payne
  I: <u>640a</u>
Barcroft, Ephriam
  II: <u>100</u>
Barcroft, William Henry
  I: <u>427</u>
Barker, Martha Ann
  I: <u>634</u>
Barnes, Kitty
  See Kitty Barnes Humphries
Barnett, Eleazer Buckner
  See Eleazer Buckner Barnett Ryley
Barrett, Lucy
  I: 731
Bartle, Samuel
  III: 23 (p. 159), 204 (p. 181), 274 (p. 189),
  455 (p. 210)
Bartleman, William
  II: 59
Barton, Benjamin
  III: 574 (p. 224), 575 (p. 224), 576a (p. 224),
  576b (p. 224)
Barton, Ellis
  I: <u>434</u>
Barton, Emeline
  I: <u>382b</u>
Barton, Mary
  III: 3 (p. 157), 574 (p. 224), 575 (p. 224),
  576a (p. 224), 576b (p. 224)
Barton, Richard C.
  III: 498 (p. 284)
Batcher, Jonathan
  I: 693
Bayliss, Daniel
  II: 337
Baynes, James Hawkins
  I: 10
Beach, Samuel
  III: 368 (p. 269), 476 (p. 281), 533 (p. 288)
Beale, Elmira
  I: 493
Beale, Frank
  II: <u>351</u>
Beale, John Francis
  II: <u>351</u>
Beale, Mary Ann
  II: <u>351</u>
Beans, Sarah

III: 459 (p. 279)
Beckley, Ann
II: 73   III: 265 (p. 188)
Beckley, Archibald
I: 172
Beckley, Betsey
I: 635
Beckley, Elizabeth
I: 638   III: 112 (p. 170), 483 (p. 282)
Beckley, Fanny
I: 635   III: 346 (p. 198)
Beckley, James R.
I: 645
Beckley, Jane Eliza
III: 100 (p. 169)
Beckley, Jesse
II: 96
Beckley, John
I: 477
Beckley, John A.
I: 364   III: 264 (p. 188), 114 (p. 240), 302 (p. 261)
Beckley, Laura
II: 112
Beckley, Mary Ann
I: 572
Beckley, Mary Ann Jackson
III: 406 (p. 204)
Beckley, Nancy
III: 99 (p. 169)
Beckley, Rozier D.
III: 126 (p. 172), 543 (p. 220)
Beckley, Thomas
II: 95
Beckley, William
I: 404, 497   III: 111 (p. 170)
Beckley, William Sr.
III: 512b (p. 217)
Bell, Albert
III: 414 (p. 205)
Bell, Amey
See Amey Bell Hackett
Bell, Britannia
I: 282, 540   III: 224 (p. 183), 335 (p. 196), 414 (p. 205)   III: 149 (p. 244)
Bell, Eleanora/Elenora
II: 208   III: 354 (p. 267)
Bell, Elizabeth
See Elizabeth Beckley
Bell, Jacob
I: 251   III: 378 (p. 201), 61 (p. 234)
Bell, James
I: 377
Bell, Jane
II: 312; see also Jane Bell Lee
Bell, John
III: 337 (p. 197)
Bell, Mary
I: 456, 574   II: 41; see also Mary Waugh
Bell, Philip A.
III: 559 (p. 291)
Bell, Robert
I: 282, 417, 460   II: 184   III: 224 (p. 183), 335 (p. 196), 149 (p. 244), 391 (p. 271) 515 (p. 286)
Bell, William
I: 633
Bellerjean, Samuel T.
I: 270
Benaugh, Eliza
III: 587 (p. 226)
Bennett, Benjamin
III: 15 (p. 158), 555 (p. 291)
Bennett, Charles
II: 23
Bennett, Daniel
III: 540 (p. 220)
Bennett, Douglass
I: 137b, 444
Bennett, Herrotus Ann
I: 600
Bennett, James
III: 568 (p. 292)
Bennett, James Waters
I: 402
Bennett, Lucy
I: 137b, 138; see also Lucy Bennett Richardson
Bennett, Martha Elizabeth
II: 169
Bennett, Mary
I: 137b, 138, 139, 401, 402   II: 169   III: 145 (p. 174)
Bennett, Mary Ann
I: 137b
Bennett, Milly
III: 10 (p. 158), 11 (p. 158)
Bennett, Sarah Ann
I: 600
Bennett, Walter
I: 137b, 139
Bennett, William
I: 137b, 138, 139
Bennett, William Douglass
I: 402
Bentley, Elizabeth
I: 188
Bentley, George
I: 477
Bentley, Nancy
I: 188
Bentley, Nelson
III: 183 (p. 179)
Berry, Ann
I: 416, 752, 753   II: 292 (p. 69)
Berry, Betsey
I: 512
Berry, Celestial/Celistia
II: 360   III: 328 (p. 264)
Berry, Charles
III: 402 (p. 273)
Berry, Ellen
II: 360   III: 326 (p. 264), 532 (p. 288)
Berry, Emily
III: 537 (p. 220)
Berry, George

I: 87   II: 290 (p. 140)
Berry, George H.
  III: 438 (p. 208)
Berry, James
  III: 521 (p. 218)
Berry, John
  III: 311 (p. 262)
Berry, Lucinda
  I: 397
Berry, Mary
  I: 223
Berry, Mary Catharine
  II: 360   III: 536 (p. 289)
Berry, Mary Margaret
  II: 120
Berry, Patsy
  II: 360   III: 206 (p. 181), 126 (p. 241, 536 (p. 289)
Berry, Patsy Elizabeth
  II: 360   III: 325 (p. 264)
Berry, Richard
  III: 142 (p. 174), 82 (p. 236), 132 (p. 242)
Berry, Sarah Jane
  II: 359   III: 122 (p. 241)
Berry, Sophia
  II: 360   III: 327 (p. 264)
Berry, Til
  I: 345
Berry, Walter
  I: 267   III: 439 (p. 208), 279 (p. 259)
Berry, William
  II: 291 (p. 140), 360   III: 94 (p. 238), 132 (p. 242)
Betzold, David
  III: 541 (p. 289)
Biggs, Darkey
  III: 52 (p. 233)
Bigsby, John
  III: 18 (p. 159), 168 (p. 246)
Billingsly, Mary Jane
  I: 759
Birch, Joseph E.
  III: 586 (p. 225), 587 (p. 226), 588 (p. 226)
Birch, Thomas
  II: 58
Birch, W. R.
  III: 406 (p. 273)
Bird, Mahala Reily
  I: 293, III: 464 (p. 211)
Black, Amy
  I: 523
Black, Ann Maria
  III: 552 (p. 221)
Black, Eliza
  III: 460 (p. 280)
Black, Harrison
  III: 197 (p. 249)
Blackburn, Amelia
  III: 348 (p. 267)
Blackburn, Betsey
  II: 279 (p. 66)
Blackburn, James
  III: 507 (p. 285)

Blackburn, Polly
  III: 507n (p. 285)
Blackburn, William
  III: 533 (p. 288)
Blackwell, David
  I: 770
Blue, Maria
  I: 282, 309, 540   III: 224 (p. 183), 335 (p. 196), 535 (p. 219), 149 (p. 244)
Bockett, Amelia
  II: 27
Bockett, Kitty
  III: 427 (p. 207), 282 (p. 259)
Boden, Martha D.
  III: 546 (p. 290)
Bombay/Bombray, Harriet
  I: 144, 556
Bombay/Bombray, Ann
  I: 556
Bond, Cornelia
  II: 285 (p. 139)
Bond, Georgiana
  II: 285 (p. 139)
Bond, Hannah
  II: 285 (p. 139)
Bond, James
  III: 43 (p. 162)
Bontz, Sarah
  III: 93 (p. 168), 94 (p. 168), 99 (p. 168)
Booth, Catharine
  III: 538 (p. 220)
Boothe, Ann
  I: 403
Bossart, Jane
  II: 314, 317
Botts, Betsy
  I: 184
Botts, Beverly
  I: 510
Botts, Catharine
  I: 576
Botts, Hannah
  I: 214
Botts, Joseph
  I: 673
Botts, Kitty
  See Kitty Botts Dogan
Botts, Nancy
  I: 566
Bounty, Harriet
  III: 459 (p. 278)
Bourbon, Dennis
  I: 521, 657   III: 279 (p. 190), 370 (p. 200), 166 (p. 246)
Bourbon, Rachel
  I: 657   III: 370 (p. 200)
Bowden, Addison
  III: 250 (p. 187)
Bowden, Alexander
  III: 153 (p. 175), 380 (p. 270)
Bowden, Cecely/Cecily
  I: 620   III: 248 (p. 186), 250 (p. 187), 377 (p. 270); see also Cecily Bowden Brooks

Bowden, Celia
　I: 625; see also Celia Bowden Rowe and Celia Bowden Ross
Bowden, Reverdy
　III: 248 (p. 186), 377 (p. 270)
Bowie, Davis
　I: 215, 234, 243, 256, 258, 259, 261, 263, 276, 281, 315, 321, I: 351, 355, 397, 425, 428, 449, 450, 543   III: 204 (p. 250)
Bowles, Betsey
　I: 771
Bowles, Charles
　II: 186   III: 337 (p. 265)
Bowles, Clarissa
　I: 234
Bowles, Eleanor
　III: 476 (p. 212)
Bowles, Elizabeth
　I: 230
Bowles, Ellen
　II: 124
Bowles, John
　I: 372, 721
Bowles, Mary
　I: 260
Bowles, Richard
　I: 644, 725
Bowles, Rosanna
　I: 379
Bowles, William
　I: 227
Bowling, Armstead
　I: 312
Bowling, Benjamin
　I: 423
Bowling, George
　I: 537
Bowling, George Henry Isaac
　I: 535
Bowling, Hannah
　I: 535
Bowling, Julia
　I: 536
Bowling, Mary
　See Mary Bowling Turner
Bowling, Moses
　I: 542
Bowling, Nancy
　I: 535
Bowling, Winny
　I: 597a
Bowman, Mary
　I: 530
Bowyer, John L.
　III: 359 (p. 268)
Braddock, Rebecca
　I: 717, 718   III: 48 (p. 232), 49 (p. 232), 50 (p. 232), 51 (p. 233)
Braddock, Robert W.
　I: 717
Braddock, Thomas
　I: 45, 718
Bradley, Joshua
　III: 9 (p. 158)
Brady, Benjamin
　III: 115 (p. 170)
Branham, Gemima
　I: 277
Branham, Josephine
　I: 313
Branham, Lorenzo
　III: 570 (p. 224), 470 (p. 281)
Branham, Rachel
　I: 313   III: 572 (p. 224)
Branham, Rosalee
　III: 571 (p. 224), 471 (p. 281)
Branham, William
　I: 313
Brannum, Angela
　III: 58 (p. 233)
Brannum, Caroline F.
　III: 401 (p. 273)
Brannum, Robert
　II: 129   III: 481 (p. 213)
Brannum, Samuel
　III: 59 (p. 233)
Brannum, Stella
　III: 57 (p. 233)
Bremont, Mary
　I: 478
Brenner, P. A.
　III: 183 (p. 248)
Brent, George
　I: 569, 665   II: 18   III: 238 (p. 254)
Brent, Martha
　I: 751, 752, 753
Brent, Nancy
　III: 39 (p. 161)
Brent, Rachel
　I: 569
Brick, Thomas
　I: 454
Briscoe, Edgar
　II: 344
Briscoe, Josephine
　II: 344
Briscoe, William
　I: 405
Broadwater, Charles L.
　I: 107
Brocchus, Amelia
　I: 239   III: 251 (p. 256)
Brocchus, Thomas
　I: 409
Brockett, F. L.
　III: 153 (p. 244), 154 (p. 244), 185 (p. 248)
Brockett, Kitty
　III: 282 (p. 259)
Brockett, Robert
　I: 33, 539   III: 160 (p. 176), 161 (p. 176), 515 (p. 217)
Brockett, Thomas
　III: 515 (p. 217)
Brook, Daniel
　I: 408
Brooke, E. Sr.

I: 57, 61
Brooke, Francis T.
   I: 1
Brooke/Brooks, John T.
   I: 1, 11
Brooks, Ann
   I: 550   II: 91, 97, 183, 194
Brooks, Ann Elizabeth
   I: <u>532</u>
Brooks, Cecily
   See Cecily Brooks Gibson
Brooks, Cecily Bowden
   III: <u>249</u> (p. 186); see also Cecily Bowden
Brooks, Desdemona
   I: <u>496</u>, 612a
Brooks, Ellen
   I: <u>612a</u>
Brooks, Fanny
   I: 667   III: 343 (p. 197), 107 (p. 239), 284 (p. 259)
Brooks, Frances
   II: <u>13</u>
Brooks, Frederick
   I: <u>667</u>   III: <u>107</u> (p. 239)
Brooks, George
   II: 339   III: <u>517</u> (p. 217), <u>272</u> (p. 258), 273 (p. 258)
Brooks, Harriet
   III: <u>409</u> (p. 205), 517 (p. 217), <u>271</u> (p. 258), 272 (p. 258)
Brooks, Mary Georgianna
   I: <u>612a</u>
Brooks, Richard
   III: <u>343</u> (p. 197), <u>284</u> (p. 259)
Brooks, Sarah
   III: <u>177</u> (p. 178)
Brooks, Sarah Jane
   I: <u>612a</u>   II: <u>61</u>
Brooks, Sydney
   II: <u>341</u>
Brown, Adeline
   III: <u>289</u> (p. 260)
Brown, Andrew
   III: <u>482</u> (p. 282)
Brown, Ann
   II: <u>144</u>, <u>181</u>   III: <u>463</u> (p. 211), <u>249</u> (p. 255); see also Ann Brown Clagett
Brown, Ann Elizabeth
   I: <u>571</u>; see also Ann Elizabeth Brown Piper
Brown, Anzy
   I: <u>320</u>
Brown, Betsey
   See Betsey Brown Washington.
Brown, Calvin
   II: <u>240</u>
Brown, Catharine
   II: <u>239</u>   III: <u>360</u> (p. 268)
Brown, Cecilia
   III: <u>529</u> (p. 219)
Brown, Celie
   I: <u>613</u>
Brown, Cornelius
   I: <u>682</u>

Brown, Daniel
   III: <u>419</u> (p. 57), <u>235</u> (p. 108)
Brown, Diana
   III: <u>77</u> (p. 11)
Brown, Dicy
   II: <u>84</u>   III: <u>338</u> (p. 122)
Brown, Elizabeth
   I: <u>104,</u> <u>739</u>   III: <u>272</u> (p. 38)
Brown, Ellen
   See Ellen Brown Mitchell
Brown, Francis
   II: <u>99</u>
Brown, Georgiana
   III: <u>525</u> (p. 146)
Brown, Harriet
   I: <u>238</u>
[Brown?], Henny
   I: <u>103</u>, 104
Brown, Henry
   III: <u>486</u> (p. 66)
Brown, James H.
   III: <u>442</u> (p. 60)
Brown, Jane
   II: <u>67</u>
Brown, John
   II: 99   III: <u>578</u> (p. 78)
Brown, John Henry
   II: <u>85</u>
Brown, John S.
   I: 559
Brown, Lenny
   II: <u>145</u>
Brown, Lucy
   See Lucy Brown Nickins
Brown, Margaret
   II: 238   III: <u>354</u> (p. 49), <u>334</u> (p. 122)
Brown, Margaret J.
   III: <u>288</u> (p. 115)
Brown, Marion R.
   III: 409 (p. 131)
Brown, Mary
   III: <u>528</u> (p. 146)
Brown, Octavia
   II: <u>385</u>
Brown, Paul
   I: <u>418</u>   II: <u>66</u>
Brown, Peter
   I: <u>442</u>
Brown, Rachel
   I: 418; see also Rachel Brown Bruce.
Brown, Samuel
   I: <u>207</u>   III: <u>499</u> (p. 68)
Brown, Sarah A.
   I: 682
Brown, Sarah Ann
   II: 85
Brown, Sarah Ann Piper
   I: <u>107</u>
Brown, Simon
   I: <u>380</u>
Brown, Susan
   I: 137b
Brown, William B.

III: 69 (p. 235)
Browne, Edmund L.
I: 245
Browne, Milley
III: 40n (p. 161)
Bruce, Charles
II: <u>55</u>   III: <u>159</u> (p. 176), <u>266</u> (p. 188)
Bruce, Clarissa Ann
II: <u>37</u>
Bruce, Daniel
III: <u>140</u> (p. 174)
Bruce, Eliza
III: <u>306</u> (p. 193)
Bruce, Eliza A.
II: <u>166</u>
Bruce, George
II: <u>108</u>
Bruce, Hannah
I: <u>727</u>   II: 70   III: <u>433</u> (p. 207)
Bruce, Hannah Ann
I: <u>727</u>   II: <u>70</u>   III: <u>434</u> (p. 208)
Bruce, Hannah Elizabeth
I: <u>727</u>
Bruce, Harriet
II: <u>103</u>
Bruce, Henrietta
See Henrietta Bruce Ford
Bruce, Laura
II: <u>166</u>
Bruce, Rachel Brown
II: <u>346</u>; see also Rachel Brown
Bruce, Robert
III: <u>393</u> (p. 203)
Bruce, Sarah Clarence
II: <u>166</u>
Bruce, William Henry
II: <u>125</u>, <u>166</u>
Bryan, Alexander
I: <u>284</u>, <u>651</u>
Bryan, Ann
I: <u>696</u>
Bryan, George
III: 13 (p. 158), 14 (p. 158), 15 (p. 158), 540 (p. 220)
Bryan, J. D.
I: 621
Bryant, Alfred
II: <u>316</u>
Bryant, Elizabeth
III: <u>35</u> (p. 231)
Bryant, George
III: <u>36</u> (p. 231)
Bryant, Joseph
III: <u>37</u> (p. 231)
Bryant, Maria
See Maria Bryant Seaton
Buck, Hannah
II: 63
Buckingham, Isaac
II: 86
Bull, Amanda
I: <u>730</u>; see also Amanda Bull Smith
Bull, Lucy Ann

I: <u>729</u>   III: <u>270</u> (p. 189)
Buller, Mary Elizabeth
II: <u>62</u>
Bumbey, Ann Maria
II: <u>375</u>   III: <u>133</u> (p. 242)
Bumbey, Bernard
II: <u>375</u>
Bumbey, Laura Virginia
II: <u>375</u>
Bumbey, Mary Elizabeth
II: <u>375</u>
Bunn, Seely
I: 217, 654b, 724
Burgess, Elizabeth Ann
I: 242
Burke, David
I: 95
Burke, Hannah
I: <u>106</u>, 484
Burke, John
III: <u>535</u> (p. 288)
Burke, Silas
III: <u>573</u> (p. 224), 578 (p. 225)
Burke, William Henry
III: <u>573</u> (p. 224)
Burns, Henry
I: <u>118</u>
Burns, Phelicia
I: <u>738</u>
Burrell, Aaron
III: <u>474</u> (p. 212)
Burrell, Charlotte
III: <u>147</u> (p. 174), <u>115</u> (p. 240)
Burrell, James
III: <u>511</u> (p. 217)
Burrell, Sarah
III: <u>356</u> (p. 268)
Burrell, Susannah
III: <u>357</u> (p. 268)
Burrell, William H.
III: <u>99</u> (p. 238)
Burton, Benjamin
I: 28
Burwell, Ellen
I: <u>541</u>
Bushbey, William
I: 112a
Butcher, Jonathan
I: 722
Butcher, Phebe
I: 458
Butler, Andrew
III: <u>27</u> (p. 160)
Butler, Charles
III: <u>380</u> (p. 201)
Butler, Chloe
I: <u>658</u>
Butler, Clarence
II: <u>161</u>
Butler, Elizabeth
I: 334   II: 161   III: <u>110</u> (p. 239)
Butler, Elizabeth Julius
III: <u>219</u> (p. 183)

Butler, Ellen
  I: 334
Butler, Evelina
  I: 215
Butler, Fanny
  III: 435 (p. 277), 436 (p. 277)
Butler, Hannah Lee
  III: 457 (p. 210)
Butler, Harriet
  I: 228   III: 241 (p. 185)
Butler, Henry
  III: 344 (p. 197)
Butler, James
  I: 235, 352, 567   III: 35 (p. 161), 334 (p. 196), 147 (p. 244)
Butler, John
  III: 436 (p. 277)
Butler, Laura
  III: 436 (p. 277)
Butler, Letty
  II: 203
Butler, Lydia Ann
  I: 637
Butler, Margaret Ann
  I: 714
Butler, Maria
  II: 16
Butler, Mary
  III: 326 (p. 195), 285 (p. 259)
Butler, Mary Eliza
  III: 40a (p. 231)
Butler, Mary Elizabeth
  III: 436 (p. 277), 566 (p. 292)
Butler, Milly
  III: 215 (p. 182)
Butler, Nathan
  III: 41 (p. 162)
Butler, Nelly Hoy
  I: 290
Butler, Phineas
  II: 161
Butler, Robert
  I: 395   III: 328 (p. 196), 392 (p. 272)
Butler, Susan
  I: 637
Butler, Susanna
  I: 593   II: 161
Buttler, Charles
  I: 713
Butts, Alexander
  I: 265
Butts, Eliza
  I: 238
Butts, James
  I: 757
Butts, Rebecca
  II: 179   III: 534 (p. 288)
Byrd, Jane F.
  I: 498
Cairns, William D.
  III: 511 (p. 286), 512 (p. 286)
Callicot, William Butler
  I: 698   III: 166 (p. 177)

Calvert, George
  II: 278 (p. 66)
Calvin, George
  I: 392
Cammel, Nicholas
  I: 11
Campbell, Betsey
  III: 192 (p. 180)
Campbell, Charles
  I: 7
Campbell, John
  I: 185   III: 191 (p. 180), 234 (p. 254)
Campbell, Lewis
  I: 203   III: 162 (p. 176)
Campbell, Lucy Ann Thornton
  II: 221   III: 419 (p. 275)
Campbell, Martha
  III: 175 (p. 247)
Campbell, Milly Julius
  III: 322 (p. 195)
Campbell, Sarah
  I: 110
Campbell, Sarah B.
  II: 2, 64
Campbell, William
  II: 19
Campbell, William Henry
  III: 508 (p. 285)
Cannon, Cassandra L.
  I: 764
Cannon, Susanna/Susannah
  I: 255, 257
Carey, Wilson M.
  I: 611
Carlin, Elizabeth
  III: 271 (p. 189)
Carlin, Wesley
  I: 528   II: 122   III: 45 (p. 232), 332 (p. 265), 333 (p. 265), 365 (p. 269), 475 (p. 281)
Carlin, William H. F.
  III: 556 (p. 222)
Carmichael, Daniel
  III: 414 (p. 274)
Carmichael, David
  III: 578 (p. 293)
Carmichael, Elizabeth
  I: 563
Carmichael, Mary Ann
  I: 563
Carmichael, Mary Elizabeth
  III: 519 (p. 287)
Carmichael, Rachael
  III: 578 (p. 293)
Carmichael, William
  I: 126, 563
Carmon, Ann
  III: 273 (p. 189)
Carpenter, Dennis
  I: 306, 370
Carr, Overton
  I: 38
Carrell, Ellen
  II: 137

Carrol, Kitty
　III: <u>24</u> (p. 229)
Carroll, Harriet Mans
　III: <u>557</u> (p. 291)
Carroll, Sicily
　I: <u>731</u>
Carson, George W.
　I: 686
Carson, Joseph
　III: <u>543</u> (p. 220)
Carson, Samuel
　I: 152　III: 385 (p. 202)
Carter, Alfred
　III: <u>412</u> (p. 274)
Carter, Charles Henry
　I: <u>608</u>
Carter, Daniel
　III: <u>554</u> (p. 291)
Carter, James
　I: <u>410</u>　III: <u>87</u> (p. 167), <u>472</u> (p. 212), <u>245</u> (p. 255)
Carter, John Lewis
　III: <u>68</u> (p. 235)
Carter, Julia A. Mandeville
　III: <u>475</u> (p. 212)
Carter, Louisa
　I: <u>256</u>
Carter, Peggy
　III: <u>185</u> (p. 248)
Carter, Richard Henry
　III: <u>80</u> (p. 166)
Carter, Robert
　I: <u>473</u>, 271
Carter, Robert C.
　II: 3
Carter, Sarah Ann
　II: <u>88</u>
Carter, Sarah Taylor
　II: <u>58</u>
Caryton/Coryton, Mrs.
　I: 722　III: 408 (p. 274)
Cash, Sarah
　II: 14
Cash, Sinah
　III: 237 (p. 185), 238 (p. 185)
Cavans, Albert
　III: <u>492</u> (p. 214)
Cavins, Henry
　III: <u>257</u> (p. 187)
Cawood, Daniel F.
　I: 87, 706　III: 175 (p. 247)
Cawood, Moses O. B.
　III: 114 (p. 170), 257 (p. 187), 263 (p. 188), 299 (p. 192)
Cazenove, Anthony Charles
　II: 81, 284 (p. 73)
Chace, George Andrew
　II: <u>227</u>　III: <u>383</u> (p. 271)
Chace, Joseph Henry
　II: <u>286</u> (p. 68)
Chace, Mary Ann Eliza
　II: <u>228</u>
Chace, Mary Elizabeth
　II: <u>279</u> (p. 71)　III: <u>178</u> (p. 247)
Chace, Samuel
　II: <u>286</u> (p. 68)
Chace, Sarah
　II: <u>286</u> (p. 68)　III: <u>287</u> (p. 260)
Chace, William Francis
　II: <u>226</u>
Chance, John
　II: 47
Chapman, Charles T.
　I: 420
Chapman, George
　II: <u>68</u>
　III: 32 (p. 230), <u>192</u> (p. 249)
Chapman, George P.
　II: <u>272</u>
　III: <u>32</u> (p. 230)
Chapman, Harriet
　II: <u>272</u>, 326
Chapman, Helen
　II: 332
Chapman, Helen Parker
　II: <u>272</u>　III: <u>194</u> (p. 249)
Chapman, Hellen Maria
　II: <u>272</u>, 327　III: <u>193</u> (p. 249)
Chapman, Lucy Ann
　See Lucy Ann Chapmen Pipsico
Chapman, Mary Ann
　II: <u>272</u>
Chapman, Mary Jane
　II: <u>272</u>, <u>325</u>
Chapman, Rebecca
　II: <u>272</u>　III: <u>293</u> (p. 260)
Chase, Cecelia/Cecilia
　I: <u>716</u>　III: <u>70</u> (p. 165)
Chase, Henry
　See Henry Tate
Chase, Mary
　See Mary Chase Digges
Chase, Samuel
　III: <u>297</u> (p. 261)
Chase, Susan
　I: <u>289</u>
Chatham, Henry
　III: 532 (p. 288)
Check, Daniel
　III: <u>426</u> (p. 276)
Check, Jackson
　III: <u>427</u> (p. 276)
Check, Lewis
　III: <u>425</u> (p. 275)
Check, Thornton
　III: <u>424</u> (p. 275)
Chichester, Daniel McCarty
　See D. McChichester
Chichester, Patsey
　II: 69, 79, 109, 257, 258, 304, 305
Childs, Gabriel D.
　III: 45 (p. 162), 220 (p. 252)
Childs, John
　I: 336　III: 418 (p. 206)
Chin, Carolus Anthony
　I: <u>273</u>

Chinn, Charles A.
  II: <u>382</u>   III: <u>88</u> (p. 237)
Chinn, Georgianna Virginia
  III: <u>17</u> (p. 159)
Chinn/Chin, Thomas
  I: <u>684</u>   III: 546 (p. 221), 547 (p. 221), 548 (p. 221)
Chinn, William Thomas
  III: <u>16</u> (p. 158)
Church, Mary Ann
  II: 363   III: 23 (p. 229)
Churchman, John
  II: 331
Clagett, Ann
  I: <u>740</u>   III: <u>95</u> (p. 238)
Clagett, Ann Brown
  II: <u>196</u>
Clagett, Horatio
  I: 294, 705
Clagett, Richard H.
  I: 388   II: 101
Clagett/Claggett, William
  I: <u>529</u>   III: <u>280</u> (p. 190), <u>96</u> (p. 238)
Claggett, James H.
  III: <u>515</u> (p. 286)
Clark, Alfred
  I: <u>308</u>
Clark, Alice
  III: <u>274</u> (p. 258)
Clark, Arberilla[Arabella?]
  I: <u>206a</u>; see also Arabella Clark Webster
Clark, Charles
  I: 14
Clark, Delia
  I: 274
Clark/Clarke, Isaac
  I: 206a, 212, 348   II: <u>182</u>   III: 212 (p. 182), 278 (p. 190), 232 (p. 253)
Clark, Nathaniel
  I: <u>662</u>   III: <u>407</u> (p. 205)
Clark, Rebecca Cole
  I: <u>149</u>
Clark, William
  I: 342
Clarke, Ambrose
  I: 212
Clarke, Eliza
  II: 160
Clarke, Mary
  I: <u>621</u>
Clarke, Sarah
  II: <u>358</u>
Coates, Frances
  III: <u>564</u> (p. 223)
Coats, Charles
  I: <u>333</u>   III: <u>340</u> (p. 266)
Coats, Samuel
  III: <u>170</u> (p. 177)
Cockrell, Harriet
  I: 229
Coke, Elisabeth
  I: 498
Colbert, Betsey/Betsy
  I: <u>701</u>   III: <u>261</u> (p. 188)
Colbert, Eleanor
  III: <u>347</u> (p. 198)
Colbert, George
  III: <u>592</u> (p. 226)
Colbert, Hannah
  I: 700, 701, 702, 703
Colbert, Hanson
  I: <u>157</u>
Colbert, Henry
  I: <u>156</u>
Colbert, John
  I: <u>700</u>   III: <u>353</u> (p. 198)
Colbert, Martha
  I: <u>703</u>   III: <u>432</u> (p. 207)
Colbert, Martha Ann
  III: <u>243</u> (p. 255)
Colbert, Mary Ann
  I: <u>702</u>   III: <u>205</u> (p. 181)
Cole, Betty
  I: 21; see also Betty Cole Roderick
Cole, Charlotte
  I: <u>148</u>
Cole, Eliza
  I: <u>403</u>   III: <u>60</u> (p. 164)
Cole, Ellen
  I: <u>200</u>, 374
Cole, Emily
  See Emily Cole Gray
Cole, Frances
  I: <u>166</u>
Cole, George
  I: <u>514</u>
Cole, George Washington
  II: <u>229</u>
Cole, James
  I: <u>245</u>   III: <u>483</u> (p. 213)
Cole, Jane
  III: <u>432</u> (p. 276), 433 (p. 277)
Cole, Jesse
  III: 421 (p. 275)
Cole, John
  I: <u>25</u>, 148, 149   III: <u>42</u> (p. 162)
Cole, John Thomas
  I: <u>262</u>
Cole, Katy
  I: <u>25</u>, 30
Cole, Louisa
  I: <u>374</u>
Cole, Lucinda
  III: <u>433</u> (p. 277)
Cole, Martha
  II: 128
Cole, Mary
  II: 290 (p. 140), 291 (p. 140), 292 (p. 140)
Cole, Mary Ann
  I: <u>167</u>, 468, 511, 512, 513, 514, 654a   II: 75, 162, 163, 172, 173, 226, 227, 228, 229, 230   III: 5 (p. 157), 6 (p. 157), 7 (p. 157), 57 (p. 164), 72 (p. 165), 73 (p. 165), 74 (p. 166), 379 (p. 270), 390 (p. 271)
Cole, Mary Ann (granddaughter of Mary Ann Cole)

III: <u>73</u> (p. 165), <u>379</u> (p. 270)
Cole, Mary Jane
II: <u>230</u>; see also Mary Jane Cole Ware
Cole, Mary Nutt
III: <u>301</u> (p. 192)
Cole, Nancy
I: 82, 148, 149; see also Nancy Cole Dudley.
Cole, Nelly
I: <u>31</u>
Cole, Polly
I: <u>104</u>
Cole, Rebecca
See Rebecca Cole Clark
Cole, Thomas
III: <u>396</u> (p. 272), 432 (p. 276), 433 (p. 277)
Cole, Violett
I: 262
Cole, Violett Day
II: <u>51</u>; see also Violett Day
Cole, William
I: <u>464</u>, <u>513</u>
Cole, William Henry
III: <u>487</u> (p. 214)
Coleman, James P.
I: 272, 287, 431 II: 41, 249, 250, 251, 252
III: 207 (p. 250), 208 (p. 250), 209 (p. 251), 410 (p. 274)
Collard, Eliza S.
I: 748
Collard, Samuel
I: 445
Collins, Ann
III: 58 (p. 164), <u>59</u> (p. 164), 64 (p. 164), 269 (p. 258), <u>270</u> (p. 258)
Collins, Ann Elizabeth
III: <u>58</u> (p. 164), <u>269</u> (p. 258)
Collins, James
III: <u>245</u> (p. 186)
Collins, James W.
III: <u>303</u> (p. 261)
Collins, Richard
III: <u>64</u> (p. 164), <u>312</u> (p. 263)
Colston, Anthony
III: <u>299</u> (p. 192)
Colston, Elizabeth
III: <u>235</u> (p. 185)
Colston, John
III: <u>584</u> (p. 225)
Colston, Thomas
III: <u>350</u> (p. 198), <u>137</u> (p. 242)
Colston, William
III: <u>412</u> (p. 205), <u>350</u> (p. 267)
Conman[?], John P.
I: 533
Conner, Dennis
I: <u>362</u>
Conner, Susan
I: 338, 339
Contee, Benjamin
III: 529 (p. 219)
Contee, Jane
II: 82, 83 III: 289 (p. 191), 172 (p. 246)
Cook, Ary
II: 211
Cook, George
I: <u>119</u>
Cook, Henry
II: 285 (p. 139)
Cook, Penny Overtal
I: <u>589</u>
Cooke, Rebecca
I: 285
Cooke, William
I: <u>611</u>
Cooper, Arthur
I: <u>78</u>
Cooper, Cornelia Ann
II: <u>321</u>
Cooper, Edward
I: <u>38</u>
Cooper, Elizabeth
I: <u>38</u>
Cooper, John Jr.
I: <u>38</u>
Cooper, Julia
III: <u>118</u> (p. 171)
Cooper, Louisa
II: <u>320</u>; see also Louisa Cooper Addison
Cooper, Mary Jane
II: <u>321</u> III: <u>157</u> (p. 245)
Cooper, Sarah Jane
II: <u>170</u>
Cooper, Thomas
I: <u>38</u>
Cooper, William
I: <u>38</u>
Corse, Wilmer
II: 274 (p. 138)
Coryell, George
I: 529 III: 280 (p. 190), 96 (p. 238)
Cotes, Frederick
II: 138, 139
Cotes, Sally
II: <u>138</u>
Cox, Julia
II: 31
Craig, Adam
I: 60
Craig, Anna
II: <u>288</u> (p. 139)
Craig, Eliza
II: <u>287</u> (p. 139)
Craig, John Henry
II: <u>289a</u> (p. 139)
Craney, George
III: <u>131a</u> (p. 172)
Craney, Maria
I: <u>304</u>
Craney, Rosetta
III: <u>62</u> (p. 164), <u>62</u> (p. 234)
Crawford, Fanny
II: <u>2</u>
Crawford, John
II: <u>64</u>
Crea, Henry W.
I: 275

305

Crease, Anthony
I: 97, 560
Crease, Anthony Jr.
I: 54
Credit, John
III: <u>57</u> (p. 164), <u>140</u> (p. 243)
Credit, Sarah Ann
III: <u>162</u> (p. 245)
Creighton, John
III: 241 (p. 185), 242 (p. 186)
Creighton, John T.
II: 237
Crier, Benjamin
II: <u>132</u>
Cross, Newman
III: <u>454</u> (p. 279)
Crupper, Robert
II: 24
Cryer, Ann
II: <u>65</u>
Cryer, Anne
II: 97
Cryer, Benjamin
I: 439
Cryer, Chloe Ann
II: <u>97</u>, <u>194</u>
Cryer, Emily
II: <u>97</u>
Cryer, Mary Jane
I: <u>736</u>
Cryer, Patsey
I: <u>439</u>
Cryer, Rebecca Frances
II: <u>97</u>
Cryer, Susan
See Susan Cryer Reed
Cryss[?], Henry
III: 521 (p. 218), 167 (p. 246)
Cupet, Robert
II: <u>26</u>
Cupid, Catharine/Catherine
III: <u>25</u> (p. 160), <u>187</u> (p. 248)
Cupid, Emanuel
III: <u>398</u> (p. 272)
Cupid, Harriet
III: <u>24</u> (p. 160)
Cupid, John
I: <u>614a</u>
Cupid, Linney/Linny
III: 24 (p. 160), 25 (p. 160), <u>26</u> (p. 160), 91 (p. 168), 170 (p. 246), <u>186</u> (p. 248), 187 (p. 248)
Cupid, Robert
III: <u>176</u> (p. 247)
Cupid, William
III: <u>91</u> (p. 168), <u>170</u> (p. 246)
Cureton, D. T.
I: 479
Currey/Currie, David
I: <u>217</u>, <u>552</u>
Currey/Currie, Elizabeth
I: <u>217</u>, <u>499</u>
Currey/Currie, Jacob
I: <u>217</u>, <u>724</u>
Currey/Currie, Mary Ann
I: <u>217</u>, <u>654b</u>
Currie, Jude
I: 217, 654b, 724
Currie, Judith
I: 458
Curtis, Adeline
III: <u>503</u> (p. 285)
Curtis, Ann M.
III: <u>502</u> (p. 284)
Curtis, Charles
III: 502 (p. 284), 503 (p. 285)
Curtis, Elizabeth
III: <u>482</u> (p. 213)
Curtis, Henry
I: <u>323</u>
Curtis, William
I: <u>366</u> III: <u>461</u> (p. 211), <u>365</u> (p. 269)
Custis, George W. P.
I: 206b, 295, 378, 668 II: 140 III: 214 (p. 182), 526 (p. 218) 57 (p. 233), 58 (p. 233), 363 (p. 268), 373 (p. 269)
Custis, W. W. P.
II: 141
Dade, Baldwin
I: 8
Dade, Daniel
I: <u>71</u>, 133
Daingerfield, Edward
III: 503 (p. 216)
Daingerfield/Dangerfield, Henry
I: 203, 330a, 617 II: 105, 275 (p. 140) III: 162 (p. 176)
Daingerfield, John B.
II: 133
Dangerfield, Maria D.
I: 124
Daniels, Felicia
III: <u>438</u> (p. 277)
Daniels, John
III: <u>388</u> (p. 202), <u>336</u> (p. 265)
Darnall, Albert F.
III: <u>516</u> (p. 217)
Darnall, George William
III: <u>216</u> (p. 182)
Darnall, James Tyler
III: <u>202</u> (p. 181)
Darnall/Darnell, John
I: <u>459</u>, 588
Darnall, Louisa
III: <u>153</u> (p. 244)
Darnall, Robert
III: <u>315</u> (p. 263)
Darnall, Wesley
III: <u>144</u> (p. 174), <u>160</u> (p. 245)
Darnell, Charles
I: <u>553</u>
Darnell, Henry
I: 314, 332, 335, 394, 459, 507b, <u>554</u> III: 86 (p. 167)
Darnell, Jane
I: <u>588</u>

Darnell, Letitia
II: <u>143</u>
Darnell, Mary Ann
I: <u>335</u>
Darnell, Priscilla
I: <u>394</u>; see also Priscilla Darnell Ware
Darnell, Sophia
II: <u>74</u>
Davey, Thomas
I: 525
Davidson, Bazil H.
I: 520, 521, 628   III: 279 (p. 190), 166 166 (p. 246)
Davis, Amelia
II: <u>323</u>, 333
Davis, Ann
III: 82 (p. 167), 484 (p. 213)
Davis, Betsey
III: 196 (p. 180), 210 (p. 182), 292 (p. 260)
Davis, Charles
I: <u>270</u>
Davis, Clarissa
I: <u>324</u>
Davis, Daniel
I: <u>429</u>   III: <u>210</u> (p. 182), <u>519</u> (p. 218)
Davis, David
I: 86
Davis, Eleanor
I: <u>54</u>
Davis, Eliza
II: <u>158</u>, 301
Davis, Emeline
I: <u>769</u>
Davis, J. H. Jr.
II: 182
Davis, Jane
I: <u>54</u>   III: <u>208</u> (p. 181)
Davis, Jeremiah
I: <u>130</u>
Davis, John
I: <u>708</u>   III: <u>391</u> (p. 203), <u>144</u> (p. 243)
Davis, Josiah H.
II: 114, 369   III: 91 (p. 168), 387 (p. 202)
Davis, Leannah
III: <u>40</u> (p. 161), <u>246</u> (p. 255)
Davis, Louisa
II: <u>176</u>
Davis, Lucy Haney
III: <u>536</u> (p. 220)
Davis, Maria
I: <u>129</u>
Davis, Mary
I: <u>48</u>, 218, <u>594</u>   II: <u>176</u>; see also Mary Davis Anderson
Davis, Milly
I: <u>54</u>
Davis, Monacai
See Monica Davis
Davis, Monica
I: 48
Davis, Moses
I: 696   II: 168
Davis, Nancy
I: <u>767</u>
Davis, Patsey
I: <u>54</u>
Davis, Rebecca
II: <u>333</u>
Davis, Richard
III: 137 (p. 173)
Davis, Sarah
I: <u>54</u>
Davis, Sarah James
I: <u>48</u>
Davis, Thomas
I: 34
Davis, Washington
I: <u>83</u>
Davis, William
I: <u>54</u>, <u>734</u>, <u>768</u>
Davis, William Henry
II: <u>176</u>, <u>301</u>, <u>333</u>
Dawson, Benjamin
I: 271
Day, Spencer
II: <u>134</u>
Day, Violett
I: <u>26</u>; see also Violett Day Cole
Deakin, Isabella
I: 329   II: 34
Dean, William
I: 646   II: 1, <u>248</u>   III: 386 (p. 202), 239 (p. 254)
Deane, John Henry
I: <u>349</u>
Deane, Nancy Hall
I: <u>592</u>
Delly, Henry
II: <u>78</u>
Delly, Roxana
II: <u>349</u>
Delly, Susan
II: <u>349</u>
Dempsey, James
II: 151, 290 (p. 142)   III: <u>294</u> (p. 260)
Dencole, Jane
I: <u>747b</u>
Dencole, Josephine
I: <u>747b</u>
Dencole, Virginia
I: <u>747b</u>
Deneale, George
I: 350
Deneale, Jane
I: <u>382a</u>
Dennison, Benjamin
III: 169 (p. 177), 170 (p. 177)
Dent, William
III; <u>539</u> (p. 289)
Denty, Mary
I: 636
Denty, Nancy
I: <u>115</u>
Derrick, Alfred
I: <u>676</u>
Derrick, Jacob

II: <u>266</u>
Derrick, James
  II: <u>261</u> III: <u>575</u> (p. 293)
Derrick, Julia
  II: <u>209</u>
Derrick, Lucinda
  I: <u>474</u> III: <u>451</u> (p. 210)
Derrick, Robert
  II: <u>264</u>
Derrick, Susan
  II: <u>263</u>
Derrick, William
  II: <u>262</u> III: <u>142</u> (p. 243)
Derricks, Jane
  I: <u>687</u>
Derricks, Maria
  II: <u>265</u>
Derricks, Nancy
  II: <u>258</u>
Deshealds, Maria
  I: 756
Deston, Isabella
  II: 34
Dibble, O. H.
  I: 469 III: 394 (p. 272)
Dickson, Moses
  I: <u>271</u>
Die, Jane
  I: <u>502</u>
Digges, Mary Chase
  III: <u>532</u> (p. 219)
Diggs, Ferdinand
  II: <u>91</u>
Diggs, John
  I: 623
Diggs, Richard
  III: <u>77</u> (p. 236)
Dilhea, Francis Montgomery
  I: <u>186</u>
Dilhea, Mary Ann
  I: <u>186</u>
Dilhea, Matilda
  I: <u>186</u>
Dixon, David
  II: <u>136</u>
Dixon, Margaret
  I: <u>2</u>
Dixon, Sally
  III: <u>547</u> (p. 290)
Dixon, Solomon
  III: <u>452</u> (p. 210)
Dixon, Turner
  II: 222 III: 53 (p. 163), 85 (p. 167), 98 (p. 168), 100 (p. 169), 111 (p. 170), 119 (p. 171), 120 (p. 171), 191 (p. 180), 199 (p. 180), 200 (p. 181), 201 (p. 181), 225 (p. 184), 226 (p. 184), 227 (p. 184), 303 (p. 193), 306 (p. 193), 345 (p. 198), 397 (p. 203), 404 (p. 204), 494 (p. 215), 495 (p. 215), 516 (p. 217), 539 (p. 289)
Dobyn, Winifred
  I: 126
Dodds, Joseph
  III: 469 (p. 212)
Dogan, Andrew
  II: <u>107</u>
Dogan, Ann
  I: <u>678</u>
Dogan, Anthony
  II: <u>277</u> (p. 141) III: <u>386</u> (p. 271)
Dogan, Catharine
  I: 576
Dogan, Charles
  II: <u>133</u> III: <u>148</u> (p. 244), <u>257</u> (p. 256)
Dogan, Cornelius
  III: <u>502</u> (p. 216)
Dogan, Elizabeth
  II: <u>275</u> (p. 140)
Dogan, Elvia
  See Elvia Taylor
Dogan, Flora
  I: 622
Dogan, Jane
  III: 150 (p. 175)
Dogan, John
  III: <u>444</u> (p. 278)
Dogan, Kitty
  I: 510, 566
Dogan, Kitty Botts
  I: 673
Dogan, Lloyd Rozier
  II: <u>160</u>
Dogan, Maria
  III: <u>50</u> (p. 163), <u>385</u> (p. 271)
Dogan/Dogans, Mary Wade
  II: <u>302</u> III: <u>387</u> (p. 271)
Dogan, Mima
  II: <u>105</u>
Dogan, Philip
  I: 576, 622
Dogan, Rebecca
  III: <u>150</u> (p. 175)
Dogan, Robert
  III: <u>158</u> (p. 176)
Dogan, Robert H.
  III: <u>63</u> (p. 164), <u>158</u> (p. 176), <u>159</u> (p. 245)
Dogan, Susannah
  III: <u>53</u> (p. 163)
Dogan, Thomas
  I: <u>622</u>
Dogans, Govenor
  III: <u>384</u> (p. 271)
Dogans, Isabella
  II: <u>303</u> III: <u>388</u> (p. 271)
Dogans, Lucinda
  II: <u>374</u>
Domain, Elizabeth
  III: 422 (p. 275)
Donaldson, John
  III: 591 (p. 226)
Donel[?], Walter
  I: 327
Dorsey, Benjamin
  II: <u>356</u> III: <u>298</u> (p. 261)
Dorsey, Edward
  III: <u>364</u> (p. 200)

Dorsey, Eliza Lee
  II: <u>281</u> (p. 138)
Dorsey, Elizabeth
  II: <u>210</u>, 356 III: <u>307</u> (p. 262)
Dorsey, James
  II: <u>40</u>
Dorsey, Julia
  II: <u>356</u>
Dorsey, Martha
  I: <u>492</u>
Dorsey, Nace
  I: <u>607</u> III: <u>308</u> (p. 262)
Dorsey, Nancy
  I: <u>492</u> II: 113
Dorsey, Sarah
  III: <u>301</u> (p. 261)
Dorsey, Sarah E.
  II: <u>356</u>
Dorsey, Townshend
  II: <u>356</u>
Dorsey, Zachariah
  II: <u>356</u> III: <u>299</u> (p. 261)
Doster, Enoch
  III: <u>436</u> (p. 208), 437 (p. 208)
Doster, John
  III: <u>443</u> (p. 209)
Doster, Margaret
  III: <u>218</u> (p. 183)
Doster, Maria
  III: <u>437</u> (p. 208)
Dougan, Ann Maria
  II: <u>43</u>
Douglas, A. O.
  III: 520 (p. 287)
Douglas/Douglass, Alexander
  III: <u>152</u> (p. 175), <u>105</u> (p. 239)
Douglas, George P.
  III: <u>4</u> (p. 227)
Douglas, Maria
  III: <u>303</u> (p. 193)
Douglas, O.
  III: 341 (p. 197)
Douglass, John
  I: 322, 614b, 709 II: 202
Dover, Betty
  I: 111
Dover, Catherine Ann
  II: <u>319</u> III: <u>121</u> (p. 241)
Dover, Celia
  I: <u>111</u>
Dover, Cloe
  I: <u>111</u>
Dover, George
  II: <u>253</u>
Dover, James
  II: <u>33</u>
Dover, Jetson
  II: 33, <u>56</u> III: <u>410</u> (p. 205), <u>81</u> (p. 236)
Dover, Lucy
  II: <u>289b</u> (p. 140) III: <u>411</u> (205)
Dover, Lydia
  I: <u>111</u>
Dover, Mary
  II: <u>89</u>
Dover, Milly
  See Milly Dover Julius
Dover, Rebecca
  See Rebecca Dover Jarbo
Dover, Samuel Sr.
  I: 111
Dover, Samuel Jr.
  I: <u>111</u>
Dover, Sarah C.
  II: <u>254</u>
Dover, Sarah Elizabeth
  II: <u>318</u>
Dover, William
  II: <u>102</u>
Drinker, George
  I: 300
Dtcher[Dutcher?], Ellen
  I: <u>258</u>
Dudley, Eliza
  II: <u>172</u>
Dudley, Elizabeth
  III: <u>74</u> (p. 166)
Dudley, James
  III: 83 (p. 167)
Dudley, Nancy
  I: <u>511</u> III: <u>72</u> (p. 165) III: <u>390</u> (p. 271)
Dudley, William
  I: <u>213</u> III: <u>79</u> (p. 166)
Duff, John
  I: <u>46</u>
Duffey, George
  III: 536 (p. 289)
Dulaney, Henry
  III: <u>55</u> (p. 163)
Dulaney, Kitty Easton
  III: <u>80</u> (p. 236); see also Kitty Easton
Dulany, Benjamin
  I: 119
Dulin, William E.
  I: 208, 209
Dunbar, Christiana
  III: <u>17</u> (p. 229)
Dundas, Laura Ann
  See Laura Ann Dundas
Dundas, Samuel
  III: <u>9</u> (p. 228)
Dunlap, Eliza
  I: 135
Dunlap, Mary
  I: 135
Dutcher, Amelia
  I: <u>315</u>
Dutcher, Ellen
  See Ellen Dtcher
Dutcher, Hannah
  I: <u>398</u>
Dutcher, William
  I: <u>276</u>, <u>543</u>
Duval, Betsey
  III: 53 (p. 163)
Duval, Elizabeth
  III: <u>49</u> (p. 163), <u>389</u> (p. 271)

Duval, Jefferson
  I: <u>565</u>
Dye, Henry
  II: <u>285</u> (p. 141), <u>286</u> (p. 142), <u>287</u> (p. 142), <u>288</u> (p. 142)
Dyer, John F.
  III: <u>127</u> (p. 172)
Dyson, Harriet Ann
  I: <u>272</u>
Dyson, Jane
  III: <u>185</u> (p. 179), <u>215</u> (p. 251)
Eaches, Eliza
  II: 124
Eaches, Mary
  II: 124
Easton, Annette
  II:. <u>205</u>
Easton, David
  I: <u>406</u>
Easton, Eliza
  I: <u>699</u>   III: <u>417</u> (p. 206)
Easton, Julia
  III: <u>493</u> (p. 214)
Easton, Kitty
  II: <u>171</u>; see also Kitty Easton Dulaney
Easton, Maria
  I: <u>407</u>
Easton, Sidney
  II: <u>204</u>
Easton, William
  I: <u>384</u>   II: <u>206</u>
Ebb, John
  I: <u>132</u>   III: <u>275</u> (p. 189), <u>310</u> (p. 262)
Ebbs, Elizabeth
  II: <u>310</u>   III: <u>123</u> (p. 241)
Edwards, Daniel
  I: <u>161</u>
Edwards, Emanuel
  I: <u>317</u>
Edwards, Haney
  III: 242 (p. 186), 322 (p. 264)
Edwards, Henrietta
  I: <u>88</u>   III: <u>424</u> (p. 206)
Edwards, Letty
  I: <u>160</u>
Edwards, Samuel M.
  I: <u>688</u>
Edwards, William
  II: <u>167a</u>
Eldred, Henry
  III: 211 (p. 251)
Ellis, George
  III: <u>352</u> (p. 198)
English, James
  I: <u>727</u>   III: 433 (p. 207)
Ennis, William
  I: <u>24</u>
Entwisle/Entwistle, James
  I: 290, 296, 376, 624   II: 196, 197, 311   III: <u>585</u> (p. 225)
Evans, Ann Augustus
  I: <u>499</u>
Evans, Catharine
  I: <u>449</u>, 661
Evans, David
  I: <u>146</u>
Evans, Edward
  I: <u>447</u>   III: <u>269</u> (p. 189), <u>372</u> (p. 269)
Evans, Elizabeth
  III: <u>510</u> (p. 216), <u>54</u> (p. 233)
Evans, Emily
  I: <u>428</u>, 623
Evans, James
  I: 164, 177, <u>504</u>, 598, 707   II: <u>69</u>, <u>92</u>, <u>233</u>   III: <u>362</u> (p. 199)
Evans, James E.
  III: <u>27</u> (p. 230)
Evans, Jane
  I: 517, 632
Evans, Jemima
  III: <u>403</u> (p. 273)
Evans, John E.
  II: <u>201</u>   III: <u>253</u> (p. 256)
Evans, Leanor
  II: <u>109</u>
Evans, Letitia
  II: <u>260</u>   III: <u>206</u> (p. 250)
Evans, Louisa C.
  III: 13 (p. 228); see also Louisa C. Evans Anderson
Evans, Mark
  I: <u>623</u>
Evans, Mary Ann
  II: <u>48</u>
Evans, Mary Frances
  III: <u>439</u> (p. 277)
Evans, Milly
  II: <u>233</u>
Evans, Monk
  II: <u>233</u>
Evans, Nancy
  I: <u>180</u>, 302, 483   II: 48
Evans, Orlando
  II: <u>173</u>
Evans, Patsey
  I: <u>482</u>
Evans, Robert
  II: <u>233</u>
Evans, Sally
  I: <u>181</u>
Evans, Samuel
  I: <u>177</u>
Evans, Sarah
  I: <u>450</u>
Evans, Sarah Ann
  I: <u>449</u>
Evans, Shimuel
  III: <u>43</u> (p. 232)
Evans, Simeon
  II: <u>308</u>
Evans, Susannah
  II: <u>257</u>
Evans, William
  I: <u>127</u>, <u>632</u>, <u>707</u>   III: <u>164</u> (p. 176), <u>277</u> (p. 259)
Ewing, Mrs.

II: 169
Fairfax, Orlando
I: 611 II: 87
Feeby, Henry
III: 499 (p. 143)
Feirel, Joseph
I: 446
Fendall, B. T.
I: 629
Fendall, Mary
I: 694
Fendall, Townshend D.
I: 461, 640a
Ferguson, Ann
II: 14
Ferguson, Dennis
I: 568
Ferguson, Elizabeth
II: 273 III: 54 (p. 163), 58 (p. 164), 113 (p. 170), 134 (p. 173), 217 (p. 183), 229 (p. 184), 230 (p. 184), 247 (p. 186), 329 (p. 196), 346 (p. 198), 468 (p. 212), 300 (p. 261), 371 (p. 269), 374 (p. 270)
Ferguson, Henry W.
III: 311 (p. 262)
Ferguson, Patty
I: 222
Ferguson, Roxaline
III: 76 (p. 166)
Feyerson, Patsey Johnson
II: 236
Field, William
III: 567 (p. 292)
Fisher, Amos
I: 33
Fisher, Charles Chapman
II: 275 (p. 138)
Fisher, Fanny
II: 23
Fisher, Henry
I: 688
Fitzgerald, Elizabeth S.
II: 304
Fitzgerald, Henny Ann
I: 302
Fitzgerald, James
I: 296
Fitzgerald, Jefferson
I: 283
Fitzgerald, Mary Jane
II: 305
Fitzhugh, Norman R.
I: 233
Fitzhugh, William H.
III: 578 (p. 225), 11 (p. 228), 535 (p. 288), 547 (p. 290)
Fletcher, Alice
I: 57
Fletcher, Betsey
I: 61, 62
Fletcher, Martha Ann
III: 51 (p. 163)
Fletcher, Mary

I: 57, 59
Fletcher, Polly
I: 57, 61
Folmare, Mary
III: 116 (p. 240), 151 (p. 244), 152 (p. 244), 376 (p. 270)
Foote, Andrew
II: 213
Foote, Ann
II: 213 III: 329 (p. 264)
Foote, Catherine
I: 758
Foote, Elizabeth
II: 213
Foote[?], Hayward
III: 573 (p. 293)
Foote, Henrietta
II: 213
Foote, Henson
II: 213
Foote, Jane Ann
III: 329n (p. 264)
Foote, Julia Ann
II: 213 III: 19 (p. 229)
Foote, Kitty
See Catherine Foote
Foote, Sarah Jane
II: 214 III: 18 (p. 229)
Forbish, William
I: 213
Ford, Armistead
III: 537 (p. 220)
Ford, Daniel
III: 138 (p. 173)
Ford, Daniel West
II: 167b
Ford, Edmonia
II: 207
Ford, Henrietta Bruce
II: 167b III: 70 (p. 235)
Ford, Judith
I: 663; see also Judith Ford Rogers
Ford, Louisa Hatton
II: 207 III: 190 (p. 179); see also Louisa Ford
Ford, William
III: 36 (p. 161), 280 (p. 259)
Ford, William Westley
II: 207
Forrest, ____
I: 11
Fortune, Jane Elizabeth
I: 484
Fowle, William H.
I: 203, 330a, 343, 695 II: 224 III: 101 (p. 169), 162 (p. 176), 437 (p. 277)
Fox, Angela
III: 480 (p. 213)
Fox, Ann
I: 28
Fox, Elin
I: 75
Fox, Eliza

I: 179
Fox, George
　III: 420 (p. 275)
Fox, Grace
　I: 300
Fox, Isaac
　I: 351
Fox, Kitty
　I: 350
Fox, Mary
　III: 115 (p. 170)
Fox, Sally
　See Sally Fox Parry
Fox, Thomas
　I: 518
Fox[?], William
　I: 377
Foy, Monica
　II: 351, 352, 353　III: 189 (p. 179), 22 (229)
Frances, Arianna
　I: 740
Franklin, Benjamin
　III: 397 (p. 203), 177 (p. 247)
Franklin, George
　III: 491 (p. 283)
Franklin, Mary
　III: 445 (p. 278)
Franklin, Nancy
　III: 376 (p. 201), 397 (p. 203)
Franklin, Phebe
　III: 404 (p. 204)
Franklin, Robert
　III: 458 (p. 279)
Frazer/Frazier, James
　I: 344　III: 147 (p. 174), 115 (p. 240)
Frazer, Jeremiah H.
　II: 12　III: 174 (p. 178)
Frazer/Frazier, Joseph
　II: 25　III: 56 (p. 163), 229 (p. 253)
Frazer, Sarah Ann
　II: 286 (p. 142)　III: 156 (p. 245)
Frazier, Fanny
　I: 242
Frazier, Frances
　III: 31 (p. 230)
Frazier, Jane
　III: 167 (p. 177), 367 (p. 269)
Frazier, Joseph Henry
　III: 471 (p. 212)
Frazier, Letty
　III: 84 (p. 167), 231 (p. 253)
Frazier, Rebecca
　III: 139 (p. 173), 230 (p. 253)
Frye, Christopher
　I: 100, 340, 426, 463　III: 141 (p. 174), 357 (p. 199), 237 (p. 254)
Frye, Margaret
　I: 601, 602
Fuddie, George
　I: 460
Fuller, Julia
　III: 134 (p. 242)
Fuller, Sally
　III: 228 (p. 184)
Fuller, Virginia
　III: 465 (p. 211), 453 (p. 279)
Fulmore, Ann
　I: 179
Gadsby, John
　I: 648
Gaines, Louisa
　I: 241
Gales, Gracey
　See Gracey Gales Snowden
Gales, Jane
　III: 181 (p. 178)
Gales, Moses
　I: 385
Gales, Sarah
　I: 281
Gander, Lewis
　I: 491
Gander, Winny
　I: 491
Gant, Agnes
　III: 575 (p. 224), 576b (p. 224)
Gant, Elizabeth Frances
　III: 576b (p. 224)
Gant, Ignatius
　I: 121
Gant, Laura C.
　III: 3 (p. 227)
Gantt, Thomas
　I: 642
Gardner, William C.
　II: 81　III: 23 (p. 159)
Garner, Margaret
　I: 500
Garner, Tristam H.
　I: 91　II: 52
Garrett, Caroline Koones
　III: 369 (p. 200); see also Caroline Koones
Garrett, David
　I: 641
Garrett, Martha
　See Martha Garrett Whiting
Garrett, Richard
　II: 86　III: 367 (p. 200)
Gaskins, Julia
　III: 468 (p. 281)
George Johnson & Co.
　I: 581
Gibbons, George
　III: 66 (p. 234)
Gibbs, Hirsley/Horsley
　III: 66 (p. 165), 53 (p. 233)
Gibbs, John G.
　I: 337
Gibbs, Lucretia
　I: 446
Gibbs, Mary
　II: 72
Gibbs, Mary Ann
　II: 323
Gibbs, William
　I: 337

Gibson, Amelia
   III: <u>540</u> (p. 289)
Gibson, Cecily Brooks
   III: <u>189</u> (p. 248)
Gibson, Charles
   III: <u>588</u> (p. 226)
Gibson, Daniel
   I: <u>411</u>   III: <u>361</u> (p. 199)
Gibson, Emily
   See Emily Gibson Hampton
Gibson, Esther
   I: <u>722</u>
Gibson, George
   I: <u>647</u>   III: <u>324</u> (p. 195)
Gibson, Henry
   II: 36
Gibson, Isaac
   I: 308
Gibson, James
   I: <u>679</u>   III: <u>102</u> (p. 238)
Gibson, John
   I: <u>237</u>
Gibson, Joseph
   II: <u>101</u>
Gibson, Louis
   III: <u>558</u> (p. 222)
Gibson, Louisa
   I: <u>517</u>
Gibson, Maria
   III: <u>508</u> (p. 216)
Gibson, Richard Henry
   II: <u>131</u>   III: <u>33</u> (p. 230)
Gibson, Sarah
   II: <u>282</u> (p. 141)
Gibson, Sarah Margaret
   III: <u>559</u> (p. 222)
Gird, John
   I: 184
Gird, Sarah
   I: <u>214</u>
Givens, Ann
   I: <u>280</u>
Giverson, Winny
   I: <u>579</u>
Glasscock, George
   II:, 276a (p. 138)
Goddard, John
   III: 376 (p. 201)
Goddard, William
   I: 119, 185, 186   III: 156 (p. 175), 191 (p. 180), 215 (p. 182), 234 (p. 254)
Godfrey, Julia
   III: <u>530</u> (p. 219), <u>97</u> (p. 238)
Goings, John
   III: <u>430</u> (p. 207), <u>316</u> (p. 263)
Gordon, Elizabeth
   I: 614a, 770   II: 132
Gordon, George
   II: <u>283</u> (p. 141)
Gordon, Mary
   II: 132
Gordon, Mary T.
   I: 614a, 650

Gordon, Sally
   I: <u>465</u>
Gover, Anthony P.
   II: 300   III: 352 (p. 198)
Gowens, Agnes
   III: 220 (p. 183)
Gowens, Catharine
   III: <u>229</u> (p. 184)
Gowens, Emily
   III: <u>230</u> (p. 184), <u>300</u> (p. 261)
Gowens, Joanna
   III: 124n (p. 172), <u>220</u> (p. 183), 229 (p. 184), 230 (p. 184), 300 (p. 261)
Grady, Joshua
   III: 495 (p. 284), 496 (p. 284)
Graham, Charles
   II: 38, 126, 127, 200, 365, 366
Graham, Fanny
   I: <u>327</u>
Graham, John
   See John Cupid
Grant, Chloe Ann
   III: <u>186</u> (p. 179)
Grant, John
   III: <u>431</u> (p. 207)
Grantt, John
   I: <u>567</u>
Gray, Alfred
   I: <u>559</u>
Gray, Amy
   I: <u>584</u>
Gray, Anna
   I: <u>585</u>
Gray, Catharine
   I: 352
Gray, Emily Cole
   II: <u>47</u>   III: <u>506</u> (p. 216)
Gray, Julia
   I: <u>274</u>
Gray, Laura Ann Dundas
   III: <u>267</u> (p. 188)
Gray, Letty
   III: <u>404</u> (p. 273)
Gray, Louisa
   III: <u>485</u> (p. 283)
Gray, Martha
   III: <u>595</u> (p. 226)
Gray, Peggy
   See Peggy Gray Jones
Gray, Richardson
   I: <u>668</u>
Gray, Sarah
   I: <u>583</u>
Gray, Thomas Shorter
   III: <u>421</u> (p. 206)
Gray, Tomason
   III: 404n (p. 273)
Gray, William
   III: <u>143</u> (p. 174), <u>497</u> (p. 284)
Gray, William Sr.
   III: <u>286</u> (p. 191)
Grayson, Henry
   I: <u>158</u>

Grayson, Jane
  I: 314
Grayson, Sarah Ann
  III: 541 (p. 289)
Grayson, Sarah Ellen
  III: 423 (p. 275)
Grayson, William
  I: 422 III: 426 (p. 207)
Green, Betsey
  III: 255 (p. 187)
Green, Eliza
  III: 22 (p. 159)
Green, Harriet
  See Harriet Green Knight
Green, James
  III: 589 (p. 226)
Green, Rebecca
  III: 521 (p. 287)
Green, Robert
  III: 574 (p. 224)
Greene, Shederick
  II: 8
Greenwood, Mary
  II: 106
Greyson, Thomas
  III: 395 (p. 272)
Grimes, Ann E.
  III: 255 (p. 256)
Grimes, James G.
  III: 448 (p. 278), 449 (p. 278), 450 (p. 278), 451 (p. 279)
Grimes, Joseph
  III: 43 (p. 162)
Grummond, Mary
  II: 299
Grymes, Ann
  I: 733
Grymes, Elizabeth Ann Waugh
  I: 544
Grymes, George Anderson
  II: 35
Grymes, George Andrew
  I: 733
Grymes, Thomas Fryer
  I: 733
Grymes, William
  I: 733
Gunnell, James S.
  I: 320
Guss, Charles
  II: 369
Hackett, Amey Bell
  III: 289 (p. 191), 172 (p. 246)
Hackett/Hacklett, Dennis
  I: 205 III: 371 (p. 200), 171 (p. 246)
Hagan, Francis
  III: 109 (p. 170), 207 (p. 181), 22 (p. 229)
Haley, Daniel
  See Daniel Smith
Hall, Betsy
  II: 80
Hall, Delilah
  III: 490 (p. 214)

Hall, Elizabeth
  II: 135 III: 222 (p. 252), 223 (p. 252), 224 (p. 252), 225 (p. 253), 469 (p. 281)
Hall, Emma
  II: 135
Hall, Fanny
  III: 68 (p. 165), 330 (p. 265)
Hall, Favorite
  I: 196
Hall, Francis
  I: 294
Hall, Isaac
  I: 150 III: 435 (p. 208)
Hall, James
  I: 150, 424
Hall, Jane
  I: 495
Hall, John
  I: 150 II: 60
Hall, John Henry
  III: 131b (p. 172)
Hall, Letitia/Letticia
  II: 135 III: 225 (p. 253)
Hall, Letty
  I: 150
Hall, Maria
  II: 174
Hall, Mary
  I: 150
Hall, Mary Elizabeth
  II: 135 III: 224 (p. 252)
Hall, Nancy
  See Nancy Hall Deane
Hall, Susan
  III: 5 (p. 227)
Hall, Theresa
  II: 178
Hall, William
  I: 150 II: 135 III: 223 (p. 252)
Halley, Alfred
  I: 371
Halley, Dennis
  III: 368 (p. 269), 476 (p. 281)
Halley, Esther
  I: 122
Halley, Jacob
  I: 354
Halley, William
  I: 354
Hallowell, Benjamin
  III: 439 (p. 277)
Hallowell, Henry
  III: 445 (p. 278), 491 (p. 283)
Hallowell, James S.
  III: 64 (p. 234), 65 (p. 234)
Hamilton, Ann
  III: 11 (p. 158)
Hamilton, Catharine
  III: 309 (p. 193), 264 (p. 257)
Hamilton, Charles
  III: 466 (p. 211), 55 (p. 233)
Hamilton, Elizabeth
  II: 82

Hamilton, Ellen
   II: 82, 83 III: 298 (p. 192) 263 (p. 257); see also Ellen Hamilton Jones
Hamilton, Jemima
   I: 93
Hamilton, Maria
   II: 198
Hamilton, Mary Ann Maria
   III: 120 (p. 171)
Hamilton, Philip
   III: 368 (p. 200), 265 (p. 257)
Hamilton, Prince
   III: 23 (p. 159)
Hamilton, Vester
   See Wesley Hamilton
Hamilton, Wesley
   I: 560
Hamilton, William
   II: 122
Hamilton, William Robert
   III: 119 (p. 171)
Hampson, Bryan
   III: 493 (p. 214)
Hampson, John L.
   I: 462, 472
Hampson, Joseph H.
   I: 726, 729, 730, 757 II: 39, 179, 203, 204, 205, 206, 341 III: 493 (p. 214)
Hampton, Emily Gibson
   II: 36
Hancock, John B.
   II: 62, 107 III: 139 (p. 173)
Handless, Betty
   I: 21, 564
Handless, Elisa
   See Betty Handless
Handless, Helin
   I: 564
Handless, Laurinda
   III: 7 (p. 157)
Handless, Nancy
   III: 96 (p. 168)
Handless, Robert
   III: 253 (p. 187)
Handless, Zachariah
   II: 75 III: 514 (p. 217)
Handy, Mary S.
   I: 606
Haney, Charles
   III: 447 (p. 209); see also Charles Haney Rhodes
Haney, Elizabeth
   III: 473 (p. 281)
Haney, Harriet
   See Harriet Haney Rhodes
Haney, Louisa
   III: 318 (p. 194); see also Louisa Haney Henderson
Haney, Lucy
   See Lucy Haney Davis
Haney, Lydia
   III: 52 (p. 163)
Haney, Mary
   See Mary Haney Johnson
Haney, Rachel
   III: 503 (p. 216)
Haney, Samuel
   III: 190 (p. 248)
Hanian, Emily
   I: 483
Hanson, Charlott
   III: 576a (p. 224)
Hanson, Sally
   II: 19
Harden, Thomas G.
   III: 188 (p. 179), 480 (p. 282)
Hardy, Mrs.
   III: 97 (p. 168), 107 (p. 169)
Hardy, Thomas S.
   II: 15, 289 (p. 142)
Harper, Sarah
   I: 429 II: 105
Harper, W. T.
   III: 99 (p. 238), 362 (p. 268), 412 (p. 274)
Harper, W. W.
   III: 483 (p. 282)
Harper, William
   II: 233
Harper, William H.
   I: 739
Harris, Alvina
   I: 706
Harris, Angelo
   II: 118
Harris, Ann
   I: 231, 561
Harris, Basheba
   III: 552 (p. 290)
Harris, Catharine
   III: 399 (p. 272)
Harris, Christopher
   I: 319
Harris, Desirlina T.
   II: 361b
Harris, Eleanor Ann
   See Eleanor Ann Harris Jenkins
Harris, Elizabeth
   III: 492 (p. 283)
Harris, Fanny
   I: 141
Harris, Harriet Jane
   I: 44
Harris, Henry
   I: 415
Harris, James
   I: 111, 174, 175, 176 II: 120, 344
Harris, Jane
   See Jane Harris Gales
Harris, Jane Elizabeth
   II: 106
Harris, Jemima
   III: 180 (p. 178), 181 (p. 178)
Harris/Harriss, John
   I: 134, 299 III: 260 (p. 188), 210 (p. 251)
Harris, Joseph
   I: 742

Harris, Kitty
I: 73
Harris, Lenobea[?]
III: 590 (p. 226)
Harris/Harriss, Louisa
II: 45 III: 210 (p. 251)
Harris, Lucretia
II: 189 III: 75 (p. 235)
Harris, Lucy
III: 214 (p. 182)
Harris, Margaret
See Margaret Harris Stepney
Harris, Nelson
I: 501
Harris, Octavia V.
II: 362 III: 34 (p. 230)
Harris, Patty
III: 348 (p. 198), 84 (p. 236)
Harris, Rachael
III: 210n (p. 251)
Harris/Harriss, Robert Oscar
III: 210 (p. 251)
Harris, Samuel
I: 742
Harris, Walter
II: 48, 80, 120, 121 III: 3 (p. 157), 365 (p. 200), 411 (p. 274)
Harris, William
I: 86
Harrison, Benjamin
I: 365
Harrison, Benoni E.
I: 167
Harrison, Charles William
III: 576 (p. 293)
Harrison, Elias
II: 190 III: 281 (p. 190), 282 (p. 190)
Harrison, John D.
I: 672 III: 415 (p. 205)
Harrison, Lucy Ann
III: 39 (p. 231)
Harrison, Polly
See Polly Blackburn
Harrison, Samuel
I: 291, 292, 293
Harriss, Edmonia
III: 211 (p. 251)
Hart, John
III: 574 (p. 293)
Hartley, Samuel
III: 523 (p. 287)
Hathaway, Kitty
See Kitty Turley
Hatton, James
I: 686
Hatton, Joseph
II: 5 III: 190 (p. 179)
Hatton, Louisa
II: 5; see also Louisa Hatton Ford
Hatton, William H.
I: 661 III: 165 (p. 177), 382 (p. 270)
Hawkins, Eliza
III: 65 (p. 165), 405 (p. 55)

Hawkins, George
II: 183, 386
Hawkins, Lydia Ann
III: 484 (p. 213)
Hawkins, Mary
II: 386; see also Mary Hawkins Ball
Hawkins, Washington
III: 28 (p. 230)
Hellen, Peter
I: 27
Helm, Catharine Stanly
III: 146 (p. 174)
Henderson, Alexander
I: 36, 172, 404
Henderson, Anne
III: 505 (p. 285)
Henderson, John
III: 372 (p. 201)
Henderson, Louisa Haney
III: 565 (p. 292); see also Louisa Haney
Henderson, Mary Ellen
III: 506 (p. 285)
Henderson, Nancy
I: 732
Henderson, Peter G.
II: 308 III: 168 (p. 177), 43 (p. 232)
Henderson, Willis E.
II: 235 III: 313 (p. 263), 314 (p. 263)
Henderson, Zilla
I: 580
Henry, Betsey
III: 75 (p. 166)
Henry, Celia
III: 29 (p. 160), 30 (p. 160), 199 (p. 249)
Henry, Charles
III: 291 (p. 191), 554 (p. 222)
Henry, Judith
III: 139 (p. 243)
Henry, Kitty
I: 582
Henry, Lucy Ann
See Lucy Ann Henry Jones
Henry, Maria
III: 395 (p. 203), 117 (p. 240)
Henry, Rebecca
III: 292 (p. 191), 551 (p. 290)
Henry, Robert
III: 103 (p. 239)
Henry, Robert Jr.
III: 32 (p. 160)
Henry, Robert Sr.
I: 247 III: 33 (p. 161), 198 (p. 249)
Henry, Rosana/Rosanna
III: 31 (p. 160), 200 (p. 250)
Henry, Sophia Lee
III: 290 (p. 191), 217 (p. 252)
Henry, Susan
III: 34 (p. 161), 201 (p. 250)
Henson, Martha
I: 175
Henson, Nancy
I: 174
Henson, Rebecca

I: 176
Hepburn, Amelia R.
III: 51 (p. 232)
Hepburn, Anderson
III: 274 (p. 189)
Hepburn, Arthur
III: 50 (p. 232)
Hepburn, John
I: 244 III: 181 (p. 247)
Hepburn, Julia A. W.
III: 49 (p. 232)
Hepburn, Latitia
I: 80
Hepburn, Lucy
I: 388
Hepburn, Moses
III: 422 (p. 206)
Hepburn, Moses G.
III: 46 (p. 232)
Hepburn, Prudence C.
III: 48 (p. 232)
Hepburn, Thomas W.
III: 47 (p. 232)
Hepburn, William
I: 129, 130, 244
Herbert, Davis
I: 724
Herbert, Eliza
II: 383
Herbert, John C.
I: 165, 199, 210, 225, 298, 333, 363, 440, 600
II: 98, 383 III: 2 (p. 157), 10 (p. 158), 11 (p. 158), 12 (p. 158), 16 (p. 158), 160 (p. 176), 161 (p. 176), 180 (p. 178), 206 (p. 181), 395 (p. 203), 532 (p. 219), 79 (p. 236), 117 (p. 240), 126 (p. 241), 340 (p. 266)
Heston, Joseph
I: 190
Hewes, Aaron
I: 20
Hewett, Emma
III: 410 (p. 274)
Hewitt, Peter
I: 447, 505, 708 III: 59 (p. 164), 64 (p. 164), 80 (p. 166), 118 (p. 171), 155 (p. 175), 158 (p. 176), 180 (p. 178), 414 (p. 205), 419 (p. 206), 303 (p. 261), 312 (p. 263), 384 (p. 271)
Hicks, N.
II: 375
Hiday, Rachal
I: 3
Hill, Thomas T.
III: 455 (p. 279)
Hinds, Maria
III: 124 (p. 172)
Hinds, Mary
III: 507 (p. 216)
Hinds, William
III: 363 (p. 200)
Hines, Alfred
I: 552

Hines, Ann
I: 387
Hines/Hinds, Elizabeth
I: 163 II: 357 III: 123 (p. 171)
Hines, Hannah
I: 279
Hines, Nathaniel
I: 330b
Hines, Peyton
I: 505
Hines, William
I: 683
Hodge, Margaret A.
II: 340
Hodge, Mary Ellen
III: 509 (p. 216)
Hoffman, Jacob
I: 65, 66, 217, 328, 522, 724
Hoffman, Peter E.
I: 553, 554, 736 II: 22, 65
Holland, Thomas
III: 268 (p. 189)
Hollinsberry, John
III: 42 (p. 162), 483 (p. 213)
Hollis, James
See James Pinn
Hones, Martha Ann
III: 406 (p. 273)
Honesty, Elizabeth
I: 357
Honesty, Henry
III: 567 (p. 223)
Honesty, James
III: 569 (p. 223)
Hooe, Bernard
I: 712, 738 II: 236, 328, 239, 240, 241, 242, 243 III: 228 (p. 184) 239 (p. 185), 240 (p. 185), 374 (p. 201), 375 (p. 201), 412 (p. 205) 334 (p. 265)
Hooff, John
III: 479 (p. 282)
Hooff, Lawrence
III: 69 (p. 165), 524 (p. 218)
Hooff, Philip H.
III: 73 (p. 235)
Hooff, William
III: 212 (p. 251)
Hopes, Delilah
III: 85 (p. 167)
Hopes, Patsey
III: 121 (p. 171)
Hopes, Richard
I: 50
Hopes, Samuel
I: 538 III; 355 (p. 199)
Hopkins, Albert
II: 291 (p. 142)
Hopkins, Catharine
II: 291 (p. 142)
Hopkins, Charles
II: 291 (p. 142)
Hopkins, Daniel
II: 291 (p. 142)

Hopkins, James
    II: <u>291</u> (p. 142)
Hopkins, Lewis
    I: 361
Hopkins, Martha
    II: <u>289</u> (p. 142)
Hopkins, Peter
    II: <u>290</u> (p. 142) III: <u>294</u> (p. 260)
Horner, R. W.
    II: 157 III: 339 (p. 266)
Horseman, Elijah
    II: 301
Horseman, Elizabeth
    III: 552 (p. 221)
Hoskins, James O. C.
    III: <u>492</u> (p. 214), 595 (p. 226)
Hough, Lawrence
    I: 697
Hough, William S.
    III: 150 (p. 244)
House, Richard
    I: 733 II: 35
Hove, Betsey
    I: <u>233</u>
Hove, Mary Frances Prior
    III: <u>553</u> (p. 290)
Howell, Charlotte
    I: 614b
Howland, Thomas H.
    I: 121
Hoy, Henry
    I: <u>376</u>
Hoy, Nelly
    See Nelly Hoy Butler
Hoye, Charles
    I: <u>624</u>
Hubball, John
    I: 20
Hughes, Benjamin
    III: <u>462</u> (p. 211)
Hughes, David
    III: <u>204</u> (p. 181)
Hughes, Jesse
    I: <u>719</u>
Hughes, Maria
    III: <u>199</u> (p. 180), 200 (p. 181), 201 (p. 181)
Hugle, Fendall
    III: 19 (p. 229)
Humphrey, Venus
    I: 494
Humphreys, Harriet
    III: <u>530</u> (p. 288)
Humphreys, Joseph
    III: 475 (p. 212)
Humphries, George
    I: <u>643</u> II: <u>296</u> III: <u>399</u> (p. 204)
Humphries, Georgeanna
    I: <u>347</u> II: <u>294</u>
Humphries, Kitty Barnes
    II: <u>293</u> (p. 142)
Humphries, Lucinda
    I: 374
Humphries, Sophia
    I: <u>347</u>
Humphries, Susanna/Susannah
    I: <u>347</u> II: <u>295</u>
Hunter, Adaline
    II: <u>241</u> III: <u>267</u> (p. 257)
Hunter, Alexander
    I: 586 III: 420 (p. 206), 457 (p. 210)
Hunter, Harriet
    See Harriet Hunter Watson
Hunter, John
    I: 204, 205, 207 III: 152 (p. 175), 371
    (p. 200), 373 (p. 201), 105 (p. 239), 171
    (p. 246), 305 (p. 262)
Hunter, Robert
    III: 103 (p. 169)
Hunter, Robert W.
    I: 620, 625, 626, 765 III: 103 (p. 169), 151
    (p. 175), 152 (p. 175), 153 (p. 175), 248
    (p. 186), 249 (p. 186), 288 (p. 191), 7
    (p. 227), 101 (p. 238), 189 (p. 248), 377
    (p. 270)
Hutchens, Ann
    I: 39, 40
Hutchin, Catharine
    III: <u>466</u> (p. 280)
Hutchin, Joseph
    III: <u>487</u> (p. 283)
Hutchins, Margaret
    I: 653 II: 386 III: 65 (p. 165)
Hutchinson, Ann
    III: <u>95</u> (p. 168), <u>358</u> (p. 268)
Hutchison, Margaret
    III: <u>454</u> (p. 279)
Hyson, Delilah
    I: <u>359</u>
Hyson, Henry
    III: <u>45</u> (p. 232)
Hyson, James Edward
    III: <u>351</u> (p. 267)
Hyson, John E.
    III: <u>499</u> (p. 284)
Hyson, Lewis
    III: <u>16</u> (p. 228)
Hyson, Louisa
    III: <u>581</u> (p. 225)
Hyson, Samuel
    I: 52, 53, 111, 135, 214, 216, 228, 326, 345,
    358 III: <u>563</u> (p. 223)
Hyson, Spenser
    III: <u>343</u> (p. 266)
Hyson, Thornton
    III: <u>580</u> (p. 225)
Hyson, Walter
    III: <u>562</u> (p. 291)
Irwin, James
    I: 609; see also James Hatton
Irwin, William H.
    I: 590, 591
Isaacs, Samuel
    I: 637, 690
Jackson, Ann
    II: <u>384</u> III: <u>52</u> (p. 233)
Jackson, Ann E.

III: 40b (p. 231)
Jackson, Betsey
   I: 723   III: 408 (p. 274)
Jackson, Catharine
   III: 542 (p. 289)
Jackson, Cecilia
   III: 8 (p. 157)
Jackson, Charlotte
   III: 416 (p. 274)
Jackson, George
   I: 23   II: 24   III: 209 (p. 182)
Jackson, Hannah
   III: 321 (p. 195)
Jackson, Harriet
   II: 222
Jackson, Harriet Medella Turner[?]
   III: 305 (p. 193)
Jackson, Henry
   II: 21
Jackson, Isaac
   III: 398 (p. 203)
Jackson, Janney
   I: 236
Jackson, John
   III: 90 (p. 167), 138 (p. 243)
Jackson, Kitty
   I: 23, 131, 626
Jackson, Laura
   II: 222
Jackson, Letty
   III: 446 (p. 209)
Jackson, Lucy
   III: 88 (p. 167), 125 (p. 241)
Jackson, Marion E.
   III: 409 (p. 274)
Jackson, Martha
   II: 113
Jackson, Mary Ann
   See Mary Ann Jackson Beckley
Jackson, Mildred
   I: 197
Jackson, Millie Julins
   I: 669b
Jackson, Nathaniel
   III: 89 (p. 167), 248 (p. 255)
Jackson, Nelly
   I: 393
Jackson, Phillis
   III: 197 (p. 180), 213 (p. 251)
Jackson, Richard
   III: 37 (p. 161)
Jackson, Robert
   III: 537 (p. 289)
Jackson, Tamer
   I: 744
Jackson, Thornton
   II: 222
Jackson, William
   I: 275
Jacob, Mary Jackson
   I: 131
Jacob, Thomas
   I: 23, 131

Jacobs, Charlotte
   II:, 188
Jacobs, Edward
   I: 589
Jacobs, Sarah
   I: 336
Jacobs, Sarah A.
   III: 46 (p. 162), 47 (p. 162), 48 (p. 162)
James, Israel
   I: 326
James, Sarah
   See Sarah James Davis
Jamieson & Anderson
   I: 120
Jamieson, Andrew
   I: 120   II: 280 (p. 138)
Jamieson, John
   I: 575
Jamieson, Robert
   I: 306, 442, 443, 446, 447, 470, 509, 562, 605, 719, 735   II: 20, 110, 129, 145, 346   III: 22 (p. 159), 325 (p. 195), 481 (p. 213), 531 (p. 219), 2 (p. 227), 71 (p. 235), 464 (p. 280)
Jamisone, David
   I: 5
Janney, Jonathan
   I: 436, 437, 502, 620, 625, 626, 655   II: 119   III: 249 (p. 186), 288 (p. 191), 101 (p. 238), 189 (p. 248)
Janney, Phinias
   II: 309
Janney, Samuel H.
   III: 223 (p. 183), 283 (p. 259)
Janney, Thomas
   III: 446 (p. 209), 515 (p. 217), 219 (p. 252)
Jarber, Rachel
   III: 105 (p. 169)
Jarbo/Jarbour, David
   I: 72, 111, 763
Jarbo/Jarbour, Rebecca Dover
   I: 111, 763
Jarboe, Mary
   II: 298
Jarboe, Samuel
   II: 298
Jarbour, Chloe
   I: 630
Jasper, Harriet
   II: 339   III: 273 (p. 258)
Jasper, Martha
   II: 339
Jasper, Mary J.
   III: 594 (p. 226)
Jefferson, Chloe Ann
   III: 129 (p. 172)
Jefferson, Elvina
   I: 716
Jefferson, Harriet
   II: 185, 271, 361a, 378, 381
Jefferson, Mary Ann
   III: 128 (p. 172)
Jefferson, Nancy
   III: 507 (p. 216)

Jeminy, Matilda
I: 183
Jenkins, Ann Eliza
I: 693
Jenkins, Eleanor Ann Harris
III: 352 (p. 267), 353 (p. 267)
Jenkins, Jemima
I: 84, 267, 345
Jenkins, Mary Jane
III: 400 (p. 204)
Jenkins, Samuel
III: 352 (p. 267)
Jennings, Hannah
I: 280   III: 401 (p. 204)
Jennings, Horatio
I: 321   III: 453 (p. 210)
Jennings, Jane
III: 579 (p. 225)
Jennings, Jesse
I: 342
Jennings, Nanthius
I: 264   III: 349 (p. 198)
Johnson, Betsey
I: 440
Johnson, Bryant
I: 118
Johnson, Charles
II: 98
Johnson/Johnston, Dennis
I: 180, 181, 294, 302
Johnson, Eliza
II: 364   III: 136 (p. 173)
Johnson, Elizabeth
I 3
Johnson, Flora
I: 671   III: 258 (p. 187), 259 (p. 188), 418 (p. 275)
Johnson, George
I: 587   II: 158, 371   III: 254 (p. 187)
Johnson, Grafton
II: 42, 336
Johnson, Hany
III: 21 (p. 159)
Johnson, Henny
I: 636
Johnson, James Edmond
II: 334
Johnson, Jane
I: 548
Johnson, Jesse
III: 290 (p. 260), 513 (p. 286)
Johnson, John
I: 636
Johnson, John T.[?]
II: 137
Johnson, Joseph
II: 86
Johnson, Joseph Nathaniel
II: 334
Johnson, Joshua
III: 291 (p. 260)
Johnson, Leannah
III: 40n (p. 161)

Johnson, Lucretia
III: 564 (p. 292)
Johnson, Lucy Ann
II: 314   III: 276 (p. 258), 319 (p. 263)
Johnson, Marcelina
II: 334
Johnson, Marcelina (daughter of Marcelina Johnson)
II: 334
Johnson, Margaret Louisa
III: 106 (p. 239)
Johnson, Martha
II: 166
Johnson, Martha Ann
II: 236
Johnson, Mary
III: 558 (p. 291)
Johnson/Johnston, Mary Ellen
II: 104, 225   III: 175 (p. 178), 306 (p. 262)
Johnson, Mary Haney
III: 319 (p. 195)
Johnson, Mary Lavinia
II: 314
Johnson, Mary Reily
I: 292
Johnson, Nancy
III: 171 (p. 177), 275 (p. 258)
Johnson, Patsey
See Patsey Johnson Feyerson
Johnson, Polly
I: 189
Johnson, Richard F.
II: 76
Johnson/Johnston, Robert
III: 114 (p. 170), 260 (p. 257)
Johnson, Sarah
II: 317   III: 129 (p. 242)
Johnson, Silvina
III: 411 (p. 274)
Johnson, Smith Alexander
III: 203 (p. 181)
Johnson, William
II: 236
Johnston, Fanny
III: 366 (p. 200)
Johnston, Reuben
I: 265, 451, 674
Johnston, Sadonia
II: 224
Jones, Aaron
II: 200
Jones, Albert
II: 270   III: 572 (p. 293)
Jones, Ann
I: 92   II: 38, 200   III: 256 (p. 187)
Jones, Ann Charlotte
II: 127
Jones, Ann Elizabeth
I: 666   II: 46
Jones, Barclay
III: 562 (p. 223)
Jones, Benjamin
I: 155   II: 270   III: 351 (p. 198), 161

(p. 245)
Jones, Calvin
  I: 353
Jones, Caroline
  II: 268
Jones, Catharine
  II: 270
Jones, Charles
  I: 374 II: 270
Jones, Cornelia
  III: 320 (p. 195)
Jones, Douglas
  III: 555 (p. 222)
Jones, Ellen Hamilton
  II: 83 III: 298 (p. 192), 263 (p. 257)
Jones, Elzy[?]
  III: 549 (p. 221)
Jones, Harriet
  III: 338 (p. 197)
Jones, Harriet Ann
  I: 508
Jones, James Henry
  III: 571 (p. 293)
Jones, Jane Eliza
  II: 270
Jones, John
  I: 373, 374 III: 500 (p. 215), 86 (p. 237), 347 (p. 267)
Jones, John L.
  II: 366
Jones, Joseph
  III: 237 (p. 185), 553 (p. 222), 570 (p. 292)
Jones, Julia
  II: 259
Jones, Kitty
  I: 316
Jones, Lauretta
  III: 26 (p. 230)
Jones, Levi
  III: 549 (p. 221)
Jones, Lucinda
  I: 715
Jones, Lucy Ann Henry
  III: 30 (p. 160)
Jones, Mary
  I: 640b
Jones, Mildred/Milly
  I: 198 III: 512a (p. 217)
Jones, Moses
  II: 199
Jones, Nancy
  III: 184 (p. 179), 271 (p. 189)
Jones, Oliver
  I: 92, 640b, 666 II: 46, 126
Jones, Olivia
  III: 256 (p. 187)
Jones, Peggy Gray
  III: 551 (p. 221), 555 (p. 222)
Jones, Roxanna
  II: 38
Jones, Sarah
  II: 270 III: 238 (p. 185)
Jones, Susan
  II: 270, 293 (p. 140) III: 247 (p. 255)
Jones, Susannah
  II: 373
Jones, Thacker
  I: 374, 596
Jones, William
  III: 184 (p. 179) 38 (p. 231)
Jones, William H.
  II: 365
Jordan, Sarah
  II: 364
Julins, Elizabeth
  I: 669b
Julins, Milly
  See Millie Julins Jackson
Julius, Elizabeth
  See Elizabeth Julius Butler
Julius, Milly Dover
  I: 111; see also Milly Julius Campbell
Julius, Thomas
  I: 123
Kane, Rebecca
  II: 175; see also Rebecca Kane Lee
Keene, Newton
  I: 571, 572
Keith, Jane Anne
  II: 82, 83
Keith, Jane[?] C.
  III: 267 (p. 188)
Keith, Margaret S.
  III: 108 (p. 170), 309 (p. 193), 264 (p. 257)
Keith, Thomas R.
  III: 267 (p. 188), 309 (p. 193), 1 (p. 227), 8 (p. 227), 9 (p. 228)
Kelsick, Mary
  See Mary Kelsick Payne
Kendall, Anna
  II: 39
Kendall, George
  III: 448 (p. 278)
Kennedy, Ann
  III: 116 (p. 171)
Kennedy, Elisa
  I: 466
Kennedy, Robert
  III: 130 (p. 172)
Kenny, John
  III: 413 (p. 274)
Kenzie, Lewis M.
  See Lewis McKenzie
Kesterson, William
  I: 213
Key, Francis
  III: 429 (p. 207)
Kilbreath, Henry
  II: 187
Kin, _____
  II: 372
King, Elizabeth
  III: 14 (p. 158), 120 (p. 240)
Kingsford, Edward
  III: 438 (p. 277)
Kinsey, Ezra

I: 111, 155
Kinsey/Kinzey, Zenas
II: 161, 218, 293 (p. 140), 297, 298, 306, 313, 329 III: 8 (p. 157), 52 (p. 163), 104 (p. 169), 105 (p. 169), 106 (p. 169), 149 (p. 175), 215 (p. 182), 245 (p. 186), 318 (p. 194), 319 (p. 195), 321 (p. 195), 354 (p. 199), 240 (p. 254), 243 (p. 255), 247 (p. 255), 250 (p. 255), 281 (p. 259), 288 (p. 260), 289 (p. 260), 453 (p. 279)
Knight, Harriet Green
I: <u>49</u>
Knight, Richard
I: <u>660</u>
Koones, Caroline
I: <u>378</u>; see also Caroline Koones Garrett
Kune[?], Thomas
I: 188
Lacey, Ann
II: 167a
Lacey, Louisa
III: <u>160</u> (p. 176)
Lamar, Harriet G.
III: <u>493</u> (p. 283)
Lambert & McKinzie
II: 274 (p. 140) III: 182 (p. 245)
Lambert, B. H.
III: <u>190</u> (p. 248)
Lambert, Benjamin
III: 51 (p. 163)
Lancaster, Richard
II: <u>367</u> III: <u>320</u> (p. 263)
Lancaster, Richard Randolph
II: <u>321</u>
Lancaster, Sarah
II: <u>321</u>
Lancaster, Sarah Moore
III: <u>19</u> (p. 159), <u>158</u> (p. 245); see also Sarah Moore
Lane, Flavus
III: <u>361</u> (p. 268)
Lane, Frances Ann
III: <u>6</u> (p. 157), <u>244</u> (p. 255), 361 (p. 268)
Lanham, Matilda
III: <u>7</u> (p. 227)
Lanphier, William Jr.
I: 542
Lanphier[?], William
II: 21
Lansdale, Mary
I: <u>19</u>
Larmour, Samuel B.
I: 91 II: 11
Latham, Hugh
III: 537 (p. 289)
Latham, Rachel
II: 159
Lawrason, James
I: 99, 119
Lawrence P. Hill & Co.
I: 581
Laws, Ann
See Ann Laws Oden

Lawson, John
II: 100 III: 223 (p. 183), 24 (p. 229)
Lay[?], Jemima
See Jemima Say[?]
Leadbeater, John
III: 150 (p. 175)
Leddy, Hugh
II: 42
Lee, Adaline
I: <u>741</u>
Lee, Adam Driver[?]
II: <u>177</u>
Lee, Albert
II: <u>177</u>
Lee, Cecelia
II: <u>281</u> (p. 141) III: <u>296</u> (p. 261)
Lee, David
II: <u>3</u>
Lee, Edmund J.
I: 427, 571
Lee, Eliza
See Eliza Lee Dorsey
Lee, Elizabeth
II: <u>280</u> (p. 141) III: <u>30</u> (p. 230)
Lee, Essen
I: <u>305</u>
Lee, Hannah
I: <u>586</u> III: <u>188</u> (p. 179), 189 (p. 179), <u>480</u> (p. 282); see also Hannah Lee Butler
Lee, Henry
III: <u>103</u> (p. 239), <u>591</u> (p. 226), <u>1</u> (p. 227)
Lee, Jane Bell
III: <u>188</u> (p. 248), <u>490</u> (p. 283); see also Jane Bell
Lee, John
I: <u>675</u> III: 458 (p. 210)
Lee, John Wesley
II: <u>177</u>
Lee, Laura Ann
II: <u>177</u>
Lee, Lewis
I: <u>479</u>
Lee, Louisa
See Louisa Lee Ruston
Lee, Lucinda
I: <u>361</u>; see also Lucinda Lee Peters
Lee, Lucy
I: 675
Lee, Luke
I: <u>204</u> III: <u>373</u> (p. 201), <u>305</u> (p. 262)
Lee, Mary
II: <u>267</u> III: <u>189</u> (p. 179)
Lee, Mary Ann
I: <u>547</u>; see also Mary Ann Lee Robinson
Lee, Michael Morris
II: <u>177</u>
Lee, Nancy
II: <u>269</u> III: <u>217</u> (p. 183)
Lee, Peter
I: <u>435</u>
Lee, Philip Andrew
II: <u>177</u>
Lee, Rachel

II: 344
Lee, Rebecca Kane
   III: 440 (p. 277); see also Rebecca Kane
Lee, Richard
   I: 705, 741
Lee, Richard K.
   III: 157 (p. 176)
Lee, Rosetta
   III: 481 (p. 282)
Lee, Sarah
   I: 221 II: 177
Lee, Sinah
   III: 454 (p. 210)
Lee, Sincai[?]
   I: 94
Lee, Sophia
   See Sophia Lee Henry
Lee, Sylvia
   III: 244 (p. 186), 113 (p. 240)
Lee, Thomas
   III: 407 (p. 273)
Lee, William
   III: 8 (p. 227)
Lee, William Fletcher
   II: 177
Legg, Elias P.
   I: 44, 227, 279
Lennett[?], Hannah B.
   III: 381 (p. 270)
Lenox, Henry
   I: 151
Leucas, Sarah
   I: 8
Lewis, Benjamin
   I: 269
Lewis, Catharine
   I: 476
Lewis, Charles
   I: 153, 154 III: 211 (p. 182), 452 (p. 279)
Lewis, Cornelia Ann
   I: 748
Lewis, Dennis
   I: 145
Lewis, Isabella
   I: 445
Lewis, Joseph
   II: 316 III: 364 (p. 268)
Lewis, Louis
   III: 327 (p. 195)
Lewis, Margaret
   II: 168
Lewis, Mary Elizabeth McQuan
   III: 358 (p. 199), 242 (p. 254)
Lewis, William
   I: 4
Lewis, William Henry
   I: 684 III: 377 (p. 201), 241 (p. 254)
Libby, Richard
   I: 94 III: 454 (p. 210)
Lightfoot, Ann
   I: 330b, 387, 552, 612b, 683 II: 17
Lindsay Hill & Co.
   I: 581

Lippitt, E. R.
   II: 123, 142
Lippitt, Mary F.
   II: 123
Litle, Richard H.
   I: 96
Lloyd, Anna H.
   II: 147
Lloyd, Harriet Mason
   I: 197, 297, 438
Lloyd, John
   III: 424 (p. 206)
Lockwood, Aquilla
   I: 95, 369, 759 II: 146
Logan, Adell
   III: 247 (p. 186), 130 (p. 242)
Logan, Christiana
   III: 54 (p. 163), 131 (p. 242)
Logan, Emeline
   I: 639
Logan, John
   III: 134 (p. 173)
Logan, Noble
   III: 371 (p. 269)
Logan, Rudolph
   III: 374 (p. 270)
Logan, Sally
   III: 133 (p. 173), 146 (p. 243)
Logan, William
   III: 329 (p. 196), 375 (p. 270), 502 (p. 284), 503 (p. 285)
Loggins, Peter
   I: 236, 414 III: 133 (p. 173), 146 (p. 243)
Loggins, Sally
   I: 414
Lomax, Ann
   III: 256 (p. 256)
Lomax, Ann Eliza
   I: 348
Lomax, Caroline
   I: 348 III: 239 (p. 185), 276 (p. 190)
Lomax, David
   I: 348
Lomax, Delilah
   I: 348 III: 489 (p. 214)
Lomax, Elias
   II: 185
Lomax, Elizabeth
   II: 361a
Lomax, Ellen
   I: 348 II: 361a III: 278 (p. 190), 488 (p. 214), 489 (p. 214), 490 (p. 214), 232 (p. 253)
Lomax, Hannah
   III: 240 (p. 185)
Lomax, Henry
   I: 481
Lomax, Hiram
   I: 348 III: 167 (p. 246)
Lomax, Julia
   I: 348 III: 490 (p. 214)
Lomax, Lucy
   III: 396 (p. 203), 74 (p. 235)

Lomax, Margaret
    I: 348   III: 488 (p. 214)
Lomax, Mary Frances
    II: 361a
Lomax, Sarah Ann
    I: 348
Lomax, Thomas
    II: 361a
Lomax, William
    III: 543 (p. 289)
Lomax, William George
    II: 361a
London, Mary
    III: 494 (p. 215)
Longster, Sarah
    III: 20 (p. 229)
Loudoun, Elizabeth
    I: 68
Loudoun, Frederick
    I: 78   III: 390 (p. 203)
Loudoun, George
    I: 69
Loudoun, Nancy
    I: 70   III: 104 (p. 169)
Loudoun, Richard
    I: 70, 412
Loudoun, William
    I: 70, 390
Lovejoy, Margaret
    III: 66 (p. 234)
Loveless, Sarah
    III: 177 (p. 178)
Lowe, John F. N.
    II: 84   III: 29 (p. 230), 338 (p. 266)
Lowry, James
    I: 419
Lucas, Monica
    III: 428 (p. 207)
Lucas, Nathaniel
    III: 439 (p. 277)
Lucas, Rebecca
    I: 649; see also Rebecca Lucas Nickens
Lucas, Sarah
    See Sarah Leucas
Lunt, Ezra
    II: 25   III: 56 (p. 163), 84 (p. 167), 167 (p. 177), 229 (p. 253), 231 (p. 253), 367 (p. 269)
Lunt, Samuel
    III: 167 (p. 177), 40a (p. 231)
Lyle, Joanna
    III: 131b (p. 172)
Lyles, Hannah Smith
    II: 192, 193   III: 252 (p. 256)
Lyles, Patterson
    I: 371
Lyles, Richard
    II: 192, III: 478 (p. 282)
Lyles, Turner
    II: 192   III: 205 (p. 250)
Lyles, William
    I: 152   II: 234   III: 385 (p. 202), 143 (p. 243)

Lyons, William
    II: 234   III: 44 (p. 232), 467 (p. 280), 561 (p. 291)
Mack, Fanny
    I: 698
Macrae, Allan
    I: 134
Madden, Scarlett
    I: 26
Madella, Cornelius
    II: 123
Madella/Medella, John
    II: 288 (p. 142)   III: 366 (p. 269)
Madella, Richard
    II: 114
Madella, Silas
    II: 287 (p. 142)
Magruder, Peter
    III: 337 (p. 197), 228 (p. 253)
Magruder, Harriet
    See Harriet McGruder
Magruder, Rachel
    III: 1 (p. 157), 111 (p. 239)
Mahoney, Robert
    III: 428 (p. 276)
Mandeville, Julia A.
    See Julia A. Mandeville Carter
Mankins, William
    III: 253 (p. 187)
Mans, Harriet
    See Harriet Mans Carroll
Marbury, F. A.
    III: 534 (p. 288)
Marbury, Leonard
    I: 211   III: 50 (p. 163), 385 (p. 271)
Mark, Ann
    II: 361b, 362, III: 34 (p. 230)
Mark, Ann H.
    II: 30
Mark, Ann S.
    I: 532   II: 29   III: 590 (p. 226)
Mark, Fanny
    III: 166 (p. 177)
Markell, Elizabeth
    II: 130
Markenheimer[?], Eliza
    I: 660
Markenheimer[?], George L.
    I: 660
Markley, Joanna
    I: 652, 653
Marrs, John
    III: 522 (p. 287)
Marsh, Phebe
    I: 63, 64
Marshall, Ann Maria
    II: 220
Marshall, Catharine
    II: 219
Marshall, Charles
    III: 589 (p. 226)
Marshall, Eldridge
    II: 219

Marshall, Louisa
II: <u>219</u>
Marshall, Louisa (daughter of Louisa Marshall)
II: <u>219</u>
Marshall, Rebecca
II: <u>115</u>
Marshall, Sarah
II: <u>219</u>
Martin, Davis
II: 105
Martin, Fanny
II: <u>4</u>
Marvel, Israel
See Israel Williams
Mason, Ann
II: 134
Mason, George
III: <u>221</u> (p. 252)
Mason, Mary
I: 146
Mason, Thompson F.
I: 106, 294 II: 233
Massies[?], John W.
II: 19
Matthews, Catherine
III: <u>434</u> (p. 277)
Mayfield, Edward A.
I: 219
Mayo, Jefferson
III: <u>429</u> (p. 207)
McCachran, Dougal
I: 182
McCartey/McCarty, John M.
I: 294, 766
McCarty, Dennis
I: <u>363</u>
McCarty, William M.
I: 294 III: 67n (p. 234)
McCatharine, D.
I: 303
McChichester, D.
III: 231 (p. 184)
McClean, Daniel
I: 87
McClean/McLean, Archibald
I: 88, 317
McCormick, John
I: 681 III: 379 (p. 201)
McCormick, Samuel M.
III: 233 (p. 185)
McCoy, Annette
II: <u>282</u> (p. 138)
McCoy, Daniel
II: <u>162</u>, 212
McCoy, Ellen
II: <u>162</u>, 163
McCoy, George Fitzgerald
II: <u>162</u>
McCoy, Laura
II: <u>282</u> (p. 138)
McCoy, Mary Ann
II: <u>163</u>

McCoy, Mary Emily
II: <u>282</u> (p. 138)
McCoy, William Henry
II: <u>162</u>, <u>282</u> (p. 138)
McDonny, George William Roy
II: <u>235</u>
McGruder, Harriet
III: <u>579</u> (p. 293)
McGuire, James
I: 93 III: 185 (p. 179), 186 (p. 179), 399 (p. 204), 215 (p. 251)
McIntosh, Ann
I: 5
McIntosh, Frankey
I: <u>5</u>
McIntosh, Julia
I: <u>338a</u>
McIntosh, Mary
I: 5
McIntosh, Molly
See Mary McIntosh
McKee, John
I: <u>635</u>
McKenzie, Anne
III: 67n (p. 234)
McKenzie/McKinzie, James
I: 649 III: 308 (p. 193), 173 (p. 247)
McKenzie, Lewis
II: 245
McKnight, Charles
I: 273, 454, 455, 648 II: 74, 382
McLean, Archibald
See McClean/McLean
McLeod, Daniel
I: 699 III: 417 (p. 206)
McLish, George
III: 129 (p. 172)
McQuan, Amy
I: <u>232</u>; see also Amey McQuan Williams
McQuan, Mary Elizabeth
See Mary Elizabeth McQuan Lewis
McQueen, Mary Elizabeth
I: <u>743</u>
McRea, Catherine
I: 163
McRea, Kitty
I: 232
Mead, Mary Ann
I: 278
Meade, Dora[?]
See Theodore Meade
Meade, Theodore
II: 72, 174, 175, 181, 186 III: 183 (p. 179), 406 (p. 204), 579 (p. 225), 134 (p. 242), 181 (p. 247), 216 (p. 252), 337 (p. 265), 348 (p. 267)
Meade, William
I: 364
Medella, Armistead
III: <u>541</u> (p. 220), <u>164</u> (p. 245); see also Betsey Payne
Medella, Betsey Payne
III: <u>165</u> (p. 246)

Medella, George
  III: 302 (p. 193)
Medella, Harriet
  See Harriet Medella Turner Jackson
Medella, Henrietta
  III: 106 (p. 169)
Medella, Lewis
  III: 25 (p. 229)
Medella, Roxana
  III: 200 (p. 181)
Medella, Susan
  III: 201 (p. 181)
Meredith, Eliza Williams
  III: 545 (p. 221), 546 (p. 221), 586 (p. 225)
Merrick, Alfred
  I: 646 III: 386 (p. 202), 239 (p. 254)
Merrick/Merricks, Rebecca
  II: 297 III: 240 (p. 254)
Merricks, Jemima Ross
  I: 396
Merricks, Louisa
  II: 1
Middleton, Alfred
  I: 737
Middleton, Chloe Ann
  I: 369 II: 121
Middleton, David
  III: 455 (p. 210), 359 (p. 268)
Middleton, Hannah
  II: 380 III: 309 (p. 262)
Middleton, Harriet Lockwood
  II: 146
Middleton, Lydia
  I: 369 II: 146
Middleton, Milly
  I: 116
Middleton, Richard
  I: 452
Middleton, Richard Henry
  I: 369
Middleton, Sarah Elizabeth
  II: 146
Middleton, Susan
  II: 7
Middleton, Thomas Irvin
  I: 369
Middleton, Ulysses
  I: 369
Milburne, B. C.
  I: 630
Miles, Bazil
  III: 333 (p. 196), 233 (p. 254)
Miles, Hannah
  III: 384 (p. 202)
Miles, Oliver
  III: 365 (p. 200)
Miller, John M.
  III: 580 (p. 294), 581 (p. 294)
Miller, Joseph H.
  II: 44
Miller, Lewis
  I: 310
Miller, Mordecai
  I: 145, 156, 157, 226, 253, 254, 313, 364, 380, 647, 679 II: 66, 131 III: 33 (p. 230), 102 (p. 238)
Miller, Mr.
  I: 418
Miller, Robert
  II: 198
Miller, Robert H.
  I: 304, 418, 432, 476, 613, 746, 747a, 748 II: 66, 101, 131, 165, 260 III: 38 (p. 161), 327 (p. 195), 39, (p. 231), 56 (p. 233), 401 (p. 273), 414 (p. 274), 576 (p. 293)
Miller, Samuel
  I: 411, 417 II: 292 (p. 142) III: 27 (p. 160), 361 (p. 199), 391 (p. 271)
Miller, Simon
  I: 386
Miller, William H.
  I: 400, 568, 684 II: 94, 101, 131, 212, 282 (p. 141) III: 377 (p. 201) 241 (p. 254)
Mills, John
  III: 579 (p. 293)
Mills, Rachel
  III: 135 (p. 173), 214 (p. 251)
Mills, William
  III: 135 (p. 173), 214 (p. 251)
Mills, William N.
  III: 197 (p. 180), 209 (p. 182), 388 (p. 202), 213 (p. 251), 336 (p. 265)
Milmer, William P.
  I: 385
Minor, Anthony
  I: 65
Minor, Daniel
  II: 213, 214 III: 18 (p. 229)
Minor, Fortune Ann
  I: 328
Minor, George
  III: 291 (p. 191), 16 (p. 228)
Minor, James
  I: 66
Minor, James Thomas
  I: 328
Minor, Letty
  I: 116, 737
Minor, Richard Henry
  I: 328
Minor, Tabitha
  I: 332
Minor, William
  I: 107, 357, 358, 359, 627, 728 III: 45 (p. 162) 479 (p. 213), 542 (p. 220), 554 (p. 222), 557 (p. 222), 558 (p. 222), 559 (p. 222), 564 (p. 223), 565 (p. 223), 566 (p. 223), 567 (p. 223), 568 (p. 223), 583 (p. 225), 60 (p. 234), 342 (p. 266), 343 (p. 266), 344 (p. 266), 345 (p. 266), 346 (p. 266), 349 (p. 267), 351 (p. 267)
Minor, William
  507b
Mitchell, Dolly Ann
  III: 574 (p. 293)
Mitchell, Ellen

I: 665 III: 238 (p. 254)
Mitchell, Ellen Brown
II: 18
Mitchell, Fanny
III: 369 (p. 269)
Mitchell, George
I: 463 III: 357 (p. 199), 237 (p. 254)
Mitchell, Joseph
III, 460 (p. 211), 324 (p. 264)
Mitchell, Lucy Ann
III: 405 (p. 273)
Mitchell, Malvina
III: 460 (p. 211), 324 (p. 264)
Mitchell, Margaret
II: 18 III: 538 (p. 289)
Mitchell, Rachel
III: 29 (p. 230)
Mitchell, Robert
I: 602
Mitchell, Sarah
I: 426
Monroe, Daniel
III: 108 (p. 170)
Monroe, Elizabeth
II: 10
Monroe, James H.
III: 524 (p. 287)
Monroe, Sarah
III: 197 (p. 180), 209 (p. 182), 388 (p. 202), 213 (p. 251), 336 (p. 265)
Moody, Penny Turner
I: 77
Moore, Alexander
I: 597b, 608, 639, 644, 714, 743
Moore, Alexander
I: 240, 347, 368, 372, 381, 406, 407, 415, 478, 541, 551, 565, 597b, 608, 639, 644, 714, 743
II: 293 (p. 142), 355 III: 181 (p. 178), 255 (p. 187)
Moore, Anne
I: 96
Moore, Joseph C.
I: 480
Moore, Sarah
I: 96 III: 116 (p. 171); see also Sarah Moore Lancaster
Moran, John
I: 704 III: 285 (p. 191)
Morgan, Ann L.
I: 166, 168
Morgan, Elizabeth
I: 122
Morgan, Flora E.
I: 764; see also Flora E. Morgan Wilson
Morgan, Mary
I: 246, 764 III: 456 (p. 210); see also Mary Morgan Reeler
Morgan, William
I: 122, 441 III: 78 (p. 166)
Morris, Adaline/Adeline
I: 484, 685
Morris, Ann Matilda
I: 484 II: 63

Morris, Cornelia
II: 32
Morris, Eliza M.
II: 255
Morris, Elizabeth
III: 218 (p. 183)
Morris, George
I: 484, 685
Morris, Henry
I: 37
Morris, Jane
I: 341; see also Jane Morris Smith
Morris, Julia
III: 339 (p. 197)
Morris, Maria
I: 309 III: 535 (p. 219)
Morris, Mary
II: 370; see also Mary Morris Nash
Morrison, William
I: 301, 441 III: 78 (p. 166)
Mortimer, Barthomew A.
I: 592
Morton, Mary Ann
I: 712
Moss, Matilda
III: 130 (p. 172), 300 (p. 192)
Muir, Mrs. William
II: 207
Mullan, Arthelia/Athelia[?]
III: 163 (p. 176), 331 (p. 265)
Munay[Murray?], George
I: 368
Muncaster[?], John
I: 246
Murray, Albert
I: 604
Murray, George
See George Munay
Murray, Gustavus
I: 240
Murray, Mary Jane
I: 381
Muse, Nancy
II: 335
Muse, Virginia
II: 335
Muse, William Henry
II: 335 III: 394 (p. 203)
Myers, John
III: 9 (p. 158), 318 (p. 263)
Myers, Louisa
III: 473 (p. 212), 370 (p. 269)
Nash, Mary Morris
III: 85 (p. 237)
Naukeley, William N.
III: 40a (p. 231)
Neale, C.
I: 582 III: 75 (p. 166), 234 (p. 185)
Neale, Christopher
I: 384, 457, 492, 531, 710 II: 3 III: 49 (p. 163), 339 (p. 197)
Negro Agnes
III: 124 (p. 172), 220 (p. 183)

Negro Amy
  I: 173
Negro Ann
  I: 137a, 218
Negro Anna
  I: 84
Negro Anne
  I: 39
Negro Anthony
  I: 90
Negro Ben
  I: 99
Negro Bet/Bett
  I: 17, 135, 440 II: 98
Negro Betty
  I: 39, 112a
Negro Billy
  I: 52, 53
Negro Caroline
  III: 67 (p. 234)
Negro Celia
  I: 33
Negro Charity
  I: 39
Negro Charles
  I: 295, 311
Negro Cincinnatus
  I: 135
Negro Clem
  I: 39
Negro Cloe
  I: 39, 112a, 112b, 113, 114
Negro Congo
  I: 14
Negro Daniel
  I: 9 III: 479 (p. 282)
Negro David
  I: 112a
Negro Delila
  I: 178
Negro Elick
  I: 27
Negro Elisha
  I: 39
Negro Emily
  I: 195
Negro Fanny
  I: 153
Negro Ferdinand
  I: 84, 85
Negro Frank
  I: 170
Negro Frederick
  I: 39
Negro George
  I: 112a, 195
Negro Hager
  I: 32
Negro Hannah
  I: 41 223
Negro Hannah Elizabeth
  I: 6
Negro Harriet
  I: 195
Negro Harry
  I: 52, 53
Negro Henry
  I: 84
Negro Hester
  I: 1
Negro Isaac
  I: 39, 42
Negro Jacob
  I: 34
Negro James
  I: 22
Negro Jane
  I: 195
Negro Janney
  I: 136
Negro Jeffery
  I: 36
Negro Jenny
  I: 6, 39
Negro Jesse
  See Negro Jeffery
Negro Joe
  I: 39
Negro Juda
  I: 39
Negro Jude
  See Jude Currie
Negro Juliann
  I: 84, 85, 114, 128
Negro Kitty
  I: 195
Negro Lem
  I: 84
Negro Letty
  I: 52, 52, 53
Negro Lilly
  I: 39
Negro Linna/Linny
  I: 84, 85, 128
Negro Little
  I: 84
Negro Lucinda
  I: 206b
Negro Lucy
  I: 6
Negro Luie
  I: 84
Negro Lydia
  I: 95, 248
Negro Marcelena
  I: 135
Negro Margery
  I: 84
Negro Maria
  I: 165, 211 II: 541 (p. 220)
Negro Mary
  I: 210
Negro Matilda
  I: 298
Negro Mayor
  I: 39

Negro Mial
  I: 84
Negro Milly
  I: <u>60</u>, 112a
Negro Molly
  I: 112a
Negro Mordecai
  I: <u>39</u>
Negro Nace
  See Ignatius Gant
Negro Nan
  I: <u>81</u>
Negro Nancy
  I: <u>16</u>, 112a
Negro Nanny
  I: <u>13</u>
Negro Ned
  I: 112a
Negro Nila
  I: 52, <u>53</u>
Negro Patty
  I: <u>39</u>, <u>199</u>
Negro Peg
  I: 440 II: 98
Negro Peter
  I: 479
Negro Priscilla
  I: <u>34</u>
Negro Priss
  I: <u>39</u>, 84
Negro Rachel
  I: <u>18</u>, <u>39</u>, <u>195</u>
Negro Rebecca
  I: <u>112b</u>
Negro Roby
  I: <u>39</u>
Negro Ruthy
  I: <u>39</u>
Negro Sally
  I: <u>84</u>, <u>85</u>
Negro Sam
  I: 84
Negro Sarah
  I: <u>39</u>
Negro Sarah Ann
  I: <u>298</u>
Negro Scipio
  I: 84
Negro Sophia
  I: <u>225</u>
Negro Sue
  I: <u>6</u>
Negro Sylvia
  I: <u>6</u>, <u>20</u>, <u>89b</u>, <u>249</u>
Negro Vina
  I: 84
Negro Wat
  I: 84
Negro Wesley
  I: <u>97</u>
Negro Will
  I: 84
Negro William
  I: <u>15</u>
Neill, Abraham
  I: 43
Nelson, Cecelia/Cecilia
  I: <u>282</u> III: <u>225</u> (p. 184), <u>124</u> (p. 241)
Nelson, Charlotte
  II: <u>271</u> III: <u>116</u> (p. 240)
Nelson, Eleanor
  I: 555, 557, 558
Nelson, George
  I: <u>282</u> III: <u>226</u> (p. 184), <u>119</u> (p. 240)
Nelson, Georgiana/Georgianna
  II: <u>271</u> III: <u>151</u> (p. 244)
Nelson, James
  I: 83
Nelson, John
  II: <u>271</u> III: <u>376</u> (p. 270)
Nelson, Martha
  I: <u>282</u> III: <u>227</u> (p. 184)
Nelson, Patty
  I: <u>282</u> II: 271 III: <u>224</u> (p. 183), 225 (p. 184), 226 (p. 184), 227 (p. 184), 119 (p. 240), 124 (p. 241), <u>149</u> (p. 244)
Nelson, Virginia
  II: <u>271</u> III: <u>150</u> (p. 244)
Nelson, William
  II: <u>271</u> III: <u>152</u> (p. 244)
Newell, Philip
  I: <u>194</u>
Newman, Attoway
  III: <u>381</u> (p. 202)
Newton, Nathaniel
  I: 345
Newton, William
  I: 399 III: 392 (p. 203)
Nicholls, Ann
  I: 35
Nicholls, Asa
  I: <u>35</u>
Nicholls, Elizabeth
  I: <u>35</u>
Nicholls, George
  I: <u>35</u>
Nicholls, Grace
  I: <u>35</u>
Nicholls, Henry
  I: <u>35</u>
Nicholls, Jane
  I: <u>35</u>
Nicholls, Jenny
  See Jane Nicholls
Nicholls, John
  I: <u>35</u>
Nicholls, John Ellison
  I: <u>35</u>
Nicholls, Kitty
  I: <u>35</u>
Nicholls, Ling
  I: <u>35</u>
Nicholls, Mary
  I: <u>35</u>
Nicholls, Rachael
  I: <u>35</u>

Nicholson/Nickolson, Margaret
  II: 215, 216, 217, 277 (p. 138)
Nickens, James Edward
  II: 350
Nickens, Jane
  I: 192
Nickens, John
  I: 191 III: 304 (p. 193), 78 (p. 236)
Nickens, John William
  II: 350
Nickens, Martha Ann
  II: 350
Nickens, Mary Francis
  II: 350
Nickens, Rebecca Lucas
  III: 308 (p. 193), 173 (p. 247)
Nickens, William
  I: 193 III: 174 (p. 247)
Nickins, Lucy
  II: 350
Nickins, Lucy Brown
  II: 197
Nickler, Marcus
  III: 300 (p. 192)
Nickles, Marcelina
  III: 254 (p. 187)
Nickols, Thomas
  I: 367
Nightingill, James
  II: 92
Nightingill, Joseph
  III: 458 (p. 279)
Nokes, Edmonia
  II: 164 III: 556 (p. 291)
Nokes, Edward
  II: 164
Nokes/Nookes, Hanson
  II: 164 III: 91 (p. 237)
Nokes, Hayes
  II: 164
Nokes, Jesse Jr.
  II: 164
Nokes/Nookes, Jesse Sr.
  II: 165 III: 90 (p. 237)
Nokes/Nookes, Malvina Pembroke
  II: 164 III: 92 (p. 237)
Nokes, Mary Ellen
  II: 164
Noland, Amelia E.
  III: 314 (p. 263)
Noland, Cecelia
  I: 255
Noland, Eliza
  III: 117 (p. 171)
Noland, Helin
  I: 255
Noland, James W.
  III: 313 (p. 263)
Noland, Jane
  I: 194, 515
Noland, Julia
  III: 13 (p. 158), 295 (p. 261)
Noland, Susan
  I: 255
Noland, William
  I: 255
Norris, Barney
  I: 430
Norris, Catharine/Catherine
  II: 378, 381; see also Catherine Norris Young
Norris, Clara
  II: 381
Norris, David
  II: 378 III: 408 (p. 205)
Norris, Eliza M.
  II: 255 III: 465 (p. 280)
Norris, Francis
  II: 378
Norris, Isaac
  II: 378
Norris, Jane
  III: 457 (p. 279)
Norris, Laura
  II: 378
Norris, Mary
  II: 381
Norris, Rachel
  II: 381 III: 550 (p. 290)
Norris, Sophia
  II: 378
Norris, William
  III: 12 (p. 228)
Nugent, Eli
  III: 154 (p. 244)
Nutt, Mary
  See Mary Nutt Cole
Nutt, Mary Ann
  I: 147
Nutt, Violet
  I: 147
Nutt, William D.
  III: 106 (p. 239)
O'Neale, Ferdinand
  III: 196 (p. 180), 210 (p. 182)
Obelton/Ovelton, Sarah
  II: 328 III: 132 (p. 173)
Obleton, Anthony
  III: 468 (p. 212)
Obleton, Ellen
  III: 469 (p. 212)
Oden, Ann Laws
  III: 178 (p. 178), 41 (p. 231)
Oden, Nathaniel
  III: 151 (p. 175), 178 (p. 178), 41 (p. 231)
Oldham, Edward
  III: 389 (p. 202), 196 (p. 249)
Oldham, Lucinda
  I: 527 III: 403 (p. 204)
Oldham, Lucy
  I: 610 III: 402 (p. 204), 195 (p. 249)
Oldham, Samuel
  I: 655 II: 119
Oscar, Thomas
  I: 520
Overtal, Penny

See Penny Overtal Cook
Padgett[?], James
    III: 538 (p. 220)
Padgett, Joseph
    III: 543 (p. 289)
Page, Ann
    II: 43
Page, Charles
    I: 60
Page, Milly
    III: 426 (p. 207), 427 (p. 207)
Page, Washington C.
    II: 287 (p. 139), 288 (p. 139), 289a (p. 139), 283 (p. 141), 342
Page, William
    II: 101, 111, 125, 167b
Page, William Byrd
    I: 7
Palmer, Eliza
    I: 695
Paris, John
    III: 323 (p. 195)
Parker, Daniel
    I: 469
Parker, Fanny
    I: 105; see also Fanny Parker Payne
Parker, George
    I: 105 II: 272 III: 194 (p. 249)
Parker, Helen
    See Helen Parker Chapman
Parker, Jenny
    I: 105
Parks, John Wilson
    I: 338
Parnell, Letty
    I: 422
Parris, George
    I: 612b
Parry, Alfred H.
    II: 93
Parry, Sally Fox
    II: 94
Pascoe/Pascol, John L.
    II: 57 III: 584 (p. 225)
Patrick, Philitia
    III: 375 (p. 201)
Patrick, William
    III: 263 (p. 188)
Patterson, Cornelia
    III: 276 (p. 190)
Patterson, Harriet
    II: 360
Payne, Ann
    See Ann Payne Barcroft
Payne, Betsey
    II: 337; see also Betsey Payne Medella
Payne, Eliza
    III: 14 (p. 228)
Payne, Fanny Parker
    III: 213 (p. 182), 89 (p. 237); see also Fanny Parker
Payne, Frederick
    III: 505 (p. 285)

Payne, Helen
    III: 529 (p. 288)
Payne, John Henry
    III: 504 (p. 285)
Payne, John W.
    III: 437 (p. 277)
Payne, Leanna
    I: 506,
Payne, Maria
    II: 180
Payne, Martha
    I: 507a
Payne, Mary Ann
    I: 519
Payne, Mary Kelsick
    III: 311 (p. 194)
Payne, Matilda
    III: 563 (p. 292)
Payne, Milly
    I: 108
Payne, Polly
    I: 201
Payne, William
    I: 526
Peach, John Gibson
    II: 225, 276b (p. 138), 334, 335, 336 III: 203 (p. 181), 394 (p. 203)
Peade, James
    I: 73
Peade, Susan
    I: 73
Pearson, Charles
    III: 546 (p. 221)
Pearson, Susannah
    III: 547 (p. 221)
Pearson, William
    III: 548 (p. 221)
Peck, Margaret
    III: 531 (p. 288)
Pembroke, Malvina
    See Malvina Pembroke Nokes
Perry, Henrietta
    I: 745 III: 221 (p. 183), 145 (p. 243)
Peters, Alexander
    III: 493 (p. 283)
Peters, Cecelia
    II: 300
Peters, Frances
    II: 300
Peters, Lucinda
    II: 300
Peters, Lucinda Lee
    III: 356 (p. 199), 268 (p. 258); see also Lucinda Lee
Peters, Sinah Ann
    III: 157 (p. 176), 163 (p. 245)
Peyton, Francis
    I: 301
Peyton, Henry
    III: 290 (p. 260)
Peyton, Lucien
    III: 487 (p. 214), 488 (p. 214), 489 (p. 214)
Peyton, Sarah A.

III: 481 (p. 282)
Phenix, Alice
II: 202
Phenix, Jack
I: 360
Phillips, Catharine
III: 356 (p. 268), 357 (p. 268)
Phillips, James
I: 645
Phillips, William H.
III: 514 (p. 286)
Phillips/Philips, Lucy
II: 277 (p. 141), 302, 303
Pickering, Sarah
II: 338 III: 191 (p. 249)
Pierce, Louisa
III: 6 (p. 227)
Piles, Nancy
III: 12 (p. 228)
Pinn, James
III: 251 (p. 187), 304 (p. 262)
Piper, Ann Elizabeth Brown
III: 393 (p. 272); see also Ann Elizabeth Brown
Piper, Edward
III: 557 (p. 222)
Piper, Elizabeth Ann
III: 502 (p. 216); see also Elizabeth Ann Piper Ramsay
Piper, Guy Henry
III: 544 (p. 221)
Piper, James E.
See James E. Piper Ramsay
Piper, Kiezey
I: 107
Piper, Margaret
See Margaret Piper Wright
Piper, Margaret Ann
III: 15 (p. 228)
Piper, Milly
I: 107
Piper, Peggy
I: 107
Piper, Sally
III: 441 (p. 277)
Piper, Sarah
III: 583 (p. 225)
Piper, Sarah Ann
See Sarah Ann Piper Brown
Piper, William Henry
See William Henry Piper Ramsay
Pipsico, Catherine
I: 51
Pipsico, Charles
I: 98
Pipsico, George
I: 286
Pipsico, John
I: 47, 98, 169
Pipsico, Lucian B. L.
II: 52
Pipsico, Lucy Ann
II: 275 (p. 138), 147

Pipsico, Lucy Ann Chapman
II: 332
Pipsico, Priscilla
I: 55
Pipsico, William
I: 47
Pipsicoe, Samuel
I: 142
Pitts, Martha
III: 505 (p. 216)
Pitts, Mary
III: 500 (p. 284)
Pitts, Sally
III: 504 (p. 216)
Pleasants, Edward
I: 219
Porter, Sinah B.
I: 311, 506, 507a, 519, 526 II: 116 III: 487 (p. 283)
Potten, George
I: 370
Potter, Lydia Ann
I: 480
Potter, Reuben
III: 369 (p. 269)
Potter, Rosetta
I: 480
Potts, John Jr.
I: 17
Powell, Joseph
I: 218
Powell, William L.
III: 2 (p. 227)
Preston, Thomas
I: 173, 325, 327
Preuss, A. W.
I: 479
Price, Argotone
I: 5
Price, Ellis
I: 147 III: 301 (p. 192)
Prichard, Sarah
I: 382b, 383, 434
Primus, Betsey
I: 454
Primus, Pompey
I: 10
Prior, Mary Frances
See Mary Frances Prior Hove
Pritchard, Ann
I: 196
Prout, William
I: 151
Quander, Felix
III: 522 (p. 218)
Quander, Gracey
III: 122 (p. 171), 278 (p. 259)
Quander, Nancy
III: 122 (p. 171)
Quanders, Jeremiah
III: 425 (p. 207)
Quin[?], Elizabeth
I: 564

Quin[?], W. H.
I: 452
Radcliff, Ann
II: 280 (p. 141), 281 (p. 141)
Ramsay, Andrew
I: 237
Ramsay, Catharine
I: 411   III: 361 (p. 199)
Ramsay, Cecelia
I: 383
Ramsay, Elizabeth Ann P[iper?]
II: 231, 232
Ramsay, James E. Piper
II: 231   III: 443 (p. 278)
Ramsay, Jane A.
II: 89, 102, 289b   III: 411 (p. 205)
Ramsay, Jane A. T.
I: 659   III: 287 (p. 191), 100 (p. 238)
Ramsay, Jesse
II: 56
Ramsay, Jesse T.
II: 253, 254
Ramsay, Mary Ann
III: 161 (p. 176)
Ramsay, W. T.
II: 15
Ramsay, William Henry Piper
II: 232   III: 442 (p. 278)
Ramswell[?], Andrew
I: 326
Ransom, Patty
I: 101
Ransom, Sally
I: 101
Rape[?], Ambrose
I: 136
Ratcliffe, Ann D.
III: 529 (p. 288)
Redman, Edward
I: 343
Redman, Maria
I: 343
Redman, Orris
I: 343   III: 101 (p. 169)
Redman, William Jr.
I: 343   III: 102 (p. 169)
Redman, William Sr.
I: 343
Reed, Benjamin F.
III: 514 (p. 286)
Reed, Hannah
III: 415 (p. 205)
Reed, Lucy Ann
I: 591
Reed, Mary
III: 475 (p. 281)
Reed, Richard Henry
I: 590
Reed, Robert S.
III: 95 (p. 168), 358 (p. 268)
Reed, Silas H.
I: 453, 529, 641, 662, 664   II: 86   III: 280 (p. 190), 367 (p. 200), 407 (p. 205), 96 (p. 238)
Reed, Susan Cryer
II: 22
Reeler, Jesse
I: 761
Reeler, Margaret
I: 761
Reeler, Mary
I: 760, 761, 762
Reeler, Mary Morgan
I: 122; see also Mary Morgan
Reeler, Samuel
I: 122, 689
Reeler, Sylvia Ann
I: 760
Reid, Hannah
I: 672
Reid, James R.
III: 432 (p. 276)
Reily, Mahala
See Mahala Reily Bird
Reily, Mary
See Mary Reily Johnson
Reily, Sarah
I: 291
Reynolds, William C.
III: 24 (p. 160) 25 (p. 160)
Rheem, John
I: 264
Rheem, John Andrew
I: 280
Rhodes, Anthony
II: 93
Rhodes, Charles Haney
I: 209
Rhodes, Harriet Haney
I: 208   III: 478 (p. 213)
Rhodes, John
III: 349 (p. 267)
Rhodes, Letitia
III: 255 (p. 256)
Rhodes, Mary
I: 551   II: 274 (p. 137)
Rhodes, Robert
II: 345
Rhodes, William
I: 21   II: 273
Richards, Caleb
III: 336 (p. 197)
Richards, Dr. John
II: 143, 282 (p. 139)
Richards, John
I: 475   II: 143
Richards, William B.
III: 501 (p. 284)
Richardson, Alice
III: 431 (p. 276)
Richardson, Catharine
III: 429 (p. 276)
Richardson, Charles W.
III: 420 (p. 206)
Richardson, Fanny
I: 711   III: 474 (p. 212)

Richardson, Harriet
   III: <u>429</u> (p. 276)
Richardson, Jane Eliza
   III: <u>429</u> (p. 276)
Richardson, John William
   III: <u>429</u> (p. 276)
Richardson, Joseph
   I: 39
Richardson, Louisa
   III: <u>429</u> (p. 276)
Richardson, Lucy Bennett
   III: <u>485</u> (p. 214); see also Lucy Bennett
Richardson, Sally
   III: <u>431</u> (p. 276)
Richardson, William P.
   I: 106
Riddle, J. R.
   II: 294, 295, 296
Riddle, Joseph
   I: 106n
Rinker, Joseph
   I: 111
Risten/Riston, Rachel
   III: 447 (p. 278), 478 (p. 282)
Riston, John
   II: 115, 219, 220
Robbins, Isaac
   I: 87
Roberts, Ann
   I: <u>259</u>
Roberts, John
   III: 409 (p. 205), 271 (p. 258)
Roberts, Julia
   II: <u>117</u>
Roberts, Kizzy
   III: <u>556</u> (p. 222)
Roberts, Sina
   I: <u>133</u>
Robey, Emily
   I: <u>690</u>
Robinson, Ann Sophia
   II: <u>283</u> (p. 139)
Robinson, Daniel
   II: <u>53</u>
Robinson, Elizabeth
   I: <u>558</u>
Robinson, George Francis
   II: <u>283</u> (p. 139)
Robinson, Harriet Elisa
   I: <u>558</u>
Robinson, Henry
   III: 581 (p. 294)
Robinson, Jane
   II: <u>283</u> (p. 139)
Robinson, Jane Eliza
   II: <u>283</u> (p. 139)
Robinson, John
   I: <u>557</u> III: <u>495</u> (p. 284)
Robinson, Louisa
   III: <u>581</u> (p. 294)
Robinson, Lucy
   III: <u>580</u> (p. 294)
Robinson, Maria
   II: <u>284</u> (p. 139) III: <u>335</u> (p. 265)
Robinson, Mary
   I: <u>557</u>
Robinson, Mary Ann Lee
   III: <u>72</u> (p. 235)
Robinson, Matthew
   I: 216, 689n III: 106 (p. 239)
Robinson, Moses
   III: <u>526</u> (p. 287)
Robinson, Nancy
   I: <u>555</u>
Robinson, Robert
   III: <u>71</u> (p. 235)
Robinson, Thomas
   III: <u>496</u> (p. 284), <u>527</u> (p. 287)
Roderick, Betty Cole
   I: 79; see also Betty Cole
Roderick, Robert
   I: <u>79</u>
Rodgers, Cornell/Corrill/Cowill[?]
   I: <u>655</u> II: 119 III: <u>194</u> (p. 180)
Rodgers, Mary Seaton
   I: <u>750</u>
Rodgers, William
   I: 655 II: <u>119</u>
Rogers, Judith Ford
   III: <u>182</u> (p. 178); see also Judith Ford
Rollings/Rollins, John
   I: 231, 366
Roman, Martha
   III: <u>423</u> (p. 206)
Rookard, Albert
   I: <u>443</u>
Roser, M. H.
   I: 29
Roseville, Emma
   I: <u>339</u>
Roseville, Jane
   I: <u>338</u>
Rose[?], Ann E.
   III: 259 (p. 188)
Ross, Charles
   I: 599
Ross, Eliza
   I: <u>252</u>
Ross, Elizabeth
   II: <u>141</u>
Ross, Henry
   II: <u>151</u>
Ross, Jane
   I: <u>250</u>, <u>462</u>
Ross, Jemima
   See Jemima Ross Merricks
Ross, John
   III: <u>387</u> (p. 202)
Ross, Jonathan
   III: 88 (p. 167), 89 (p. 167), 90 (p. 167), 144 (p. 174), 202 (p. 181), 216 (p. 182), 400 (p. 204), 138 (p. 243)
Ross, Lucretia
   II: <u>141</u>
Ross, Mary Jane
   II: <u>285</u> (p. 141) III: <u>155</u> (p. 244)

Ross, Rebecca
  I: 396
Ross, Sally
  I: <u>492</u> II: <u>343</u>
Ross, William
  II: <u>11</u>
Rowe, Celia Bowden
  III: <u>288</u> (p. 191), <u>101</u> (p. 238)
Rowe, Henry
  I: <u>659</u> III: <u>287</u> (p. 191), <u>100</u> (p. 238)
Roxbury, Jacob
  III: <u>315</u> (p. 263)
Roy, George William
  See George William Roy McDonny
Russell, J. B. F.
  I: 734
Russell, John
  II: 8
Rustin, Mary
  II: <u>245</u>
Rustin, Moses
  II: <u>245</u>
Ruston, Louisa Lee
  I: <u>615</u>
Rye, Jane
  II: 356, 357, 358 III: 121 (p. 171), 176 (p. 178), 235 (p. 185), 407 (p. 273)
Ryley, Eleazer Buckner Barnett
  I: <u>43</u>
Sales, Harriet
  I: 670
Sales, Henry
  I: <u>670</u>
Sales, John
  III: <u>561</u> (p. 222)
Sales, Mary E.
  I: <u>257</u>
Sanford, Thomas
  II: 37, 55 III: 266 (p. 188)
Santford, Louisa
  I: <u>243</u>
Sarey[?], Charity
  I: <u>628</u>
Sargent, Margaret
  I: 46
Sargent, Sarah Waugh
  I: <u>287</u>
Savoy, Polly
  I: <u>539</u> III: <u>383</u> (p. 202)
Savoy, William
  I: <u>629</u> III: <u>332</u> (p. 196)
Say[?], Jemima
  I: 578
Scholfield, William A.
  I: 475
Scott, Charles
  I: 670, 720 II: 281 (p. 138) III: 81 (p. 166)
Scott, James S.
  III: 466 (p. 211), 477 (p. 213), 68 (p. 235)
Scott, Jesse
  I: 727 III: 433 (p. 207)
Scott, Margaret
  III: <u>486</u> (p. 283)
Scroggins, Stephen
  I: <u>190</u>
Seals, Ann
  III: <u>168</u> (p. 177), <u>378</u> (p. 270)
Seals, Miriam
  I: <u>609</u>
Seals, Spencer
  I: <u>581</u>
Seals, Susan
  III: 168 (p. 177), 378 (p. 270)
Sears, Susan
  II: <u>237</u>
Seaton, Adolphus
  I: <u>749</u> II: <u>187</u>
Seaton, Ann Maria
  I: 275
Seaton, Catharine
  See Catharine Seaton Williams
Seaton, George
  I: 749, 750, 752, 753 III: <u>176</u> (p. 178)
Seaton, George Lewis
  I: <u>749</u>
Seaton, Hannah Ann
  I: <u>753</u> III: <u>312</u> (p. 194)
Seaton, John Andrew
  III: <u>317</u> (p. 194)
Seaton, John Andrew Thomas
  I: <u>749</u>
Seaton, Laura
  I: <u>749</u>
Seaton, Laura Virginia
  III: <u>315</u> (p. 194)
Seaton, Louisa
  I: 275
Seaton, Lucinda
  I: <u>749</u>, 749, 750, <u>751</u>, 752, 753 III: <u>313</u> (p. 194)
Seaton, Lucinda Sr.
  III: <u>316</u> (p. 194)
Seaton, Maria Bryant
  III: <u>467</u> (p. 211)
Seaton, Martha
  I: <u>749</u>
Seaton, Martha Ann
  III: <u>314</u> (p. 194), <u>518</u> (p. 286)
Seaton, Mary
  See Mary Seaton Rodgers
Seaton, Sarah
  I: <u>749</u>
Seaton, ____
  I: 11
Selden, Clarissa
  I: <u>140</u>
Selden, Wilson Carey
  I: 137a III: 560 (p. 222)
Semmes, Agnes Virginia
  III: <u>10</u> (p. 228)
Semmes, Elizabeth
  III: 122 (p. 171)
Semmes, Margaret
  III: 272 (p. 189)
Semmes, William H.
  III: 62 (p. 164), 131a (p. 172), 62 (p. 234)

Servoy, Jane Elizabeth
  II: <u>249</u> III: <u>209</u> (p. 251)
Servoy, Laura V.
  II: <u>252</u> III: <u>208</u> (p. 250)
Servoy, Louisa S.
  II: <u>251</u>
Servoy, Mary C.
  II: <u>250</u> III: <u>207</u> (p. 250)
Sewall, Joseph
  I: 600
Seymour, Charlotte
  III: <u>341</u> (p. 197)
Seymour, Mary Ellen
  III: <u>520</u> (p. 287)
Seyton, William H.
  III: 68 (p. 165)
Shackleford, John
  II: 286 (p. 139), 279 (p. 141) III: 178 (p. 247)
Shakes, John
  I: 593
Shavers, Landon
  III: 550 (p. 221)
Shavers, Lavinia
  III: <u>550</u> (p. 221)
Shields, Ann Elizabeth
  II: <u>352</u>
Shields, Emma Shorter
  II: <u>353</u>
Shields, James
  I: <u>159</u> III: <u>69</u> (p. 235)
Shields, James Henry
  II: <u>353</u>
Shields, John
  III: <u>501</u> (p. 284)
Shields, John Randolph
  II: <u>353</u>
Shields, Matilda
  II: 99 III: <u>156</u> (p. 175)
Shields, Nora Jenifer
  II: <u>353</u>
Shields, _____
  II: 353
Shinn, J. A.
  III: 398 (p. 272)
Shinn, Stephen
  I: 527, 610 II: 27, 338 III: 402 (p. 204), 403 (p. 204), 191 (p. 249), 195 (p. 249)
Shirley, Margaret A.
  II: 148, 149, 150
Short/Shortt, Nelly
  III: <u>163</u> (p. 176), <u>331</u> (p. 265)
Shorter, Ann
  I: <u>28</u>
Shorter, Barrett
  I: <u>29</u>
Shorter, Belinda
  I: <u>29</u>
Shorter, Catharine
  I: <u>29</u>
Shorter, John
  I: <u>29</u>
Shorter, Kitty
  I: 178
Shorter, Matilda
  I: <u>29</u>
Shorter, Rachael
  I: <u>29</u>
Shreve, Isaac
  I: 471
Shreve, Margaret
  III: 169 (p. 177), 542 (p. 220), 14 (p. 228), 477 (p. 282), 560 (p. 291)
Shreve, Samuel
  III: 477 (p. 282)
Shryer, Daniel
  II: 152, 153, 154, 155
Sidebottom, Ann
  II: 283 (p. 139), 284 (p. 139) III: 338 (p. 197), 335 (p. 265)
Simmons, Mary
  II: 7
Simms, Ann
  III: 40n (p. 161)
Simms, Elizabeth
  III: 425 (p. 207), 522 (p. 218)
Simms, George
  III: <u>195</u> (p. 180), <u>509</u> (p. 285)
Simms, Helen
  I: <u>669a</u> III: 198 (p. 180), <u>510</u> (p. 286)
Simms, John D.
  I: 577
Simms, William
  I: 676
Simpson, Adeline
  I: <u>355</u> III: <u>204</u> (p. 250)
Simpson, Delia
  I: 713 III: 110 (p. 170), 126 (p. 172)
Simpson, Gilbert
  III: <u>472</u> (p. 281)
Simpson, James H.
  III: 504 (p. 285)
Simpson, James W.
  III: 466 (p. 280)
Simpson, Jane Elizabeth
  I: <u>297</u>
Simpson, Linney
  I: <u>117</u>
Simpson, Mary
  I: <u>438</u>
Simpson, Priscilla
  I: 395, 497 II: 73, 95, 96
Sims, Margaret
  III: 457 (p. 279)
Skidmore, Isaac
  III: 416 (p. 274)
Skidmore, Jesse
  I: 583, 584, 585 III: 125 (p. 172), 143 (p. 174), 320 (p. 195)
Skidmore, John William
  III: 476 (p. 212), 416 (p. 274)
Skidmore, William
  III: 485 (p. 283)
Skinner, Daniel
  III: <u>243</u> (p. 186)
Skinner, Hannah Frances

II: <u>284</u> (p. 141)
Skinner, Mary Jane
  II: <u>309</u>
Skinner, Sarah
  II: <u>81</u>
Slade, William
  I: <u>516</u>
Slater, Jane Eliza
  II: <u>31</u>
Slater, Margaret Ellen
  II: <u>140</u>
Slater, Susan
  II: <u>140</u>
Slatford, Thomas
  I: 771 III: 192 (p. 180)
Sleymaker, Junius
  III: 15 (p. 228)
Smart[?], James
  II: 32
Smith, Amanda Bull
  III: <u>513</u> (p. 217)
Smith, Ann
  I: <u>616</u> II: <u>128</u> III: <u>539</u> (p. 220), <u>98</u> (p. 238)
Smith, Ann Cornelia
  III: <u>345</u> (p. 266)
Smith, Ann Maria
  I: <u>331</u>
Smith, Benjamin
  I: <u>220</u>
Smith, Betsey
  III: <u>137</u> (p. 173)
Smith, Daniel
  I: <u>540</u>
Smith, Daniel H.
  III: <u>335</u> (p. 196)
Smith, Delia
  III: <u>444</u> (p. 209), 445 (p. 209)
Smith, Ellen
  III: <u>495</u> (p. 215)
Smith, Francis L.
  II: 208 III: <u>593</u> (p. 226), 354 (p. 267)
Smith, George
  III: <u>477</u> (p. 213), <u>542</u> (p. 220)
Smith, Griffith
  III: <u>64</u> (p. 234)
Smith, Hannah
  I: 220, 221; see also Hannah Smith Lyles
Smith, Hugh
  I: 90 II: 307 III: <u>93</u> (p. 237), <u>400</u> (p. 273), <u>488</u> (p. 283), <u>489</u> (p. 283)
Smith, Jane Morris
  III: <u>330</u> (p. 196)
Smith, John
  II: <u>278</u> (p. 141) III: <u>445</u> (p. 209)
Smith, John L.
  II: 67 III: <u>461</u> (p. 280), 462 (p. 280), 463 (p. 280)
Smith, John W.
  I: 530, 715 II: 221 III: 10 (p. 228)
Smith, John W. (Mrs.)
  II: 375
Smith, Joseph
  I: 333 II: 368

Smith, Kitty
  I: <u>458</u> III: <u>61</u> (p. 164)
Smith, Leme
  III: <u>332</u> (p. 265)
Smith, Lerue
  I: <u>528</u>
Smith, Margaret V.
  III: <u>560</u> (p. 291)
Smith, Martha
  II: <u>191</u> III: <u>447</u> (p. 278)
Smith, Mary
  II: <u>276a</u> (p. 138)
Smith, Mordecai
  I: 81
Smith, Nancy
  I: <u>226</u>
Smith, Philip
  I: <u>578</u>
Smith, Philip A.
  III: <u>246</u> (p. 186)
Smith, Philip Andrew
  II: <u>276</u> (p. 140)
Smith, Randolph
  II: <u>274</u> III: <u>182</u> (p. 248)
Smith, Sarah
  II: <u>276</u> (p. 140)
Smith, Sidney
  II: 199
Smith, Slighter
  I: 712, 739 II: 10, 241, 242 III: 266 (p. 257), 267 (p. 257)
Smith, Susan
  II: <u>306</u> III: <u>281</u> (p. 259)
Smith, Susan Louisa
  II: <u>276</u> (p. 140)
Smith, Thomas Daniel
  II: <u>276</u> (p. 140)
Smith, William Wilson
  II: <u>276</u> (p. 140)
Smoot, Charles C.
  I: 607 II: 40, 278 (p. 138), 279 (p. 138) III: <u>297</u> (p. 261), 298 (p. 261), 299 (p. 261), 301 (p. 261), 308 (p. 262)
Smoot, James E.
  I: 607 III: 308 (p. 262)
Smyth, Edward
  II: 88
Snowden, Edgar
  II: 76, 112
Snowden, Gracey Gales
  III: <u>491</u> (p. 214)
Snyder, Elizabeth
  II: 16
Snyder, Matthias
  I: 570
Snyder, Matthias Sr.
  II: 45
Soloman/Solomon, William
  I: <u>100</u>, 601, 602 691, 692 II: <u>152</u>, 153, 313 III: <u>360</u> (p. 199)
Soloman/Solomon, William
  III: 440 (p. 208), <u>226</u> (p. 253)
Solomon, Caroline

III: <u>258</u> (p. 256)
Solomon, Charles
III: <u>56</u> (p. 233)
Solomon, George
I: <u>340</u> III: <u>141</u> (p. 174)
Solomon, James
II: <u>155</u>
Solomon, Jane Ann
III: <u>259</u> (p. 257)
Solomon, John Thomas
I: <u>691</u>
Solomon, Kitty
I: 691, 692 II: 313
Solomon, Mary Ellen
I: <u>691</u> II: <u>313</u> III: <u>261</u> (p. 257)
Solomon, Robert Henry
I: <u>692</u>
Solomon, Sarah Ann
III: <u>233</u> (p. 185)
Solomon, Sinah
I: <u>344</u> III: <u>232</u> (p. 184)
Solomon, Susan
II: <u>154</u> III: <u>227</u> (p. 253), 258 (p. 256), 259 (p. 257)
Solomon, Townsend
II: <u>153</u> III: <u>226</u> (p. 253)
Solomon, Wilson
III: <u>459</u> (p. 210), <u>180</u> (p. 247)
Sombay, Mordecai
I: <u>303</u>
Somers, Hannah
III: <u>302</u> (p. 193), 305 (p. 193)
Somers, Joseph R.
III: 25 (p. 229)
Southson, Richard
III: 347 (p. 267)
Spencer, Robert
II: <u>149</u>
Spencer, Sarah Jane
II: <u>148</u>
Stabler, Edward
I: 501 III: 501 (p. 215)
Stabler, Mary
I: 501
Stabler, Richard H.
III: 456 (p. 279), 577 (p. 293)
Stabler, William
I: 501, 573, 574, 603 II: 118 III: 214 (p. 182), 416 (p. 206), 523 (p. 218), 570 (p. 224), 571 (p. 224), 572 (p. 224)
Stanly, Catharine
See Catharine Stanly Helm
Stanton, Elihu
III: 37 (p. 161)
Stark, Margaret
I: <u>420</u>
Starks, Catharine
I: <u>424</u>
Starks, Fanny
III: <u>458</u> (p. 210)
Steele, Elijah
III: <u>430</u> (p. 276)
Steele, Emma

III: <u>430</u> (p. 276)
Steele, Sarah
III: <u>430</u> (p. 276)
Steele, Winney
III: <u>430</u> (p. 276)
Stepney, Emeline
I: <u>606</u>
Stepney, John William
III: <u>107</u> (p. 169)
Stepney, Margaret
III: <u>75</u> (p. 235)
Stepney, Salina
III: <u>97</u> (p. 168)
Stepney, Stephen
III: <u>127</u> (p. 172)
Stepney, William
I: <u>472</u>
Stevens, Elizabeth
II: 170
Stewart, Charles J.
II: 209, 210
Stewart, James
II: 13
Stewart, Mary Ann
III: <u>479</u> (p. 213), <u>60</u> (p. 234)
Stone, Olivia
III: 27 (p. 160, 28 (p. 160), 29 (p. 160), 30 (p. 160), 31 (p. 160), 32 (p. 160), 34 (p. 161), 41 (p. 162), 103 (p. 239), 199 (249), 291 (p. 260)
Stone, Penelope
III: 368 (p. 269), 476 (p. 281)
Stoutely, Mary Ann
I: <u>120</u>
Strange, Jacquelin
III: <u>523</u> (p. 287)
Stuart, Cornelia
III: <u>139</u> (p. 243)
Stuart, James M.
I: 408
Sullivan, Mary
III: 40b (p. 231)
Sumby Lucy
I: <u>254</u>, 746, 747a
Sumby, Fanny
I: <u>183</u>
Sumby, George L.
I: <u>747a</u>
Sumby, James
I: <u>432</u>
Sumby, John
I: <u>765</u> III: <u>450</u> (p. 209), <u>179</u> (p. 247)
Sumby, Mark Anthony
I: <u>471</u>
Sumby, Mary
I: <u>253</u> II: <u>90</u> III: <u>470</u> (p. 212)
Sumby, Philip
I: <u>182</u>
Sumby, Robert
III: <u>149</u> (p. 175)
Sumby, Samson
I: <u>400</u> III: <u>534</u> (p. 219)
Sumby, William

I: <u>746</u>
Summers, Simon
   I: 579
Swain, George
   III: 310 (p. 194)
Swann, Frances
   I: 121
Swann, Mary
   III: 548 (p. 290)
Swann, William T.
   I: 121
Swayne, Thomas
   I: 642
Swift, Ann
   I: 222
Swink, Sally
   III: 406 (p. 273)
Syphax, Amelia
   II: <u>363</u>
Syphax, Austin
   III: <u>373</u> (p. 269)
Syphax, Bertha Ellen
   III: <u>523</u> (p. 218)
Syphax, Charles
   III: <u>526</u> (p. 218)
Syphax, Cornelia
   III: <u>363</u> (p. 268)
Syphax, Daniel
   II: <u>315</u>
Syphax, David
   III: <u>456</u> (p. 279)
Syphax, Douglas/Douglass
   II: <u>379</u>   III: <u>577</u> (p. 293)
Syphax, Eliza
   II: <u>379</u>
Syphax, Frances
   II: <u>315</u>
Syphax, Judy
   II: <u>50</u>
Syphax, Lewis
   II: <u>379</u>   III: <u>472</u> (p. 281)
Syphax, Maria
   III: <u>416</u> (p. 206)
Syphax, Sally
   II: <u>49</u>
Syphax, William
   I: <u>409</u>   II: 49, 50, 315, 379   III: <u>501</u> (p. 215)
Talbert, Mary
   I: <u>766</u>
Talbot, Francis
   I: <u>681</u>   III: <u>379</u> (p. 201)
Talbot, Sally
   I: 688
Tate, Cassandra
   I: <u>457</u>   III: <u>4</u> (p. 157)
Tate, Eliza
   III: <u>20</u> (p. 159)
Tate, Garret
   II: <u>59</u>
Tate, Henrietta
   II: <u>348</u>
Tate, Henry
   III: <u>2</u> (p. 157), <u>79</u> (p. 236)

Tate, Hetty
   I: <u>503</u>
Tate, James
   III: <u>340</u> (p. 197)
Tate, James H.
   III: <u>527</u> (p. 219)
Tate, Margaret Ann
   I: <u>457</u>   III: <u>413</u> (p. 205)
Tate, Martha
   II: <u>116</u>
Tate, Mary
   I: <u>694</u>   II: <u>311</u>   III: <u>422</u> (p. 275)
Tate, Nanny
   I: 125
Tate, Simeon/Simon Jr.
   I: <u>457</u>   II: <u>322</u>
Tate, Simeon/Simon Sr.
   I: <u>125</u>, 457   II: <u>324</u>
Tate, William E.
   II: <u>71</u>   III: <u>187</u> (p. 179), <u>262</u> (p. 188)
Tate, William M.
   II: <u>142</u>
Tatsepaugh, Henry
   III: 208 (p. 181)
Tatsepaugh, John
   I: <u>634</u>   III: <u>420</u> (p. 275)
Taylor, Alice Ann
   III: <u>202</u> (p. 250)
Taylor, Ann
   II: 347
Taylor, Ann Maria
   II: <u>10</u>
Taylor, Anna Maria
   III: <u>183</u> (p. 248)
Taylor, Caroline Rebecca
   II: <u>347</u>
Taylor, Christy
   I: <u>614b</u>
Taylor, Cornelia
   II: <u>215</u>   III: <u>128</u> (p. 241)
Taylor, Cornelius
   III: 135 (p. 173)
Taylor, Cynthia
   I: <u>451</u>
Taylor, Daniel
   I: 148, 149, <u>82</u>
Taylor, Elias
   II: <u>277</u>
Taylor, Elisa
   I: <u>650</u>
Taylor, Elizabeth
   III: <u>484</u> (p. 282)
Taylor, Elvia
   I: <u>677</u>
Taylor, Gertrude Eugenia
   II: <u>256</u>
Taylor, Henrietta
   I: <u>493</u>   III: <u>172</u> (p. 177)
Taylor, Jane
   I: <u>603</u>
Taylor, John
   I: 74
Taylor, Josephine Frances

II: 347
Taylor, Joshua
  III: 28 (p. 160)
Taylor, Lawrence B.
  II: 4, 68   III: 91 (p. 237), 192 (p. 249)
Taylor, Louisa
  II: 256
Taylor, Lydia Ann
  II: 54   III: 173 (p. 177)
Taylor, Martha Ann
  II: 104
Taylor, Martha Ellen
  II: 256
Taylor, Mary Ann
  II: 10
Taylor, Nelly
  I: 614b
Taylor, Nora
  II: 184
Taylor, Philitia
  III: 374 (p. 201), 184 (p. 248)
Taylor, Phillis
  II: 10
Taylor, Rebecca
  II: 137 216, 223   III: 127 (p. 241)
Taylor, Robert J.
  I: 107, 515, 516, 758
Taylor, Sandy
  I: 709
Taylor, Sarah
  See Sarah Taylor Carter
Taylor, William
  I: 74   II: 217   III: 87 (p. 237)
Taylor, William Montgomery
  III: 524 (p. 218)
Tenley, Robert
  I: 605
Territt, Hannah B.
  III: 148 (p. 174)
Thomas, Benjamin
  III: 561 (p. 222)
Thomas, David
  I: 285
Thomas, Fanny
  I: 191, 192, 193
Thomas, Gustavus
  I: 216
Thomas, Joanna
  III: 484 (p. 282)
Thomas, Minty
  I: 587
Thomas, Oscar
  III: 560 (p. 222), 362 (p. 268), 362 (p. 268)
Thomas, Sally
  II: 90   III: 470 (p. 212)
Thomas, Spencer
  I: 4
Thomas, Whiting
  II: 383
Thomas, _____
  II: 372
Thompson, Eloyius
  I: 310, 386

Thompson, James
  II: 342
Thompson, Jane
  II: 368
Thompson, Jonah
  I: 9
Thompson, Margaret
  I: 150, 171, 424   II: 60   III: 436 (p. 208), 443 (p. 209), 444 (p. 209), 445 (p. 209)
Thompson, Martha
  II: 340
Thompson, Mary C.
  III: 112 (p. 170)
Thompson, Sarah
  II: 329
Thompson, Sylvia
  II: 331
Thomson, Elias
  III: 155 (p. 175)
Thornton, Jane Weeks
  III: 252 (p. 187); see also Jane Weeks
Thornton, John
  III: 110 (p. 170), 83 (p. 236)
Thornton, Lucy Ann
  See Lucy Ann Thornton Campbell
Thornton, Robert
  III: 494 (p. 284)
Thornton, William
  III: 331 (p. 196)
Toler, Henry
  I: 126
Townsend/Townshend, Caroline
  I: 490   III: 294 (p. 192), 295 (p. 192)
Townsend, Catharine
  III: 296 (p. 192)
Townsend, Eliza
  II: 247
Townsend/Townshend, James
  I: 455, 490   III: 293 (p. 192), 294 (p. 192)
Townsend, Sarah Frances
  III: 297 (p. 192)
Townsend, Sophia
  III: 295 (p. 192)
Townsend, William
  II: 246
Tracey, Louisa
  I: 570
Tracy, Henry
  I: 597b
Trammell, George W.
  III: 74 (p. 235)
Triplett, Alfred
  I: 433
Triplett, Betsey
  I: 322
Triplett, Milly
  II: 255   III: 465 (p. 280)
Triplett, Prince Wesley
  II: 255
Tubman, James
  III: 76 (p. 235)
Tucker, James O.
  III: 580 (p. 225), 581 (p. 225), 582 (p. 225)

Turley, Charles Gardney
  II: <u>280</u> (p. 138)
Turley, Dorcas
  I: <u>436</u>
Turley, George
  III: <u>464</u> (p. 280)
Turley, George W.
  II: <u>188</u> III: <u>262</u> (p. 257)
Turley, Harriet
  III: <u>273</u> (p. 189)
Turley, Henson
  III: <u>148</u> (p. 174), <u>381</u> (p. 270)
Turley, Jane
  I: <u>562</u>
Turley, John M.
  III: <u>531</u> (p. 219)
Turley, Kitty
  III: <u>231</u> (p. 184)
Turley, Maria
  I: <u>437</u>
Turley, Maria Ann
  I: <u>735</u>
Turly, Thomas
  II: <u>110</u>
Turner, Ann
  III: <u>3</u> (p. 157)
Turner, Catharine
  I: <u>76</u>
Turner, Daniel
  III: <u>477</u> (p. 282)
Turner, Dick
  I: <u>534</u>
Turner, Eleanor
  III: <u>234</u> (p. 185)
Turner, Elizabeth
  I: 284
Turner, Hannah
  I: <u>534</u>
Turner, Harriet
  See Harriet Medella Turner Jackson
Turner, John B.
  I: 19
Turner, Lucy Ann
  III: <u>520</u> (p. 218), <u>63</u> (p. 234)
Turner, Mary Bowling
  I: <u>534</u>
Turner, Penny
  See Penny Turner Moody
Turner, Rebecca
  I: <u>537</u>
Tyler, Henry
  I: 251
Tyler, Phebe Ann
  II: <u>44</u> III: <u>342</u> (p. 197), <u>104</u> (p. 239)
Upton, Charles H.
  III: 477 (p. 213)
Vaccari, Frederick
  I: 416
Valentine, Caesar
  I: 346
Valentine, Lydia
  II: <u>292</u> (p. 142)
Valentine, Priscilla
  III: <u>333</u> (p. 265)
Valentine, Sarah
  I: <u>12</u>
Valentine, William
  I: <u>346</u>
Vanhavre, T. M. A.
  I: 115
Vansant, James
  II: 144, 180, 350
Vasse, Ambrose
  I: 375, 433
Vasse, Eveline
  I: <u>375</u>
Vaughn, Robert Jr.
  I: <u>102</u>, <u>224</u>
Vaughn, Robert Sr.
  I: 102, 224
Veitch, Alexander
  I: 747b
Veitch, Richard
  I: 230, 379, 413
Veitch, Will
  I: 260
Veitch, William
  II: 168
Vernon, Sally
  III: 492 (p. 283)
Vernon, Sarah
  II: 189 III: 76 (p. 166), 77 (p. 166), 333 (p. 196), 75 (p. 235)
Violett, E. R.
  II: 256
Violett, John
  I: 49
Violett, Robert
  II: 201
Vowell, John C.
  I: 618, 619 II: 11
Vowell, John D.
  I: 343
Vowell, Thomas
  I: 324, 594, 595, 767, 768, 769 II: 11
  III: 39 (p. 161)
Walker, Francis M.
  II: 246, 247
Walker, George W.
  III; <u>524</u> (p. 287)
Walker, Henry
  III: <u>549</u> (p. 290)
Walker, Marian/Marion
  II: 370 III: 293 (p. 191), 295 (p. 192), 296 (p. 192), 297 (p. 192)
Walker, Rachel
  I: <u>461</u>
Walsh, John J.
  III: 544 (p. 289), 545 (p. 290)
Walton, Hannah
  III: 154 (p. 175)
Walton, Lucinda
  III: 22 (p. 159)
Walton, William
  I: 96
Wanton, Hannah S.

II: 54, 176, 347
Ward, Catharine
  I: 143 II: 103
Ward, Charles
  III: 11 (p. 228)
Ward, John
  III: 562 (p. 223)
Ward, Jonathan
  II: 272, 275 (p. 138), 325, 326, 327
Ward, Zachariah
  I: 89a
Ware, Adeline
  III: 212 (p. 251)
Ware, Betsey
  I: 261
Ware, Caroline
  I: 697 III: 69 (p. 165)
Ware, John Kinzey/McKinsey
  II: 178 III: 218 (p. 252)
Ware, Kinsey
  I: 561, 575 III: 44 (p. 162)
Ware, Mary Jane Cole
  III: 446 (p. 278)
Ware, Philip
  III: 73 (p. 235)
Ware, Priscilla Darnell
  III: 86 (p. 167)
Warner, Charlotte
  I: 202
Warner, Hannah Ann
  III: 282 (p. 190)
Warner, Jane
  III: 281 (p. 190)
Warner, Loudon
  I: 162
Warner, Mary
  II: 218 III: 250 (p. 255)
Warner, Matilda
  I: 756
Washington, Bendett
  I: 633
Washington, Betsey Brown
  I: 497
Washington, Betty
  I: 500
Washington, Elizabeth
  I: 360
Washington, Francis
  I: 467
Washington, General George
  I: 14, 52, 53, 350, 750, 751, 752 II: 14
  III: 122n (p. 171), 124 (p. 172), 184 (p. 179),
  220 (p. 183), 238 (p. 185), 316 (p. 194),
  404n (p. 273), 507n (p. 285)
Washington, George
  III: 528 (p. 219), 585 (p. 225), 460 (p. 280)
Washington, Harriet
  III: 12 (p. 158)
Washington, Henry
  I: 710
Washington, Jane C.
  I: 663
Washington, John
  III: 417 (p. 275)
Washington, John A.
  I: 362
Washington, Joshua
  I: 742
Washington, Martha
  I: 52, 53, 350
Washington, Mary
  I: 745 III: 221 (p. 183), 145 (p. 243)
Washington, Robert P.
  I: 277
Waters, Ann Sophia
  III: 345 (p. 198)
Waters, Benjamin
  I: 170, 426 II: 377 III: 344 (p. 197), 364
  (p. 200), 157 (p. 245), 320 (p. 263)
Waters, Daniel
  III: 113 (p. 170)
Waters, Jonathan
  I: 389 III: 71 (p. 165)
Waters, Maria
  III: 112 (p. 170)
Waters, Sarah
  II: 278 (p. 141)
Watkins, Eliza
  I: 263
Watson, Ann
  I: 229, 680 III: 92 (p. 168)
Watson, Cornelius
  I: 704
Watson, Edgar
  II: 243
Watson, Harriet Hunter
  II: 242, 243 III: 266 (p. 257)
Watson, Henry
  III: 259 (p. 188), 418 (p. 275)
Watson, James
  III: 76 (p. 235)
Watson, John
  II: 243
Watson, Josiah
  I: 341 III: 330 (p. 196)
Watson, Sarah
  II: 243
Watson, Thomas
  I: 680
Watts, Ellen Maria
  III: 548 (p. 290)
Watts, John
  I: 19, 356
Waugh, Alexander
  I: 631 II: 53
Waugh, Catharine
  I: 288
Waugh, Daniel
  I: 288 II: 20
Waugh, Elizabeth Ann
  I: 288; see also Elizabeth Ann Waugh
  Grymes
Waugh, George
  I: 288
Waugh, James R.
  I: 288

Waugh, Jane
I: <u>573</u>
Waugh, John Thomas
I: <u>288</u>, <u>656</u>
Waugh, Lettia
I: <u>288</u>
Waugh, Mary
I: <u>574</u> III: <u>533</u> (p. 219); see also Mary Bell
Waugh, Mary E.
II: <u>211</u>
Waugh, Mary Roderick
I: 288
Waugh, Sarah
See Sarah Waugh Sargent
Waugh, Townshend
I: 250
Waugh, William
I: <u>288</u>, <u>431</u>
Weaver, Charles Henry
III; <u>545</u> (p. 290)
Weaver, Eliza
III: <u>93</u> (p. 168), 94 (p. 168), 98 (p. 168)
Weaver, Emanuel
I: <u>399</u> III: <u>392</u> (p. 203)
Weaver, Hannah Ann
III: <u>544</u> (p. 289)
Weaver, Joanna
III: <u>98</u> (p. 168)
Weaver, Letty
II; <u>17</u> III: <u>382</u> (p. 202), <u>109</u> (p. 239)
Weaver, Sarah Ann
III: <u>94</u> (p. 168)
Weaver, William
III: <u>38</u> (p. 161), <u>108</u> (p. 239)
Webster, Addison
III: <u>489</u> (p. 283)
Webster, Arabella Clark
II: 195 III: <u>212</u> (p. 182); see also Arberilla Clark
Webster, Araminta
I: <u>124</u>
Webster, Caroline C.
II: <u>195</u>
Webster, Charles E.
II: <u>195</u>
Webster, Daniel
I: 89a
Webster, Daniel C.
II: <u>195</u>
Webster, George H.
I: 278
Webster, Henrietta
II: <u>299</u>
Webster, Isaac A.
II: <u>195</u>
Webster, James
III: <u>284</u> (p. 190), <u>310</u> (p. 194), <u>141</u> (p. 243), <u>321</u> (p. 264), <u>400</u> (p. 273)
Webster, John
I: 278
Webster, Julia G.
II: <u>195</u>
Webster, Letitia
III: <u>242</u> (p. 186), <u>322</u> (p. 264)
Webster, Lucy
I: 89a II: <u>299</u>
Webster, Oliver
II: <u>299</u>
Webster, Orlando
II: <u>299</u>
Webster, Patty
II: <u>307</u> III: <u>93</u> (p. 237)
Webster, Rosalia Eugenia
II: 164 III: 92 (p. 237)
Webster, Susanna
III: <u>5</u> (p. 157)
Webster, William
III: <u>488</u> (p. 283)
Webster, William Armstrong
I: <u>89a</u>
Webster, William Henry
II: <u>195</u>
Wedge, Elijah
III: <u>449</u> (p. 209)
Wedge, Mary
II: <u>372</u> III: <u>136</u> (p. 242)
Weeks, Henry
I: <u>187</u>
Weeks, Jane
I: <u>268</u>; see also Jane Weeks Thornton
Weeks, Sally
I: 187, 268
Weemes, William
I: 82
Wells, Cornelius
I: 334
West, G. W.
I: 107
West, Harriet
I: 448 II: 29, 30
West, James
I: <u>448</u> II: <u>30</u>
West, John
I: 103, <u>171</u>, 173, 392, 523 III: 473 (p. 281)
West, Lewis
I: <u>674</u>
West, Ottaway
I: <u>448</u> II: <u>29</u>
West, Robert
I: <u>448</u>
West, Simon
I: 580
Weston, Sarah
I: <u>325</u>
Weston, William Henry
I: <u>489</u>
Whaley, John
III: 530 (p. 219)
Wheat, Benoni
I: 52, 89b, 547, 615 II: 269 III: 103 (p. 169)
Wheeler, Betsy
I: <u>550</u>
Wheeler, Ignatius
I: 267
Wheeler, Jabez

II: 384, 385 III: 423 (p. 206)
Wheeler, John
  III: <u>48</u> (p. 162)
Wheeler, Lydia Ann
  III: <u>47</u> (p. 162)
Wheeler, Martha Ann
  III: <u>498</u> (p. 215)
Wheeler, Mary
  II: 380 III: <u>497</u> (p. 215)
Wheeler, Medora
  III: <u>46</u> (p. 162)
Wheeler, Minny
  I: 318, 550
Wheeler, Rachael
  I: 84, 85, 128, 267, 345 III: <u>228</u> (p. 184)
Wheeler, Richard H.
  I: <u>725</u>
Wheeler, Rosetta
  III: <u>45</u> (p. 162), 46 (p. 162), 47 (p. 162), 48 (p. 162), <u>220</u> (p. 252)
Wheeler, Samuel
  I: 331, 409, 423, 534, 535, 536, 597a
White, Elizabeth
  I: <u>599</u>
White, Elizabeth Ann
  I: 622
White, Faith
  I: <u>468</u>
White, Kitty
  III: <u>325</u> (p. 195)
White, Nancy
  III: <u>154</u> (p. 175)
White, Samuel
  I: <u>654a</u>
White, Thomas M.
  III: 339 (p. 197), 132 (p. 242), 325 (p. 264), 326 (p. 264), 327 (p. 264), 328 (p. 264)
Whiting, Eliza
  II: <u>376</u>
Whiting, Elizabeth
  II: <u>15</u>
Whiting, John
  I: 144, 198, 200, 316, 373, 374, 596 III: 500 (p. 215), <u>500</u> (p. 215), 512a (p. 217), <u>86</u> (p. 237), 86 (p. 237); see also John Jones
Whiting, John T.
  II: <u>291</u> (p. 142)
Whiting, Martha Garrett
  II: 15
Whiting, Matthew
  I: 57, 61
Whiting, Virginia
  II: <u>291</u> (p. 142)
Whitler, Eli/Ely
  III: <u>207</u> (p. 181), <u>236</u> (p. 254)
Whitler, John F.
  III: <u>22</u> (p. 229)
Whitler, Randolph
  III: <u>498</u> (p. 284)
Whitley, Susan
  III: <u>109</u> (p. 170)
Whitington, Thomas
  I: 143

Whittington, Henry
  III: <u>438</u> (p. 208), 439 (p. 208), 279 (p. 259)
Wiggins, Lavinia
  II: <u>223</u>
Wiley, Catharine
  III: <u>372</u> (p. 201)
Wiley, Hugh
  II: 259
Wiley, Margaret
  II: 267
William L. Powell & Son
  III: 417 (p. 275)
Williams, Amey McQuan
  III: <u>359</u> (p. 199)
Williams, Ann Maria
  III: <u>344</u> (p. 266)
Williams, Basil/Bazil
  III: <u>424</u> (p. 275), 425 (p. 275), 426 (p. 276), 427 (p. 276), 429 (p. 276), 430 (p. 276), 431 (p. 276), 435 (p. 276), 436 (p. 277)
Williams, Catharine
  III: <u>236</u> (p. 185), <u>573</u> (p. 293)
Williams, Catharine Seaton
  I: <u>752</u>
Williams, Celia
  I: <u>453</u> <u>720</u> III: <u>81</u> (p. 166), 83 (p. 167)
Williams, Charles
  III: <u>125</u> (p. 172), <u>317</u> (p. 263)
Williams, Cordelia
  III: <u>450</u> (p. 278)
Williams, Daniel
  III: <u>582</u> (p. 225), <u>118</u> (p. 240)
Williams, David
  I: <u>525</u>
Williams, Dolly
  III: 117 (p. 171)
Williams, Eliza
  See Eliza Williams Meredith
Williams, Elizabeth
  I: <u>728</u>
Williams, Francis
  I: 154 III: <u>211</u> (p. 182), <u>452</u> (p. 279)
Williams, Georgeanna/Georgiana
  II: <u>355</u> III: <u>23</u> (p. 229)
Williams, Gustavus
  I: <u>617</u>
Williams, Hannah
  I: <u>627</u>
Williams, Israel
  I: <u>239</u> III: <u>251</u> (p. 256)
Williams, James
  I: <u>509</u> III: <u>216</u> (p. 252)
Williams, Jane
  I: <u>595</u> III: <u>346</u> (p. 266)
Williams, Jesse
  I: <u>421</u>
Williams, John
  III: <u>342</u> (p. 266), <u>449</u> (p. 278), <u>569</u> (p. 292)
Williams, John Rozier
  II: <u>355</u>
Williams, Joseph
  I: <u>664</u>
Williams, Julia Ann

II: 355
Williams, Junus
  I: 453
Williams, Laura Virginia
  II: 355
Williams, Letitia
  III: 83 (p. 167)
Williams, Lewis
  II: 157 III: 339 (p. 266)
Williams, Marcellus
  III: 566 (p. 223)
Williams, Mary
  III: 82 (p. 167), 451 (p. 279)
Williams, Nancy
  I: 531 III: 496 (p. 215), 568 (p. 223)
Williams, Samuel
  II: 338 III: 336 (p. 197), 191 (p. 249)
Williams, Samuel T.
  I: 553
Williams, Sanford
  III: 565 (p. 223)
Williams, Sarah Elizabeth
  II: 355
Williams, Thomas
  III: 21 (p. 229), 397 (p. 272)
Williams, William
  III: 179 (p. 178), 203 (p. 250)
Williams, William A.
  I: 474
Williams, William M.
  II: 111
Williams, Winifred
  II: 191, 192, 193 III: 252 (p. 256)
Willis, Judy
  I: 38
Wilmer, Ann B.
  I: 722 III: 408 (p. 274)
Wilmer, William H.
  I: 744 II: 78 III: 199 (p. 180), 302 (p. 193), 305 (p. 193), 541 (p. 220), 164 (p. 245)
Wilson, Albert
  I: 549
Wilson, Alice
  I: 58, 546
Wilson, Cornelius
  III: 285 (p. 191)
Wilson, Flora E. Morgan
  III: 441 (p. 208); see also Flora E. Morgan
Wilson, Henry
  I: 58
Wilson, James
  I: 56, 549, 598
Wilson, James Jr.
  I: 58, 545
Wilson, James Sr.
  I: 58
Wilson, John
  III: 384 (p. 202)
Wilson, Mary
  I: 58
Wilson, Presley
  II: 79
Wilson, Richard
  III: 286 (p. 260)
Wilson, Robert
  I: 549
Wilson, Samuel
  I: 546
Wilson, Samuel Bee
  I: 164
Wilson, William
  I: 11, 601 III: 440 (p. 208)
Windsor, George William
  II: 330
Windsor, John Thomas
  I: 278
Windsor, Maria
  II: 330
Winter, Elisabeth B.
  I: 495
Wise, George
  I: 638
Wise, John
  I: 275
Wood, John
  I: 312, 525 III: 77 (p. 236)
Wood, Mary
  I: 89
Wren, John
  I: 22, 41
Wright, Charles
  I: 469 II: 371
Wright, Charles Henry
  III: 461 (p. 280)
Wright, Dennis
  I: 469
Wright, Francis
  I: 469 II: 371 III: 462 (p. 280)
Wright, Joseph
  II: 371 III: 463 (p. 280)
Wright, Lavinia/Livinia
  I: 469 II: 371 III: 394 (p. 272)
Wright, Margaret Piper
  I: 109
Wright, Martha Ann
  I: 577
Wright, Mary Jane
  I: 577
Wright, Moses
  III: 2 (p. 227)
Wyatt, Fendall
  II: 34 III: 415 (p. 274)
Wyatt, Malinda
  I: 619
Wyatt, Peggy
  I: 329, 618
Wyatt, Sarah
  I: 329
Yates/Yeates, Cassa/Cassy
  I: 726 III: 222 (p. 183)
Yates, John
  I: 247, 148 III: 33 (p. 161), 198 (p. 249)
Yeates, William
  II: 12
Yeaton, W. C.
  II: 376

Yeaton, William
  I: 508 II: 164
York, Charlotte
  II: 190
Yorpp, Betty
  I: 413 II: 244
Yorpp, Mary
  II: 244
Young, Ann
  I: 652, 653
Young, Catherine Norris
  III: 323 (p. 264); see also Catharine Norris
Young, Elizabeth
  I: 652
Young, Hannah Ann
  II: 130
Younger, Edward
  I: 38
Zimmerman, Reuben
  II: 367

www.ingramcontent.com/pod-product-compliance
Lightning Source LLC
Chambersburg PA
CBHW080726300426
44114CB00019B/2500